The **Rough Guide** to

New England

written and researched by

Sarah Hull, Stephen Keeling, and Zhenzhen Lu

ROUGH
GUIDES

NEW YORK · LONDON · DELHI

www.roughguides.com

Contents

Literary New England
color section following
p.176

**New England food
and drink** color section
following p.368

◀◀ Vermont farm ◀ Cape Elizabeth, Maine

Introduction to

New England

The states of Massachusetts, Rhode Island, Connecticut, Vermont, New Hampshire, and Maine – collectively known as New England – often regard themselves as the repository of all that is intrinsically American. And though nostalgia does play a big part in the tourist trade here, this is undeniably one of the most historic parts of the United States.

Boston especially is celebrated as the birthplace of American independence – so many of the seminal events of the Revolutionary War took place here, or nearby at Lexington and Concord – and the coastal towns of Massachusetts, Rhode Island, and Maine, though now geared almost entirely towards seasonal visitors, still bear plenty of traces of the region' early settlements. This is, after all, where the first permanent European colonies in the New World were established, their survival aided by groups of Native Americans whose legacy is reflected in place names throughout the region.

Not everything is about historical legacy, though. Indeed, above all New England packs an enormous amount of variety into what is by American standards a relatively small area. Its attractions are many and sundry, taking in sites both cerebral – fine collections of art and Americana, the homes of many seminal figures of American literature (Henry David Thoreau, Mark Twain, and Emily Dickinson, among legions

> **Though nostalgia does play a big part in the tourist trade here, this is undeniably one of the most historic parts of the United States.**

of others), and the country's most influential academic institutions – and active, including excellent opportunities for skiing, hiking, cycling, and beaching, not to mention eating and drinking or just watching the leaves

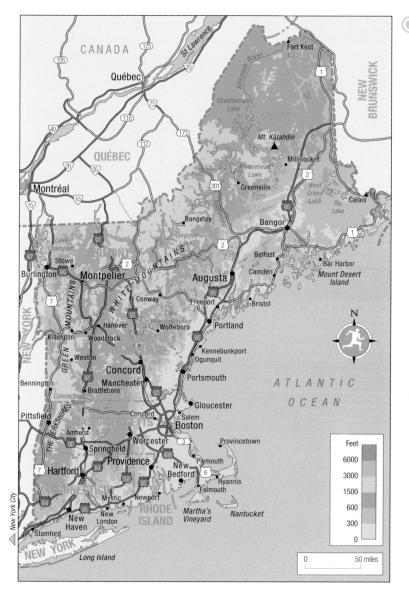

change color and drop from the trees. The landscape is surprisingly diverse as well, ranging from sandy beaches and rocky bluffs to green rolling hills and even snowy mountains.

The **landscape**, in particular, has had a major impact on the character of the region's inhabitants. Inland, its thin soil and harsh

Fact file

- Boston is the only New England city to rank among the top 100 in population in the US.

- The highest point in the region is New Hampshire's Mount Washington, 6288ft above sea level.

- Cambridge is home to the oldest college in the US, Harvard, founded in 1636.

- The Thanksgiving holiday is often traced back to a harvest celebration that took place in Plymouth back in 1621, though direct correlations are not certain.

- Vermont produces around seventy million pounds of cheese a year.

- Maine has around 3500 miles of shoreline and, at more than 30,000 square miles, is by far the largest state in the region. Rhode Island, at little more than 1000 square miles, is not only the smallest state in the region, but in the entire country.

▼ Nautical shop, Portland

climate have traditionally made it difficult to sustain an agricultural way of life, while the manufacturing prosperity of the nineteenth and early twentieth centuries is now only a distant memory. The whaling and shipbuilding industries of the coastline, too, had their heyday in the nineteenth century. Over time, these circumstances have produced a tough, hearty "Yankee" spirit. Indeed, the region's traditional role as home to the country's cultural elite is due more to the vagaries of history and ideology than economic realities – there are pockets of northern New England that are as poor as anywhere in the US, and the southern states suffer all the problems normally associated with urban and suburban settings.

Despite the geographic diversity, New England is compact and well defined, and quite easy **to get around**; only Maine, the region's largest and most rural state, takes any real time to navigate. Connecticut, Massachusetts, and Rhode Island are more urban and historic and, where nature intervenes, it is usually along the spectacular coastline. Further north, the lakes and mountains of Vermont, New Hampshire, and particularly Maine offer **wilderness** to rival any in the nation.

Where to go

Boston is the undisputed capital of New England, perhaps America's most historic city, and certainly one of its most elegant, full of enough colonial charm and contemporary culture, including a fine array of restaurants and bars, to satisfy most appetites. Together with its energetic student-oriented neighbor, **Cambridge**, Boston merits a visit of at least a few days. It also makes a good base for day-trips out to historic Lexington and Concord, the rocky North Shore, where the witch sights of **Salem** probably hold the most interest, and **Cape Cod** – a charming but usually very crowded peninsula, with delightful, quirky **Provincetown** at its outermost tip. Ferries head from the Cape to the popular summer retreats of **Martha's Vineyard** and **Nantucket**.

> New England packs an enormous amount of variety into what is by American standards a relatively small area.

West of Boston, there's the collegiate **Pioneer Valley**, which gives way to the **Berkshires**, a scenic if somewhat twee retreat for the East Coast's cultural elite. Southwest of Boston, along the coast, tiny Rhode Island's two main attractions are energetic **Providence** and wealthy **Newport**, beyond which you can take in the better parts of the Connecticut coast: the seaport of **Mystic**, and, further on, likeable **New Haven**, home to Yale University.

▲ Charles River, Boston

In Vermont, outside of relaxed, urbane **Burlington**, you're best off just wandering the state's backroads in search of country inns and dairy farms – unless, of course, you're making the pilgrimage to **Ben & Jerry's** in Waterbury. If you've come for winter sports, resorts like **Killington** and **Stowe** rank among the best in the Northeast. Over in New Hampshire, the rugged glory of the **White Mountains** is the state's most dramatic lure, with the highest peaks in the region; indeed, if you enjoy camping or hiking you won't want to miss this area. Coastal **Portsmouth** is crammed with historic mansions and enticing restaurants.

Finally, there's Maine, which has perhaps New England's most extreme blend of seaside towns (**Portland**, **Bar Harbor**) and untamed interior wilderness, in which you can spot moose outside of **Rangeley**, whitewater raft near **Moosehead Lake**, and do some remote hiking in **Baxter State Park** along the Appalachian Trail, which runs through all three of New England's northern states.

When to go

New England is at its most beautiful during the **fall**, when the foliage is magnificent, but it's also one of the most popular times to visit the region, so accommodation is usually packed and prices high. The region gets quite cold and snowy during the **winter** months, but they're a perfect time to visit if you want to ski or take part in other winter sports. **Summer** is high season, when most tourist attractions – especially along the coasts of Cape Cod, Maine, and Rhode Island, and inland in the Berkshires – really kick into high

Fall foliage

New England is undoubtedly a year-round destination, but nothing really compares to how towns and tourist bureaus alike treat the **fall foliage season**. In a way it might seem unbelievable that such a thriving industry can be predicated on watching leaves turn color, but that's how spectacular the display is. If you plan on heading to the region during the prime times – much of October, though with some variance depending on where you are – be sure to make reservations long in advance, and be prepared to pay a bit more than normal. Then take a drive into the mountains or along some river valley (preferably in the Berkshires, White Mountains, or almost anywhere in Vermont), and admire the fiery reds, yellows, and oranges of the maples, birches, and poplars.

gear, and things can get crowded. On balance, late **spring** is probably the best time to come: the temperature is generally agreeable, if a little unpredictable, the crowds are more dispersed, and prices have yet to go up for the tourist season.

Average daytime temperatures and rainfall in New England

	Jan	Feb	Mar	Apr	May	Jun	Jul	Aug	Sep	Oct	Nov	Dec
Bangor, ME												
max (°F)	27	28	37	52	63	73	79	75	68	57	45	30
max (°C)	-3	-2	3	11	17	23	26	24	20	14	7	-1
min (°F)	9	10	21	34	43	52	57	55	48	39	30	16
min (°C)	-13	-12	-6	1	6	11	14	13	9	4	-1	-9
rain (in)	3.0	2.9	3.2	3.3	3.5	3.3	3.3	3.3	3.4	3.4	4.6	3.9
rain (mm)	76.2	73.7	81.3	83.8	88.9	83.8	83.8	83.8	86.4	86.4	116.8	99.1
Boston, MA												
max (°F)	36	37	45	57	66	77	82	81	72	63	52	39
max (°C)	2	3	7	14	19	25	28	27	22	17	11	4
min (°F)	23	25	32	41	50	59	64	64	57	46	39	27
min (°C)	-5	-4	0	5	10	15	18	18	14	8	4	-3
rain (in)	3.6	3.6	3.7	3.6	3.3	3.1	2.8	3.2	3.1	3.3	4.2	4.0
rain (mm)	91.4	91.4	94.0	91.4	83.8	78.7	71.1	81.3	78.7	83.8	106.7	101.6
Burlington, VT												
max (°F)	25	27	37	54	66	75	81	79	70	57	45	30
max (°C)	-4	-3	3	12	19	24	27	26	21	14	7	-1
min (°F)	9	9	21	34	45	54	59	57	48	39	30	16
min (°C)	-13	-13	-6	1	7	12	15	14	9	4	-1	-9
rain (in)	1.8	1.6	2.2	2.8	3.1	3.5	3.6	4.1	3.3	2.9	3.1	2.4
rain (mm)	45.7	40.6	55.9	71.1	78.7	88.9	91.4	104.1	83.8	73.7	78.7	61.0

21

things not to miss

It's not possible to see everything that New England has to offer in one trip — and we don't suggest you try. What follows is a selective taste of the region's highlights: dramatic scenery, picturesque villages, colonial relics, and unusual museums. They're arranged in five color-coded categories, which you can browse through to find the very best things to see and experience. All highlights have a page reference to take you straight into the Guide, where you can find out more.

01 **The houses of Beacon Hill** Page **89** • Be on the lookout for purple-tinted windowpanes and bow-fronted town houses as you stroll Boston's most elegant neighborhood.

02 Skiing Stowe Page **367** • Fine slopes abound in Vermont and New Hampshire, but the oldest resort of Stowe is still one of the best.

03 Eating in Portsmouth Page **400** • There are a raft of surprisingly upscale restaurants in this seafront New Hampshire town, including some enticing ones right on the water.

04 Saint-Gaudens National Historic Site Page **420** • Soak up the exuberant work of one of the nation's greatest sculptors, set within the tranquil buildings and gardens of his former New Hampshire home.

05 A baseball game at Fenway Park Page **103** • The country's oldest Major League ballpark is home to the beloved Red Sox, the 37-foot-tall "Green Monster," and lots of legendary baseball lore.

06 **Burlington** Page **374** • One of New England's most purely enjoyable towns, with an assured sense of vitality, plenty of culture, and a lovely setting on Lake Champlain in Vermont.

07 **Block Island's inns** Page **278** • Watch the sun set from any of a number of grand Victorian inns perched along the island's Old Harbor.

08 **Acadia National Park, ME** Page **505** • Although it's petite, this national park packs a beautiful punch – rugged, varied, and dramatic.

09 **Shelburne Museum** Page **381** • Outside of Burlington, this illuminating collection of Americana re-creates daily life over the past two centuries in exact detail.

10 Mass MoCA Page **247** • The far corner of Western Massachusetts is an unlikely place for a first-class contemporary art museum, but that only adds a special thrill to seeing its strange exhibits.

11 Mystic Seaport Page **289** • So what if it's a bit of a tourist trap? It's still the easiest way to experience New England's maritime life in the late 1800s.

12 Hiking the Long Trail Page **348** • The region is perfect for hikers, with one of the most rewarding (and challenging) treks running through Vermont's mountainous interior.

13 Litchfield Hills Page **321** • If you're looking for scenic villages and manicured town squares, amidst some surprisingly rural patches, this Connecticut alternative to the Berkshires should do the trick.

14 **Apple-picking** Page **147** • Pick your own apples and enjoy freshly pressed cider in the fall, when orchards in Massachusetts open their gates to visitors.

15 **Nantucket** Page **203** • This lovely, tiny island boasts wild beauty, accessible beaches, and a rich whaling legacy that inspired *Moby Dick*.

16 **Tracing colonial history** Pages **72**, **143** & **144** • Very much where America began, New England has all sorts of emblems of its birth, from the sights along Boston's Freedom Trail to the battlegrounds at Lexington and Concord.

17 **Portland** Page **464** • Maine's cultural heart, Portland has all the tempting museums, boutiques, and restaurants of a larger metropolis, only without all the hustle and bustle.

18 **Harvard Square** Page **109** • The epicenter of Cambridge, Harvard Square buzzes with youthful activity day and night.

19 **Summer festivals in the Berkshires** Page **237** • Tanglewood is the most celebrated outdoor venue of all, but there are plenty of places to take in music, drama, and much more in the Berkshires.

20 **Newport's mansions** Page **266** • Such ostentation was called "conspicuous consumption" in Thorstein Veblen's day; in ours, you don't have to be self-conscious at all to gawk at the folly.

21 **Cape Cod National Seashore** Page **182** • Enjoy raw, untouched beaches, craggy dunes, and wickedly tempting clam shacks in this fragile but protected national park.

Basics

Basics

Getting there

The primary point of arrival into New England is Boston, Massachusetts, the region's largest city. All the major airlines operate direct flights to Boston's Logan International Airport from the US, Canada, and Europe (those coming from points west typically connect with domestic flights in California). Within North America, trains are a second (but not particularly cheap) option for getting to regional cities like Boston, Portland, and Providence, while for budget travelers, the Greyhound, Concord Coach Lines, and Peter Pan bus companies make a good alternative, and are also useful for reaching smaller towns. Really, though, the best way to get to New England is by car, especially if you're looking to cover a lot of ground. Boston is an important exception to this rule, however, as the city's antiquated roads make driving a nightmare; it's recommended you park your car during a visit to Boston.

From North America

Getting to New England **from anywhere in North America** is only problematic – via any kind of transport – in the winter, when roads get icy and airports occasionally close due to inclement weather.

By air

Direct **flights** to Boston's Logan International Airport are available from all the major hubs in North America (including Canadian cities Toronto, Montréal, Vancouver, and Ottawa), though you may find yourself connecting through Chicago, New York, or another large East Coast city. Some of the discount domestic airlines use other New England cities as hubs: Southwest flies to Providence's T.F. Green Airport and Manchester's Manchester–Boston Airport, and JetBlue flies to Burlington (VT) and Portland (ME) in addition to Boston. Smaller airports in Portland (ME), Bangor (ME), and Windsor Locks (near Hartford, CT) are serviced less regularly by smaller aircraft, though some have international terminals as well. It's also worth checking flights to New York City, as these are often cheap enough to make taking a bus or train the rest of the way to New England worth the inconvenience.

East Coast arrivals have the best access to the region, as frequent **shuttles** to Boston originate from New York's LaGuardia, JFK, and Newark airports (JetBlue, Delta, and US Airways), and Washington, DC's Reagan

National Airport (JetBlue and US Airways); most of these fly hourly during the week and every couple of hours on the weekend. Southwest also runs a near-hourly shuttle from Baltimore's BWI Airport (near DC) to Providence for just over $100 each way.

Generally, the most expensive time to fly is from mid-May to early September; note, though, that regional flights can continue to stay pricey well into November thanks to the popularity of the fall foliage season (mid-Sept to mid-Nov). The winter season – with the exception of Thanksgiving, Christmas, and New Year's – is the cheapest time to fly. **Fares** are lowest in the heavily trafficked Northeast corridor; a round-trip fare from New York can cost as little as $90–100, although $150–200 is more typical; from Washington, DC and Miami, the range is usually $225–300; from Chicago, $300–350. Round-trip fares from LA, San Francisco, or Seattle typically cost $500–600, though these can go as low as $350. From **Canada**, be prepared to pay around $800 from Toronto and Montréal, and closer to $850 from Vancouver.

By train

If you don't mind taking your time getting to New England, then an **Amtrak train** (☎1-800/USA-RAIL, ⊛www.amtrak.com) may be just the thing. Train travel is most convenient for those traveling to New England from Washington, DC and

Airports in New England

Connecticut
Bradley International Airport I-91, Exit 40, Windsor Locks (near Hartford)
☎860/292-2000 or 1-888/624/1533, ⊛www.bradleyairport.com.

Maine
Portland International Jetport 1001 Westbrook St, Portland ☎207/874-8877,
⊛www.portlandjetport.org.

Massachusetts
Barnstable Municipal Airport 480 Barnstable Rd, Hyannis ☎508/775-2020,
⊛www.flycapeair.com.
Logan International Airport East Boston ☎1-800/235-6426, ⊛www.massport.com.

New Hampshire
Manchester–Boston Airport Brown Avenue, Manchester ☎603/624-6556, ⊛www
.flymanchester.com.

Rhode Island
T.F. Green Airport, 2000 Post Rd, Warwick ☎401/737-8222 or 1-888/268-7222,
⊛www.pvdairport.com.

Vermont
Burlington International Airport 1200 Airport Drive, South Burlington ☎802/863-1889, ⊛www.burlingtonintlairport.com.

New York, though · unless you're taking local commuter services, it's not much less expensive than air travel. The Amtrak trains that serve the Northeast corridor are the fleet's most reliable, which means that they sometimes stick to their official schedules. **Fares** from New York to Boston range from $118 to $224 round-trip – trains that leave late at night are the least expensive, while the Acela Express is the most expensive, but will shave only about forty minutes off the normal travel time (4hr 30min). From Washington, DC, the regular train runs just shy of eight hours ($236 round-trip) while the Acela Express takes 6hr 30min ($338 round-trip). Amtrak does offer several good-value **rail passes** that allow unlimited travel in certain areas, and the website also offers special **deals** and weekly sales.

Visitors approaching the region **from Canada** on Via Rail (☎1-888/842-7245, ⊛www.viarail.ca) can connect with Amtrak in Toronto or Montréal. The rail journey can take anywhere from twelve to twenty hours from Toronto and Montréal, and over three days from Vancouver. Fares start at around Can$250 round-trip from the closer points.

By bus

Considering how expensive rail travel can be in the US, getting to New England by **bus** can be an appealing option. **Greyhound** (☎1-800/231-2222, ⊛www.greyhound.com) has an extensive network of destinations in New England. As with air and train routes, Boston is the best-served destination, especially if you're coming from New York or Washington, DC; trips typically take 4hr 30min from New York and 10hr 30min from DC; round-trip **fares** cost around $70 and $132, respectively (book online for the best deals). Another way to travel from New York to Boston (and vice versa) is via the **Chinatown bus**, which, although a bit dodgy, will get you there very cheaply. The two Chinatown bus companies are Fung Wah (☎212/925-8889, ⊛www.fungwahbus.com) and Lucky Star (☎1-888/881-0887, ⊛www.luckystarbus.com), both of which charge $15 each way, leave hourly from a designated pick-up spot in New York's Chinatown, and arrive at Boston's South Station. The **Bolt Bus** (⊛www.boltbus.com) offers service between New York and Boston, and New York, Philadelphia, and Washington DC, with the added bonus of wireless internet on board. Tickets are cheap ($1–25), especially if booked online beforehand.

Coming **from Canada**, the new wi-fi-enabled NeOn bus runs direct from New York City to Toronto for as little as $1; tickets are only available online (ⓦwww.greyhound.com). Several daily buses from Toronto reach Boston with at least one only changeover, contributing to a minimum fourteen-hour ride (Can$170 round-trip). Buses from Montréal to Boston, with a transfer, run around Can$189 round-trip. In all cases, contact Greyhound (ⓣ1-800/231-2222, ⓦwww.greyhound.ca).

By car

Renting a car in North America involves the usual steps of phoning the local branch, or checking the website, of one of the major companies (see "Getting around," p.24); most have offices at destination airports. Also worth considering are fly-and-drive deals, which give cut-rate (and sometimes free) car rental when buying an air ticket. A car rented in Canada can normally be driven across the border into the US, but you will pay a much higher fee if you do not return it to its country of origin. Most of the larger companies have offices in Canada. To rent a car you must be **over 21** years old, and drivers under 25 are charged a per-day surcharge of approximately $30.

It's very easy to get to New England via car, with several **major highways** transecting the region: I-95, which runs along the Atlantic coast south from Canada and circumscribes the Boston area; I-90 (the Massachusetts Turnpike or "Mass Pike"), which approaches Massachusetts from the west; and I-91,

which heads south from Québec and rims Vermont and New Hampshire before hitting Amherst, Massachusetts, and Hartford, CT. Drivers planning on hitting downtown Boston during their New England tour should be prepared for its confusing road layout, poor signage, and crazy drivers. Other than that, driving should be straightforward.

From the UK and Ireland

There are plenty of direct flights **from Britain and Ireland** to Boston, fewer to other regional cities. Keep in mind that the first place the plane lands on American soil is your point of entry into the US, which means you'll have to collect your bags and go through customs and immigration, even if you're continuing on to other regional points.

Fares hover around £250 in low season (Nov to mid-Dec & Jan–March), £350 in spring and fall, and over £400 in high season (May–Sept). Flights from Ireland (Shannon) can ring in at over £550.

From Australia, New Zealand, and South Africa

There are no direct flights to Boston **from Australia** or **New Zealand** – most visitors from those countries reach the eastern US by way of cities such as Los Angeles and San Francisco. However you do it, it's a long trip (about 14hr to the West Coast, and another 6hr to New England).

Fares to LA and San Francisco from eastern **Australian** cities cost the same, while from Perth they're about Aus$400 more. There are daily nonstop flights from Sydney to LA and San Francisco on United Airlines and to LA on Qantas, for around Aus$1800 in low season (Oct–Nov & Jan–March); figure another Aus$1000 to continue

New England driving times

From Boston

To Burlington, VT 3hr 40min
  (216 miles)

To Concord, NH 1hr 15min (68 miles)

To Hartford, CT 1hr 35min (101 miles)

To Hyannis, MA 1hr 20min (70 miles)

To New Haven, CT 2hr 10min
  (137 miles)

To Newport, RI 1hr 15min
  (71 miles)

To Northampton, MA 1hr 35min
  (103 miles)

To Portland, ME 2hr (107 miles)

To Providence, RI 1hr (50 miles)

To Provincetown, MA 3hr (116 miles)

Fly less – stay longer! Travel and climate change

Climate change is perhaps the single biggest issue facing our planet. It is caused by a build-up in the atmosphere of carbon dioxide and other greenhouse gases, which are emitted by many sources – including planes. Already, **flights** account for three to four percent of human-induced global warming: that figure may sound small, but it is rising year on year and threatens to counteract the progress made by reducing greenhouse emissions in other areas.

Rough Guides regard travel as a **global benefit**, and feel strongly that the advantages to developing economies are important, as are the opportunities for greater contact and awareness among peoples. But we also believe in traveling responsibly, which includes giving thought to how often we fly and what we can do to redress any harm that our trips may create.

We can travel less or simply reduce the amount we travel by air (taking fewer trips and staying longer, or taking the train if there is one); we can avoid night flights (which are more damaging); and we can make the trips we do take "climate neutral" via a carbon offset scheme. **Offset schemes** run by climatecare .org, carbonneutral.com, and others allow you to "neutralize" the greenhouse gases that you are responsible for releasing. Their websites have simple calculators that let you work out the impact of any flight – as does our own. Once that's done, you can pay to fund projects that will reduce future emissions by an equivalent amount. Please take the time to visit our website and make your trip climate neutral, or get a copy of the *Rough Guide to Climate Change* for more detail on the subject.

www.roughguides.com/climatechange

on to Boston. There are also several airlines that fly via Asia, which involves either a transfer or stopover in their home cities. The best deal is on JAL (Aus$4000), which includes a night's stopover accommodation in Tokyo or Osaka in the fare. If you don't want to spend the night, Cathay Pacific and Singapore Airlines can get you there, via a transfer in their home cities of Hong Kong and Singapore, for around Aus$1750, while Korean Air (via Seoul) is sometimes a few dollars cheaper.

From **New Zealand**, most flights are out of Auckland (add about NZ$200–250 for Christchurch and Wellington departures). The best deals are on Air New Zealand, to Los Angeles or San Francisco either nonstop or via Honolulu, Fiji, Tonga, or Papeete; or on United Airlines, also nonstop to LA or San Francisco; Air Pacific via Fiji; and Qantas via Sydney (though direct is cheaper). Via Asia, Singapore Airlines offers the best connecting service to LA and San Francisco, while JAL offers another option with either a transfer or stopover in Tokyo. A two-tiered flight (non-stop to the West Coast and nonstop again to Boston) costs NZ$3000–3500 in high season.

Flights from Johannesburg, South Africa generally have one to two layovers (in Paris, Dakar, or New York), with prices hovering at around US$1250 round-trip.

Round-the-world flights

If you intend to take in New England as part of a world trip, a **round-the-world** (RTW) ticket offers the greatest flexibility. In recent years, many of the major international airlines have aligned themselves with one of two globe-spanning networks: the "Star Alliance," which links Air New Zealand, Ansett Australia, United, Lufthansa, Thai, SAS, Varig, and Air Canada; and "One World," which combines routes run by American, British Airways, Canadian Airlines, Cathay Pacific, LAN Chile, and Qantas. Both offer RTW deals with three stopovers in each continental sector you visit, with the option of adding additional sectors relatively cheaply. Fares depend on the number of sectors, but a 21-day advance ticket from Australia to Boston, Burlington, Hartford, or Providence usually starts at around Aus$3000 (low season) for a US–Europe–Asia–home itinerary.

Airlines, agents, and operators

Online booking

🌐 www.expedia.co.uk (in UK), 🌐 www.expedia
.com (in US), 🌐 www.expedia.ca (in Canada)
🌐 www.lastminute.com (in UK)
🌐 www.opodo.co.uk (in UK)
🌐 www.orbitz.com (in US)
🌐 www.travelocity.co.uk (in UK), 🌐 www
.travelocity.com (in US), 🌐 www.travelocity
.ca (in Canada), 🌐 www.travelocity.co.nz (in
New Zealand)
🌐 www.travelonline.co.za (in South Africa)
🌐 www.zuji.com.au (in Australia)

Airlines

Aer Lingus Republic of Ireland ☎ 0818/365 000,
New Zealand ☎ 1649/3083355, South Africa
☎ 1-272/2168-32838, UK ☎ 0870/876 5000,
US & Canada ☎ 1-800/IRISH-AIR; 🌐 www
.aerlingus.com.
Air Canada US & Canada ☎ 1-888/247-2262, UK
☎ 0871/220 1111, Republic of Ireland ☎ 01/679
3958, Australia ☎ 1300/655 767, New Zealand
☎ 0508/747 767; 🌐 www.aircanada.com.
American Airlines and **American Eagle** US
& Canada ☎ 1-800/433-7300, UK ☎ 020/7365
0777, Republic of Ireland ☎ 01/602 0550, Australia
☎ 1800/673 486, New Zealand ☎ 0800/445 442;
🌐 www.aa.com.
Air France US ☎ 1-800/237-2747, Canada
☎ 1-800/667-2747, UK ☎ 0870/142 4343,
Australia ☎ 1300/390 190, South Africa
☎ 0861/340 340; 🌐 www.airfrance.com.
Air New Zealand New Zealand ☎ 0800/737000,
Australia ☎ 0800/132 476, UK ☎ 0800/028
4149, Republic of Ireland ☎ 1800/551 447, US
☎ 1-800/262-1234, Canada ☎ 1-800/663-5494;
🌐 www.airnz.co.nz.
British Airways US & Canada ☎ 1-800/AIRWAYS,
UK ☎ 0844/493 0787, Republic of Ireland
☎ 1890/626 747, Australia ☎ 1300/767 177, New
Zealand ☎ 09/966 9777, South Africa ☎ 114/418
600; 🌐 www.ba.com.
Cape Air US ☎ 1-800/352-0714, 🌐 www
.flycapeair.com.
Continental US & Canada ☎ 1-800/523-3273, UK
☎ 0845/607 6760, Republic of Ireland ☎ 1890/925
252, Australia ☎ 1300/737 640, New Zealand
☎ 09/308 3350, International ☎ 1800/231 0856;
🌐 www.continental.com.
Delta Airlines and **Delta Shuttle** US & Canada
☎ 1-800/221-1212, UK ☎ 0845/600 0950,

Republic of Ireland ☎ 1850/882 031 or 01/407
3165, Australia ☎ 1300/302 849, New Zealand
☎ 09/9772232; 🌐 www.delta.com.
Frontier US ☎ 1-800/432-1359, 🌐 www
.frontierairlines.com.
Japan Airlines (JAL) US & Canada
☎ 1-800/525-3663, UK ☎ 0845/774 7700,
Republic of Ireland ☎ 01/408 3757, Australia
☎ 1-300/525 287 or 02/9272 1111, New Zealand
☎ 0800/525 747 or 09/379 9906, South Africa
☎ 11/214 2560; 🌐 www.jal.com or www
.japanair.com.
JetBlue US ☎ 1-800/538-2583, 🌐 www.jetblue
.com.
Midwest Airlines US ☎ 1-800/452-2022,
🌐 www.midwestairlines.com.
Northwest US ☎ 1-800/225-2525, 🌐 www.nwa
.com.
Qantas US & Canada ☎ 1-800/227-4500, UK
☎ 0845/774 7767, Republic of Ireland ☎ 01/407
3278, Australia ☎ 13 13 13, New Zealand
☎ 0800/808 767 or 09/357 8900, South Africa
☎ 11/441 8550; 🌐 www.qantas.com.
Southwest US ☎ 1-800/435-9792, 🌐 www
.southwest.com.
United US ☎ 1-800/864-8331, UK ☎ 0845/844
4777, Australia ☎ 13 17 77; 🌐 www.united.com.
US Airways, Shuttle, and **Express** US & Canada
☎ 1-800/428-4322, UK ☎ 0845/600 3300,
Republic of Ireland ☎ 1890/925 065; 🌐 www
.usair.com.
Virgin Atlantic US ☎ 1-800/821-5438, UK
☎ 0870/574 7747, Australia ☎ 1300/727 340,
South Africa ☎ 11/340 3400; 🌐 www
.virgin-atlantic.com.

Travel agents

Adventure World Australia ☎ 02/8913 0755,
🌐 www.adventureworld.com.au; New Zealand
☎ 09/524 5118, 🌐 www.adventureworld.co.nz.
Agents for a vast array of international adventure
travel companies that operate trips to every
continent.
Airtech US ☎ 212/219-7000, 🌐 www.airtech.com.
Stand-by seat broker.
American Holidays Northern Ireland ☎ 028/9031
0000, Republic of Ireland ☎ 01/673 3840; 🌐 www
.american-holidays.com. Offers tour packages from
Ireland to North America.
Bon Voyage UK ☎ 0800/316 3012, 🌐 www
.bon-voyage.co.uk. Tailor-made trips to the US.
British Airways Holidays UK ☎ 0870/850
9850, 🌐 www.baholidays.co.uk. Packages and
independent itineraries for both long trips and
shorter breaks.

ebookers UK ☎0800/082 3000, Republic of Ireland ☎01/488 3507; ⊛www.ebookers.com. Low fares on an extensive selection of scheduled flights and package deals.
Exodus US ☎1-800/843-4272, UK ☎020/8675 5550; ⊛www.exodus.co.uk. Adventure and activity-oriented vacation packages focusing on low-impact tourism.
Explore Worldwide UK ☎0870/013 1537, ⊛www.explore.co.uk. Hundreds of group tours, including everything from short weekend trips to activity-oriented family adventures.
North America Travel Service UK ☎020/7569 6710, ⊛www.northamericatravelservice.co.uk. Luxurious travel packages. Their 13-day "Grand Autumn Tour" takes in Boston and some of New England's prettiest spots (beginning at £2415 per person).
North South Travel UK ☎01245/608 291, ⊛www.northsouthtravel.co.uk. Friendly, competitive travel agency, offering discounted fares worldwide;

profits are used to support projects in the developing world, especially sustainable tourism.
STA Travel US ☎1-800/777-0112 or 1-800/781-4040, Canada ☎1-888/427-5639, UK ☎0870/1630 026, Australia ☎1300/733 035, New Zealand ☎0508/782 872; ⊛www.statravel .com. Worldwide specialists in independent travel; also student IDs, travel insurance, car rental, railpasses, and more.
Trailfinders UK ☎0845/058 5858, Republic of Ireland ☎01/677 7888, Australia ☎1300/780 212; ⊛www.trailfinders.com. One of the best-informed and most efficient agents for independent travelers.
Trek America US ☎1-800/TREKUSA, ⊛www .trekamerica.com; UK ☎0845/330-6095, ⊛www .trekamerica.co.uk. Trekking company geared to 18–38-year-olds offering one- to two-week day-camping and hiking tours through the eastern US (from $800).

Getting around

Although rural areas can be nearly impossible to access if you don't have a car, getting from one city to another in New England on public transportation is seldom much of a problem – good bus links and reasonable, though limited, train services are nearly always available. If you want to visit every small town, though, or be able to travel without being tied to a schedule, renting your own car is highly recommended.

By car

Driving is the best way to get around New England. Away from the cities and major towns, many places are almost impossible to reach without your own wheels. National and state parks and forests, especially, are served infrequently by public transportation, usually only as far as the main visitors' center.

Drivers wishing to **rent cars** should be over 21 and are supposed to have held their licenses for at least one year (though this is rarely checked); people **under 25 years old** but older than 21 will have to pay higher rates. In general, $300 a week is a fairly standard base rate for a subcompact. Always be sure to get free **unlimited mileage**, and be aware that returning the car in a different city from the

one in which you rented it can incur a charge. Also, don't automatically go for the cheapest rate, as there's some difference in the quality of cars from company to company; industry leaders like Hertz and Avis tend to have newer, lower-mileage cars, and they also may have fewer hidden add-on charges than firms that initially seem less expensive.

Car-rental agencies

Alamo US ☎1-800/522-9696, ⊛www.alamo.com.
Avis US ☎1-800/331-1212, Canada ☎1-800/879-2847, UK ☎0844/581 8181, Republic of Ireland ☎021/428 1111, Australia ☎13 63 33 or 02/9353 9000, New Zealand ☎09/526 2847 or 0800/655 111, South Africa ☎11/923 3660; ⊛www.avis.com.

Budget US ☎1-800/527-0700, Canada
☎1-800/268-8900, UK ☎0870/156 5656,
Australia ☎1300/362 848, New Zealand
☎0800/283 438; ⓦwww.budget.com.
Dollar US ☎1-800/800-3665, Canada
☎1-800/229 0984, UK ☎0808/234 7524, Republic
of Ireland ☎1800/515 800; ⓦwww.dollar.com.
Enterprise Rent-a-Car US & Canada
☎1-800/261-7331, UK ☎0870/350 3000,
Republic of Ireland ☎1890/227 999; ⓦwww
.enterprise.com.
Hertz US & Canada ☎1-800/654-3131, UK
☎0870/040 9000, Republic of Ireland ☎01/870
5777, Australia ☎13 30 39, New Zealand
☎0800/654 321, South Africa ☎21/935 4800;
ⓦwww.hertz.com.
National US ☎1-800/227-7368, UK ☎0870/400
4588, Australia ☎0870/600 6666, New Zealand
☎03/366 5574; ⓦwww.nationalcar.com.
Thrifty US & Canada ☎1-800/847-4389, UK
☎01494/751 540, Republic of Ireland ☎1800/515
800, Australia ☎1300/367 227, New Zealand
☎0800/737 070; ⓦwww.thrifty.com.

Motoring organizations

American Automobile Association ☎1-800/222-
4357, ⓦwww.aaa.com. Each state has its own club
– check the website for local addresses and phone
numbers.
Canadian Automobile Association
☎613/247-0117, ⓦwww.caa.ca. Each region has
its own club – check the website for local addresses
and phone numbers.

Roads

There are several types of roads in New
England. The best for covering long
distances quickly are the straight, fast
interstate highways, usually at least six
lanes and always prefixed by "I" (eg, I-95);
these are marked on maps by a red, white,
and blue shield bearing the number. Even-
numbered interstates run east–west and
those with odd numbers run north–south.
Though most roads are free, some of
the more traveled highways, known as
turnpikes, charge anywhere from $0.75 to
several dollars to cruise down their broad
lanes. You'll be warned in advance that a
toll booth is coming. A grade down are the
state highways (eg, Hwy-1) and the US
highways (eg, US-395). Some major roads in
cities are technically state highways but are
better known by their local names (Hwy-1

Hitchhiking

The usual advice given to **hitchhikers**
is that they should use their common
sense; in fact, of course, common
sense should tell anyone that
hitchhiking in the US is a **bad idea**.
We do not recommend it under any
circumstances; nor do we recommend
picking up hitchhikers.

in Brunswick, Maine, for instance, is better
known as Mill St). In rural areas, you'll also
find much smaller county roads, which are
known as routes (eg, Rte-1).

Rules of the road

UK, Canadian, Australian, and New Zealand
citizens can all drive in the US provided they
have a regular driver's license; International
Driving Permits are not required.

Although the law says that drivers must
keep up with the flow of traffic, which is often
hurtling along at 75 miles per hour (mph), the
maximum speed limit in New England is
65mph, with lower posted limits – usually
around 25–35mph in built-up areas. The
default speed limit in most cities is 25mph,
so if you don't see a sign, you'd probably do
well to adhere to this limit.

If you are flagged down by the police, don't
get out of the car, and don't reach into the
glove compartment (the officer may think you
are reaching for a gun). Simply sit still with
your hands on the wheel. If you are signaled
to pull over at night on a deserted stretch
of road, know that it's within your rights to
proceed to the next well-lit area before pulling
over; you should put your right turn signal on
(indicating you intend to pull over) and drive
slowly until you feel comfortable about a
place to stop.

By air

New England is small enough that traveling
around by **plane** is generally unnecessary.
It can be useful for long trips – from Providence, RI to Burlington, VT, for example – but
in those cases the routes are usually not well
traveled so the tickets can be expensive. At
off-peak times, flights between Boston and
Portland, ME, cost around $200.

By train

Amtrak's four main routes in New England provide decent, though limited, **rail** connections between the few major cities in western New England, as well as some of the minor ones. Probably the prettiest route is the *Vermonter*, which winds from Washington, DC through New York City and then western Connecticut, western Massachusetts, and all the way north through Vermont. The other major north–south Amtrak routes in and around New England – the *Ethan Allen* (Washington, DC to Rutland, VT) and the *Acela Regional* (Washington, DC to Boston, MA) – are almost as scenic, as is the *Downeaster* (Boston, MA to Portland, ME). There's also a route called the *Lake Shore Limited* that travels the length of Massachusetts (from Chicago, IL) to Boston.

For all information on Amtrak fares and schedules in the US, call the toll-free number (☎1-800/USA-RAIL) or visit the Amtrak website (⊛www.amtrak.com). International travelers can cut fares greatly by using one of several Amtrak **rail passes**, which give unlimited travel within certain time periods. All comers should look out for the special deals and sales advertised on the website.

By bus

If you're traveling on your own, and making a lot of stops, **buses** are by far the cheapest way to get around. There are several main bus companies (see below) linking the major cities and many smaller towns in New England. Out in the country, buses are fairly scarce, sometimes appearing only once a day, so you'll need to plot your route with care. As for **fares**, bus tickets are consistently less than train or airline tickets.

To avoid possible hassle, lone female travelers in particular should take care to sit as near to the driver as possible, and to arrive during **daylight hours**, as many bus stations are in fairly unsafe areas. It used to be that any sizeable community would have a bus station; in some places, now, the post office, a convenience store, or a gas station doubles as the bus stop and ticket office.

New England bus companies

C&J Trailways ☎1-800/258-7111 or 603/430-1100, ⊛www.ridecj.com. Service from Logan Airport and Boston's South Station through northern MA to southern NH.

Concord Coach Lines ☎1-800/639-3317, ⊛www.concordcoachlines.com. Good coverage of New Hampshire and Maine, with connecting services to Logan Airport.

Greyhound ☎1-800/231-2222, ⊛www .greyhound.com. Nationwide coverage; the contact number can fill you in on routes, times, and addresses of local terminals.

Peter Pan ☎1-800/343-9999, ⊛www .peterpanbus.com. Relatively frequent and extensive service between Boston and New York, via Springfield and Hartford as well as service to Rhode Island and New Hampshire.

Plymouth and Brockton ☎508/746-0378, ⊛www.p-b.com. Comprehensive service to Cape Cod from Boston.

Cycling

If you have the stamina for it, **cycling** is one of the best ways to see New England. Some of the larger cities have cycle lanes and local buses equipped to carry bikes (strapped to the outside), and even the bustle of Boston can be easily escaped in half an hour by bicycle.

Bus passes

One good bus deal is the **Greyhound Discovery Pass**, offering unlimited travel within a set time limit: most travel agents can oblige or you can order online at ⊛www.discoverypass.com. They come in several durations, all between seven days ($329) and sixty days ($750). The first time you use your pass (which becomes the commencement date of the ticket), it will be dated by the ticket clerk, and your destination is written on a page that the driver will tear out and keep as you board the bus. Repeat this procedure for every subsequent journey. Also, make sure to check timetables other than Greyhound's – the pass is valid on some participating lines like Peter Pan and Bonanza.

Bikes can be **rented** for around $25 a day, or $90–100 a week, from most bike stores; local visitors' centers will have details (we've listed rental options where applicable throughout the *Guide*). Many states also have **rail trails**, old railway routes that have been paved and turned into bike paths. These are great because they are scenic and tend to take steep hills gradually. A good source for cycling **information** in New England, including trail and bike store locations, is the New England Mountain Bike Association (℡1-800/576-3622, ⓦwww.nemba.org). Meanwhile, the Adventure Cycling Association (℡406/721-1776 or 1-800/755-2453, ⓦwww.adventurecycling.org) sells detailed biking maps of routes that travel along smaller roads and bike paths, as well as information about camping en route.

Accommodation

Accommodation standards in New England are high, and costs inevitably form a significant proportion of the expenses for any trip to the area. It is possible to haggle, however, especially in the chain motels, and if you're on your own, you can possibly pare down costs by sleeping in dormitory-style hostels. However, groups of two or more will find it only a little more expensive to stay in the far more plentiful budget motels and hotels. By contrast, the lone traveler will have a hard time of it: "singles" are usually double rooms at only slightly reduced rates. Prices quoted by hotels and motels are almost always for the whole room rather than for each person using it.

Hotel and motel rooms in New England in general adhere to a uniform standard of comfort – double beds with bathroom, TV, and phone. A growing number of New England hotels provide a **complimentary breakfast**. Generally, this will be no more than a cup of coffee and a doughnut, but in cities and business hotels it is increasingly likely to comprise fruit, cereals, muffins, and toast, even made-to-order entrees in the pricier spots. In most places you'll be able to find cheap hotels and motels simply by keeping your eyes open – they're usually advertised by roadside signs. Alternatively, there are a number of chains whose rooms start at $60–70, such as Econolodge, Motel 6, and Travelodge. Mid-priced options include Best Western, Howard Johnson, and Ramada – though if you can afford to pay this much ($80–140) there's normally somewhere nicer to stay.

Most hotels require a credit card to make a reservation, though this does not mean that you'll have to pay by card. Since cheap accommodation in the cities and on the popular sections of the coast is snapped up fast, book ahead whenever possible. Reservations are only held until 5 or 6pm unless you've told the hotel that you'll be arriving late.

Discounts and reservations

During off-peak periods many motels and hotels struggle to fill their rooms, so you may be able to negotiate a few dollars off the asking price. If possible, see if you can find a better price on a search engine (such as ⓦwww.expedia.com or ⓦwww.kayak.com) before your arrival. Also, note that room rates range wildly depending on the season and the day – it's worth calling to investigate the current price. Staying in the same place for more than one night may bring further reductions. Hotels may also make their rooms available to online booking consolidators like

Accommodation price codes

Throughout this book, accommodation has been assigned a price code according to the average cost of the least expensive **double room** in high season. Note that the high and low seasons for tourists vary across the region, so there can be a great deal of fluctuation in room rates – for example, in areas like the Berkshires, prices can rise drastically during the popular fall foliage season; as well, many establishments charge more on Friday and Saturday nights, while big-city business hotels often slash their prices on weekends. We've listed specific prices rather than codes for hostels, apartments, and campgrounds. Only where we explicitly say so do the price codes include local taxes, which range from seven to thirteen percent.

❶ $30 and under
❷ $31–50
❸ $51–75

❹ $76–100
❺ $101–125
❻ $126–150

❼ $151–175
❽ $176–250
❾ $251 and above

hotels.com, where the rate can be much lower than even the hotel is allowed to offer. For motels in particular, note also that you might be able to get a **discount** by presenting a membership card from a motoring organization like AAA (see p.25).

B&Bs

Bed-and-breakfast inns (B&Bs) are ubiquitous in New England – nearly every town with any tourist traffic at all will have one. Typically, **B&Bs** are restored old buildings with fewer than ten rooms and plenty of antique furnishings, although recent years have seen a range of chic and contemporary B&Bs opening up throughout New England. **Prices** vary greatly: anywhere from $90 to $350 depending on location, season, and facilities. Most fall between $125 and $150 per night for a double, a little less for solo travelers.

New England B&B contacts

B&B Cape Cod ☎1-800/541-6226, ⓦwww .bedandbreakfastcapecod.com. A good resource, but does not allow you to contact B&Bs directly.
B&B Online ☎1-800/215-7365, ⓦwww.bbonline .com. A good selection of New England lodging is organized geographically on this nationwide site.
Boston Area B&B Reservations ☎617/964-1606 or 1-800/832-2632, ⓦwww.bbreserve.com. Includes limited listings for Maine, New Hampshire, and Vermont, as well as Boston.
New England Inns and Resorts ☎603/964-6689, ⓦwww.newenglandinnsandresorts.com. Represents properties all over New England.
Nutmeg B&B ☎1-800/727-7592, ⓦwww .nutmegbb.com. Connecticut listings only.

Passport to New England ☎1-800/981-3275, ⓦwww.passporttonewengland.com. A partnership of upscale regional inns.

Hostels

At an average of $25–30 per night per person, **hostels** are the cheapest accommodation option in New England other than camping. There are three main kinds of hostel-type accommodation in the US: YMCA/YWCA (known as "Ys"), offering accommodation for both sexes or, in a few cases, women only; official HI-AYH (☎301/495-1240, ⓦwww .hiusa.org); and the growing AAIH (American Association of Independent Hostels) organization. There is a fairly good concentration of hostels in New England, at least compared with the rest of the US. HI-AYH are the most prevalent, though there are many unaffiliated hostels as well. For a complete listing of the hostels in the region, check out ⓦwww .hostels.com.

Prices in **YMCAs** range from around $25 for a dormitory bed to $40 for a single or double room. You'll find **HI-AYH** hostels (the prefix is usually shortened to HI in listings) in major cities and popular hiking areas, including national and state parks, mostly in Vermont and Massachusetts. Most urban hostels have 24-hour access, while rural ones may have a curfew and limited daytime hours. Rates at HI hostels range from around $25–30 for a dorm bed and around $45 for a private room. The **independent hostels** in the AAIH group are usually a little less expensive than their HI counterparts, and have fewer rules. The quality is not as consistent, though; some can be quite poor, while others are absolutely wonderful. There is often no curfew and, at some, a party atmosphere is encouraged.

One good New England **hosteling information service** is the Eastern New England Council in Boston (☎617/718-7990, ⓦwww.usahostels.org), which can tell you which hostel you're nearest, whether it's open or booked, and also sell you a membership card.

Youth hostel information

In the US and Canada

Hosteling International–American Youth Hostels ☎301/495-1240, ⓦwww.hiusa.org
Hosteling International Canada ☎1-800/663-5777 or 613/237-7884, ⓦwww.hihostels.ca.

In the UK and Ireland

Hostelling International Northern Ireland ☎028/9032 4733, ⓦwww.hini.org.uk.
Irish Youth Hostel Association ☎01/830 4555, ⓦwww.anoige.ie.
Scottish Youth Hostel Association ☎0870/155 3255, ⓦwww.syha.org.uk.
Youth Hostel Association (YHA) England and Wales ☎01629/592700, ⓦwww.yha.org.uk.

In Australia and New Zealand

Australia Youth Hostels Association ☎02/9261 1111, ⓦwww.yha.com.au.
Youth Hostelling Association New Zealand ☎0800/278 299 or 03/379 9970, ⓦwww.yha.co.nz.

Camping

New England **campgrounds** range from the primitive (a flat piece of ground that may or may not have a water tap) to places more like open-air hotels, with shops, pools, game rooms, restaurants, and washing facilities. Naturally enough, **prices** vary accordingly, from nothing for the most basic plots to $55 a night for something comparatively luxurious. Call ahead for **reservations** at the bigger parks, or anywhere at all during national holidays or the summer. Many save a number of sites for same-day arrivals, but to claim one of these you should plan on arriving early in the day – before 9am to be safe.

Contact the local chamber of commerce for information on land usage and **wilderness camping**. In other designated public lands you can camp rough pretty much anywhere you want provided you first obtain a wilderness permit (either free or about $5) and, usually, a campfire permit; these can be procured from the nearest park ranger's office. You should also take the proper precautions: carry sufficient food and drink to cover emergencies, inform the park ranger of your travel plans, and watch out for bears and the effect your presence can have on their environment. For more information on these undeveloped regions – which are often protected within either national parks or national forests – contact the **US Forest Service** (☎1-800/832-1355, ⓦwww.fs.fed.us).

Reserving a campground

Kampgrounds of America (KOA; ☎406/248-7444, ⓦwww.koakampgrounds.com) privately oversees many **campgrounds** all over New England; although these are largely for RVs, there are one-room "Kabins" available at almost all their sites. More tent-friendly (and aesthetically pleasing) sites can be found in the state parks and public lands. To reserve a site at public campgrounds, contact the individual state's division of parks and recreation: CT (☎860/424-3200), MA (☎1-877/422-6762), ME (☎207/287-3821), NH (☎603/271-3556), RI (☎401/222-2632), and VT (☎802/879-6565). The Appalachian Mountain Club (AMC) also has some very well-maintained camping areas and mountain huts; call their headquarters in Boston for reservation information (☎617/523-0655, ⓦwww.outdoors.org).

Food and drink

Food in New England is difficult to categorize, though there is certainly a tradition of hearty Yankee cooking permeating the landscape.

Traditional American cooking – burgers, steaks, salads, and baked potatoes – is served all over New England. **Seafood** is particularly abundant along the coast, where it is prepared in both upscale expensive gourmet restaurants and no-nonsense harborside shacks. Many fishing towns in New England have large **Portuguese** and growing Brazilian communities – Portuguese restaurants in these areas are on the whole authentic and inexpensive.

In terms of regional specialities, the seafood is excellent and well loved, and wherever you go you'll be tempted by fresh oysters, clams, fish, and lobsters. Any of these ocean creatures can also be part of a traditional New England **clambake**, a delicious way of enjoying the fruits of the sea. Keep an eye out, too, for the prized lobster roll – lobster meat mixed with a bit of mayonnaise and lemon, and served on a grilled hot-dog bun – and **clam chowder**, a thick, creamy shellfish soup. Signature Boston baked beans, a salty stewed mix of pork, onions, and beans, are still found on more nostalgic New England menus. The region also offers a vast range of **produce**: corn, apples, pears, strawberries, blueberries, peaches, plums, and cranberries are all grown locally. **Maple syrup** is a big product here and every state produces at least some amount of the sweet liquid. Vermont is probably the most culinarily distinct of the states, and is well known for its quality **dairy** products: cow, sheep, and goat's cheese, milk, and yogurt – not to mention Ben and Jerry's ice cream (see p.364). For more about the region's culinary delights, see the "*New England food and drink*" color section, following p.368.

Meals

For the price (on average $7–12), **breakfast** is the best-value and most filling meal of the day. Diners, cafés, and coffeeshops all serve breakfast until at least 11am, with some places serving it all day. Between 11am and 3pm look for excellent-value **lunchtime set menus** – Chinese, Indian, and Thai restaurants frequently have help-yourself buffets, and many Japanese restaurants give you a chance to eat sushi much more cheaply ($10–12) than usual. Most diners are decently priced all the time: you can get a good-sized lunch for $8–10. Along the coast, many seafood restaurants and shacks sell all manner of breaded and fried fish and various shellfish. Country inns and B&Bs that serve dinner are good bets for high-quality food in a romantic setting; many have professional chefs on staff.

Drinking

Bars and cocktail lounges are prevalent across New England. The bars in Boston are particularly lively, while other younger and more tourist-driven towns like Portland, ME, Portsmouth, NH, Burlington, VT, and Providence, RI, hold most of New England's worthwhile pubs and microbreweries.

To **buy and consume alcohol** in the US you need to be 21, and in New England you will be asked for ID even if you look much older. Bars and nightclubs are likely to be fully licensed, while restaurants may only have half-licenses allowing them to serve beer and wine but no hard liquor. It is sometimes permitted to take your own wine into a restaurant, where the corkage fee will be around $10. You can buy beer, wine, or spirits more cheaply and easily in supermarkets, delis, and liquor stores.

An alternative to drinking dens, **coffeeshops** play a vibrant part in New England's social scene. It's worth looking beyond the ubiquitous *Starbucks* to smaller, local joints, where the ambience will be more enjoyable and the coffee most likely much better. In larger towns and cities, cafés will boast of the quality of the roast, and offer a full array of cappuccinos, lattes, and the like. Herbal teas and light snacks are often on the menu, too.

The media

Since being the birthplace of America's first newspaper, *Publick Occurrences*, which was published in Boston in 1690, New England today continues to have a number of well-executed, if generally left-leaning, media strongholds. You'll find local listings in a slew of leftist weeklies, while the local paper of record is the liberal *Boston Globe* (Ⓦ www.bostonglobe.com).

Newspapers

Boston's oldest **newspaper**, the *Boston Globe* ($0.75; Ⓦ www.bostonglobe.com) remains the region's best general daily; its fat Sunday edition ($2.50) includes substantial sections on art, culture, and lifestyle. The *Boston Herald* ($0.75; Ⓦ www.bostonherald .com) is the *Globe's* conservative tabloid competitor and is best for getting your gossip and local sports coverage fix. The two stalwarts are complemented by smaller papers like the *Hartford Courant* (Ⓦ www .courant.com), the *Portland Press Herald* (Ⓦ www.pressherald.com), Vermont's *Seven Days* (Ⓦ www.7dvt.com), and the *Providence*

Journal (Ⓦ www.projo.com), which tend to excel at local coverage, but typically rely on agencies such as the Associated Press (AP) for foreign and even national news stories.

Radio

Radio stations are abundant, and run up and down both the FM and AM dials; the latter is strong on news and talk, while the former carries some of the region's best stations, including National Public Radio (NPR) and college broadcasts of jazz, classical, world music, and other genres neglected by mainstream radio.

Festivals

Someone, somewhere is always celebrating something in New England, although, apart from national holidays, few festivities are shared throughout the entire region. Instead, there is a multitude of local events: arts-and-crafts shows, county fairs, ethnic celebrations, music festivals, parades, and more. Local tourist offices can provide full lists, or you can just phone ahead to the visitors' center in a particular region to ask what's coming up. The calendar below provides an overview of unusual or particularly noteworthy area festivals. For information on public holidays, see p.46.

January	February
Stowe Winter Carnival Stowe, VT, third week; ☎ 1-800/GOSTOWE, Ⓦ www.stowewintercarnival .com. Hard-partying celebration of all things winter – also includes movie nights, ice carving, and a snow volleyball tournament.	**Railroad Show** West Springfield, MA, first weekend (or last weekend in Jan); ☎ 860/243-0811, Ⓦ www.railroadhobbyshow .com. An extravaganza of trains, both model and real.

Winter Festival Burlington, VT, first weekend; ☏802/864-0123, ⊛www.enjoyburlington.com. Ice sculptures, a penguin plunge (volunteers brave an icy Lake Champlain for charity), and general merry-making.

Winter Festival Newport, RI, second week; ☏401/847-7666, ⊛www.newportevents.com. Discounts at area shops and restaurants with the purchase of a festival button, plus hayrides, concerts, and ice sculpting.

March

Mardi Gras Bretton Woods, NH, weekend before Ash Wed (sometimes in Feb); ☏1-800/314-1752. A masquerade ball held in the historic *Mount Washington Hotel* (see p.441) is the apex of this traditional celebration.

Saints and Spirits Celebration Rockport/ Camden, ME, mid-March; ☏207/236-4404). St Patrick's Day parties and Irish singalongs meant to dispel the "mud season blues."

St Patrick's Day Parade South Boston, MA, March 17; ☏617/258-7955. Very Irish South Boston does Saint Patty proud with spectators, families, and pub-crawlers alike all turning the streets into a sea of green.

April

Boston Marathon Boston, MA, third Mon; ☏617/236-1652, ⊛www.bostonmarathon.org. Perhaps the premier running event in the US; really fun for spectators as well.

Vermont Maple Festival St Albans, VT, last full weekend; ☏802/524-5800, ⊛www .vtmaplefestival.org. Maple-related exhibits/ demonstrations, food contests, and, of course, pancake breakfasts.

May

Moose Mainea Greenville, ME, mid-May to mid-June; ☏207/695-2702. Moose-watching, boat and bike races, and family activities.

Open Studios VT (statewide), last weekend; ☏802/223-3380. Artists open their homes and studios to the public.

June

Ethan Allen Days Manchester, VT, mid-June; ☏802/362-1788. Revolutionary battle enactments along Vermont's Ethan Allen Highway (Rte-7A).

Revels North Norwich, VT, late June; ☏1-866/556-3083, ⊛www.revelsnorth.org. Music, food, and puppets from 5pm until dark on the Sat closest to the longest day of the year (June 21).

July

Fourth of July Celebration Boston, MA ☏1-888/484-7677, ⊛www.july4th.org. The largest Fourth of July celebration in the country. The main attraction is a Boston Pops concert at the Hatch Shell, accompanied by an awesome fireworks display. People arrive early in the morning, or even the night before to get prime seats for the concert, while others line up in boats along the Charles River. The Pops perform an identical program (minus the fireworks and the 1812 Overture) on the evening of July 3.

Fourth of July Celebration Bristol, RI; ☏401/253-0445, ⊛www.july4thbristolri.com. The small seaside town operates the oldest Fourth of July festival in the country, including an impressive parade, fireworks, and weeks of events leading up to the occasion.

Moxie Festival Lisbon Falls, ME, second weekend; ☏207/783-2249, ⊛www.moxiefestival.com. Activities, fireworks, and entertainment in celebration of the old-fashioned, odd-tasting soda in a bright orange can.

Revolutionary War Festival Exeter, NH, mid-month; ⊛www.independencemuseum.org. Mock battles by local militia buffs and costumed locals wander the town.

August

Maine Lobster Festival Rockland, ME, first weekend; ☏207/596-0376, ⊛www .mainelobsterfestival.com. Eight tons of boiled lobster. Enough said.

Newport Folk Festival Newport, RI, early Aug; ⊛www.festivalnetwork.com. This three-day festival has been drawing big names since 1959 – it's where Bob Dylan first caused an outrage by going electric. Get tickets in advance.

Narragansett Powwow Charlestown, RI, second weekend; ☏401/364-1100. Native American dancing, music, crafts, and food.

Crane Beach Sand Blast! Ipswich, MA, late Aug; ☏978/356-4351. Sandcastle-building contest.

Union Fair and Blueberry Festival Union, ME, mid-month; ⊛www.unionfair.org. One of the oldest traditional fairs in the state, with music, rides, animals, and blueberry pies.

September

Windjammer Weekend Camden, ME, first weekend; ☏207/236-4404, ⊛www .windjammerweekend.com. Maine's largest windjammer gathering, with a schooner parade, fireworks, contests, and concerts in Camden's beautiful harbor.

The Big E West Springfield, MA, last two weeks of Sept; ☎413/737-2443, ⊛www.thebige .com. The largest fair in the northeast, with agricultural competitions, horse shows, and really good cream puffs.
Oyster Festival Norwalk, CT, second weekend; ☎203/838-9444, ⊛www.seaport.org. Seaport Association extravaganza, featuring tall ships, a juried craft show, and oysters every which way.
World's Fair Tunbridge, VT, second weekend; ☎802/889-5555, ⊛www.tunbridgefair.com. Agricultural fair with butter-churning, cheese-making, sheep-shearing, and the like.

October

Renaissance Faire Hebron, CT, last weekend in Sept and first two weekends in Oct, including Columbus Day; ☎860/478-5954, ⊛www.ctfair.com. King Arthur comes to Connecticut with a small realm of archers, merchants, elves, and court entertainers.
Cranberry Harvest Celebration Wareham, MA, first weekend; ☎508/759-1041 ext. 13, ⊛www .cranberries.org. Harvest festival that includes helicopter rides over the flooded red fields of berries ($25), harvest tours, and cooking demonstrations.
Topsfield Fair Topsfield, MA, first week; ☎978/887-5000, ⊛www.topsfieldfair.org. The country's oldest agricultural fair (dating to 1818) with a bee-keeping show, pie-baking contest, and lots of cute farm animals.
Head of the Charles Regatta Cambridge, MA, mid-month; ☎617/868-6200, ⊛www.hocr.org. One of the largest rowing events in the world, with over six hundred teams participating.
Haunted Happenings Salem, MA, late Oct, ☎877/SALEM-MA, ⊛www.hauntedhappenings .org. Visit the haunted houses and historic hotspots

of this pretty town in the foliage-filled days leading up to Halloween.
Wellfleet OysterFest Wellfleet, MA, second weekend; ⊛www.wellfleetoysterfest.org. This weekend includes concerts, art fairs, shellfish education and tasting, and – oddly – a spelling bee.

November

Antiquarian Book Fair Boston, MA, mid-month; ⊛www.bostonbookfair.com. Tons of old books on display and for sale, plus author panels and signings.
Thanksgiving at Plimoth Plantation Plymouth, MA, fourth Thursday; ☎508/746-1622, ⊛www .plimoth.org. Roast turkey, gravy, mashed potatoes, and all the T-Day trimmings, served near the site of America's first Thanksgiving.

December

Victoria Mansion's Holiday Gala Portland, ME, first weekend; ☎207/772-4841. Gape at the holiday finery decking out one of New England's most dazzling historic homes.
Christmas Town Festival Bethlehem, CT, first weekend; ☎203/266-5557. Caroling, crafts, and the lighting of the town tree by Santa himself.
Christmas in Newport Newport, RI, month-long; ☎401/849-6454, ⊛www.christmasinnewport .org. Events all over town, including concerts, make-your-own-gifts workshops, "The Nutcracker," and the Santa Train.
First Night various cities, Dec 31. Many regional cities host First Night festivals on New Year's Eve, lasting generally all day and into the night. A button will grant you admission into venues throughout the town that have concerts and activities. Check local papers or call city councils for details.

Culture and etiquette

New Englanders are often caricatured as standoffish, but this analysis isn't really fair. While not as exuberant as their warm-weather counterparts, they are a polite, hearty crew, and quick to help a person in need. Small-town New England in particular is quite community-minded – don't be surprised if strangers wave at you, or generally go out of their way to welcome you into the neighborhood fold.

Smoking

Smoking is as much frowned upon in New England as in the rest of the US. Cinemas are non-smoking, smoking is prohibited on public transportation and flights, and all New England states have banned smoking in restaurants and bars. Cigarettes are sold in almost any food shop, convenience store, drugstore, or bar, though a pack of twenty costs upwards of $9.

Tipping

Tipping is expected for all bar and restaurant service. Expect to tip about fifteen percent of the bill before tax to waiters in most restaurants (unless the service is truly wretched) and twenty percent for good service. In the US, this is where most of a waiter's income comes from, and not leaving a fair amount is seen as an insult. About fifteen percent should be added to taxi fares; round up to the nearest $0.50 or dollar, as well. A hotel porter should get $1–2 per bag. Housekeeping gets $1–2 per guest per day (you can leave it under the pillow); valet attendants get $2.

Sports

Boston is the only city in New England with major professional sports teams – excepting football, they have one team in each of the primary sports (baseball, hockey, and basketball); the region's only professional football team is based slightly afield, in Foxboro, MA. Boston is undeniably a sports town, but until fairly recently New England residents suffered a lot of team-related angst – the New England Patriots (football) had never won a Super Bowl, and the beloved Boston Red Sox (baseball) had not won a World Series since 1918. All that has changed now – the Sox clinched their first Series in 86 years in 2004 (and then they won again in 2007), while the Patriots were victorious in the 2002, 2004, and 2005 Super Bowls. The Boston Celtics (basketball) have also had their share of glory lately, winning the 2008 NBA championship. Unfortunately, there's still not a lot of happy news for the Boston Bruins (hockey), although their fan base remains quite strong. Soccer is also catching on – the New England Revolution ("Revs") claimed a championship title at the 2007 US Open and again at SuperLiga 2008.

Baseball

Baseball has a relaxed pace and seemingly Byzantine rules, and is often called "America's pastime." Games are played (162 each season) almost every day from April to September, with the league championships and the World Series, the final best-of-seven playoff, lasting through October. Watching a game is always a pleasant day out, augmented by drinking beer and eating hot dogs; in the unshaded bleachers beyond the outfield, tickets are comparatively cheap ($18–20) and the crowds usually sociable.

Teams and tickets

All Major League Baseball (MLB) teams play in either the **National League** or the **American League**, each of which is split into three divisions, East, Central, and West. New England's Major League team is the American League East **Boston Red Sox**, who play at Fenway Park (see p.103). The Sox's two "farm teams" – minor league clubs that are training grounds for future stars – are also located in New England. The Pawtucket Red Sox (known as the Pawsox) play just minutes from Providence, RI (see p.260), while the Portland Sea Dogs are based out of Maine (see p.473). Tickets to farm team games are almost never sold out, and are much cheaper than Major League games, around $15. **Tickets** to see the Red Sox (☎617/267-9440, ⊛www.redsox.com) cost $20–325 per seat but are difficult to come by, since Red Sox viewing borders on a religious experience for many regional residents.

Football

Football in America attracts the most obsessive and devoted fans of any sport, perhaps because there are fewer games played – only sixteen per team in a season, which lasts through the fall and into mid-winter. Games consist of four fifteen-minute quarters, with a fifteen-minute break at halftime. Time is only counted when play is in progress, however, so matches can take up to three hours to complete. With quick skirmishes and military-like movements up and down the field, the game is ideal for television; never is this more apparent than Sunday or Monday nights, when televised games feature prominently at national bars.

Teams and tickets

All teams play in the **National Football League** (NFL), which divides the teams into two conferences, the National Football Conference (NFC) and the American Football Conference (AFC). The football season begins in late summer and lasts through the end of January. **Tickets** for New England's only team, the Patriots, who play at Gillette Stadium in Foxboro, MA (☎1-800/543-1776, ⊛www.gillettestadium.com), cost $65–169, but are nearly impossible to procure: home games have been sold out for years, and are already pre-sold for years to come. When they are available, ticket sales are handled by Ticketmaster (☎617/931-2000, ⊛www.ticketmaster.com); for more current **information**, call or visit the Patriots' website (☎508/543-1776, ⊛www.patriots.com). If you're desperate to see a live game, you can always try to buy tickets from a scalper outside of the stadium on game day – though be aware that you're sure to pay very inflated prices, and that buying tickets from a scalper is technically illegal.

Basketball

Basketball is played by athletes of phenomenal agility – seven-foot-tall giants who float through the air over a wall of equally tall defenders, seemingly change direction in mid-flight, then slam-dunk the ball in the hoop. Games last for 48 minutes of play time, around two hours total from start to finish.

Teams and tickets

While New England's National Basketball Association (NBA) team, the **Boston Celtics** (☎617/523-6050, ⊛www.nba.com/celtics), had their most iconic days in the 1980s with Larry Bird and company, they have recently seen a hard-earned resurgence with an NBA championship win in 2008. Call Ticketmaster (☎617/931-2000, ⊛www.ticketmaster.com) for available seating and pricing ($10–85). College basketball is also extremely popular in the US. In New England, the University of Connecticut, the University of Massachusetts, Boston College, and Providence College all field perpetually competitive teams. Additionally, in recent years quite a lot of buzz has been generated around the University of Connecticut **women's basketball** team, the Huskies, who were the 2000, 2002, and 2004 NCAA (National Collegiate Athletic Association) champions. **Tickets** cost around $25 for college games. Call each school's athletic department for game and ticket info: UConn ☎1-877/288-2666; UMass ☎413/545-0810; Boston College ☎617/552-GoBC; Providence College ☎401/865-4672.

Ice hockey

Ice hockey is popular in New England, not least because the cold winter weather is so conducive to the sport. Many children grow up playing it and go on to compete at the area's highly competitive colleges and universities; a very small percentage go on to play in the professional **National Hockey League** (NHL). In Boston, college hockey is huge, culminating with February's wildly popular Boston Beanpot (ⓦwww.beanpothockey.com), when men's and women's teams from Boston University,

Boston College, Harvard University, and Northeastern University all compete for city bragging rights.

Teams and tickets

New England has one NHL team, the **Boston Bruins** (ⓦwww.bostonbruins.com), and it's blessed with a strong fan base. **Tickets** start at about $25. Call Ticketmaster (☎617/931-2000) for more information. Tickets cost around $25 for college games. In Boston, call each school's athletic department for game and ticket info: Boston University ☎617/353-GoBU; Harvard University ☎1-877/GO-HARVARD; Boston College ☎617/552-GoBC; Northeastern University ☎617/373-GoNU.

Outdoor activities

New England has some fabulous backcountry and wilderness areas, and there's plenty to keep you out of breath here. The most popular activities include skiing and snowboarding, hiking, fishing and hunting, and camping, though mountain-biking and kayaking fall right behind.

Skiing and snowboarding

Skiing and **snowboarding** are the region's biggest mass-market participant sports, with downhill resorts all over northeastern New England. In fact, the mountains ringing the northern ends of Maine, New Hampshire, and Vermont offer the best skiing in the eastern US. Bigger resorts are more expensive, but they also have the best snow-making facilities, making skiing possible even in cold but dry winters. In **Maine**, Sugarloaf and Sunday River are good spots, while **Vermont's** best are Killington, Mount Snow, Stowe, Stratton, and Okemo. Though **New Hampshire's** mountains are less tall and steep, you can still get a good day of skiing in at Waterville Valley. Smaller mountains can be great learning spots, and are often less crowded. You can **rent** equipment for about $65 a weekend, and lift tickets for the best locations

top out at around $75 a day. The internet is a great source for additional **information**: each state detailed above has its own website with links to mountains and weather reports (ⓦwww.skimaine.com, ⓦwww.skivermont .com, and ⓦwww.skinh.com). A number of companies run all-inclusive ski trips (including transportation, lift tickets, equipment, and accommodation) from the larger cities. In addition to convenience, these outfits usually offer good deals.

A cheaper alternative to downhill is **cross-country skiing**. A number of backcountry ski lodges offer a range of rustic accommodation, equipment rental, and lessons, from as little as $30 a day for skis, boots, and poles, up to about $250 for an all-inclusive weekend tour. For additional information, consult ⓦwww.nensa.net, an exhaustive reference to the sport in New England.

Hiking

Hiking is huge, especially in the northern areas of New England, although you'll find good places to get out into nature just about anywhere outside of the main cities. Most state and federally operated parks maintain good trails, not least the famous **Appalachian Trail**, which originates in Georgia and winds through the backcountry of New England before traversing New Hampshire's White Mountains and terminating in northern Maine.

Wilderness areas start close to the main areas of national parks. There is normally no problem entering the wilderness for day walks, but overnight trips require **wilderness permits**. In peak periods, a quota system operates for the most popular paths, so if there's a hike you specifically want to do, obtain your permit well ahead of time (at least two weeks in advance, or more).

The **Appalachian Mountain Club** (AMC; ☎617/523-0655, ⓦ www.outdoors.org) offers a range of backcountry hikes into otherwise barely accessible parts of the wilderness, with food and guide provided. The hikes take place at all times of the year, cost anywhere from $0 to $800, last from a day to two weeks, and are heavily subscribed, making it essential to book well in advance. Club members pay around $20 less, though you'll also have to pay $50 to join. AMC also has some very well-maintained camping areas and mountain huts; call their headquarters in Boston (see number above) for information on how to make reservations.

Hunting and fishing

Hunting and **fishing** are two of the most popular outdoor pursuits in New England. Duck, deer, and sometimes even the mighty moose are all popular targets, though hunting and gun-carrying laws are strict and you'll need a **permit** (ask the local chamber of commerce how you can get one). Streams, lakes, ponds, and rivers fill up with fishermen in season, though, as with hunting, permits are required and laws are strict.

Camping

Protected areas in the US fall into a number of categories. Most numerous are **state parks**, owned and operated by the individual states. These include state beaches, state historic parks, and state recreational areas, which are often centered around sites of geological or historical importance and not necessarily in rural areas. Daily **fees** are usually less than $5, though beaches in high season can charge as much as $20 per car.

Acadia National Park in Maine (ⓦ www .nps.gov/acad; see p.505) is the only national park in New England, operated by the federal government. The federal government also operates national recreation areas, where campgrounds and equipment-rental outlets are available, though not always in adequate numbers. New England's two **national forests**, the Green Mountain National Forest in Vermont (see p.348) and the White Mountain National Forest in New Hampshire (see p.431), are huge, covering fifty percent of all public land in Vermont and an area larger than the state of Rhode Island in New Hampshire. They are federally administered by the US Forest Service (ⓦ www.fs.fed.us), but with much less protection than national parks. More roads run through national forests, and often there is some limited logging and other land-based industry operated on a sustainable basis.

All the above forms of protected land can contain **wilderness areas**, which aim to protect natural resources in their most native state. In practice this means there's no commercial activity at all; buildings, motorized vehicles, and bicycles are not permitted, nor are firearms and pets. Overnight camping is allowed, but wilderness permits (free to $5) must be obtained in advance from the land management agency responsible. In New England, the White and Green mountains both have large wilderness areas, with only the regions near roads, visitors' centers, and buildings designated as less stringently regulated "front country."

When camping, check that **fires** are permitted before you start one; if they are, use a stove in preference to local materials – in some places firewood is scarce, although you may be allowed to use deadwood. No open fires are allowed in wilderness areas, where you should also try to camp on previously used sites. Where there are no toilets, bury human waste at least four inches into

Outdoor dangers and wildlife

You're likely to meet many kinds of **wildlife** and come upon unexpected **hazards** if you head into the wilderness, but with due care, many potential difficulties can be avoided.

Bugs and pests

Hiking in the foothills should not be problematic but you should check your clothes frequently for **ticks** – blood-sucking, burrowing insects known to carry **Lyme disease**, a health hazard especially in southern New England. One early sign of Lyme disease is a bull's-eye rash that forms around a bite – if you develop one of these, seek treatment immediately. Less harmful but more prevalent are **mosquitoes**; bring along insect repellent to keep them at bay. **Black flies** also come out in force in the warm summer months, and, with a tenacious appetite for human heads, ears, and faces, and a perpetual buzz, can be tremendously annoying; again, carry insect repellent.

Bears

You're highly unlikely to encounter a **bear** in New England, though the American black bear is native to the region, and prevalent in the northern wilderness areas. To reduce whatever likelihood there is of running into one, make noise as you walk. If you do come across a bear, keep calm, and make sure it is aware of your presence by clapping, talking, or making other sounds. Black bears may **charge** with no intention of attacking when attempting to steal food or if they feel threatened. Don't run, just slowly back away.

If a bear visits your camp, it will be after your food, which should be stored in airtight containers. Some campgrounds are equipped with bear-proof lockers, which you are obliged to use to store food when not preparing or eating it. Elsewhere, you should hang both food and garbage from a high branch some distance from your camp. **Never feed a bear**: it will make the bear dependent on humans for food and increase the risk of attacks on humans in the future.

Mountain lions and coyotes

You probably won't run into a **mountain lion** or **coyote** in New England (and if you do, they will probably just slink away), but there have been recent sightings in the region. While both animals generally keep pretty much to themselves, it's possible that they would take an interest in you (or more probably, your pets), as they are known to attack livestock. If by some small chance you run into one of these

the ground and a hundred feet from the nearest water supply and camp. Always carry away your **trash**.

One potential problem while camping is **giardia**, a water-borne protozoan causing an intestinal disease, symptoms of which are diarrhea, abdominal cramps, fatigue, and loss of weight; if you contract it, you will require treatment. To avoid catching it, **never drink** from rivers and streams, however clear creatures and sense they are about to attack, shout, wave your arms, and throw rocks at them.

Moose

Moose, which live in the lush, unpopulated regions near the Canadian border, seldom attack unless provoked. The largest member of the deer family, they can be up to nine feet tall and weigh as much as 1200 pounds. They are mostly active at night, but can also be seen at dusk and dawn, when they may gather to feed near lakes and streams. Though they may seem slow, tame, and passive, moose can be unpredictable, especially during the mating season in September and October. If you happen upon one in the forest, move slowly, avoid making any loud noises, and keep your distance. The best place to view a moose is from your automobile, although you should be careful speeding along northern country roads, especially at night – there are 700 moose-to-vehicle collisions each year in Maine alone.

Poison ivy

Poison ivy is recognizable by its configuration of three leaves to a stem, which can be matte or shiny, green or, in the fall, yellow and red. Plants can be low-growing or can climb as vines to surround trees, and both forms are found in open woods or along stream banks throughout much of New England. It's highly allergenic, so avoid touching it. If you do, washing with strong soap, taking frequent dips in the sea, and applying cortisone cream usually helps to relieve the symptoms; in extreme cases, see a doctor. Whatever you do, don't touch your face or eyes.

Avalanches and meltwaters

In the mountains, your biggest dangers have nothing to do with the flora or fauna. **Spring snows** are common, giving rise to the possibility of **avalanches** and **meltwaters**, which make otherwise simple stream-crossings hazardous. Drowning in fast-flowing meltwater rivers is one of the biggest causes of death in New England wilderness areas. The riverbanks are often strewn with large, slippery boulders, so keep clear unless you are there for river activities. Sudden changes in the weather are also common in mountainous regions, when temperatures can fluctuate wildly and high winds and storms appear out of nowhere; be sure to have warm clothing with you at all times, and check with park rangers before long backcountry treks.

and inviting they may look. Water that isn't from taps should be boiled for at least five minutes, or cleansed with an iodine-based purifier (such as Potable Aqua) or a giardia-rated filter, available from camping or sports stores. Finally, don't use ordinary **soaps** or detergents in lakes and streams; you can buy special ecological soap for washing needs.

Travel essentials

Costs

Accommodation is likely to be your biggest single expense in New England. Few hotel, motel, or B&B rooms cost under $90 a night; you're likely to pay more than $150 for anything halfway decent in a city, and rates in rural areas are not much cheaper. In Boston, it may well be difficult to find anything at all for less than $200 a night. On the plus side, these prices are almost invariably for a double room, so you will save money if you can split the cost with a travel companion. Hostels offering dorm beds – usually for $25–30 a night – are available, but they are by no means everywhere, and save little money for two or more people traveling together. Camping, of course, is cheap (anywhere from free to $25 per night), but rarely practical in the big cities. As for **food**, $25 a day is enough for an adequate life-support diet – while $35–40 is more reasonable.

The rates for **getting around** New England, especially on buses, and to a lesser extent on trains and planes, may look inexpensive on paper, but the distances involved mean that costs soon mount up. For a group of two or more, renting a car can be a very good investment (see "Getting around", p.24), not least because it enables you to stay in the ubiquitous budget motels along the interstate highways instead of relying on expensive downtown hotels.

Remember that a **sales tax** of between five and seven percent is added to virtually everything you buy in stores except for groceries, but will not be included as part of the marked price. Exceptions to this rule are that there is no sales tax in New Hampshire, and clothing is exempt in Massachusetts and Rhode Island. Finally, many accommodations apply a **hotel tax**, which can add as much as fourteen percent to the total bill.

Crime and personal safety

New England is a very safe place to visit. In the more risky areas, common sense and a certain degree of caution should be enough to avoid most problems. For instance, seek local advice before exploring unfamiliar and run-down parts of a city, avoid walking along deserted streets at night, leave valuables in hotel safes, don't leave luggage clearly visible in cars (especially rental cars), and don't resist violent theft.

The **emergency number** for police is ☎911; phone numbers for lost or stolen credit cards, traveler's checks, and the like can be found on p.46.

Identification should be carried at all times. Two pieces will satisfy any inquiry, one of which should have a photo: a driving license, passport, and credit card(s) are your best bets. Not having your license with you while driving is an arrestable offense.

Drugs

Possession of under an ounce of marijuana is a misdemeanor in every New England state except Massachusetts and Maine, and will result in a fine that varies from $200 or $400 in Maine to a whopping $2000 in New Hampshire. Being caught with more than an ounce, however, means facing a criminal charge for dealing, and a possible prison sentence – stiffer if caught anywhere near a school. Of the New England states, Massachusetts has the most lenient stance on marijuana, passing a measure in 2008 that charges people a mere $100 fine if they are caught with less than an ounce. Other drugs are, of course, completely illegal.

Winter driving

Driving in the **winter** is actually less perilous than some may expect. As long as you don't drive *during* a snowstorm or icestorm and take care in the mountains, there's not too much to worry about.

In general, it's smart to check road and weather conditions before setting out and keep your gas tank two-thirds full to prevent the vehicle's fuel line from freezing. Drive slowly, and don't ever slam on the brakes (apply a consistent tapping motion instead), as slamming can cause your vehicle to slide if there's any ice present. Consider getting snow tires or tire chains, or carrying an **emergency car-care kit** on trips in difficult weather conditions. Such a kit typically contains antifreeze, windshield washer fluid, shovel, ice scraper, jumper cables, flares or reflectors, blankets, non-perishable food, and a first-aid kit. Lastly, there are **emergency phones** stationed along freeways at regular intervals, though you won't find these on quieter roads.

Electricity

Electrical outlets use 120V AC, and plugs are generally two-pronged; most foreign-made appliances will need both a voltage converter and a plug adapter. A good reference for all things electric is Ⓦwww.kropla.com/electric.

Entry requirements

Under the **Visa Waiver Program**, citizens of the UK, Ireland, Australia, and New Zealand – as well as citizens of many other countries – visiting the US for a period of less than ninety days at a minimum need an onward return ticket, a machine-readable passport, and a visa waiver form. The latter will be provided either by your travel agency, by the airline before check-in, or on the plane, and must be presented to immigration upon arrival. The same form covers entry across the borders with Canada and Mexico, whether by land or by air. However, those eligible for the scheme must apply for a visa if they intend to work, study, or stay in the country for more than ninety days. Under no circumstances are visitors who have been admitted under the Visa Waiver Program allowed to extend their stays beyond ninety days. Doing so will bar you from future use of the program. The best place for up-to-date US visa information is online at Ⓦwww.travel.state.gov.

Canadian citizens, who have not always needed a passport to get into the US, should have their passports on them when entering the country. If you're planning on staying for more than ninety days, you'll need a visa, which can be applied for by mail through the US embassy or nearest US consulate. If you cross the US border by car, be prepared for US Customs officials to search your vehicle. Remember, too, that without the proper paperwork, Canadians are barred from working in the US.

Prospective visitors from parts of the world not covered by the Visa Waiver Program, and those without machine-readable passports, often require a valid passport and a **non-immigrant visitor's visa**. How you obtain a visa depends on what country you're in and your status when you apply, so telephone the nearest US embassy or consulate (see the list on p.42). You'll need to provide a passport valid for at least six months beyond your intended stay and two passport photos, as well as the appropriate fee. Expect the process to take up to three weeks.

Immigration

The standard immigration regulations apply to all visitors, whether or not they are using the Visa Waiver Program. During the flight, you'll be handed an **immigration form** (and a customs declaration; see below), which must be presented at immigration control once you land. The form requires that you cite your proposed length of stay and to list an address where you'll be staying, at least for your first night. Previously, "touring" was a satisfactory entry here, but since 2001 controls have become more stringent and a verifiable address is now required.

You probably won't be asked unless you look disreputable in the eyes of the official on duty, but you should be able to prove that you have a **return air ticket** (if flying in) and enough money to support yourself while in the US; anyone revealing the slightest intention of working while in the country is likely to be refused admission. Around $300–400 a week is usually considered sufficient to support yourself – waving a credit card or two may do the trick. You may also experience difficulties if you admit to being HIV-positive or having AIDS or TB. Part of the immigration form will be attached to your passport, where it must stay until you leave, when an immigration or airline official will detach it.

Customs

Upon arrival in the US, **customs** officers will take your customs declaration and check to see if you're carrying any banned items, such as animals, plants, fresh foods, and so on.

You'll also be asked if you've visited a farm in the last month – if you have, you may well have your shoes taken away for inspection. As well as food and anything agricultural, it's prohibited to carry into the country any articles from Afghanistan, Cuba, Iran, Libya, North Korea, Serbia, and Sudan, or obscene publications, drug paraphernalia, lottery tickets, and switchblades. Prescription drugs should be labeled and accompanied by a prescription or doctor's note explaining that the drug is for use under his or her direction.

US embassies and consulates abroad

Australia

ⓦ usembassy-australia.state.gov
Canberra Moonah Place, Yarralumla, ACT 2600 ⓣ 02/6214 5600, ⓕ 6214 5970.
Melbourne 553 St Kilda Rd, PO Box 6722, Vic 3004 ⓣ 03/9526 5900, ⓕ 9510 4646.
Perth 16 St George's Terrace, 4th floor, WA 6000 ⓣ 08/9202 1224, ⓕ 9231 9444.
Sydney MLC Centre, 59th floor, 19–29 Martin Place, NSW 2000 ⓣ 02/9373 9200, ⓕ 9373 9125.

Canada

ⓦ ottawa.usembassy.gov
Ottawa 490 Sussex Drive, ON K1N 1G8 ⓣ 613/688-5335, ⓕ 688-3082.
Calgary 615 Macleod Trail SE, 10th floor, AB T2G 4T8 ⓣ 403/266-8962, ⓕ 264-6630.
Halifax Purdy's Wharf Tower II, suite 904, 1969 Upper Water St, NS B3J 3R7 ⓣ 902/429-2480, ⓕ 423-6861.
Montréal 1155 St Alexandre St, Québec B 1Z1 ⓣ 514/398-9695, ⓕ 398-0973.
Quebec City 2 Place Terrace Dufferin, QC G1R 4T9 ⓣ 418/692-2095, ⓕ 692-4640.
Toronto 360 University Ave, ON M5G 1S4 ⓣ 416/595-1700, ⓕ 595-0051.
Vancouver 1075 W Pender St, BC V6E 2M6 ⓣ 604/685-4311, ⓕ 685-5285.
Winnipeg 201 Portage Ave, Suite 860 MB R38 3K6 ⓣ 204/940-1800, ⓕ 940-1809.

Ireland

Dublin 42 Elgin Rd, Ballsbridge, Dublin 4 ⓣ 01/668 8777, ⓕ 668 9946, ⓦ dublin.usembassy.gov.

New Zealand

ⓦ newzealand.usembassy.gov
Wellington 29 Fitzherbert Terrace, Thorndon ⓣ 04/462 6000, ⓕ 499 0490.

Auckland Citibank Building, 3rd floor, 23 Customs St ⓣ 09/303 2724, ⓕ 366 0870.

South Africa

ⓦ southafrica.usembassy.gov
Pretoria 877 Pretorius St, Arcadia, Pretoria ⓣ 012/431 4000, ⓕ 342 2299.
Cape Town 2 Reddam Ave, Westlake 7945 ⓣ 021/702 7300, ⓕ 702 7493.
Durban Old Mutual Building, 303 West St, Durban 4001 ⓣ 031/305 7600, ⓕ 305 7691.
Johannesburg 1 River St, Killarney ⓣ 011/644 8000, ⓕ 646 6916.

UK

ⓦ www.usembassy.org.uk
London 24 Grosvenor Square, W1A 1AE ⓣ 020/7499 9000, visa hotline (£1.20 per min) ⓣ 09042-450100.
Belfast Danesfort House, 223 Stranmillis Rd, Belfast BT9 5GR ⓣ 028/9038 6100, ⓕ 9068 1301.
Edinburgh 3 Regent Terrace, EH7 5BW ⓣ 0131/556 8315, ⓕ 557 6023.

Embassies and consulates in New England

All of the following, with the exception of New Zealand, are located in Boston. South Africa's embassy is in Washington, DC.
Australia 22 Thomson Place ⓣ 617/261-5555.
Canada 3 Copley Place, suite 500 ⓣ 617/262-3760.
Ireland 535 Boylston St ⓣ 617/267-9330.
New Zealand 57 North Main St, PO Box 1318, Concord, NH ⓣ 603/225-8228.
South Africa 3051 Massachusetts Ave NW, Washington, DC ⓣ 202/232-4400.
UK 1 Memorial Drive, Cambridge ⓣ 617/245-4500.

Gay and lesbian travelers

Go to the right places, and New England can be a very enjoyable destination for gay and lesbian visitors. The region possesses some firm favorites on the gay North American travel circuit, and gay-friendly accommodations can be found dotted all over the region. However, go to the wrong places – mainly rural areas – and you will find that the narrow-minded attitudes of "small town America" are still alive. Be cautious, then, with open displays of affection. As difficult and frustrating as this may be, it's usually the most effective way to keep the bigots at bay.

There are sizeable predominantly gay areas in almost all of the New England states. The **South End** of Boston is what Greenwich Village and Chelsea are to New York and the Marais is to Paris. Other "gay" cities in Massachusetts include **Provincetown**, one of the world's premier gay beach resorts, and **Northampton**, well known for its large lesbian community. Elsewhere, the Rhode Island city of **Providence** has a vibrant gay scene, while **Ogunquit** is the quieter, Maine version of Provincetown. **Vermont** is notoriously liberal, and even traditionally conservative **New Hampshire** has recently joined other New England states in passing anti-discrimination laws.

Contact the International Gay & Lesbian Travel Association (☎954/630-1637, ⓦwww .iglta.org), for a list of gay- and lesbian-owned or -friendly **tour operators**. Meanwhile, gaytravel.com (☎1-800/GAY-TRAVEL, ⓦwww .gaytravel.com) is a good online travel agency where you can make bookings and get help with travel planning, and Now Voyager (☎1-800/255-6951, ⓦwww.nowvoyager.com) is a gay and lesbian travel consolidator with Boston-based package tours.

Getting married

In July of 2000, **Vermont** became the first state in the Union to legally recognize **civil unions** for same-sex couples. This groundbreaking move has made Vermont, always one of the country's more gay-friendly states, a prime destination for gay and lesbian couples looking to get married. Hotels, inns, and B&Bs have caught on to the trend, and have begun to offer their premises for civil wedding ceremonies. For more information on how to enter into a civil union in Vermont with your partner, call the Secretary of State's office on ☎1-802/828-2363; another good resource is ⓦwww .vermontgaytravel.com. New Hampshire has since followed suit, legalizing civil unions in June of 2007. Further steps were taken in **Massachusetts** and **Connecticut** in 2004 and 2008, when, respectively, they became the only states in the nation to recognize **gay marriages** (which differ from civil unions, and are considered more of the "real thing").

Publications

There are a number of **publications** covering New England's various gay scenes. *Bay Windows* (☎617/266-6670, ⓦwww .baywindows.com) is the region's largest gay and lesbian weekly, with cultural listings for the region's six states. The bimonthly *Metroline Magazine* (☎860/231-8845, ⓦwww.metroline-online.com) has information on the gay scene in Connecticut, with additional news pertaining to greater New England. Some tourist information centers stock the free *Pink Pages* (☎1-866/943-PINK, ⓦwww.linkpink.com), a complete listing of gay- and lesbian-friendly businesses and community organizations in the New England states – although about half of the book is devoted to Boston.

For additional research try one of many **online publications**, such as gay and lesbian travel resources like ⓦwww.qtmagazine .com, or something more specific to New England, such as ⓦwww.outinboston.com, ⓦwww.vermontgaytravel.com, and ⓦwww .gayinmaine.com.

Health

Visitors from Europe, Australia, New Zealand, and Canada don't require any vaccinations to enter the US. All travelers will be comforted to know that if you have a serious accident while you're in New England, emergency services will get to you sooner and charge you later. For emergencies, dial toll-free ☎911 from any phone. If you have medical or dental problems that don't require an ambulance, most hospitals will have a walk-in emergency room: for the nearest hospital, check with your hotel or dial information at ☎411.

Should you need to see a **doctor**, lists can be found in the *Yellow Pages* under "Clinics" or "Physicians and Surgeons" (or Google those listings according with the name of your location). Be aware that even simple consultations are costly, usually around $75–100 each visit, which is payable in advance. Keep receipts for any part of your medical treatment, including prescriptions, so that you can claim against your insurance once you're home. (See "Insurance", p.44, for more).

For minor ailments such as headache or the common cold, stop by a local **pharmacy**; some are open 24hr, especially in the larger cities. Foreign visitors should note that many medicines available over the counter at home – codeine-based painkillers, for one – are available by prescription only in the US.

Medical resources for travelers

CDC ⓦ www.cdc.goc/travel. Official US government travel health site.
International Society for Travel Medicine ⓦ www.istm.org. Full listing of travel health clinics.

Insurance

Getting travel insurance is highly recommended, especially if you're coming from abroad and are at all concerned about your health – prices for medical attention in the US can be exorbitant. A secondary benefit is that most policies also cover against theft and loss, which can be useful if you're toting around an expensive camera or any high-tech gear. Before paying for a new policy, though, check to see if you're already covered: some home insurance policies may cover your possessions while overseas, and many private medical schemes include cover when abroad.

Canadians are covered for medical mishaps overseas by their provincial health plans. If you only need trip cancellation/interruption coverage (to supplement your existing plan) this is generally available at about $6 per $100.

Internet

Public internet access in New England is still mostly the reserve of public libraries and universities – there are very few designated internet cafés, since most people have service at home. That said, every major city will have a number of coffee shops that provide free wi-fi, as well as a few 24 hour Kinkos copy shops, which usually provide internet access for around $0.30 a minute. Many hotels offer free or cheap high-speed internet access. While libraries and universities have more limited hours (usually Mon–Fri 9am–5pm, Sat 10am–noon, closed Sun) and time constraints (around 15min per person), their major advantage is that the service is free to everyone; if you have your own laptop, wi-fi here is free and available for unlimited use.

Laundry

Laundromats are pretty easy to find in the larger cities – check in with the hotel's staff or look online to see what's available in your area. For more rural spots, ask a local or stop in at the chamber of commerce. Generally, a load of laundry costs about $3 (paid for in quarters – a good laundromat will have a change machine) and $1.50 for an hour of drying time.

Mail

Post offices are usually open Monday through Friday from about 9am to 5pm, and in some cases on Saturday from 9am to noon; there are also **blue mailboxes** on many street corners, into which you can deposit already-stamped mail.

Ordinary mail within the US costs $0.42 for a letter weighing up to an ounce; addresses must include the five-digit zip code (postal code), and a return address should be written

Rough Guides travel insurance

Rough Guides has teamed up with Columbus Direct to offer you **travel insurance** that can be tailored to suit your needs. Products include a low-cost **backpacker** option for long stays; a **short break** option for city getaways; a typical **holiday package** option; and others. There are also annual **multi-trip** policies for those who travel regularly. Different sports and activities (trekking, skiing, etc) can be usually be covered if required.

See our website (ⓦ www.roughguides.com/website/shop) for eligibility and purchasing options. Alternatively, UK residents should call ☏ 0870/033 9988; Australians should call ☏ 1300/669 999 and New Zealanders should call ☏ 0800/55 9911. All other nationalities should call ☏ +44 870/890 2843.

New England state abbreviations

Connecticut: CT
Maine: ME
Massachusetts: MA

New Hampshire: NH
Rhode Island: RI
Vermont: VT

on the upper left corner of the envelope; postcards cost $0.27 to mail. **Air mail** between New England and Europe generally takes about a week to arrive. International postcards and letters weighing up to one ounce cost $0.94.

Note that if you want to send any **parcels** out of the country, they must be packaged and sealed accordingly, and you'll need to fill out a green customs declaration form, available at the post office.

For all things mail, head to the US Postal Service's website at ⓦwww.usps.com; it's especially helpful for looking up zip codes.

Maps

Most of the tourist offices we've mentioned here or throughout the Guide can supply you with good **maps**, either free or for a small charge; supplemented with the ones in this book, these should be enough for general sightseeing and touring. If you need more specific detail, pick up our full-size, tear-proof *Rough Guide New England Map*, available at most bookstores or from ⓦwww.roughguides.com. For driving or cycling through **rural** areas, Maine-based DeLorme (ⓦwww.delorme.com) publishes its valuable *Atlas & Gazetteer* for each of the New England states ($19.95 each), with marked campgrounds and national park and forest information. For detailed **hiking** maps, check with ranger stations in parks and wilderness areas or with camping stores.

Measurements and sizes

Measurements are in inches, feet, yards, and miles; weight is in ounces, pounds, and tons. American pints and gallons are about four-fifths of imperial ones. Clothing sizes are two figures less than what they would be in Britain – a British women's size 12 is a US size 10 – while British shoe sizes are 1.5 sizes below American ones for women, and one size below for men.

Money

US currency comes in bills of $1, $5, $10, $20, $50, and $100. The dollar is made up of 100 cents with coins of 1 cent (known as a penny), 5 cents (a nickel), 10 cents (a dime), and 25 cents (a quarter).

A combination of **cash** and an **ATM** or **debit card** are the best way to carry and obtain money while in New England. You'll find ATMs ("automated teller machines") on nearly every corner in big cities, and they shouldn't be too difficult to locate in rural areas, either. Any ATM or debit card issued in the US should work in all ATMs, while travelers from abroad should make sure their card is part of the Cirrus or Plus network. Keep in mind that you'll usually be charged $1–2 every time you make a withdrawal from an ATM not operated by your home bank.

If you'd rather not carry around a lot of cash, you might want to supplement your dollars with **traveler's checks**, which offer the security of knowing that lost or stolen checks will be replaced. Don't forget to keep the receipt and a record of the serial numbers safe and separate from the checks themselves; in the event that checks are lost or stolen, the issuing company will expect you to report the loss forthwith (see p.46 for phone numbers), and will require these serial numbers. Traveler's checks can be used same as cash in virtually all shops, restaurants, and gas stations – though in the hinterlands they might provoke a moment of head-scratching and manager-consulting before being accepted.

It's a good idea to carry a **credit card** or two in case of emergency; the major companies (MasterCard, Visa, and American Express) will work anywhere in America, no matter where the card was issued. A compromise between plastic and traveler's checks is **Visa Travel-Money**, a disposable prepaid debit card with a PIN which works in all ATMs that accept Visa cards. You load up your account with funds before leaving home, and when they run out, you simply throw the card away. The card is available in most countries from branches of Thomas Cook and Citicorp. For more information, check the Visa TravelMoney website at ⓦ www.usa.visa.com.

Banks are generally open from 9am until 5pm Monday to Thursday, and 9am to 6pm on Friday. Some have limited hours on Saturdays, and ATMs are usually accessible 24 hours a day. Most major banks change foreign traveler's checks and currency as well. **Exchange bureaus**, found at airports, tend to charge less commission than banks: Thomas Cook and American Express are the biggest names. If your traveler's checks and/or credit cards are stolen or if you need to find the nearest bank that sells a particular brand of traveler's check, or to buy checks by phone, call one of the following numbers: American Express (℡ 1-800/221-7282), Traveler's check Customer Service (℡ 1-800/645-6556), MasterCard International/Thomas Cook (℡ 1-800/223-7373), or Visa (℡ 1-800/227-6811).

Wiring money

Having money **wired** from home is never convenient or cheap, and should be considered a last resort. The two largest money-wiring companies in the US are MoneyGram (℡ 1-800/MONEYGRAM, ⓦ www.moneygram .com) and Western Union (℡ 1-800/325-6000, ⓦ www.westernunion.com); call or visit either company's website to find the location nearest you.

Youth and student discounts

Once obtained, various **youth/student ID cards** soon pay for themselves in savings. Full-time students are eligible for the International Student ID Card (ISIC; ⓦ www .isiccard.com), which entitles the bearer to special air, rail, and bus fares, as well as discounts at museums, theaters, and other attractions. For Americans there's also a health benefit, providing up to $3000 in emergency medical coverage and $100 a day for sixty days in the hospital, plus a 2 hour hotline to call in the event of a medical, legal, or financial emergency. The card costs $22 for Americans, Aus$18 for

Australians, NZ$20 for New Zealanders, and £9 in the UK.

You have to be 26 or younger to qualify for the **International Youth Travel Card**, which costs US$22/£9 and carries the same benefits. Teachers qualify for the **International Teacher Card**, offering similar discounts and costing US$22, Aus$18, and NZ$20. All of these cards are available online or from student-oriented travel agents in North America, Europe, Australia, and New Zealand.

Opening hours and public holidays

Shops and services are generally open Monday to Saturday from 8 or 9am until 5 or 6pm. Many stores are also open on Sundays, and larger towns and cities will invariably have 24-hour supermarkets and pharmacies. For banking and post office hours, see above and p.44, respectively.

On the national, or federal, **public holidays** listed in the box below, banks and offices (and many shops) are liable to be **closed** all day. The traditional summer season for tourism runs from Memorial Day to Labor Day, and some tourist attractions are open only during that period.

Phones

With respect to calling abroad from the US, you've got several options, the most convenient of which is using your **credit card** – most pay phones now accept them. A cheaper option is using a **prepaid phone**

Public holidays

Jan 1 New Year's Day

Third Mon in Jan Martin Luther King Jr's Birthday

Third Mon in Feb Presidents' Day

Last Mon in May Memorial Day

July 4 Independence Day

First Mon in Sept Labor Day

Second Mon in Oct Columbus Day

Nov 11 Veterans' Day

Fourth Thurs in Nov Thanksgiving Day

Dec 25 Christmas Day

Useful phone numbers and codes

Emergencies and information

Emergencies ☏911; ask for the appropriate emergency service: fire, police, or ambulance.

Directory information ☏411

Directory inquiries for toll-free numbers ☏1-800/555-1212

Long-distance directory information ☏1-(area code)/555-1212

Operator ☏0

New England area codes

Connecticut northern Connecticut ☏860/959; southern Connecticut ☏203

Maine ☏207

Massachusetts Boston ☏617/857; suburban Boston ☏781/339; Cape Cod ☏508/774; northern MA ☏978/351; western MA ☏413

New Hampshire ☏603

Rhode Island ☏401

Vermont ☏802

International calling codes

Calling TO New England from abroad your country's international access code + 1 + area code + seven-digit number

Calling FROM New England

To Australia ☏011 + 61 + city code

To Canada ☏1 + area code

To New Zealand ☏011 + 64 + city code

To the Republic of Ireland ☏011 + 353 + city code

To South Africa ☏011 + 27 + city code

To the UK and Northern Ireland ☏011 + 44 + city code (minus the initial zero)

---

card, sold at many convenience stores in denominations that begin at $5.

Mobile phones

If you're from overseas and you want to bring your **mobile phone** (referred to as "cell phones" in the US) with you, you'll need to check with your phone provider about whether it will work abroad, what the roaming charges will be, or if you can use a local SIM card in it (though this will change your number to an American one). If you find your phone won't work in the States, you might consider renting one.

Senior travelers

For many senior citizens, retirement brings the opportunity to explore the world in a style and at a pace that is the envy of younger travelers. As well as the obvious advantages of being free to travel for longer periods during

the quieter – and less expensive – seasons, anyone over the age of 62 (with suitable ID) can enjoy a tremendous variety of discounts. Amtrak, Greyhound, local buses, and many US airlines offer (smallish) percentage reductions on fares to older passengers. In addition, museums, art galleries, and even hotels offer small discounts, and since the definition of "senior" can drop to as low as 55, it is always worth asking.

In addition, any US citizen or permanent resident aged 62 or over is entitled to free admission to all national parks, monuments, and historic sites using a **Golden Age Passport**, for which a once-only fee of $10 is charged; it must be issued in person at any such site, and proof of age is required. This free entry also applies to any accompanying car passengers or, for those hiking or cycling, the passport-holder's spouse and children. It also gives a fifty percent reduction on fees for camping, parking, and boat launching. The individual states also offer senior citizen **discounts** on admission to state-run parks, beaches, and historic sites; these give $1 off parking and $2 off family camping in state-operated parks, except where the fee is less than $2. Finally, several states offer special senior citizen general discount passes – contact the relevant state's tourist information center for details (see below).

The **American Association of Retired Persons** (AARP; ☎202/434-2277 or 1-800/424-3410, ⊛www.aarp.org), organizes group travel for senior citizens and can provide discounts on accommodation, car rental, air travel, and vacations with selected tour operators. Annual membership (which includes a subscription to their excellent *Modern Maturity* magazine) is available to anyone over 50, costing $12.50 ($29.50 for three years) for US residents, $17 for Canadians, and $28 for those living abroad.

There are a number of Boston-based **tour operators** specializing in vacations for seniors. Elderhostel, 11 Ave de Lafayette (☎1/800-454-5768, ⊛www.elderhostel .org), runs an extensive worldwide network of educational and activity programs for people over 55 (companions may be younger). Trips range anywhere from their Boston "Day of Discovery with Boston Lyric Opera" ($154) to those that last a week or more, and costs are on the whole in line with those of commercial tours. There are numerous programs offered in New England, with themes ranging from brush painting in Massachusetts to sea-kayaking off the Maine coast. In the UK, Saga Holidays (☎0130/377 1111 or 0800/096 0078, ⊛www.saga.co.uk/travel) is the country's biggest and most established specialist in vacations aimed at older people. New England tours include most of the major sights, and are conducted during the popular "fall foliage" season.

Time

New England runs on **Eastern Standard Time (EST)**, five hours behind GMT in winter and three hours ahead of the US West Coast. East Coast daylight savings time (4hr behind GMT) runs from the first Sunday in April to the last Sunday in October.

Tourist information

Advance information for a trip to New England can be obtained by calling the appropriate state's information center (see below). A publicly funded firm called Discover New England (☎802/253-2500, ⊛www .discovernewengland.org) also exists to provide advance information on all six New England states.

Once you've arrived, you'll find most towns have **visitors' centers** of some kind – often called the Convention and Visitors Bureau (CVB) or the Chamber of Commerce: many are listed within the *Guide*. The essential difference between the two types of visitors' centers is that the former deals exclusively with tourism-related businesses, while the latter represents all types of commerce. Either one will give out detailed information on the local area, however, and can often help with finding accommodation. Additionally, free newspapers in most places carry news of events and entertainment. Of the several **publications** with travel information specific to New England, check out the range of magazines published by Yankee Publishing (⊛www.yankeemagazine.com). *Yankee Magazine* is published ten times a year, and contains travel features and coverage of the latest New England living trends. Their annual *Yankee Magazine Travel Guide to New England* also contains travel features, accompanied by plenty of useful practical information. The *Yankee Magazine's Bed & Breakfast and Inn Directory*, meanwhile, features more than six hundred places to stay in New England. Lastly, *Boston* magazine (⊛www.bostonmagazine .com) is a fine monthly publication which has feature articles on its title town as well as the rest of New England.

State information centers

Connecticut One Financial Plaza, 755 Main St, Hartford, CT 06103 ☎860/256-2800 or 1-888/288-4748, ⊛www.ctvisit.com

Maine 59 State House Station, Augusta, ME 04333 ☎1-888/624-6345, ⊛www.visitmaine.com

Massachusetts 10 Park Plaza, suite 4510, Boston, MA 02116 ☎617/973-8500 or 1-800/227-MASS, ⊛www.massvacation.com

New Hampshire 172 Pembroke Rd, Concord, NH 03302 ☎603/271-2665, ⊛www.visitnh.gov

Rhode Island 315 Iron Horse Way, Suite 101, Providence, RI 02908 ℡ 1-800/250-7384, ⓦ www.visitrhodeisland.com

Vermont Vermont Dept. of Tourism and Marketing National Life Bldg, 6th floor, Montpelier, VT 05620 ℡ 802/828-3237 or 1-800/VERMONT, ⓦ www.vermontvacation.com

Websites

Though we've listed relevant **websites** for accommodation, organizations, major sights, and so on throughout this guide, the following might help you pursue a few special areas of interest in preparation for your visit.

AlpineZone ⓦ www.alpinezone.com. Check up on ski and hiking trail reports in the northeast, as well as accommodation on all the mountains.

Boston Online ⓦ www.boston.com. General info on the city, local news, entertainment, and goings-on.

New England History ⓦ www.newenglandhistory.info. Well-organized site for limited historical background on each state, plus some good old images and notable quotes.

New England Lighthouses ⓦ www.lighthouse.cc. Organized by state, with photos, history, and pretty much everything you might need to find out about your favorite lighthouse.

New England for Visitors ⓦ gonewengland.about.com. Links to all sorts of fairly mainstream info, including tour operators, major ski resorts, and the like.

Travelers with children

New England is a great place to bring kids, as so many of the region's historical sights – ships, lighthouses, recreated colonial villages with character actors – are actually more fun with a wide-eyed youngster to show around. In addition, there are several zoos, aquariums, and children's museums in the area.

Check the internet and you'll find that in addition to commercial attractions catering to children – mini-golf, water slides, arcades, and the like – many states also have apple **orchards** for picking in the fall and farms with strawberries and raspberries for picking in the spring and summer. All destination **ski areas** in New England have reputable and licensed ski schools for children that include lessons, lift tickets, and meals. Most restaurants offer children's menus and booster chairs, and all but the nicest boutique hotels are child-equipped and friendly.

In **Boston**, the Children's Museum (see p.80), the Museum of Science (see p.93), and the Aquarium (see p.80) are all world-class sights geared towards children. In nearby Acton, the Discovery Museums (℡978/264-4200, ⓦ www.discoverymuseums.org) are well worth a trip out of the way for a day with younger kids. In Connecticut the Mystic Seaport and Aquarium (see p.288) and Dinosaur State Park (see p.319) outstrip the area's museums in excitement for kids. One good resource is the Association for Children's Museums website (ⓦ www.childrensmuseums.org), which has a state-by-state breakdown of kid-oriented museums.

Amusement parks in New England are not destination sights the way they are in Florida, though the area does have a smattering of small-town carnivals. If the kids are clamoring for a roller coaster, consider Six Flags New England (ⓦ www.sixsflags.com), StoryLand in New Hampshire (ⓦ www.storylandnh.com), or Funtown/Splashtown USA in Maine (ⓦ www.funtownsplashtownusa.com) – though note that a day out at any of these parks can be fairly pricey.

Travelers with disabilities

Travelers with mobility problems or other physical disabilities are likely to find New England – as with the US in general – to be much more in tune with their needs than anywhere else in the world. All public buildings must be wheelchair-accessible and have suitable toilets; most city street corners have dropped curbs; subways have elevators; and most city buses are able to kneel to make access easier. Most hotels, restaurants, and theaters (certainly any built in the last ten years or so) also generally have excellent wheelchair access. Most obstacles can usually be overcome – or avoided altogether – if you call 48 hours or so before your arrival at a bus or train station, airport, hotel, restaurant, park, or other such facility.

Contacts

In the US and Canada

Mobility International USA ℡541/343-1284, ⓦ www.miusa.org. Information and referral services, access guides, tours, and exchange programs.

Society for the Accessible Travel and Hospitality (SATH) ☎ 212/447-7284, ⓦ www .sath.org. Non-profit educational organization which has actively represented travelers with disabilities since 1976.

In the UK and Ireland

Disability Action Group Belfast ☎ 028/9029 7880, ⓦ www.disabilityaction.org. **Irish Wheelchair Association** Dublin ☎ 01/818 6400, ⓦ www.iwa.ie. Useful information provided about traveling abroad with a wheelchair. **Tourism for All** Andover ☎ 0845/124 9971, ⓦ www .holidaycare.org.uk or www.tourismforall.info.

Provides information on all aspects of travel for the disabled and elderly.

In Australia and New Zealand

Disabled Persons Assembly ☎ 04/801 9100, ⓦ www.dpa.org.nz. New Zealand resource center with lists of travel agencies and tour operators for people with disabilities. **NDS (National Disability Services)** ☎ 02/6283 3200, ⓦ www.nds.org.au. Lists of travel agencies and tour operators.

Guide

Guide

Boston

CHAPTER 1 # Highlights

* **North End** You'll find some of Boston's most famed sights, plus its best cannoli, in its most authentic Italian neighborhood. See p.82

* **Beacon Hill** Long the neighborhood of choice for the city's elite, with stately red-brick Federalist townhouses and gaslights lining the narrow, cobblestoned streets. See p.89

* **Newbury Street** This swanky promenade of designer boutiques and cafés will tempt you to break the bank. See p.98

* **A Red Sox game at Fenway** Watch one of baseball's most storied teams play in one of the country's classic ballparks. See p.103

* **Isabella Stewart Gardner Museum** Styled after a fifteenth-century Venetian palace, this delightful museum boasts an eclectic collection and a sublime central courtyard. See p.106

* **Arnold Arboretum** The crown jewel of Boston's Emerald Necklace is a botanist's delight and one of the finest arboretums in North America. See p.109

* **Harvard Square** Cambridge's buzzing heart is steps from the ivy-covered walls of Harvard University and close to the Colonial mansions of Brattle Street. See p.109

▲ Beacon Hill

Boston

BOSTON is about as close to the Old World as the New World gets: staunchly American, the city nonetheless proudly trades on its colonial past. Occasionally it takes things a bit too far – what's a faded relic elsewhere is a plaque-covered sight here – but nowhere else will you get a better feel for the events and the personae behind the birth of a nation. This is not to say the city is lacking in modern attractions: its cafés, shops, nicely landscaped public spaces, and diverse neighborhoods are just as alluring as its historic sites. Indeed, the new millennium has brought a major renaissance to Boston: the completion of the Big Dig project, the glamorous new Institute of Contemporary Art, the expanding Seaport District, and the Red Sox World Series victories in 2004 and 2007 have all contributed to the feeling that Boston's future may be even stronger than its past.

A visit to Boston is the highlight of any trip to New England. The city's relatively small size – both physically and in terms of population (tenth among US cities) – and its provincial feel are actually to its great advantage. Though it has expanded since it was first settled in 1630 through landfills and annexation, it has never lost its center, a tangle of streets clustered around Boston Common. Groups of Irish and Italian descent have carved out authentically and often equally unchanged communities in areas like the North End, Charlestown, and South Boston, and the districts around the Common exude an almost small-town atmosphere. Even as Boston has evolved from busy port to the rejuvenated place it is today, it has remained, fundamentally, a city on a human scale.

Some history

Boston's first permanent settlement was started by **William Blackstone**, who split off from a camp in Weymouth for more isolated territory in 1630. He was rapidly joined by Puritan settlers, to whom he sold most of the land he had claimed; then called the Shawmut Peninsula, it was soon renamed by the Puritans after their hometown in England: Boston.

Early Bostonians enjoyed almost total political autonomy, but with the restoration of the British monarchy in 1660, the Crown began appointing governors to oversee the colony. The colonists clashed frequently with these appointees, their resentment growing with a series of acts over the next ninety years that restricted certain civil and commercial liberties. This culminated in such skirmishes as the Boston Massacre and the Boston Tea Party, events that helped ignite the **Revolutionary War**, which effectively started in Lexington (see p.143), just outside Boston.

Post-Revolution, Boston emerged as a leading port city, eventually moving on to prominence in textiles and other industries. Its success in these fields brought waves

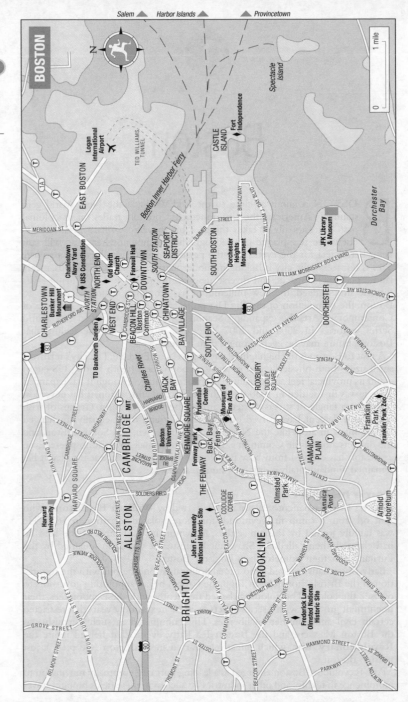

BOSTON

Salem ▲   Harbor Islands ▲   ▲ Provincetown

N

1 mile
0

Logan International Airport

TED WILLIAMS TUNNEL

EAST BOSTON

1A

MERIDOAN ST

Spectacle Island

CASTLE ISLAND

Fort Independence

Dorchester Bay

Boston Inner Harbor Ferry

E. BROADWAY

STREET

WILLIAM J DIX BLVD

SUMMER

SOUTH BOSTON

Dorchester Heights Monument

JFK Library & Museum

SEAPORT DISTRICT

SOUTH STATION

DOWNTOWN

CHINATOWN

Faneuil Hall

Old North Church

USS Constitution

Charlestown Navy Yard

NORTH END

NORTH STATION

CHARLESTOWN
Bunker Hill Monument

RUTHERFORD AVE

CAMBRIDGE ST

WEST END

Boston Common

Beacon Hill

BAY VILLAGE

SOUTH END

TREMONT STREET

WASHINGTON STREET

ROXBURY

DUDLEY SQUARE

DUDLEY ST

MASSACHUSETTS AVENUE

WILLIAM MORRISSEY BOULEVARD

DORCHESTER

DORCHESTER AVE

93

90

COLUMBIA ROAD

BLUE HILL AVENUE

TD Banknorth Garden

93

STORROW DR

Charles River

BACK BAY

MEMORIAL DRIVE

MIT

CAMBRIDGE

HARVARD BRIDGE

MAGAZINE STREET

MAIN STREET

BROADWAY

PROSPECT STREET

CAMBRIDGE STREET

KIRKLAND STREET

HARVARD SQUARE

Harvard University

ALLSTON

MASSACHUSETTS TURNPIKE

SOLDIERS FIELD RD

COOLIDGE AVENUE

3

GROVE STREET

MOUNT AUBURN STREET

BELMONT STREET

Boston University

BU BRIDGE

COMMONWEALTH AVE

SOLDIERS FIELD

WESTERN AVENUE

BRIGHTON

N. BEACON STREET

CAMBRIDGE STREET

MARKET STREET

COMMONWEALTH AVENUE

FOSTER ST

BEACON STREET

TREMONT ST

Prudential Center

Museum of Fine Arts

KENMORE SQUARE

Fenway Park

Back Bay Fens

THE FENWAY

HUNTINGTON AVE

COLUMBUS AVENUE

28

RIVERWAY

JAMAICAWAY

JAMAICA PLAIN

CENTRE STREET

Olmsted Park

Jamaica Pond

Arnold Arboretum

Franklin Park

Franklin Park Zoo

COLUMBUS AVENUE

WASHINGTON STREET

John F. Kennedy National Historic Site

COOLIDGE CORNER

BEACON STREET

BROOKLINE

CHESTNUT HILL AVE

RESERVOIR ROAD

BOYLSTON STREET

HAMMOND STREET

PARKWAY

NEWTON STREET

LA GRANGE ST

GROVE STREET

CLYDE ST

WARREN ST

LEE ST

GODDARD AVENUE

Frederick Law Olmsted National Historic Site

9

of immigrants – notably Irish, Italian, and Chinese – in the nineteenth century; all three groups still have sizeable communities in the city and the region. Additionally, the city gained a reputation as the center of the American university system, with more than sixty institutes of higher learning in the area. This academic connection has also played a key role in the city's left-leaning political tradition. But despite a strong history of progressive thought, the city was less successful when it came to integration, and **racial tensions** flared up frequently in the twentieth century, most notoriously with the advent of public school busing in the 1970s. Race relations have improved of late, with community revitalization efforts that have strengthened the business centers of African-American neighborhoods, and more symbolically, with the election of Massachusetts's first black governor, Deval Patrick, in November 2006. In addition, the Big Dig has completely rejuvenated the look of the city – most notably with the elegant, skyline-boosting Zakim Bridge, the central Rose Kennedy Greenway, and the beautification of the HarborWalk – and with these changes, a renewed sense of confidence has taken hold.

Arrival, information, and city transport

Boston is the unchallenged travel hub of New England. Conveniently, all **points of arrival** are located inside the city boundaries, none more than a few miles away from downtown, and all are well connected to public transport.

By air

Busy **Logan International Airport** (☎1-800/23-LOGAN, ⊛www.massport .com/logan) services both domestic and international flights. It has four terminals (A, B, C, and E), which are connected by shuttle buses. You'll find car rental desks, internet access, information booths, and ATMs in all of them, and currency exchange in terminals B and E.

Taxis from the airport are convenient but expensive – it will cost around $30, plus an extra $7.50 or so in tolls, to most downtown destinations. The subway, or, as it's known in Boston, the **T** (see p.60 for details), is the cheapest way to reach downtown Boston from Logan. The Airport subway stop is a short shuttle-bus ride from the airport proper; catch the shuttle from outside the arrivals level of any of the four terminals. From the Airport station, you can take the Blue Line to State or Government Center, both in the heart of downtown, and transfer to the Red, Orange, or Green lines to reach other points; the ride to downtown lasts about fifteen minutes. Another alternative is to take the Silver Line (see p.61), a speedy bus posing as a subway line that stops at the airport and continues on to South Station, the Seaport District, and the South End.´

Just as quick, and a lot more fun, is the **water taxi** (☎617/422-0392, ⊛www .citywatertaxi.com), which whisks you across the harbor to numerous points around Boston. From the airport, courtesy bus #66 will take you to the pier. The water taxis don't run on a set schedule; if there isn't a boat waiting in the harbor, contact them via the checkerboard call box at the Logan dock (April–Nov Mon–Sat 7am–10pm, Sun 7am–7pm; $10).

By bus or train

The main terminus for both **buses** and **trains** to Boston is **South Station**, in the southeast corner of downtown at Summer Street and Atlantic Avenue. Amtrak trains arrive at one end of the station, which has an information booth, newsstands, a food court, and several ATMs, while buses arrive at the clean and modern terminal next door. Moving on, there is a subway stop (the Red Line) down a level from the Amtrak station. It's a bit of a trek from the bus station; those with sizeable baggage will find the walk particularly awkward, as there are no porters or handcarts. Trains also stop at **Back Bay Station**, 145 Dartmouth St, on the **T**'s Orange Line – this station has two ATMs and a number of food stalls, but little else in the way of amenities.

By car

Driving into Boston is the absolute worst way to get there, and will likely put a damper on your trip. Boston drivers are notorious for their aggressive, impatient style, and the learning curve for navigating the city by car is so steep that even local residents sometimes still have trouble.

If you insist on driving, two highways provide direct access to the city: **I-90**, known locally as the Mass Pike or The Pike, and **I-93**, known as the Central Artery. The latter cuts north–south through the heart of Boston and provides the most majestic entrance to the city, courtesy of the impressive Zakim Bridge. If you're coming from western Massachusetts, I-90 is the most direct route. Once you reach Boston, **Storrow Drive** is the main local drag, running alongside the Charles River and providing access to the core of the city. A third highway, **I-95**, circumnavigates the greater Boston area, affording entry points for its many suburbs.

Information

Boston's main public tourist office is the **Boston Common Visitor's Information Center**, on Boston Common (Park Street **T**; daily 9am–5pm; ℡617/426-3115). You'll find loads of maps and brochures here, plus information on historical sights, cultural events, accommodation, restaurants, and bus trips. The National Park Service maintains an excellent **visitors' center** across the street from the Old State House, at 15 State St (daily 9am–5pm; ℡617/242-5642); it too has plenty of free brochures, plus bathrooms and a bookstore. In Back Bay, there is a visitor **kiosk** in the Prudential Center, 800 Boylston St (daily 9am–5pm). Visitors to **Cambridge** can get all the information they need from the Cambridge Office of Tourism (℡617/441-2884 or 1-800/862-5678, ⊛www.cambridge-usa.org), which maintains a kiosk outside the subway station in Harvard Square (Mon–Sat 9am–5pm). For advance information, the best sources are the Greater Boston Convention & Visitors Bureau (GBCVB; ⊛www.bostonusa.com) and the *Boston Globe* (⊛www.bostonglobe.com).

The **Boston CityPass** (available online or at the attractions that accept it; $44; ⊛citypass.net) is a ticket booklet that covers admission to the Prudential Skywalk Observatory, the John F. Kennedy Presidential Library & Museum, the Museum of Fine Arts, the New England Aquarium, the Harvard Museum of Natural History, and the Museum of Science; if you plan to visit all or most of these sights, you'd do well to pick one up.

The city's oldest **newspaper**, *The Boston Globe* ($0.75; ⊛www.bostonglobe.com), is still its principal general daily; its hefty Sunday edition ($2.50) includes meaty sections on art, culture, and lifestyle. The *Boston Herald* ($0.75; ⊛www.bostonherald.com) is the *Globe*'s tabloid competitor, best for local gossip and sports coverage. The rest of the city's print media are primarily **free weeklies**. The *Boston Phoenix* (free; ⊛www.bostonphoenix.com), available at sidewalk newspaper stands around town, offers extensive entertainment **listings** as well as good feature articles. Other freebies like *Boston's*

Guided tours of Boston

One of the best ways to orient yourself in Boston, aside from walking, is by taking a tour, of which there are many variations available.

Narrated trolley tours

Beantown Trolley ☎1-800/343-1328 or 781/986-6100, ⓦwww.beantowntrolley .com. One of the oldest and most popular tours, covering the gamut from waterfront wharfs to Beacon Hill Brahmins and Fenway area museums, with multiple pick-up and drop-off points around town. $29.

Old Town Trolley Tours ☎617/269-7010, ⓦwww.trolleytours.com. Another hop-on, hop-off tour, this one on orange-and-green trolleys with thematic routes like the "Chocolate Tour" and "Ghosts and Gravestones," in addition to the standard day tour. $34; online discounts.

Other city tours

Boston by Foot ☎617/367-2345, ⓦwww.bostonbyfoot.org. Informative 90min walking tours that focus on the architecture and history of different Boston neighborhoods. Also has "Boston by Little Feet" tours, geared towards the Freedom Trail's smaller pedestrians. $8–14.

Boston Duck Tours ☎617/267-DUCK, ⓦwww.bostonducktours.com. Excellent tours that take to the streets and the Charles River in restored World War II amphibious landing vehicles. Tours depart every half-hour from the Prudential Center at 101 Huntington Ave and the Museum of Science at Science Park; reservations advised in summer. $29.

Boston National Historical Park Visitor Center Freedom Trail Tours ☎617/242-5642. Ranger-led tours centering on a number of Freedom Trail hotspots and the Black Heritage Trail. Tours (90min) begin at the Visitor Center (15 State St) April–Nov Mon–Fri 2pm, Sat–Sun 10am, 11am & 2pm. In summer, get there 30min early – the tours are first-come, first-served. Free.

Brush Hill Grayline Tours ☎1-800/343-1328 or 781/986-6100, ⓦwww.brushhilltours .com. Day-long bus tours to surrounding towns such as Concord, Lexington, Plymouth, and Salem. Late March to Nov; some tours summer only. $32–55.

Gondola di Venezia ☎617/876-2800, ⓦwww.bostongondolas.com. So it's not really Venice, but who cares when you can woo your sweetie on a straight-from-Venice gondola (complete with chocolates and a live accordion player)? $99–229 per couple.

North End Market Tours ☎617/523-6032, ⓦwww.northendmarkettours.com. Award-winning walking and tasting tours of the North End's Italian *salumerias* and the bustling markets of Chinatown. Often booked up, so reserve well in advance. $48–60.

Super Duck Excursions ☎1-877/34DUCKS, ⓦwww.superduckexcursions.com. This up-and-coming duck tour company starts and ends its tours at the Charlestown Navy Yard, showing off Boston sites en route. Daily, 11am–3pm on the hour. They also have a trolley and double-decker bus city tour. $29 and $34.

Weekly Dig (ⓦwww.weeklydig.com) and *The Improper Bostonian* (ⓦwww .improper.com) have listings of new and noteworthy goings-on about town. *Bay Windows* (ⓦwww.baywindows.com), a small weekly catering to the **gay and lesbian** population, is available free in the South End (the city's primary gay neighborhood). The lone monthly publication, *Boston Magazine* ($3.99; ⓦwww.bostonmagazine.com), is a glossy lifestyle **magazine** with good restaurant reviews and a yearly "Best of Boston" roundup.

City transport

Much of the pleasure of visiting Boston comes from being in a city built long before cars were invented. Walking around the narrow streets can be a joy; conversely, driving around them is a nightmare. If you have a car, you're best off parking it for the duration of your trip (see p.137) and getting around either by **foot** or **public transit** – a system of subway lines, buses, and ferries run by the Massachusetts Bay Transportation Authority (MBTA; ☎1-800/392-6100, ⓦwww.mbta.com).

Subway (the T)

Boston's **subway** is cheap, efficient, and, when you're not in a terrific hurry, charmingly antiquated – its Green Line was America's first underground train, built in the late nineteenth century. Four train lines transect Boston and continue

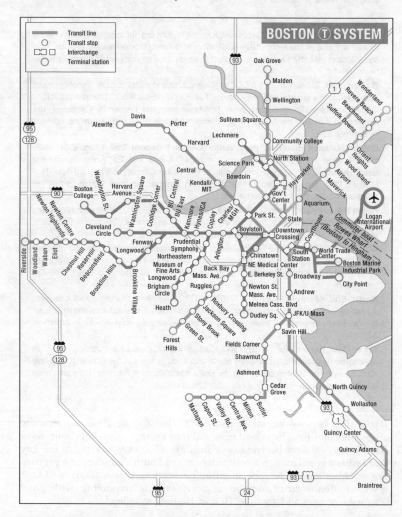

out into some of its more proximate neighbors. Each line is color-coded and passes through downtown before continuing on to other districts. The **Red Line**, which serves Harvard, runs most frequently, intersecting South Boston and Dorchester to the south and Cambridge to the north. The **Green Line** hits Back Bay, Kenmore Square, the Fenway, and Brookline. The **Blue Line** heads into East Boston and is most useful for its stop at Logan Airport. The **Orange Line** traverses the South End and continues down to Roxbury and Jamaica Plain. The four lines are supplemented by a bus rapid transit (BRT) route, the **Silver Line**, which runs above ground along Washington Street from Downtown Crossing **T** and has additional access to the airport and the Seaport District. More of a fast bus than a subway, the line cuts through the South End.

All trains travel either **inbound** (towards the quadrant made up of State, Downtown Crossing, Park Street, and Government Center stops) or **outbound** (away from the quadrant). If you're confused about where you're going, the train's terminus is also designated on the train itself; for instance, trains to Harvard from South Station will be on the "Inbound" platform, and labeled "Alewife."

Boston has recently installed a new and somewhat confusing system for subway **fares**. Within the city, the standard fare is $2, payable by the purchase of a "CharlieTicket" (presumably named for the Kingston Trio recording of the *MTA Song*, which tells the story of a man named Charlie who never returned from his train ride due to an exorbitant subway exit fare), which can be purchased at any of the ATM-like machines in the station. If you buy a "CharlieCard" – with more of a credit-card thickness and a longer lifespan – your fare begins at only $1.70 per ride. Your safest (and simplest) bet is the **LinkPass**, which covers all subway and local bus journeys (as well as the ferry to Charlestown) at a cost of $9 a day or $15 a week.

The biggest drawback to the **T** is its **hours** (Mon–Sat 5.15am–12.30am, Sun 6am–12.30am); the 12.30am closing time means you'll be stuck taking a taxi home after last call at the bar. Free transit **maps** are available at any station.

Buses

The MBTA also manages a whopping 170 **bus routes** both in and around Boston. The buses run less frequently than the subway and are harder to navigate, but they bear two main advantages: they're cheaper ($1.50, exact change only) and they provide services to many more points – see the website for route maps. If you're transferring from the **T**, you'll have to pay the full fare; transferring between buses is free, however, as long as you have a transfer from your original bus. Note that the **T**'s LinkPass (see above) includes unlimited bus access for one to seven days. Most buses run from 5.30am to 1am.

Ferries

Of all the MBTA transportation options, the Inner Harbor **ferry** is by far the most scenic: $1.70 gets you a 10-minute boat ride with excellent views of downtown Boston. The boats navigate several waterfront routes by day, though the one most useful to visitors is that connecting Long Wharf with the Charlestown Navy Yard (every 15min Mon–Fri 6.30am–8pm, every 15min Sat & Sun 10am–6pm).

Bikes

In and around Boston are some eighty miles of **bike trails**, making it an excellent city to explore on two wheels. Bicycles can be rented from Boston Bicycle, 842 Beacon St (☏617/236-0752; ⊛www.cambridgebicycle.com), or their sister location, Cambridge Bicycle, 259 Massachusetts Ave, near MIT (☏617/876-6555, ⊛www.cambridgebicycle.com), and from Boston Bike

Tours and Rentals, near the Visitor Information Center on Boston Common (☎617/308-5902; ⓦwww.bostonbiketours.com). Rentals are around $25 per day. Urban Adventours (☎1-800/979-3370, ⓦwww.urbanadventours.com) can take you around for a couple of fun and easy-going hours by bike. A copy of *Boston's Bike Map* ($5.95) is available at any decent bike store and will help you find all the trails and bike-friendly roads in the area.

Taxis

Given Boston's small scale and the efficiency of its public transport, **taxis** aren't as necessary – or as prevalent – as in bigger cities. You can generally hail one along the streets of downtown or Back Bay, though competition gets pretty stiff after 1am, when the subway has stopped running and bars and clubs begin to close; in this case just call the cab company directly. In Cambridge, taxis mostly congregate around Harvard Square. Boston Cab (☎617/536-5010) and Metro Cab (☎617/782-5500) have 24-hour service and accept major credit cards. In Cambridge, call Yellow or Ambassador Cab (☎617/547-3000). As a general rule, the rate starts at $2.80 and goes up by $0.40 per 1/7 mile.

Accommodation

For such a popular destination, Boston has a surprisingly limited range of well-priced **accommodation**. There are still bargains to be found, but prices at many formerly moderate **hotels** have inched into the expense-account range. Even if the city's hotels are not suited to all budgets, however, they do cater to most tastes, and range from the usual **chains** to some excellent independent hotels, the best of which are in Back Bay.

A surprising number of **B&Bs** are tucked into renovated brownstones in Back Bay, Beacon Hill, and the South End, as well as Cambridge and Brookline. The industry is thriving, largely because it is so difficult to find hotel accommodation for less than $150 a night – and many B&Bs offer just that. You can make reservations directly with the places we've listed; there are also numerous B&B **agencies** that can do the booking for you (see box below).

Short-term **furnished apartments**, spread throughout the city, are another option, though most have two-week minimums. There are also a handful of decent **hostels** if you're looking for real budget accommodation, though definitely book ahead, especially in summer. Hotels and B&Bs are listed below by neighborhood, with hostels listed separately; you'll find their locations plotted on the corresponding neighborhood maps.

B&B agencies and short-term accommodation

Bed & Breakfast Agency of Boston 47 Commercial Wharf ☎617/720-3540 or 1-800/248-9262, UK ☎0800/895 128, ⓦwww.boston-bnbagency.com; Aquarium **T**. Can book you a room in a brownstone, a waterfront loft, or even on a yacht. Nightly, weekly, or monthly options.

Bed & Breakfast Associates Bay Colony ☎781/449-5302 or 1-888/486-6018, ⓦwww.bnbboston.com. Features some real finds in Back Bay and the South End.

Bed & Breakfast Reservations ☎617/964-1606, ⓦwww.bbreserve.com. Lists B&Bs in Greater Boston, on the North Shore, and on Cape Cod.

Boston Reservations/Boston Bed & Breakfast ☎781/547-5427, ⓦwww.bostonreservations.com. Competitive rates at B&Bs as well as at leading hotels.

Downtown

Courtyard Boston Tremont Hotel 275 Tremont St ☎617/426-1400, ⊛www.marriott.com; NE Medical Center **T**. If you want to be in the Theater District you can't do better than this Marriott-managed 1925 hotel, the former national headquarters of the Elks Lodge. The opulent lobby somewhat compensates for the smallish rooms. ❾

Four Seasons 200 Boylston St ☎617/338-4400 or 1-800/332-3442, ⊛www.fourseasons.com; Arlington **T**. The tops in city accommodation, with all 288 rooms offering quiet, contemporary comfort. It's also home to the tempting *Aujourd'hui* restaurant (see p.121). ❾

Harborside Inn 185 State St ☎617/723-7500, ⊛www.harborsideinnboston.com; State **T**. This small hotel is housed in a renovated 1890s mercantile warehouse across from Quincy Market. The rooms – with exposed brick, hardwood floors, and cherry furniture – are a welcome surprise for this part of town, which can lean toward a chain hotel mentality. ❽

Hyatt Regency 1 Ave de Lafayette ☎617/912-1234, ⊛www.regencyboston.hyatt.com; Chinatown **T**. The Hyatt is just one of the reasons for Downtown Crossing's regeneration in recent years. The plush hotel is beautifully furnished with antiques, and there's a fantastic array of services. Wi-fi available. ❾

Langham 250 Franklin St ☎617/451-1900 or 1-800/543-4300, ⊛www.langhamhotels.com; State **T**. This stern granite building in the heart of the Financial District is the former Federal Reserve Bank of Boston. The spacious rooms all feature cable TV, internet access, and Italian marble bathrooms. Be sure and check out their Saturday chocolate bar (see p.118). ❽

Marriott Custom House 3 McKinley Square ☎617/310-6300 or 1-888/236-2427, ⊛www.marriott.com; Aquarium **T**. All the rooms at this downtown landmark-turned-hotel are one-bedroom suites with spectacular Boston Harbor and city views. ❾

Millennium Bostonian Hotel 26 North St, Faneuil Hall Marketplace ☎617/523-3600 or 1-866/866-8086, ⊛www.millenniumhotels.com; Government Center **T**. This hotel, in the heart of downtown, has splendid rooms, some with fireplaces and en-suite balconies. Common areas have wi-fi. ❾

Nine Zero 90 Tremont St ☎617/772-5800, ⊛www.ninezero.com; Park St **T**. Executive-class hotel with 190 polished rooms equipped with cushy beds, high-speed and wireless internet, CD players, and a complimentary morning paper. Amazing central location. ❾

Omni Parker House 60 School St ☎617/227-8600 or 1-800/843-6664, ⊛www.omniparkerhouse.com; Park **T**. No one can compete with the *Omni Parker House* in the history department: it's the oldest continuously operating hotel in the US. Though the present building only dates from 1927, the lobby, decorated in dark oak with carved gilt moldings, recalls the splendor of the original nineteenth-century building that once housed it. Although the rooms are small, they have been recently renovated. ❾

Radisson Hotel Boston 200 Stuart St ☎617/482-1800, ⊛www.radisson.com; Arlington **T**. Pleasingly located in the Theater District just one block from the Common, this cozy, chic Radisson garners great reviews for its spacious rooms and nice amenities like free wi-fi and private balconies. ❽

XV Beacon 15 Beacon St ☎617/670-1500 or 1-877/XVB-EACON, ⊛www.xvbeacon.com; Park St **T**. Luxurious boutique hotel across from the Boston Athenæum, with 61 spectacular rooms equipped with marble bathrooms, high-speed internet, Kiehl's toiletries, CD players, decadent upholstery, and working gas fireplaces. Rates include use of a chauffeured Lexus. ❾

Waterfront

Boston Harbor Hotel 70 Rowes Wharf ☎617/439-7000, ⊛www.bhh.com; South Station **T**. Opulent accommodation in an atmosphere of studied corporate elegance, right on the water. There's a health club, pool, gracious concierge staff, and rooms with harbor and city views; the former are substantially pricier. ❾

InterContinental Hotel 510 Atlantic Ave ☎617/747-1000, ⊛www.intercontinentalboston.com; South Station **T**. Swanky hotel that caused quite a buzz when it opened in 2006 because it was seen as a harbinger of the waterfront's rejuvenation. It offers deluxe amenities (including a fitness center with a 45ft heated pool) and spacious, modern rooms in a nice location close to South Station. Also home to *Miel*, a 24hr brasserie. ❾

Marriott Long Wharf 296 State St ☎617/227-0800 or 1-888/236-2427, ⊛www.marriott.com; Aquarium **T**. Many of the rooms here boast harbor views, but the stunning, vaulted lobby is what really makes this Marriott stand out. ❾

Seaport Hotel 1 Seaport Lane ☎617/385-4000 or 1-877/SEAPORT, ⊛www.seaportboston.com; World Trade Center **T**. A luxurious Boston newcomer out in the Seaport District, this hotel offers access to the Institute of Contemporary Art and Convention Center, as well as business travel standards like cozy linens and internet access. ❾

Westin Boston Waterfront 425 Summer St
ⓣ617/532-4600, ⓦwww.westinbostonwaterfront
.com; World Trade Center **T**. Over the bridge in the
Seaport District, this stylish new hotel, connected
to the Convention Center, is mainly favored by
business folks, but its relatively reasonable rates
are beginning to tempt other happy patrons. ⑧

North End

La Cappella Suites 290 North St
ⓣ617/523-9020, ⓦwww.lacappellasuites
.com; Haymarket **T**. Accommodation has finally
come to the North End with this lovely new arrival
– three cozy, modern rooms with wi-fi, cable TV,
and a nice public seating area. Two of the rooms
have private balconies. Be prepared for a five-floor
walk up to the rooms. ⑥–⑧

Charlestown

Bed & Breakfast Afloat 28 Constitution Rd
ⓣ617/241-9640, ⓦwww.bedandbreakfastafloat
.com; Community College **T**. Guests at this B&B
stay on a houseboat, sailboat, or yacht, right in
Boston Harbor. All vessels come with Continental
breakfast and access to the marina pool; the fancier
ones also have DVD players and hot tubs. ⑦–⑨
Constitution Inn 150 3rd Ave ⓣ617/241-8400 or
1-800/495-9622, ⓦwww.constitutioninn.org; North
Station **T**. This inn, from which downtown is but a
ferry ride away, has 150 rooms equipped with
cable TV, a/c, and private baths, in addition to an
on-site weight-room, sauna, and pool. ⑧
Residence Inn Marriott Boston Harbor 34–44
Charles River Ave ⓣ617/242-9000, ⓦwww
.residenceinnboston.com; Community College **T**.
The Marriott's all-suite *Residence Inn* is close to
some of the main sights along the Freedom Trail.
The amazing views of Boston's skyline over the
river more than make up for the slightly sterile
atmosphere. Wi-fi available. ⑨

Beacon Hill

Beacon Hill Hotel 25 Charles St ⓣ617/723-7575
or 1-888/959-BHHB, ⓦwww.beaconhillhotel.com;
Charles **T**. Pampered luxury in the heart of
Beacon Hill, these thirteen sleek chambers come
with flat-screen TVs and high-speed internet. The
hotel is also home to a fantastic bistro and
fireplace bar. ⑨
Charles Street Inn 94 Charles St ⓣ617/314-8900,
ⓦwww.charlesstreetinn.com; Charles **T**. Intimate,
romantic inn with rooms named after Boston
luminaries: the "Isabella Stewart Gardner" features a
Rococo chandelier, while the "Oliver Wendell
Holmes" boasts a king-sized sleigh bed. All rooms
come with working fireplaces. ⑨

Holiday Inn Boston at Beacon Hill 5 Blossom St
ⓣ617/742-7630, ⓦwww.hisboston.com; Charles
or Bowdoin **T**. Somewhat misleadingly named – it's
located in the West End – this Holiday Inn property
has pretty rooms and all the modern accoutrements, including a weight room and pool. ⑨
The John Jeffries House 14 David G.
Mugar Way ⓣ617/367-1866, ⓦwww
.johnjeffrieshouse.com; Charles **T**. This little gem
has some of the best prices in town, and clean
and tasteful rooms to match. A mid-scale hotel at
the foot of Beacon Hill, it features Victorian-style
decor, cable TV, wi-fi, and kitchenettes in most
rooms. ⑤–⑦
Liberty Hotel 215 Charles St
ⓣ617/224-4000, ⓦwww.libertyhotel.com;
Charles **T**. The *Liberty Hotel* has taken over the
labyrinthine digs of an 1851 prison in Beacon Hill and
fashioned it with stylish furnishings and lush details
such as a fitness and business center, phenomenal
views, same-day laundry service, and overnight
shoe-shines. They also have the *Scampo* restaurant
and the *Alibi* lounge (see p.126), currently the places
to see and be seen in Boston. ⑨

West End

Bulfinch Hotel 107 Merrimac St ⓣ617/624-0202,
ⓦwww.bullfinchhotel.com; North Station **T**. A
beautiful and fresh addition to the West End, this
sleek hotel is housed in a vintage triangular building.
The pretty, neutral-toned rooms are brightened with
contemporary paintings, and there's high-speed
internet and an exercise room; the *Bulfinch* also plays
host to the fabulous *Flatiron Tapas Bar & Lounge*. ⑧
Onyx Hotel 155 Portland St ⓣ617/557-9955,
ⓦwww.onyxhotel.com; North Station **T**. The stark,
glass-paneled front of this small luxury hotel belies
an opulent interior, though avoid the "Britney
Spears" room – designed by her mom, it looks as
you would have expected the singer's childhood
room to look, complete with pink Bible and fairy
statuettes.Very pet-friendly, and the in-hotel *Ruby
Room* bar is great for a nightcap. ⑨

Back Bay

463 Beacon Street Guest House 463 Beacon St
ⓣ617/536-1302, ⓦwww.463beacon.com; Hynes
T. The good-sized, no-frills rooms in this renovated
brownstone in the heart of Back Bay are available
by the night, week, or month, and come equipped
with kitchenettes, cable TV, and various hotel
amenities (though no maid service); some have a/c,
hardwood floors, and ornamental fireplaces. There
are some less expensive rooms with shared baths.
Ask for the top-floor room, which has a nice view
from its balcony. ④

Boston Park Plaza Hotel & Towers 50 Park Plaza at Arlington St ☏617/426-2000 or 1-800/225-2008, ⓦwww.bostonparkplaza.com; Arlington **T**. The *Plaza's* old-school elegance and hospitality – plus its central location – make it stand out; the high-ceilinged rooms, complete with high-speed internet, are quite comfortable, too. ⑨

Charlesmark Hotel 655 Boylston St ☏617/247-1212, ⓦwww.thecharlesmark .com; Copley **T**. Forty smallish, contemporary rooms with cozy beechwood furnishings, good rates, a lively bar, and modern amenities like wi-fi and CD players (the sound system is hooked into your bathroom so you can sing as you shower). ⑦–⑨

The Colonnade 120 Huntington Ave ☏617/424-7000 or 1-800/962-3030, ⓦwww .colonnadehotel.com; Prudential **T**. The *Colonnade* has recently been reinvented with deluxe details such as high-thread-count bed linens, modern bathrooms, wi-fi in all rooms, flat-screen HDTVs, and iPod alarm clocks. Rooms are spacious, and in summer months there's access to a rooftop pool – the only one in Boston. ⑨

Copley Inn 19 Garrison St ☏617/236-0300 or 1-800/232-0306, ⓦwww.copleyinn.com; Prudential **T**. Comfortable rooms with full kitchens, a friendly staff, and a great location. A fine budget option in Back Bay, especially since if you stay six days, the seventh night is free. ⑤

Copley Square Hotel 47 Huntington Ave ☏617/536-9000 or 1-800/225-7062, ⓦwww .copleysquarehotel.com; Copley **T**. This historic spot is currently rejuvenating its 143 rooms to have wi-fi, contemporary decor, iPod docks, twice-a-day housekeeping services, and "anything, anytime, delivered within a reasonable amount of time." ⑨

Eliot 370 Commonwealth Ave ☏617/267-1607 or 1-800/442-5468, ⓦwww.eliothotel.com; Hynes **T**. West Back Bay's answer to the *Ritz*, this plush, nine-floor hotel has sizeable rooms with kitchenettes, Italian marble baths, huge beds with Egyptian cotton sheets, and wi-fi. ⑨

Fairmont Copley Plaza 138 St James Ave ☏617/267-5300 or 1-800/795-3906, ⓦwww .fairmont.com; Copley **T**. Built in 1912, this pretty, iconic spot right by the city's main library boasts Boston's most elegant lobby. Even if you don't stay here, you should at least have a martini in the fabulous *Oak Bar* (see p.126). ⑨

Hotel 140 140 Clarendon St ☏617/585-5600, ⓦwww.hotel140.com; Back Bay **T**. Completely renovated in 2005, this 54-room boutique hotel offers accommodation that ranges from budget to "superior," as well as some twin-bed options – a welcome respite from many Back Bay prices

– although with its youthful clientele and location inside the YWCA headquarters building, its "budget" aspect is felt. ⑦

Jurys Boston 350 Stuart St ☏617/266-7200, ⓦwww.jurysboston.com; Arlington **T**. Set in a 1920s building that used to be Boston Police headquarters, the 220 smallish rooms here have huge beds, marble bathrooms, multi-head showers, and heated towel racks. The function rooms are named after celebrated Irish writers Shaw, Yeats, Beckett, Joyce, and Wilde; displays in the lobby show old police memorabilia. ⑨

The Lenox 61 Exeter St ☏617/536-5300 or 1-800/225-7676, ⓦwww.lenoxhotel.com; Copley **T**. Billed as Boston's version of the *Waldorf-Astoria* when its doors first opened in 1900, *The Lenox* is a far cry from that now, though it's still one of the most comfortably upscale hotels in the city, with recently renovated rooms that garner positive reviews from patrons. ⑨

Mandarin Oriental 776 Boylston St ☏617/535-8888, ⓦwww.mandarinoriental .com/boston; Copley **T**. Boston is all abuzz with the opening of this glamorous, extremely expensive Back Bay hotel. Spacious rooms offer such luxuries as silk window treatments, personal trainers, and an indulgent spa. *L'Espalier* restaurant (see p.121), long a darling of Boston's restaurant scene, will be moving from its landmark brownstone digs into the hotel. ⑨

Newbury Guest House 261 Newbury St ☏617/437-7666, ⓦwww.newburyguesthouse .com; Copley **T**. Big Victorian brownstone with 32 rooms that run the gamut from cramped chambers with overstuffed chairs to spacious bay-windowed quarters with sleigh beds. Continental breakfast included, wi-fi throughout, and a really great location. Still, you'll feel the fact that it's a budget option – the decor feels tired in spots. ⑦

Taj Boston 15 Arlington St ☏617/536-5700 or 1-800/241-3333, ⓦwww.tajhotel.com; Arlington **T**. Replacing (albeit lovingly) the city's historic *Ritz-Carlton* flagship, *Taj Boston* is the ultimate in luxurious, old-school Boston accommodation, with wood-burning fireplace suites, gilded antique furniture, and a not-to-be-beat location across from the Public Garden. ⑨

South End

82 Chandler Street 82 Chandler St ☏617/482-0408 or 1-888/482-0408, ⓦwww.82chandler.com; Back Bay **T**. Basic rooms in a restored 1863 brownstone that sits on an up-and-coming street in the South End. Wi-fi available throughout. ⑥

Chandler Inn 26 Chandler St ☏617/482-3450, ⓦwww.chandlerinn.com; Back Bay **T**.

Contemporary, comfortable European-style boutique hotel above the popular *Fritz* bar (see p.133); perks like satellite TV, in-room wi-fi, and Continental breakfast are included in the rates. ⑧

Clarendon Square Inn 198 W Brookline St ☎617/536-2229, ⓦwww.clarendonsquare.com; Back Bay **T**. Gorgeous, well-loved B&B on a pretty South End side street with indulgent perks like heated bathroom tiles, limestone floors, and a 24hr roof-deck hot tub. ⑥–⑨

Encore B&B 116 West Newton St ☎617/247-3425, ⓦwww.encorebandb.com; Back Bay **T**. On a pleasant South End side street, you'll get pampered at this cheerful B&B with contemporary decor, wi-fi, and a sitting area or balcony in all three of their rooms. ⑥–⑧

Kenmore Square and the Fenway

The Buckminster 645 Beacon St ☎617/236-7050 or 1-800/727-2825, ⓦwww.bostonhotelbuckminster .com; Kenmore **T**. Though renovated not so long ago, the 1897 *Buckminster* retains the feel of an old Boston hotel with its antique furnishings. It's also within easy walking distance of Fenway Park and Boston University. Breakfast included. ⑦

Gryphon House 9 Bay State Rd ☎617/375-9003 or 1-877/375-9003, ⓦwww.innboston.com; Kenmore **T**. This hotel-cum-B&B around the corner from Fenway has eight budget yet stylish suites equipped with working gas fireplaces, cable TV, VCR, CD player, and high-speed internet. Free parking. ⑧

Hotel Commonwealth 500 Commonwealth Ave ☎617/933-5000, ⓦwww .hotelcommonwealth.com; Kenmore **T**. Old-world charm mixed with modern decor make this a welcome addition to Boston's hotel scene. Nice touches include choice linens and L'Occitaine products. The hotel also hosts the fabulous *Eastern Standard* bar (see p.127), *Great Bay* restaurant (see p.122), and *Foundation Lounge* (see p.127). ⑨

Oasis Guest House 22 Edgerly Rd ☎617/267-2262, ⓦwww.oasisgh.com; Symphony **T**. Sixteen comfortable, budget rooms, some with shared baths, in a renovated brownstone near Symphony Hall. ④

Brookline

Beech Tree Inn 83 Longwood Ave ☎617/277-1620, ⓦwww.thebeechtreeinn.com; Longwood **T**. Just two blocks from the **T**, this welcoming Victorian has ten brightly decorated rooms, scrumptious breakfasts, and baked goods throughout the day. ⑤–⑦

On The Park B&B 88 Columbia St ☎617/277-0910, ⓦwww.onthepark.net; Griggs St or Winchester St **T**.

A little off the beaten path, this 100-year-old home has three lovely bedrooms decked out in warm tones with a nice mix of contemporary and antique furnishings. ⑥

Cambridge

Blue's Bed and Breakfast 82 Avon Hill St ☎617/354-6106, ⓦwww.bluesbedandbreakfast .com; Porter or Harvard **T**. Two sunny, folk-art filled bedrooms in a cozy B&B that's near Harvard Square and is blessed with welcoming, world-traveling innkeepers. Free wi-fi, great breakfasts. ⑤

Cambridge Bed and Muffin 267 Putnam Ave ☎617/576-3166, ⓦwww.bedandmuffin.com; Central or Harvard **T**. Just one block from the Charles River and close to Harvard and Central squares, this tranquil B&B has endearing, cheerful little rooms and a friendly owner. No en-suite bathrooms, and no TVs, but plenty of books and quiet. ④

Charles Hotel 1 Bennett St ☎617/864-1200 or 1-800/882-1818, ⓦwww.charleshotel.com; Harvard **T**. Clean, bright rooms – some overlooking the Charles River – that have a good array of amenities: cable TV, minibar, Shaker furniture, and access to the adjacent WellBridge Health Spa. There's also an excellent jazz club, *Regattabar* (see p.129), and two great restaurants, *Henrietta's Table* (see p.123) and *Rialto*. ⑨

Harding House 288 Harvard St ☎617/876-2888, ⓦwww.cambridgeinns.com; Harvard **T**. This cozy Victorian home has 14 bright rooms with hardwood floors, throw rugs, TVs, a/c, and shared or private bath. Rates include breakfast, and there is free parking. ⑤–⑥

Hotel Marlowe 25 Edwin H Land Blvd ☎617/868-8000, ⓦwww.hotelmarlowe.com; Lechmere or Kendall **T**. The funky decor at this hotel is cozy and plush, with faux-leopard-print rugs and bright, boutiquey designs in the rooms. Internet access available. ⑨

Inn at Harvard 1201 Massachusetts Ave ☎617/491-2222 or 1-800/458-5886, ⓦwww.theinnatharvard.com; Harvard **T**. Harvard University owns this red-brick hotel, which is set right on campus. Its four-story atrium was inspired by a Venetian piazza, and its rooms, while small, have huge writing desks and look out onto the Square. ⑥–⑨

Irving House 24 Irving St ☎617/547-4600, ⓦwww.cambridgeinns.com; Harvard **T**. Excellent, friendly option near Harvard Square that shares the same management with the *Harding House* (see above). Laundry facilities (coin-operated) and tasty breakfasts are included; both shared and private baths. ⑤–⑨

Kendall Hotel 350 Main St ☎617/577-1300, ⓦwww.kendallhotel.com; Kendall **T**. This hotel near MIT occupies a former 1894 fire station. Its 65 quaint rooms are country-chic with quilts and reproduction antiques; modern amenities include internet and gym access. ❾

Le Meridien 20 Sidney St ☎617/577-0200, ⓦwww.lemeridien.com; Kendall Square **T**. Contemporary hotel anchoring an office tower near MIT. The modern rooms have muted color schemes, and come with internet access, both wired and wi-fi. ❾

Lotus Place Bed and Breakfast 208 Prospect St ☎617/201-4528, ⓦwww.lotusplace .com; Central **T**. Three charming, modern rooms with beautiful linens and contemporary bathrooms. The suite sleeps 2 to 4, and there are cheaper rates for singles. ❺–❽

Hostels

Berkeley Residence YWCA 40 Berkeley St ☎617/375-2524, ⓦwww.ywcaboston.org /berkeley; Back Bay **T**. Clean and simple rooms next door to a police station. All rates include breakfast; dinner is an additional $7.50. Singles ($60), doubles ($90), and triples ($105) in a convenient South End location. Longer-term accommodation only available to women.

HI–Boston 12 Hemenway St ☎617/536-1027, ⓦwww.bostonhostel.org; Hynes **T**. In the Fenway area, close to the hip end of Newbury St and the Lansdowne St clubs, this hostel features standard dorm accommodation, but stands out for its fun management, internet access, and Sunday pancake breakfasts. Dorm beds $32–39 a night. In summer, book ahead or check in at 8am.

HI–Boston at Fenway 575 Commonwealth Ave ☎617/536-9455, ⓦwww.bostonhostel.org; Kenmore **T**. A summer-only hostel (June 1 to mid-Aug) that functions as a BU dorm in winter months. Spacious rooms and a great location within walking distance of nightclubs and Fenway Park. Members $36, non-members $39.

YMCA of Greater Boston 316 Huntington Ave ☎617/536-7800, ⓦwww.ymcaboston.org /huntington; Northeastern **T**. Good budget rooms, and access to the Y's health facilities (pool, weight room, etc). Singles are $50, but you can get a four-person room for $100. Co-ed June–Sept, otherwise men-only. Ten-day maximum stay.

The City

Boston is small for an American city, but it nonetheless encompasses many diverse neighborhoods, almost all of which are easy to explore on foot. The **downtown** area is situated on a peninsula that juts into Boston Harbor; most of the other neighborhoods branch out south and west from here. Downtown really begins with Boston Common, a large public green that holds many of the city's major historical sights either on or near its grounds. A ten-minute walk east of the Common, historic Faneuil (pronounced "Fan-yoo-el") Hall, the so-called "Cradle of Liberty," goes a long way in capturing the spirit of downtown Boston, and nearby Quincy Market bustles with office workers in search of lunch. Across Surface Street and the Rose Kennedy Greenway (formerly I-93) from the marketplace is the **North End**, the city's Little Italy, while just across Boston's Inner Harbor is **Charlestown**, the home of the world's oldest commissioned warship, the USS *Constitution*. Southeast of the North End lies the **waterfront**, beautified since the Big Dig opened up the area by sending I-93 underground. These structural changes have also inspired development on the other side of the water, in the **Seaport District** and **Fort Point Channel** neighborhoods. Always a haven for artists' studios, they're also now a mecca for sleek boutiques, restaurants, and the Institute of Contemporary Art.

North of the Common are the vintage gaslights, red-brick Federalist townhouses, and narrow streets of **Beacon Hill**, the city's most exclusive residential neighborhood. Charles Street runs south along the base of the hill and separates Boston Common from the Public Garden, which marks the beginning of **Back Bay**. This similarly well-heeled neighborhood of opulent rowhouses is also home to modern landmarks like the John Hancock Tower, New England's tallest skyscraper. South of Back Bay is the gay enclave of the **South End**, known for its hip restaurants and residents. The student domains of **Kenmore Square** and the **Fenway** are west of Back Bay: the former has some of the area's best nightlife, while the latter is home to the Museum of Fine Arts, the Isabella Stewart Gardner Museum, and hallowed Fenway Park. Southwest of all these neighborhoods are Boston's vast **southern districts**, which boast some links in Frederick Law Olmsted's series of parks known as the "Emerald Necklace," such as the dazzling Arnold Arboretum and Franklin Park, home to the city zoo. Across the Charles River from Boston lies **Cambridge**, a must for its excellent bookstore-and-funky-café scene and, above all, Harvard University.

Downtown Boston

Boston's **downtown** encompasses both its colonial heart and contemporary core. An assemblage of red-brick buildings and modern office towers, the area's glamor factor doesn't quite rival that of other big-city centers, but it's still quite attractive. It is also home to a number of the best reasons – both historical and modern – for visiting the city.

The best place to start exploring downtown is **Boston Common**, a king-sized version of the tidy green space at the core of innumerable New England villages. If you want to learn about the city's past, follow the **Freedom Trail**, a self-guided walking tour (see box, p.72), out of the Common. Probably the most popular stop on the Trail is bustling **Faneuil Hall Marketplace**, but there are other areas of interest as well: **King's Chapel**, on Tremont Street, and the nearby **Old State House** mark the periphery of Boston's earliest town center, while **Spring Lane**, a tiny pedestrian passage off Washington Street, recalls the location of one of the bigger springs that lured early settlers over to the Shawmut Peninsula from Charlestown. The most evocative streets, however, are those whose character has been less diluted over the years – **School Street**, **State Street**, and the eighteenth-century enclave known as **Blackstone Block**, near Faneuil Hall. East of the Common is the **Financial District**, where the short streets follow the tangled patterns of colonial village lanes; south of here is the small but vibrant **Chinatown** and adjacent **Theater District**.

During the day, when the streets are full of office workers and tourists, the whole downtown area is quite lively, but come nightfall the crowds thin out substantially. Chinatown, the Theater District, and Quincy Market are exceptions to this, as is the **waterfront**, which is seeing a renaissance following the completion of the Big Dig. The latter area is particularly pleasant, illuminated by the twinkling lights of moored ships.

Boston Common and around

Boston's premier open space is **Boston Common**, a fifty-acre green that effectively separates historic, workaday downtown from its posh neighbors, the Beacon Hill and Back Bay districts. Established in 1634 as "a trayning field" and "for the feeding of cattell" – or so a tablet opposite the central Park Street **T** station relates – the Common is still more of a functional space than a decorative one, used both by pedestrian commuters on their way to downtown's office towers and by tourists seeking the **Boston Common Visitor's Information Center** (see p.58), the official starting-point of the Freedom Trail. While not as well manicured as the adjacent **Public Garden** (see p.94), it nonetheless offers plenty of benches and lawn space if you are looking to take a breather.

The Common has served many roles and had many faces over the years. Even before John Winthrop and his fellow Puritan colonists earmarked the land for public use in 1634, it was used as pasture by the Reverend William Blackstone, Boston's first European settler. Not long after, it disintegrated into little more than

▲ Boston Common

a town gallows. Newly elected president George Washington made an appearance on the Common in 1789, as did his aide-de-camp, the Marquis de Lafayette, several years later. In the nineteenth century, iron fencing encircled the entire park, where it stayed until World War II, when the majority of it was used for scrap metal: it is said to be at the bottom of Boston Harbor.

While often unnoticed by passers-by, the **Central Burying Ground** has occupied the southeast corner of the Common, near the intersection of Boylston and Tremont streets, since 1754. The gravestones are worth a meander; artist Gilbert Stuart (see p.273), best known for his portraits of George Washington, died penniless and was interred in Tomb 61. Among other notable residents are members of the largest family to take part in the Boston Tea Party, various soldiers of the Revolutionary Army, and Redcoats killed in the Battle of Bunker Hill.

It's a short walk from the graveyard to **Flagstaff Hill**, the highest point on the Common, crowned with the Civil War **Soldiers and Sailors Monument**, which is topped by a bronze statue of Lady Liberty and encircled by four plaques displaying scenes of cap-wearing sailors and bayonet-toting soldiers. A repository of gunpowder in colonial days, the hill overlooks the **Frog Pond**, once home to legions of unusually large amphibians and the site of the first water pumped into the city. These days it's a simple kidney-shaped pool, used for wading in summer and ice-skating in winter; there's also a really great playground nearby. A path east of the pond leads to the elegant, two-tiered **Brewer Fountain**, an 1868 bronze replica of one from the Paris Exposition of 1855; the scantily clad gods and goddesses at its base are watched over by the cherubs above.

Park Street

The 1809 **Park Street Church**, just across from the Common at the corner of Park and Tremont streets (mid-June to Aug daily 8.30am–3pm; rest of year by appointment; free; ☎617/523-3383; Park Street **T**), is a large and rather uninteresting building, though its 217-foot-tall white telescoping **steeple** is undeniably impressive. The church's reputation rests not on its aesthetic, however, but on the events that took place inside: this is where William Lloyd Garrison delivered his first public address calling for the nationwide abolition of slavery, and where the song *America* ("My country 'tis of thee …") was first sung, on July 4, 1831.

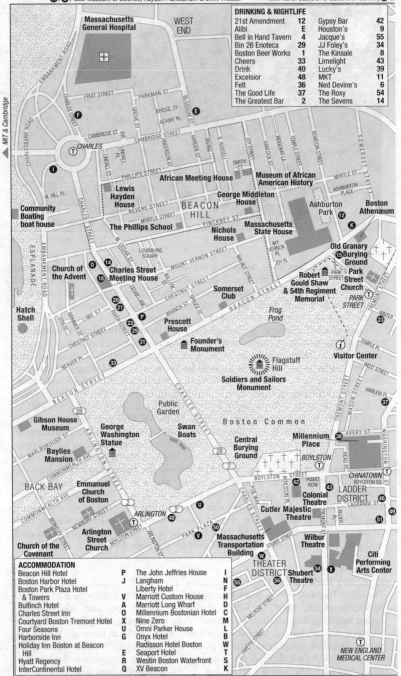

DRINKING & NIGHTLIFE

21st Amendment	12	Gypsy Bar	42
Alibi	E	Houston's	9
Bell in Hand Tavern	4	Jacque's	55
Bin 26 Enoteca	29	JJ Foley's	34
Boston Beer Works	1	The Kinsale	8
Cheers	33	Limelight	43
Drink	40	Lucky's	39
Excelsior	48	MKT	11
Felt	36	Ned Devine's	6
The Good Life	37	The Roxy	54
The Greatest Bar	2	The Sevens	14

ACCOMMODATION

Beacon Hill Hotel		The John Jeffries House	I
Boston Harbor Hotel	P	Langham	N
Boston Park Plaza Hotel	J	Liberty Hotel	F
& Towers	V	Marriott Custom House	H
Bulfinch Hotel	A	Marriott Long Wharf	D
Charles Street Inn	O	Millennium Bostonian Hotel	C
Courtyard Boston Tremont Hotel	X	Nine Zero	M
Four Seasons	U	Omni Parker House	L
Harborside Inn	G	Onyx Hotel	B
Holiday Inn Boston at Beacon		Radisson Hotel Boston	W
Hill	E	Seaport Hotel	T
Hyatt Regency	R	Westin Boston Waterfront	S
InterContinental Hotel	Q	XV Beacon	K

▼ South End

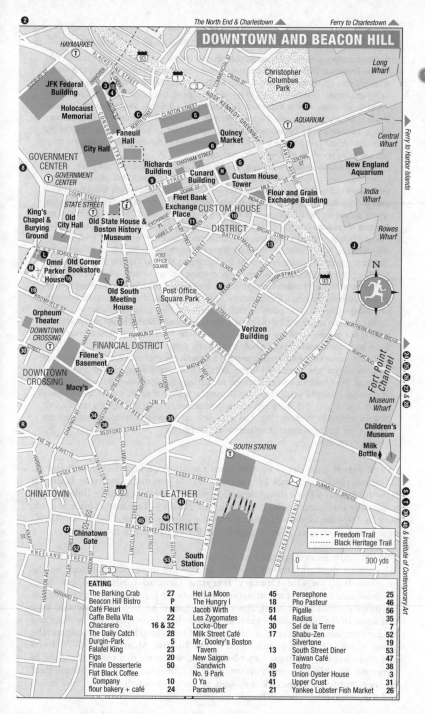

DOWNTOWN AND BEACON HILL

The North End & Charlestown ▲   Ferry to Charlestown ▲

EATING

The Barking Crab	27	Hei La Moon	45	Persephone	25
Beacon Hill Bistro	P	The Hungry I	18	Pho Pasteur	46
Café Fleuri	N	Jacob Wirth	51	Pigalle	56
Caffe Bella Vita	22	Les Zygomates	44	Radius	35
Chacarero	16 & 32	Locke-Ober	30	Sel de la Terre	7
The Daily Catch	28	Milk Street Café	17	Shabu-Zen	52
Durgin-Park	5	Mr. Dooley's Boston		Silvertone	19
Falafel King	23	Tavern	13	South Street Diner	53
Figs	20	New Saigon		Taiwan Café	47
Finale Desserterie	50	Sandwich	49	Teatro	38
Flat Black Coffee		No. 9 Park	15	Union Oyster House	3
Company	10	O Ya	41	Upper Crust	31
flour bakery + café	24	Paramount	21	Yankee Lobster Fish Market	26

The Freedom Trail

Boston's history is remarkably accessible, thanks largely to tourist-friendly contrivances like the **Freedom Trail**. The path originated after World War II, when Boston experienced an economic slump as people migrated to the suburbs; in response, resident William Schofield came up with the idea of a trail highlighting the city's sights to lure visitors – and their money – back into town. Delineated by a 2.5-mile-long red-brick (or paint) stripe in (or on) the sidewalk, the trail stretches from Boston Common to Charlestown, linking sixteen points "significant in their contribution to this country's struggle for freedom." About half the sights on the trail are related to the Revolution itself; the other half are more germane to other times and topics.

In the Revolution-relevant column, there's the **Old North Church** (see p.84), whose lanterns warned of the British troop movements in 1775; **Faneuil Hall** (see p.74), where opposition to the Brits' proposed tea tax was voiced; the **Old South Meeting House** (see p.77), wherein word came that said tax would be imposed; the **Old State House**, which served as the Boston seat of British government (see p.75); and the site of the **Boston Massacre** (see p.76). Other stops on the trail include the **USS Constitution** (see p.87), which failed to sink under British cannon fire in the War of 1812, earning her the nickname "Old Ironsides"; the **Park Street Church** (see p.69), site of William Lloyd Garrison's seminal oration in favor of abolition; and the **Old Corner Bookstore** (see p.76), a publishing house for American (and some British) writers. You'll also find two instances of British dominion along the trail: the **Bunker Hill Monument** (see p.89), an obelisk commemorating a British victory, albeit in the guise of a moral one for America, and **King's Chapel** (see opposite), built to serve the King's men stationed in Boston. Finally, you can check out the gilt-domed **Massachusetts State House** (see p.91) after visiting the gravesites of the Boston luminaries who fought for it – they lie interred in three separate **cemeteries** (see below, opposite, and p.86).

Though some of the touches intended to accentuate the trail's appeal move closer to tarnishing it (the costumed actors outside some of the sights, the pseudo-old signage), the Freedom Trail remains the easiest way to orient yourself downtown, and is especially useful if you'll only be in Boston for a short time, as it does take in many "must-see" sights. For more info and an interactive timeline of Boston's history, visit Ⓦwww.thefreedomtrail.org. You can also pick up a detailed National Park Service **map** of the trail from the visitors' center at 15 State St.

Park Street itself slopes upward from the church along the edge of Boston Common toward the State House (see p.91). It was once known as **Bulfinch Row** for its many brick townhouses designed by architect Charles Bulfinch, but today only one remains, the bay-windowed **Amory–Ticknor House** at no. 9, built in 1804 for George Ticknor, the first publisher of *The Atlantic Monthly*; it's now home to the excellent restaurant *No. 9 Park* (see p.118 for review).

Old Granary Burying Ground

Adjacent to the Park Street Church is one of the more peaceful stops on the Freedom Trail, the **Old Granary Burying Ground** (daily 9am–5pm; free), the final resting place for numerous Revolutionary leaders. The entrance, an Egyptian Revival arch, fronts Tremont Street, and it's from the sidewalk here that some of the most famous gravesites can be best appreciated: the boulder and plaque commemorating revolutionary James Otis; Samuel Adams's tomb; and the group grave of the five people killed in the **Boston Massacre** of 1770. From any angle you can see the stocky **obelisk** at dead center that marks the grave of Benjamin Franklin's parents. Further inside are the graves of Peter Faneuil, **Paul Revere**, and **John Hancock**, although, as the rangers will tell you, "the stones and the bones may not match up."

The Boston Athenæum

Around the block from the Old Granary Burying Ground, the venerable **Boston Athenæum**, 101/2 Beacon St (Mon 8.30am–8pm, Tues–Fri 8.30am–5.30pm, Sat 9am–4pm; free; ☏617/227-0270, ⊛www.bostonathenaeum.org; Park Street **T**), was established in 1807, and is one of the oldest and most ornate independent research libraries in the country. In naming their library, the founders demonstrated not only high-minded classicism but also marketing sensibility, as its growing stature was a potent enough force to endow Boston with a lofty sobriquet – the "Athens of America" – that has stuck. Best known today are its special collections, including the original holdings of the library of King's Chapel, which contained the 1666 edition of Sir Walter Raleigh's *History of the World*, and its prominent artworks – an impressive array of sculptures, coupled with paintings by the likes of Sargent and Stuart. During the nineteenth century, the Athenæum's art collection was the most significant in New England, and provided the underpinnings for the initial collection at the Museum of Fine Arts. It's well worth popping inside to experience the atmosphere of studious refinement. However, unless you're a member, you'll be confined to the first floor. To get a better sense of the collection, take a docent-led art and architecture tour (Tues & Thurs 3pm; reservations required; free; ☏617/227-0270 ext 279).

King's Chapel and Burying Ground

Just a block or so east from the Athenæum is Boston's oldest cemetery, the atmospheric **King's Chapel Burying Ground**, 58 Tremont St (daily: June–Oct 9.30am–4pm; Nov–May 10am–4pm; hours may fluctuate; free; Park Street **T**), and its accompanying church, both well worth a wander. One of the chief pleasures of walking here is to examine the ancient tombstones, many beautifully etched with winged skulls and contemplative seraphim. The burying ground was one of the favorite Boston haunts of author **Nathaniel Hawthorne**, who drew inspiration from the grave of a certain Elizabeth Pain to create the famously adulterous character of Hester Prynne for his novel *The Scarlet Letter*.

The most conspicuous thing about the **chapel** that stands on the grounds (June–Sept Mon–Sat 10am–4.30pm, Sun 1.30–4pm; free) is its absence of a steeple (there were plans for one, just not enough money). The gray, foreboding building was completed in 1754, with the pillar-fronted portico added in 1789; the belfry boasts the biggest bell ever cast by Paul Revere. The current structure replaced an earlier wooden chapel, which had been constructed amid some controversy: in 1686, King James II revoked the Massachusetts Bay Colony's charter, installed Sir Edmund Andros as governor, and gave him orders to found an Anglican parish – a move that didn't sit too well with Boston's Puritan population. While hardly ostentatious, the elegant Georgian interior, done up with wooden Corinthian columns and lit by chandeliers, provides a marked contrast to the minimalist adornments of Boston's other old churches. It also features America's oldest pulpit, dating from 1717, and many of its original pews. Few visitors go past the entrance, but it is worth peeking inside, ideally during one of the weekly chamber music concerts (Tues 12.15–12.45pm; $3 suggested donation).

Government Center

Most visitors pass through **Government Center**, due north of King's Chapel Burying Ground and west of Faneuil Hall, at some point during their time in Boston, as it's a travel hub. That said, passing through is just about all there is to do, although this wasn't always the case: today's government buildings stands on the former site of **Scollay Square**, once Boston's red-light district. Scollay was razed in the early 1960s, and all traces of its salacious past eliminated; indeed, the only thing that remains from the area's steamier days is the Oriental Tea Company's Steaming Kettle advertisement. The plaza is now overlaid with concrete, thanks to a plan by I.M. Pei, and towered over by two monolithic edifices: Boston City Hall, on the east side, and the John F. Kennedy Federal Building, on the north. One pretty face stands out from all the concrete, however: the graceful nineteenth-century **Sears Crescent** building, former publishing house for the abolitionist journal *The Christian Freeman*.

Faneuil Hall Marketplace and around

Between the Financial District and the North End is **Faneuil Hall Marketplace**, a bustling public gathering ground popular with tourists and locals alike. Built as a market during colonial times, it declined during the nineteenth century and, like the area around it, was pretty much defunct until the 1960s, when it was successfully reinvented as a restaurant and shopping mall.

The much-hyped **Faneuil Hall** (daily 9am–5pm; ☎617/242-5642, ⓦwww .nps.gov; State Street **T**) doesn't appear particularly majestic from the outside: it's a four-story brick structure with a golden grasshopper weathervane. Nevertheless, this is where revolutionary firebrands such as Samuel Adams and James Otis whipped up popular support for independence by protesting British tax legislation. The first floor currently houses a panoply of tourist shops, which make for a less than dignified memorial; you'll also find an information desk, a post office, and a BosTix kiosk (see p.131) here. The second floor is more impressive, with an auditorium that has been preserved to reflect modifications made by Charles Bulfinch in 1805. Its focal point is a massive canvas depicting an embellished version of "The Great Debate," during which Daniel Webster argued against South Carolina Senator Robert Hayne for the concept of the United States as one nation. While the debate was an actual event in 1830, the painting contains a number of nineteenth-century luminaries, such as Nathaniel Hawthorne and Alexis de Toqueville, who certainly weren't in attendance – the artist simply thought this would help him sell his painting.

The three oblong markets just behind Faneuil Hall were built in the early eighteenth century to contain the trade that quickly outgrew the hall. The center building, known as **Quincy Market** (Mon–Sat 10am–9pm, Sun noon–6pm; ☎617/523-1300, ⓦwww.faneuilhallmarketplace.com; State Street **T**), holds a super-extended corridor lined with stands vending a variety of take-out treats – it's the mother of all food courts. To either side of Quincy Market are the **North and South markets**, which hold restaurants and popular chain clothing stores, as well as specialized curiosity shops (one sells only purple objects, another nothing but vests). There's not much to distinguish it from any other shopping complex, save a few good restaurants and some surrounding bars, but sitting on a bench on a summer day, eating ice cream while mobs of people mill about, is a quintessential (if slightly absurd) Boston experience.

If you walked here from Government Center, you might have noticed **Dock Square**, immediately at the back of Faneuil Hall, and so named for its original location directly on Boston's waterfront; carvings in the pavement indicate the shoreline in 1630. The square's center is dominated by a statue of **Samuel Adams**, notable for its hyperbolic caption: "A Statesman, incorruptible and fearless." A narrow corridor known as Scott's Alley heads north from here to Creek Square and **Blackstone Street**, the eastern edge of a tiny warren of streets. The uneven cobblestones and low brick buildings stretching west from here to Union Street have remained largely untouched since the 1750s; many of them, especially those along Union, now house restaurants and pubs. If in the area on a Friday or Saturday afternoon, follow Blackstone Street to Hanover to witness one of Boston's best-known open-air markets, the **Haymarket**. Here, produce sellers heckle patrons, and happy shoppers haggle right back.

The corner of Union and North streets marks the location of the former home of **William Dawes**, one of the riders who joined Paul Revere on his midnight ride. Unlike Revere, his house has not been favorably preserved – it's now a *McDonald's* – but you can view a plaque commemorating the site. Just north on Union you'll see six tall hollow glass pillars erected as a **memorial** to victims of the **Holocaust**. Built to resemble smokestacks, the columns are etched with six million numbers recalling the tattoos the Nazis gave their victims. Steam rises from grates beneath each of the pillars to accentuate their symbolism.

The Custom House District

South of the Faneuil Hall Marketplace, the wedge of downtown between State and Broad streets and Atlantic Avenue is the unfairly overlooked **Custom House District**, dotted with some excellent architectural examples, chief among them the **Custom House Tower** (now a Marriott hotel; see p.63), built in 1847 and surrounded by 32 huge Doric columns; the thirty-story Greek Revival tower itself was added in 1915. Though no longer the tallest skyscraper in New England (a status it held for forty-nine years), it still has plenty of character and terrific views – you can check them out from the 360-degree observation deck (weather permitting tours Mon–Thurs & Sat–Sun 2pm; free; ☎617/310-6300).

State Street originally extended into Boston Harbor, and the area still retains glimpses of its maritime past. Get a look at the elaborate cast-iron facade of the **Richards Building** at no. 114 – a clipper ship company's office in the 1850s – and the **Cunard Building** at no. 126, its ornamental anchors recalling Boston's status as the North American terminus of the first transatlantic steamship mail service. Another landmark, just a block south from the Custom House Tower, is the **Flour and Grain Exchange Building**, 177 Milk St, a fortress-like construction with a turreted, conical roof that evokes the Romanesque Revival style of prominent local architect H.H. Richardson.

Old State House

That the graceful, three-tiered tower of the red-brick **Old State House**, at the corner of Washington and State streets (daily 9am–5pm; $5; ☎617/720-1713, ⓦ www.bostonhistory.org; State Street **T**), is dwarfed by skyscrapers amplifies, rather than diminishes, its colonial-era dignity. For years this was the seat of the Massachusetts Bay Colony, and consequently the center of British authority in New England. Later it served as Boston's city hall, and in 1880 it was nearly demolished so that State Street traffic might flow more freely. Fortunately, the Boston Historical Society was formed in 1881 specifically to rally for the building's preservation, and was ultimately successful in converting it into a museum.

Downtown vistas

Whether from in or out of town, people can't seem to get enough of Boston's skyline – its pastiche of brownstone churches and glass-paneled skyscrapers framing Massachusetts Bay ranks among the country's finest. You can check out Boston from every angle by ascending the **Marriott Custom House** (see p.63), the **Prudential Tower** (see p.100), the office building at **470 Atlantic Ave**, and the **Bunker Hill Monument** (see p.89). The best lay of the land, though, is had from the water – board the **Charlestown ferry** (see p.87) or visit the **Harbor Islands** (see p.81) and watch the city recede.

The Boston Massacre

Directly in front of the Devonshire Street side of the Old State House, a circle of cobble-stones embedded in a small traffic island marks the site of the **Boston Massacre**, the tragic outcome of escalating tensions between Bostonians and the British Redcoats that occupied the city. This riot of March 5, 1770, began when a young wigmaker's apprentice began heckling an army officer over a barber's bill. The officer sought refuge in the Custom House, which stood opposite the Old State House at the time, but a throng of people had gathered, including more soldiers, at whom the mob flung rocks and snowballs. When someone threw a club that knocked a Redcoat onto the ice, he rose and fired. Five Bostonians were killed in the ensuing fracas. Two other patriots, John Adams and Josiah Quincy, actually defended the offending eight soldiers in court; six were acquitted, and the two guilty were branded on their thumbs.

The building has certainly seen its share of history. An impassioned speech in the second-floor Council Chamber by James Otis, a Crown appointee who resigned to take up the colonial cause, sparked the quest for independence from Britain fifteen years before it was declared; legend has it that on certain nights you can still hear him hurling his anti-British barbs. In addition, the **balcony** overlooking State Street was the place from which the Declaration of Independence was first read publicly in Boston, on July 18, 1776. Two hundred years later, Queen Elizabeth II – the first British monarch to set foot in Boston – made a speech from the balcony as part of the American Bicentennial activities. As for the **museum**, the permanent ground-level exhibit, titled "Colony to Commonwealth," has a number of well-designed displays chronicling Boston's role in inciting the Revolutionary War, including tea from the infamous party, a flag that the Sons of Liberty used to announce their meetings, a jacket belonging to John Hancock, and Paul Revere's propagandistic **print** of the Boston Massacre.

Adjacent to the Old State House, at 15 State St, is the downtown **visitors' center** for the National Park Service (daily 9am–5pm; free; ☎617/242-5642, ⓦwww.nps.gov/bost; State Street **T**), which is chock-full of maps, facts, and particularly helpful park rangers. There are also uncrowded bathrooms.

Washington Street shopping district

The **Washington Street shopping district** takes up much of downtown proper, and holds some of the city's most historic sights, but it tends to shut down after business hours. The stops can be seen in half a day, though you'll need to allow more time if shopping is on your agenda; the stretch around **Downtown Crossing** is full of stylish diversions.

Across School Street from King's Chapel is the legendary **Omni Parker House**. It was in this hotel that Boston cream pie – really a layered cake with custard filling and chocolate glaze on top – was concocted in 1855. On a more bizarre note, both Ho Chi Minh and Malcolm X used to work here, the former in the kitchen and the latter as a busboy.

Only one block long, School Street offers up some of the best of Boston's charms, beginning with the antique gaslights that flank the western wall of King's Chapel. Just beyond is a grand French Second Empire building that served as **Boston City Hall** from 1865 to 1969. A few doors down on the left, the gambrel-roofed former **Old Corner Bookstore** anchors the southern end of School as it joins Washington. In the nineteenth century, the stretch of Washington from here to Old South Meeting House was Boston's version of London's Fleet Street, with a convergence of booksellers, publishers, and newspaper headquarters. The bookstore itself – once home to the publishing house Ticknor & Fields – was

Boston's hottest literary salon, with the likes of Emerson, Longfellow, and even Dickens and Thackeray all part of their author list.

At the corner of School and Washington is the **Irish Famine Memorial**, commemorating the Irish refugees who emigrated to Boston in the 1840s as a result of the fungal potato crop that claimed one million lives in their home country. Its focus is an unsettling pair of statues, one depicting an Irish family holding their hands out for food, the other, a (presumably) Bostonian family ignoring them.

Old South Meeting House

Washington Street's big architectural landmark is the **Old South Meeting House**, at no. 310 (daily: April–Oct 9.30am–5pm; Nov–March 10am–4pm; $5, kids $1; ⊤617/482-6439, ⓦwww.oldsouthmeetinghouse.org; Downtown Crossing **T**), a charming brick church recognizable by its tower – a separate, but attached, structure that tapers into an octagonal spire. Put up in 1729, this is the second oldest church building in Boston, after Old North Church in the North End. The venue saw its share of anti-imperial rhetoric while it was still young. The day after the Boston Massacre, outraged Bostonians assembled here to demand the removal of the troops that were ostensibly guarding the town. More momentously, on the morning of December 16, 1773, nearly five thousand locals met here, awaiting word from Governor Thomas Hutchinson on whether he would permit the withdrawal of three ships in Boston Harbor containing taxed tea. When a message was received that the ships would not be removed, Samuel Adams announced, "This meeting can do no more to save the country!" His simple declaration triggered the **Boston Tea Party** (see box below).

Before becoming the **museum** it is today, the Meeting House served as a stable, a British riding-school, and even a bar. One of the things lost in the transition was the famous original high pulpit, which the British tore out during the Revolution and used as firewood; the ornate one standing today is a replica from 1808. Note the exterior **clock**, the same one installed in 1770. While the real draw here is the chance to experience a historical hotspot, if you take the audio tour, included in the admission price, you will hear campy re-enactments of a Puritan church service and the Boston Tea Party debates, among other more prosaic sound effects.

The Boston Tea Party

The first major act of rebellion preceding the Revolutionary War, the **Boston Tea Party** was far greater in significance than it was in duration. On December 16, 1773, a long-standing dispute over colonial taxation came to a dramatic head. At nightfall, a group of five thousand waited at Old South Meeting House to hear the governor's ruling regarding three ships full of tea (one of many imports from England bearing a Crown-imposed tax in the colonies) moored in Boston Harbor. Upon receiving word that the Crown would not lift the tax, the throng converged on Griffin's Wharf. Around one hundred of them, most dressed in Indian garb, boarded the brigs and threw their cargo of tea overboard. The partiers disposed of 342 chests of tea, each weighing 360 pounds; the total amount discarded was worth more than one million dollars by today's standards. While it had the semblance of spontaneity, the event was in fact planned beforehand, and the mob was careful not to damage anything but the offending cargo. In any case, the Boston Tea Party transformed protest into revolution. The ensuing British sanctions, colloquially referred to as the "Intolerable Acts," and the colonists' continued resistance, further inflamed the tension between the Crown and its colonies, which eventually exploded at Lexington and Concord (see p.143).

South of the Meeting House, pedestrian-friendly **Downtown Crossing**, an outdoor mall area centered on the intersection of Washington and Summer streets, brims with department stores and smaller shops that mostly cater to budget shoppers. Its nucleus is **Filene's Basement**, home to the legendary "Running of the Brides" event, in which brides-to-be claw their way to marked-down gowns. The everyday shopping experience is calmer.

The Financial District

Boston's **Financial District** hardly conjures the same image as those of New York or London, but it continues to wield influence and is not entirely devoid of historic interest – though this is generally more manifest in plaques rather than actual buildings. Like most of America's business districts, the area runs on an office-hours-only schedule, and many of its little eateries and Irish pubs are closed on weekends, though some brave new restaurants are beginning to appear. The generally immaculate streets follow the same short, winding paths as they did three hundred years ago, only now thirty- and forty-story skyscrapers have replaced the wooden houses and churches that used to clutter the area.

The most dramatic approach is east from Washington via Milk Street. A bust of **Benjamin Franklin** surveys the scene from a recessed niche above the doorway at 1 Milk St, across from the Old South Meeting House. The site marks Franklin's birthplace, although the building itself only dates from 1874. Further down Milk, the somber, 22-story **John W. McCormack Federal Courthouse** building formerly housed one of Boston's larger post offices, giving the adjacent **Post Office Square** its name. The plaza's pretty triangular layout and cascading fountains are popular with area professionals at lunchtime. A prime Art Deco specimen is nearby at 185 Franklin St, the head office of communications company **Verizon**. The step-top building was a 1947 design; more recently the phone booths outside were given a Deco makeover. **Exchange Place**, 53 State St, is a mirrored-glass tower rising from the facade of the old Boston Stock Exchange; the *Bunch of Grapes* tavern, a favorite watering hole of revolutionary rabble-rousers, once stood here. Behind it is tiny **Liberty Square**, once the heart of Tory Boston and now home to *Aspirations for Liberty*, a sculpture honoring the Hungarian anti-Communist uprising of 1956. The statue is an elegant depiction of rebels rising to hold up a (presumably rebellious) baby.

Chinatown

Boston's **Chinatown** lies wedged into just a few square blocks between the Financial and Theater districts – what it lacks in size it makes up in activity. Lean against a pagoda-topped payphone on the corner of **Beach and Tyler streets** and watch the way life here revolves around the food trade: by day, merchants barter over the price of produce, while by night Bostonians arrive in droves to linger at Chinatown's restaurants. Walk down either of those streets – the neighborhood's two liveliest – and you'll pass most of the restaurants, bakeries, and markets, in whose windows you'll see the usual complement of roast ducks hanging from hooks and aquariums filled with future seafood dinners. At the corner of Tyler and Beach streets is a plaque marking the site where John Wheatley purchased **Phillis Wheatley** to serve as his slave in 1761; twelve years later she become the first published African-American woman with "Poems on Various Subjects, Religious and Moral." Chinatown has two cool outdoor spaces: the impressive **Chinatown Gate**, a red-and-gilt monolith guarded by four Fu dogs, which overlooks the intersection of Hudson and Beach streets; and **Chinatown Park**, in front of the gate that's based on the ideals of Feng Shui and incorporates stones, streams, and waterfalls. Chinatown is at its most vibrant during its festivals, especially **Chinese (Lunar) New Year** in January (sometimes early Feb). At the **Festival of the August Moon**, there's a bustling street fair. Call Chinatown Main Street, a neighborhood cultural organization, for more info (℡617/350-6303).

The Leather District

Just east of Chinatown, the six square blocks bounded by Kneeland, Atlantic, Essex, and Lincoln streets designate the **Leather District**, which takes its name from the nineteenth-century days when the shoe industry was a mainstay of the New England economy, and the leather needed to make the shoes was shipped through the warehouses here. The leather industry in Boston has pretty much disappeared now, and the Financial District has horned in on its former territory, but some of the warehouses still have their signs on them, like the Boston Hide & Leather Co, at 20 East St. Apart from its leathery past, this petite area is known for sleek eateries and a number of galleries, well situated within lofty warehouses. Nearby **South Station** is Boston's main train and bus terminus.

The Theater District

Just south of Boston Common is the slightly seedy **Theater District**, the chief attractions of which are the flamboyant buildings that lend the area its name. Not surprisingly, you'll have to purchase tickets in order to inspect their interiors (see p.131), but it's well worth a quick walk along Tremont Street to admire the facades of the Wilbur, Colonial, and Cutler Majestic theaters. The **Citi Performing Arts Center** – formerly the Wang Center for the Performing Arts and the Schubert Theatre – is just around the corner from **Piano Row**, a section of Boylston Street between Charles and Tremont that was the center of American piano manufacturing and music publishing in the nineteenth and early twentieth centuries. There are still a few piano shops around, but the hip restaurants and clubs in the area are of greater interest. A number of these are tucked between Charles and Stuart streets around the mammoth **Massachusetts Transportation Building**, and cater to the theater-going crowd.

The waterfront

Boston's urban renewal program, sparked by the beginning of the Big Dig in the early 1990s, has resulted in a resurgence of its **waterfront** area, which stretches from the North End to South Station. The recent underground routing of the

---

The Harborwalk

The **Harborwalk** officially begins in Dorchester, curving eastwards into the beaches of South Boston (a whopping 47 miles in all). Though visitors shouldn't expect to see the whole thing, it's quite pleasant to walk the portion that meanders through the wharves alongside the Boston waterfront. Start at Lewis Wharf, where a gravel path leads to a pretty circular garden. Continue south, passing by Christopher Columbus Park and the Aquarium. Before arriving at the vaulted *Boston Harbor Hotel*, check out David von Schlegell's "Untitled Landscape" on India Wharf, two pairs of fifteen-foot L-shaped bends of metal which seem to magnetically compel children (and adults, too) to run between them. Throughout, there are peaceful harbor vistas, complete with sailboats drifting on the water, but the best scenery of the walk is contained between Lewis Wharf and 470 Atlantic Ave, former site of the Boston Tea Party and current home to a fantastic fourteenth-floor observation deck (free; daily 10am–5pm). For more information, visit the Harborwalk's extensive website (𝖶 www.bostonharborwalk.com).

John Fitzgerald Expressway (I-93), which had separated the waterfront from the rest of downtown since the 1950s, has allowed the city to reconnect with the sea through a series of projects such as the expansion of the New England Aquarium and the conversion of wharf buildings into housing. As you cross Surface Street, which separates Faneuil Hall Marketplace from the North End, take note of the **Rose Kennedy Greenway**, a thirty-acre public park occupying the strip that used to be I-93.

While the waterfront that's concentrated around **Long Wharf** is quite touristy (it's occupied by vendors selling T-shirts, furry lobsters, and the like), strolling the atmospheric **Harborwalk** (see box, p.79) that edges the water affords unbeatable views of Boston, and is a pleasant respite from historic sites. You'll also find plenty of diversion if you've got little ones in tow at the **New England Aquarium**. Otherwise, you can do some watery exploring on a number of **boat tours** or escape the city altogether by heading out to the **Harbor Islands**. The rapidly up-and-coming **Fort Point Channel** and the **Seaport District**, meanwhile, are two spacious harborside areas across the Congress Street Bridge from downtown. Accessible by the Silver Line **T**, the two neighborhoods are full of lofty old warehouse spaces, restaurants, and two compelling museums.

Long Wharf

The best place to start when visiting the waterfront is **Long Wharf**, which was built in 1710 and is still the area's hub. This is also the main point of departure for **harbor cruises**, whale-watching trips, and ferries to Cape Cod and Salem. As you might expect, summer is its most active season, when the wharf comes alive with vendors selling souvenirs and ice cream, although it's perhaps most enjoyable – and still relatively safe – at night, when even the freighters appear graceful against the moonlit water. Walk out to the end for an excellent view of **Boston Harbor**.

New England Aquarium

Next door to Long Wharf is the waterfront's main draw, the **New England Aquarium** (July–Aug Mon–Thurs 9am–6pm, Fri–Sun 9am–7pm; Sept–June Mon–Fri 9am–5pm, Sat & Sun 9am–6pm; $19.95, children $11.95; ☎617/973-5200, ⓦwww.neaq.org; Aquarium **T**). Especially fun for kids, the aquarium has plenty of good exhibits, like the penguins on the bottom floor; be sure to play with the device that maneuvers a fish-shaped point of light around the bottom of their pool – the guileless waterfowl mistake the light for a potential meal and follow it around hopefully. In the center of the aquarium's spiral walkway is an impressive collection of marine life: a three-story, 200,000-gallon cylindrical tank packed with sea turtles, moray eels, sharks, stingrays, and other ocean exotica. The Aquarium also runs **whale-watching** trips (April–Oct; 3hr 30min–5hr, call for times; $36, children $30; ☎617/973-5206) and is home to a **3D IMAX theater** (daily 9.30am–10.30pm; $9.95, children $7.95), which, at more than six stories high, has the largest screen in New England.

Situated between Long Wharf and Commercial Wharf, **Christopher Columbus Park** is a pretty green space bisected by a wisteria-laden trellis. This leisurely park also features a rose garden and kid-sized fountain, well loved in the summer months.

Children's Museum

It's hard to miss the larger-than-life **Hood Milk Bottle**, one of Boston's best-loved icons, across the Congress Street Bridge in the Fort Point Channel. It's estimated that if the bottle was filled with milk, it would hold 58,000 gallons. Just behind the bottle at 300 Congress St, the expanded **Children's Museum**

(Mon–Thurs, Sat & Sun 10am–5pm, Fri 10am–9pm; $10, children $8, Fri 5–9pm $1; ☎617/426-8855, ⓦwww.bostonkids.org; South Station **T**), comprises three floors of educational exhibits, designed to trick kids into learning about an array of topics, from musicology to the engineering of a humungous bubble. Before you leave, be sure to check out the Recycle Shop, where industrial leftovers are transformed into craft-fodder.

Institute of Contemporary Art

The pearl in the Seaport District's oyster is the newly opened **Institute of Contemporary Art**. Looking like a glamorous ice-cube perched above Boston Harbor, the museum, at 100 Northern Ave (Tues & Wed 10am–5pm, Thurs & Fri 10am–9pm, Sat & Sun 10am–5pm; $12, children ages 17 and under free; free on Thurs 5–9pm, and free for families the last Sat of the month; ☎617/478-3100, ⓦwww.icaboston.org; Courthouse Station **T**), gives you a show before you've even crossed the threshold. Once inside, the permanent collection and gallery space, located on the fourth floor, features works by late twentieth- and twenty-first-century artists such as photography by Nan Goldin, sculptural textiles by Mona Hatoum, and figures by Louise Bourgeois. Ongoing temporary exhibitions are also on view. One standout piece is Cornelia Parker's "Hanging Fire"; a suspended sculpture comprised of floating charcoal shapes that the artist uncovered at an arson crime site. Complementing the artwork is the building's dramatic cantilever shape, extending eighty feet over the water. From the interior, this section functions as the "Founders Gallery," a meditative ledge where, if you look down, you'll find yourself standing directly above the harbor.

The second floor houses an innovative theater space whose glass walls alter their transparency in order to accommodate for lighting; shows here range from modern dance performances to "The Matrix"; also, in summer the museum's gorgeous front deck offers live music shows and dance nights. Check the museum website for more information.

The Harbor Islands

Extending across Massachusetts Bay from Salem to Portsmouth, NH, the 34 islands that comprise the bucolic **Harbor Islands** served as defense points during the American Revolution and Civil War. They were transformed into a national park in 1996, with the result that six are now easily accessible by ferry from Long Wharf (see opposite), and a seventh, Little Brewster, has a ferry that leaves from Fan Pier.

The most popular and best served of the lot, **George's Island**, saw heavy use during the Civil War, as evidenced by the remains of **Fort Warren** (May to mid-Oct daily dawn–dusk; free), a battle station covering most of the island. Mostly used as a prison for captured Confederate soldiers, its musty barracks and extensive fortress walls have an eerie feel, although the parapets offer stunning views. You'll get more out of a visit by taking a park ranger tour (free). George's Island often holds performances, be it jazz, children's theater, or a vintage baseball game; check the Harbor Islands website (ⓦwww.bostonislands.com) for scheduling.

The Harbor Islands have seen major renovations of late, including faster ferries and, most notably, the addition of **Spectacle Island** as an accessible spot. Spectacle has outgrown its murky past (it was a horse rendering plant, then a city dump) to become an environmentally savvy green space. In cleaning up the island, engineers solved two civic headaches at once – they used the Big Dig's dirt (3.7 million cubic yards) to cap Spectacle's landfill. The island now features a small lifeguarded beach, a snack bar, a green visitors' center (complete with self-composting bathrooms), and pretty trails.

Island-bound

A fifteen-minute ferry ride connects Long Wharf with central **George's Island** or **Spectacle Island** (May to mid-Oct daily on the hour 9am–4pm, weekends every 30min, call to confirm times; $12, children $7; ☎617/223-8666, ⓦwww .bostonislands.com; Aquarium **T**), the hubs from which water taxis (free) shuttle visitors to the other four. Aside from George's and Spectacle, the more remote islands lack a freshwater source, so be sure to bring **bottled water** with you. The same goes for food – if you're traveling beyond George's or Spectacle, you should also consider packing a picnic lunch, though the former two islands offer low-key **snack bars** or – for a small snack – go **berry-picking** on Grape and Bumpkin islands. In the interest of preserving island ecology, no bicycles or in-line skates are allowed. You can **camp**, for a nominal fee, on three of the islands (May to mid-Oct; Lovells, Bumpkin, and Grape ☎1-877/422-6762); you'll need to bring your own supplies. The Harbor Islands **information** kiosk, at the foot of Long Wharf, keeps a detailed shuttle **schedule** and stocks excellent **maps**. Visit ⓦwww.bostonislands.com and ⓦwww .nps.gov/boha for more information.

If you're interested in seeing one of the other Harbor Islands, it's best to make a full day of it, as the shuttle service is a little irregular. The densely wooded **Lovells** is a good bet, hosting tidepools and sand dunes near the remains of Fort Standish, an early twentieth-century military base. The largest of all, the 134-acre **Peddocks**, is laced with hiking trails connecting the remains of Fort Andrews, used from 1904 to 1945, with a freshwater pond and wildlife sanctuary. **Bumpkin** was once the site of a children's hospital whose ruins, along with those of an old farmhouse, lie along raspberry-fringed pathways. More berries grow on **Grape**, an ideal bird-watching spot.

The most intriguing of the islands is the one furthest at sea – **Little Brewster** – home to the 1783 Boston Light, the oldest light station in the country, and the only one that still has a Coast Guard-staffed keeper on site. Excellent tours to Little Brewster are run daily (late June to mid-Oct) from Fan Pier by the National Park Service (3hr; bring a boxed lunch, and prepare for the 76-step walk up; $38, children $29; ☎617/223-8666, ⓦwww.bostonislands.com; South Station **T**).

The North End

Hemmed in nearly all around by Boston Harbor, the small, densely populated **North End** is Boston's Little Italy. The narrow streets here are chock-a-block with Italian bakeries and restaurants, and also hold some of Boston's most storied sights. Despite the fact that the above-ground highway that once separated the area from downtown has been removed (and replaced by the Rose Kennedy Greenway), and that the Haymarket **T** station isn't far away, the area still has a bit of a detached feeling, which makes it all the more charming.

The North End's insular quality goes back to colonial times, when it was actually an island, joined by short bridges to the mainland. Though landfill eventually ended the district's physical isolation, the North End remained very much a place apart. Irish immigrants poured in after the potato famine of 1845–48, followed by Eastern European Jews in the 1850s and southern Italians in the early twentieth century. The latter have for the most part stayed, and the North End is still Boston's most authentically Italian neighborhood. In recent years, however, yuppies have begun to overtake the area's waterfront, making inroads into rehabilitated tenements, and boutiques have cropped up along Hanover and Salem streets. Though you still see laundry dangling from windows and grandmothers chattering in Italian, it's feared that it won't be long before the neighborhood loses its distinctive character. In the meantime, however, everyone seems to be getting on splendidly.

Hanover Street and around

Hanover Street has long been the main connector between the North End and the rest of Boston, and it is along here – and small side streets like Parmenter and Richmond – that many of the area's traditional *trattorias*, cafés, and bakeries lie. It's also where you'll find, in its first few blocks, perhaps Boston's most authentically European flavor: although there are a handful of chain stores in the neighborhood, the majority of businesses remain refreshingly independent.

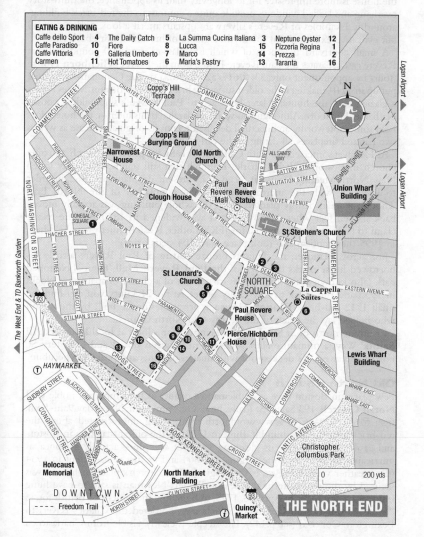

EATING & DRINKING

Caffe dello Sport	4	The Daily Catch	5	La Summa Cucina Italiana	3	Neptune Oyster	12
Caffe Paradiso	10	Fiore	8	Lucca	15	Pizzeria Regina	1
Caffe Vittoria	9	Galleria Umberto	7	Marco	14	Prezza	2
Carmen	11	Hot Tomatoes	6	Maria's Pastry	13	Taranta	16

THE NORTH END

The little triangular wedge of cobblestones and gaslights known as **North Square**, one block east of Hanover between Prince and Richmond, is among the most historic and attractive pockets of Boston. Here the eateries recede in deference to the **Paul Revere House**, the oldest residential address in the city, at no. 19 (mid-April to Oct daily 9.30am–5.15pm; Nov to mid-April Tues–Sun 9.30am–4.15pm; $3; T617/523-2338, Wwww.paulreverehouse.org). The three-story post-and-beam structure, which dates from about 1680, stands on the former site of the home of Puritan heavyweight Increase Mather, which burned down in the Great Fire of 1676. The building, in which Revere lived from 1770 to 1800, was restored in 1908 to reflect its seventeenth-century appearance; prior to that it served variously as a grocery store, tenement, and cigar factory. Though the house is more impressive for its longevity than its appearance, the third-story overhang and leaded windows provide quite a contrast to the red-brick buildings around it. Examples of Revere's silverware upstairs merit a look, as does a small but evocative exhibit about the mythologizing of his famed horseback ride.

A small courtyard, the focus of which is a glass-encased 900-pound bell that Revere cast, separates the Paul Revere House from the **Pierce/Hichborn House** (tours by appointment only; $3; T617/523-2338), a simple Georgian-style house put up in 1710, making it the oldest surviving brick house in Boston. Moses Pierce, a glazier, built the house; it later belonged to Paul Revere's shipbuilding cousin, Nathaniel Hichborn. Although you won't be dazzled by its interior, the house does hold some noteworthy architectural details: it retains its original staircase as well as two painted fireplaces, all dating to the early 1700s.

At Hanover's intersection with Clark Street is **St Stephen's Church**, the only church in Boston built by Charles Bulfinch that still stands. Originally called New North Meeting House, it received its present-day name in 1862, in order to keep up with the increasingly Catholic population of the North End. Though it seems firmly planted today, the whole building was actually moved back sixteen feet when Hanover Street was widened in 1870. A more recent claim to fame is that the funeral for JFK's mother, Rose Kennedy, was held here in 1995 (her baptism also took place here, 104 years prior).

Just across Hanover, the famous bronze **statue** of Paul Revere astride his borrowed horse marks the edge of the **Paul Revere Mall**. The cobblestoned park (also known as the Prado) was carved out of a chunk of apartment blocks in 1933 and runs back to tiny Unity Street. At no. 21 Unity you can find the small 1712 red-brick **Clough House**, a private residence built by the mason who helped lay the brick of the nearby Old North Church.

Continue north of St Stephen's on Hanover for a look at local landmark **All Saints' Way**, a miniature alley squeezed in between nos. 4 and 6 Battery St. Folksy and sweet, it's decked out with images of saints and peaceful cherubim.

Old North Church

Few places in Boston have as emblematic a quality as the simple yet noble **Old North Church**, 193 Salem St (daily: June–Oct 9am–6pm; Nov–May 9am–5pm; free; T617/523-6676, Wwww.oldnorth.com), rising unobstructed above the red-brick apartments around it. Built in 1723, it's the oldest structure in Boston, and easily recognized by its gleaming 191-foot **steeple** – actually a replica, as hurricanes toppled both the original in 1804 and its first replacement in 1954 (the weather vane, however, is the original). The church's place in history was secured by the two lanterns that sexton Robert Newman is said to have hung inside it on the night of April 18, 1775, to signal the movement of British forces "by sea" from Boston Common (which then bordered the Charles River) to Lexington–Concord (see p.142). The steeple is clearly visible from Charlestown

▲ Old North Church

across the water and even from downtown, lending a certain credence to this story. Still, some historians speculate that the lanterns were actually hung from another church, the North Meeting House, which occupied the spot in North Square (no. 12) where the **Sacred Heart Italian Church** now stands; that Tories burned that one for firewood in 1776 adds fuel to the theory. In any case, the spotlessly white interior here contains the oldest functioning clock in an American public building, made in 1726. The timber on which the box pews rest is supported by 37 basement-level crypts. Of the 1100 bodies resting therein, one is that of John Pitcairn, a British major killed in the Battle of Bunker Hill. His remains were tagged for Westminster Abbey, but didn't make it back.

Some of Old North's greatest charms are actually outside the church itself, notably the diminutive **Washington Memorial Garden**, the brick walls of which are bedecked with commemorative plaques honoring past church members, and the inviting **Eighteenth-Century Garden**, planted with floral varieties that were popular in that century.

Copp's Hill Burying Ground and Terrace

Up Hull Street from Old North Church, atmospheric **Copp's Hill Burying Ground** (daily dawn–dusk), with its eerily tilting slate tombstones and stunning harbor views, holds the highest ground in the North End. Among the ten thousand interred here are nearly a thousand men who had lived in the "New Guinea Community," a long-vanished colonial enclave of free blacks at the foot of the hill. The most famous gravesite, however, is that of the Mather family, just inside the wrought-iron gates on the Charter Street side. Increase Mather and son Cotton were dominant clerics in Boston's congregational meeting houses, a fact not at all reflected in the rather diminutive, if appropriately plain, tomb. You'll notice that many gravestones have chunks missing, the consequence of British soldiers using them for target practice during the 1775 Siege of Boston; the grave of one Captain Daniel Malcolm, in the third row of gravestones (starting at the left), bears particularly strong evidence of this.

The granite **Copp's Hill Terrace**, a plateau separated from the burial ground by Charter Street, was the place from which British cannons bombarded Charlestown during the Battle of Bunker Hill. Just over a century later, in 1919, a 2.3-million-gallon tank of molasses exploded nearby, creating a syrupy tidal wave thirty feet high that engulfed entire buildings and drowned 21 people and a score of horses. Old North Enders claim you can still catch a whiff of the stuff on exceptionally hot days. Lastly, across the street from Copp's Hill is Boston's **narrowest house**, at 44 Hull St. It really *is* narrow – nine- and a-half feet wide – and that's about it, as it's a private residence and you can't go in.

Salem and Prince streets

While the Old North Church is **Salem Street**'s star attraction, in the lower blocks between Prince and Cross streets, Salem is arguably the North End's most colorful thoroughfare. The actual street – whose name is a corruption of "Shalom Street," as it was known to its European Jewish settlers – is so narrow that the buildings seem to lean into one another, and light traffic makes it a common practice to walk right down the middle of the road. Along here you'll find an agreeable assemblage of Italian grocers, aromatic *pasticcerias*, and cafés.

Meanwhile, serpentine **Prince Street** cuts through the heart of the North End on an east–west axis, linking Salem and Hanover streets. Like most thoroughfares in the neighborhood, this appealing artery also has its share of restaurants, but it tends to be more social – locals typically pass the day along the pavement here on folding chairs brought from home. At the corner of Hanover Street, **St Leonard's Church**, 14 N Bennet St (Mon–Fri 9am–1pm; ☎617/523-2110), was supposedly the first Italian Catholic church in New England. The ornate interior is a marked contrast to the city's stark Protestant churches, while the so-called "Peace Garden" in front, with its prosaic plantings and tacky statuary, is – in a sense – vintage North End.

Charlestown

Charlestown, across Boston Harbor from the North End via the Charlestown Bridge, is a very pretty, quietly affluent neighborhood that's quite isolated from the city. Most visitors only make it over this way for the historic frigate the

USS **Constitution**, which is too bad, because the neighborhood's meandering byways, lined with elegant Colonial- and Federal-style rowhouses, make for pleasant exploration. It's a 20-minute stroll over the bridge to many of the area's sights (follow the Freedom Trail's strip of red paint). A fun alternative is to take the ferry ($1.70; ☎617/227-4321) from Long Wharf to the Charlestown Navy Yard.

The earliest Puritan settlers had high hopes for developing Charlestown when they arrived in 1629, but an unsuitable water supply pushed them over to the Shawmut Peninsula. Charlestown grew slowly after that, and had to be completely rebuilt after the British burned it down in 1775. The mid-1800s witnessed the arrival of the so-called "lace-curtain Irish," somewhat better off than their East Boston brethren, and the district remains Irish at heart. Longtime locals have acquired a reputation for being standoffish, due to episodes such as their resistance to school desegregation in the 1970s, but relations have been vastly improved since then. As you make the uphill climb to the **Bunker Hill Monument** – Charlestown's other big sight – look toward the water for jaw-dropping views of the Zakim Bridge and Boston at large.

USS Constitution

The sprawling **Charlestown Navy Yard** was one of the first and busiest US naval shipyards – riveting together an astounding 46 destroyer escorts in 1943 alone – though it owes most of its present liveliness to the **USS Constitution**, at Constitution Wharf (April to late Oct Tues–Sun 10am–5.50pm; Nov–March Thurs–Sun 10am–3.50pm; free; ☎617/242-5671, ⓦwww.ussconstitution.navy .mil). President Nixon decommissioned the Yard in 1974, and it became part of the Boston National Historical Park, but its focal point remains the *Constitution*, the oldest commissioned warship afloat in the world. Launched two centuries ago to safeguard American merchant vessels from Barbary pirates and the French and British navies, she earned her nickname during the War of 1812, when cannonballs fired from the British HMS *Guerrière* bounced off the hull (the "iron sides" were actually hewn from live oak, a particularly sturdy wood), leading to the first and most dramatic naval conquest of that war. The ship went on to win 33 battles – never losing one – before it was retired from service in 1830.

Authentic enough in appearance, the *Constitution* has certainly taken its hits – roughly ninety percent of the ship has been reconstructed. Even after extensive renovations, though, Old Ironsides is still too frail to support sails for extended periods of time, and the only regular voyages it makes are annual Fourth of July turnarounds in Boston Harbor. There's often a line to visit the ship – especially in the summer – but it's worth the wait to get a close-up view of its physique, which is as tall as a twenty-story building, and three hundred feet long. After ambling about the main deck, scuttle below, where you'll find an impressive array of cannons. Though most are replicas, two functional models face downtown from the bow, from where they mark mast-raising and -lowering daily. Were they to fire the 24-pound balls for which they were originally cast, they'd topple the Custom House Tower across the bay.

Adjacent to the ship, the National Park Service runs a worthy new visitors' center detailing the history of the naval yard. Here you will find vintage photographs as well as forging tools, nautical treasures, and artifacts, such as the pleasingly named "Warner-Swasey Twister-Winder." Used for twisting rope, the machine's shape seems almost provocative.

Charlestown Navy Yard

Housed in a substantial granite building a short walk from Old Ironsides and across from Pier 1, the **USS Constitution Museum** (daily: mid-April to late

Oct 9am–6pm; Nov to early April 10am–5pm; free; ☎617/426-1812, ⓦwww
.ussconstitutionmuseum.org) is well worth a visit. The downstairs covers the
history of the ship, including the story of how, in the 1920s, US schoolchildren
contributed $154,000 in pennies toward its preservation. Upstairs is perhaps
more fun, with hands-on exhibits putting you in the role of a sailor: determine
whether your comrades have scurvy or gout and attempt to balance yourself
on a footrope.

Berthed in between Old Ironsides and the ferry to Long Wharf is the hulking
gray mass of the World War II destroyer **USS Cassin Young** (same hours as the
Constitution; free). You can stride about the expansive main deck and check out
some of the cramped chambers below, but it's mostly of interest to World War II
history buffs. At the northern perimeter of the Navy Yard is the **Ropewalk
Building**. Between 1830 and 1970 every single strand of rope for the US Navy
was made in this granite building, the only one of its kind still standing in the
country; unfortunately it's not open to the public.

City Square to the Bunker Hill Monument

Toward Charlestown's center, there's a wealth of eighteenth- and nineteenth-
century townhouses, many of which you'll pass on your way from the Navy Yard
to the Bunker Hill Monument. John Harvard, the English minister whose library
and funds launched Harvard University after his death, lived in Charlestown and
left a legacy of street names here: directly behind **City Square**, Harvard Street
curves through the small **Town Hill** district, site of Charlestown's first settled

The Battle of Bunker Hill

The Revolutionary War was at its bloodiest on the hot June day in 1775 when
British and colonial forces clashed in Charlestown. In the wake of the battles at
Lexington and Concord two months before, the British had assumed full control
of Boston, while the patriots had the upper hand in the surrounding countryside.
The British, under the command of generals Thomas Gage, William Howe, and
"Gentleman Johnny" Burgoyne, intended to sweep the area clean of "rebellious
rascals." Americans intercepted the plans and moved to fortify **Bunker Hill**, the
dominant hill in Charlestown. However, when Colonel William Prescott arrived on
the scene, he chose to occupy **Breed's Hill** instead, either due to confusion – the
two hills were often confused on colonial-era maps – or tactical foresight, based
on the proximity of Breed's Hill to the harbor. Whatever the motivation, more than
a thousand citizen-soldiers arrived during the night of June 16, 1775, and fortified
the hill with a 160-foot-long earthen redoubt by morning.

Spotting the Yankee fort, the Redcoats, each carrying 125 pounds of food and
supplies on their backs, rowed across the harbor to take the rebel-held town. On the
patriots' side, Colonel Prescott ordered that his troops not fire "'til you see the whites
of their eyes" – such was their limited store of gunpowder. When the enemy's approach
was deemed near enough, the patriots opened fire; though vastly outnumbered, they
successfully repelled two full-fledged assaults. Some British units lost more than ninety
percent of their men, and what few officers survived had to push their men forward with
their swords to make them fight on. By the third British assault, the Redcoats had shed
their gear, reinforcements had arrived, and the Americans' gunpowder was dwindling –
as were their chances of clinching victory. The rebels continued to fight with stones and
musket butts; meanwhile, British cannonfire from Copp's Hill in the North End was
turning Charlestown into an inferno. Despite the eventual American loss, the patriots
were invigorated by their strong showing, and the British, who lost nearly half of their
men who had fought in the battle, became convinced that victory over the rebels would
only be possible with a much larger army.

community. You'll also find Harvard Mall and adjacent Harvard Square (not to be confused with the one in Cambridge).

At the corner of Main and Warren streets is the **Warren Tavern**, a small wooden structure built after the British burned Charlestown in the Battle of Bunker Hill, and named for Dr Joseph Warren, who was killed in combat. From the tavern, Devens Street to the south and Cordis Street to the north are packed with historic houses; the most imposing is the Greek Revival mansion at **33 Cordis Street**. West on Main Street, at Thompson Square, the landmark **Five Cents Savings Bank Building**, with its steep mansard roof and Victorian Gothic ornamentation, looms above the convenience stores. Further west is the **Phipps Street Burying Ground**, which dates from 1630. While many Revolutionary soldiers are buried here, it's not part of the Freedom Trail – perhaps even more of a reason to make the detour.

Double back and head up Monument Avenue, toward the Bunker Hill Monument. The red-brick townhouses that you'll pass are some of the most eagerly sought residences in town. Nearby is **Winthrop Square**, Charlestown's unofficial common, just south of the monument. The prim rowhouses overlooking it form another upscale enclave.

Bunker Hill Monument

Commemorating the Battle of Bunker Hill is the **Bunker Hill Monument** (daily 9am–4.30pm; free), a gray, dagger-like obelisk that's visible from just about anywhere in Charlestown, thanks to its position atop a butte confusingly known as Breed's Hill (see box opposite). It was here that the New England militia built a fort on the night of June 16, 1775, to wage what was ultimately a losing battle, despite its recasting by US historians as a great moral victory. The tower is centrally positioned in **Monument Square** and fronted by a statue of Colonel William Prescott, who commanded the Americans. Inside, 294 steps wind the 221 feet to the top; hardy climbers will be rewarded with sweeping views of Boston, the harbor, and surrounding towns – and, to the northwest, the stone spire of the **St Francis de Sales Church**, which stands atop the real Bunker Hill.

A new **museum** at the base of the monument (daily 9am–4.30pm; free) has well-executed exhibits on the battle, the history of Charlestown, and some cool ephemera, such as the drawings that were submitted in the contest to determine the monument's design.

Beacon Hill

No visit to Boston would be complete without an afternoon spent strolling around **Beacon Hill**, a dignified stack of red brick rising over the north side of Boston Common. This is the Boston of wealth and privilege, one-time home to numerous historical and literary figures – including John Hancock, John Quincy Adams, Louisa May Alcott, and Oliver Wendell Holmes – and still the address of choice for the city's elite. Its narrow, hilly byways are lit with gaslights and lined with nineteenth-century-style townhouses, all part of an enforced preservation that prohibits modern buildings, architectural innovations, or anything else that might disturb the cultivated atmosphere of urban gentility.

It was not always this way. In colonial times, Beacon Hill was the most prominent of three peaks known as the Trimountain, which formed Boston's geological backbone. The sunny south slope was developed into prime real estate and quickly settled by the city's elite, while the north slope was closer in spirit to the **West End**, a tumbledown port district; indeed, the north slope was home to so much salacious activity that outraged Brahmins termed it "Mount Whoredom." By the end of the twentieth century, this social divide was almost entirely eradicated, though today it can still be seen in the somewhat shabbier homes north of Pinckney Street and in the occasional reference to the south slope as "the good side." Still, both areas have much to offer, if of very different character: on the south slope, there's the grandiose **Massachusetts State House**, attractive boulevards like **Charles Street** and the **Beacon Street Promenade**, and the residences of past and present luminaries. More down to earth are the north slope's **Black Heritage Trail** sights, such as the **African Meeting House**, and some vestiges of the old West End.

Beacon Street

Running along the south slope of Beacon Hill above the Common, **Beacon Street** was once described by Oliver Wendell Holmes as Boston's "sunny street for the sifted few." This lofty character remains today: a row of stately brick townhouses, fronted by ornate iron grillwork, presides regally over the area.

The elegant bow-fronted 1808 **Prescott House**, at no. 55 (May–Oct Wed, Thurs & Sat noon–4pm, tours every 30min; $5; ☏617/742-3190, ⓦwww .nscda.org/ma; Park St **T**), is still worth a visit. Designed by an understudy of Charles Bulfinch, the house's most distinguished inhabitant was historian William Hickling Prescott, whose family occupied it from 1845 to 1859. Hung above the Federalist and Victorian furniture inside are a photograph of two crossed swords that once belonged to Colonel William Prescott and British Captain John Linzee, the historian and his wife's respective grandfathers. The men fought against each other at Bunker Hill (see box, p.88), and the sight of their munitions here inspired William Thackeray, a frequent visitor, to write *The Virginians*.

Across the street, the **Founder's Monument** commemorates Boston's first European settler, William Blackstone, a Cambridge-educated loner who moved from England to a piece of wilderness he acquired for next to nothing from the Shawmut Indians – the site of present-day Boston. A stone bas-relief depicts the moment in 1629 when Blackstone sold most of his acreage to a group of Puritans from Charlestown (and marks the year, 1630, when Boston was founded).

Back on the north side of Beacon Street, and a few steps past Spruce Court, is the last of a trio of **Charles Bulfinch** houses (see box below) commissioned by lawyer and future Boston mayor Harrison Gray Otis over a ten-year period; the four-story Classical house has been home to the American Meteorological Society since 1958. Just east of here, it's hard to miss the twin-swelled granite building at no. 42–43, built for Colonel David Sears' family by Alexander Parris,

---

The architecture of Charles Bulfinch

Charles Bulfinch was America's foremost architect of the late eighteenth and early nineteenth centuries, and his distinctive style – somewhere between Federal and Classical – remains Boston's most recognizable architectural motif. Mixing Neoclassical training with New England practicality, Bulfinch built residences characterized by their rectilinear brick structure and pillared porticoes – examples remain throughout Beacon Hill, most notably at 87 Mount Vernon St and 45 Beacon St. Although most of his work was residential, Bulfinch made his name designing various government buildings, such as the 1805 renovation of **Faneuil Hall** and the **Massachusetts State House**, whose dome influenced the design of state capital buildings nationwide. His talents extended to urban planning as well, including the layout of Boston's **South End**, and an area known as Tontine Crescent, a half-ellipse planned around a park; the remaining vestiges of the latter are found around the Financial District's Franklin and Arch streets.

of Quincy Market fame. Its stern Greek Revival facade has welcomed members of the exclusive **Somerset Club** since 1872.

Farther up the street, on the edge of the Common facing the Massachusetts State House, is a majestic monument honoring the **54th Massachusetts Regiment**, the first all-black company to fight in the Civil War, and its leader, Robert Gould Shaw, scion of a moneyed Boston Brahmin clan. Isolated from the rest of the Union army, given the worst of its resources, and saddled with menial or terribly dangerous assignments, the regiment performed bravely; most of its members, including Shaw, were killed in a failed attempt to take Fort Wagner from the Confederates. Augustus Saint-Gaudens' 1897 bronze sculpture depicts the regiment's farewell march down Beacon Street, and the names of the soldiers killed in action are listed on its reverse side (though these were only added in 1982). Robert Lowell won a Pulitzer Prize for his poem, *For the Union Dead*, which took its inspiration from the monument; the regiment's story was also depicted in the 1989 film *Glory*.

Massachusetts State House

Across the street from the 54th Massachusetts Memorial rises the large gilt dome of the Charles Bulfinch-designed **Massachusetts State House** (Mon–Fri 10am–4pm, last tour at 3.30pm; free; ☎617/727-3676; Park Street **T**). Though only three stories high, it seems taller, sitting at the confluence of the steep grade of Park and Beacon streets. Of the current structure, only the central section was part of Bulfinch's original design; the wings jutting out on either side and the section extending up Bowdoin Street were all added later. An all-star team of Revolution-era luminaries contributed to its construction: built on land purchased from John Hancock, its cornerstone was laid by Samuel Adams, and the copper for its dome was rolled in Paul Revere's foundry (though it was covered over with gold leaf in the 1870s).

Inside the labyrinthine interior, the central hallway, up one flight, is the only section of any real interest to visitors. Best is the sober and impressive **Memorial Hall**, a circular room surrounded by tall columns of Siena marble; it contains transparencies of the original flags carried into battle by Massachusetts soldiers and is lit by a stained-glass window bearing the state seal. On the third floor, a carved wooden fish known as the **Sacred Cod** hangs above the public gallery in the House of Representatives. The politicos take this symbol so seriously that when it was stolen by Harvard pranksters in the 1930s, the House didn't reconvene until it was recovered.

Behind the State House on Bowdoin Street lies grassy **Ashburton Park**, centered on a pillar that is a replica of a 1789 Bulfinch work. The column indicates the hill's original summit, which was sixty feet higher and topped by a 65-foot post with the warning light – an iron pot filled with combustibles – that gave Beacon Hill its name.

Nichols House

The only Beacon Hill residence open year-round to the public is **Nichols House**, at 55 Mount Vernon St (April–Oct Tues–Sat 11am–4pm; Nov to late March Thurs–Sat 11am–4pm; $7; ☎617/227-6993, ⊛www.nicholshousemuseum.org; Park Street **T**). It's yet another Bulfinch design, and was most recently the home of landscape designer and pacifist Rose Standish Nichols, the niece of sculptor Augustus Saint-Gaudens (the man behind the 54th Regiment Memorial; see p.420). Full of pieces from the seventeenth to the twentieth centuries, the interior isn't too gripping unless you have an interest in antique furnishings; it's best to go to get perspective on the life of leisure led by Beacon Hill's elite.

Louisburg Square and around

A bit further west, between Mount Vernon and Pinckney streets, **Louisburg Square** forms the gilded, geographic heart of Beacon Hill. The central lawn, surrounded by wrought-iron fencing and flanked by statues of Columbus and Aristides the Just, is owned by local residents, making it the city's only private square. On either side of this oblong green are rows of brick townhouses, though the square's distinction is due less to its architecture than to its residents. Among those to call the area home have been novelist Louisa May Alcott and members of the Vanderbilt family; it's currently home to former presidential candidate Senator John Kerry and his wife, ketchup heiress Teresa Heinz.

Just south of Louisburg Square, between Willow and West Cedar streets, narrow **Acorn Street** still has its original early nineteenth-century cobblestones. Barely wide enough to accommodate a car, it was originally built as a byway lined with servants' residences. It's often referenced (or photographed) for being the epitome of Beacon Hill quaint. One more block south, **Chestnut Street** features some of the most intricate facades in Boston, particularly Bulfinch's **Swan Houses**, at nos. 13, 15, and 17, with their recessed arches, Doric columns and wrought-iron balconies.

Smith Court and the African Meeting House

On the north side of the slope, Joy Street intersects with tiny **Smith Court**, once the center of Boston's substantial pre-Civil War black community and now home to a few stops on Boston's Black Heritage Trail (see box below). The **African Meeting House**, at no. 8 (Mon–Sat 10am–4pm; donations welcome; ☎617/725-0022, Ⓦwww.afroammuseum.org; Park Street **T**), is the oldest black church in the country, and in its heyday served as the spiritual and political center for Boston's black residents. It is also the birthplace of abolitionism: in 1832, William Lloyd Garrison founded the New England Anti-Slavery Society here, the first group of its kind to call for the immediate end of slavery. The place is currently being remodeled to look as it did in 1854, but its exterior (and character) is well represented on the Trail.

At the end of Smith Court, you can walk along narrow **Holmes Alley**, once part of the Underground Railroad, a loose network of abolitionist homes used to protect escaped slaves. Built in 1843, the **Abiel Smith School**, 46 Joy St, was the first public building in the country established for the purpose of educating black children. Today, it houses the **Museum of African American History** (Mon–Sat 10am–4pm; donations welcome; ☎617/725-0022, Ⓦwww .afroammuseum.org; Park Street **T**) and rotates a number of well-tailored exhibits centered on abolitionism and African-American history.

The Black Heritage Trail

In 1783, Massachusetts became the first state to declare slavery illegal. Not long after, a large community of free blacks and escaped slaves grew up in Beacon Hill. The **Black Heritage Trail** traces the neighborhood's key role in local and national black history – and is the most important historical site in America devoted to pre-Civil War African-American history and culture. Starting from the **54th Massachusetts Memorial** (see p.91), the 1.6-mile loop takes in fourteen sights, detailed in a **guide** available at the **Museum of African American History** and at the Boston National Historical Park **visitors' center** at 15 State St. The best way to experience the trail is by taking a National Park Service **walking tour** (Mon–Sat 10am, noon & 2pm, call to reserve; free; ☎617/742-5415 or 617/242-5642, Ⓦwww.nps.gov/boaf; Park Street **T**).

Charles Street and the Esplanade

Headed towards the river, pretty **Charles Street** is the commercial center of Beacon Hill, lined with scores of restaurants, antique shops, and speciality boutiques. A jaunt west off Charles down **Mount Vernon Street** brings you past some of Beacon Hill's most beautiful buildings – none of which you can enter, unfortunately – including the Federal-style **Charles Street Meeting House**, at the corner of the two streets, now repurposed as an office building, and the vegetation-shrouded Victorian Gothic **Church of the Advent**, at Mount Vernon's intersection with Brimmer.

Connected to Charles Street at its north end by a footbridge and spanning nine miles along the Charles River, the **Esplanade** is yet another of Boston's well-manicured public spaces. The stretch alongside Beacon Hill is the nicest, providing a picturesque way to appreciate the Hill from a distance. Just below the Longfellow Bridge (which connects to Cambridge) is the Community Boating Center, the point of departure for sailing, kayaking, and windsurfing outings on the Charles (April–Oct Mon–Fri 1pm–sunset, Sat & Sun 9am–sunset; two-day visitor's pass $100; must be able to prove sailing abilities; ☏617/523-1038, Ⓦwww.community-boating.org; Charles Ⓣ). The white half-dome rising from the riverbank just south is the **Hatch Shell**, a public performance space best known for its Fourth of July celebration, which features a free concert by the Boston Pops (a pared-down, snappy version of the Boston Symphony Orchestra) and a massive fireworks display over the river (see p.32). Free movies and jazz concerts occur almost nightly in summer; call ☏617/227-0627 or visit Ⓦwww.hatchshell.com for a schedule of events.

The West End

North of Cambridge Street, the tidy rows of townhouses give way to a spread of office buildings and old brick structures, signaling the start of the **West End**. Once Boston's main port of entry for immigrants and transient sailors, this area has seen its lively character pretty much disappear, though a vestige remains in the small tangle of byways behind the buildings of **Massachusetts General Hospital**, where you'll see urban warehouses interspersed with Irish bars, which swell to a fever pitch after Celtics basketball and Bruins hockey games. Those games take place nearby at the **TD Banknorth Garden**, 150 Causeway St (formerly the Boston Garden; see p.138 for ticket details). Within the arena is the affable **Sports Museum** (daily 11am–5pm; admission on the hour at 11pm, 12pm, 1pm, 2pm with last tour at 3pm; hours fluctuate according to events; $6; ☏617/624-1234, Ⓦwww.sportsmuseum.org; North Station Ⓣ), where visitors can glimpse statues of Boston sports legends like Celtic Larry Bird and Bruin Bobby Orr, as well as the American League Championship banner won by the Red Sox in 2004. There are also old uniforms and equipment, but best of all is the hockey penalty box from the old Boston Garden, which you are invited to climb into.

Back along Cambridge Street, at no. 141, the brick **Harrison Gray Otis House** (Wed–Sun 11am–4.30pm, tours every 30min; $8; ☏617/227-3956, Ⓦwww.historicnewengland.org; Charles Ⓣ), originally built for the Otis family in 1796, sits incongruously among modern stores and office buildings. Its first two floors have been painstakingly restored – from the wallpaper right down to the silverware sets – in the Federal style.

Situated on a bridge over the Charles, Boston's beloved **Museum of Science** (July to early Sept Mon–Thurs, Sat & Sun 9am–7pm, Fri 9am–9pm; Sept–June Mon–Thurs, Sat & Sun 9am–5pm, Fri 9am–9pm; $19, children $16; ☏617/723-2500, Ⓦwww.mos.org; Science Park Ⓣ) consists of several floors of interactive exhibits illustrating basic principles of natural and physical science. The best exhibit is the Theater of Electricity in the Blue Wing, a darkened room full of optical illusions and glowing displays on the presence of electricity in everyday life. The museum also houses a five-story IMAX theater as well as the Charles Hayden Planetarium (call for show times; $9, children $7; ℡617/723-2500, Ⓦwww.mos .org); along with the standard starry productions, the latter also features a number of laser shows, including the infamous "Laser Floyd: Dark Side of the Moon." The museum's new **3D Theater** ($4 in addition to museum admission) provides a chance to wear those retro-cool 3D glasses.

Back Bay

Beginning at Charles Street and the **Public Garden**, **Back Bay**, a meticulously planned neighborhood of elegant, angular streets, looks much as it did in the nineteenth century, right down to the original gaslights and brick sidewalks. Boston's most cosmopolitan area, it buzzes with chic eateries, trendy shops, and an aura of affluence. Its other main draw is its trove of Gilded Age rowhouses, specifically their fanciful architectural details.

Starting abreast the Charles River, the east–west thoroughfares of Back Bay are **Beacon** and **Marlborough** streets, **Commonwealth Avenue**, and **Newbury** and **Boylston** streets. These are transected by eight shorter streets, so fastidiously laid out that not only are their names in alphabetical order, but trisyllables are deliberately intercut by disyllables: Arlington, Berkeley, Clarendon, Dartmouth, Exeter, Fairfield, Gloucester, and Hereford, until you get to Massachusetts Avenue. The grandest townhouses are on Beacon Street and Commonwealth Avenue, though Marlborough, between the two, is more atmospheric and Boylston and Newbury are the commercial streets. In the middle of it all is a small open space, **Copley Square**, surrounded by the area's main sights: **Trinity Church**, the **Boston Public Library**, and the **John Hancock Tower**.

The Public Garden

Some of the highest property values in Boston are those in proximity to the lovingly maintained **Public Garden**, a 24-acre park first earmarked for public use in 1859. Of the garden's 125 types of trees, many identified by little brass placards, most impressive are the weeping willows that ring the picturesque man-made **lagoon**, around which you can take a fifteen-minute ride in a **swan boat** (April to late June daily 10am–4pm; late June to early Sept daily 10am–5pm; early to mid-Sept Mon–Fri noon–4pm, Sat & Sun 10am–4pm; $2.75; ℡617/522-1966, Ⓦwww.swanboats.com; Arlington **T**). There's often a line to hop on board

From swamp to swank: the building of Back Bay

The fashioning of **Back Bay** occurred in the mid-nineteenth century, when a shortage of living space in Boston prompted developers to revisit a failed dam project on the Charles River, which had made a swamp of much of the area. **Arthur Gilman** manned the huge landfill project, which began in 1857. Taking his cue from the grand boulevards of Paris, Gilman decided on an orderly street pattern extending east to west from the Public Garden. By 1890, the cramped peninsula of old Boston was flanked by 450 new acres. You'll notice that, with a few exceptions, the brownstones get fancier the farther from the Garden you go, a result of architects and those who employed them trying to one-up each other. The exteriors of most of the buildings remain unaltered, although visually that's as far as you'll usually get, unless the place has been converted into a shop, salon, or gourmet eatery; in that case, step inside and hang onto your wallet.

▲ Mrs Mallard and Her Eight Ducklings, in the Public Garden

– instead of waiting, you can get just as good a perspective on the park from the tiny suspension bridge that crosses the lagoon. The park's other big family draw is the cluster of bronze bird sculptures collectively called **Mrs Mallard and Her Eight Ducklings**, installed to commemorate Robert McCloskey's 1941 children's tale *Make Way for Ducklings*, which was set here. Of the many statues and monuments throughout the park, the oldest and oddest is the 30-foot-tall **Good Samaritan** monument, a granite and red-marble column that is a tribute to, of all things, the anesthetic qualities of ether; controversy as to which of two Boston men invented the drug led Oliver Wendell Holmes to dub it the "Either Monument." Finally, a dignified equestrian statue of **George Washington**, installed in 1869 and the first of the general astride a horse, watches over the Garden's Commonwealth Avenue entrance.

Commonwealth Avenue

The garden leads into the tree-lined median of **Commonwealth Avenue**, the 220-foot-wide showcase street of Back Bay. The mall here forms the first link in Frederick Law Olmsted's so-called **Emerald Necklace** (see box, p.104), which begins at Boston Common and extends all the way to the Arnold Arboretum in Jamaica Plain. "Comm Ave," as locals call it, is at its prettiest in early May, when the magnolia and dogwood trees are in full bloom.

On the street proper, the **Gamble Mansion**, at no. 5, now houses the Boston Center for Adult Education, but slip inside for a look at the opulent ballroom built expressly for the owner's daughter's debutante ball. You'll have to be content to see the **Ames–Webster House**, at 306 Dartmouth St, from the outside. Built in 1872 for railroad tycoon, Massachusetts governor, and US congressman Frederick Ames, it features a two-story conservatory, central tower, and imposing chimney. Farther down Commonwealth, at no. 314, is the 1899 **Burrage House**, a synthesis of Vanderbilt-style mansion and the French chateau of Chenonceaux. The exterior is a riot of gargoyles and cherubim; inside it's less riotous, serving as a retirement home.

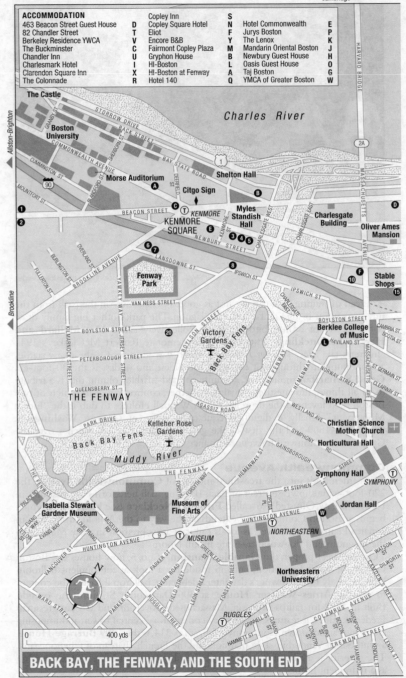

ACCOMMODATION

463 Beacon Street Guest House	D	Copley Inn	S	Hotel Commonwealth	E
82 Chandler Street	T	Copley Square Hotel	N	Jurys Boston	P
Berkeley Residence YWCA	V	Eliot	F	The Lenox	K
The Buckminster	C	Encore B&B	Y	Mandarin Oriental Boston	J
Chandler Inn	U	Fairmont Copley Plaza	M	Newbury Guest House	H
Charlesmark Hotel	I	Gryphon House	B	Oasis Guest House	O
Clarendon Square Inn	X	HI-Boston	L	Taj Boston	G
The Colonnade	R	HI-Boston at Fenway	A	YMCA of Greater Boston	W
		Hotel 140	Q		

The Castle

Boston University

Charles River

STORROW DRIVE

GRANBY ST
BACK STREET
COMMONWEALTH AVENUE
BAY STATE ROAD

CUMMINGTON ST

BLANDFORD ST
SHERBORN ST
DEERFIELD ST

Morse Auditorium **Ⓐ**

Shelton Hall **Ⓑ**

Citgo Sign

MOUNTFORT ST

Ⓞ①
②

BEACON STREET **Ⓣ** KENMORE

KENMORE SQUARE

Myles Standish Hall

KENMORE ST
CHARLESGATE WEST

Charlesgate Building

Ⓓ

Oliver Ames Mansion

Ⓔ ③④⑤

NEWBURY STREET

OVERLAND AVENUE

BROOKLINE AVENUE

⑥⑦

LANSDOWNE ST

⑧

Ⓕ⑩

Stable Shops ⑮

FULLERTON ST
BURLINGTON ST

Fenway Park

IPSWICH ST

IPSWICH ST

CHARLESGATE EAST

MASSACHUSETTS AVENUE

HARVARD BRIDGE

Cambridge

2A

1

B

VAN NESS STREET

BOYLSTON STREET

Berklee College of Music **Ⓛ**

CAMBRIA ST
SCOTIA ST

KILMARNOCK STREET
JERSEY STREET

BOYLSTON STREET

⑳

BOYLSTON STREET

Victory Gardens

Back Bay Fens

HAVILAND ST

Ⓞ

ST GERMAIN ST
CLEARWAY ST

PETERBOROUGH STREET

NORWAY STREET

Mapparium

THE FENWAY

QUEENSBERRY ST

AGASSIZ ROAD

WESTLAND AVE

MASSACHUSETTS AVE

Christian Science Mother Church

PARK DRIVE

Kelleher Rose Gardens

SYMPHONY RD

GAINSBOROUGH STREET

HEMENWAY ST

Horticultural Hall

Back Bay Fens

Muddy River

THE FENWAY

FORSYTH ST
FORSYTH WAY

Symphony Hall **Ⓣ**
SYMPHONY

THE FENWAY

ST STEPHEN
OPERA PL

Isabella Stewart Gardner Museum

Museum of Fine Arts

Jordan Hall

PALACE RD

FELTON
EVANS WAY
LOUIS PRANG ST

MUSEUM RD

HUNTINGTON AVENUE

Ⓦ

NORTHEASTERN

VANCOUVER ST

EVANS WAY

9 **Ⓣ** MUSEUM

PARKER ST

GREENLEAF ST

WATSON ST

HUNTINGTON AVENUE

TAVERN ROAD
FIELD STREET
LEON STREET
FORSYTH STREET

DILWORTH ST

Northeastern University

CONNER'S STREET

N

WARD STREET

PARKER ST

RUGGLES STREET

Ⓣ
RUGGLES

GRINNELL ST
CUNARD ST

COLUMBUS AVENUE
DAVENPORT ST
BURKE ST
BENTON ST
WHITTIER ST

HAMMET ST
KENDALL ST

LENOX ST
TREMONT STREET

0 ——— 400 yds

BACK BAY, THE FENWAY, AND THE SOUTH END

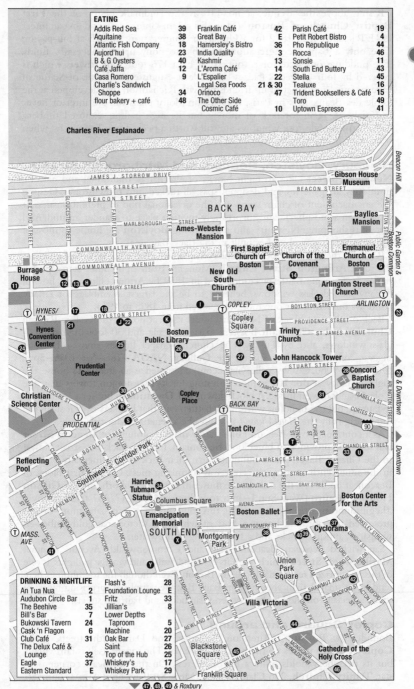

EATING

Addis Red Sea	39	Franklin Café	42	Parish Café	19
Aquitaine	38	Great Bay	E	Petit Robert Bistro	4
Atlantic Fish Company	18	Hamersley's Bistro	36	Pho Republique	44
Aujord'hui	23	India Quality	3	Rocca	46
B & G Oysters	40	Kashmir	13	Sonsie	11
Café Jaffa	12	L'Aroma Café	14	South End Buttery	43
Casa Romero	9	L'Espalier	22	Stella	45
Charlie's Sandwich		Legal Sea Foods	21 & 30	Tealuxe	16
Shoppe	34	Orinoco	47	Trident Booksellers & Café	15
flour bakery + café	48	The Other Side		Toro	49
		Cosmic Café	10	Uptown Espresso	41

Charles River Esplanade

JAMES J. STORROW DRIVE

Gibson House Museum

BACK STREET
BEACON STREET

BACK BAY

MARLBOROUGH STREET

Baylies Mansion

COMMONWEALTH AVENUE

Ames-Webster Mansion

COMMONWEALTH AVENUE

Burrage House

First Baptist Church of Boston

Church of the Covenant

Emmanuel Church of Boston

NEWBURY STREET

New Old South Church

Arlington Street Church

BOYLSTON STREET

HYNES/ICA

COPLEY

ARLINGTON

BOYLSTON STREET

Hynes Convention Center

Boston Public Library

Copley Square

PROVIDENCE STREET

Trinity Church

ST JAMES AVENUE

Prudential Center

John Hancock Tower

STUART STREET

Concord Baptist Church

Christian Science Center

Copley Place

STANHOPE STREET

BACK BAY

CHANDLER STREET

PRUDENTIAL

Reflecting Pool

Tent City

CORTES ST

Southwest Corridor Park

CARLETON ST

LAWRENCE STREET

APPLETON STREET

Harriet Tubman Statue

DARTMOUTH PL

GRAY STREET

Boston Center for the Arts

Emancipation Memorial

Columbus Square

Boston Ballet

MASS. AVE

SOUTH END

Montgomery Park

MONTGOMERY ST

Cyclorama

Union Park Square

SHAWMUT AVENUE

Villa Victoria

TREMONT STREET

Blackstone Square

Franklin Square

WASHINGTON STREET

Cathedral of the Holy Cross

DRINKING & NIGHTLIFE

An Tua Nua	2	Flash's	28
Audubon Circle Bar	1	Foundation Lounge	E
The Beehive	35	Fritz	33
Bill's Bar	7	Jillian's	8
Bukowski Tavern	24	Lower Depths	
Cask 'n Flagon	6	Taproom	5
Club Café	31	Machine	20
The Delux Café &		Oak Bar	27
Lounge	32	Saint	26
Eagle	37	Top of the Hub	25
Eastern Standard	E	Whiskey's	17
		Whiskey Park	29

47, 48, 49 & Roxbury

Rising above the avenue, at no. 110, is the landmark belfry of the **First Baptist Church of Boston** (Mon–Fri 11am–3pm), designed by architect H.H. Richardson in 1872 for a Unitarian congregation, though at bill-paying time only a Baptist congregation was able to pony up the necessary funds. The puddingstone exterior is topped off by a 176-foot **bell tower**, which is covered by four gorgeous friezes by Frederic-Auguste Bartholdi, of Statue of Liberty fame, a product of his friendship with Richardson that developed at the Ecole des Beaux Arts in Paris. Richardson's lofty plans for the interior never materialized, again for lack of money, but its high ceiling, exposed timbers, and Norman-style rose windows are still worth a peek if you happen by when someone's in the church office.

Newbury, Boylston, Beacon, and Marlborough Streets

Newbury Street takes in eight blocks of alternately traditional and eclectic boutiques, art galleries, and designer spas, all tucked into brownstones. Despite the encroachment of chain stores and the occasional nod to pretentiousness, it remains an atmospheric and surprisingly inviting place to wander around. And not all is shopping: Newbury and neighboring **Boylston** are home to most of the old schools and churches built in the Back Bay area.

Right on the corner of Boylston and Arlington streets is Back Bay's first building, the squat **Arlington Street Church** (Mon–Fri 10am–5pm, Sun 10am–3pm), a minor Italianesque masterpiece designed in 1859 by Arthur Gilman; its host of Tiffany stained-glass windows, believed to be the largest assemblage of Tiffany windows unified under one roof, were added from 1898 to 1933.

Back on the first block of Newbury Street itself, at no. 67, the Gothic Revival **Church of the Covenant** boasts a soaring steeple and 30-foot-high stained-glass windows, also by Tiffany. The church's chapel houses one of Boston's biggest contemporary art spaces, the **Gallery NAGA** (Tues–Sat 10am–5pm; ℡617/267-9060, Ⓦwww.gallerynaga.com). Designed as an architect's house, the flight-of-fancy at **no. 109** is more arresting for its two donjon towers than the Cole-Haan footwear inside. A block down, **271 Dartmouth** houses a *Papa Razzi* restaurant, but the building with mock battlements that hunkers over it steals the show: originally the *Hotel Victoria*, it looks like a Venetian–Moorish castle.

As a continuation of Beacon Hill's stately main thoroughfare, **Beacon Street** was long the province of blueblood Bostonians. It is the Back Bay street closest to the Charles River, yet its buildings turn their back to it, principally because in the nineteenth century the river was a stinking mess. On the first block of Beacon, at no. 137, is the only house museum in the neighborhood, the **Gibson House Museum** (Wed–Sun 1–3pm, tours hourly; $7; ℡617/267-6338, Ⓦwww.thegibsonhouse.org). Built in 1859, this rowhouse has an ornate, more-or-less preserved interior, and boasts a host of whimsical Victoriana: gold-embossed wallpaper, antique clocks and a functioning dumbwaiter.

Sandwiched between Beacon Street and Commonwealth Avenue is quiet **Marlborough Street**, which, with its brick sidewalks and vintage gaslights, is one of the most prized residential locales in Boston. Even though the townhouses here tend to be smaller than elsewhere in Back Bay, they display a surprising range of styles, especially on the blocks between Clarendon and Fairfield streets.

Copley Square and around

Bounded by Boylston, Clarendon, St James, and Dartmouth streets, petite **Copley Square** makes up the heart of Back Bay. The square itself is fairly plain, but its periphery holds quite a bit of interest. On the northeast corner is its star, **Trinity Church**, 206 Clarendon St (Mon–Sat 9am–6pm, Sun 1–6pm; $6, includes guided tour, call for times; ☎617/536-0944, ⓦwww.trinityboston.org; Copley **T**), whose original interior design concept was to create the experience of "walking into a living painting." The result is H.H. Richardson's 1877 Romanesque masterpiece, a polychromatic display fashioned by artist John La Farge. The majestic central tower reaches ten stories, and is situated between sweeping arches and a glamorous golden chancel. While it's all quite lovely, Trinity's finest feature is La Farge's aquamarine *Christ in Majesty* triptych, a bold, multidimensional stained-glass window. Aim to make your visit while the sun is setting and the stained glass is at its most brilliant, or during one of the free organ recitals (Fri 12.15pm). A **farmers' market** materializes opposite the *Fairmont Copley Plaza Hotel* on Tuesday and Friday mornings from May through October.

The **Boston Public Library** (Mon–Thurs 9am–9pm, Fri & Sat 9am–5pm, Oct–May Sun 1–5pm; ☎617/536-5400, ⓦwww.bpl.org) anchors the sidewalk opposite the square. It's the largest public research library in New England, and the first one in America to lend books. Architects McKim, Mead & White built the Italian Renaissance Revival structure in 1895; the massive inner bronze doors were designed by Daniel Chester French (sculptor of the Lincoln Memorial in Washington, DC). Inside, check out the imposing **Bates Reading Room**, with its barrel-vaulted ceiling and oak paneling. The library's most remarkable facet is tucked away on the top floor, however, where the darkly lit **Sargent Hall** is covered with more than fifteen murals painted by John Singer Sargent. Entitled the *Triumph of Religion*, the panels range from the brazen *Pagan Gods* to the serene scenes of *Heaven*. After viewing, you can take a breather in the library's open-air central **courtyard**, modeled after that of the Palazzo della Chancelleria in Rome.

Opposite the library is one of Boston's most attractive buildings, the **New Old South Church** (Mon–Fri 9am–5pm), a name to which there is actually some logic: the congregation at downtown's Old South Meeting House (and church) outgrew those premises and decamped here in 1875 – hence, the "New" Old South Church. The names of former Old South members reads like a who's who of historical figures: Benjamin Franklin, Phillis Wheatley, Samuel Adams, and even Mother Goose all worshipped here. You need not be a student of architecture to be won over by the Italian Gothic design, most pronounced in the ornate, 220-foot bell tower, its copper roof lantern replete with metallic dragons. The interior is an alluring assemblage of dark woods set against a rose-colored backdrop, coupled with fifteenth-century English-style stained-glass windows.

John Hancock Tower

At 62 stories, the **John Hancock Tower**, 200 Clarendon St, is the tallest building in America north of New York City, and in a way Boston's signature skyscraper – first loathed, now loved, and taking on startlingly different appearances, depending on your vantage point. In Back Bay, the angular edifice is often barely perceptible, due to designer I.M. Pei's deference to adjacent Trinity Church and the old brownstones nearby. From Beacon Hill, it appears broad-shouldered and stocky; from the South End, taller than it really is; from across the Charles River, like a crisp metallic wafer. Though the building serves as an office tower, visitors were, until recently, allowed to ascend to its sixtieth-floor **observatory** for some of the most stunning views around – but security concerns have prompted its closure; now, you'll have to head instead to the Prudential Skywalk (see p.100) for Boston vistas. Next door to the tower is the *old* Hancock Tower, which cuts a distinguished profile with its truncated step-top roof.

Prudential Tower

Nothing can cloak the funkiness of the **Prudential Tower** at 800 Boylston St, just west of Copley Square. This 52-story gray intruder in the Back Bay skyline is one of the more unfortunate by-products of the urban renewal craze that gripped Boston and most other American cities in the 1960s. That said, it's now a Boston landmark, and the fiftieth-floor **Skywalk** (Nov–Feb daily 10am–8pm; March–Oct 10am–10pm; $11; Ⓣ617/859-0648, Ⓦwww.prudentialcenter.com; Prudential Ⓣ) does offer a stunning 360-degree view of Boston, complemented by a fun audio tour. If you're hungry (or just thirsty) you can avoid the admission charge by ascending two more floors to the *Top of the Hub* restaurant (see p.126); your bill may well equal the money you just saved, but during daytime hours it's fairly relaxed, and you can linger over coffee or a drink. If shopping is your thing, the Prudential also doubles as the city's best mall (see "Shopping," p.136), and it's worth a browse here after visiting the Skywalk.

Christian Science buildings

People gazing down from the top of the Prudential Tower are often surprised to see a 224-foot-tall Renaissance Revival basilica at its base. This rather artificial-looking structure is the central feature of the world headquarters of the **First Church of Christ, Scientist**, at 75 Huntington Ave (Mon–Sat 10am–4pm; free; Ⓦwww.tfccs.com; Hynes Ⓣ), which dwarfs the earlier Romanesque **Christian Science Mother Church** just behind it, built in 1894. The center's 670-foot-long red-granite-trimmed reflecting pool makes a good spot for lunchtime lounging.

The highlights of a visit here, though, are on the ground floor of the **Mary Baker Eddy Library**, in the Christian Science Publishing building at 200 Massachusetts Ave (Tues–Sun 10am–4pm; $6; Ⓣ1-888/222-3711, Ⓦwww.marybakereddylibrary.org; Hynes Ⓣ). The library's original Art Deco lobby has been transformed into the grandly named Hall of Ideas, home to a glass and bronze fountain that appears to cascade with words rather than water; the sayings – a collection of inspiring tidbits – are projected from the ceiling for a near-holographic effect. Tucked behind the Hall of Ideas is the equally marvelous **Mapparium**, a stained-glass globe whose thirty-foot diameter you can cross on a glass bridge. The technicolor hues of the panels, illuminated from behind, reveal the geopolitical realities of the world in 1935, when the globe was constructed, as evidenced by country names such as Siam, Baluchistan, and Transjordan. Intended to symbolize the worldwide reach of journalism, the Mapparium has a more immediate payoff: thanks to the spherical glass surface, which absorbs no sound, you can whisper, say, "What's Tanganyika called today?" at one end of the bridge and someone on the opposite end will hear it clear as a bell – and perhaps proffer the answer (Tanzania).

Bay Village

Back near the Public Garden, one of the oldest sections of Boston, **Bay Village**, bounded by Arlington, Church, Fayette, and Stuart streets, functions now as a small atmospheric satellite of Back Bay, filled with a warren of gaslights and tiny brick houses. The area is popular with Boston's **gay community**, who moved in over a decade ago, before the nearby South End came into favor.

Bay Village's overall resemblance to Beacon Hill is no accident: many of the artisans who pieced that district together built their own, smaller houses here throughout the 1820s and 1830s. A few decades later, water displaced in the creation of Back Bay threatened to turn the district back into a swamp, but Yankee ingenuity led to the lifting of houses and shops onto wooden pilings eighteen feet above the water level. Backyards were raised only twelve feet, and when the water receded many residents designed sunken gardens. You can still see some of these in the alleys behind Melrose and Fayette streets. A more unusual remnant is the **fortress** at the intersection of Arlington and Stuart streets and Columbus Avenue, complete with drawbridge and fake moat, that was built for the **First Corps of Cadets**, a private military organization.

Bay Village's proximity to the Theater District made it a prime location for **speakeasies** in the 1920s, not to mention a natural spot for actors and impresarios to take up residence; indeed, the building at **48–50 Melrose Street** originally housed a movie studio. Around the corner at 17 Piedmont St is the site of the 1942 Cocoanut Grove Fire, in which 492 people tragically perished in a nightclub.

The South End

The trendy **South End**, a predominantly residential neighborhood extending below Back Bay from Huntington Street to I-93, and loosely cut off from downtown by I-90, is almost always modified by the term "quaint" – though for once, the tag fits. The neighborhood boasts a spectacular concentration of **Victorian architecture**. The sheer number of such houses earned the South End a National Landmark District designation in 1983, making the 500-acre area the largest historical neighborhood of its kind in the country. The South End is also known for its well-preserved **ironwork**; a French botanical motif known as Rinceau adorns many stairways and windows. Details like these have made the area quite popular with upwardly mobile Bostonians (particularly gay folks), who have been moving into the neighborhood over the past decade. The result is some of the most upbeat and happening **streetlife** in town – most clustered on Tremont and on pockets of Washington, a few blocks below the Back Bay **T**, the neighborhood's only **T** stop.

Dartmouth Street to Columbus Avenue

Dartmouth Street, anchored by Copley Place on the far side of the road, gets tonier the closer it gets to Tremont Street, a few blocks southeast. Immediately below Copley Place, at 130 Tremont, is **Tent City**, a mixed-income housing co-op that owes its name to a 1968 sit-in protest – tents included – staged on the formerly vacant lot by residents concerned about the neighborhood's dwindling low-income housing. Their activism thwarted plans for a parking garage, and the result is a fine example of environmental architecture planning.

Columbus Avenue, which intersects Dartmouth below Tent City, is lined with handsome Victorian houses, though the main interest is a tiny wedge of parkland known as **Columbus Square**, four blocks southwest of Dartmouth, between Pembroke and West Newton streets. The space is the repository of two outstanding bronze relief sculptures commemorating Boston's role as part of the Underground Railroad. The **Harriet Tubman "Step on Board" Memorial** depicts the abolitionist leading weary slaves to safety, while the nearby 1913 **Emancipation** statue is a more harrowing portrait of slaves' plight: the three figures here are achingly thin and barely clothed.

Appleton and Chandler streets

Cobblestoned **Appleton Street** and quiet **Chandler Street**, which jut off to the northeast from Dartmouth below Columbus Avenue, are the most sought-after South End addresses. The tree-lined streets here are graced with flat- and bow-fronted rowhouses that would easily be at home in London's Mayfair. If you're here in October, you can catch the South End Historical Society's (☏617/536-4445, ⓦwww.southendhistoricalsociety.org) **house tour** for a better perspective on the area.

The Cyclorama and the Stanford Calderwood Pavilion

The heart of the South End is at the intersection of Clarendon and Tremont streets, where some of the trendiest restaurants operate. That said, the area's only real sights are a collection of performance spaces, chief among which is the domed **Cyclorama**, at 539 Tremont, which was built in 1884 to house an enormous, 360-degree painting of the Battle of Gettysburg (since moved to Gettysburg itself). Later used as a carousel and even a boxing ring, the repurposing continued until 1972, when its current tenant, the **Boston Center for the Arts** (Ⓣ617/426-5000, Ⓦwww.bcaonline.org), moved in, providing a home for more than a dozen low-budget theater troupes. Right next door to the Cyclorama is the **Stanford Calderwood Pavilion** (Ⓣ617/266-0800, Ⓦwww.huntingtontheatre.org), home to two brand-new theater spaces – the first new theaters to be built in Boston in over 75 years. These vary widely in design: the Wimberly is a luxurious proscenium theater favored for contemporary productions, while the Roberts Studio employs a black-box setup and is generally used for smaller productions.

Villa Victoria and the SoWa District

North from Blackstone and Franklin squares lies **Villa Victoria**, a housing project serving 3000 members of the community. If you're in the area, check out **Plaza Betances,** the enclave's central square (on W. Dedham and Washington sts), where the **Ramón Betances Mural** occupies a wall measuring a whopping 45 feet long by 14 feet high. Created in 1977 by 300 teenagers, the brightly colored mosaic has less to do with its namesake (a leader in Puerto Rico's fight for independence from Spain) than with simple hope, as demonstrated by the cheerful faces and flowers that surround a massive sun; a Spanish inscription asserts "let us know how to fight for our honor and our liberty." Meticulously executed, it may be Boston's best piece of public art.

Around the intersection of **Harrison** and **Thayer** streets, near the eastern edge of the South End, a handful of **art galleries** have showrooms. Wandering around this up-and-coming **SoWa** ("South of Washington") district could easily distract you for an hour or so. The best time to visit is on **First Fridays** (first Fri of month 5–9pm; Ⓣ617/482-2477, Ⓦwww.sowaartistsguild.com), when the galleries ply visitors with wine and spaces are abuzz with artists and fans.

Kenmore Square

Kenmore Square, at the junction of Commonwealth Avenue and Beacon Street, is the primary point of entry to Boston University, one of the country's larger private institutions. The unofficial playground for BU students, the square is a lively stretch of youth-oriented bars and casual restaurants. Many of the buildings on its north side have been snapped up by BU, such as the bustling six-story Barnes & Noble mall, 660 Beacon St, on top of which is perched the monumental **Citgo Sign**, Kenmore's main landmark. This 60-square-foot neon advertisement, a pulsing red-orange triangle (the oil company's logo), has been a popular symbol of Boston since it was placed here in 1965.

The main **Boston University** campus runs alongside the Charles River, on the narrow stretch of land between Commonwealth Avenue and Storrow Drive. The school has made inventive reuse of old buildings, such as the dormitory **Myles Standish Hall**, at 610 Beacon St, a scaled-down version of New York's Flatiron Building that was once a hotel. **Shelton Hall**, behind Standish on Bay State Road, is another hostelry-turned-dorm where playwright Eugene O'Neill undramatically made his long day's journey into night. **Bay State Road** was the westernmost extension of Back Bay, evidenced by its wealth of turn-of-the-century brownstones, most of which now house BU graduate institutes and smaller residence halls. An ornate High Georgian Revival mansion at no. 149 houses the office of the university president. The street ends at **The Castle**, an ivy-covered Tudor mansion now used for university functions and housing a BU-only pub. Continuing the theme back on Commonwealth is the domed **Morse Auditorium**, formerly a synagogue. One long block down is the closest thing the BU campus has to a center, **Marsh Plaza**, with its Gothic Revival chapel and memorial to Martin Luther King, Jr, who graduated from the school.

The Fenway

The Fenway spreads out south of Kenmore Square like an elongated kite, taking in sights disparate enough to please almost any visitor. Lansdowne Street marks the northern edge of the district, and it is here that you'll find many of Boston's nightclubs. Just around the corner from the clubs, the district starts in earnest with **Fenway Park**, the venerable home to the Boston Red Sox. This is quite removed, however, from the highbrow spaces of Fenway's eastern perimeter, dotted with some of Boston's finest cultural institutions: **Symphony Hall**, the **Museum of Fine Arts**, and the **Isabella Stewart Gardner Museum**. Running down the neighborhood's spine is the **Back Bay Fens**, a huge green space designed by Frederick Law Olmsted, urban landscaper extraordinaire.

Fenway Park

Baseball is treated with reverence in Boston, so it's appropriate that the city's team, the Red Sox, plays in one of the country's most storied ballparks, **Fenway Park**, 24 Yawkey Way (in-season daily 9am–4pm, off-season daily 9am–3pm, tours every hour on the hour but call ahead, as times vary according to game schedule;

The Curse: reversed!

With the Boston Red Sox having won baseball's coveted World Series titles in both 2004 and 2007, the "curse" that once hung over the team is quickly becoming a distant memory. In 1903, the **Boston Pilgrims** (as they were then called) became the first team to represent the American League in baseball's World Series, upsetting the heavily favored Pittsburgh Pirates to claim the championship; their continued financial success allowed them to build a new stadium, **Fenway Park**, in 1912. During their first year there, Boston won the Series again, and repeated the feat in 1915, 1916, and 1918, led in the latter years by the young pitcher **George Herman "Babe" Ruth**, who also demonstrated an eye-opening penchant for hitting home runs. The team was poised to become a dynasty when its owner, Harry Frazee, began a fire sale of the team to finance a Broadway play that was to star his girlfriend. Most of the players went for bargain prices, including Ruth, who was sold to the New York Yankees, which went on to become the most successful professional sports franchise ever, with the Babe at the forefront.

After Ruth's departure, the Red Sox embarked upon a long period in the **wilderness**, with 86 demoralizing years without a World Series win. This drought began, over the years, to be blamed on "**the Curse of the Bambino**" (aka Babe Ruth) – punishment meted out by the baseball gods for selling off one of the game's greatest players. After coming maddeningly close to the title many times – most notably in 1986, when the Sox were one strike away from clinching the Series before a ground ball rolled through the legs of first baseman Bill Buckner – the team finally broke the curse in 2004: after losing the first three games of a best-of-seven series to the Yankees, the Red Sox won four in a row, then went on to sweep the St Louis Cardinals for the **World Series** crown. In 2007, the Red Sox began a new tradition of World Series sweeps, beating the Colorado Rockies in four straight games to win their second championship in four years.

$12, children $10; tour info line ☏617/226–6666, ⓦ www.redsox.com; Kenmore or Fenway **T**). One of the oldest ballparks in the country, Fenway was constructed in 1912 in a tiny, asymmetrical space just off Brookline Avenue, resulting in its famously awkward dimensions, which include an abnormally short right-field line (302ft) and a fence that doesn't at all approximate the smooth arc of most outfields. The 37-foot-tall left-field wall, aka the **Green Monster**, is another quirk (it was originally built because home runs were breaking local windows); that it is so high makes up for some of the park's short distances.

Tours of the ballpark are fun and deservedly popular, but your best bet is to come see a game. The season runs from April to October, and **tickets** are fairly reasonable, though often very hard to come by: since clinching the 2004 and 2007 World Series titles, Red Sox hysteria has ascended to previously unknown heights. Call ☏617/267–1700 or visit ⓦ www.redsox.com for ticket info.

The Back Bay Fens

The Fenway gets its name from the **Back Bay Fens** (daily 7.30am–dusk; ⓦ www.emeraldnecklace.org/fenway.htm), a snakelike segment of Frederick Law Olmsted's Emerald Necklace that takes over where the prim Commonwealth Avenue Mall leaves off. The Fens were fashioned from marsh and mud in 1879, a fact reflected in the name of the waterway that still runs through them today – the **Muddy River**. In the northern portion of the park, local residents maintain small garden plots in the unmanicured **Victory Garden**, the oldest community garden in the US. Nearby, below Agassiz Road, the more formal **Kelleher Rose Garden** boasts colorful hybrid species bearing exotic names like Marmalade Skies and Climbing White Iceberg. Though pretty, the Fens get a bit dodgy as night falls, so it would behoove you to leave before it gets dark.

Berklee College of Music and Symphony Hall

Not far from the Fens' northern tip, the renowned **Berklee College of Music** makes its home on the busy stretch of Massachusetts Avenue south of Boylston Street, an area with several budget-friendly eateries. In addition to coordinating the BeanTown Jazz Festival every September, there's nearly always something

---

Frederick Law Olmsted and the Emerald Necklace

The string of urban parks that stretches through Boston's southern districts, known as the **Emerald Necklace**, grew out of a project conceived in the 1870s, when landscape architect **Frederick Law Olmsted** was commissioned to create for Boston a series of urban parks like those he had done in New York and Chicago. A Romantic naturalist, Olmsted conceived of nature as a way to escape the ills wrought by society, and considered his urban parks a means for city-dwellers to escape the clamor of their everyday lives. He converted much of Boston's remaining open space, which was often disease-breeding marshland, into a series of fabulous, manicured parks beginning with the Back Bay Fens, including the Riverway along the Boston–Brookline border, and proceeding through Jamaica Pond and the Arnold Arboretum to Roxbury's Franklin Park (see p.108). While Olmsted's original skein of parks was limited to these, further development linked the Fens, via the Commonwealth Avenue Mall, to the Public Garden and Boston Common, all of which now function as part of the Necklace. This makes it all the more impressive in scale, though the Necklace's sense of pristine natural wonder has slipped in the century since their creation – the more southerly links in the chain, starting with the Fens, have grown shaggy and are unsafe at night. The **Boston Park Rangers** (9am–5pm; ☏617/635-7383) organize free walking tours covering each of the Necklace's segments from Boston Common to Franklin Park.

musical going on in the Berklee environs – check Ⓦwww.berklee.edu/events for a list of (often very inexpensive) performances. A few short blocks south, **Symphony Hall** (Ⓣ1-888/266-1200, Ⓦwww.bso.org; Symphony **T**), home to the Boston Symphony Orchestra, anchors the corner of Massachusetts and Huntington avenues. The inside of the 1900 McKim, Mead & White design is apparently just the right shape to provide the hall with perfect acoustics.

Museum of Fine Arts

Rather inconveniently located in south Fenway – but absolutely worth the trip – the **Museum of Fine Arts**, at 465 Huntington Ave (Mon & Tues 10am–4.45pm, Wed–Fri 10am–9.45pm, Sat & Sun 10am–4.45pm; Thurs–Fri West Wing and select galleries only after 4.45pm; $17, additional charge for Gund Gallery exhibits, Wed after 4pm suggested donation only; Ⓣ617/267-9300, Ⓦwww.mfa.org; Museum **T**), is New England's premier art space, and home to one of the most distinctive collections in the country. Founded in 1870 in Copley Square, the museum moved to its permanent home in 1909. It is currently undergoing an ambitious renovation that will include a new wing and a glass pavilion for the central courtyard. While great news for the long run, at the time of writing locating long-standing pieces of art was a bit difficult. Be prepared for gallery closings, but don't worry, the museum puts on a great show no matter what is on display.

Art of the Americas and the Musical Instruments gallery

On the first floor, a marvelously rich **American collection** features a number of John Singleton Copley portraits of revolutionary figures, plus his gruesome narrative *Watson and the Shark*. Romantic naturalist landscapes from the first half of the nineteenth century – such as Albert Bierstadt's quietly majestic *Buffalo Crossing* – dominate several rooms; and from the latter half of the century there are several seascapes by Winslow Homer; Whistler's *Harmony In Flesh and Colour*; and works from the Boston school, notably Childe Hassan's gauzy *Boston Common at Twilight* and John Singer Sargent's spare *The Daughters of Edward Darley Boit*.

Highlights of the **Latin American** holdings include Fernando Botero's voluptuous *Venus*, bold sentinel of the West Wing's second floor, and Claudio Bravo's introspective *At the Gallery* and *Interior with Landscape Painter*, both unfairly hidden in the *Bravo* restaurant.

Across the hall from the Huntington Street entrance, it's worth popping into the **Musical Instruments** gallery, even if just to glimpse item #12 – one of the world's first saxophones, made by Adolphe Sax himself.

Impressionist Room

The second-floor **Impressionist** room contains a lot of the museum's best-loved pieces, including Van Gogh's *Postman Joseph Roulin*, Monet's *Water Lilies* and *Rouen Cathedral (Morning Effect)*, although the real show-stopper, his tongue-in-cheek *La Japonaise*, is around the corner in the Rosenburg gallery. Degas figures prominently here with his *Pagans and Degas' Father* and a bronze cast of the *14-Year-Old Dancer*, as does Renoir, whose *Dance at Bougival* faces Gauguin's sumptuous display of existential angst *Where Do We Come From? What Are We? Where Are We Going?*.

Shapiro Rotunda and other galleries

Between the second-floor Egyptian and Asian galleries is the outstanding **Shapiro Rotunda**, its dome and en-suite colonnade inset with murals and bas-reliefs by John Singer Sargent, who undertook the commission following his work in the Boston Public Library (see p.99). Operating under the belief that mural painting was the key to "artistic immortality," this installation certainly guaranteed the artist a lasting place in the MFA, and some controversy to boot: when the project was completed shortly before his death in 1925, his Classical theme was falling out of vogue and his efforts were considered the "frivolous works of a failing master." The rotunda leads to the **Koch Gallery**, which ranks among the museum's more spectacular showings. Designed to resemble a European palace hallway, its walls are hung two-high with dozens of portraits and landscapes of varying sizes, including three pieces by El Greco.

For those in the know, the MFA's **Asian galleries** are a highlight. The Chinese, Indian, Southeast Asian, and Islamic collections are excellent, but the standout is the museum's **Japanese collection**, quite simply one of the best in the world, in part because of the MFA's partnership with the Foundation for the Arts, Nagoya. The first floor is filled with samurai swords, lacquer boxes, and kimonos, while the second floor's temple room, peacefully arranged with tranquil Buddha statues, feels like a marvelous museum secret. There's also an astounding collection of hanging vibrant, bloom-filled scrolls and *ukiyo-e* woodblock prints.

Isabella Stewart Gardner Museum

Less broad in its collection, but more distinctive and idiosyncratic than the MFA, is the nearby **Isabella Stewart Gardner Museum**, 280 The Fenway (Tues–Sun 11am–4.45pm; $12, free admission for those named "Isabella"; ⊤617/566-1401, Ⓦwww.gardnermuseum.org; Museum **T**). Dynamic Boston socialite Gardner collected and arranged more than 2500 objects in her four-story home (which she designed herself), making this the only major museum in the country that is entirely the creation of a single individual. It's a hodgepodge of works from around the globe, presented without much attention to period or style; Gardner wanted the setting of her pieces to "fire the imagination." Your imagination does get quite a workout – there's art everywhere you look, with many of the objects unlabeled, placed in corners or above doorways, for an effect that is occasionally chaotic, but always striking. To get the most out of a visit, aim to join the hour-long **tour** (Tues–Fri 2.30pm; free), but get there early as only fifteen people are allowed, on a first-come, first-served basis. Alternatively, the **gift shop** sells a worthwhile **guide** ($6) detailing the location and history of every piece on display.

▲ Isabella Stewart Gardner Museum

The Gardner is best known for its spectacular central **courtyard**, styled after a fifteenth-century Venetian palace, where flowering plants and trees bloom year-round amid statuary and fountains. The courtyard also shows off Ms Gardner's sense of humor: note the tiled, snake-haired Medusa at its center, from whom one glance – according to Greek myth – turned onlookers to stone (hence all the statues). The museum's greatest success is the **Spanish Cloister**, a long, narrow corridor which perfectly frames John Singer Sargent's ecstatic representation of flamenco dance, *El Jaleo*, and also contains fine seventeenth-century Mexican tiles and Roman statuary and sarcophagi. The **Gothic Room** on the third floor holds another Sargent show-stopper – a stunning portrait of Isabella herself. Although mild by today's standards, the Gardners feared its near-erotic quality was too scandalous for public consumption, and the painting was not exhibited publicly until after her death. Also on the third floor are sixteenth-century Italian choir stalls and stained glass from Milan and Soissons cathedrals, as well as Paul-César Helleu's moody *Interior of the Abbey Church of Saint-Denis*.

The **Titian**, **Veronese**, and **Raphael rooms** comprise a strong showing of Italian Renaissance and Baroque work, including Crivelli's *St George and the Dragon*. What is still a first-rate array of seventeenth-century Northern European works was debilitated in 1990 by the biggest art heist in history: three Rembrandts and a Vermeer were among thirteen artworks stolen – you can spot the missing works by their empty frames, kept up as placeholders for their return.

The second floor's magnificent **Tapestry Room,** hung with mid-sixteenth-century Brussels tapestries, makes a sumptuous backdrop for the weekend chamber orchestra concerts, lectures, and other events that are held here (☎617/278-5150).

Brookline

The leafy, affluent town of **BROOKLINE**, south of Boston University and west of The Fenway, is centered on bustling **Coolidge Corner**, at the intersection of Beacon and Harvard streets. Close by is the **John F. Kennedy National Historic Site**, at 83 Beals St (Wed–Sun 10am–4.30pm; $3; ☎617/566-7937), the outwardly unremarkable house where JFK was born on May 29, 1917. The inside is rather plain, too, though a narrated voiceover by the late president's mother, Rose, adds some spice to the roped-off rooms. Along Brookline's southern fringe is the **Frederick Law Olmsted National Historic Site**, 99 Warren St (Fri–Sun 10am–4.30pm; free; ☎617/566-1689, Ⓦwww.nps.gov /frla), which doubled as Olmsted's family home and office; it's currently closed for renovations until 2010. To reach Brookline, take the Green Line's C branch to Coolidge Corner.

Boston's southern districts

The parts of Boston that most visitors see – downtown, Beacon Hill, Back Bay, the North End – are actually only a tiny part of the city. To the south lies a vast spread of residential neighborhoods, including largely Irish **South Boston**, hip **Dorchester**, historic **Roxbury**, and pleasant **Jamaica Plain**, which count among them Jamaica Plain's **Arnold Arboretum** and Dorchester's **John F. Kennedy Presidential Library and Museum**. All of these areas are fairly accessible on the **T** from downtown (although not always safe to walk around, especially after dark), with a neighborhood-like feel that's not necessarily exciting for out-of-towners. Jamaica Plain (popularly known as "JP") might be the exception to this; Centre Street there has boomed into one of the hippest eating and shopping strips in the city.

Castle Island and Fort Independence

South Boston ("Southie") narrows to an end in Boston Harbor on a strip of land called **Castle Island**, off the end of William J. Day Boulevard, a favorite leisure spot for residents. The island, reachable by bus #9 or #11 from the Broadway **T**, is covered by parks and beaches. At its tip is **Fort Independence** (guided tours Sat & Sun noon–3.30pm; free), a stout granite edifice that was one of the earliest redoubts in the Americas, originally established in 1634; what you see today is actually a thicker rendition of the 1801 version. Its walls aren't much to look at, although supposedly a gruesome incident that happened inside served as inspiration for Edgar Allan Poe's *The Cask of Amontillado*.

John F. Kennedy Presidential Library and Museum

The **John F. Kennedy Presidential Library & Museum** (daily 9am–5pm; $10; ℡1-866/JFK-1960, ⊛www.jfklibrary.org; JFK/UMass **T**; free shuttle every 20min), at Columbia Point, is spectacularly situated in an I.M. Pei-designed building overlooking Boston Harbor. The campaign exhibits are most interesting for their television and radio ads, which illustrate the squeaky-clean self-image America possessed at that time. The section on the Kennedy administration is more serious, highlighted by a 22-minute film on the Cuban Missile Crisis that evokes the tension of the event, if exaggerating Kennedy's heroics. The final section of the museum is perhaps the best: an atrium overlooking the harbor, with excerpts from Kennedy's *Profiles on Courage* – affecting enough to move even the most jaded JFK critic. Oddly enough, the museum is also the repository for Ernest Hemingway's original manuscripts. Call to make an appointment to see them (℡1-866/JFK-1960).

Dorchester Heights Monument

Back at the convergence of South Boston and Dorchester rises **Dorchester Heights**, whose northernmost point, Thomas Park, is crowned by a stone **tower** commemorating George Washington's bloodless purge of the Brits from Boston. After the Continental Army had held the British under siege in the city for just over a year, Washington wanted to put an end to the whole thing. On March 4, 1776, he amassed all the artillery he could get his hands on and placed it on towering Dorchester Heights, so the tired Redcoats could get a good look at the patriots' firepower. Intimidated, they swiftly left Boston – for good. The park, generally empty and pristinely kept, still commands the same sweeping views of Boston and its southern communities that it did during the Revolutionary War. The best vista is from the top of the tower itself, though it's only open by appointment (free; ℡617/242-5642).

Franklin Park

Roxbury's **Franklin Park** (Forest Hills **T**), the southernmost link in the Emerald Necklace, was one of Olmsted's proudest accomplishments, due to the sheer size of the place. Its scale is indeed astounding – 527 acres of green space, with trails for hikers, bikers, and walkers. A lot of the park has grown shaggy from lack of upkeep, however, so take care – and be especially careful not to get caught out here at night, as it borders some of Boston's more dangerous areas.

The **Franklin Park Zoo**, at 1 Franklin Park Rd in Franklin Park (April–Sept Mon–Fri 10am–5pm, Sat & Sun 10am–6pm; Oct–March daily 10am–4pm; $12, kids $7; ℡617/541-LION, ⊛www.zoonewengland.com), has little besides its backdrop to distinguish it from other zoos, though it does boast the impressively recreated African Tropical Forest, the largest indoor open-space zoo design in North America, housing bats, warthogs, and gorillas. Check out Bird's World, too, a charming relic from the days of Edwardian zoo design: a huge wrought-iron cage you can walk through while birds fly overhead.

Jamaica Plain and the Arnold Arboretum

Diminutive **Jamaica Plain** is one of Boston's more successfully integrated neighborhoods, with a mix of students, immigrants, and families. Located between Roxbury and the section of the Emerald Necklace known as the Muddy River Improvement, the area's activity focuses on **Centre Street**, home to some inexpensive cafés and restaurants.

Jamaica Plain's star attraction – and really the only must-see sight in all the southern districts – is the 265-acre **Arnold Arboretum**, at 125 Arborway (daily sunrise–sunset; donations welcome; ☎617/524-1718, ⓦwww.arboretum .harvard.edu; Forest Hills **T**), the most vital link in the Emerald Necklace. Its collection of flowering trees, vines, and shrubs has benefited from more than one hundred years of careful grooming and ample funding, and is now one of the finest in North America. The plants are arranged along a series of paths enjoyed by everyone from dog-walkers to serious botanists. The array of Asian species – the best in the world outside of Asia – is highlighted by the **Larz Anderson Bonsai Collection**, and is brilliantly concentrated along the Chinese Path, a walkway near the center of the park. It's best to visit during spring, when magnolias, crab apples, and lilacs complement the greenery with dazzling chromatic schemes. "**Lilac Sunday**," a celebration held on the third Sunday in May, sees the Arboretum at its most vibrant, when its collection of lilacs – the second largest in the US – is in full bloom.

Cambridge

Walk down almost any street in **CAMBRIDGE** – just across the Charles River from Boston, but a world apart in atmosphere and attitude – and you will pass plaques and monuments honoring literati and revolutionaries who lived and worked in the area as early as the seventeenth century. But along its Colonial-period brick sidewalks and narrow, crooked roads, Cambridge vibrates with a vital present: starched business people bustle past punk rock kids; clean-cut college students coexist with the homeless; and tourists look on as street vendors purvey goods and perform music. It's all enough to make Cambridge an essential stopover on your trip.

The city is loosely organized around a series of squares – confluences of streets that are the focus of each area's commercial activity. By far the most important of these is **Harvard Square**, location of the eponymous university and the top draw for visitors. The area around it is home to the city's main sights, particularly the stretch of Colonial mansions in **Old Cambridge**. Blue-collar **Central Square** is less touristy but no less urban than its collegiate counterpart, while farther east along the Charles is **Kendall Square**, home to the **Massachusetts Institute of Technology** (MIT), one of the world's premier science and research institutions, and some peculiar architecture and an excellent museum.

Harvard Square and the University

Harvard Square – a buzzing public space in the shadow of Harvard Yard – radiates out from the **T** stop along Massachusetts Avenue, JFK Street, and Brattle Street. A small **tourism kiosk** run by the Cambridge Tourism Office (daily 9am–5pm; ☎617/441-2884 or 1-800/862-5678, ⓦwww.cambridge-usa .org) faces the station exit, but more of the action is in the adjacent sunken area known as **The Pit**, a triage center for alternative culture. Moody youths spend entire days sitting here admiring each other's green hair and body piercings while homeless locals hustle for change. This is also the focal point of the city's **street music scene**, at its most frenetic on Friday and Saturday nights and Sunday afternoons, when all the elements converge: crowds mill about; evangelical demonstrators engage in shouting matches; and bands perform on every corner.

North of Harvard Square along Massachusetts Avenue lies one of Cambridge's first cemeteries, the **Old Burying-Ground**, whose style and grounds have scarcely changed since the seventeenth century. The gravestones are adorned in a style somewhere between Puritan austerity and medieval superstition: inscriptions praise the simple piety of the Christian deceased, but are surrounded by death's-heads carved to ward off evil spirits. You're supposed to apply to the sexton of

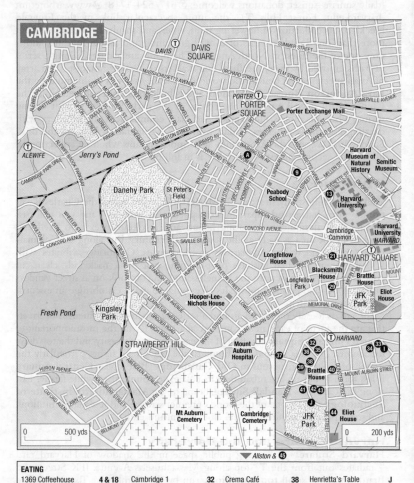

▼ *Allston &* **45**

EATING

1369 Coffeehouse	**4 & 18**	Cambridge 1	**32**	Crema Café	**38**	Henrietta's Table
Algiers Coffeehouse	**39**	Central Kitchen	**20**	Darwin's Ltd	**14 & 29**	Helmand
Bartley's Burger Cottage	**34**	Chez Henri	**9**	East Coast Grill	**3**	Hungry Mother
Beantowne Coffeehouse		Christina's Homemade		Emma's Pizza	**12**	LA Burdick Chocolate
and Café	**8**	Ice Cream	**5**	The Garage	**40**	Olé Mexican Grill
Blue Room	**11**	Craigie on Main	**17**	Harvest	**37**	Oleana

Christ Church for entry, but if the gate at the path behind the church is open (as it frequently is), you can enter – just be respectful.

Dawes Park, a triangular wedge of concrete squeezed into the intersection of Massachusetts Avenue and Garden Street, is named for William Dawes, one of the patriots who rode to alert residents that the British were marching on Lexington and Concord in 1775. While Longfellow chose to commemorate Revere's midnight ride, Cambridge's citizens must have appreciated Dawes' contribution just as much. Actually, there was a third rider, Dr Samuel Prescott, who's generally credited as the only one to complete the ride. Bronze hoofmarks in the sidewalk mark the event, and placards behind the pathway provide information on the history of the Harvard Square/Old Cambridge area.

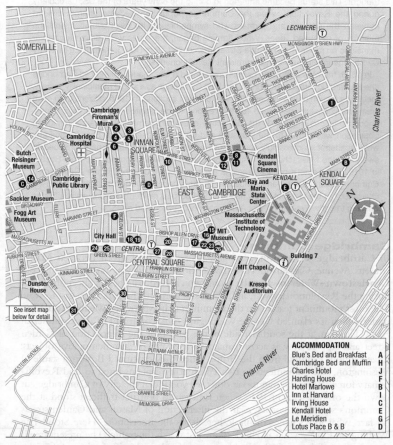

ACCOMMODATION	
Blue's Bed and Breakfast	A
Cambridge Bed and Muffin	H
Charles Hotel	J
Harding House	F
Hotel Marlowe	B
Inn at Harvard	I
Irving House	C
Kendall Hotel	E
Le Meridien	G
Lotus Place B & B	D

		DRINKING & NIGHTLIFE					
Punjabi Dhaba	6	Cantab Lounge	19	Great Scott	45	Phoenix Landing	27
Salts	16	Charlie's Kitchen	42	Lizard Lounge	13	Plough & Stars	24
Tealuxe	35	Club Passim	36	Middle East	28	Regattabar	43
Toscanini's	22	Cuchi Cuchi	15	Middlesex	26	River Gods	30
Upstairs on the Square	41	Enormous Room	20	Miracle of Science	23	Shay's	44
Veggie Planet	36	Grafton Street	33	People's Republik	25	T.T. the Bear's Place	28
						Western Front	31

A history of Cambridge

Cambridge began inauspiciously in 1630, when a group of English immigrants from Charlestown founded **New Towne** village on the narrow, swampy banks of the Charles River. These Puritans hoped New Towne would become an ideal religious community; to that end, they founded a college in 1636 for the purpose of training clergy. Two years later, the college took its name in honor of a local minister, **John Harvard**, who bequeathed his library and half his estate to the nascent institution. New Towne was eventually renamed Cambridge for the English university where many of its figureheads were educated, and became a publishing center after the importation of the printing press in the seventeenth century. Its printing industry and university established Cambridge as a bastion of intellectual activity and political thought. This status became entrenched during the early years of the US, particularly during the Revolution, when the Cambridge population became sharply divided between the artisans and farmers who sympathized with the Revolution and the minority of moneyed Tories. When fighting began, the Tories were driven from their mansions on modern-day Brattle Street (then called "Tory Row"), their place taken by Cambridge intelligentsia and prominent Revolutionaries.

In 1846, the Massachusetts Legislature granted a city charter linking Old Cambridge (the Harvard Square area) and industrial East Cambridge as a single municipality. Initially, there was friction between these two very different sections; in 1855, citizens from each area unsuccessfully petitioned for the regions to be granted separate civic status. Though relations improved, the distinctive characters remained. A large immigrant population was drawn to the industrial and commercial sectors of East Cambridge, while academics increasingly sought out Harvard, whose reputation had continued to swell, and the Massachusetts Institute of Technology, which moved here from Boston in 1916. The district's political leanings are less liberal today than in the 1960s, when Cambridge earned the name "Moscow on the Charles" due to its unabashedly Red character, but the fact that nearly half of its 90,000-plus residents are university affiliates ensures that it will remain one of America's most opinionated cities.

Cambridge Common

In **Cambridge Common**, a roughly square patch of green between Massachusetts Avenue, Garden Street, and Waterhouse Street, you can retrace the old **Charlestown–Watertown path**, along which Redcoats beat a sheepish retreat during the Revolutionary War, and which still transects the park from east to west. The most prominent feature on the Common is, however, the **Washington Elm**, under which it's claimed George Washington took command of the Continental Army. The elm, at the southern side of the park near the intersection of Garden Street and Appian Way, is accompanied by a wealth of commemorative objects: three cannons captured from the British when they evacuated Boston, a statue of Washington, and monuments to two Polish army captains hired to lead Revolutionary forces. What the memorials don't tell you is that the city of Cambridge cut down the original elm in 1946 when it began to obstruct traffic; it stood at the Common's southwest corner, near the intersection of Mason and Garden streets (in fact, what looks like a manhole here bears the inscription "Here Stood The Washington Elm" – you can check it out, just watch the traffic). The present tree is the offspring of the original, raised from one of its branches. To further confuse the issue, the Daughters of the American Revolution erected a monument commemorating the south*east* corner of the park as the spot where Washington did his thing, and recently, historians have suggested that Washington actually commissioned the troops at Wadsworth House in Harvard Yard. Safe to explore by day, the Common can be sketchy after dark – try to avoid it at night.

Harvard University

The transition from Harvard Square to **Harvard Yard** – the proper center of the university – is brief and dramatic: in a matter of only several feet, the buzz of car traffic and urban life gives way to grassy lawns, towering oaks, and an aura of intellectualism. The atmosphere is more illusory than real, however, as the Yard's narrow footpaths are constantly plied by preoccupied students and camera-clicking tour groups, who make the place seem more like an amusement park than an university campus. You can join the hullabaloo by taking a free one-hour guided tour from the **Holyoke Center Arcade**, 1350 Massachusetts Ave (June–Aug Mon–Sat 10am, 11.15am, 2pm & 3.15pm; Sept–May Mon–Fri 10am & 2pm, Sat 2pm; ☎617/495–1573). The Center also provides limited free internet use, as well as **maps** and brochures detailing everything Harvard-related.

Enter through Johnston Gate, across Massachusetts Avenue from the Common, and you're in the **Old Yard**, a large, rectangular area enclosed by freshman dormitories. Opposite the gate, in front of marble-hued University Hall, is the Yard's trademark icon, the **John Harvard statue**, around which tour groups gather to hear the story of the statue's three lies (it misdates the college's founding; erroneously identifies John Harvard as the college's founder; and isn't really a likeness of John Harvard). While it's a popular spot for visitors to take pictures, male students at the college covet the statue as a site of public urination. You might want to stay away from rubbing the toe (supposedly good luck).

The architectural contrast between modest, 1762 **Hollis Hall**, north of Johnston Gate, and its grandiose southern neighbor, **Matthews Hall**, built around a hundred years later, mirrors Harvard's transition from a quiet training ground for ministers to a cosmopolitan university. The indentations in Hollis's front steps also hold some historical interest: students used to warm their rooms by heating cannonballs, and, when it came time to leave for the summer, they would dispose of them by dropping them from their windows.

East of the Old Yard lie the grander buildings of Tercentenary Theater, where a vast set of steps leads up to the enormous pillars of **Widener Library**. Named after Harvard grad and *Titanic* victim Harry Elkins Widener, whose mother paid for the project, it's the center of the largest private library collection in the US,

▲ Harvard Square

boasting 65 miles of bookshelves. At the opposite side of the yard is **Memorial Church**, whose narrow, white spire strikes a balancing note to the pillared front of Widener.

North of Harvard Yard, across Cambridge Street, lies the main quad of **Harvard Law School**, focusing on the stern gray pillars of **Langdell Hall**, the imposing edifice on its western border. Above Langdell's entrance is a Latin inscription encapsulating the Western ideal of the rule of law, tinctured with an unusual degree of religiosity: "*Non sub homine, sed sub deo et lege*" ("Not under man, but under God and law").

It's hard to miss the conspicuously modern **Carpenter Center** as you walk past down Quincy Street, a slab of gray amidst Harvard's ubiquitous brick. Completed in 1963 as a center for the study of visual art, the Carpenter Center is the only building in America designed by French architect Le Corbusier. Be sure to traverse its trademark feature, a walkway through its center, meant to reflect the path worn by students on the lot on which the center was built. The basement of the building houses the **Sert Gallery** (free; ☎617/495-3251), curated jointly by the university art museums and visual arts students.

Harvard Art Museum

Harvard's three **art museums** (the Fogg, the Sackler, and the Busch-Reisinger) have benefited from years of scholarly attention and donors' financial generosity. Unfortunately, all three are currently closed for a major renovation, which will merge them into one large collection at 32 Quincy St; this is not slated to reopen until 2013. Once open, the new **Harvard Art Museum** will encompass over 150,000 works of art, including highlights of Harvard's substantial gathering of Western art, a small yet excellent selection of German Expressionists and Bauhaus works, and sensuous Buddhas and gilded bodhisattvas from its Asian and Islamic art collections. During the renovation, you can check out a selection of the university's holdings at 485 Broadway, the former home of the **Arthur M. Sackler Museum** (Mon–Sat 10am–5pm, Sun 1–5pm; $9, free on Sat before noon; ☎617/495-9400).

Museum of Natural History, Peabody Museum, and Harvard Semitic Museum

North of the Sackler Museum is the **Harvard Museum of Natural History**, 26 Oxford St (daily 9am–5pm; $9, includes entry to the Peabody Museum, free to MA residents Sun 9am–noon; ☎617/495-3045, ⓦwww.hmnh.harvard.edu), a nineteenth-century Victorian museum with well-executed exhibits. Start your visit at **Minerals, Gems, and Meteorites**, a visual feast of rocks and gemstones, with a spectacular 1600-pound amethyst-encrusted cavity as its centerpiece. The adjacent gallery houses the museum's *pièce de resistance*, the stunning **Ware Collection of Glass Models of Plants**. This project began in 1886 and terminated in 1936, leaving the museum with an absolutely unique and visually awesome collection of flowers constructed entirely from glass; it's really not to be missed. Down the hall, the **zoological galleries** are home to some freakishly huge fossils, including a 42-foot-long prehistoric marine reptile, the *Kronosaurus*. Around the corner is the *Glyptodont*, which looks like an inflated armadillo.

The Museum of Natural History is connected to the **Peabody Museum**, 11 Divinity Ave (same hours and cost as above; ☎617/496-1027, ⓦwww.peabody.harvard.edu), which displays archeological and ethnographic materials, many culled from Harvard University expeditions. The Peabody also features interesting exhibits on North American Native Americans, though the strength of the museum lies in its collection of pieces from Mesoamerica. Best are the enormous, carved Copan stelæ on which births, deaths, and bloodlettings are all recorded in ancient Maya.

Facing the Peabody is the **Harvard Semitic Museum**, 6 Divinity Ave (Mon–Fri 10am–4pm, Sun 1–4pm; free; ⓦwww.fas.harvard.edu/~semitic), which lacks the magnetism of its neighbors but holds some Near Eastern archeological artifacts that are worth a look. Seek out the second floor's set of Egyptian amulet and funerary figurines.

Old Cambridge

After the outbreak of the American Revolution, Cambridge's patriot dissidents ran their Tory neighbors out of town, but left their sumptuous houses along "Tory Row" (now **Brattle Street**, the main drag of **Old Cambridge**) more or less unharmed. The area has remained a neighborhood of stately mansions, although only two of the houses are open to the public; the rest you'll have to view from across their expansive, impeccably kept lawns.

Longfellow House

One house you can visit for more than just a look is the **Longfellow House**, 105 Brattle St (June–Oct Wed–Sun 10am–4.30pm, tours hourly 10.30–11.30am & 1–4pm; $3; ⓣ617/876-4491, ⓦwww.nps.gov/long; Harvard **T**), where poet Henry Wadsworth Longfellow lived while serving as a professor at Harvard. The house was erected for Loyalist John Vassall in 1759, who promptly vacated it on the eve of the Revolutionary War; it was later used by George Washington as his headquarters during the siege of Boston. In 1837 it became home to Longfellow, who initially moved in as a boarder. After he married Fanny Appleton, her father purchased the house for them as a wedding gift, and the poet lived here until his death in 1882. The house is preserved in an attempt to portray it as it was during his residence. The halls and walls are festooned with Longfellow's furniture and art collection; most surprising is the wealth of nineteenth-century pieces from the Far East, amassed by Longfellow's son Charlie on his world travels. Just outside, a lovely garden features labyrinthine shrubs, snapdragons, and roses all laid out with historical accuracy from plans dating to 1904.

Hooper-Lee Nichols House

The second of the Brattle Street mansions open to the public, half a mile west of the Longfellow House and worth the trip if you've got the stamina, is the **Hooper-Lee-Nichols House**, at no. 159 (Tues & Thurs 2–5pm, tours at 2 & 3pm; $5; ⓣ617/547-4252, ⓦwww.cambridgehistory.org), one of the oldest residences in Cambridge. The house began as a post-medieval farmhouse, and underwent various renovations until it became the Georgian mansion it is today. Tour guides open secret panels to reveal centuries-old wallpaper and original foundations; otherwise, you'll see rooms predictably restored with period writing tables and canopy beds.

Mount Auburn Cemetery

At the terminus of Brattle Street is **Mount Auburn Cemetery**, an unexpected treasure. Laid out in 1831 as America's first "garden cemetery," its 175 acres of stunningly landscaped grounds, complete with ponds and fountains, provide a gorgeous contrast with the many spare "burying grounds" in the city. Resting here are painter Winslow Homer and art patron Isabella Stewart Gardner, among others. Pick up a **map** at the visitors' center at the entrance to find out who's where, and get a sense of the cemetery's scope by ascending the **tower** that lies smack in its center – from here, you can see all the way to downtown Boston.

Central and Inman squares

Working-class **Central Square**, as you might expect, is located roughly in the geographical center of Cambridge, and is appropriately the city's civic center, home to its government buildings. It's a good place to shop and eat, and is home to some of the best nightlife in Cambridge (see p.127 & p.129).

Overshadowed by Cambridge's busier districts, **Inman Square** is a quiet area directly north of Central Square, centered on the confluence of Cambridge, Beacon, and Prospect streets. It's a pleasant, mostly residential neighborhood where much of Cambridge's Portuguese-speaking population resides, though it has become more cosmopolitan of late, and there are some good shopping and eating opportunities here as well. The lone landmark is the charming **Cambridge Firemen's Mural**, at the corner of Cambridge and Hampshire streets, a work of public art commissioned to honor the men in red.

Massachusetts Institute of Technology

Eastern Cambridge is mostly taken over by the **Massachusetts Institute of Technology** (MIT), which occupies over 150 acres alongside the Charles River and provides an intellectual counterweight to the otherwise working-class character of the area. Originally established in Back Bay in 1861, MIT moved across the river in 1916 and has since risen to international prominence as a major center for theoretical and practical research in the sciences.

The campus buildings and geography reflect the quirky character of the institute, emphasizing function and peppering it with a peculiar notion of form. Behind the massive pillars that guard the entrance of **Building 7**, 77 Massachusetts Ave, you'll find a labyrinth of corridors through which you can traverse the entire east campus without ever going outside – it's known to Techies as the **Infinite Corridor**. Just inside the entrance you'll find the **MIT Information Center** (Mon–Fri 9am–5pm, campus tours 10.45am & 2.45pm; ☎617/253-4795), while atop the nearby MacLaurin Building (aka "Building 10") is MIT's best-known architectural icon, a massive gilt hemisphere called the **Great Dome**.

MIT has drawn the attention of some major twentieth-century architects, who have used the university's progressiveness as a testing ground for some of their more experimental works. Two of these are located in the courtyard across Massachusetts Avenue from **Building 7**. The **Kresge Auditorium**, designed by Finnish architect Eero Saarinen, resembles a large tent, though its real claim to fame is that it rests on three, rather than four, corners; the architect allegedly designed it over breakfast by cutting into his grapefruit. In the same courtyard, another Saarinen work, the red-brick **MIT Chapel**, is shaped like a stocky cylinder with an abstract sculpture of paper-thin metal serving as a spire; inside, a delicate metal screen scatters light patterns across the floor. The I.M. Pei-designed Wiesner Building is home to the **List Visual Art Center** (Tues–Thurs, Sat & Sun

364.4 Smoots (+ 1 Ear)

If you walk from Boston to Cambridge across the scenic Harvard Bridge (which leads directly into MIT's campus), you might wonder about the graffiti partitioning the sidewalk. Doled out into "smoots," it records the height of Oliver R. Smoot, a MIT Lambda Chi Alpha fraternity pledge in 1958. The shortest member of the group, part of Smoot's initiation process was to have his body used as a tape measure, all down the Harvard Bridge – resulting in the conclusive "364.4 Smoots + 1 Ear" at the bridge's culmination. The marks are lovingly repainted by LCA pledges every year, the Smoot has gone so far as to be included as an official measurement in the Google Calculator, and the act has gone down in history as one of the school's best "hacks."

noon–6pm; free), which displays contemporary artworks utilizing a wide range of media. Of perhaps more interest, down Massachusetts Avenue at no. 265, the **MIT Museum** (daily 10am–5pm; $7.50; ☎617/253-5927, ⓦweb.mit.edu/museum) has a number of standout displays, including "Holography: the Light Fantastic," a collection of seriously cool eye tricks; there is also an exhibit of mini-machines, such as a walking wishbone.

Eating

Boston is loaded with places to eat – everything from cafés that serve full meals to bars and pubs that double as restaurants to higher-end dinner-only options. In most places, save certain areas of downtown, you won't have a problem finding somewhere to grab a **quick bite,** whether it's a diner, deli, or some other kind of snack joint. In addition to all the places listed below, see the bars listed on p.124, many of which offer food.

Boston's **café** scene offers a limited range of places to hang out; there are a number of sleek, laptop-worthy spots around Back Bay's **Newbury Street** and over in the **South End**. Value is better in the **North End**, but the liveliest cafés are in **Cambridge**.

Cafés

Although the *Starbucks* invasion has done some real damage to the **café** scene in Boston and Cambridge, there are still lots of independent places where you can relax with a book and a hot drink. At many cafés, you can just as easily get an excellent full meal as you can a cup of coffee.

Downtown

Flat Black Coffee Company 50 Broad St ☎617/951-1440; State **T**. This Australian-inspired place (in Australianese, a "flat white" is a particular blend of steamed milk and espresso) offers up freshly brewed, free-trade coffee to happy Financial District patrons. Not too loungey, but there are tasty pastries on offer as well as free wi-fi.

North End

Caffé dello Sport 308 Hanover St ☎617/523-5063; Haymarket **T**. A continuous stream of Rai Uno soccer matches is broadcast from the ceiling-mounted TV sets, making for an agreeable din amongst a very local crowd. Along with espresso, beer, wine, and sambuca are served.
Caffé Paradiso 255 Hanover St ☎617/742-1768; Haymarket **T**. Simple but great little neighborhood hangout with rugby and soccer matches on the TV. Drink options include espresso, wine, and cocktails, but come for the tasty pastries and wicked good gelato.

Beacon Hill

Caffe Bella Vita 30 Charles St ☎617/720-4505; Charles **T**. A casual café with fine coffees, tasty

pastries, and good gelato. Also doubles as a great lunch or casual dinner spot, with low-key salads and soups.

Back Bay

L'Aroma Café 85 Newbury St ☎617/412-4001; Copley **T**. This amiable café has a friendly staff, good paninis, and tasty cappuccinos for refueling while shopping along Newbury St.
Tealuxe 108 Newbury St ☎617/927-0400; Copley **T**. A sister shop to the Harvard Square original (see p.118), this charming little tea haven has all the varieties of hot, iced, and bubble teas you might ever need to satisfy your pick-me-up needs.

The South End

Uptown Espresso 563 Columbus Ave ☎617/236-8535; Ruggles **T**. Often voted "Best of Boston," this lovely space in a South End brownstone features free wi-fi, tasty sandwiches and pastries, and of course, fabulous espresso, best lingered over in their sunroom or outdoor patio.

Cambridge

1369 Coffeehouse 757 Massachusetts Ave ☎617/576-4600; Central **T**. The *1369*'s relaxed environment attracts both earnest thirty-something leftists and youthful hipsters; your best bets are the standard array of caffeinated beverages and particularly exquisite desserts. Its original location is at 1369 Cambridge St, in Inman Square (⊤617/576-1369; #69 bus).

Algiers 40 Brattle St ⊤617/492-1557; Harvard **T**. North African café popular with Harvard's artsy set; there are few more atmospheric places in which to sip first-rate coffee.

Crema Café 27 Brattle St ⊤617/876-2700; Harvard **T**. You can drink your coffee here with Harvard students at rustic, communal tables on a pretty outdoor patio. Free wi-fi.

L.A. Burdick's 52D Brattle St ⊤617/491-4340; Harvard **T**. Simply breathing in the aromas at this fabulous *chocolaterie* is an exercise in indulgence:

iced chocolate, chocolate mousse cake, and little chocolate mice and penguins, all waiting to be consumed.

Tealuxe 0 Brattle St ⊤617/441-0077; Harvard **T**. Now a chain, this is the original, and still a great spot. The place is smaller than a teacup, but they manage to stock over a hundred varieties of tea, including Crème de la Earl Grey, reported to taste like birthday cake.

Jamaica Plain

Canto 6 3346 Washington St, Jamaica Plain ⊤617/983-8688; Green St **T**. Tasty espresso drinks and life-changing pastries like the "Bostok," a brioche with orange blossom cream, or the "Sleepy Hollow," a roll filled with egg and gruyère and baked to crispy perfection.

Restaurants

As far as the city's culinary landscape goes: **Italian** restaurants and bakeries cluster in the **North End**, mainly on Hanover and Salem streets; **Chinatown** packs in all types of Asian fare; and the trendiest restaurants, usually of the **New American** variety, tend to cluster in the **South End** and **Back Bay**. **Cambridge** dining life centers on Harvard, Inman, and Central squares.

Boston Common and Downtown Crossing

Chacarero 101 Arch St ⊤617/542-0392 and 26 Province St ⊤617/367-1167; Park St **T** or Downtown Crossing **T**. Fabulous and fresh, the *chacarero* is a Chilean sandwich built of warm, soft bread and filled with avocado, chicken, green beans, muenster cheese, and hot sauce; good veggie sandwich version, too. Mon–Fri 8am–6pm; cash only.

Falafel King 48 Winter St, Ste 1 ⊤617/338-8355; Park St **T**. You'll know you've found this gem, nestled within an otherwise unappealing food court, when you come across the long line of regulars waiting for cheap and tasty traditional shawarma sandwiches ($5.50; even better with pickles). Closed weekends; cash only.

Locke-Ober 3 Winter Place ⊤617/542-1340; Park St **T**. A Boston legend, this blue-blooded institution consists of traditional fancy fare like steak tartare and oysters on the half shell. Patrons should dress to impress and prepare to spend a wad of cash. Reservations required.

🏃 **No. 9 Park** 9 Park St ⊤617/742-9991; Park St **T**. Excellent restaurant with sedate green walls and plates busy with Southern French and Italian entrees. A seven-course tasting menu ($90, with wine $150) allows you to try almost everything.

Silvertone 69 Bromfield St ⊤617/338-7887; Park St **T**. Nostalgia runs high at this bustling basement bar and eatery serving standout comfort foods like mashed potatoes and meatloaf and mac and cheese. *Silvertone* also has cocktails and a good selection of beer on tap. Closed Sun.

Faneuil Hall and around

Durgin-Park 340 Faneuil Hall Marketplace ⊤617/227-2038; Government Center or State **T**. A Boston landmark in operation since 1827, *Durgin-Park* has a no-frills Yankee atmosphere and a waitstaff known for their surly charm. It's a good place to go for iconic New England foods like roast beef, baked beans, and warm Indian pudding. The downstairs bar is cheaper and livelier.

Union Oyster House 41 Union St ⊤617/227-2750; State **T**. The oldest continuously operating restaurant in America has two big claims to fame: French king Louis-Philippe lived over the tavern during his youth, and the toothpick was first used here. It's a bit of a tourist trap, but the antiquated ambience is very cool; go for the raw bar.

Financial District

Café Fleuri 250 Franklin St, in the *Langham Hotel* ⊤617/451-1900 ext 7125; State **T**. Foremost a fancy Mediterranean brasserie, *Café Fleuri* is best known for one thing: chocolate. On Sat mornings (Sept–June; $38, kids $20) the restaurant literally flows with the stuff – their chocolate bar is equipped with a fountain, crêpes, cakes, and puddings. There is also a great Sunday jazz brunch. Reservations recommended.

Milk Street Café 50 Milk St ⊤617/542-3663; State **T**. Kosher and quick are the key words at this downtown eatery, popular with suits and vegetarians for their large designer sandwiches and salads. Cash only.

Mr. Dooley's Boston Tavern 77 Broad St ⊤617/338-5656; State **T**. One of the many Irish pubs downtown, though with a quieter and more atmospheric interior than the rest. Also known for its live music acts and Traditional Irish Breakfast Sundays – nice, especially since finding anything open around here on Sun is a challenge.

Radius 8 High St ⊤617/426-1234; South Station **T**. Housed in a former bank, this ultramodern French restaurant injects a dose of minimalist industrial chic to the cautious Financial District. The tasty nouvelle cuisine is complemented by an extensive wine list, although some would say that a trip here is wasted if you don't order the burger, considered the best in town.

Theater District

Finale Desserterie 1 Columbus Ave ⊤617/423-3184; Arlington **T**. Devilishly good desserts are the mainstay at this sweet emporium; the top-notch wines and cordials are a treat, too. There's another location in Harvard Square (30 Dunster St; ⊤617/441-9797; Harvard **T**).

Jacob Wirth 31–37 Stuart St ⊤617/338-8586; Boylston **T**. A German-themed Boston landmark, around since 1868; even if you don't like bratwurst washed down with a hearty lager, something is sure to please. There are singalongs on Fri.

Pigalle 75 Charles St S ⊤617/423-4944; Boylston **T**. Breeze into one of *Pigalle's* chocolate-colored booths and settle in for a romantic evening of indulgent French fare. For a perfect conclusion to a night at the theater, try their roasted beet rolls with mint and horseradish cream ($12) or go for the classic steak *frites* ($29).

Teatro 177 Tremont St ⊤617/778-6841; Boylston **T**. A gorgeous space with high arched ceilings and serene blue lighting, *Teatro* bustles with patrons enjoying pre- and post-show Italian fare, or indulgent antipasti ($8–24) and drinks. Be sure to partake of the calamari with lemon aioli ($14). Although it gets noisy, it's still a great date spot.

Chinatown

Hei La Moon 88 Beach St ⊤617/338-8813; Chinatown **T**. Just outside Chinatown proper, *Hei La Moon* is a local favorite for dim sum, with

authentic dishes like shrimp *shumai* and barbecued pork buns as well as more adventurous fare like chicken feet. Expect a long wait on Sun.

New Saigon Sandwich 696 Washington St ⊤617/542-6296; Chinatown **T**. Super cheap ($2.50) Vietnamese *banh mi* sandwiches (tofu, spicy chicken, and the like) and good bubble tea.

Pho Pasteur 682 Washington St ⊤617/482-7467; Chinatown **T**. Very popular Vietnamese restaurant offering a multitude of tasty variations on *pho* noodle soup.

Shabu-Zen 16 Tyler St ⊤617/292-8828; Chinatown **T**. This fun and healthy spot lets you cook your own thinly sliced meats and veggies tableside. Entrees include rice or noodles, a side of raw veggies, and dessert; the chicken platter is $11.

Taiwan Café 34 Oxford St ⊤617/426-8181; Chinatown **T**. Devotees swoon over this busy, authentic Taiwanese eatery serving mustard greens with edamame, clams with spicy black bean sauce, and steamed pork buns done just right. Open until midnight. Cash only.

Leather District

Les Zygomates 129 South St ⊤617/542-5108; South Station **T**. Busy French bistro with good wine selections and gourmet *frites*. Try the duck confit for dinner, and for dessert indulge in wine with chocolate fondue. They also own *Sorriso Trattoria* next door at 107 South St (⊤617/259-1560) serving rustic Italian food.

O Ya 9 East St ⊤617/654-9900; South Station **T**. The portions here are petite and the prices sky high, but patrons swoon over *O Ya's* exquisite sushi – try the wild bluefin tuna *tataki* and roasted beet sashimi. One of Boston's greatest foodie hangouts, in a sleek, intimate space.

South Street Diner 178 Kneeland St ⊤617/350-0028; South Station **T**. The stools at the counter have been spinning since 1947, when this cheap and tasty Boston landmark opened its doors. Now known as more of a late-night hangout with burgers, sandwiches, and the like, they're open 24hr on the weekend, Mon–Fri 5pm–5am.

Waterfront

The Barking Crab 88 Sleeper St, at the Northern Ave Bridge ⊤617/426-CRAB; South Station **T**. This endearing, touristy seafood shack aims to please with its comfortable atmosphere (it looks like a circus tent) and unpretentious, inexpensive menu, centered on anything they can pull from the ocean. Excellent city skyline views – plus it's right on the harbor.

🏃 **flour bakery + café** 12 Farnsworth St ☎617/338-4333; South Station **T**. An offshoot of the well-loved South End institution (see p.122), this low-key eatery is tucked inside a brick warehouse around the corner from the Children's Museum. Positively bursting with fantastic pastries, sandwiches, and salads, they're best known for their BLTs and house-made raspberry seltzer. Top it off with a home-made peanut butter Oreo cookie.

Persephone 283 Summer St ☎617/695-2257; South Station **T**. One of the Fort Point Channel's brave new upstarts, this trendy yet unpretentious place serves local New American cuisine (think grass-fed leg of lamb for two; $32) amidst their clothing boutique Achilles Project.

Sel de la Terre 255 State St ☎617/720-1300; Aquarium **T**. The less-expensive sister to upscale *L'Espalier* (see opposite), *Sel de la Terre* honors its name ("Salt of the Earth") with rustic Provençale fare like hearty bouillabaisse, and perhaps the best french fries in Boston. They also have a new location adjacent to *L'Espalier* (774 Boylston St ☎617/266-8800; Copley **T**).

Yankee Lobster Fish Market 300 Northern Ave ☎617/345-9799; Silver Line Way Station **T**. Right on the water in the Seaport District, this low-key lobster shack serves up fresh seafood (the lobster roll is particularly noteworthy) from its takeout window. It's a hike from downtown – you might want to hop on the Silver Line.

The North End

Carmen 33 North Square ☎617/742-6421; Haymarket **T**. With its intimate size and exposed brick walls, *Carmen* is perhaps the North End's most romantic spot. No dessert, but their signature plates such as the roasted red beets with mint and ricotta ($6) or entrees like the *crespelle bolognese* ($20) make sure you don't leave hungry.

The Daily Catch 323 Hanover St ☎617/523-8567 (Haymarket **T**); 2 Northern Ave ☎617/772-4400 (South Station **T**). Ocean-fresh seafood, notably calamari and shellfish – Sicilian-style, with loads of garlic – draws big lines to this tiny storefront restaurant. The spacious Seaport location offers a solid alternative to the touristy Yankee clam chowder thing.

🏃 **Galleria Umberto** 289 Hanover St ☎617/227-5709; Haymarket **T**. North End nirvana: There are fewer than a dozen items on the menu, but the lines are consistently to the door for Umberto's perfect pizza and savory *arancini* (rice balls). Lunch only, until 2.30pm, but get there earlier as they almost always sell out.

Hot Tomatoes 261 North St ☎617/557-0033; Haymarket **T**. Created by the people who own *Carmen* (see above), this North End newcomer

offers fantastic salads and sandwiches like the "Green Monster" (mozzarella, arugula, artichokes, eggplant, yellow sqash and pesto; $8.50).

La Summa Cucina Italiana 30 Fleet St ☎617/523-9503; Haymarket **T**. If you simply want Italian food as good as your *nona* used to make, then look no further than *La Summa,* named for the chef-owner's grandma, who taught her to cook while growing up right here in the North End. Their baked manicotti ($16) will make your day. Reservations recommended on weekends.

Marco 253 Hanover St ☎617/742-1276; Haymarket **T**. Although it's on bustling Hanover St, this stylish eatery's intimate, second-floor location has the feel of a hidden speakeasy. Excellent, pricey Italian entrees served amidst exposed brick walls and rustic wooden ceilings and tabletops.

Neptune Oyster 63 Salem St ☎617/742-3474; Haymarket **T**. Snazzy little raw bar filled with devoted fans who swoon over the fantastic shucked shellfish and locally famed lobster rolls.

Pizzeria Regina 111/2 Thacher St ☎617/227-0765; Haymarket **T**. Visit *Regina* for tasty, cheap pizza, served in a neighborhood feed station where the wooden booths haven't budged since the 1940s. Don't be fooled by chains bearing the *Regina* label in other parts of town – this is the original, vastly superior location. Cash only, and be prepared for a wait.

Prezza 24 Fleet St ☎617/227-1577; Haymarket **T**. Named for the chef's grandma, who hails from Prezza, Italy, this minimalist hotspot offers decadent dishes like sweet rock shrimp and risotto with shaved black truffles. *Prezza* is also known for its lovingly prepared wine list (dad's a wine guy). A two-course meal will cost around $50.

Taranta 210 Hanover St ☎617/720-0052; Haymarket **T**. *Taranta* is a mix of Italian and Peruvian flavors, which translates into dishes such as pork chops with sugar cane and giant Peruvian corn ($30) and lobster ravioli with mascarpone cherry tomato sauce ($25). It's on busy Hanover St, but *Taranta* remains a bit of a secret among locals.

Charlestown

Navy Yard Bistro & Wine Bar Sixth St, at the corner of First Ave ☎617/242-0036; Community College **T**. Very close to the USS *Constitution* but still a bit tricky to find, this casually elegant local spot has tasty favorites like lamb chops ($22) and seared sea scallops ($22) served amidst exposed brick walls and an open kitchen. You can also eat outside.

Sorelle Bakery and Café 100 City Square (☎617/242-5980) and 1 Monument Ave (☎617/242-2125); Community College **T**. Two locations: one a welcome oasis after crossing the

Charlestown Bridge, the other more tucked away, with a delightful hidden patio. Both have phenomenal muffins and cookies, plus lemonade and other lunch fare.

Tangierino 83 Main St ☎617/242-6009; Community College **T**. Super-romantic Moroccan restaurant with authentic entrees like *ka'dra* lamb with figs and cheese-filled eggplant ($27). Next door, patrons puff contentedly on hookahs and ogle the belly dancers at their *Casbah Lounge*.

Beacon Hill

Beacon Hill Bistro 25 Charles St, in the *Beacon Street Hotel* ☎617/723-1133; Charles **T**. Sleek New American and French bistro with an upscale neighborhood feel. Short ribs with prunes share counter space with cod with capers and tomatoes; breakfast is traditional American. They also have a gorgeous bar – go for the blood-orange martinis and killer mojitos.

Figs 42 Charles St ☎617/742-3447; Charles **T**. This noisy, popular offshoot of *Olives* has excellent thin-crust pizzas, topped with such savory items as figs and prosciutto or caramelized onions and arugula.

The Hungry I 71½ Charles St ☎617/227-3524; Charles **T**. Pricey but romantic, the food here is delectable and features a changing menu of classic American fare with creative twists. If you come on a night when the signature venison with *poivre noir* is served, prepare for food heaven.

Paramount 44 Charles St ☎617/720-1152; Charles **T**. The Hill's neighborhood diner serves Belgian waffles and *frittatas* to brunch regulars by day, and decent American standards like hamburgers and meatloaf by night.

Upper Crust 20 Charles St ☎617/723-9600; Charles **T**. A popular pizza joint with fresh and tasty offerings; there's generally a slice of the day (such as spinach with pesto and tomato; $3). There are other locations at 222 Newbury St (☎617/262-0090; Copley **T**), 683 Tremont St (☎617/927-0090; Prudential **T**), and 49b Brattle St (☎617/497-4111; Harvard **T**).

Back Bay

Atlantic Fish Company 761 Boylston St ☎617/267-4000; Copley **T**. Easy to find on bustling Boylston St, this classy seafood spot has an interior resembling the fine lines of a yacht, complemented by tastefully executed entrees. Open for lunch and dinner; try the lobster salad.

Aujourd'hui 200 Boylston St, in the *Four Seasons* ☎617/351-2037 or 1-800/332-3442; Arlington **T**. Dine on roasted Maine lobster – accompanied by crabmeat wontons, pineapple compote, and

fenugreek broth – from antique china while enjoying the view out over the Public Garden. Your best bet is their Sunday brunch, which has the view without the price tags.

Café Jaffa 48 Gloucester St ☎617/536-0230; Hynes **T**. One of Back Bay's best inexpensive dining options, with great Middle Eastern fare served up in an inviting space. They're known for their falafel and locally famous lamb chops, but you can't really go wrong here.

Casa Romero 30 Gloucester St ☎617/536-4341; Hynes **T**. Well-loved Mexican spot whose subterranean location will make you feel like you've stumbled upon a romantic hideaway. Entrees start at $15.

Kashmir 279 Newbury St ☎617/536-1695; Hynes **T**. The food and decor are equally inviting at Newbury St's only Indian restaurant, and one of Boston's best.

L'Espalier 774 Boylston St ☎617/262-3023; Copley **T**. A ravishing French restaurant now happily situated in its new location at the swanky *Mandarin Oriental* hotel. The food is first-rate, but the lofty prices suggest that the buzz is factored into your bill.

Legal Sea Foods 26 Park Place (☎617/426-4444; Arlington **T**); 100 Huntington Ave, level two, Copley Place (☎617/266-7775; Copley **T**); 800 Boylston St, Prudential Center (☎617/266-6800; Prudential **T**); 255 State St (☎617/742-5300; Aquarium **T**), 5 Cambridge Center (☎617/864-3400; Kendall **T**). The *Starbucks* of the sea: it seems you can't turn a corner in Boston without encountering one of these eateries. As they claim, the seafood is fresh, and their clam chowder is loved by many.

The Other Side Cosmic Café 407 Newbury St ☎617/536-8437; Hynes **T**. This ultra-casual hipster hangout on "the other side" of Newbury Street offers gourmet sandwiches, tasty salads, fresh juices, and pitchers of good beer. Open late.

Parish Café 361 Boylston St ☎617/247-4777; Arlington **T**. The ambience isn't much, but who cares when you're eating the best sandwiches in Boston? *Parish Café* formed when chefs from Boston's best restaurants created a fancy rotating sandwich selection, such as the "Blue Ginger" (rare tuna with teriyaki glaze and avocado wasabi aioli; $13).

Sonsie 327 Newbury St ☎617/351-2500; Hynes **T**. This Newbury Street staple is good for contemporary bistro fare, particularly the swanky sandwiches, pastries, and chocolate bread pudding. In the summertime, aim for their Sunday brunch – the restaurant opens onto the street, jazz filters lazily through the air, and of course the food is fabulous.

Trident Booksellers & Café 338 Newbury St
☎617/267-8688; Hynes **T**. Great little bookstore
café (see p.135), featuring a "perpetual breakfast,"
free wi-fi, and tasty lunches and dinners.

South End

Addis Red Sea 544 Tremont St ☎617/426-8727;
Back Bay **T**. A lovely, intimate Ethiopian eatery
where you sit on carved wooden stools and eat
injera (a warm, spongy bread) and *gomen wat*
(collard greens with onions and garlic; $8) over a
petite, communal table.

Aquitaine 569 Tremont St ☎617/424-8577;
Back Bay **T**. This swanky French brasserie is
the place to be and be seen; settle into a
marvelous leather banquette, gape at the aston-
ishing array of wine, and feast on the best *steak
frites* and foie gras in town. They also have a
snazzy and more affordable brunch (the *prix-fixe*
option is $10).

B & G Oysters 550 Tremont St ☎617/423-0550;
Back Bay **T**. If you can manage to get a table at
this tiny, pearlescent restaurant, you're in luck. The
oysters (from $2.25 each) are simply the best
Boston has to offer.

Charlie's Sandwich Shoppe 429 Columbus Ave
☎617/536-7669; Back Bay **T**. A little diner-style
hole-in-the-wall offering some of the best breakfasts in the entire city. Standouts include the
decadent banana and pecan griddlecakes and their
justly famous turkey hash. Closed Sun, cash only,
and beware – no customer toilets.

flour bakery + café 1595 Washington St
☎617/267-4300; Back Bay **T**. Quite possibly the
best café in town, this stylish South End spot has a
drool-worthy array of *brioche au chocolat*, old-
fashioned sour cream coffee cake, gooey caramel
nut tarts, rich cakes, savory sandwiches, and
home-made breads. They also have another
location in the Fort Point Channel (see p.120).

Franklin Café 278 Shawmut Ave ☎617/350-
0010; Back Bay **T**. New American cuisine at very
reasonable prices, enjoyed by a hip, unpretentious
clientele. There are only eleven tables – be
prepared to wait at the bar for at least two
martinis. Open late.

Hamersley's Bistro 553 Tremont St
☎617/423-2700; Back Bay **T**. *Hamersley's* is
widely regarded as one of the best restaurants in
Boston, and with good cause. Every night star
chef (and owner) Gordon Hamersley dons a Red
Sox cap and takes to the open kitchen, where
he dishes out unusual – and unforgettable –
French-American seasonal fare.

🏃 **Orinoco** 477 Shawmut Ave ☎617/369-7075;
Mass Ave **T**. Off the beaten South End path,
this tiny, beloved tapas spot is hidden no more, with
lines out the front for its authentic Venezuelan
cuisine. If you can stand the wait, head for their
scrumptious weekend brunch.

Pho Republique 1415 Washington St
☎617/262-0005; Back Bay **T**. Hip Indochine
restaurant that attracts a young, stylish clientele
for its hearty *pho* (noodle soup) and lemongrass
martinis.

Rocca 500 Harrison Ave ☎617/451-5151;
Back Bay **T**. In the artsy SoWa district, this
spacious Italian newcomer keeps things
buzzing with home-made *panzotti* pasta ($16)
and fish stew with shrimp and crostini ($25).
Free parking.

Stella 1525 Washington St ☎617/247-7747; Back
Bay **T**. Fantastic, fancy-pants Italian fare served in
a beautiful white interior. Nice outdoor seating in
the summer. Open late.

South End Buttery 314 Shawmut Ave
☎617/482-1015; Back Bay **T**. Impossible to
resist, this adorable neighborhood café offers
egg sandwiches on home-made biscuits,
house-made soups and sandwiches, foamy
cappuccinos, and terrific cupcakes named for
the owner's dogs.

🏃 **Toro** 1704 Washington St ☎617/536-4300;
Back Bay **T**. A hip and lively tapas bar
brimming with white and red sangria and inventive
plates such as grilled corn with lime and cheese.

Kenmore Square and the Fenway

Great Bay 500 Commonwealth Ave, in the
Hotel Commonwealth ☎617/532-5300;
Kenmore **T**. This stellar seafood restaurant more
than lives up to its reputation. Pancetta-wrapped
swordfish ($27), and wolf-fish with artichoke
ragout ($26) are both sublime, and their clam
chowder is considered the best of the best ($11).
Entrees are complemented by soft, colorful lighting
and whimsical wood-paneling, reminiscent of
a ship.

India Quality 484 Commonwealth Ave St
☎617/267-4499; Kenmore **T**. Despite the
strange name, this is considered one of the best
Indian spots in town, with great food augmented
by really good service in a fairly upscale, sit-
down surrounding.

Petit Robert Bistro 468 Commonwealth Ave
☎617/375-0699; Kenmore **T**. This French bistro
boasts a chalkboard menu that's been priced for
the little guy; entrees, such as *coq au vin* with
buttered noodles, run $14–20. There's also another
location at 480 Columbus Ave (☎617/867-0600;
Back Bay **T**).

Brookline

Anna's Taqueria 1412 Beacon St, Brookline Ⓣ617/739-7300; Coolidge Corner **T**. Exceptional tacos, burritos, and quesadillas are the only things on the menu at this extremely cheap Mexican eatery – but they're so good branches have opened at 446 Harvard St (Coolidge Corner **T**), 822 Somerville Ave (Porter **T**), 84 Mass Ave (Kendall **T**), and 236A Elm St (Davis **T**).

Matt Murphy's 14 Harvard St, Brookline Ⓣ617/232-0188; Brookline Village **T**. Authentic Irish comfort food such as warm potato and leek soup with brown bread and shepherd's pie with a crispy potato crust. The place is tiny, and you may have to wait, but it's well worth it. They also have occasional live music. Cash only.

Jamaica Plain

Ten Tables 597 Centre St, Jamaica Plain Ⓣ617/524-8810; Green St **T**. This inviting little spot with exposed brick walls was designed to feel like an intimate dinner party – there really are only ten tables. The French and American fare (entrees $15–20), made from local ingredients, is sure to please. Though the menu changes according to the season, locals rave about the four-course vegetarian tasting menu (every night except Wed; $25), a landmark that's here to stay.

Cambridge: Harvard Square and around

Bartley's Burger Cottage 1246 Massachusetts Ave Ⓣ617/354-6559; Harvard **T**. A Cambridge must-visit. The names of the dishes poke fun at politicians of the hour, while the food itself is artery-clogging joy in the form of a juicy burger and raspberry lime rickey. Good veggie burgers, too. Cash only, and expect funky hours.

Cambridge 1 27 Church St Ⓣ617/576-1111; Harvard **T**. Swanky, thin-crust pizza spot in a vintage firehouse right in the heart of Harvard Square. There's also another location in the Fenway at 1381 Boylston St (Ⓣ617/437-1111; Fenway **T**).

Chez Henri 1 Shepard St Ⓣ617/354-8980; Harvard or Porter **T**. Chef Paul O'Connell's experiment in fusion brings Modern French together with Cuban influences, best sampled in the light salads and excellent Cuban crab cake appetizers. If you're looking to spend less cash, head to the adjacent bar for their Cuban pressed sandwich.

Darwin's Ltd 148 Mt Auburn St (Ⓣ617/354-5233) and 1629 Cambridge St (Ⓣ617/491-2999); both Harvard **T**. Two locations, both offering wonderful sandwiches (roast beef, sprouts, and apple slices), as well as fresh salads and baked goods. Cash only.

The Garage 36 JFK St (no phone); Harvard **T**. A sort of "mall" with hipster stores (records, tattoos, and hemp clothing), this landmark spot also has good cheap eats – pizza, Mexican, Vietnamese, and ice cream.

Harvest 44 Brattle St Ⓣ617/868-2255; Harvard **T**. White-tablecloth Harvard Square institution with a seasonal menu of New American cuisine; the outdoor courtyard is another fine feature.

Henrietta's Table 1 Bennett St, in the *Charles Hotel* Ⓣ617/661-5005; Harvard **T**. One of the only restaurants in Cambridge that serves classic New England fare. Some might say, however, that a trip to *Henrietta's* is wasted if it's not for their brunch (Sun noon–3pm; $39 per person), which allows unlimited access to farm-fresh treats from around New England.

Upstairs on the Square 91 Winthrop St Ⓣ617/864-1933; Harvard **T**. Amidst a whimsical decor of animal-striped carpet patterns, glorious green walls, and winged light bulbs, *Upstairs on the Square* serves equally inventive food, falling somewhere between New American and Old Colonial. They also have a rosy wooden bar, a lovely Saturday tea, and Sunday brunch.

Veggie Planet 47 Palmer St Ⓣ617/661-1513; Harvard **T**. This subterranean, very casual eatery underneath *Club Passim* (see p.129) has tasty and creative vegetarian and vegan pizzas, soups, and salads. Try the vegan peanut curry (tofu, broccoli, peanuts, and Thai red peanut curry sauce; $11) on their slow-rise organic dough.

Cambridge: Central Square and around

Central Kitchen 567 Massachusetts Ave Ⓣ617/491-5599; Central **T**. Hip Central Square bistro with a delightful chalkboard menu offering European classics (*moules frites*) and contemporary American twists (mushroom ragout with ricotta dumplings) in an intimate, stylish setting. The inviting *Enormous Room* bar (see p.127) is upstairs.

Craigie on Main 853 Main St Ⓣ617/497-5511; Central **T**. Locals are thrilled about *Craigie's* recent move to Central Square. Family-owned and operated, they're known for their "refined rusticity," creating new menus daily based on what's available (entrees begin at $22). Patrons are treated like family, and the place is perpetually packed. Reservations recommended.

Salts 798 Main St Ⓣ617/876-8444; Central **T**. Elegant, contemporary American newcomer that has foodies awhirl with its merging of local and organic ingredients and exquisite French technique and presentation. Patrons are absolutely crazy about the glazed duck for two ($65) – you almost need to order it in advance – but you can't really go wrong with anything on the menu.

Toscanini's 899 Main St ☎617/491-5877; Central **T**. The inventive, ever-changing ice-cream list here includes original flavors like "chocolate sluggo," which mixes light- and dark-chocolate ice cream, ganache, chocolate chips, almonds, and Hydrox cookies. Great coffee drinks as well.

Cambridge: Kendall Square and around

Bean Towne Coffee House and Café 1 Kendall Square ☎617/621-7900; Kendall **T**. Café right by MIT with bulging sandwiches, fresh salads, and coffee served up by friendly baristas.

Blue Room 1 Kendall Square ☎617/494-9034; Kendall **T**. Unpretentious restaurant with superlative grilled fusion cuisine; pan-seared skate ($21) and braised lamb ($23) are common, but what accompanies them – cumin and basmati yogurt or tomatillos – isn't. The menu changes with what ingredients are available, so the food is always fresh and innovative.

Emma's Pizza 40 Hampshire St ☎617/864-8534; Kendall **T**. This local pizzeria has signature thin pies and slices featuring fun toppings like roasted sweet potatoes and ricotta. Consistently listed at or near the top of "best in Boston" lists.

Hungry Mother 233 Cardinal Medeiros Ave ☎617/499-0090; Kendall **T**. A whimsical, carefully executed mix of comfort-meets-soul food, this popular little dinner spot has fun menu items like boiled, salted peanuts ($3) and cornmeal catfish with collard greens ($17).

Cambridge: Inman Square and around

Christina's Homemade Ice Cream 1255 Cambridge St ☎617/492-7021; Harvard or Central **T**. Inspiring well-deserved devotion amongst a legion of fans, *Christina's* is the kind of place

people brace rush hour traffic over just to get their hands on a scoop of her Adzuki bean, burnt sugar, or honey lavender flavors – procured from the owner's spice shop right next door.

East Coast Grill 1271 Cambridge St ☎617/491-6568; Harvard or Central **T**. A festive and funky atmosphere – think *Miami Vice* – in which to enjoy fresh seafood (there is a raw bar tucked into one corner) and Caribbean side dishes such as grilled avocado, pineapple salsa, and fried plantains. The Sunday serve-yourself Bloody Mary bar is reason enough to visit.

Olé Mexican Grill 11 Springfield St ☎617/492-4495; Harvard or Central **T**. Widely regarded as one of Boston's best Mexican eateries, this pricier-than-a-taqueria spot is worth it for the *tacos de atún asado* (rare tuna steak in handmade tortillas; $19) and jicama salad ($8.75).

Oleana 134 Hampshire St ☎617/661-0505; Central **T**. If you can, secure a table on the wisteria-laden patio, where you can linger over lamb steak with fava bean moussaka ($25) and Armenian bean and walnut pâté with home-made string cheese ($4). Be sure to save room for the stellar baked Alaska, served with coconut ice cream and passion fruit-caramel sauce ($14).

Punjabi Dhaba 225 Hampshire St ☎617/547-8272; Central **T**. This unassuming, no-frills Indian eatery inspires almost maniacal devotion among its fans, who trek across Cambridge for quick and cheap *palak paneer* and chicken *tikka masala*.

East Cambridge

Helmand 143 1st St ☎617/492-4646; Lechmere **T**. The interior won't win any style awards, but this beloved Afghan dinner spot is favored by everyone from Harvard students to families to couples on a first date. Don't miss the *kaddo borawni* (baked baby pumpkin seasoned with sugar and served on yogurt garlic sauce; $7.50).

Drinking

Despite – or perhaps because of – the lingering Puritan anti-fun ethic that pervades Boston, people here seem to **drink** more than in most other American cities. The most prevalent place to nurse a pint is the **Irish pub**, of which there are high concentrations in the **West End** and downtown around **Quincy Market**. More upscale are the bars and lounges of **Back Bay**, along Newbury and Boylston streets. The rest of the city's neighborhood bars, pick-up joints, and yuppie hotspots are differentiated by their crowds: **Beacon Hill** tends to be older and a bit stuffy; **downtown**, mainly around Quincy Market and the Theater District, draws a healthy mix of tourists and locals; while **Kenmore Square** and **Cambridge** are fairly student-oriented. **Bars** in

Boston stop serving at 2am (at the latest), and most strictly enforce the drinking–age minimum of 21.

Downtown

Bell in Hand Tavern 45 Union St ☏617/227-2098; State or Government Center **T**. The oldest continuously operating tavern in Boston draws a fairly exuberant mix of tourists and professionals.

Felt 533 Washington St ☏617/350-5555; Downtown Crossing **T**. An upscale pool hall and dance lounge, *Felt* is full of young and beautiful people willing to pay $14 an hour for a table. One of the new places to see and be seen in town.

The Good Life 28 Kingston St ☏617/451-2622; Downtown Crossing **T**. This stylish bar generates quite a buzz, owing as much to its inventive martinis as to nights dedicated to the likes of old-school hip-hop and deep house music. Choose between tasty full meals ($12–25), dozens of vodkas, or getting your groove on downstairs.

Houston's 60 State St ☏617/573-9777; State St **T**. Part of a swanky restaurant chain, *Houston's* doubles as the sleekest bar in Faneuil Hall. In summer, a deck opens close enough to feel the energy from Faneuil Hall, but far enough removed so you can drink in peace.

JJ Foley's 21 Kingston St ☏617/695-2529; Downtown Crossing **T**. Attended by bike messengers and businessmen during the day, this little Irish gem plays host to a casual scene of locals and students by night. Friendly and recommended.

The Kinsale 2 Center Plaza ☏617/742-5577; Government Center **T**. Shipped brick by brick from Ireland to its current location, this outrageously popular Irish pub is as authentic as it gets; the menu even lists beer-battered fish and hot pastrami on a "bulkie" (a sandwich bun).

Limelight 204 Tremont St ☏617/423-0785; ⓦwww.limelightboston.com; Boylston **T**. Nearly unbelievable karaoke utopia where you can either opt for the stage ($5 cover) and perform in *American Idol*-esque environs (you can even choose your own background imagery), or the studios ($10 per hr) where you and your friends can belt out *Like A Virgin* in privacy.

MKT 130 Water St ☏617/367-0658; State **T**. Fairly fancy, new lounge and bar spot over in the Financial District that's favored by suit-wearing sorts of men and ladies in heels. If you're looking for something that's a step above anything in Faneuil Hall, *MKT* is a nice alternative.

Waterfront

Drink 348 Congress St ☏617/695-1806; South Station **T**. This sleek, signless, subterranean spot features a zigzagging bar and fancy, well-made cocktails from three different eras (1800s, 1900s, and today) served beneath delicately hanging light bulbs. No cocktail menus, but the expert bartender-therapists will lend an ear to your drinking desires and procure the perfect beverage.

Lucky's 355 Congress St ☏617/357-5825; South Station **T**. Over the water and quite a walk from the subway, this subterranean lounge is one of Boston's best-kept secrets – mainly because it's off the beaten path (there's no sign out front). Inside is a '50s pad complete with martini-swilling patrons and live jazz; on Sundays, Frank Sinatra impersonators get the locals swinging.

North End

Caffe Vittoria 290-296 Hanover St ☏617/227-7606; Haymarket **T**. A Boston institution, the *Vittoria's* atmospheric original section, with its dark-wood paneling, pressed-tin ceilings, murals of the Old Country, and Sinatra-blaring Wurlitzer, is vintage North End. It's only open at night, though a street-level addition next door is open by day for excellent cappuccinos.

Fiore 250 Hanover St ☏617/371-1176; Haymarket **T**. Two words: rooftop bar. In summer, the outdoor patio buzzes with patrons lingering over martinis while enjoying the pretty view.

Lucca 226 Hanover St ☏617/742-9200; Haymarket **T**. This sleek and stylish restaurant serves overpriced, fancy Northern Italian dinner fare, but it's worth stopping in for a glass of wine from the fantastic wine list.

Charlestown

Tavern on the Water 1 Eighth St, Pier 6 ☏617/242-8040; Community College **T**. Located right on the water (the USS *Constitution* is anchored nearby), the *Tavern* sports what is possibly Boston's best skyline view. The food is forgettable; stick with whatever's on tap.

Warren Tavern 2 Pleasant St ☏617/241-8142; Community College **T**. An atmospheric place to enjoy a drink, and the oldest standing structure in Charlestown. The *Warren* also has a generous menu of good tavern food.

Beacon Hill

21st Amendment 150 Bowdoin St ☏617/227-7100; Bowdoin **T**. This dimly lit, down-home watering hole, which gets its name from the amendment that repealed Prohibition, is a favorite haunt of legislators from the adjacent State House and students from nearby Suffolk University – you might even run into John Kerry.

Alibi 215 Charles St, in the *Liberty Hotel* ☎857/241-1144; Charles **T**. Currently *the* place to see and be seen in Boston, and there's generally a line out front. A young, dressed-up clientele soaks in the vibe amidst lengthy leather seating, candlelight, and celebrity mug shots.

Bin 26 Enoteca 26 Charles St ☎617/723-5939; Charles **T**. This classy wine bar has up to 250 bottles in its rotation and 50–60 varieties available by the glass. Helpful servers can aid you in matching your drink up with its perfect food counterpart, perhaps a marinated olive plate ($7) or a slice of gorgonzola ($6).

Cheers 84 Beacon St ☎617/227-9605; Arlington **T**. If you don't already know, and if the conspicuous banners outside don't tip you off, this is the bar that served as the inspiration for the TV show *Cheers*. If you've gotta go, be warned – it's packed with tourists, the inside bears little resemblance to the NBC set, and the food, though cutely named ("eNORMous burgers"), is pricey and mediocre. Plus, it's almost certain that nobody will know your name.

The Sevens 77 Charles St ☎617/523-9074; Charles **T**. While the tourists pack into *Cheers*, you can drop by this cozy wood-paneled joint to watch the game or shoot darts in an authentic Boston neighborhood bar.

The West End

Boston Beer Works 112 Canal St ☎617-896-BEER; North Station **T**. Originally a Fenway spot, this Boston institution has since opened up additional digs by the TD Banknorth Garden, With over 15 micro-beers on tap (made on the premises), billiards, and tasty bar food, it makes for a great spot to kick back and watch the game.

Greatest Bar 262 Friend St ☎617/367-0544; North Station **T**. Directly across from TD Banknorth Garden, this lively newcomer in the West End constitutes four floors of action, including two floors of spinning DJs – but to be honest the energy centers on sports watching: it's a great place to catch a Celtics or Red Sox game. Occasionally there's a cover charge.

Back Bay

Bukowski Tavern 50 Dalton St ☎617/437-9999; Hynes **T**. Arguably Boston's best dive bar, this watering hole has views over the Mass Pike and such a vast beer selection that a home-made "wheel of indecision" is spun by waitstaff when patrons can't decide. There's a smaller, equally cool location at 1281 Cambridge St in Inman Square (☎617/497-7077; #69 bus).

Excelsior 272 Boylston St ☎617-426-7878; Arlington **T**. Technically a restaurant offering imaginative modern American cuisine, *Excelsior* is more famous among Bostonians for its posh and happening bar scene and impressive muddled cocktails.

Flash's 310 Stuart St ☎617/574-8888; Back Bay **T**. A nice, laid-back alternative for Back Bay. with a low-key, beer-drinking crowd and lots of tempting girly drinks on offer, such as the "Nordic Nectar" (vodka, fresh orange juice, Cointreau, and a splash of champagne; $8). Easy to find by its lovely retro neon sign.

Oak Bar 138 St James Ave, in the *Fairmont Copley Plaza* ☎617/267-5300; Copley **T**. Rich wood paneling, high ceilings, and excellent martinis (including the engagement martini, replete with diamond ring and deluxe suite; $12,750) make this a genteel spot to drink in Back Bay.

Top of the Hub 800 Boylston St ☎617/536-1775; Prudential **T**. An atmospheric space on the 52nd floor of the Prudential Center, *Top of the Hub* features a snazzy jazz lounge, swanky cocktails, and fancy food. A great date spot, although you have to go through an unromantic security check first.

Whiskey Park 64 Arlington St, in the *Park Plaza* ☎617/542-1482; Arlington **T**. Owned by Randy Gerber (aka Mr Cindy Crawford), this lounge's chic chocolate-brown design was conceived by Michael Czysz, the guy behind Lenny Kravitz's swinging Miami pad. The prices match the celebrity name-dropping, but there's hardly a better place in town to grab a cocktail.

Whiskey's 885 Boylston St ☎617/262-5551; Hynes **T**. A real-life beer commercial: young guys wearing baseball caps, sports on TV, and a pervasive smell of booze. Still, it's not a bad place to watch a Sox game.

The South End

The Beehive 541 Tremont St ☎617/423-0069; Back Bay **T**. Snuggled inside the Boston Center for the Arts is this spacious newcomer to Boston's bar scene. With chandeliers dripping from the ceiling, a red-curtained stage, and knock-you-down cocktails, the *Beehive* exudes a vaudeville vibe, complete with jazz, cabaret, or burlesque shows nearly every night.

The Delux Café & Lounge 100 Chandler St ☎617/338-5258; Back Bay **T**. This retro hideaway has all the fixings of a great dive spot: fantastic kitschy decor, constant cartoon viewing, and a Christmas-lit Elvis shrine. The menu is funky American fusion blended with old standbys like grilled-cheese sandwiches and split-pea soup. Cash only.

Kenmore Square

Audubon Circle 838 Beacon St ☎617/421-1910; Kenmore **T**. Sleek bar where a well-dressed crowd gathers for cocktails and fancy, tasty bar food before and after games at Fenway Park.

Cask 'n Flagon 62 Brookline Ave ☎617/536-4840; Kenmore **T**. An iconic neighborhood bar right by Fenway Park, the *Cask 'n Flagon* is a popular place for the Red Sox faithful to warm up before games and celebrate after.

Eastern Standard 528 Commonwealth Ave ☎617/532-9100; Kenmore **T**. Set inside a gorgeous, spacious dining room, this Boston favorite pulls in a nice mix of clientele, both age- and style-wise. The bartenders really know what they're doing, and are just as quick to make you a swanky highball as they are to pull you a pint. There's also a nice patio in the summer.

Foundation Lounge 500 Commonwealth Ave, in the *Hotel Commonwealth* ☎617/859-9900; Kenmore **T**. Spacious, upscale marble bar amidst a hip (but not hipper-than-thou) clientele. A more discreet Red Sox-viewing ambience.

Lower Depths Taproom 476 Commonweath Ave ☎617/266-6662; Kenmore **T**. A welcome newcomer to the ballpark scene, this pub is known for their extensive beer selection (16 on tap, plus plenty in bottles) and excellent pretzels and $1 hot dogs. Cash only; beer and wine only.

Jamaica Plain

James's Gate 5–11 McBride St, Jamaica Plain ☎617/983-2000; Forest Hills **T**. Beat Boston's harsh winter by sipping Guinness by the blazing fireplace in this cozy pub, or by trying the hearty fare in the excellent restaurant out back.

Cambridge: Harvard Square

Charlie's Kitchen 10 Eliot St ☎617/492-9646; Harvard **T**. While downstairs is a well-loved burger joint, upstairs is a buzzing bar, at its rowdiest on Tues karaoke nights. Fifteen beers on tap, a rocking jukebox, and a good mix of patrons. They've recently expanded to include an outdoor beer garden.

Shay's 58 JFK St ☎617/864-9161; Harvard **T**. Unwind with grad students over wine and quality beer at *Shay's*, a relaxed contrast to the student-oriented bars elsewhere in the Square.

Grafton Street 1230 Massachusetts Ave ☎617/497-0400; Harvard **T**. Modern, breezy Irish pub atmosphere hosting an older, well-dressed set that enjoys smooth drafts and equally good food.

Cambridge: Central Square

Cuchi Cuchi 795 Main St ☎617/864-2929; Central or Kendall **T**. Linger over fantastic cocktails at the bar and soak in *Cuchi Cuchi's* Gatsby-esque fabulousness. The waitresses are decked out in vintage flapper dresses, and gilded mirrors and painted lampshades abound.

Enormous Room 567 Massachusetts Ave ☎617/491-5550; Central **T**. Walking into this comfy, tiny lounge tucked above *Central Kitchen* (see p.123 for review) is tantamount to entering a swanky slumber party. The clientele lounges, sans shoes (these are discreetly placed in cubbies), along myriad plush couches. DJs nightly.

Middlesex 315 Massachusetts Ave ☎617/868-6739; Central **T**. A slightly hipper-than-thou vibe, but with good reason – the gorgeous space makes you want to dress to impress. You can create your own drinking environs with the lush lounge chairs on wheels and movable minimalist tables. "Hearthrob," on the second and fourth Tues of every month, has lines out the door for its electro-retro beat dance heaven ($5 cover).

Miracle of Science 321 Massachusetts Ave ☎617/868-ATOM; Central **T** or #1 bus. Surprisingly hip despite its status as an MIT hangout. There's noir decor and a laid-back, unpretentious crowd, though the place can get quite crowded on weekend nights. The bar stools will conjure up memories of high school chemistry class.

People's Republik 876 Massachusetts Ave ☎617/491-6969; Central or Harvard **T**. Smack dab between MIT and Harvard, *People's Republik* attracts a good mix of technocrats and potential world-leaders. It takes its Communist propaganda seriously – with its posters on the walls, anyway; the range of tap offerings is positively democratic.

Phoenix Landing 512 Massachusetts Ave ☎617/576-6260; Central **T**. The *Phoenix* is about the only place in Cambridge you'll still catch European sporting events on TV, but it's best known for its nightly dance parties. Tues is karaoke and Wii night.

Plough & Stars 912 Massachusetts Ave ☎617/576-0032; Central or Harvard **T**. Under-the-radar neighborhood spot that's very much worth a visit for its animated cribbage games, quality pub grub, or nightly live music.

River Gods 125 River St ☎617/576-1881; Central **T**. Though a bit of an underground spot, it's worth the trip. An Irish bar with a twist, they serve good cocktails alongside Guinness, fantastic food, and DJs spinning good tunes; patrons lounge in throne-like chairs.

Nightlife

In recent years the city's **nightlife** has received something of a wake-up call. **Lansdowne Street**, adjacent to Fenway Park, remains the queen of the clubbing scene, although a few spots have also been moving into **Downtown Crossing**. Boylston Place – which links Boston Common with the Theater District and is known locally as "The Alley" – is where most of the action is found. Though Boston is by no means a 24-hour city, these spots have given a bit of fresh air to a scene that lived in the shadow of the city's so-called high culture.

The **live music** scene plays perhaps a bigger part in the city's nightlife. Many of the bars and clubs, especially around Kenmore Square and Central Square, are just as likely, if not more, to have a scruffy garage band playing for only a nominal cover as they are to have a slick DJ spinning house tunes. And Boston has spawned its share of enormous **rock** acts, from the ever-enduring Aerosmith to a smattering of indie rock favorites such as the Pixies and Sebadoh. Boston is also home to a number of well-loved **jazz** and **blues** joints; you can usually find something cheap and to your liking almost any day of the week. For **club and music listings**, check Thursday's *Boston Globe* "Calendar," the *Boston Phoenix*, or *Boston's Weekly Dig*; the two best websites are Ⓦ www.boston.com and Ⓦ www.stuffatnight.com.

Nightclubs

Boston's **nightclubs** are mostly clustered in downtown's Theater District and around Kenmore Square, with a few prominent ones in Back Bay and the South End. Many of the Back Bay and South End venues are **gay clubs**; for a listing of these, see p.133. Otherwise, a number of the clubs below have special gay nights. **Cover charges** are generally in the $5–10 range, though sometimes there's no cover at all.

An Tua Nua 835 Beacon St, Kenmore Square Ⓣ617/262-2121; Kenmore **T**. Despite its Gaelic name ("the new beginning"), this popular neighborhood hangout is just as much dance bar as it is Irish pub. Thursday is college nights (with a lot of hip-hop and Top 40) get especially crowded with BU and Northeastern undergrads. Wed is salsa night.

Gypsy Bar 116 Boylston St, Theater District Ⓣ617/482-7799; Boylston **T**. Very posh lounge popular with the European set; you can watch jellyfish pulsing peacefully behind the bar while ordering a cocktail. Prepare to dress snappy – no sneakers or sleeveless tees, as well as (weirdly) no polo shirts. DJ dance beats Frid & Sat; occasional cover charges.

Jillian's 145 Ipswich St, Kenmore Square Ⓣ617/437-0300; Kenmore **T**. Massive entertainment club complex housing an arcade, a raucous, spacious dance club, and a bowling alley.

Milky Way 405 Centre St, Jamaica Plain Ⓣ617/524-3740; Stony Brook **T**. "Lanes and lounge" – this is a bowling alley-cum-nightclub, in the heart of JP. The lovely retro space features low-key local bands, cheap beer, old-school Galaga and Ms Pac Man and seven vintage lanes.

Ned Devine's 200 Quincy Market Bldg, at Faneuil Hall Marketplace Ⓣ617/248-9900; Government Center **T**. Irish pub and rowdy nightclub, populated by fun-loving tourists and dancing oglers.

The Roxy 279 Tremont St, Theater District Ⓣ617/338-7699, Ⓦ www.roxyboston.com; Boylston **T**. Cavernous singles' scene nightclub in an old-fashioned dance hall.

Saint 90 Exeter St, Back Bay Ⓣ617/236-1134; Copley **T**. Upscale lounge and club with lush decor and chi-chi drinks – the tables tend to be occupied by people more famous or well-off than you, however.

Live music

The strength of Boston's **live music** is its diversity – the city's venues host both superstar performers and small, experimental acts on a regular basis.

Rock and pop

Bank of America Pavilion Fan Pier, 290 Northern Ave ℗ 617/728-1600, Ⓦ www.livenation.com; South Station **T**. During the summer, concerts by well-known performers are held here under a huge white tent at Boston Harbor's edge.

Bill's Bar 51⁄2 Lansdowne St, Kenmore Square ℗ 617/421-9678; Kenmore **T**. This self-titled "dirty rock bar" books a "sleazy" line-up that includes rock, metal, and indie bands as well as reggae Sundays. There are also a number of 18+ shows; cover generally costs around $10.

Great Scott 1222 Commonwealth Ave, Allston ℗ 617/566-9014; Harvard Ave **T**. Popular with students and older hipsters alike, this well-loved space plays host to local and national (read: national acts you probably haven't heard of) rock and indie bands. Cheap drinks, and a pleasant patio where you can kick back and play groupie.

Lizard Lounge 1667 Massachusetts Ave, Cambridge ℗ 617/547-0759; Harvard or Porter **T**. This, the downstairs portion of the restaurant & bar *Cambridge Common*, has rock and jazz acts pretty much nightly, for a fairly nominal cover charge (around $8).

Middle East 472 Massachusetts Ave, Cambridge ℗ 617/354-8238, Ⓦ www.mideastclub.com; Central **T**. Local and regional progressive rock acts regularly stop in at this Cambridge institution. Downstairs hosts bigger bands; smaller ones ply their stuff in a tiny upstairs space. They also have *ZuZu*, a tasty little lounge.

Museum of Fine Arts 465 Huntington Ave, Fenway ℗ 617/369-3300, Ⓦ www.mfa.org; Museum **T**. Better known for their jazz and classical acts, the *MFA* is steadily gaining a strong collection of indie rock fans thanks to their bookings of bands like The Sea and the Cake and Mates of State. Intimate, pared-down performances are held in the Remis Auditorium; tickets run about $20.

Orpheum Theatre 1 Hamilton Place, Boston Common ℗ 617/931-2000; Park St or Downtown Crossing **T**. Once an old-school movie house, it's now a vintage venue for big-name bands. The small space means you're closer to the action, and its retro environs are a refreshing change from corporate theaters.

Paradise Rock Club 967–969 Commonwealth Ave, Allston ℗ 617/562-8800; Ⓦ www.thedise.com;

Pleasant Street **T**. One of Boston's classic rocking venues. Lots of greats have played here – Blondie, Elvis Costello, and Tom Waits, to name a few. It's still as happening as it was 25 years ago, only now it also has a restaurant-cum-rock lounge next door.

TD Banknorth Garden 50 Causeway St, West End ℗ 617/624-1750, tickets ℗ 617/931-2000, Ⓦ www.tdbanknorthgarden.com; North Station **T**. This arena, in the West End, attracts a decent number of big-name acts – when the Celtics or Bruins aren't playing, that is.

T.T. the Bear's 10 Brookline St, Cambridge ℗ 617/492-2327, Ⓦ www.ttthebears.com; Central **T**. A downmarket version of *Middle East*: lesser-known bands, but in a space with a grittiness and intimacy its neighbor lacks. Mostly punk, rock, and electronica.

Jazz, blues, and folk

Cantab Lounge 738 Massachusetts Ave, Cambridge ℗ 617/354-2685; Central **T**. Although from the outside it looks like the kind of sleazy place your mother wouldn't want you to enter, it's actually one of the few truly bohemian spots in town, with hopping live jazz and blues.

Club Passim 47 Palmer St, Cambridge ℗ 617/492-7679, Ⓦ www.clubpassim.org; Harvard **T**. Folkie hangout where Joan Baez and Suzanne Vega got their starts. There's also world music and spoken word performances.

Regattabar 1 Bennett St, in the *Charles Hotel*, Cambridge ℗ 617/661-5000, Ⓦ www .regattabarjazz.com; Harvard **T**. *Regattabar* draws top national jazz acts, although, as its location in the swish *Charles Hotel* might suggest, the atmosphere is a bit sedate. Dress nicely and prepare to pay at least $25 cover.

Wally's Cafe 427 Massachusetts Ave, Roxbury ℗ 617/424-1408, Ⓦ www.wallyscafe.com; Massachusetts Avenue **T**. Founded in 1947, this is one of the oldest jazz clubs around. Refreshingly unhewn, they host lively jazz and blues shows that draw a vibrant crowd. No cover.

Western Front 343 Western Ave, Cambridge ℗ 617/492-7772; Central **T**. The *Front* puts on rollicking jazz, blues, hip-hop, and reggae shows for a dance-crazy audience. Drinks are cheap, and the Jamaican food served on weekends is delectably authentic.

Performing arts and film

Boston's **cultural scene** is famously vibrant, with many first-rate artistic institutions. Foremost among them is the **Boston Symphony Orchestra**, which gave its first concert in 1881; in fact, Boston is arguably at its best in the **classical** music department, and there are many smaller but internationally known chamber and choral music groups to shore up that reputation. The **Boston Ballet** is also considered world-class, though it's probably best known for its annual production of *The Nutcracker*.

The **theater** here is quite active too. Boston remains a try-out city for Broadway productions in New York City, and smaller companies have increasingly high visibility. It's a real treat to see a play or musical at one of the opulent old theaters such as the **Citi Performing Arts Center** (formerly the Wang Center) or the **Cutler Majestic**. For current productions, check the listings in the *Boston Globe*'s Thursday "Calendar" section or the *Boston Phoenix*.

The **film** scene is dominated by the Sony/Loews conglomerate, which runs several multiplexes featuring major first-run Hollywood movies. For foreign, independent, classic, or cult cinema, you'll have to look to other municipalities – Cambridge is best, though Brookline has some arthouse movie theaters as well.

Classical music

Boston prides itself on being a sophisticated city, and nowhere does that show up more than in its proliferation of **orchestras** and **choral groups**. This is helped in no small part by the presence of three of the nation's foremost music academies: the Peabody and New England conservatories, and the Berklee College of Music.

Symphonies and chamber music ensembles

Alea III ℡617/353-3340 and **Boston Musica Viva** ℡617/354-6910, ⓦwww.bmv.org. Two regulars at BU's Tsai Performance Center (see opposite).

Boston Baroque ℡617/484-9200, ⓦwww .bostonbaroque.org. The country's first permanent baroque orchestra is now a resident ensemble at Jordan Hall and Sanders Theatre.

Boston Camerata ℡617/262-2092, ⓦwww .bostoncamerata.com. Regular performances of choral and chamber concerts, from medieval to early American, at various locations in Boston.

Boston Chamber Music Society ℡617/349-0086, ⓦwww.bostonchambermusic.org. The society has soloists who perform in Jordan Hall (Fri) and Sanders Theatre (Sun).

Boston Philharmonic ℡617/236-0999, ⓦwww.bostonphil.org. Vibrant, almost exuberant orchestra whose conductor prefaces performances with a discussion of the evening's compositions. Performances take place at Jordan Hall (Sat) and Sanders Theatre (Sun).

Boston Pops ℡617/266-1492, ⓦwww.bso.org. A subsection of the Boston Symphony Orchestra, the Pops are considered to be lighter and "poppier" than their more formal counterpart, and are best known for their dynamic July 4 performance on the Esplanade.

Boston Symphony Chamber Players ℡1-888/266-1200, ⓦwww.bso.org. The only permanent chamber group sponsored by a major symphony orchestra and made up of its members; they perform at Jordan Hall as well as other venues around Boston.

Boston Symphony Orchestra ℡617/266-1492, ⓦwww.bso.org. Boston's world-renowned orchestra performs in Fenway's acoustically perfect Symphony Hall; in summer, they ship out to Tanglewood Festival in gorgeous Lenox, Massachusetts (see p.240).

The Cantata Singers & Ensemble ℡617/868-5885, ⓦwww.cantatasingers.org. Boston's premier choral group, which also performs at Jordan Hall.

Handel & Haydn Society ℡617/266-3605, ⓦwww.handelandhaydn.org. Performing chamber and choral music since 1815, these distinguished artists can be heard at Symphony Hall, Jordan Hall, and the Cutler Majestic.

Pro Arte Chamber Orchestra ℡617/779-0900, ⓦwww.proarte.org. Cooperatively run chamber orchestra in which musicians have full control. Gives Sun afternoon performances at Harvard's Sanders Theatre.

Venues

Berklee Performance Center 136 Massachusetts Ave ℡617/747-8890 (concert information) or 617/747-2261 (box office), ⓦwww.berkleebpc .com; Symphony **T**. Berklee College of Music's main performance center, known for its quality contemporary repertoire.

Isabella Stewart Gardner Museum 280 The Fenway ☎617/278-5156, ⓦwww.gardnermuseum .org; Museum **T**. Chamber and classical concerts, including many debuts, are held regularly at 1.30pm on weekends (Sept–May) in the museum's decadent Tapestry Room; there are also shows on Thurs evenings, including jazz. The $23 ticket price includes museum admission.

Jordan Hall 30 Gainsborough St ☎617/585-1260, ⓦwww.newenglandconservatory.edu; Symphony **T**. The impressive concert hall of the New England Conservatory, just one block west from Symphony Hall, is the venue for many chamber music performances as well as those by the Boston Philharmonic (☎617/236-0999).

Museum of Fine Arts 465 Huntington Ave ☎617/369-3300 or 617/267-9300, ⓦwww.mfa .org; Museum **T**. During the summer, the MFA's jazz, folk, and world music "Concerts in the Courtyard" take place each Wed at 7.30pm; a variety of indoor performances are also scheduled for the rest of the year.

Sanders Theatre 45 Quincy St, Cambridge ☎617/496-2222; Harvard **T**. Dating to 1875, this 1166-seat venue has an intimate 180-degree design and excellent acoustics perfect for showing off its Boston Philharmonic and Boston Chamber Music Society performances.

Symphony Hall 301 Massachusetts Ave ☎1-888/266-1492 (concert information) or 1-888/266-1200 (box office), ⓦwww.bso.org; Symphony **T**. This is the regal, acoustically perfect venue for the Boston Symphony Orchestra; the famous Boston Pops concerts happen in May and June; in July and Aug, the BSO retreats to Tanglewood, in the Berkshires (see p.240).

Tsai Performance Center 685 Commonwealth Ave ☎617/353-TSAI (event information) or 617/353-8725 (box office), ⓦwww.bu.edu/tsai; Boston University **T**. Improbably tucked into BU's School of Management, this hall is a frequent venue for chamber music performances, prominent lecturers, and plays; events are often affiliated with BU and thus are inexpensive.

Dance

The city's longest-running **dance** company is the **Boston Ballet** (☎617/ 695-6950 or 1-800/447-7400, ⓦwww.bostonballet.org), with an unparalleled reputation in America and beyond; their biggest blockbuster, the holiday performance of *The Nutcracker*, boasts an annual attendance of more than 140,000. In addition, there are smaller dance troupes, like chub-loving **Big Moves** (ⓦwww .bigmoves.org), which perform in less traditional venues like the Institute of Contemporary Art. The **Boston Dance Alliance** has an informative website centered on Boston's local dance scene (ⓦwww.bostondancealliance.org).

Theater

It's quite possible to pay dearly for a night at the **theater**. Tickets to bigger shows range from $25 to $100 depending on the seat, and there is, of course, the potential of a pre- or post-theater meal (see p.119 for restaurants in the Theater District). Your best option is to pay a visit to **BosTix**, a half-price, day-of-show ticket booth with two outlets: Copley Square at the corner of Dartmouth and Boylston streets, and Faneuil Hall Marketplace, by Abercrombie & Fitch (both Mon–Sat 10am– 6pm, Sun 11am–4pm; ☎617/482-2849); tickets go on sale at 10am (11am on Sun; Faneuil Hall location closed Mon) and only cash is accepted, although you can now get the same deals through their website (ⓦwww.bostix.org). Full-price tickets can be had through **Ticketmaster** (☎617/931-2000, ⓦwww.ticketmaster .com) or by contacting the relevant theater directly. If you have a valid school ID or ISIC card, a number of theaters offer cheaper **student rush** tickets on the day of the performance; call the venue in question for more information. The **smaller venues** tend to showcase more offbeat and affordable productions, and shows can cost under $10 – though you shouldn't bank on that.

Major venues

American Repertory Theatre 64 Brattle St, at the Loeb Drama Center ☎617/547-8300,

ⓦwww.amrep.org; Harvard **T**. Excellent, fairly avant-garde theater near Harvard Square known for staging plays by the likes of Shaw, Wilde, and

Stoppard. They also have a flexible performance space, Zero Arrow, at the corner of Mass Ave and Arrow St in Harvard Square.

Boston University Theatre 264 Huntington Ave ☎617/266-0800, ⊛www.huntingtontheatre.org; Symphony **T**. The largest non-touring playhouse in Boston, known for their phenomenal sets. Productions here range from the classic to the contemporary.

Charles Playhouse 74 Warrenton St ☎617/ 426-6912, ⊛www.blueman.com; Boylston **T**. The Charles is more or less the permanent home of *Shear Madness* (⊛www.shearmadness.com; $40), a participatory, comic murder mystery, and *Blue Man Group* (⊛www.blueman.com; $48– 58), an eye-opening, edgy multimedia show performed by three bald and blue-painted men. They also host a select number of other big-name performances.

Colonial Theatre 106 Boylston St ☎617/426-9366, ⊛www.bostonscolonialtheatre.com; Boylston **T**. Built in 1900 and since refurbished, this is the doyenne of Boston theaters, known primarily for its Broadway-scale productions.

Citi Center for the Performing Arts 270 Tremont St ☎617/482-9393, ⊛www.citicenter.org; Boylston **T**. Formerly the Wang Center and the Schubert Theatre, these two old theaters have been rebranded under the Citi Center's moniker. The Wang is the biggest performance center in Boston, and the city's grande dame, a movie house of palatial proportions – its original Italian marble, gold leaf ornamentation, crystal chandeliers, and 3800 seats – dating to 1925 – all remain. The Schubert, dubbed the city's "Little Princess" is a 1680-seat theater that has been restored to its pretty early 1900s appearance, with white walls and gold leaf accents.

Cutler Majestic Theatre 219 Tremont St ☎1-800/233-3123, ⊛www.maj.org; Boylston **T**. This lavish venue, with soaring ceilings and Neoclassical friezes, has recently had extensive renovations; it hosts productions of the Emerson Stage company and the Boston Lyric Opera.

The Opera House 539 Washington St ☎617/259-3400, ⊛www.broadwayacrossamerica .com; Downtown Crossing **T**. Built in 1928, this opulent theater recently reopened after a major restoration. It hosts large-scale traveling productions (such as *Wicked*), as well as the Boston Ballet's Christmas-time production of *The Nutcracker*.

Wilbur Theatre 246 Tremont St ☎617/931-2000, ⊛www.ticketmaster.com; Boylston **T**. *A Streetcar Named Desire*, starring Marlon Brando and Jessica Tandy, debuted in this small Colonial Revival theater before going to Broadway, and the Wilbur has been trying to live up to that production ever since. A beloved Boston landmark, the Wilbur is unfortunately on the market, making its future uncertain.

Small venues

Boston Center for the Arts 539 Tremont St ☎617/426-5000, ⊛www.bcaonline.org; Back Bay **T**. Several theater troupes, many experimental, stage productions at the BCA, which incorporates a series of small venues on a single South End property. These include the Cyclorama and the Stanford Calderwood Pavilion (see p.102).

Hasty Pudding Theatre 12 Holyoke St, Cambridge ☎617/495-5205, ⊛www.hastypudding.com; Harvard **T**. Harvard University's all-male Hasty Pudding Theatricals troupe, one of the country's oldest, mounts one show per year (usually a musical comedy; Feb & March) at this theater, then hits the road, after which the Cambridge Theatre Company moves in.

Institute of Contemporary Art 100 Northern Ave, Seaport District ☎617/478-3100, ⊛www .icaboston.org; Courthouse Station **T**. Boston's leading venue for all things cutting-edge.

Lyric Stage 140 Clarendon St, Back Bay ☎617/585-5678, ⊛www.lyricstage.com; Back Bay **T**. Both premieres and modern adaptations of classic and lesser-known American plays take place at this intimate theater within the renovated YWCA building.

Film

In Boston, as in any other large American metropolis, it's easy enough to catch general release **films**. If you're looking for out-of-the-ordinary fare, however, you'll have to venture out a bit from the center. Whatever you're going to see, admission will cost you about $10, though matinees (before 6pm) can be cheaper. You can call ☎617/333-FILM for automated listings.

Brattle Theatre 40 Brattle St, Cambridge ☎617/876-6837, ⊛www.brattlefilm.org; Harvard **T**. A historic basement indie cinema that pleasantly looks its age. They have thematic

film series plus occasional author appearances and readings.

Coolidge Corner Moviehouse 290 Harvard St, Brookline ☎617/734-2500, ⊛www.coolidge.org;

Coolidge Corner **T**. Film buffs flock to this classic theater for foreign and independent movies. The interior is adorned with Art Deco murals.

Harvard Film Archive Carpenter Center, Cambridge 24 Quincy St ⓣ617/495-4700, ⓦwww.harvardfilmarchive.org; Harvard **T**. Artsy, foreign, and experimental films.

Institute of Contemporary Art 100 Northern Ave ⓣ617/478-3100, ⓦwww.icaboston.org; Courthouse Station **T**. The ICA screens films like Japanese and New England animation as well as bigger box office films amongst its gorgeous, glassy environs.

Kendall Square Cinema 1 Kendall Square, Cambridge ⓣ617/499-1996, ⓦwww .landmarktheatres.com; Kendall **T**. All the neon decoration, cramped seating, and small screens of your average multiplex, but this one has the area's widest selection of first-rate foreign and independent films. It's actually located on Binney St near Cardinal Medieros Ave.

Museum of Fine Arts Theater 465 Huntington Ave ⓣ617/267-9300, ⓦwww.mfa.org/film; Museum **T**. Well-executed art films and documentaries often accompanied by lectures from the filmmaker, in addition to hosting several showcases like the Jewish Film and the French Film festivals.

Gay and lesbian Boston

Boston is a gay-friendly city. Indeed, in 2004 it became one of only two states in the nation to honor gay marriage (the other is Connecticut, which followed suit in 2008). The center of the **gay scene** is the South End, a largely residential neighborhood whose businesses, mostly restaurants and cafés, are concentrated on a short stretch of Tremont Street above Union Park. Adjacent to the South End, on the other side of Arlington Street, is tiny **Bay Village**, which has several gay bars and clubs. The **lesbian scene** is pretty well mixed in with the gay scene, and there are few exclusively lesbian bars or clubs.

Boston's two free **gay newspapers** are *in newsweekly* (ⓦwww.innewsweekly .com) and *Bay Windows* (ⓦwww.baywindows.com). The latter is one of two good sources of **club information**, the other being the *The Boston Phoenix*. All can be found in various venues and bookstores, notably Calamus Bookstore, 92B State St (ⓣ617/338-1931), and the Center for New Words, 7 Temple St, Cambridge (ⓣ617/876-5310). Both vestibules have gay and lesbian community bulletin boards, with postings for apartment rentals, club happenings, and so forth.

Bars and clubs

Boston has a good variety of gay **bars** and **clubs**, ranging from the sophisticated (*dbar*) to the low-key (*Fritz*) – and of course a number of bumping dance clubs (*Machine*). For night owls who haven't gotten their fill of dancing at closing time, ask around for an invite to Boston's on the down-low after-hours private party, "Rise," at 306 Stuart St (ⓣ617/423-7473); this members-only event for gays and straights gets going at 2am.

Club Café 209 Columbus Ave ⓣ617/536-0966, ⓦwww.clubcafe.com; Back Bay **T**. This combination restaurant/video bar popular among South End yuppies has a back lounge, *Moonshine*, showing the latest videos. They make a wide selection of martinis with fun names like "Pouty Princess" and "Dirty Birdie."

dbar 1236 Dorchester Ave, Dorchester ⓣ617/265-4490; Savin Hill **T**. Although *dbar* is a bit out of the way, it's well worth the trip – most locals think it's the best gay bar in town. Set amidst an inlaid mahogany interior, *dbar* serves fancy fusion fare from 5–10pm; after that it's all about honeysuckle *caiparinhas* and getting your groove on.

Eagle 520 Tremont St ⓣ617/542-4494; Back Bay **T**. Generally tends to be the last stop of the night, with a cruisey, divey flavor. Prepare for salty bar service.

Fritz 26 Chandler St ⓣ617/482-4428; Back Bay **T**. South End sports bar likened to the gay version of *Cheers* because of its friendly staff and mix of casually attired locals and visitors.

Jacque's Cabaret 79 Broadway ☎617/426-8902; Arlington **T**. Priscilla, Queen of the Desert invades New England at this drag dream, where past-it divas lip-synch *I Love the Nightlife*. There's a nice melting pot of patrons; it's quite popular for bachelorette parties. Showtime is Fri 10pm, Sat 7.45pm & 10pm, other shows nightly. Cover $10; bar is cash only.
Machine 1254 Boylston St ☎617/536-1950, ⒲www.machine-boston.com; Kenmore **T**.

A favorite with the gay crowd on Fri and Sat when the club's large dancefloor and top-notch music has the place pumping. The adjacent pool tables and bar let you take a breather from dancing while you soak up the scene. Cover around $10.
Milky Way 405 Centre St, Jamaica Plain ☎617/524-3740; ⒲www.dykenight.com; Stony Brook **T**. The fourth Fri of the month, a lesbian dance and bowling night gets its groove on.

Shopping

Boston is an extremely pleasant place to **shop**, with attractive stores clustered on atmospheric streets like Charles in Beacon Hill, and Newbury in Back Bay. Harvard Square is another excellent place for a window-shopping wander, with especially good **bookstores**. Otherwise, most of the action takes place downtown, first and foremost at the **Faneuil Hall Marketplace**. There's also thrifty Downtown Crossing, at Washington and Summer streets, centered on Filene's Basement, a bargain-hunter's delight. The North End, historically the go-to spot for cooking ingredients, has more recently become a hotspot for hip clothing boutiques, while the gay-savvy South End always has something cool to seek out, be it clothing, artworks, or sleek home decor.

▲ Newbury Street boutique

Books

Boston is a literary city. This is well reflected in the quality and diversity of **bookstores** to be found both in Boston and neighboring Cambridge.

Barnes & Noble 800 Boylston St, Prudential Center ☎617/247-6959 (Prudential **T**); 660 Beacon St ☎617/267-8484 (Kenmore **T**); Two large outposts of the national bookstore chain. The one on Beacon St is capped by the neon Citgo sign (see p.102).

Brattle Book Shop 9 West St ☎617/542-0210; Park St **T**. One of the oldest antiquarian bookstores in the country. You can buy a book for $1 outside, or find one for $10,000 inside (they recently sold a first-edition *Walden* for a few grand).

Brookline Booksmith 279 Harvard St, Brookline ☎617/566-6660; Coolidge Corner **T**. This cozy shop doesn't seem to have a particular specialty, but its friendly staff makes it perfect for browsing.

Calamus Bookstore 92B South St ☎617/338-1931; South Station **T**. Boston's only gay bookstore, with a good selection of reasonably priced books and cards, plus a vast community bulletin board at the entrance.

Grolier Poetry Bookstore 6 Plympton St, Cambridge ☎617/547-4648; Harvard **T**. With 14,000 volumes of verse, this tiny shop has gained an international following among poets and their fans. Frequent readings.

Harvard Book Store 1256 Massachusetts Ave ☎617/661-1515; Harvard **T**. Three huge rooms of new books upstairs, a basement for used volumes, and an award-winning remainder department downstairs. Academic and critical work in the humanities and social sciences dominate, with a healthy dose of fiction thrown in.

Raven Used Books 52-B JFK St ☎617/441-6999; Harvard **T**. Readers rave about Raven, and rightly so. This delightful, well-kept little bookstore stocks scholarly (but not pretentious) reads covering everything from anarchism and poetry to jazz and physics.

Trident Booksellers & Café 338 Newbury St ☎617/267-8688; Hynes **T**. One of the last great independent bookstores in Boston. Has a bit of an alternative vibe; buy an obscure magazine and pretend to read it over coffee in the café (see review p.122). Free wi-fi.

Food and drink

Eating out in Boston may prevail, but should you choose to cook your own **food**, or get provisions for a picnic, you won't do so badly either. There are also some excellent spots to pick up pastries, pies, and other dessert–oriented items, especially in the North End.

Formaggio Kitchen 244 Huron Ave, Cambridge ☎617/354-4750; Harvard **T**; 268 Shawmut Ave, South End ☎617/350-6996; Back Bay **T**. Although regarded as one of the best cheese shops in Boston, the gourmet meats, salads, sandwiches, and baked goods here are also worth sampling.

Maria's Pastry 46 Cross St ☎617/523-1196; Haymarket **T**. The best pastries in the North End, and inexplicably under-rated. *Maria's* chocolate cannoli with fresh ricotta filling will change your life and make your day.

Mike's Pastry 300 Hanover St ☎617/742-3050; Haymarket **T**. Iconic and touristy, yet still attended by locals, in many way's *Mike's is* the North End. Love it or hate it, lining up for one of their twine-wrapped boxes of heavenly pastries is a quintessential Boston experience.

Modern Pastry 257 Hanover St ☎617/523-3783; Haymarket **T**. You can't miss *Modern's* glorious vintage sign out front, nor would you want to – inside is fresh *torrone, cannoli*, little marzipan fruits and some of the North End's best pastries. Family-owned for seventy years.

Polcari's Coffee 105 Salem St ☎617/227-0786; Haymarket **T**. Vintage, well loved and brimming with coffees, as well as every spice you can think of. Worth going in for the aroma alone, or just to hear the local gossip from the men behind the counter. In summer, don't miss the home-made lemon ice ($1.50).

Salumeria Italiana 151 Richmond St ☎617/523-8743; Haymarket **T**. Arguably the best Italian grocer this side of Roma, this shop stocks only the finest cheeses, meats, and more.

Savenor's 160 Charles St ☎617/723-6328; Charles **T**. Known for its meats, this small gourmet food shop in Beacon Hill also has a produce selection, in addition to prepared foods – ideal for taking to the nearby Charles River Esplanade for an impromptu picnic.

Malls and department stores

Boston's **malls** are widely scattered about, and are good places to visit if you need to pick up a number of diverse items. In addition, they also contain most of the city's biggest **department stores**, though a few unattached ones stand out around Downtown Crossing.

CambridgeSide Galleria 100 Cambridgeside Place ☎617/621-8666; Kendall **T**. Not too different from any other large American shopping mall. The haze of neon and packs of teens can be exhausting, but there's no similarly dense and convenient conglomeration of shops in Cambridge.

Copley Place 100 Huntington Ave ☎617/369-5000; Copley **T**. This ambitious, upscale office-retail-residential complex features more than a hundred stores and the tempting Barney's New York.

Faneuil Hall Marketplace Faneuil Hall ☎617/523-1300; Government Center **T**. The city's most famous market, with a hundred or so shops, plus Quincy Market next door. It's tourist-oriented, but still worth a trip.

Filene's Basement 426 Washington St ☎617/542-2011; Downtown Crossing **T**. Discounted merchandise from Macy's upstairs and other big-name department stores, plus a few Boston boutiques. Temporarily closed for renovations.

The Harvard Coop 1400 Massachusetts Ave ☎617/499-2000; Harvard **T**. Harvard's local department store, with a wide selection of insignia clothing, books, and the like.

The Heritage on the Garden 300 Boylston St ☎617/426-9500; Arlington **T**. Not so much a mall as a very upscale mixed-use complex across from the Public Garden that consists of condos, restaurants, and boutiques.

Louis Boston 234 Berkeley St ☎617/262-6100; Arlington **T**. Occupying a stately, freestanding building from 1863 that once housed Boston's Museum of Natural History (which became the Museum of Science), this is the city's classiest and most expensive clothes emporium. A Boston landmark, and worth a visit, despite the price tags.

The Shops at Prudential Center 800 Boylston St ☎617/236-3100; Prudential **T**. A hundred or so mid-market shops, heavily patronized by local residents and conventioneers who genuinely enjoy buying commemorative T-shirts and ties.

Music

The best places for new and used **music** in Boston are on Newbury Street in Back Bay, around Massachusetts Avenue near Kenmore Square, and up in Harvard Square – as you might expect, basically all the places students can be found hanging about.

Looney Tunes 1106 Boylston St ☎617/247-2238; Hynes **T**. The way a record store should be – walls bedecked with sultry vintage jazz records, a great selection of CDs and vinyl, and a hip staff that's not snooty.

Newbury Comics 332 Newbury St ☎617/236-4930; Hynes **T**. Boston's biggest alternative record store carries lots of independent labels you won't find at the national chains along with a substantial array of vinyl, posters, zines, and kitschy T-shirts. It's also a good place to pick up fliers on local club happenings. There's a branch in Cambridge at the Garage mall, 36 JFK St (☎617/491-0337; Harvard **T**).

Nuggets 486 Commonwealth Ave ☎617/536-0679; Kenmore **T**. American jazz, rock, and R&B are the strong suits at this venerable new and used record store.

Planet Records 54B JFK St, Cambridge ☎617/492-0693; Harvard **T**. Unpretentious and well priced with a good selection of used CDs. It doesn't get more rock 'n' roll than the charred guitar they have hanging by the register – a remnant from the fire that decimated their former location.

Skippy White's 538 Massachusetts Ave, Cambridge ☎617/491-3345; Central **T**. Excellent collection of jazz, blues, R&B, gospel, funk (all manners), and hip-hop. Hum a few bars and the salesfolk will guide you to the right section.

Underground Hip Hop 234 Huntington Ave ☎617/262-0200; Symphony **T**. One of the best selections of hip-hop here or anywhere. It's well organized too – sit on a comfy stool, listen all you want to the tunes on their extensive website (ⓦwww.undergroundhiphop.com), and then they'll grab what you want from the back.

Speciality shops

Bobby from Boston 19 Thayer St ⊤617/423-9299; NE Medical or Broadway **T**. Long adored by local rockers and movie wardrobe professionals, Bobby's South End loft is, hands down, the best place to find men's vintage clothing from the 1920s–60s as well as a great spot for fabulous female finds. Cash or check only.

Bodega 6 Clearway St ⊤617/421-1550; Hynes **T**. Out front stocks your favorite bodega mainstays (think Cheerios and toilet paper); walk towards the vending machine door to reveal a secret backroom filled with covetous designer sneakers and stylish hip-hop wear.

The London Harness Company 60 Franklin St ⊤617/542-9234; Downtown Crossing **T**. Chiefly known for its high-quality luggage goods, this atmospheric shop reeks of traditional Boston – indeed, Ben Franklin used to shop here. They also vend a wide array of items like chess sets, clocks, candlesticks, and inlaid decorative boxes.

Shake the Tree Gallery 95 Salem St ⊤617/742-0484; Haymarket **T**. A good spot for a little retail therapy – bright, chunky gemstone necklaces, funky sock monkeys, designer jeans, yuppie candles, and other modern, pretty *objets* that you will never need but must have.

Listings

Banks and currency exchange Bank of America is Boston's largest, with branches and ATMs throughout the city. Bureaux de change are not very prevalent. You can find locations at Logan Airport Terminal E; Travelex, 745 Boylston St; and many Bank of America branches.

Consulates Canada, 3 Copley Place, suite 500 (⊤617/262-3760); UK, 1 Memorial Drive Cambridge (⊤617/245-4500); Ireland, 535 Boylston St (⊤617/267-9330); Australia, 55 Thomson Place (⊤617/261-5555).

Hospitals Massachusetts General Hospital, 55 Fruit St (⊤617/726-2000, ⊛www.massgeneral .org; Charles/MGH **T**); Beth Israel Deaconess Medical Center, 330 Brookline Ave (⊤617/667-7000, ⊛www.bidmc.org; Longwood **T**); Tufts Medical Center, 800 Washington St (⊤617/636-5000, ⊛www.tuftsmedicalcenter.org; NE Medical **T**); Brigham & Women's Hospital, 75 Francis St (⊤617/732-5500 or 1-800/BWH-9999, ⊛www .brighamandwomens.org; Longwood or Brigham Circle **T**); Children's Hospital, 300 Longwood Ave (⊤617/355-6000, ⊛www .childrenshospital.org; Longwood **T**).

Internet Pop into a local university and use one of their free public computers. Harvard's Holyoke Center Arcade, at 1350 Massachusetts Ave in Cambridge, has a couple of stations with 10min access maximum. The same goes for MIT's Building 7 at 77 Massachusetts Ave (also in Cambridge). Boston's main public library, 700 Boylston St, has free 15min internet access. See p.117 for coffee shops with free wi-fi. There is also the ubiquitous FedEx/Kinko's; try the 24hr location (Fri and Sat it closes at 11pm) at 187 Dartmouth St (⊤617/262-6188; Copley **T**).

Laundry Appleton St Laundromat, 9 Appleton St (daily 7am–8.30pm; ⊤617/338-8887; Back Bay **T**), is a good, clean bet; drop-off service starts at $10.

Parking A nightmare. The best parking secret is the Parcel 7 garage, at 136 Blackstone St (⊤617/973-6954). The posted rates won't mention it, but if you get your ticket validated at a North End business the rates are only $1 an hour for the first three hours (after that it goes way up). Another good spot is after 4pm or on weekends at the Garage at Post Office Square ($9 day, weekday in after 4pm and out before 5am $9; ⊤617/423-1500). You can also park and ride at the safe and cheap Alewife **T** stop in Cambridge (at the intersection of US-2 and Cambridge Park Drive; $5 a day; ⊤1-800/392-6100) or try for a metered spot in Back Bay. The parking limit at nonmetered spots is two hours, whether posted or not.

Pharmacies The CVS drugstore chain has locations all over the city, though not all have pharmacies. For those, try the branches at 155–157 Charles St, in Beacon Hill (open 24hr; ⊤617/227-0437, pharmacy ⊤617/523-1028), and 35 White St, in Cambridge's Porter Square (open 24hr; ⊤617/876-4037, pharmacy ⊤617/876-5519).

Police In case of emergency, get to a phone and dial ⊤911.

Post office The most central post office downtown is at 31 Milk St in Post Office Square (Mon–Fri 7.30am–7pm); Cambridge's central branch is at 770 Massachusetts Ave, in Central Square (Mon–Fri 7.30am–6pm, Sat 7.30am–2pm); the General Post Office, 25 Dorchester Ave, behind South Station, is open 24hr. Call ⊤1-800/ASK-USPS for further information.

1

Sports Baseball: Red Sox (☏1-877/REDSOX9, ⓦwww.redsox.com) play at Fenway Park, seats $20–325. Basketball: Celtics (☏1-800/4NBATIX, ⓦwww.nba.com/celtics) play at the TD Banknorth Garden, 150 Causeway St, in the West End, seats $10–85. Hockey: Bruins (☏617/931-2000, ⓦwww .bostonbruins.com), also at the TD Banknorth Garden, seats $27–200.

Travel agents STA Travel, 65 Mt Auburn St, Harvard Square, Cambridge (☏617/576-4623), specializes in student and youth travel; American Express Travel, 170 Federal St (☏617/439-4400), provides general services.

Eastern
Massachusetts

CHAPTER 2 # Highlights

* **Walden Pond** Think transcendentalist thoughts, or just take a relaxing walk and swim at this historically significant and physically beautiful spot. See p.146

* **Clam shacks** Fried, juicy belly clams and fresh lobster are a treat all along the Massachusetts coast. See p.161 & 163

* **Cape Cod biking** The Rail Trail is great for touring, while the Province Lands bike path takes a more scenic route through the dunes. See p.181 & p.191

* **Hit the beach** The region's bountiful beaches make a fine excuse to laze about. See p.184

* **Provincetown** Perhaps the lone must-see on the Cape, a lively town with great beaches, tasty seafood, and an anything-goes mentality. See p.187

* **Nantucket** Leaf through Melville's *Moby Dick* while admiring the digs of one-time whaleboat captains in Nantucket Town, the *Pequod's* port of call. See p.203

▲ Cape Cod National Seashore beach

Eastern Massachusetts

A
s the cradle of much of early American development, **Eastern Massa-chusetts** has quite a bit to offer in the way of history. Just inland from Boston, and easily visited as day-trips from that city, are the towns of **Lexington** and **Concord**, where the Revolutionary War began in 1775, and **Lowell**, the birthplace of America's Industrial Revolution. The state's deceptively long and once influential coast, meanwhile, can be divided into four sections, each of which is linked to Boston by a network of major highways: the **North Shore**, which stretches from the city's bland northern suburbs to the New Hampshire border, includes the "witch" town of **Salem** and rocky **Cape Ann**, home to the old fishing ports of **Gloucester** and **Rockport**; the **South Shore**, which extends from the southern outskirts of Boston towards **Plymouth**, where the Pilgrims landed in 1620, past the partially restored whaling port of **New Bedford**, all the way to the Rhode Island border; the outstretched arm of **Cape Cod**, which reaches more than seventy miles into the Atlantic, and is dotted with a range of popular resorts, none better than bohemian **Provincetown**; and the relaxed, upmarket holiday islands of **Martha's Vineyard** and **Nantucket**.

As with much of New England, there are seasonal factors to take into consideration when visiting this part of the state. While the inland towns can be visited at any time, the coast is best experienced in the summer or early fall, when the sun and water are at their warmest – though beautiful in winter, the beach towns can also be somewhat desolate, with many hotels, restaurants, and attractions shut up until spring. The nicest way to vacation in this part of the state is to pick a beach town on the Cape or the islands, and plant yourself for a week of summer activities – the sights won't take more than a few days to tour, and then you can relax and enjoy the swimmable beaches, clam shacks, and fun neighborhood bars.

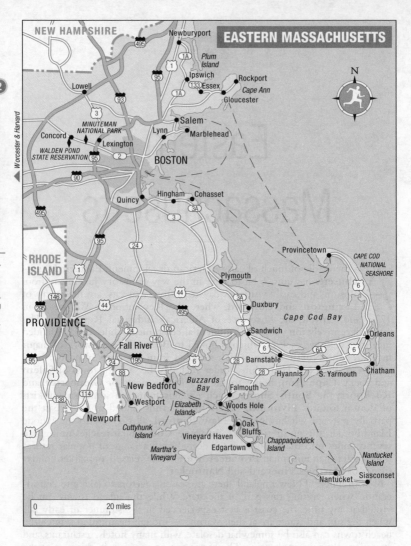

NEW HAMPSHIRE

EASTERN MASSACHUSETTS

N

495 Newburyport

1A Plum Island

1 Ipswich

95 133 Essex Rockport

Lowell 1A Cape Ann

93 Gloucester

3 Salem

MINUTEMAN NATIONAL PARK

Concord Lynn Marblehead

WALDEN POND STATE RESERVATION Lexington

95 2 BOSTON

90

Quincy Hingham Cohasset

495 3A

3

95 Provincetown CAPE COD NATIONAL SEASHORE

24 6

Plymouth

RHODE ISLAND

1 44 3A Duxbury

146 Cape Cod Bay

235 44 3

PROVIDENCE 24 105 495 Sandwich Orleans

140 6 6A 6

95 Fall River 6 Barnstable Chatham

1 24 195 28 S. Yarmouth

88 28 Hyannis

138 114 New Bedford Buzzards Bay Falmouth

Westport Elizabeth Islands Woods Hole

Newport Cuttyhunk Island Oak Bluffs

Vineyard Haven Chappaquiddick Island Nantucket Island Siasconset

Martha's Vineyard Edgartown

Nantucket

0   20 miles

Around Boston

The American Revolution (see box opposite) began at **Concord** and nearby
Lexington in April 1775 with what has become known as "the shot heard
round the world." Both towns have been cashing in on this history-altering
event ever since, with each skirmish, Revolutionary hero, and colonial house
commemorated with monuments and visitors' centers full of scale models and
remnant musketry. Close to Concord are the towns of **Lincoln** and **Harvard**,

home to some smaller museums of equal interest, while north of Boston is the industrial city of **Lowell**, now undergoing a renaissance. All these towns are best visited as day-trips from Boston.

Lexington and around

Modern **LEXINGTON**, long since absorbed by Boston's urban sprawl, is a relatively posh commuter suburb, and it won't take more than an afternoon to see all the sights on offer. The meticulously manicured **Battle Green** in the center of town is fronted by Henry Kitson's diminutive but dignified statue *The Minute Man*, a musket-bearing figure of Captain John Parker (an American commander fatally wounded at the battle). The **Lexington Visitor Center**, 1875 Massachusetts Ave, on the eastern periphery of the Green (daily: April–Nov 9am–5pm; Dec–March 10am–4pm; free; ☎781/862-2480, ⊛ www.lexingtonchamber.org), has a diorama that shows the detail of the battle, while in the Minute Men's headquarters at the **Buckman Tavern**, facing the Green at 1 Bedford St (daily April–Oct 10am–4pm; guided tour every 30min; $6; ☎781/862-5598), a bullet hole from a British rifle has been preserved in an inner door near the first-floor tap room. A couple of blocks north, at 36 Hancock St, a plaque affixed to the exterior of the **Hancock-Clarke House** (☎781/862-1703; call for hours) reminds us that this is where "Samuel Adams and John Hancock were sleeping when aroused by Paul Revere." Closed for a comprehensive renovation at the time of writing, it should re-open in 2009.

South of town, at the intersection of Massachusetts Avenue (Rte-4) and Rte-2A, a contemporary building houses the **National Heritage Museum** (Mon–Sat 10am–5pm, Sun noon–5pm; free; ☎781/861-6559, ⊛ www.monh.org), which tries to be just that, with rotating displays on all facets of American history, daily life, and culture, plus a permanent exhibit on the Battle of Lexington.

Revolutionary history

The first battle of the **American Revolution** began in Lexington on April 19, 1775, when British troops were intercepted as they headed to Concord to seize American munitions. The British plans were hardly a secret; upon their departure from Boston Common, Paul Revere and William Dawes rode off on separate routes to sound the alarm. Within minutes, church bells were clanging throughout the countryside, signaling the rebels – called "Minute Men" because they were prepared to fight at a moment's notice – to head for **Lexington Green**. Revere gave the final alarm to John Hancock and Samuel Adams at the Hancock-Clarke House (see above).

With only 77 Americans pitted against seven hundred British regulars, the clash in Lexington was more a show of resolve than a hope for victory. Eight Americans were killed; the British suffered no casualties, and continued marching the three miles further west to **Concord**. By the time they arrived, hundreds more Minute Men had massed on a farm behind **North Bridge** (see p.146). When a British officer accidentally set fire to a building, the Americans, believing that the town was going up in smoke, fired on the British – the "shot" immortalized by Ralph Waldo Emerson in his *Concord Hymn*. Now outnumbered four to one, the British suffered heavily in the ensuing battle, which continued all the way back to Boston, where the Redcoats retreated.

Practicalities

Lexington is only eleven miles from downtown Boston. By **car**, take Rte-2 out of the city towards Arlington, then follow the signs to Lexington. The MBTA (☎617/222-3200, Ⓦwww.mbta.com) also runs buses (15min; $1.50) to Lexington from Cambridge's Alewife Station. Once in town, Liberty Ride (daily 10.30am–4.30pm; $20 for 2 days; ☎781/862-0500 ext 702, Ⓦwww.libertyride.us), operates a hop-on, hop-off **trolley bus service** between the National Heritage Museum and the North Bridge in Concord (see p.146), stopping at all the main sights.

Eating options in town are fairly unexceptional; try *Via Lago*, near the Visitor Center at 1845 Massachusetts Ave (closed Sun; ☎781/861-6174), a casual counter-service spot serving decent pastas, sandwiches, and salads, or head to nearby Boston-chain *Vinny T's*, 20 Waltham St (☎781/860-5200), for heaping portions of reliable Italian fare like fennel sausage lasagna and spaghetti bolognese.

Minute Man National Historical Park

Forming a corridor between Lexington and Concord, the **Minute Man National Historical Park** (sunrise–sunset; ☎978/369-6993, Ⓦwww.nps.gov /mima) preserves, in almost obsessive detail, every inch of the **Battle Road**, along which the British forces were pushed back towards Boston on April 19, 1775.

The park follows Rte-2A, beginning just beyond the intersection with I-95, two miles west of Lexington. The best place to get oriented is the **Minute Man Visitor Center** (daily: late March to late Oct 9am–5pm, late Oct to late Nov 9am–4pm; ☎978/318-7832), a short drive past the intersection. From here Rte-2A (which becomes Lexington Rd), winds past most of the attractions, though it's far more pleasant to follow the five-mile **Battle Road Trail** from the visitor center on bike or foot. Highlights include the monument marking where **Paul Revere** was captured by the British, ending his famous ride, and the **Hartwell Inn** (end May to end Oct daily 9.30am–5.30pm; free) the local hostelry in 1775 and now the focus for some historical re-enactments.

The park ends at the outskirts of Concord and the seventeenth-century **Wayside**, 455 Lexington Rd (tours only: May–Oct Wed–Sun 11am, 1pm, 3pm & 4.30pm; $5; ☎978/318-7826), home of Samuel Whitney, muster man for the Minute Men, but better known today as a literary landmark: Louisa May Alcott lived in the house as a teenager in the 1840s, and Nathaniel Hawthorne lived and wrote here between 1852 and 1870. Among the antique furnishings inside, the most evocative is the slanted desk in the fourth-floor "tower," at which Hawthorne wrote, standing up.

Alcott penned *Little Women* at **Orchard House**, next door at no. 399 (April–Oct Mon–Sat 10am–4.30pm, Sun 1–4.30pm; Nov–March Mon–Fri 11am–3pm, Sat 10am–4.30pm, Sun 1–4.30pm; closed Jan 1–15; entry by guided tour only, $9; ☎978/369-4118, Ⓦwww.louisamayalcott.org), where she and her family lived from 1858 to 1877. The guided tour is well worth your time; although it focuses heavily on the differences between Alcott's life and her most famous book, it is also the best way to get a good impression of the area's strong nineteenth-century literary, intellectual, and liberal activist community (see box opposite).

Concord and around

The Revolutionary War theme continues in earnest in **CONCORD**, though the town's literary associations are just as much, if not more, of a draw. Like Lexington, it's little more than an upscale suburb of Boston these days, though far more successful at retaining the feel of a tree-filled New England country town than its urban neighbor, even when visitors swamp the center in peak season.

The Town

Driving into Concord from Lexington, the first place of interest beyond Orchard House, at the intersection of Rte-2 and Rte-2A, is the **Ralph Waldo Emerson House** (mid-April to Oct Thurs–Sat 10am–4.30pm, Sun 1–4.30pm; $8; ℡978/369-2236), where the essayist and poet lived from 1835 until his death in 1882. The creaking interior – bedrooms, kitchen, and dining rooms – have been preserved as they would have looked in Emerson's day, though the precious contents of his study were donated to the absorbing **Concord Museum**, 200 Lexington Rd (Jan–March Mon–Sat 11am–4pm, Sun 1–4pm; April–Dec Mon–Sat 9am–5pm, Sun noon–5pm; $10; ℡978/369-9763, ⓦwww.concordmuseum.org), across the street. The museum, which stands on the former site of Emerson's apple orchard, has more than a dozen galleries displaying period furnishings from eighteenth- and nineteenth-century Concord, including a sizeable collection of Thoreau's personal effects, such as the bed from his hut at Walden Pond. More interesting, however, are the Revolutionary War artifacts, including one of the signal lanterns from Boston's Old North Church.

Concord's business district hugs **Main Street**, which intersects Monument Street right by the historic **Colonial Inn**, an atmospheric place to stay or just to eat lunch. Main Street crosses Lexington Road at the **Hill Burying Ground**, from the top of which you can survey much of the town. A few blocks behind the grounds, off Rte-62, lies **Sleepy Hollow Cemetery**, where Concord literati Ralph Waldo Emerson, Nathaniel Hawthorne, Henry David Thoreau, and Louisa May Alcott are interred atop "Authors' Ridge."

Concord and transcendentalism

A half-century after independence, Concord became the center of a revolution in American thinking known as **transcendentalism**. The transcendentalists, many of them Harvard-educated Unitarian ministers unhappy with their church's conservatism, denied the existence of miracles and stressed the conviction that insight and intuitive knowledge were the ways to enhance the relationship between man, nature, and the "over-soul." These beliefs were born of a passion for rural life, liberty, and intellectual freedom. Indeed, the free thinking that transcendentalism unleashed put writers at the vanguard of American literary expression.

In 1834, **Ralph Waldo Emerson** moved into the Old Manse (see p.146), the house his grandfather had built near the North Bridge; there, in 1836, he wrote the book that would signal the birth of the movement, *Nature*, in which he argued for the function of nature as a visible manifestation of invisible spiritual truths. His stature as an intensely pensive, learned scribe drew other intellectuals to Concord, notably Henry David Thoreau, Nathaniel Hawthorne, Bronson Alcott (father of Louisa May), and Margaret Fuller. These Concord authors formed a close-knit group. In 1840, Emerson and Fuller co-founded *The Dial*, the literary magazine which became the movement's semi-official journal. Nathaniel Hawthorne, a native of Salem, rented the Old Manse for three years, returned to his hometown, then moved back to Concord permanently in 1852. Meanwhile, Emerson financed Thoreau's Walden Pond sojourn and the Alcotts lived in Orchard House, on Lexington Road. The largely wholesome literary movement spawned several short-lived utopian farming ventures, including Bronson Alcott's Fruitlands (see p.147). Its effects were longer lasting than these communities, however, as its proponents played an important role in the abolitionist and feminist movements.

The most vaunted spot in Concord is the **North Bridge Area**, slightly removed from the town center. This was the site of the armed resistance that halted the British march in 1775. The focal point of the area is the bridge, which, though photogenic, looks a bit too groomed to provoke much patriotic sentiment – indeed, it's a 1954 replica of an earlier replacement. A short walk from here takes you to the **North Bridge Visitor Center**, 174 Liberty St (daily: late March to late Oct 9am–5pm; late Oct to late Nov 9am–4pm; Dec to late March 11am–3pm), where a diorama of the battle is displayed along with assorted military regalia.

Literally a stone's throw from the North Bridge (on the other side of the Concord River from the Visitor Center), is the **Old Manse** (mid-April to Oct Mon–Sat 10am–5pm, Sun noon–5pm; guided tours only, every 30min; $8; ☎978/369-3909), a house built for Ralph Waldo Emerson's grandfather, the Reverend William Emerson, who witnessed the hostilities from his window. Of the numerous rooms in the house, all with period furnishings intact, the most interesting is the small upstairs study where Nathaniel Hawthorne, who rented the house in the early 1840s, wrote *Mosses from an Old Manse*, a rather obscure text that endowed the place with its name.

Practicalities

You'll find ample **parking** (free) in the center of Concord, behind the visitors' center on Main Street, though the lot can fill up fast in the summer. Driving from Boston, you can skip Lexington and the Minute Man National Historical Park by taking Rte-2 straight to Concord. The MBTA (☎617/222-3200, ⓦwww.mbta .com) operates trains from Boston's North Station to Concord Depot (40–45min; $6.25 one-way), a stiff 1.5-mile walk from the center. The Chamber of Commerce, 15 Walden St (hours vary, call ahead; ☎978/369-3120, ⓦwww .concordchamberofcommerce.org), offers one hour thirty minute guided **walking tours** for $20 (mid-March to Nov Mon & Fri at 1pm, Sat & Sun 11am & 1pm) from its central **visitors' center** at 58 Main St (daily April–Oct 10am–4pm).

For somewhere to **stay**, the upscale *Colonial Inn*, 48 Monument Square (☎1-800/370-9200 or 978/369-9200, ⓦwww.concordscolonialinn.com; ❽), is a 56-room hotel that still manages to feel like a B&B, while *Amerscot House B&B*, nine miles west in Stow, 61 W Acton Rd (☎978/897-0666, ⓦwww .amerscot.com; ❻), offers attentive hospitality in a restored 1734 farmhouse. The inexpensive *Concordian Motel*, a few miles west of downtown Concord on Rte-2 at 71 Hosmer St in Acton (☎978/263-7765, ⓦwww.concordianmotel .com; ❸–❹), has 52 comfortable air-conditioned rooms. If you're looking for a bite to **eat**, try the *Cheese Shop*, 29 Walden St (closed Sun & Mon; ☎978/369-5778), a great place for picnic fixings. For an inexpensive sit-down meal, head to *Main Streets Market Café*, 42 Main St (☎866/413-3981), which offers home-made soups, chowders, and sandwiches, with an ice cream take-out at the back in summer and a wide range of live music (mostly jazz, blues, or folk) most nights.

Walden Pond State Reservation

The tranquility savored by Henry David Thoreau at **Walden Pond**, just south of Concord proper off Rte-126 (7am to sunset; parking $5; ☎978/369-3254), is for the most part gone, thanks to the masses of tourists who pour in to retrace his footsteps (and in the summer, to swim). The place itself, however, has remained much the same since the author lived here from 1845 to 1847, essentially attempting to put transcendentalist philosophy into practice, an experiment he later documented in his 1854 book *Walden*. A reconstructed single-room hut is situated near the parking lot, while the site of his cabin, closer to the pond, is marked out with stones. If you take the footpath that meanders around the pond you'll find smaller trails to the water that are rarely crowded and good spots for contemplation.

Lincoln

Two miles south of Walden Pond, the affluent suburban town of **LINCOLN** is home to several worthy diversions, notably the **DeCordova Museum and Sculpture Park**, 51 Sandy Pond Rd (Tues–Sun 10am–5pm; $12, sculpture park free when museum is closed; ☎781/259-8355, ⓦwww.decordova.org). All manner of impressive contemporary sculptures (mainly by American, particularly regional, artists) peppers the museum's expansive grounds. Most fascinating are the bigger works, like John Buck's *Dream World* and Paul Matisse's *Musical Fence*, which look like they've simply tumbled into their present positions. The museum, somewhat overshadowed by the garden, hosts eye-catching special exhibits with an emphasis on contemporary multimedia art.

Also in Lincoln, the **Gropius House**, 68 Baker Ridge Rd (June to mid-Oct Wed–Sun 11am–5pm; mid-Oct to May Sat & Sun 11am–5pm; tours on the hour; $10; ☎781/259-8098), was designed in 1937 by the German founder of the influential **Bauhaus school** of architecture, when he came to teach at Harvard University. The house's unattractive exterior belies the more pleasant, if utilitarian, interior, still containing items belonging to the family and a valuable collection of Bauhaus-inspired furniture designed by fellow Modernist Marcel Breuer.

Harvard

Thirteen miles west of Concord, the small town of **HARVARD** is home to the **Fruitlands Museum**, 102 Prospect Hill Rd (mid-May to Oct Mon–Fri 11am–4pm, Sat & Sun 11am–5pm; $10; ☎978/456-3924, ⓦwww.fruitlands .org), once the site of one of the transcendentalists' agricultural communities, headed by **Bronson Alcott**. Aiming to create a "New Eden," Alcott started the idealistic commune here with his English friend Charles Lane in 1843, espousing vegetarianism, freedom of expression, and celibacy (the latter after siring four daughters, including Louisa May), but talk of living off the "fruits of the land" proved much easier in theory than practice, and the experiment was short-lived. The original farmhouse now houses a **museum** with exhibits on the transcendentalist movement, including letters and memorabilia of Alcott, Emerson, and Thoreau, and there are two hundred acres of woodlands and meadows on the site, which you can explore on four well-marked trails.

There are also three smaller galleries in the museum grounds: the **Shaker Gallery** has displays of furniture, crafts, and artifacts retrieved from a Shaker

---

Cider and wine

The Harvard area is well known for its **apples** and apple products. You can pick your own at **U-Pick Phil's Apples**, 24 Prospect Hill Rd (Sept–Nov daily 8am–6pm; ☎978/456-3361, ⓦwww.philsapples.com), where you can also make **cider** at the weekends. **The Nashoba Valley Winery**, on Wattaquadoc Hill Rd (daily 11am–5pm, tours on weekends 11am–4pm; $6; ☎978/779-5521, ⓦwww.nashobawinery.com), near **Bolton**, approximately fifteen miles west of Concord, offers peach-, plum-, apple-, and berry-picking (seasonal), as well as samples of their award-winning wines and microbrews. Complete the experience at on-site *J's Restaurant* (closed Mon & Tues, dinner not served Sun; reservations recommended; ☎978/779-9816).

▲ Indian Museum at Fruitlands

community that once existed here; the **Picture Gallery** features a collection of American art, including New England landscape paintings by Hudson River School artists Thomas Cole and Frederick Edwin Church; and an **Indian Museum** highlights Native American handicrafts, clothing, headdresses, pottery, dolls, and carvings. Sitting atop Prospect Hill, the whole site affords spellbinding views of the surrounding country, best appreciated at the 🎋 *Tea Room*, which serves a full range of salads and light lunches, as well as speciality teas.

Lowell

The mighty red-brick mills of **LOWELL**, thirty miles northwest of Boston on the Merrimack River, were once at the heart of the American Industrial Revolution. The town is named for entrepreneur **Francis Cabot Lowell**, who in 1814 established the first textile mill in America to use power looms (in Waltham, outside Boston), after memorizing the necessary technology (a secret at the time) on an earlier visit to England; Lowell, which utilized the power of the Merrimack, was a larger venture founded in 1822. By the 1840s, it was one of the most productive cities in the world, turning out almost one million yards of cotton cloth every week. The city hit hard times during the Great Depression, and the last mill closed in the 1950s; like many former industrial towns in the region, Lowell today remains proudly working-class and relatively neglected. However, the city center has been preserved as an absorbing and powerful memorial to the city's role in American history. As you explore, you'll also come across mentions of the city's most famous son, author **Jack Kerouac** (see box, p.150), who was born and raised here; the city makes several appearances in his novels, and Jack was buried here in 1969.

The City

Still very much a working city center, much of the downtown area has been incorporated within the **Lowell National Historical Park** (Ⓦ www.nps.gov /lowe), a collection of restored mill buildings, museums, and shops.

In addition to the national park sights, there are also a handful of other worthy diversions in the center. The **National Streetcar Museum**, 25 Shattuck St, (Thurs–Sun 11am–4pm; $2; Ⓦ www.trolleymuseum.org/lowell) is a small exhibit about the history of public transit in Lowell (primarily the trolleys), while the **Revolving Museum**, 22 Shattuck St (Tues–Sun 11am–4pm; free; Ⓣ 978/937-2787, Ⓦ www.revolvingmuseum.org), shows temporary exhibits of bold, contemporary artwork. Further up the street, the **New England Quilt Museum**, 18 Shattuck St (Tues–Sat 10am–4pm; May–Dec also Sun noon–4pm; $5; Ⓣ 978/452-4207 ext 15, Ⓦ www.nequiltmuseum.org), houses vintage and contemporary quilts, which will appeal mainly to aficionados. Across the canal, the **Whistler House Museum of Art**, 243 Worthen St (Wed–Sat 11am–4pm; $5; Ⓣ 978/452-7641, Ⓦ www.whistlerhouse.org), is the birthplace of **James McNeil Whistler** (1834–1903). The controversial artist actually renounced his hometown, spending most of his life in London, where he became associated with the Aesthetic Movement and early Modernism. This gallery houses a small but impressive collection of nineteenth- and early twentieth-century New England artists, as well as some of Whistler's own etchings.

Lowell National Historical Park

Begin your tour of the historical park at the modern **visitors' center** (daily 9am–5pm; Ⓣ 978/970-5000), in the heart of the vast Market Mills complex. Multimedia presentations covering the history of the city (and less frequently, Jack Kerouac) screen regularly in the theater, while exhibits fill in the gaps and rangers are on hand to provide maps and advice. Walking is the best way to explore – with the exception of Wannalancit Mills, everything is within a few minutes of the visitors' center – but there's also a **trolley bus** that runs to all the park's main sights (March–Nov every 30–45min, more frequently at weekends; free). Illuminating **tours** via trolley bus are given at least once daily (free), as well as boat trips along the Merrimack's branch canals ($8–10; call or see the website for schedule).

The highlight of the park, the **Boott Cotton Mills Museum** (daily 9.30am–5pm; $6), lies at the end of John Street, fifteen-minutes' walk north of the visitor center. A beautifully restored mill building dating from the 1830s, it's one of the most memorable sights in the state. Inside, you'll find a vast room of ninety whirring looms from the 1920s. Only seven run at one time, yet the noise produced is still deafening – it's hard to imagine what it would have been like to work here with all of them pounding away. Upstairs, a comprehensive history

On the trail of Jack Kerouac

Jack Kerouac, one of America's most influential modern authors, is best known for his seminal novel *On the Road* (1957), which established him as the father of the Beat Generation. Though much of his adult life was spent wandering the country, Kerouac was born in Lowell in 1922 (at 9 Lupine Rd); his parents were French-Canadian immigrants from Québec and he grew up in what was known as Little Canada (east of the city center), becoming a successful athlete at Lowell High School (still on Kirk St). The national historical park commemorates the city's most famous son with documentaries shown at the visitors' center (see p.149), and a few bits and pieces displayed at the Mill Girls exhibit (see below), including Jack's typewriter and backpack. Fans should also check out the **Jack Kerouac Commemorative**, a collection of stones and pillars inscribed with excerpts from his writings, west of Boott Mills in Kerouac Park, and Jack's simple **grave**, in the Sampas family plot at Edson Cemetery on Gorham Street, two miles south of the intersection with the Lowell Connector. Returning to Lowell in 1967, Jack wrote the last book published before his death, *Vanity of Duluoz*, and hung out at *Nicky's Bar* at 112 Gorham St (now a café). Finally, if you visit in the fall, check out **"Lowell Celebrates Kerouac!"** (℡1-877/KEROUAC, ⓦlckorg.tripod.com), a three-day festival of readings, exhibits, and special events.

of Lowell is laid out in chronological order, enhanced by video dramatizations, testimony of actual workers (the accidents section is especially sobering), and exhibits such as a spinning frame from 1839.

In addition to the revolutionary power loom, Francis Cabot Lowell also broke new ground with his employees: young women from New England farming communities, who became known as "mill girls." To get a deeper sense of what life was like for them, wander up the street to the Mogan Cultural Center and its poignant **Mills Girls & Immigrants Exhibit** (daily 1.30–5pm; free), a recreation of a mill boardinghouse for unmarried girls circa 1830. Though nineteenth-century life here was grim by modern standards, it was nonetheless an improvement on Britain's "dark satanic mills." Things got worse after the middle of the nineteenth century, when Irish immigrants began to replace the local girls, and were treated far more poorly.

Further east along Suffolk Street and the Northern Canal, **Wannalancit Mills** (end June–Aug daily 1–4.30pm; free) is home to the "River Transformed" exhibition, which showcases original nineteenth-century turbines and explains how the Merrimack River was used to power the whole city.

The industrial theme is continued at the **American Textile History Museum**, 491 Dutton St (Thurs & Fri 9am–4pm, Sat & Sun 10am–5pm; $8; ℡978/441-0400, ⓦwww.athm.org), south of the visitors' center. The museum was given a jazzy makeover in 2008, including a new permanent exhibit titled "Textile Revolution: An Exploration through Space and Time." Especially fun for kids, it highlights the history of textiles with interactive spinning, weaving, designing, and recycling displays.

Practicalities

Driving into Lowell from Boston is straightforward: take US-3 (N) to I-495 (N) and then the Lowell Connector; signs direct you to the visitors' center on Dutton Street, where you can **park** for free.

The city is best experienced as a day-trip, though there are a couple of reasonable business **hotels** on the outskirts; the best is the *Courtyard by Marriott*, 30 Industrial Ave, in East Lowell (℡978/458-7575; ⓞ). You'll find plenty of

places to eat near the museums downtown, with several restaurants and Irish pubs along Market Street opposite the visitors' center, and al fresco dining on nearby Palmer Street – *Fortunato's* at no. 44 (℡978/454-9800) is a smart Italian place serving sandwiches as well as all the usual favorites. The city has a sizeable Greek community, whose heritage is kept alive at *Athenian Corner*, 207 Market St (dinner daily, lunch Mon–Fri only; ℡978/458-7052), offering succulent baked lamb ($12) and stuffed grape leaves ($11), while ♣ *Urban Oasis Organic Café*, 194 Middle St (℡978/453-1311) is part café, part health store, with a huge range of herbal teas and tasty organic and vegetarian meals like "the Goddess," a blend of carrots, beets, broccoli, tofu, ginger sauce, and brown rice ($9). Set within a grand 1859 building, *Cobblestones*, 91 Dutton St (closed Sun; ℡978/970-2282) boasts a friendly bar and a menu of more traditional New England fare: plenty of seafood, grills, and wild game (in fall and winter).

The North Shore

The **North Shore**, which extends from Boston to the New Hampshire border, takes in some of Massachusetts' most disparate geography and culture. Outside the city a series of glum working-class suburbs – Revere, Saugus, Lynn – gradually yield to such bedroom communities as Swampscott and Beverly Farms, then to the charming waterfront town of **Marblehead** and nearby **Salem**, known for its infamous witch trials. Just north of here juts scenic **Cape Ann**, the so-called "other Cape"; with its lighthouses, seafood shanties, and rocky shores, it's a scaled-down version of the Maine coast. Highlights include the fishing port of **Gloucester** and the laid-back oceanfront village of **Rockport**. Further up the coast, the land flattens out a bit, with acres of salt marshes and some of the finest white sands in New England, particularly on **Plum Island** and near the sleepy villages of **Essex** and **Ipswich**. Closer to the New Hampshire border, the elegant old fishing burg **Newburyport** is of some historical interest, with scores of Federal mansions and a commercial district dating to the early 1800s. Any of these towns can be reached in an easy day-trip from Boston, and none should take more than a day to explore.

Marblehead

Just fifteen miles north of downtown Boston, affluent **MARBLEHEAD** sits on a peninsula thrusting out into Massachusetts Bay, its shoreline cliffs overlooking a wide natural harbor. This advantageous position has long been the town's greatest asset: founded by hardy fishermen from the English West Country in 1629, Marblehead quickly became a thriving **port**, especially in the years leading up to the Revolution. During the war, the Marblehead militia was commissioned to lease the first US warship, local schooner *Hannah*; four subsequent made-in-Marblehead vessels formed what would become the US Navy. Today boating, especially yachting, remains the lifeblood of the town, and Marblehead is at its most animated during the annual **Race Week** (the last week of July).

The Town

The streets that wind down to the Marblehead waterfront are lined with old clapboard houses, most of them quite modest with tiny gardens – a reminder that fishermen, not farmers, lived here in the Colonial period. A bit further back from the ocean, along **Washington Street**, are the larger homes of the merchants who prospered here before the Revolution. Among them is the 1768 **Jeremiah Lee Mansion** at no. 161 (June–Oct Tues–Sat 10am–4pm; $5; ☎781/631-1069), the Georgian home of the eponymous shipping magnate, who imported all his interior decorations, including English wallpaper and South American mahogany. In fact, Lee's wallpaper is the only eighteenth-century hand-painted paper in existence today. Nearby, at the early eighteenth-century **King Hooper Mansion**, 8 Hooper St (Tues–Sat noon–4pm, Sun 1–5pm; free; ☎781/631-2608, ⓦwww.marbleheadarts.org), you can contrast the slave quarters with the lavish ballroom, and see some local art as well. While in the area, stop by **Abbot Hall** on Washington Square (summer Mon, Tues & Thurs 8am–5pm, Wed 7.30am–7.30pm, Fri 8am–5pm, Sat 10am–5pm, Sun 11am–5pm; winter open weekdays only and Fri till 1pm; free; ☎781/631-0000), Marblehead's town hall, which houses Archibald Willard's famous painting *The Spirit of '76*.

To get a sweeping view of the port, head to the end of Front Street and **Fort Sewall**, the remnants of fortifications built by the British in 1644 and later enlarged to protect the harbor from French cruisers; these defenses also shielded the USS *Constitution* in the War of 1812. Closer to the center of town, but with similar views, is **Old Burial Hill** on Orne Street, the resting place of more than six hundred Revolutionary War soldiers.

Practicalities

The Chamber of Commerce maintains an **information booth** at the corner of Pleasant and Essex streets (late May to early Sept Mon–Fri 9am–5pm, Sat & Sun 10am–6pm; ☎781/639-8469) and an **office** at 62 Pleasant St (Mon–Fri 9am–5pm; ☎781/631-2868, ⓦwww.visitmarblehead.com). Of the places to **stay** in Marblehead, most of which are B&Bs, best is the central *Harbor Light Inn*, 58 Washington St (☎781/631-2186, ⓦwww.harborlightinn.com; ⑥–⑨); it's elegant, if a little stuffy, and has a heated outdoor pool in summer. More casual is the *Pheasant Hill B&B*, 71 Bubier Rd (☎781/639-4799, ⓦwww.pheasanthill .com; ⑦), with three private rooms with water views. It's not surprising that seafood headlines the town's **dining** options. Try *Flynnie's on the Avenue*, 28 Atlantic Ave (☎781/639-2100), for inexpensive fish and chips, or *Lime Rickey's* (☎781/631-6700), right on Devereux Beach towards the end of Ocean Avenue, for lobster rolls ($17) and fried clams ($18). Alternatively, *The Landing*, 81 Front St (☎781/639-1266), serves pricier seafood in a room with harbor views. You can also tuck into fresh lobster on an outdoor terrace at *The Barnacle*, 141 Front St (☎781/631-4246).

Salem

The witch trials of 1692 put **SALEM** on the map, and the coastal town, four miles north of Marblehead, has done little since to distance itself from its macabre history; indeed, most of its attractions focus on fairly kitsch witch-related activities. It's all a bit misleading, considering Salem was the site where the **Massachusetts Bay Colony** was first established – with the most elevated of intentions – and also for years an immensely prosperous port.

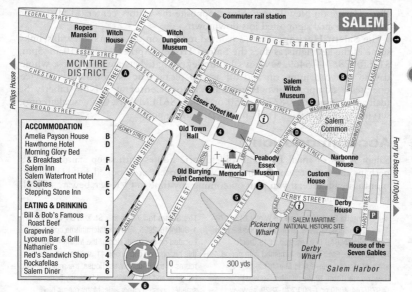

ACCOMMODATION

Amelia Payson House	B
Hawthorne Hotel	D
Morning Glory Bed & Breakfast	F
Salem Inn	A
Salem Waterfront Hotel & Suites	E
Stepping Stone Inn	C

EATING & DRINKING

Bill & Bob's Famous Roast Beef	1
Grapevine	5
Lyceum Bar & Grill	2
Nathaniel's	D
Red's Sandwich Shop	4
Rockafellas	3
Salem Diner	6

Some history

In 1626, a deep, well-protected harbor lured a handful of English settlers here, a place known by the local Massachusetts Indians as **Naumkeag**. In 1628 John Endecott arrived as the first governor of the Massachusetts Bay Colony, formally chartered the following year. When John Winthrop turned up with 1000 colonists in 1630, the focus of the colony moved south to Boston, but Salem grew steadily nonetheless. **Elias Derby**, said to be America's first millionaire, built his fortune by running privateers from the town during the Revolutionary War; afterwards, when British ports barred American vessels, he directed his ships to China and the East Indies.

Of the many goods on Salem's outbound ships, the most lucrative by far was **cod**, which found a huge market in Europe. Salem's "merchant princes" brought back everything from spices to olive oil to fine china, for a while monopolizing the luxury goods trade in the young country. But by the mid-1800s, the California Gold Rush, the Civil War, and the silting up of the harbor all conspired to rob Salem of its prosperity. Today the harbor is still home to hundreds of boats, though most are pleasure craft. Ironically, Salem's **witch heritage** (see box, p.155) has proved to be its ultimate salvation: were it not for the town center, which capitalizes on the trials, this once proud port might look as unsightly as many of its North Shore neighbors.

Arrival, information, and local transport

MBTA commuter **trains** run hourly (30min; $5.25 one-way) between Boston's **North Station** and Salem, and there's also a regular MBTA **bus** service (50min; $3.50) from Haymarket Square. A high-speed **ferry** ($9-12; ℡978/741-0220, Ⓦwww.salemferry.com), runs around every two hours from Central Wharf in Boston to Salem's Blaney Street Dock.

Traveling by **car** from Boston, Rte-1A is the most direct but congested choice; taking I-93, I-95, and Rte-128 is usually faster. You can **park** in the Museum

Place Garage on New Liberty Street, opposite the visitors' center ($1.50/hr), or in one of several signposted lots downtown.

The **Salem Heritage Trail**, a painted red line on the town's sidewalks, links some of the key sights, as does the **Salem Trolley** (April–Oct daily 10am–5pm; $12; ☎978/744-5469, ⓦwww.salemtrolley.com); tickets are valid for a whole day, so you can jump on and off as you please. The National Park Service operates a comprehensive **Regional Visitor Center** at 2 New Liberty St (daily 9am–5pm; ☎978/740-1650 or 1-877/SALEM-MA, ⓦwww.salem.org), serving as the Heritage Trail's unofficial starting point.

Accommodation

Salem is full of small **B&Bs** in old historic houses with steep staircases. It is perhaps the only town in America where **hotels** are booked for Halloween months in advance; if you plan on coming any time in October, beware of high prices and full houses.

Amelia Payson House 16 Winter St ☎978/744-8304, ⓦwww.ameliapaysonhouse.com. Small, friendly B&B in a restored 1845 Greek Revival home. Each room is furnished with period antiques. Closed mid-Nov to March. ⑥–⑦

Hawthorne Hotel 18 Washington Square W ☎978/744-4080 or 1-800/729-7829, ⓦwww.hawthornehotel.com. Right in the heart of things, this full-service hotel is a Salem landmark with reasonable prices and a respectable restaurant and pub. The owners also run the 1808 *Suzannah Flint House* on Essex St, with three beautifully renovated rooms. ⑤–⑨

Morning Glory Bed and Breakfast 22 Hardy St ☎978/741-1703, ⓦwww.morningglorybb.com. This three-room 1808 Federal townhouse down by the water (and the House of the Seven Gables) has a friendly owner, and a roof deck and porch with water views. ⑥–⑦

The Salem Inn 7 Summer St ☎978/741-0680 or 1-800/446-2995, ⓦwww.saleminnma.com. Located on the south side of the McIntire District, this historic inn comprises 41 well-maintained rooms in the Captain West House, the main central building, and the Curwen and Peabody houses, smaller ones on either side. Many rooms have working fireplaces. ⑥–⑨

Salem Waterfront Hotel and Suites 225 Derby St ☎978/740-8788, ⓦwww.salemwaterfronthotel.com. This brand-new Best Western branch adds 86 much-needed rooms to the center of town near the water. It's a standard large hotel – minimalist design, heated indoor pool – with prices to match. ⑧

The Stepping Stone Inn 19 Washington Square N ☎978/741-8900 or 1-800/338-3022, ⓦwww.thesteppingstoneinn.com. An unassuming B&B in an 1846 building across from Salem Common and next to the Witch Museum. Rooms are restored in gracious, nineteenth-century style. ④–⑥

The Town

You're never far from the Puritans' woeful legacy in Salem, with its plethora of tacky witch museums, exhibits, and memorials. Don't waste money on the storefront "museums" that line the streets; they're nothing more than glorified waxworks with spooky lighting and gift shops. The Witch House and Salem Witch Museum are better, though the town's real highlights – the Peabody Essex Museum and the old waterfront – focus on its maritime history.

Essex Street Mall and around

The **Essex Street Mall** – a car-free, boutique-filled stretch of Essex Street – is the closest thing Salem has to a main drag. At its northern end, the **Salem Witch Museum**, Washington Square North (daily: July–Aug 10am–7pm; Sept–June 10am–5pm; $8; ☎978/744-1692, ⓦwww.salemwitchmuseum.com), provides some entertaining, if kitschy, orientation on the witch trials. Though really just a sound-and-light show that uses wax figures to depict the events, it's still better than the other "museums" in town. In front of the house is an imposing statue of **Roger Conant**, founder of Salem's first Puritan settlement.

The hokey **Witch Dungeon Museum**, on the west side of town at 16 Lynde St (daily April–Nov 10am–5pm; $7; ☎978/741-3570, ⊛www.witchdungeon .com), occupies a nineteenth-century church situated on the site of the prison where the accused witches were held. Inside you're again treated to reconstructions of key events, though this time by real people. Afterwards the actors escort you to a re-created "dungeon," where you can see that some of the cells were no bigger than a telephone booth. If all this feels a bit too theatrical, head to the simple and moving **Witch Trials Memorial**, at Charter and Liberty streets, a series of stone blocks etched with the names of the hanged. The memorial is wedged into a corner of the **Old Burying Point Cemetery**, where one witch judge, **John Hathorne**, forebear of Salem's most famous son, Nathaniel Hawthorne, is buried. The author of *The Scarlet Letter* added a "w" to his name in an attempt to exorcise the shame.

The Salem witch trials

By their quantity alone, Salem's witch memorials speak of the magnitude of the hysteria that gripped the town for much of 1692 and 1693. The colony was already in turmoil, experiencing something of an identity crisis: Salem Village, slightly inland, was a struggling community of Calvinist farmers mired in land disputes and personality clashes, while Salem Town was an affluent port. Those caught up in the intrigue lived in Salem Village (which separated to form the town of Danvers in 1752), while the actual trials took place in Salem Town, known today simply as Salem.

The first casualties were the Village's young teenage girls, who reported as truth tales of the occult they had heard from **Tituba**, a West Indian slave woman. Their fun took a sinister turn when the daughter and niece of a clergyman, Samuel Parris, experienced convulsions and started barking. It's unknown if the cause of the fits was epilepsy or the adverse effects of eating moldy bread, but other girls began to copy them, and when the Village doctor failed to diagnose the problem, the accusations of witchcraft began to be taken seriously.

The trials that ensued pitted neighbor against neighbor, even husband against wife. "Confessing" to witchcraft spared you the gallows but meant castigation. Mary Lacy of Andover, for instance, reported that "me and Martha Carrier did both ride on a stick when we went to a witch meeting in Salem Village." Another accused, Giles Cory, first testified that his wife was a witch, then refused to accept the court's authority. To coerce him, he was staked on ground under planks while stones were pressed on top of him. He lasted two days, and died without confessing.

The trials were also marked by the girls' crazed ravings: in a scene re-enacted at the Witch Dungeon Museum (see above), Ann Putnam claimed that Sarah Good, a pipe-smoking beggar woman, was biting her, right in front of the judge. Such **"spectral evidence"** was accepted as fact, and the trials soon degenerated into the definitive case study of guilt by association. More than 150 villagers were accused and imprisoned (this in a village of 500), nineteen were hanged and four died in jail. Tituba, who readily confessed to sorcery, was not among them.

The most grisly day in Salem's history was **September 22, 1692**, when eight villagers were hanged. Though the hysteria continued for a while unabated, with another 21 people tried in January 1693, the court's legitimacy, shaky from the start, was starting to wear thin. Appalled by the sordid state of affairs, the new royal governor, **William Phipps**, intervened after his wife was accused, and forbade the use of spectral evidence as proof. All of the accused were acquitted that May, and families of the victims eventually awarded damages. The whole affair was immortalized in the 1950s by **Arthur Miller's** *The Crucible*, written at the height of the similarly paranoid McCarthy trials.

Peabody Essex Museum

The best sight in Salem is the newly renovated **Peabody Essex Museum**, at 161 Essex St (daily 10am–5pm; $15; ☎978/745-9500, ⓦwww.pem.org), the oldest continuously operating museum in the US. Its vast, modern space incorporates more than thirty galleries displaying art and artifacts from around the world that illustrate Salem's past importance as a trading point between East and West. Founded by ship captains in 1799 to exhibit the items they obtained while overseas, the museum also boasts the biggest collection of nautical paintings in the world. Other galleries hold Chinese and Japanese art; Asian, Oceanic, and African ethnological artifacts; American decorative arts; and, in a preserved house that the museum administers, documents from the witch trials. A creatively curated whaling exhibit features not only the requisite scrimshaw but also Ambrose Garneray's 1835 painting, *Attacking the Right Whale*, as well as the gaping lower jaw of a sperm whale. The museum's prize possession, however, is **Yin Yu Tang**, a sixteen-room Qing dynasty house that the museum purchased, dismantled, and rebuilt here. Admission is an additional $4, and you must reserve a time at the front desk to see it – advance reservations are recommended (online or at ☎877/736-8499).

Salem Maritime National Historic Site

Little of Salem's original waterfront remains, although the two-thousand-foot-long **Derby Wharf** is still standing, fronted by the imposing Federalist-style **Custom House**. These two, and ten other buildings, comprise the **Salem Maritime National Historic Site**, which maintains a **visitors' center** at 174 Derby St (daily 9am–5pm; ☎978/740-1650, ⓦwww.nps.gov/sama). The chief sights – Narbonne House, Derby House, Customs House, and the *Friendship* cargo vessel – can only be visited on daily one-hour tours ($5). Nathaniel Hawthorne worked as chief executive officer at the Custom House for three years, a stint which he later described as "slavery." The office-like interior is rather bland, as is the warehouse in the rear, with displays of tea chests and such. Millionaire Elias Derby received the nearby **Derby House** in 1762 as a wedding gift from his father; its position overlooking the harbor allowed him to monitor his shipping empire. The interior has been immaculately restored in all its eighteenth-century finery. At **Narbonne House**, one of the oldest houses here (dating from 1675), the rooms show how the building's structure changed over the years. The original East Indiaman *Friendship* was launched in 1797 and captured by the British in 1812; the impressive replica on the wharf was built by the Park Service and offers a fascinating insight into life at sea in the nineteenth century. Next to Derby House, the **West India Goods Store** emulates a nineteenth-century supply shop by peddling nautical accoutrements like fishhooks and ropes, as well as supplies like molasses candy and "gunpowder tea," a tightly rolled, high-grade Chinese green tea.

The House of the Seven Gables

The most famous sight in the waterfront area is undoubtedly the **House of the Seven Gables**, at 54 Turner St (daily: July–Oct 10am–7pm, Nov–June 10am–5pm, closed first half of Jan; $12; ☎978/744-0991, ⓦwww.7gables .org), a rambling mansion by the sea that served as inspiration for Hawthorne's eponymous novel. Standard tours of the 1668 house – the oldest surviving wooden mansion in New England – cover the building's history and architecture. The author's birthplace, the **Nathaniel Hawthorne House**, a small, nondescript circa 1750 structure, was moved here from Union Street in 1958.

The McIntire District

The witch attractions pick up again at the so-called **Witch House**, west of the Essex Mall at 310 Essex St (May to early Nov daily 10am–5pm; $8, guided tours $10; ℡978/744-0180, ⊛www.corwinhouse.org). The well-preserved former home of Judge Jonathan Corwin, this is where the preliminary examinations of the accused took place. This museum offers more history than most in town, with some real artifacts as well as reconstructed ones. It's also a good point of departure for exploring the **McIntire District**, a square mile of sea captains' homes west of downtown between Federal and Broad streets. The most picturesque stretch of these mansions, built after the Revolutionary War, is along **Chestnut Street**. Of these, the **Phillips House**, at no. 34 (June–Oct Tues–Sun 11am–4pm; Nov–May Sat & Sun 11am–4pm; $5; ℡978/744-0440, ⊛www.phillipsmuseum.org), is the only one open to the public, via half-hour tours. Built by Elias Derby's son-in-law in 1821, it's a welcome break from the supernatural, and worth seeing for its trove of bric-a-brac from around the world.

Eating and drinking

Salem has a decent range of places to **eat** and **drink**, though nothing too out of the ordinary. Most of the top seafood spots are situated near the harbor.

Bill & Bob's Famous Roast Beef 9 Bridge St (Rte-1A), just south of the Essex Bridge ℡978/744-9835. The North Shore has been famous for its hot roast beef sandwiches since the 1950s, and this local chain, a short drive north of the center, is the best place to try one ($4.25).

Grapevine 26 Congress St ℡978/745-9335. Top-notch restaurant with creative dishes like brook trout pasta, exceptional local cod, and great vegetarian options (entrees $21– 27).

Lyceum Bar and Grill 43 Church St ℡978/745-7665. Affordable Yankee cooking with modern updates. Try their fish chowder ($6.50), fresh oysters ($2.25), and good-value lunch plates (from $10).

Nathaniel's At the *Hawthorne Hotel*, 18 Washington Square ℡978/825-4311. One of two restaurants in the hotel, with an excellent Sunday jazz brunch ($29) and menu of solid grills and New England fare – live piano adds class in the evenings. Try the other hotel restaurant, the *Tavern*, for less expensive food.

Red's Sandwich Shop 15 Central St ℡978/745-3527. Hearty and downright cheap breakfasts and lunches served in the old London Coffee House (built in 1698); the hamburger special costs a mere $2.50. Probably the most popular tourist eatery in town. Mon–Sat closes at 3pm, Sun at 1pm.

Rockafellas 231 Essex St ℡978/745-2411. Standard, reasonably priced American fare, including pizza, ribs, large salads, and prize-winning clam chowder (entrees $11–26). The bar serves creative cocktails, and there's live music nearly every night.

Salem Diner 70 Loring Ave (Rte-1A), south of the center ℡978/741-7918. This historic diner in an original 1941 Sterling Streamliner car (one of only four remaining in the US) is a must-visit for road-trip aficionados. Try the Spanish omelet, meat loaf, or "American chop suey," all costing around $5.

Cape Ann and the north coast

Low-key **Cape Ann**, some forty miles north of Boston, draws plenty of visitors, mainly on account of its salty air and seafood restaurants. There aren't many sights per se, and the best thing about the place is its unspoiled scenery and rocky headlands. From I-95, Rte-128 (E) will take you all the way to **Gloucester**, then it's either Rte-127 or scenic Rte-127A to **Rockport**. Continuing north along the coast you come to **Essex**, notable for its fried clams, and the sleepy towns of **Ipswich** and **Newburyport**, both with compact historic districts worth exploring.

Gloucester

Founded in 1623, **GLOUCESTER** is the oldest fishing port in Massachusetts, though recent years of over-fishing in the Atlantic have robbed the town of any aura of affluence. Yet the fact that Gloucester remains one of the few genuine working towns on the coast is what makes it so appealing. The struggles of the town's near-legendary fishermen are at the center of Mark Kurlansky's gripping history, *The Last Fish Tale* (2008), while the movie *The Perfect Storm* (2000) followed the true-life tragedy of local swordfishing boat *Andrea Gail*. Gloucester also has an artistic identity, established by the painter **Winslow Homer**, who spent summers here in 1873 and 1880, and the bevy of artists who set up a colony on **Rocky Neck**.

Arrival and information

Gloucester is just over an hour by **commuter rail** from Boston's North Station ($7.25 one-way; ☎617/222-3200, ⓦwww.mbta.com); trains arrive about half a mile from the harbor. You'll find **parking** (free) in St Peter's Square, right on the harbor near the **Cape Ann Chamber of Commerce**, 30 Commercial St (Mon–Fri 9am–6pm, Sat 10am–6pm, Sun 10am–4pm; ☎978/283-1601, ⓦwww.capeannchamber.com), which dispenses local information and maps; there's also a **visitors' center** out of town near the beach at Stage Fort Park, Rte-127 (May to mid-Oct Mon–Wed & Sun 9.30am–5.30pm, Thurs–Sat 9am–6pm; ☎978/281-8865), which can give you a map detailing area **beaches**.

Accommodation

Only a handful of motels and B&Bs serve the area, but you'll rarely have trouble finding a room.

Cape Ann Motor Inn 33 Rockport Rd ☎978/281-2900, ⓦwww.capeannmotorinn.com. One of the better motels in the area, right on Long Beach. All rooms come with kitchenettes and stunning ocean views (try and get up for sunrise). Simple breakfast served on the outdoor deck. ➏

The Harborview Inn 71 Western Ave ☎978/283-2277 or 1-800/299-6696, ⓦwww.harborviewinn .com. This B&B is quiet, friendly, and minutes from all of Gloucester's attractions. Rooms are vividly decorated with a Victorian theme, most with harbor views. ➏–➑

Julietta House 84 Prospect St ☎978/281-2300, ⓦwww.juliettahouse.com. Another relatively tranquil option, offering simple but comfortable Georgian-style rooms decked out with antique beds and furnishings. ➏

The Town

Driving into town on Rte-127 you'll pass one of Gloucester's sources of pride, the 1923 bronze *Man at the Wheel* – it's an over-hyped statue of a fisherman at the wheel of a ship. Downtown Gloucester is dominated by its scruffy waterfront brightened somewhat by a handful of sights on the Harbor Loop, off Rogers Street. The **Gloucester Maritime Heritage Center** (mid-May to late Oct daily 10am–5pm; ☎978/281-0470; ⓦwww .gloucestermaritimecenter.org) is a worthy ongoing attempt to preserve the dock area, comprising a small outdoor aquarium and marine exhibits ($5), the main pier, boathouse, restored marine railway, gift shop (daily 10am–5pm), and quirky **Diving Locker Museum** (Mon–Wed & Fri–Sat 9.30am–5pm, Sun 1–5pm; free), with antique diving suits. Much of *The Perfect Storm* was filmed around here, though the real *Crow's Nest* bar is further up the road (see p.160). Nearby you'll also find the **Whale Center of New England** (see box opposite).

Whale-watching off Cape Ann

One of the most popular and exhilarating activities along this stretch of coast is **whale-watching**: trips depart from Gloucester, Salem, and Newburyport to the important whale feeding grounds of Stellwagen Bank and Jeffreys Ledge, where an abundance of plankton and small fish provide sufficient calories (around one million a day) to keep fifty-foot, 25-ton humpbacks happy. Most boats claim at least a 99 percent sighting record, though this does not necessarily mean that you're going to see a whale breaching just a few feet away – sometimes you may catch no more than a glimpse of a tail. Most companies also have a guarantee that if you don't see a whale you'll get a free pass to come back anytime.

The best place to begin is Gloucester, home to the **Whale Center of New England**, 24 Harbor Loop, with a **museum** (July–Sept daily 11am–7pm; Oct–June Mon–Fri 9am–5pm; free; ☎978/281-6351, ⓦwww.whalecenter.org) featuring a 28ft humpback whale skeleton. Gloucester whale-watching companies include the Yankee Fleet, 37 Commercial St (☎978/283-0313 or 1-800/WHALING, ⓦwww.yankeefleet.com); Captain Bill & Sons (☎978/283-6995 or 1-800/339-4253, ⓦwww.captbillandsons.com) in the Whale Center building; and Cape Ann Whale Watch, at Rose's Wharf (☎1-800/877-5110, ⓦwww.caww.com). During July and August, each company offers two daily trips (around $42; May–June & Sept–Oct just two a day Sat & Sun, and one a day Mon–Fri).

To learn a bit more about the town's past, walk into the center on Duncan and Pleasant streets to the **Cape Ann Historical Museum**, 27 Pleasant St (Tues–Sat 10am–5pm, Sun 1–4pm; $8; ☎978/283-0455, ⓦwww.capeannhistoricalmuseum .org), where the history of Gloucester and Cape Ann is well documented through photographs, fishing implements, and paintings by a variety of artists, including Winslow Homer. Across the road, **City Hall**, 9 Dale Ave (usually open Mon–Fri 8.30am–5pm), is worth a look for its sea-themed murals, and the roll of honor on the main staircase, where the names of town fishermen lost at sea are inscribed. Nearby **Middle Street** is home to Gloucester's oldest houses, including the **Sargent House Museum** at no. 49 (mid-May to late Oct Fri–Sun 11am–4pm; guided tours only, $7.50; ☎978/281-2432, ⓦwww.sargenthouse.com), built in 1782 for Judith Sargent Murray, an early feminist writer. The restored interior holds a fine collection of Chinese porcelain, Revere silver, period furniture, and artwork by John Singer Sargent.

Rocky Neck and Beauport

The **Rocky Neck Art Colony** (ⓦwww.rockyneckartcolony.org), a two-mile drive around the southern side of the harbor, was established in the 1850s, and its salt-box shacks have been attracting artists ever since. Stop in at the **North Shore Arts Association** on East Main St (May–Oct Mon–Sat 10am–5pm, Sun noon–5pm; ☎978/283-1857, ⓦwww.northshoreartsassoc.org) for information on the thirty or so galleries in the area, and then park (free) at the causeway on Rocky Neck Avenue before exploring on foot.

Keep driving down East Main Street to Eastern Point and **Beauport** (tours hourly: June to mid-Oct 10am–4pm; $10; ☎978/283-0800), a 45-room mansion perched on the rocks overlooking the harbor. Started in 1907 as a summer retreat for interior designer Henry Davis Sleeper, the house evolved over the following 27 years into an elaborate villa filled with European, American, and Asian objects. The tour, which meanders through all this, provides a fascinating view of the lifestyles of the early twentieth-century rich and famous.

Hammond Castle Museum

More unusual is the **Hammond Castle Museum**, 80 Hesperus Ave (off Rte-127), on the harbor's southwestern corner (May–Oct Tues–Sun 10am–4pm; $10; ☎978/283-2080, ⓦwww.hammondcastle.org). It was built in the 1920s by eccentric financier and inventor John Hays Hammond Jr, who wanted to bring medieval European relics back to the US. He succeeded: the austere fortress is brimming with them, from armor and tapestries to the elaborately carved wooden facade of a fifteenth-century French bakery – not to mention the partially crushed skull of one of Columbus's shipmates.

Eating and drinking

As you'd expect, Gloucester is an excellent place for **seafood**, with several unpretentious, venerable old restaurants and diners.

Captain Carlo's 27–29 Harbor Loop ☎978/283-6342. Wharfside institution where fresh lobsters, clams, haddock, swordfish, shrimp, and calamari feature prominently on the menu; the clam chowder ($6) is almost as good as the hype suggests. Live music most nights.

The Crow's Nest 334 Main St ☎978/281-2965. Long a fisherman's hangout, this bar featured heavily in *The Perfect Storm*, though it cashes in with T-shirts and caps, ordering a beer before lunch is more likely to endear you to the locals than mentioning the movie. Also offers accommodation for $65.

Elliott's at the Blackburn 2 Main St ☎978/282-1919. Cozy restaurant in the inn where Winslow Homer spent the summer of 1873. Decent steaks and grills accompany the ubiquitous seafood, and there's live music most nights. Dinner only, closed Mon.

Lobsta Land 10 Causeway St ☎978/281-0415. Exquisite shellfish (the eponymous lobster takes center stage) and a vast menu of beautifully cooked fish at one of the best restaurants on the North Shore. Take Exit 13 off Rte-128, and head north; Causeway St is the first right.

Madfish Grille 77 Rocky Neck Ave, Rocky Neck ☎978/281-4554. Another restaurant with stellar views of the harbor, and a menu of fresh salads,

burgers, and seafood such as clam chowder, lobster cakes, and grilled fish – the clam bake is exceptional. The bar features live music (rock, reggae, and blues) Thurs–Sun. Closed Nov–April.

Pleasant Street Tea Co 7 Pleasant St ☎978/283-3933. This alluring café is close to the museum and City Hall, with comfy couches, drapes, and a menu of refreshing teas, soups, and wholesome sandwiches. Free wi-fi.

Smokin' Jim's Bar-B-Q 121 E Main St ☎978/283-1055. It's worth making a trip out towards Rocky Neck to this popular roadside wood and charcoal grill with finger-licking Southern-style pulled pork, brisket, and smoked chicken – most orders are $8–10, while a full rack of ribs is $21. Closed Mon & Tues, and when it rains.

Studio Restaurant 51 Rocky Neck Ave, Rocky Neck ☎978/283-4123. Though this small seafood restaurant is a little touristy, it has a lovely deck right on the water, and tasty pastas ($14–21). Formerly the studio of artist Hugh Breckenridge. Closed Nov–April.

Virgilio's Bakery 29 Main St ☎978/283-5295. This tiny deli and bakery has been serving locals since 1961. A great place to stock up on fresh semolina loaves, Portuguese sweet-breads, and fat sandwiches such as the Italian-inspired "St Joseph" and veggie "Northeaster."

Rockport

Like Gloucester, the town of **ROCKPORT**, just five miles north, began as a fishing village. From early on, though, its picturesque harbor attracted summer vacationers and artists, and now the village of clapboard houses and fishing huts – many of them converted to shops, ice-cream stalls, galleries, bars, and clam shacks – feels a world away.

Works by contemporary local artists, some of them terribly kitsch, can be seen at the **Rockport Art Association**, 12 Main St (mid-May to mid-Oct Mon–Sat 10am–5pm, Sun noon–5pm; Oct–Dec & March to mid-May Tues–Fri 10am–4pm, Sat 10am–5pm, Sun noon–5pm; free; ☎978/546-6604, ⓦwww.rockportartassn .org). Main Street ends at a thin peninsula known as **Bearskin Neck**, a photogenic street of old fishermen's cottages. The neck rises as it reaches the sea, and there's a dazzling view of the harbor from its end. Though squarely aimed at tourists, it's still a beguiling place to hang out and grab a bite to eat.

Just north of Rockport on Rte-127 (turn left on Curtis St), everything inside the unique and aptly named **Paper House**, on Pigeon Hill St (daily April–Oct 9am–6pm; $1.50), is made of shellacked paper – even the desk fashioned from the *Christian Science Monitor*. It's the result of a project undertaken in 1922 by a local engineer who "always resented the daily waste of newspaper."

Practicalities

Rockport is the **last stop** on the Rockport Line from Boston's North Station ($7.75 one-way; T617/222-3200, Wwww.mbta.com). The town has plenty of **accommodation**, mostly in inns and B&Bs. The *Pleasant Street Inn*, at no. 17 (T978/546-3916 or 1-800/541-3915, Wwww.pleasantstreetinn.net; ⑤–⑥), is a gracious Victorian perched on a knoll overlooking the village; there's a carriage house with two bedrooms, and a newer cottage with three. The *Addison Choate Inn*, 49 Broadway (T978/546-7543 or 1-800/245-7543, Wwww.addisonchoateinn .com; ⑥–⑦), a Greek Revival house, has a lovely porch, homey rooms, and complimentary breakfast buffet. The *Bearskin Neck Motor Lodge* (T1-877/507-6272, Wwww.rockportusa.com/bearskin; ⑦) offers simple rooms at the best location in town: it's right at the end of the spit with most of the shops and restaurants.

Rockport's **restaurants** serve moderately priced fresh seafood; the added bonus of a waterfront view is often the only distinction between them. The simplest but most inviting is *Roy Moore Lobster Company*, a 1918 fish shack on Bearskin Neck (T978/546-6696) offering lobster by the pound, clam chowder ($4), stuffed clams ($1), fish cakes ($1.50), and a sunny back porch; you can have a sit-down meal at the related *Fish Shack Restaurant* (T978/546-6667) at nearby Dock Square. Farther down Bearskin Neck is the more upscale *My Place by the Sea* (T978/546-9667), with a stupendous waterfront setting to complement the delicate entrees. Sweet addicts should check out *Tuck's Candies* (T800/569-2767), 15 Main St, selling velvety chocolates since 1929.

Essex

The former shipbuilding town of **ESSEX**, seven miles northwest of Gloucester along Rte-133, is a major antiques center these days, but should be visited primarily for the splendid **Essex Shipbuilding Museum** at 66 Main St (June–Oct Wed–Sun 10am–5pm; Nov–May Sat & Sun 10am–5pm; $7; T978/768-7541, Wwww.essexshipbuildingmuseum.org), where more than four thousand ships have been constructed over the years, including schooners, steamers, and yachts. The museum traces their history through models, tools, and old photographs.

Practicalities

Among the few places to **stay** in these parts is the *George Fuller House*, 148 Main St (T978/768-7766 or 1-800/477-0148, Wwww.cape-ann.com /fuller-house; ⑤–⑦), a rambling old Federal home with attractive, air-conditioned rooms, some featuring views over the marshes, and a full breakfast. Essex is one of the best places to **eat** on the North Shore. *Woodman's*, 121 Main St (T978/768-6057), claims to be the first restaurant in America to serve fried clams (in 1916); order them before grabbing a table (fried plates from around $11). Less famous, but certainly no less good, is *J. T. Farnham's Seafood and Grill*, 88 Eastern Ave (Rte-133), just before the main village (T978/768-6643; closed Dec–March), with a similar line-up of fried clams, as well as lobster.

Ipswich

Little **IPSWICH**, five miles northwest of Essex, is worth a stop for its pretty historical district and the stunning **Crane's Beach**, four miles of enticing sands lining Ipswich Bay at the end of Argilla Road (daily 8am–sunset; ☎978/356-4354). There's a large parking lot that fills up during the summer (Mon–Fri $15 per car, Sat & Sun $22).

Ipswich's other claim to fame is that it has more pre-1725 houses than any other community in the country. Probably built in the 1670s, the **John Whipple House**, 1 South Village Green (May to mid-Oct Wed–Sat 10am–4pm, Sun 1–4pm; $5, $7 with John Heard House; ☎978/356-2811), was one of the nation's first homes to be restored – in 1898 – and is filled with a variety of antiques and Arthur Wesley Dow paintings; an outdoor herb garden contains some fifty varieties of medicinal plants. Admission includes entry to the nearby **John Heard House**, 54 S Main St (same hours as Whipple), an 1800 sea captain's home filled with Chinese and early American furnishings and a collection of carriages.

Practicalities

You can grab a local map at the **visitors' center**, 36 S Main St/Rte-1A (mid-May to late Oct Mon–Sat 9am–5pm, Sun noon–5pm), in the red Hall-Haskell House. One of the cheaper places to **stay** is the *Whittier Motel*, 120 County Rd/Rte-1A (☎978/356-5205 or 1-877/418-0622, ⓦwww.whittiermotel.com; ❺), an aging roadside inn close to the local attractions. The centrally located *Ipswich Inn*, 2 East St (☎978/356-2431, ⓦwww.ipswichinn.com; ❻) is much more appealing – a stately Victorian B&B with eight cozy rooms. For a treat, try the ⚞ *Inn at Castle Hill* (☎978/412-2555, ⓦinnatcastlehill.thetrustees.org; ❽), a beautiful house on the Crane Estate (two miles along Argilla Rd, just before the beach) that has been transformed into a B&B with ten spotless and TV-less rooms, each with its own character and some with water views.

▲ Crane's Beach

Ipswich is lauded for its clams, so you'd be remiss not to **eat** at the incredible 🔥 *Clam Box*, 246 High St (☎978/356-9707), which has been knocking out fried clams ($14) and various seafood since 1938; it's two miles north of town on Rte-1A. To try some of the North Shore's equally renowned hot beef sandwiches, make a stop at *Chick's Roast Beef*, 44 Central St/Rte-1A (☎978/356-5536), or for a more upscale meal visit *1640 Hart House*, 51 Linebrook Rd (☎978/356-1640), which offers chicken, pasta, and steak dishes. It's also north of town, off Rte-1A.

Newburyport and around

Just south of the New Hampshire border, **NEWBURYPORT** is Massachusetts' smallest city and one of its most rewarding, a pleasant mix of upscale boutiques and historic homes that still functions as a fishing port. Ironically, though, while Newburyport gives off a historical air, the **Market Square Historic District**, with its brick sidewalks, old lampposts, and upscale shops and eateries, is not quite as old as you'd think – a fire destroyed the area in 1811, and everything had to be rebuilt.

The **visitors' center**, 38 Merrimac St (Mon–Sat 10am–4pm, Sun noon–4pm; ☎978/462-6680) can help with local maps and information. To get a taste for the city, simply stroll the streets in the center of town, especially **State** and **High**; sample some incredibly fresh seafood; and watch the boats from the Waterfront Park and Promenade, which faces the Merrimack River. You're better off skipping the town museums in favor of milling about the eerie **Old Hill Burying Ground**, adjacent to the beautiful Bartlett Mall on High Street, where many Revolutionary War veterans and prominent sea captains are interred.

Plum Island

Plum Island, an eleven-mile barrier beach just south of Newburyport on Rte-1A, is mostly occupied by the remote **Parker River National Wildlife Refuge** (daily dawn–dusk; $5 per car, $2 walk-in; ⊛ www.fws.gov/northeast /parkerriver), a bird-watching sanctuary on the migratory route of a vast number of different species. In summer the refuge is populated by great blue herons, glossy ibises, and snowy egrets; the array is less impressive the rest of the year. Just outside the refuge, at the end of Fordham Way, there is a nice beach (free; parking $10). It gets better, and less developed, the further south you go.

Practicalities

If you don't have your own transport, Newburyport is accessible by MBTA **rail** from Boston's North Station (1hr 5min; $7.75 one-way); the train station is less than a mile from the center of town. Though Newburyport is really best for spending an afternoon or stopping over for dinner, there are a couple of good places to **stay**. Dating from 1803, the *Clark Currier Inn*, 45 Green St (☎978/465-8363 or 1-800/360-6582, ⊛ www.clarkcurrierinn.com; ❻), features antique-laden rooms with canopy beds, and plenty of common areas in which to relax, while *The Essex Street Inn*, 7 Essex St (☎978/465-3148, ⊛ www.essexstreetinn.com; ❺), is an attractive Colonial-style house right off the main drag with a wide choice of elegant rooms at a range of prices.

Two of the more reliable spots in town for a **meal** that won't break the bank are *Glenn's*, 44 Merrimac St (closed Mon; ☎978/465-3811), where you can savor big portions of grilled seafood, and *Agavé*, 50 State St (☎978/499-0428), an excellent Mexican bistro with both traditional and seafood-oriented dishes. On Plum Island, try the 🔥 *Plum Island Grille* on Sunset Blvd (dinner only; ☎978/463-2290), which serves upscale, fresh fish (entrees $22–34).

The South Shore

The **South Shore** makes a clean sweep of the Massachusetts coast from suburban **Quincy**, home of second president **John Adams**, to the former whaling port of **New Bedford**. **Plymouth** is the only really tourist-driven place along this stretch, on account of its **Pilgrim** associations; if you're not interested in reliving the coming of the *Mayflower*, the town, while pleasant enough, will probably not merit more than a few hours' exploration. **New Bedford** has fewer sights, one of which is a well-conceived whaling museum, but they all feel a bit more authentic.

Quincy

Though very much a part of Boston's urban sprawl, **QUINCY** nonetheless bills itself rather imperiously as the "City of Presidents" – it was the birthplace of **John Adams** and his son **John Quincy**, the second and sixth presidents of the United States. Traditionally one of the least popular founding fathers, the elder Adams drew new attention in 2008 thanks to an HBO mini-series, with the irascible politician finally receiving some of the credit that he believed he always deserved. The Adams sights here are well worth a visit for anyone interested in the family's role in early America.

The long Adams presence in town is preserved as the **Adams National Historic Site**, a collection of three buildings associated with the family until the 1940s, when the properties and everything inside them were donated to the National Park Service. The site can only be visited as part of an illuminating guided **tour** (2hr; $5; last tour 3.15pm); to get tickets stop by the **visitors' center**, 1250 Hancock St (mid-April to mid-Nov daily 9am–5pm; ☎617/770-1175, ⓦwww.nps.gov/adam), in the center of town (there's a parking garage behind it). A convenient **trolley bus** runs between the visitors' center and the tour's main sites.

First you'll be taken to the **John Adams Birthplace**, a creaky wooden frame salt-box built in 1681, and purchased by John Adams' father in 1720. Adams himself was born inside in 1735, and lived here until he married the indomitable Abigail in 1764, when he moved into the building next door, now the **John Quincy Adams Birthplace**. The sixth president was born in this house in 1767, and it was here that John Adams ran his law practice and wrote the state constitution – it was also here that Abigail composed her now-famous letters to her husband during his long wartime absences.

In 1788 the family moved across town to the farm of Peacefield, now known as the **Old House**. Incredibly, everything inside once belonged to the family, and most of it dates back to the time of John and Abigail. John Quincy inherited the house after his father's death in 1826, but his greatest legacy is the magnificent **Stone Library**, in the garden. Built in 1870 to house the over 14,000 volumes owned by the sixth president, it contains such precious tomes as the Bible presented to John Quincy by the *Amistad* Africans in 1841 – his defense of the group to the Supreme Court, during which he condemned the institution of slavery, was dramatized in the 1997 movie *Amistad*.

After the tour, pop into the **United First Parish Church** (Mon–Sat 9am–5pm, Sun 1–5pm; free), near the visitors' center, where both presidents are buried.

Practicalities

Quincy can be reached on the **T** red line from Boston (☎617/222-3200, Ⓦwww
.mbta.com). There's nowhere really to **stay** here besides a few large chain hotels
and motels which straddle the expressway to Boston. There are, however, some
decent places to **eat**: *Tullio's*, 150 Hancock St (☎617/471-3400), does delectable
pastas, while fiery Tex-Mex fare – including fresh salsa, plump burritos, and potent
margaritas – is available at *La Paloma*, 195 Newport Ave, just off Rte-3A north of
Quincy in Newport Center (closed Mon; ☎617/773-0512).

Plymouth

Nowhere are the origin myths of the United States more sharply exposed than
in **PLYMOUTH**, the first permanent settlement established by the English
Pilgrims in December 1620. Revered for centuries as "America's hometown"
(a designation that ignored several older English, French, and Spanish settlements), in actuality Plymouth was rapidly overshadowed by the Massachusetts
Bay Colony, and has remained a backwater since the 1650s. In recent decades,
the town has grappled with different perspectives of the Colonial period: in 1970
Native Americans established the "**National Day of Mourning**," challenging
the traditional **Thanksgiving** story, and today more attention is being paid
in museums to the area's indigenous inhabitants, the **Wampanoags**, than the
Pilgrims. Yet despite all this, the virtuous, hard-working Pilgrims retain an icy
grip on the American imagination – many still believe that it was here, in the
1620s, that America really got started.

Arrival and information

Plymouth & Brockton **buses** (☎508/746-0378, Ⓦwww.p-b.com) run from
Boston ($14), stopping at the Park and Ride lot at Exit 5 off Rte-3, where a
local shuttle runs into town and to Plimoth Plantation (May–Aug Fri–Sun; $2).
By car, aim for the waterfront; there's plenty of metered **parking** along Water
Street and near the **visitors' center**, 170 Water St (daily: summer 8am–8pm;
winter 9am–5pm; ☎508/747-7525, Ⓦwww.visit-plymouth.com), which stocks
plenty of local information.

Accommodation

By the Sea 22 Winslow St
☎508/830-9643 or 1-800/593-9688,
Ⓦwww.bytheseabedandbreakfast.com. One of the
better but less expensive options in town, this B&B
offers three spacious suites with private bath and
harbor views. ⑦–⑧
Governor Bradford 98 Water St ☎508/746-6200,
Ⓦwww.governorbradford.com. Standard, modern
hotel overlooking the water, with comfy but

uninspiring doubles and small complimentary
breakfast. ⑥
John Carver Inn 25 Summer St ☎508/746-7100
or 1-800/274-1620, Ⓦwww.johncarverinn.com.
The best accommodation in Plymouth, a modern
79-room inn with plush, beautifully finished rooms
and an indoor pool, close to the waterfront and all
the downtown attractions. ⑥

The Town

Plymouth is a fairly ordinary town, despite its origins. Its few attractions lie in the
center, along the waterfront, or in the historic district. The most famous of these
is **Plymouth Rock**, sheltered by a pseudo-Greek temple on the seashore where
the Pilgrims are said to have first touched land. It is really of symbolic importance

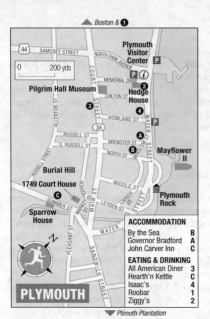

▲ Boston & ❶

Plymouth Visitor Center

Pilgrim Hall Museum

Hedge House

Mayflower II

Burial Hill

1749 Court House

Plymouth Rock

Sparrow House

PLYMOUTH

▼ Plimoth Plantation

ACCOMMODATION	
By the Sea	B
Governor Bradford	A
John Carver Inn	C

EATING & DRINKING	
All American Diner	3
Hearth'n Kettle	C
Isaac's	4
Roobar	1
Ziggy's	2

only: the rock was identified in 1741, and the Pilgrims had in fact already spent several weeks on Cape Cod before coming here. The **Pilgrim Hall Museum**, 75 Court St (Feb–Dec daily 9.30am–4.30pm; $7; ☎508/746-1620, ⊛www .pilgrimhall.org), offers a thoughtful and well-balanced introduction to the Pilgrim story, embellishing exhibits with paintings, displays, and artifacts that may have come over on the *Mayflower*.

For a sense of the town's post-Pilgrim past, visit the nearby 1809 **Hedge House**, 126 Water St (June–Aug Wed–Sun 2–6pm, $5; ☎508/746-0012), a Federal-style mansion built by sea captain William Hammatt. The beautifully restored rooms feature period furnishings, paintings, and objects from China obtained by its former merchant owners.

At the other end of Water Street, **Leyden Street**, the original main street of the Pilgrim settlement, runs from the waterfront into the historic district, though there's nothing left here from the seventeenth century. The oldest building in Plymouth is actually a short walk further up the hill: **Sparrow House**, 42 Summer St (April–Dec Thurs–Tues 10am–5pm; $2; ☎508/747-1240, ⊛www .sparrowhouse.com), built in the 1630s by Richard Sparrow, who arrived from England in 1633. The ground-floor gallery contains local pottery and crafts, while the upper rooms are decorated in the threadbare style of early settlers.

Mayflower II

The best sight in Plymouth is the replica of the *Mayflower*, called the **Mayflower II**, docked at the State Pier on Water Street (April–Nov daily 9am–5pm; $10, combo ticket with Plimoth Plantation $28; ☎508/746-1622, ⊛www.plimoth .org). Built in Britain by craftsmen who followed the detailed and historically accurate plans drawn up by a naval architect at MIT, the *Mayflower II* was given to America as a gesture of goodwill in 1957 (exhibits outline the tension in US–UK relations at the time). This version meticulously reproduces the brown hull and red strapwork that were typical of a seventeenth-century merchant vessel – which is what the original *Mayflower* was, before being outfitted for passengers prior to its horrendous 66-day journey across the Atlantic. Notice the hawthorn, or English mayflower, carved into the stern; whether the original ship was so adorned is unclear. On board, modern-day crew members and role-playing "interpreters" in period garb, meant to be representatives of the Pilgrim passengers, field questions. Below the main deck, you can have a look at the "tween decks" area, where the Pilgrims' cramped cabins would have been.

Plimoth Plantation

Similar in approach and authenticity is the **Plimoth Plantation**, three miles south of town off Rte-3 (April–Nov daily 9am–5pm; $24, combo ticket with

Mayflower II $28; ☎508/746-1622, 🌐www.plimoth.org). An introductory film and exhibitions at the **visitors' center** offer an insight into the early Colonial period, beginning with the culture of the Wampanoag people; the genesis of Thanksgiving is also examined in detail.

Beyond here, a recreation of "Plimoth" circa 1627, as well as a Wampanoag settlement, have been built using traditional techniques. At the English village, visitors are expected to participate in a charade – you're to pretend to have stepped back into the seventeenth century – which can be a bit tiresome, but the sheer depth of detail ultimately wins you over. Exchanges in the Wampanoag village are less structured, with the Native American staff wearing traditional clothes (but not role-playing), keen to chat about native customs.

Other attractions include the **Crafts Center**, where artisans not only weave baskets (historically accurate), but also make pottery and ceramics (not accurate – the Pilgrims imported that stuff from England), and the **Nye Barn**, where the plantation's rare-breed livestock program is introduced.

Eating and drinking

All American Diner 60 Court St ☎508/747-4763. Great choice for breakfasts and standard diner fare, open daily till 2pm.

Hearth 'n Kettle At the *John Carver Inn*, 25 Summer St ☎508/746-710. Smart local chain, and a safe bet for well-priced New England specialties like Cape scrod (white fish), seafood cakes, and lobster pie (entrees $15–20).

Isaac's Restaurant 114 Water St ☎508/830-0001. Locals moan that standards have fallen somewhat at this classy, romantic joint, but it remains a great choice for ocean views and a time-tested menu of seafood, steaks, and pastas.

🏃 **Roobar** 10 Cordage Park ☎508/746-4300. Not only is this Cape Cod chain one of the best places for wood-fired pizzas in the region, but its stylish, funky interior and popular bar also make it a great place for a drink – try the tangy martinis. It's just off Rte-3A, north of the center.

Ziggy's 120 Water St ☎508/746-5411. No-frills waterfront shack selling cheap but tasty ice cream, shakes, and fast food.

New Bedford and around

Though **NEW BEDFORD** is still a working-class city – the former whaling port, 45 miles south of Boston, remains home to one of the nation's largest fishing fleets – efforts at restoration have heightened the place's aesthetic appeal. The mercantile buildings, nineteenth-century houses, and cobblestone streets in the city center now more clearly conjure up the setting that inspired Herman Melville to set the early pages of *Moby Dick* here.

Much of the downtown area is preserved within the **New Bedford Whaling National Historic Park**, a collection of old buildings, art galleries, and antique stores, the centerpiece of which is the impressive **visitors' center**, 33 Williams St (daily 9am–5pm; ☎508/996-4095). Here films and displays recount the history of the town; the emphasis is squarely on the achievements of whaling as a commercial enterprise in the eighteenth and nineteenth centuries, but other aspects of local history are also highlighted – the Underground Railroad went through here, with **Frederick Douglass** as its biggest success – and you can grab maps of nearby **mansions**, remnants of the town's whale-derived wealth.

Just around the corner, the main attraction in town is the **New Bedford Whaling Museum**, 18 Johnny Cake Hill (daily 9am–5pm, every second Thurs of the month open to 9pm; $10; 🌐www.whalingmuseum.org), housed in a former church. This remarkable museum features the world's largest ship model and a half-scale version of the whaling vessel *Lagoda*, as well as scrimshaw, harpoons, international artifacts retrieved by whalers, and a full-size replica of a ship's forecastle. A smaller section of the museum holds the roster of the whaling ship *Acushnet*, which shows Melville as one of its crew. There's also a modern building that houses the 66-foot skeleton of a juvenile blue whale accidentally struck and killed by a tanker in 1998, and a sperm whale skeleton, which washed ashore in Nantucket in 2002.

Immediately opposite the museum stands the **Seamen's Bethel**, the "Whale-man's Chapel" built in 1832 and described in *Moby Dick* (mid-May to late Oct Mon–Fri 10am–4pm; free; ℡508/992-3295). It features a rather small replica of the ship-shaped pulpit described in Melville's book. More evocative are the memorials to those who died at sea lining the walls.

You can also take a look inside one of the town's historic mansions, the Greek Revival **Rotch-Jones-Duff House & Garden Museum**, 396 County St (Mon–Sat 10am–4pm, Sun noon–4pm; $5; ⓦwww.rjdmuseum.org). Built by a Quaker whaling captain in 1834, it retains many of its original decorations and furnishings, including decadent marble fireplace mantles and oriental rugs. The formal gardens, laid out in their original style, with boxwood hedges, roses, and wildflowers, occupy an entire city block.

Practicalities

If you want to **stay** in New Bedford, *Melville House* is an atmospheric B&B at 100 Madison St (℡508/990-1566, ⓦwww.melvillehouse.net; ⑥); it was the home of Melville's sister. Across the street from the visitors' center, *Freestone's*, 41 Williams St (℡508/993-7477), serves excellent chowder and microbrews in a restored 1877 bank. If you're looking for local flavor, try the authentic Portuguese dishes at *Antonio's*, 267 Coggeshall St (℡508/990-3636). Finally, ⚔ *Café Balena*, 24 N Water St (closed Mon–Tues; ℡508/990-0061), offers top-notch Italian classics, enhanced by the highly gifted singing wait staff.

Cuttyhunk Island

If you're really desperate to get away from the crowds, take a one-hour boat trip from 66B State Pier in New Bedford out to minuscule **Cuttyhunk Island**, an entirely uncommercial isle with beaches lined with wildflowers. Two of the best are **Channel Beach**, just a short walk from the ferry dock, and **Church's Beach**, on the other side of the island, ideal for swimming. The outermost of the **Elizabeth Islands**, which stretch for sixteen miles from Buzzards Bay, Cuttyhunk was the site of one of the first English settlements in the northeast: a 22-day sojourn in 1602 which resulted in the building of a stockade and the planting of a medicinal garden. A small stone tower on an island in **Gosnold Pond**, at Cuttyhunk's western end, honors the event.

Get here via the Cuttyhunk Ferry Company, which runs to the island and back at least once daily (usually 9am and 4pm, call for exact times; same-day round-trip $40; ℡508/992-1432, ⓦwww.cuttyhunkferryco.com). **Bicycles** – which you can rent in New Bedford at Yesteryear Cyclery, 330 Hathaway Rd (closed Sun; $18 per day; ℡508/993-2525, ⓦwww.yesteryearcyclery.com), and take over on the ferry (extra $5) – are the best way to get around the tiny island. There are only a couple of **restaurants** here, so you're best off bringing your own lunch. A few commercial establishments – gift shops and markets – are located at **Four Corners**, the island's hub. If you want to **stay** the night, the *Cuttyhunk Fishing Club*, close to where the ferry lets off (℡508/992-5585, ⓦwww.cuttyhunkfishingclub.com; ⑦; closed in winter), is an inn with clean and comfortable rooms in an idyllic setting.

Fall River

The fate of **FALL RIVER**, a glum fishing and industrial town about fifteen miles west of New Bedford, will forever be linked to the trial of **Lizzie Borden**, who was accused (and later acquitted) of the ax murders of her father and stepmother in 1892. The town plays up the associations: the **Fall River Historical Society**, 451 Rock St (April to mid-Nov Tues–Fri 9am–4.30pm; June–Sept weekends also 1–5pm; tours on the hour; $6; ☎508/679-1071, ⓦwww.lizzieborden.org), contains exhibits of the affair, including photographs of the Borden family, as well as information about the city. There's also a **museum** at the **Lizzie Borden B&B**, 92 Second St (tours daily on the hour 11am–3pm; $12.50; ☎508/675-7333), where the deeds were done.

More impressive than the remnants of the trial is **Battleship Cove**, accessible from I-195 Exit 5 at the Braga Bridge (daily: end June to Aug 9am–5pm; Sept–June 9am–4.30pm; $14; ⓦwww.battleshipcove.org), the site of an impressive assemblage of World War II naval craft. The USS *Massachusetts*, or "Big Mammie," as she was known to the troops, is enormous, with bunks under the deck stacking five high. Visitors are really given the run of the ship, a welcome change from tours of historic houses, and more fun for children. Of the other boats on hand, the submarine USS *Lionfish* is also worth seeing.

Practicalities

Fall River's Chamber of Commerce provides **tourist information** at 200 Pocasset St (Mon–Fri 10am–4pm; ☎508/676-8226, ⓦwww.fallriverchamber .com), but a safer bet (if you're driving) might be the **Massachusetts Gateway Tourist Information Center** (daily 9am–5pm, Sat & Sun May–Oct to 8pm; ☎508/675-5515, ⓦwww.bristol-county.org), between exits 2 and 3 on I-195 eastbound in neighboring Swansea.

One of the few places to **stay** in Fall River is the campily spooky *Lizzie Borden B&B*, 92 Second St (☎508/675-7333, ⓦwww.lizzie-borden.com; ❼). Macabre as it sounds, you can stay in the rooms where Lizzie's parents were found, savor the kind of breakfast they ate the day they were murdered, and load up on memorabilia in the gift shop.

Fall River is home to a large Portuguese population, a fact reflected in its proliferation of Portuguese **restaurants**. The best of these is *Sagres*, 181 Columbia St (☎508/675-7018), a casual, well-priced place with a good wine list and live Fado music on Friday and Saturday nights at 8pm. The International Institute of Culinary Arts is in town as well, and good upscale food can be found at their restaurant *Giorgio's The Steak House*, 30 Third St (☎508/672-8242; dinner only, closed Sun & Mon).

Cape Cod and the islands

One of the most celebrated slices of real estate in America, **Cape Cod** boasts a consistently stunning quality of light and some of the best beaches in New England. The slender, crooked Cape gives Massachusetts an extra three hundred miles of coastline, though access to much of this is prevented by shore-hugging summer houses. Those parts of the Cape that haven't fallen prey to overdevelopment have been preserved as the snug villages they were a hundred or more years ago. Only **Provincetown**, at the Cape's very tip, successfully manages to mesh the past with the present; its unique art galleries, shops, and restaurants make it far and away the destination of choice. It's also perched on the best stretch of the **Cape Cod National Seashore**, so there's no need to go elsewhere, though tiny upscale towns like **Sandwich**, **Brewster**, and **Chatham** make for scenic stops along the way. In recent years local chambers of commerce have been trying to lure tourists in the off season by touting the region's "historical attractions," but for most the beaches still reign supreme.

Just off the south coast of Cape Cod, the islands of **Martha's Vineyard** and **Nantucket** have long been some of the most popular and prestigious vacation destinations in the US. Both mingle an easy-going cosmopolitan atmosphere with ornate mansions and museums harking back to the golden age of whaling. Be prepared for crowds in the summer, when day-trippers swamp both places, especially on weekends.

Some history

Martha's Vineyard and the Cape received their English designations in 1602, when explorer **Bartholomew Gosnold** visited the area; he named the island after his daughter, while the arm's moniker was inspired by the profusion of white fish in local waters. The Royalist presence in the area remained strong through the Revolutionary War; indeed, during the conflict many residents sided with the Crown. By the early 1800s, **whaling** had become the Cape's primary industry, with the towns of the Outer Cape doing particularly well; fishing and agricultural ventures, including the harvesting of **cranberries**, were also lucrative.

Cape Cod's rise as a **tourist destination** is mainly attributable to the development of the railroad in the nineteenth century (Provincetown was connected to Boston by rail in 1873). Wealthy Bostonians and New Yorkers were, for the first time, able to get to the Cape with relative ease, and many purchased land to build summer homes. Today, the Cape's population more than doubles in the summer, when more than 80,000 cars a day cross the **Cape Cod Canal**.

For the foreseeable future, however, nature will be the real arbiter of the Cape's fate. Without the rocky backbone of other parts of the coast, the land is particularly vulnerable to **erosion**: between Wellfleet and Provincetown the

---

The Cape Cod Canal

Between 1909 and 1914 a **canal** was dug across the westernmost portion of Cape Cod, effectively making the Cape an island. Initial work began in 1880, under the auspices of the Cape Cod Canal Company. In 1899 New York businessman Augustus Belmont took over the project; ten years later, state-of-the-art earth-moving equipment was introduced, and the canal was finally completed in 1914, though it was too shallow and narrow to allow anything but one-way traffic. In 1928 the federal government purchased the waterway, and enlarged it as a WPA project during the Great Depression. By 1940 the canal was the widest in the world. Take a closer look on a **boat trip** with Hy-Line Cruises (June–Oct; $14–20; ☏ 508/295-3883, ⓦ www.hy-linecruises.com), which runs a variety of trips ranging from straightforward tours to jazz outings from Onset Town Pier off routes 6 and 28. You don't have to be on the water to enjoy it, though; the views of the canal from the **Sagamore** and **Bourne bridges** are some of the dramatic on the East Coast. There is also a bike trail on either side of the waterway.

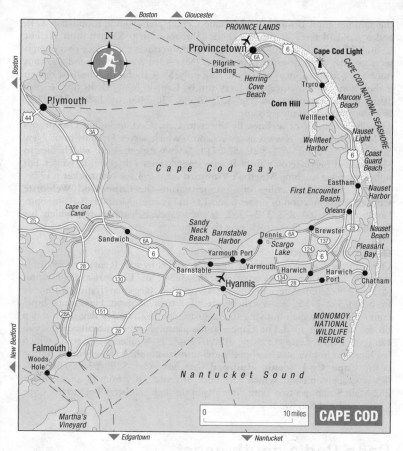

land is scarcely one mile wide, and narrowing all the time. The one benefit of the environmental situation is that it keeps development in check, especially in the vicinity of the protected **National Seashore**.

Arrival and information

The most direct way to reach the Cape is by **car**. On a fairly quiet day it takes under two hours to get from downtown Boston to the Sagamore Bridge via Rte-3, but expect this to double on summer weekends and holidays. Beyond the Cape Cod Canal, which marks the start of the Cape near the town of Sandwich, Rte-6 is particularly congested throughout the summer; it's also remarkably dull. If you're heading directly to Falmouth, note that it's faster to aim for the Bourne Bridge, three miles south of Sagamore, and take Rte-28.

Peter Pan Bus Lines subsidiary Bonanza (℡888/751-8800, ⓦwww.peterpanbus .com) operates **buses** from Boston (one-way $26) and New York (one-way $73) to Woods Hole and Falmouth, while Plymouth & Brockton (℡508/746-0378, ⓦwww.p-b.com) has a more complete set of Cape destinations (one-way Boston to Hyannis $19, to Provincetown $29).

You can also take **ferries** to **Provincetown**: Bay State Cruise Company (℡617/748-1428, ⓦwww.baystatecruisecompany.com) runs a daily fast ferry in the summer from Boston's World Trade Center pier (90min; round-trip $71), and a standard ferry at the weekends (3hr; round-trip $33); Boston Harbor Cruises (☎617/227-4320, ⓦwww.bostonharborcruises.com), does two express services a day from Boston's Long Wharf (May–Oct; 90min; $71), and also runs once a day from Gloucester (July & Aug only; $80). By far the cheapest option is the Plymouth–Provincetown ferry, run by Captain John's Boats (July & Aug 10am daily; 90min; round-trip $37; ☎508/746-2400 or 1-800/242-2469, ⓦwww.provincetownferry.com).

Finally, a number of **airlines** fly direct to Cape Cod, including US Airways (☎1-800/428-4322, ⓦwww.usairways.com), which serves Hyannis from New York, and Cape Air (☎1-800/352-0714, ⓦwww.capeair.com), which flies to Hyannis and Provincetown from Boston several times a day, even in winter. For information on reaching **Martha's Vineyard** see p.194, for **Nantucket** p.177.

The Cape Cod Chamber of Commerce runs the **Cape Cod Welcome Center**, at the junction of routes 6 and 132 in Hyannis (Mon–Fri 8.30am–5pm, Sat 9am–5pm; ☎1-888/332-2732, ⓦwww.capecodchamber.org), which has information about all the towns on the Cape.

Getting around

Once on the Cape, the best way to get around is by **car**. Rentals are available through Thrifty, in Orleans (☎508/255-2234), or Enterprise, in Hyannis (☎508/778-2205). Alternatively, the Cape Cod Regional Transit Authority (☎1-800/352-7155, ⓦwww.thebreeze.info) runs frequent Flex route buses connecting the Cape's outlying towns (6am–8pm; $2); simply flag them down on the side of the road. The Cape also has plentiful and scenic **bike** paths; you can rent at Bike Zone ($20/day; ☎508/775-3299, ⓦbikezoneinc.com), which has locations in Hyannis, Mashpee, and South Yarmouth. A more touristy option is the **Cape Cod Scenic Railroad** (late May–Oct; $20; ☎508/771-3800, ⓦwww.capetrain.com), which runs once or twice a day from Hyannis Depot, 252 Main St, along a two-hour circuit west through cranberry bogs to the Cape Cod Canal and Sandwich.

Cape Cod's south coast

From the Bourne Bridge, **Rte-28** runs south to Falmouth then hugs the Nantucket Sound until it merges with routes 6 and 6A in Orleans. This is certainly not the most attractive or scenic route on the Cape: much of it is lined with motels and strip malls, and it can get seriously clogged with traffic during the summer. Nonetheless, it runs through a number of important hubs along the south coast, notably **Falmouth** and **Hyannis**, and at its end is the handsome town of **Chatham** and the blissfully quiet **Monomoy National Wildlife Refuge**.

Falmouth

Boasting more coastline than any other Cape Cod town, **FALMOUTH** has no fewer than fourteen harbors among its eight villages. At the center of these is **Falmouth Village**, with a prim central green surrounded by Colonial, Federal, and Greek Revival homes. Typical of New England, a number of these old sea captains' houses are now B&Bs, and are complemented by a touristy mix of T-shirt shops, ice-cream parlors, and real estate offices.

The Falmouth Historical Society runs the only real attractions in town, the **Museums on the Green** at 55 Palmer Ave, at the western end of Main Street (mid–June to mid–Oct Tues–Fri 10am–4pm, Sat 10am–1pm; $5; ☎508/548-4857, ⓦwww.falmouthhistoricalsociety.org). Get oriented at the small visitors' center in **Hallett Barn**, which provides an introduction to the site, essentially two eighteenth-century houses crammed with period furniture, art, and displays on town history. The oldest, the 1760s **Conant House**, also has a room dedicated to local girl **Katherine Lee Bates**, who composed the song *America the Beautiful*; she was born in 1859 at 16 Main St. The 1790 **Julia Wood House** next door was a doctor's home; one room is set up as a clinic, with a horrifying display of primitive dental utensils. The adjacent Colonial-style flower garden, herb garden, and Memorial Park are pleasant places to stroll or picnic (open year-round; free).

Information

The Falmouth bus depot occupies the old train station on Depot Avenue, at the western end of Main Street, around 1.5 miles from the harbor and ferry to Martha's Vineyard (see p.194); you'll find the latter clearly signposted at the eastern end of Main Street. The **Falmouth Chamber of Commerce**, 20 Academy Lane, Rte-28 (June–Aug Mon–Fri 8.30am–5pm, Sat 10am–4pm; Sept–May Mon–Fri 8.30am–5pm, Sat 9.30am–5pm; ☎508/548-8500, ⓦwww.falmouthchamber.com) runs a useful **visitors' center** just off Main Street; they also have maps covering the four-mile **Shining Sea Bikeway**, which leads to Woods Hole.

Accommodation

Falmouth has some lovely **accommodation** options that make it a good base for exploring the Cape and catching the **ferry** to Martha's Vineyard.

Beach Breeze Inn 321 Shore St ☎508/548-1765, ⓦwww.beachbreezeinn.com. This 1858 Victorian offers heaps of character, arresting views, beautiful grounds, and clean rooms, just 100 yards from Surf Drive Beach. ❽–❾

Beach Rose Inn 17 Chase Rd, West Falmouth, off Rte-28A ☎508/540-5706 or 1-800/498-5706, ⓦwww.thebeachroseinn.com. Superb B&B dating from the 1860s, in a tranquil setting. The exquisite breakfast is served on a lovely outdoor deck. Also has a massage room and free wi-fi. ❽–❾

Cape Wind Waterfront Resort 34 Maravista Ave Extension ☎508/548-3400 or 1-800/267-3401, ⓦwww.capewind.com. Perfect for families, this waterfront resort has well-equipped cottages steps away from the Great Pond inlet and a host of free attractions, including a great pool, paddleboats, and even bocce. ❽

Inn on the Sound 313 Grand Ave ☎508/548-3786 or 1-800/682-0565, ⓦwww.innonthesound.com. A stunning location (45ft above the bay), mesmerizing views, and gourmet food make this posh B&B a real treat; luxury linens and a well-stocked library mean you may not want to venture out at all. ❽

Mostly Hall 27 Main St ☎508/548-3786 or 1-800/682-0565, ⓦwww.mostlyhall.com. This amiably run 1849 mansion has queen-sized canopy beds in each of its six rooms. ❻–❾

Eating and drinking

Betsy's Diner 457 Main St ☎508/540-0060. An authentic 1950s diner serving no-nonsense fare and beckoning you to "Eat Heavy." Closes at 2pm Sun.

Chapaquiot Grill 410 Rte-28A, West Falmouth ☎508/540-7794. Popular roadside restaurant serving wood-fired pizzas and grilled fish from $13.

The Clam Shack 227 Clinton Ave ☎508/540-7758. A local institution. Enjoy heaping plates of fried seafood (including the eponymous clams, of course) on outside picnic tables or the smashing rooftop deck with prime waterfront views. Closed early Sept–late May.

Liam Maguire's Irish Pub 273 Main St ☎508/540-0060, ⓦwww.liammaguire.com. The best place in town for a drink; it's not a great place to eat, but if you stick to basics like bangers and mash or corned beef and cabbage you can't go wrong. There's live Irish folk music most nights.

Woods Hole

The salty drop of a town that is **WOODS HOLE** owes its name to the water passage, or "hole," between Penzance Point and Nonamesset Island, linking Vineyard Sound and Buzzards Bay. Most people come here for the ferry to Martha's Vineyard (see p.194), and it's little more than a clump of casual restaurants and convenience stores clustered around the harbor. Nearby you'll find the **Woods Hole Oceanographic Institute**, 15 School St (May–Oct Mon–Sat 10am–4.30pm; Nov–Dec Tues–Fri 10am–4.30pm; $2; ☏508/457-2034, ⓦwww .whoi.edu), which houses an exhibit on the 1986 rediscovery of the *Titanic*, a project the institute spearheaded, and some neat submarine capsules that children will enjoy. In July and August the Institute offers twice-daily **tours** (Mon–Fri 10.30am & 1.30pm; reserve in advance) of their otherwise off-limits research labs. Also worthwhile are the informative, hands-on cruises run from the harbor by **OceanQuest**: lobster and scallop traps are pulled up for inspection, and those on board can handle the marine life (July–Aug Mon–Fri 10am, noon, 2pm & 4pm, Sat noon & 2pm; $22; ☏1-800/37-OCEAN, ⓦwww.oceanquestonline.org).

Back on land, examples of the marine life that lurks off the Cape's shores are kept behind glass at the National Marine Fisheries Service, at the corner of Albatross and Water streets (June–Aug Tues–Sat 11am–4pm, Sept–May Mon–Fri 11am–4pm; free; ☏508/495-2001, ⓦwww.nefsc.noaa.gov), which maintains America's oldest **aquarium**. The displays are mostly limited to cod, lobster, and other piscine creatures that are more appealing on a plate; the main exception, the seals, give visitors a thrill at feeding time (daily 11am & 4pm). Note that adults need picture ID to enter the aquarium.

Practicalities

Buses arriving in Woods Hole drop off at the ferry terminal, which also has plenty of parking ($8–12). The best place to stay around here is *Woods Hole Passage*, 186 Woods Hole Rd (☏508/548-9575, ⓦwww.woodsholepassage.com; ❻–❽), with brightly painted bedrooms in a red-shingled carriage house set in spacious grounds. For a bite to eat, try *Fishmonger's Café*, 56 Water St (☏508/540-5376), a laid-back natural-foods eatery with a number of vegetarian dishes in addition to seafood standards.

▲ Woods Hole Oceanographic Institute

Hyannis

One of the Cape's biggest and liveliest towns, **HYANNIS** is mainly visited for its transportation links (the ferry to Nantucket; see box, p.177) and commercial options. There's little in the way of sights, though there are some pleasant public beaches, quaint B&Bs, and plenty of places to eat and drink, especially in summer. The little glamour the town can claim derives from the **Kennedy Compound**, the family's summer home in **Hyannisport**, a private, upscale residential section of town a couple of miles southwest of Hyannis proper. It's best glimpsed, if you must, from the water: Hy-Line Cruises, at the Ocean Street Docks, runs cruises that pass by (April to late Oct; $15.50; ☎1-800/492-8082, Ⓦwww.hy-linecruises.com).

If it's the Kennedy legacy you've come to see, probably the best place to start is the **John F. Kennedy Hyannis Museum**, 397 Main St (mid-April to mid-May Mon–Sat 10am–4pm, Sun noon–4pm; mid-May to late Oct Mon–Sat 9am–5pm, Sun noon–5pm; Nov, Dec & mid-Feb to mid-April Thurs–Sat 10am–4pm, Sun noon–4pm; $5; ☎508/790-3077, Ⓦwww.jfkhyannismuseum.org), which displays the expected nostalgia, mainly in the form of black-and-white photographs. It's not a comprehensive history, focusing instead on Kennedy's relationship with Cape Cod. For a non-presidential diversion, take a self-guided tour of the **Cape Cod Potato Chip Factory**, on Breed's Hill Road (Mon–Fri 9am–5pm; free; ☎508/775-7253, Ⓦwww.capecodchips.com). The tasty chips, once a local phenomenon but now found almost everywhere, are hand-cooked in kettles; you only get to peer in on the chip-making process, but there are delicious free samples. You'll find the factory off Independence Drive, which leads north from Rte-132 just outside town.

Arrival and information

Hyannis is only twenty miles east of Falmouth along Rte-28, but is approached much faster from Boston via the north side of the Cape and Rte-6. Rte-132 into town is often heavily congested in summer. The **ferry terminals** lie around the main harbor, at the eastern end of Main Street (see p.177). **Buses** arrive at the Hyannis Transportation Center, at the intersection of Main and Center streets, around fifteen-minutes' walk from the harbor.

The local Chamber of Commerce maintains an **information center** inside the JFK museum on Main Street (April–Oct Mon–Sat 9am–5pm, Sun noon–5pm; Nov–March Thurs–Sat 10am–4pm, Sun noon–4pm; ☎1-877/492-6647, Ⓦwww.hyannis.com).

Accommodation

Hyannis has no shortage of places **to stay**: chain motels line Rte-132, and there's a cluster of bland hotels along Main Street in the center.

Saltwinds B&B 319 Sea St ☎508/771-7213, Ⓦwww.saltwindsbb.com. Options close to the beach include this elegant Victorian, whose friendly owners will usually drop you off at the ferry. ❺

Sea Beach Inn 388 Sea St ☎508/775-4612, Ⓦcapecodtravel.com/seabeach. Another solid choice close to the beach, this family-oriented B&B boasts small but neat rooms, free pick-up service, wi-fi, and Continental breakfast. ❹–❺

Sea Coast Inn 33 Ocean St ☎1-800/466-4100, Ⓦwww.seacoastcapecod.com. The best choice in the center of town, offering clean and functional motel-style accommodation close to the ferry docks; the helpful owners throw in free breakfast and internet use. ❺–❻

Simmons Homestead Inn 288 Scudder Ave ☎508/778-4999 or 1-800/637-1649, Ⓦwww.simmonshomesteadinn.com. This is the only B&B in Hyannisport, with thirteen creatively themed rooms in an 1820 sea captain's home. ❽

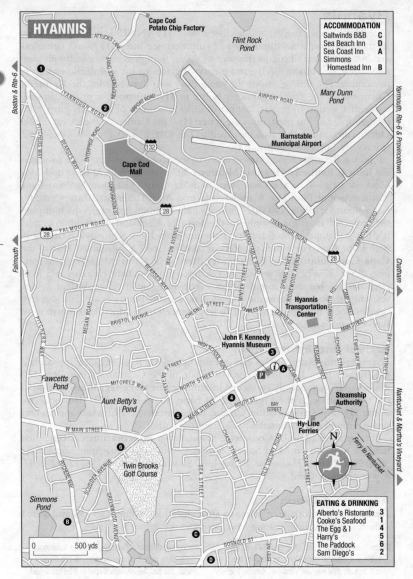

HYANNIS

Cape Cod
Potato Chip Factory

Flint Rock
Pond

ATTUCKS LANE

IYANNOUGH ROAD

INDEPENDENCE DRIVE

AIRPORT ROAD

AIRPORT ROAD

Mary Dunn
Pond

ACCOMMODATION	
Saltwinds B&B	C
Sea Beach Inn	D
Sea Coast Inn	A
Simmons Homestead Inn	B

PITCHERS WAY

ENTERPRISE ROAD

BEARSES WAY

CORPORATION ST

132

Cape Cod
Mall

Barnstable
Municipal Airport

28

FALMOUTH ROAD

28

BEARSES WAY

28

YANNOUGH ROAD

BARNSTABLE ROAD

SPRING STREET

RIDGEWOOD AVENUE

CANE STREET

YARMOUTH RD

WALTON AVENUE

WINTER STREET

MEGAN ROAD

BRISTOL AVENUE

CHESNUT STREET

CHARLES ST

HIGH SCHOOL ROAD

CENTRAL AVE

Hyannis
Transportation
Center

MAIN STREET

LEWIS BAY RD

BAY VIEW STREET

PITCHERS WAY

STEVENS STREET

MITCHELS WAY

NORTH STREET

John F. Kennedy
Hyannis Museum

3

SCHOOL STREET

PLEASANT STREET

Fawcetts
Pond

i A

P

Aunt Betty's
Pond

5

MAIN STREET

4 SOUTH ST

BAY STREET

Steamship
Authority

W MAIN STREET

CHASE STREET

SEA STREET

Hy-Line
Ferries

OLD COLONY ROAD

N

6

SCUDDER AVENUE

GREENWOOD AVENUE

Twin Brooks
Golf Course

OCEAN STREET

Ferry to Nantucket

Simmons
Pond

B

PITCHERS WAY

C

0   500 yds

GOSNOLD ST

D

ESTEY AVE

EATING & DRINKING	
Alberto's Ristorante	3
Cooke's Seafood	1
The Egg & I	4
Harry's	5
The Paddock	6
Sam Diego's	2

Eating and drinking

Alberto's Ristorante 360 Main St ☎508/778-1770.
Reasonably priced option for northern Italian dishes
and home-made pasta (lunch entrees from $13).
Cooke's Seafood 1120 Iyanough Rd/Rte-132
☎508/775-0450. It's hard to go wrong here with
the fresh broiled and fried seafood – especially the
clams ($10.50). Open daily March–Nov.

The Egg & I 521 Main St ☎508/771-1596.
Perfect spot for big breakfasts, with large portions,
addictive home fries, and an outdoor deck.
Harry's 700 Main St ☎508/778-4188. Cajun spot
serving spicy jambalaya, barbecued ribs, and live
blues music most days of the week – it can get
fairly raucous on summer nights.

Literary New England

Perhaps fitting for a region dominated by institutions of higher learning, New England has an incredibly rich literary heritage. In some ways this is where American literature began, spurred by the religious sermons of Cotton Mather and the Puritan histories of William Bradford in the 1600s but truly coming into its own and asserting a dominant influence throughout the nineteenth and twentieth centuries. During this period Boston was the publishing center of the US, and the regional writers that now figure most prominently in the American literary canon were hard at work. More contemporary authors such as Donald Hall and Stephen King have kept the tradition very much alive.

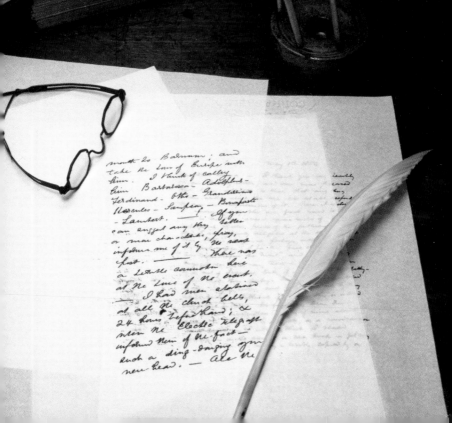

Louisa May Alcott ▲

Title page from Walden ▼

WALDEN;

OR,

LIFE IN THE WOODS.

By HENRY D. THOREAU,

AUTHOR OF "A WEEK ON THE CONCORD AND MERRIMACK RIVERS."

I do not propose to write an ode to dejection, but to brag as lustily as chanticleer in the morning, standing on his roost, if only to wake my neighbors up. — Page 92.

Copy 7

BOSTON:

TICKNOR AND FIELDS.

M DCCC LIV.

Transcendentalist writings

The **transcendentalist movement** of the 1830s and 1840s, spearheaded by **Ralph Waldo Emerson**, was born of a passion for rural life, intellectual freedom, and belief in experience as a way to enhance the relationship between man, nature, and the "over-soul." Much of the rhetoric came from the movement's founding document, Emerson's 1836 essay *Nature*, written not long after he moved to Concord, Massachusetts. The movement put local writers at the vanguard of American literary expression; articles by **Henry David Thoreau**, **Louisa May Alcott**, **Bronson Alcott** (Louisa's father), and other members of the Concord coterie filled the pages of *The Dial*, the transcendentalist journal founded by Emerson and edited by **Margaret Fuller**. An early feminist, Fuller also wrote prodigiously, while Alcott penned the classic *Little Women*.

A literary tour

You can visit many of the region's literary sources, including the homes where Longfellow (Cambridge; see p.115), Alcott (Orchard House in Concord; see p.144), Dickinson (Amherst; see p.228), Twain (Hartford; see p.314), Wharton (The Mount, near Lenox; see p.241), and many more notables were either born, reared, or spent their time writing. It's also possible to see sites made famous by the works themselves, like the House of the Seven Gables in Salem (see p.156), or the Seamen's Bethel in New Bedford, from *Moby Dick* (see p.168). Whether meditating by Walden Pond (see p.146) or stopping in the snowy woods near Robert Frost's farm in Derry, New Hampshire (see p.407), you're sure to feel some spirit move you.

The most famous work from that time remains *Walden*, Thoreau's study in solitude, covering the two years he spent living in a hut near Walden Pond.

The Gothic tradition

While some New England authors have viewed nature as a benevolent force, others have seen it less benignly. Salem (Massachusetts) resident Nathaniel Hawthorne wrote moralistic stories that occasionally approximated Gothic horror, and often cast a suspicious eye on nature and society. *The House of the Seven Gables*, a story alluding to the Salem Witch Trials, treats the disintegrating house itself as a force of nature, capable of destroying those within it. These were just the kind of themes taken up by horror writers H.P. Lovecraft and Stephen King. Lovecraft was born in Providence, Rhode Island, in 1890 and spent nearly all his life in New England until his death in 1937. Lovecraft's stories have all the classic motifs of horror fiction, but mix with them a local sensibility and evocations of ancient and sinister New England landscapes.

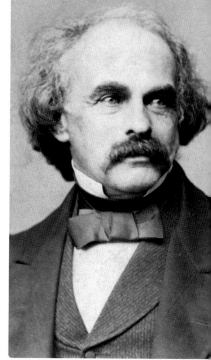
▲ Nathaniel Hawthorne

▼ Stephen King

One of the most popular writers of the modern day, King is the creator of nearly fifty horror novels and plenty more short stories, most of them set in New England towns not unlike Bangor, Maine, where he was born. Favorites include *The Stand* and *The Dead Zone*, though perhaps the most appropriate convergence of landscape and regional pride comes in *The Girl Who Loved Tom Gordon*, in which a girl gets lost in the woods and keeps herself sane by imagining she's talking to (then) Boston Red Sox pitcher Tom Gordon.

Robert Frost's farm ▲

Emily Dickinson Museum ▼

Illustration from Moby Dick ▼

New England poetry

"Listen my children and you shall hear/ Of the midnight ride of Paul Revere." Schoolchildren have been hearing the opening couplet of "The Midnight Ride of Paul Revere," by **Henry Wadsworth Longfellow** – for decades. The author of such lyric poems as "The Song of Hiawatha," Longfellow was born in Portland, Maine, and lived much of his adult life in Cambridge, Massachusetts. While he celebrated heroic Americans in his verses, **Emily Dickinson** wrote much more personal lines at her family's home in Amherst, Massachusetts, although they weren't published until after the reclusive poet's death in 1886. **Robert Frost**, who owned a number of farms throughout the region, might be considered the prototypical New England poet, for his pastoral evocations and philosophical musings ("The Road Less Traveled"). Former US poet laureate **Donald Hall**, who makes his home in New Hampshire, is also known for using New England imagery in his works, which include the essay collection *String Too Short to Be Saved* and children's book *Ox-Cart Man*.

Maritime writing

New England's tradition of maritime writing began with the iconic 1840 *Two Years Before the Mast*, written by a young seaman, Richard Dana, though the best known ocean-going title is definitely Herman Melville's *Moby Dick*, a heroic allegory which also works as an almost encyclopedia-like introduction to the whaling industry. Every year on January 3, the anniversary of Melville's first whaling trip, fans gather in New Bedford for a marathon reading of the American classic.

Ferries to Nantucket

Hyannis is the principal ferry port for **Nantucket** (see p.203). Both the Steamship Authority (South Street Dock; ☎508/447-8600, ⓦ www.islandferry.com) and Hy-Line Cruises (Ocean Street Dock; ☎508/778-2600 or 1-800/492-8082, ⓦ www.hy-linecruises .com) run year-round passenger services to the island, though only the Steamship Authority's boats take cars ($130–190 per vehicle, not including passenger tickets; make summer car reservations months in advance – spots for July and Aug fill up as early as Jan).

Both companies have fast ferries (1hr; $32.50–39 one-way; reservations recommended). The Steamship Authority's regular car ferry (2hr 15min) costs $16.50 one-way for passengers; the Hy-Line's traditional passenger ferry (around 2hr) is $19.50 per person. Passengers can bring bikes onto fast and traditional ferries – both companies charge an additional $6 one-way.

Parking at the official ferry lots is usually $12–15 per day, but if you're just heading to the island for the day, you can also leave your car at the free parking lot behind the JFK museum, a 10-minute walk from the terminals.

The Paddock 20 Scudder Ave ☎508/775-7677. The best place in town to splurge, with an upscale, club-like interior and menu of fabulous seafood such as pan-seared Cape sea scallops and hearty seafood stew (entrees from $17). Open daily April–Nov for lunch and dinner.

Sam Diego's 950 Iyanough Rd/Rte-132 ☎508/771-8816. Dependable, casual restaurant serving Mexican, Southwestern, and barbecue fare – you'll pay less than $10 for lunch dishes.

Chatham

The only town on the South Shore really worth visiting is genteel **CHATHAM**, eighteen miles east of Hyannis on Rte-28. Though it becomes just as tourist-driven as any other Cape town during the summer, it also manages to maintain something of a small-town atmosphere (thanks largely to strict zoning laws).

Arrival and information

Buses drop off at the Chatham Rotary, where Rte-28 becomes Main Street, right in the middle of town. Tour and bike **maps** of Chatham are available from the **information booth** at 533 Main St (May–Oct Mon–Sat 10am–5pm, Sun noon–5pm; ☎508/945-5199, ⓦ www.chathamcapecod.org) or the **Visitor Information Center**, 2377 Main St (Mon–Sat 10am–5pm, Sun noon–3pm).

The Town

The town's focal point is **Main Street** in **Chatham Village**, which begins on Rte-28 before branching off towards the ocean, and is home to upscale boutiques, sophisticated restaurants, and charming inns. The town's finest historical attraction, the **Atwood House Museum**, 347 Stage Harbor Rd (June & Sept to mid-Oct Tues–Sat 1–4pm; July & Aug 10am–4pm; $5; ☎508/945-2493, ⓦ www.chathamhistoricalsociety.org), is a short walk south. A sea captain's home dating from 1752, the house now contains eight galleries designed to highlight life on Cape Cod since the seventeenth century, with displays of seafaring artifacts, art, antique dolls, seashells, and toys. The adjacent Mural Barn houses the rather gaudy *Stallknecht Murals*, a triptych painted between 1932 and 1945 by Alice Stallknecht Wight that depicts 130 Chathamites listening to a contemporarily dressed Christ.

At the southern end of Main Street, a few-minutes' drive from the center, is the 1877 **Chatham Light**, which stands guard over a windswept bluff and the "Chatham Bars," a series of sandbars. The cause of many a shipwreck, these sandbars nonetheless protected the town from Atlantic storms until January 1987, when a Nor'easter broke through, forming the **Chatham Break** and leaving the town exposed to the vagaries of the ocean. Right below the lighthouse is a nice beach, but the parking is limited to thirty minutes, so you're best off biking over from town. A mile north on Rte-28, the **Fish Pier** on Shore Road provides a spot to wait for the town's fleet to come back in the mid-afternoon. To catch the water taxi to **Monomoy Island**, a 7600-acre wildlife refuge (see box below), drive south from the lighthouse along Morris Island Road.

Accommodation

Chatham is well endowed with tasteful **accommodation**, with **B&Bs** that are a bit more upscale (and pricey) than those elsewhere on the Cape. Reservations are strongly advised year-round.

The Captain's House Inn 369–371 Old Harbor Rd ☏ 508/945-0127 or 1-800/315-0728, ⓦ www.captainshouseinn.com. Easy elegance prevails at this sumptuously renovated 1839 Greek Revival whaling captain's home; most rooms have fireplaces, and rates include delicious breakfasts and afternoon tea with fresh-baked scones. ⑨
The Carriage House Inn 407 Old Harbor Rd ☏ 508/945-4688, ⓦ www.thecarriagehouseinn.com. This year-round B&B with young, friendly owners provides seven modern but welcoming rooms and slightly lower prices than the surrounding inns. ⑧
Chatham Bars Inn 297 Shore Rd ☏ 508/945-0096 or 1-800/527-4884, ⓦ www.chathambarsinn.com. The *grande dame* of Cape Cod's seaside resorts,

with 205 rooms and cottages decorated in country-chic style spread out over a 22-acre oceanfront property. Even for this, though, the prices are high – you're really paying for the fantastic setting. ⑨
Chatham Tides Waterfront Motel 394 Pleasant St, South Chatham ☏ 508/432-0379, ⓦ www.chathamtides.com. Choose between standard hotel rooms or self-catering townhouse suites at this pricey motel right on the beach. Closed Nov to mid-May. ⑧–⑨
Chatham Wayside Inn 512 Main St ☏ 508/945-5550 or 1-800/391-5734, ⓦ www.waysideinn .com. This 56-room refurbished 1860 sea captain's home is one of the finer inns in the area. Great food, too. ⑨

Monomoy National Wildlife Refuge

Stretching out to sea for nine miles south of Chatham, the desolate **Monomoy National Wildlife Refuge** is a fragile barrier island. Attached to the mainland until breached by a storm in 1958, the beach was divided in half by another storm in 1978; today the islands are accessible only by boat. The refuge spreads across 7600 acres of sand and dunes, tidal flats and marshes, with no roads, no electricity, and no human residents. Indeed, the only man-made buildings on the islands are the South Monomoy Lighthouse and the lightkeeper's house.

The refuge is a stopover point for almost three hundred species of shorebirds and migratory **waterfowl**, including many gulls and endangered piping plovers, for whose protection several sections of the refuge have been fenced off. In addition, the islands are home to white-tailed deer, and harbor and gray seals are frequent visitors in winter. Several organizations conduct island **tours**, among them Monomoy Island Ferry, a small boat run by Keith Lincoln (☏ 508/945-5450, ⓦ www .monomoyislandferry.com); walking tours of the island are led by a naturalist (call for rates), seal boat tours are $30, and bird-watching tours are $20. Make sure you stop in at the headquarters of the Wildlife Refuge, located on Morris Island, which also has a **visitors' center** (Mon–Sat 8am–4pm; ☏ 508/945-0594) offering small displays and leaflets on Monomoy.

Eating and drinking

Chatham abounds in upmarket **restaurants**, as well as the more casual eateries typical in these parts.

Carmine's Pizza 595 Main St ☎508/945-5300. Casual checked-tablecloth joint serving inexpensive and tasty pizzas with an accent on spice – the "Pizza from Hell" combines garlic, red pepper, jalapeños, and pineapple slices.

Chatham Bars Inn 297 Shore Rd ☎508/945-0096 or 1-800/527-4884. The hostelry's formal dining room offers expensive New England cuisine with wonderful ocean views, while the bar is one of the most fashionable on the Cape.

Chatham Squire 487 Main St ☎508/945-0945. This informal and affordable spot has a raw bar, a seafood menu embellished with pastas and barbecue dishes, and karaoke on Tues.

The Impudent Oyster 15 Chatham Bars Ave ☎508/945-3545. Popular upscale bistro with generous portions of inventively prepared fresh seafood.

Marion's Pie Shop 2022 Main St (Rte-28) ☎508/432-9439. Popular with locals and tourists alike for delicious sweet apple pies, savory chicken pies, and yummy breakfast cinnamon rolls. Closed Mon Sept–May.

Vining's Bistro 595 Main St (upstairs) ☎508/945-5033. Imaginative offerings at this appealing dinner spot range from Portuguese-style Chatham scrod to warm lobster tacos (entrees $17–30). Dinner only; closed Jan–March.

Cape Cod's north coast

The meandering stretch of Rte-6A that parallels the Cape Cod Bay shoreline between Sandwich and Orleans is among the most scenic roads in New England, affording glimpses of the Cape Cod of popular imagination: salt marshes, crystal-clear ponds, ocean views, and tiny villages. There are hundreds of historic buildings along the 34-mile stretch, a large number of which have been turned into antiques shops or B&Bs; the towns of **Sandwich** and **Brewster** have the highest concentration of well-preserved homes. If you're traveling by car, it's worth ditching your wheels temporarily to bike the **Cape Cod Rail Trail**, a totally flat path running from **Dennis**, about fifteen miles past Sandwich, through Brewster to **Wellfleet**, about twenty miles up the Cape.

Sandwich

Overlooked **SANDWICH** kicks off Rte-6A with little of the crass commercialization common to so many Cape towns, probably in part because it is so close to the mainland. Take Rte-130 into the town's old **village center**: a little village green, white steepled church, a smattering of B&Bs, antiques shops, and a general store. Near the junction of Main (Rte-130) and Water streets, the **Shawme Pond** and adjacent **Dexter's Grist Mill**, built in 1654, make for a pleasant, peaceful stop, especially if you want to hear about (and maybe even see in progress) the milling process (mid-June to mid-Oct Mon–Sat 10am–4.30pm, Sun 1–4.30pm; $3; ☎508/888-5144). Across the road, at 129 Main St, the **Sandwich Glass Museum** (Feb–March Wed–Sun 9.30am–4pm; April–Dec daily 9.30am–5pm; $5; ☎508/888-0251, ⓦwww.sandwichglassmuseum.org) contains fourteen galleries housing artifacts from the Boston & Sandwich Glass Company, which set up shop here in 1825. Besides thousands of functional and decorative pieces, the museum has a working glassblowing studio, with presentations every hour.

The other museums around town are only really recommended for those with an abiding passion for Americana. The **Heritage Museums and Gardens** at Grove and Pine streets (mid-May to Nov daily 9am–6pm; Nov–April Wed–Sun 10am–4pm; $12; ☎508/888-3300, ⓦwww.heritagemuseumsandgardens.org) features a load of Currier and Ives prints, old firearms, a working 1912 carousel, replicas of US flags, and a collection of antique cars. The seventy-plus-acre **gardens** are beautiful in season, especially July when the rhododendrons are in bloom.

Sandwich's attractions also include several miles of **beach**, though the water (like at all the Cape's bayside beaches) is several degrees cooler than on the Nantucket Sound side. It will cost you $10 to park at **Town Neck Beach**; take Tupper Road off Rte-6A, then the first right, up Town Neck Road.

Practicalities

You can pick up local maps and **information** from the Town Hall (Mon–Fri 9am–4pm) on Main Street near the pond, or from the Sandwich Chamber of Commerce (April–Oct Mon–Fri 10am–4pm, Sun 1–4pm; ℡508/833-9755, Ⓦwww.sandwichchamber.com), further along the pond at 4 Water St.

The place to **stay** in Sandwich is the *Dan'l Webster Inn*, 149 Main St (℡508/888 -3622 or 1-800/444-3566, Ⓦwww.danlwebsterinn.com; Ⓞ), a rambling Colonial-style hostelry modeled on a building that was a haunt of Revolutionary patriots, with hotel-style rooms and charming courtyards. The hotel also does some of the best **meals** in town: top-notch, classic American dishes (most entrees $28–35); they also serve breakfast and lunch in a sunlit conservatory. *Twin Acres Ice Cream Shoppe*, 21 Rte-6A, just outside the village (℡508/888-0566), is the best of several ice cream shacks in these parts.

Barnstable

BARNSTABLE, ten miles east of Sandwich on Rte-6A, was, after Sandwich, the second town to be founded on Cape Cod, in 1639. Early prosperity was attained through the whaling industry, and Barnstable's harbor was the busiest port on the Cape until it silted up last century. Today the beautiful **Sandy Neck Beach Park** (May to mid-Oct daily 8am–9pm; mid-Oct to April 8am–6pm; ℡508/362-8300), a six-mile barrier beach, is probably your main reason for checking out the town. Follow Sandy Neck Road (which splits off Rte-6A, just over the Sandwich line) to get here. **Parking** is $15 (free May–Sept after 3.30pm and Oct–April).

A few miles from the turning to the beach, in West Barnstable, the majestic 1717 Neoclassical **West Parish of Barnstable**, at 2049 Meetinghouse Rd (Rte-149, south of Rte-6A), is the oldest surviving Congregationalist church in the US, and its bell tower contains a bell cast by Paul Revere. Further evidence of Barnstable's earlier prosperity can be seen in several imposing buildings, including many sea captains' houses, in the leafy **village center**, another five miles along Rte-6A.

Practicalities

If you want to **stay** overnight, *Beechwood*, 2839 Rte-6A (℡508/362-6618, Ⓦwww .beechwoodinn.com; Ⓞ), an 1853 Queen Anne-style house, has six romantic rooms decorated in Victorian style. Another lovely option is the ⚑ *Honeysuckle Hill Bed & Breakfast*, 591 Old King's Hwy/Rte-6A (℡508/362-8418, Ⓦwww .honeysucklehill.com; Ⓞ), with four rooms and one suite in a quintessential Cape Cod 1810 home. For something to **eat**, try the *Barnstable Restaurant & Tavern*, 3176 Main St (℡508/362-2355), offering fine local seafood and an extensive menu of Italian dishes. Stellar waterfront views and more classic seafood can be had at the *Mattakeese Wharf*, 271 Millway Rd (℡508/362-4511; closed Nov–April).

Yarmouth Port

Three miles east of Barnstable along Rte-6A is **YARMOUTH PORT**, a delightful hamlet marked by a series of sea captains' houses that have been converted into B&Bs. Along one two-mile stretch, no building has been constructed since 1900, which has created something of a time-warp effect. This is augmented by **Hallet's**, 139 Hallet St (Rte-6A), a general store that started as a pharmacy in 1889, and still boasts its original counter and soda fountain. Hours have been erratic in recent years; check Ⓦhallets.net for details. Nearby, on the town green (off Rte-6A at 11 Strawberry Lane), the **Captain Bangs Hallet House** (June to mid-Oct Thurs–Sun 1–3pm; tours hourly; $3; Ⓦwww.hsoy.org) is a 1740 Greek Revival mansion built by one of the town's founders, though its name comes from the sea captain who lived here in the late 1800s. Tours take in the original kitchen, complete with beehive oven, and fine views from the back of the house.

In decent weather, you might walk amongst the 53 acres of the **Nature Trails**, entered right behind the post office on Rte-6A, before Hallet's (trails open year-round during daylight hours; suggested donation $0.50). This tranquil park contains oak and pine woods and a wealth of other flora. At the gatehouse, the left-hand trail leads 100 yards to **Kelley Chapel**, a seaman's bethel built in 1873.

Practicalities

There's no reason to **stay** here, except to get a dose of old-fashioned seafaring days. If this sounds appealing, the *Liberty Hill Inn*, 77 Main St (Ⓣ508/362-3976, Ⓦwww.libertyhillinn.com; ⑥–⑧), offers a quintessential country inn ambience in six rooms with canopy beds and fireplaces. You can **eat** Italian fare at *abbicci*, 43 Main St/Rte-6A (Ⓣ508/362-3501), which serves excellent and pricey seafood as well as more traditional meat and pasta dishes. Yarmouth Port is also home to one of the Cape's best Japanese restaurants, *Inaho*, 157 Main St/Rte-6A (closed Sun; Ⓣ508/362-5522), for those looking for a break from fried seafood.

Dennis

In **DENNIS**, four miles down the road from Yarmouth Port, a trip to the beach means pristine **Scargo Lake**, just off Rte-6A. The best place for a dip is **Princess Beach**, which has restrooms and a picnic area; to find it, turn right off Rte-6A along Old Bass River Road, then turn left on Scargo Hill Road. The town itself, named after its founder, Reverend Josiah Dennis, retains a colonial feel, notably in places like the clergyman's home, the **Josiah Dennis Manse**, 77 Nobscusset Rd (late June–Aug Tues 10am–noon, Thurs 2–4pm; small donation requested; Ⓣ508/385-2232), a short way off Rte-6A. Built in 1736, it's set up to reflect life in the Reverend's day. There's also a one-room schoolhouse dating from 1770 on the grounds.

One of the most famous summer theaters in the US, the **Cape Playhouse**, on Rte-6A between Nobscusset and Corporation roads (late June to early Sept daily except Sun; Ⓣ508/385-3911, Ⓦwww.capeplayhouse.com), was a Unitarian meeting house until its purchase in 1927 by Raymond Moore, who had intended to start a theater company in Provincetown but found that town too remote. The complex also contains an art cinema, (tickets $8.50; Ⓣ508/385-2503, Ⓦwww.capecinema.com), modeled after a Congregational church. On the ceiling is a stunning astrological mural designed by Rockwell Kent and Jo Mielziner. Also on site, the **Cape Museum of Fine Arts** (Mon–Sat 10am–5pm, Sun 1–5pm; mid-Oct to April closed Mon; $8; Ⓣ508/385-4477, Ⓦwww.cmfa.org) showcases works by local artists, many of whom seem to have a penchant for seascapes and marine life portraits, though the gallery often has good contemporary fare as well.

For cycling enthusiasts, the **Cape Cod Rail Trail**, a tarred bicycle path on the bed of the Old Colony Railroad, extends 26 miles from Dennis to Wellfleet (beginning in South Dennis on Rte-134 south of Rte-6). Barbara's Bike &

Sports, at 430 Rte-134 in South Dennis (☎508/760-4723), near the start of the trail, and also in Brewster further along, rents bikes for about $24 a day and stocks copies of trail maps. Check out ⓦwww.capecodbikeguide.com.

Practicalities

If you're looking to **stay** in Dennis, the *Isaiah Hall B&B Inn*, 152 Whig St (☎508/385-9928 or 1-800/736-0160, ⓦwww.isaiahhallinn.com; ⑤–⑧), is an 1857 Greek Revival farmhouse with ten attractive rooms and two suites, all equipped with VCRs and wi-fi, within walking distance of village and beach. For more resort-like accommodation, check into the *Lighthouse Inn*, 1 Lighthouse Inn Rd, West Dennis (☎508/398-2244, ⓦwww.lighthouseinn.com; ⑨), an expansive compound with private beach, mini-golf, tennis, and shuffleboard. You can **eat** generous portions of fried clams, clam cakes, and fish and chips ($11) at *Captain Frosty's Fish & Chips*, 219 Rte-6A (☎508/385-8548), or try the justifiably celebrated lobster rolls at ⚓ *Sesuit Harbor Café*, 375 Sesuit Neck Rd (☎508/385-6134), which has outdoor tables off Rte-134 in East Dennis, overlooking Sesuit Harbor.

Brewster

BREWSTER is yet another agreeable, if anodyne, Cape Cod town, known as a leading antiques center. The 1834 **First Parish Church**, 1969 Main St (Rte-6A), has one of New England's more fascinating legends attached to (or buried within) it: one of the gravestones bears the names of two men lost at sea: Captain David Nickerson and his adopted son, Captain René Rousseau. The story goes that Nickerson was in Paris during the French Revolution when a woman handed him the infant René; locals maintain he was the son of Louis XVI and Marie Antoinette. More picturesque is the town's last remaining windmill, the 1795 **Higgins Farm Windmill**, 785 Rte-6A (July–Sept Thurs–Sat 1–4pm; free; ☎508/896-9521), with a roof resembling a capsized dory, and the still-functioning waterwheel at the **Stony Brook Mill and Museum**, just off Rte-6A at 830 Stony Brook Rd (June–Aug Sat & Sun 10am–2pm; free), built on the site of an earlier mill that churned out cloth, boots, and ironwork for over a century; the second-story museum displays local bric-a-brac.

Cape Cod National Seashore

The protected **Cape Cod National Seashore** extends along much of the Cape's Atlantic side, stretching forty miles from Chatham to Provincetown. It's a fragile environment: three feet of the lower Cape is washed away each year. Environmentalists are hoping that a program of grass-planting will help prevent further erosion.

It was on these shifting sands that the **Pilgrims** made their first home in the New World: they obtained their water from Pilgrim Spring near Truro, and at Corn Hill Beach they uncovered a cache of corn buried by the Wampanoag Indians, who had been living on the Cape for centuries – a discovery which kept them alive their first winter, before they moved on to Plymouth.

Displays and films at the **Salt Pond Visitor Center**, on Rte-6 just north of Eastham (daily 9am–4.30pm; ☎508/255-3421, ⓦwww.nps.gov/caco), trace the geology and history of the Cape. A pretty road and hiking/cycling trail head east to the sands of **Coast Guard Beach** and **Nauset Light Beach**, both of which offer excellent swimming. You can also catch a free shuttle ride there from the visitor center in summer. Another fine beach is **Head of the Meadow**, halfway between Truro and Provincetown. Beach entrance fees are collected from late June through early September: $15 for cars and $3 for pedestrians and cyclists.

Farther down Rte-6A at 869 Main St, the **Cape Cod Museum of Natural History** (June–Sept daily 9.30am–4.30pm; Oct–Dec, & Feb–March Wed–Sun noon–4pm; April & May Wed–Sun 10am–4pm; $8, trails free; ℡508/896-3867, Ⓦwww.ccmnh.org) makes for a enlightening diversion – especially for kids – with exhibits on the fragile Cape environment, whales, other marine life, and short but captivating nature trails that straddle cranberry bogs and salt marshes before continuing on to the bay.

Practicalities

The best place to **stay** – and **eat** – in Brewster is the *Bramble Inn*, 2019 Main St (℡508/896-7644, Ⓦwww.brambleinn.com; ⓐ), a lovely old place that takes in two rustic homes with upscale country-style fittings. Its **restaurant** (dinner only; closed Jan–March), one of the Cape's finest, does pricey seafood such as seafood curry (with lobster) and pumpkin seed-encrusted fish of the day. Another good lodging option is *Brewster by the Sea*, 716 Main St/Rte-6A (℡508/896-3910, Ⓦwww.brewsterbythesea.com; ⓑ), an upscale, eight-room B&B offering spa services and the like, as well as a delicious breakfast and an outdoor pool in the summer. For superb contemporary French cuisine, try ⚑ *Chillingsworth*, 2449 Rte-6A (℡508/896-3640), which also boasts a sumptuous setting; if you're going to splurge, their seven-course table d'hôte menu (about $75) can't be beat, but the bistro menu is much cheaper.

The Outer Cape

North of Orleans, the Outer Cape narrows considerably; beyond **Wellfleet** the land is scarcely one mile wide, and the coastline becomes increasingly wild and fragile, much of it protected within the **Cape Cod National Seashore** (see box opposite). Aside from the beaches and coastal attractions, lively **Provincetown**, at the very tip of the Cape, provides the biggest allure.

Eastham

Largely undiscovered **EASTHAM**, on Rte-6 as the Cape begins to curve toward Provincetown, is home to fewer than five thousand residents, most of whom are content to sit and watch the summer traffic pass by on its way north. Though the sum of the town's commercial facilities is little more than a small strip of shopping malls and gas stations along Rte-6, if you veer off the highway you will glimpse some authentic Cape flavor.

The first detour is the **Fort Hill** area, part of the Cape Cod National Seashore, which has a scenic overlook with views of **Nauset Marsh**, a former bay that became a marsh when **Coast Guard Beach** was formed ($15 parking; free shuttle buses to the beach). North of Coast Guard, at the corner of Ocean View Drive and Cable Road, is the red-and-white **Nauset Light**, originally located in Chatham but installed here in 1923 and moved back 350 feet a decade ago when it was in danger of falling into the sea. In 1838, this spot was home to three brick lighthouses, known as the "Three Sisters." In 1892, erosion necessitated their replacement by wooden towers; two were moved away in 1918 and the last in 1923. Acquired by the National Park Service, they now stand in the woods, well away from the coast.

On Eastham's bayside, **First Encounter Beach**, at the end of Samoset Road, refers to the first meeting between Pilgrims and Native Americans in 1620. It was hardly a cordial rendezvous; with the *Mayflower* anchored in Provincetown,

Cape Cod beaches

With over three hundred miles of coastline, Cape Cod certainly doesn't lack **sand**. What it does lack, however, is facilities; the few beaches that have services (restrooms, lifeguards, snack bars) are, not surprisingly, usually busiest. **Parking** across the Cape is also a bit of a crapshoot: your best bet, if you're planning on hitting the beach frequently, is to visit the local town hall and inquire about non-resident parking permits (which can range from $30 for three days to $60 for a week). These town beaches are most often on a bay or pond, whereas the best ocean beaches are pay as you go. In terms of water conditions, the Cape's southern stretches (facing Nantucket Sound) tend to be calmer and warmer than the Atlantic side. You'll find details of some of the best beaches in the relevant sections of the guide, but these are also worth checking out:

Around Hyannis

Craigville Beach Off Craigville Beach Road in Centerville, just west of Hyannis. Well-oiled and toned sun-worshipers flock to this broad expanse of sand, nicknamed "Muscle Beach."

Kalmus Beach Off Gosnold Street in central Hyannis. A big wind-surfing destination at the mouth of the busy harbor, with full facilities and an urban feel.

Brewster

Breakwater Beach Off Breakwater Road. Shallow-water beach with restrooms close to town.

Paines Creek Beach Off Paines Creek Road. One-and-a-half-mile bay beach with great body-surfing when the tide comes in.

Dennis

Corporation Beach Off Rte-6A. One of the best-maintained beaches on the Cape, with wheelchair-accessible boardwalks, a children's play area, lifeguards, and full facilities.

Mayflower Beach Off Rte-6A. Popular family spot with natural tidal pools.

---

an exploration party led by Myles Standish came ashore, only to meet a barrage of arrows. Things settled down after a few gunshots were returned, and since then the beach has been utterly tranquil.

Practicalities

The place to **stay** in Eastham is the *Whalewalk Inn*, 220 Bridge Rd (℡508/255-0617 or 1-800/440-1281, ⓦwww.whalewalkinn.com; ❻–❾), where immaculate guestrooms and tasty breakfasts are the big draws; the cottages are more spacious than the rooms in the main building. There's also a **hostel**, *Mid-Cape American Youth Hostel*, 75 Goody Hallet Drive (℡508/255-2785, ⓔmidcape@usahostels.org; dorms $32 non-members, cabins $140; open mid-May to mid-Sept), in a collection of woodsy cabins. For something to **eat**, *Arnold's Lobster & Clam Bar*, 3580 Rte-6 (℡508/255-2575), provides generous portions of fried seafood, while *Box Lunch*, 4205 Rte-6 (℡508/255-0799), as its name suggests, is the place to go for picnic fixings.

Wellfleet

WELLFLEET, with a year-round population of just 2500, is one of the least developed towns on the Cape. Once the focus of a thriving oyster-fishing industry, today it is a favorite haunt of writers and artists who come to seek inspiration from the unsullied landscape. Despite the fact that a number of

Falmouth

Old-Silver Beach Off Rte-28A in North Falmouth. Popular, calm beach with great sunsets; college kids and young families alike gather here, the latter drawn to its natural wading pool.

Surf Drive Beach Off Shore Street. Another family favorite; a shallow tidal pool between jetties is known as "the kiddie pool."

Orleans

Nauset Beach Off Rte-28. Over in East Orleans is one of the Cape's best beaches, a nine-mile-long wedge of sand at the end of Beach Road ($15 parking fee); don't miss the onion rings at *Liam's* snack bar – they're legendary.

Provincetown

Herring Cove Beach Off Rte-6. Easily reached by bike or through the dunes, and famous for sunset-watching, this beach is actually more crowded than those nearer town, though never unbearably so.

Province Lands Off Race Point Road. Beautiful vast, sweeping moors and bushy dunes are buffeted by crashing surf.

Wellfleet

Cahoon Hollow Beach Off Ocean View Drive. Good surfing and full facilities make this town-run beach popular with the thirty-something set. Don't miss the delicious oysters at the *Beachcomber* shack (see box, p.186).

White Crest Off Ocean View Drive. The main distinction between White Crest and neighboring Cahoon Hollow is the clientele – here, it's a predominantly young college crowd.

---

art galleries have surfaced – most of them along **Main** or **Commercial** streets – the town remains remarkably unpretentious, with many of the galleries themselves resembling fishing shacks and selling distinctive original works. Pick up a guide to the galleries at the **information booth** at the corner of Rte-6 and LeCount Hollow Road (summer daily 9am–6pm; fall and spring Sat & Sun 10am–6pm; ☎508/349-2510). The **Wellfleet Historical Society Museum**, 266 Main St (late June to early Sept Tues & Fri 10am–4pm, Wed, Thurs & Sat 1–4pm; free; ⓦ www.wellfleethistoricalsociety.com), has an interesting collection of furniture, nautical artifacts, and photographs, as well as exhibits on the local oyster industry.

The most scenic part of town is actually outside the center, at the bluff-lined **Marconi Station Site**, east off Rte-6 in South Wellfleet, where Guglielmo Marconi issued the first transatlantic radio signal on January 18, 1903, announcing greetings from President Roosevelt to King Edward VII. Nothing remains of Marconi's radio towers, but there are some scale models beneath a gazebo-type structure overlooking the ocean. A short trail up the cliffside leads to a vantage point from which you can see across the entire Cape – just a mile wide at this point. Take the same turning off Rte-6 for sandy **Marconi Beach** (then bear right at the first junction), where you'll find facilities and parking ($15) that rarely fills to capacity.

Oyster shucking

No visit to Wellfleet would be complete without a taste of the town's famous oysters. In fact, the little mollusks are so abundant here that the French explorer Samuel de Champlain named the town "Port aux Huîtres" (or Oyster Port) when he disembarked in 1606. One of the best places to dive into a plate of the raw variety is the rowdy 🍖 *Beachcomber*, Cahoon Hollow Beach (mid-May to early Sept; ☎508/349-6055), a fun beach shack with awesome waterfront views. You can also attend the Wellfleet **Oyster Weekend** (every mid- to late October; ⓦ www.wellfleetoysterfest.org), complete with raw bars and shucking contests.

Practicalities

If you want to **stay** the night in Wellfleet, try the laid-back *Holden Inn*, 140 Commercial St (open May–Oct; ☎508/349-3450, ⓦwww.theholdeninn .com; ❻–❽), a farmhouse-style structure with 27 rooms, some with shared baths, or the charming *Inn at Duck Creeke*, 70 Main St (open May–Oct; ☎508/349-9333, ⓦwww.innatduckcreeke.com; ❺), a cozy country inn situated on five woodland acres. Tiny though Wellfleet is, there are a number of casual seafood **restaurants** worth checking out, such as *Mac's Shack*, 91 Commercial St (dinner only, May–Oct; ☎508/349-6333), an old oyster shack that has a superb raw bar and sushi, and *Moby Dick's*, on Rte-6 across from Gull Pond Road (May–Oct; ☎508/349-9795), which offers family seafood dining. *Finely JP's*, 554 Rte-6 (dinner only; ☎508/349-7500), is a deceptively plain roadside shack that serves tasty oysters and other delicious dishes at a good price; try the oysters Bienville, a baked extravaganza of mushrooms, parmesan, cream, and white wine.

Truro

Most of the sprawling town of **TRURO** falls within the boundaries of the Cape Cod National Seashore, allowing it to preserve the kind of natural beauty that has attracted artists, writers, and even politicians over the years.

It was here that **Myles Standish** and his companions from the *Mayflower* found the cache of Indian corn that helped them survive their first New England winter in 1620; a plaque at **Corn Hill** marks the exact spot. It wasn't until 1697, however, that the first permanent settlement was established. In 1797 Truro became the site of Cape Cod's first lighthouse, powered by whale oil. Today a golf course flanks the lighthouse's 1857 replacement, the **Cape Cod Light** (late May to Oct daily 10am–5.30pm; $4; ☎508/487-1121) at the end of Lighthouse Road (take S Highland Rd from Rte-6A). Also known as the Highland Light, in 1996 it was moved back 453ft from the eroding shoreline. The interpretive center inside has a short video about the site, but the real treat is the view from the top – you can compare it with the equally stunning views from the nearby observation deck, perched on one of the highest cliffs on the Cape. A short walk inland on Lighthouse Road, the **Highland House Museum** (June–Sept Mon–Sat 10am–4.30pm, Sun 1–4.30pm; $4; ☎508/487-3397, ⓦwww.trurohistorical.org) is a 1907 hotel that's now home to some rather prosaic historical artifacts, such as fishing and whaling implements, old photographs, and seventeenth-century firearms; better are the objects obtained from the many shipwrecks that have occurred offshore, as well as the second-floor rooms done up in Victorian style.

Practicalities

Places to **stay** in Truro are mainly confined to a strip that hugs the bay shoreline west of Shore Road (Rte-6A) in North Truro. All of the following are open only in **summer**. *Kalmar Village* (☏508/487-0585, Ⓦwww.kalmarvillage.com; ❻) consists of 45 spacious and well-kept one- and two-bedroom cottages in an oceanfront community. In July and August, these can only be rented by the week; at other times, nightly rentals are possible. The *Top Mast*, 209 Shore Rd (Rte-6A), North Truro (☏508/487-1189, Ⓦwww.topmastresort.com; ❺), looks like three adjacent motels; the rooms are unattractive but the price and beachside location are right. Truro is also home to one of the Cape's two HI **hostels** at 111 North Pamet Rd (☏508/349-3889, ✉truro@usahostels.org; dorms $29). A former Coast Guard station near the beach, it offers both co-ed and private rooms ($120). For something to **eat**, *Adrian's*, 535 Rte-6, North Truro (☏508/487-4360), serves breakfasts and dinners with an Italian touch, while *Blackfish*, 17 Truro Center Rd, off Rte-6A (summer only; ☏508/349-3399), offers fine contemporary American food (entrees $19–33).

Provincetown

The fishing burg of **PROVINCETOWN**, at the very tip of Cape Cod, has long been a popular summer destination, with the excellent beaches, art galleries, and welcoming atmosphere attracting bohemians, artists, and fun-seekers alike. Over the past few decades, however, it has become known most famously as a **gay** resort destination, complete with frequent festivals and theme weekends. P-town, as the coastal community is often called, also has a drop of **Portuguese** culture, after a smallish population of fishermen began settling here in the mid-1800s; their legacy is now celebrated in an annual June **festival** complete with music and Portuguese soup-tasting competitions. Throughout the summer, P-town's population swells into the tens of thousands, and there's often a carnival atmosphere in the bustling streets.

Some history

The Pilgrims came ashore here and stayed for five weeks in 1620, signing the **Mayflower Compact**, before sailing across Cape Cod Bay to Plymouth. Provincetown was incorporated in 1727, and soon became a thriving fishing, salt-processing, and whaling port; by 1880, the town was the richest per capita in Massachusetts. Fishing retains its importance here, but the town's destiny as one of the East Coast's leading **art colonies** was assured in 1899, when painter

---

Tours in Provincetown

Provincetown claims the title of first **whale-watching** spot on the East Coast; the best company is the Dolphin Fleet, 132 Bradford St (April–Oct; $37; ☏508/240-3636 or 1-800/826-9300, Ⓦwww.whalewatch.com), with cruises leaving frequently from MacMillan Wharf. If you want to take a **boat ride**, Viking Princess Cruises, MacMillan Wharf (☏508/487-7323, Ⓦwww.capecodecotours.com), run one-hour trips round the bay several times a day in season ($14–21), while Flyer's Boat Rentals, 131A Commercial St (☏508/487-0898 or 1-800/750-0898, Ⓦwww.flyersboats.com), rents kayaks ($50/day), Sunfish sailboats ($60 per day), and powerboats (from $130 per day). You can also opt to ramble about the dunes in a four-wheel-drive vehicle with **Art's Dune Tours**, at 4 Standish St (April–Oct 10am–dusk, tours 1hr; $25; ☏508/487-1950, Ⓦwww.artsdunetours.com). Finally, Race Point Aviation (☏508/873-2342, Ⓦwww.racepointaviation.com) offers mesmerizing twenty-minute flights over the Cape for just $80, from the airport on Race Point Road.

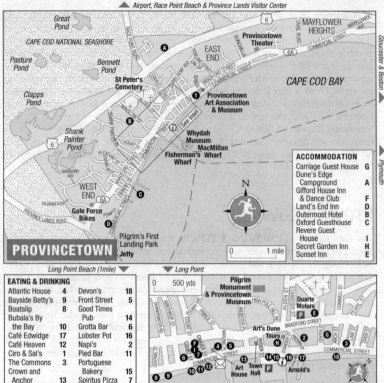

▲ Airport, Race Point Beach & Province Lands Visitor Center

ACCOMMODATION

Carriage Guest House	G
Dune's Edge Campground	A
Gifford House Inn & Dance Club	F
Land's End Inn	D
Outermost Hotel	B
Oxford Guesthouse	C
Revere Guest House	I
Secret Garden Inn	H
Sunset Inn	E

EATING & DRINKING

Atlantic House	4	Devon's	18
Bayside Betty's	9	Front Street	5
Boatslip	8	Good Times Pub	14
Bubala's By the Bay	10	Grotta Bar	6
Café Edwidge	17	Lobster Pot	16
Café Heaven	12	Napi's	2
Ciro & Sal's	1	Pied Bar	11
The Commons	3	Portuguese Bakery	15
Crown and Anchor	13	Spiritus Pizza	7

Charles W. Hawthorne founded the **Cape Cod School of Art**. By the early 1900s, many painters had begun to ply their trade in abandoned shacks by the sea, and by 1916 there were six art schools here. The natural beauty and laid-back atmosphere also began to seduce young writers like Mary Heaton Vorse, who established the **Provincetown Players** theater group in 1915. **Eugene O'Neill** joined the company in 1916, premiering his *Bound East for Cardiff* in a waterfront fish house. Today, thanks in part to strict **zoning laws** designed to protect Provincetown's fragile environment, major development has been kept at bay, preserving the flavor of the old town.

Arrival, information, and local transport

Parking can be problematic in summer, so get here early; try the waterfront lot near MacMillan Wharf ($2.50 per hr), or the Duarte Motors Parking Lot, Bradford St at Standish St (first hr $5, $1 per hr thereafter; $15 per day).

Taking the **ferry** here from Boston, Gloucester, or Plymouth (see p.165) is a pricey but stress-free alternative to driving, and you can also take a **bus** from Boston, which stops right in the middle of town near MacMillan Wharf. The **Chamber of Commerce** is next to the bus stop, 307 Commercial St (May–Oct daily 9am–5pm, limited winter hours; ☎508/487-3424, Ⓦwww.ptownchamber .com). A good online resource is Ⓦwww.provincetown.com; gay travelers may also want to check Ⓦwww.gayprovincetown.com.

Provincetown is a very **walkable** place, though **bicycles** can come in handy, especially if you want to venture a bit further afield. For rentals, Arnold's, 329 Commercial St (☎508/487-0844), right in the center of town, is open from mid-April to mid-October, as is Gale Force Bikes, 144 Bradford St Ext (daily 8am–8pm; ☎508/487-4849, ⓦwww.galeforcebikes.com). Bikes at both places go for about $20 per day.

Accommodation

Many of the most picturesque cottages in town are **guesthouses**, some with spectacular views over Cape Cod Bay – unsurprisingly, many are run by gay couples and are generally gay-friendly. The best area to be is the quiet West End, though anything on Bradford Street will also be removed from the summertime racket. Prices are generally very reasonable until mid-June, and off season you can find real bargains. In addition, there are a few **motels**, mostly on the outskirts of town towards the Truro line. The welcoming *Dune's Edge Campground*, on Rte-6 just east of the central stoplights (May–Sept; ☎508/487-9815, ⓦwww.dunes-edge .com), charges $30–40 for one of its wooded sites.

Carriage Guest House 7 Central St ☎508/487-8855, ⓦwww.thecarriagehse .com. Fabulously maintained rooms, some with private decks, and all with VCRs and CD players; stylish breakfasts and large hot tub and sauna are soothing extras. ❾

Gifford House Inn & Dance Club 9 Carver St ☎1-800/434-0130, ⓦwww.giffordhouse.com. Affordable and popular gay resort with lobby piano bar, restaurant, and dancefloor; Continental breakfast included. ❺

Land's End Inn 22 Commercial St ☎1-800/276-7088 or 508/487-0706, ⓦwww.landsendinn.com. Meticulously decorated rooms and suites, many with sweeping ocean views, in a fanciful turreted house; Continental breakfast and daily wine and cheese tasting included. ❽

Outermost Hostel 28 Winslow St ☎508/487-4378, ⓦwww.outermosthostel.com. Hostel with the cheapest rates in town: thirty $25 beds in five cramped dorm cabins. Rates include kitchen access and parking. Closed Nov–April. Office open 8–9.30am & 5.30–9.30pm.

Oxford Guesthouse 8 Cottage St ☎508/487-9103, ⓦwww.oxfordguesthouse .com. Seven rooms and suites elegantly decorated in English "country style," with classical drapes and patterned wallpaper adding to the vintage ambience – you get Continental breakfast, cookies in the afternoons, and a civilized "wine hour" every evening. CDs, DVDs and wi-fi available. ❼

Revere Guest House 14 Court St ☎508/487-2292 or 1-800/487-2292, ⓦwww.reverehouse.com. This pleasant B&B has a garden patio and antiques-accented rooms, one with shared bath. ❽

Secret Garden Inn 300a Commercial St ☎1-866/786-9646 or 508/487-9027, ⓦwww .secretgardenptown.com. This place is a relative bargain, with seven quaint rooms done up in country furnishings, but with modern touches like TVs and a/c, in a house with a veranda; country breakfast included. ❺

Sunset Inn 142 Bradford St ☎508/487-9810, ⓦwww.sunsetinnptown.com. Clean, quiet rooms in an 1850 captain's house with double or queen beds and private or shared bath. Closed Jan–March. ❺

The Town

The town center is essentially two three-mile-long streets, **Commercial** and **Bradford**, that follow the harbor and are connected by about forty tiny lanes of no more than two blocks each. **Fisherman's Wharf**, and the more touristy **MacMillan Wharf**, busy with whale-watching boats, yachts, and colorful old Portuguese fishing vessels, split the town in half.

MacMillan Wharf also houses the **Whydah Museum**, no. 16 (May & Sept–Oct daily 10am–5pm; June–Aug daily 10am–8pm; $10; ☎508/487-8899, ⓦwww .whydah.com), which displays some of the bounty from the 1717 shipwreck of the pirate vessel *Whydah* off the coast of Wellfleet. The lifelong quest of native Cape Codder Barry Clifford to recover the treasure from the ship – holding loot from more than fifty others when it sank – paid off royally in the summer of 1983, when thousands of coins, gold bars, pieces of jewelry, and weapons were retrieved, ranging from odds and ends like silver shoe buckles and flintlock pistols to rare African gold jewelry. The most evocative display in the museum, though, is the ship's **bell**, a little rusty but not so corroded that you can't read "The Whydah Galley – 1716."

Two blocks north of the piers, atop Town Hill, is the 252-foot granite tower of the **Pilgrim Monument & Provincetown Museum** (daily: April to mid-June & mid-Sept to Nov 9am–5pm; mid-June to mid-Sept 9am–7pm; $7; ☏508/487-1310, ⒲www.pilgrim-monument.org). Completed in 1910 to commemorate the Pilgrims' landing here on November 21, 1620, the tower was modeled on the Torre del Mangia in Siena, Italy, despite the lack of historical relevance. It's 116 steps to the observation deck; on a clear day you can see all the way to Boston. In the museum at its base, a series of exhibits give a fairly romantic account of the Pilgrim story and subsequent history of the town, from fishing and whaling port (including a section on the **HMS Somerset**, a British battleship that ran aground here during the Revolutionary War), to art and theater colony. You can park here for two hours for free ($10 deposit).

Back on the main drag, the **Provincetown Art Association and Museum**, 460 Commercial St (mid-May to Sept Mon–Thurs 11am–8pm, Fri 11am–10pm, Sat & Sun 11am–5pm; Oct to mid-May Thurs–Sun noon–5pm; $5; ☏508/487-1750, ⒲www.paam.org), rotates works from its two-thousand-strong collection, with equal prominence given to both upcoming and well-known local artists such as Peter Busa (1914–85), though you might find the cleverly designed, eco-friendly galleries more interesting than the art on display.

At Commercial Street's western end, the Pilgrim **landing place** is marked by a modest bronze plaque on a boulder. Nearby, just past the *Provincetown Inn*, is the **Breakwater Trail**, a mile-long **jetty** that cuts across to **Long Point Beach**, a great place to watch the sun set; you can also take the **shuttle** across Cape Cod Bay out here (mid-June to mid-Sept; $10 one-way, $15 round-trip), from MacMillan Wharf.

▲ Provincetown street scene

Around one and a half miles north of town along Race Point Road, the Province Lands **visitors' center** (May–Oct daily 9am–5pm; ☎508/487-1256), is part of the Cape Cod National Seashore, with videos and displays highlighting the exceptionally fragile environment here. From the center you can take off into the dunes; nearby **Race Point Beach** has lifeguards and miles of sand. Province Lands is also home to the best **bike path** on Cape Cod, roaming through the dunes and without a building in sight.

Eating

Eating in Provincetown is fun but can be expensive; the snack bars around MacMillan Wharf are particularly pricey. Still, there are some real treats to be had, and they need not break your budget – look out in particular for the town's **Portuguese** restaurants. In summer, try to arrive early or make a reservation; in winter, most eateries **close**, though some remain open on weekends.

Bayside Betty's 177 Commercial St ☎508/487-6566. Funky waterfront eatery with hearty breakfasts and seafood dinners – try the perfect lobster roll ($17). Come evening, it's also a popular martini bar.

Bubala's by the Bay 183 Commercial St ☎508/487-0773. This local institution offers casual outdoor eating, with a vast menu providing something for everyone; top picks are fish and chips ($17), and the market-priced fresh shellfish.

Café Edwidge 333 Commercial St ☎508/487-2008. Breakfast is the thing at this popular second-floor spot; try the home-made Danish pastries and fresh-fruit pancakes. Creative bistro fare at dinner (entrees $20–36). Closed Tues.

Café Heaven 199 Commercial St ☎508/487-9639. Massive breakfast plates (served through the afternoon), baguette sandwiches, and local art make this a popular daytime choice, but it's the juicy hamburgers that really make it stand out. Open 'til late.

Ciro & Sal's 4 Kiley Court ☎508/487-6444. Traditional Northern Italian cooking with plenty of veal and seafood; a bit on the pricey side, with pastas from $17 and entrees from $23, but well worth it. Dinner only.

The Commons 386 Commercial St ☎508/487-7800. French bistro food and tasty pizzas from a wood-fired oven make this a popular spot.

Devon's 401 1/2 Commercial St ☎508/487-8200. This cute fishing shack has been converted into a fine dining outpost with just 37 seats and an open kitchen by Devon Ruesch – try and reserve a table on the patio. The menu features French/American fusion cuisine, paring items like local sea scallops with truffle zabaglione; the desserts and breakfasts are also spectacular.

Front Street 230 Commercial St ☎508/487-9715. Popular Italian and Continental restaurant in a Victorian house. The menu changes weekly, but you might find dishes like butternut ravioli and mojito-grilled swordfish. Entrees $19–30. Closed Tues.

Lobster Pot 321 Commercial St ☎508/487-0842. Its landmark neon sign is like a welcome mat for those who want ultra-fresh crustaceans. Affordable (lobster ravioli $11; clam chowder $5–6) and family-oriented, with a great outdoor deck. Closed Dec–March.

Napi's 7 Freeman St ☎508/487-1145. Popular dishes at this art-strewn spot include pastas and soups like thick Portuguese fish stew and clam chowder (from $6). They have a less expensive menu on week nights, and lots of veggie options (entrees from $17). Free parking at no. 5.

Portuguese Bakery 299 Commercial St ☎508/487-1803. This old stand-by is the place to come for cheap breakfasts and baked goods, particularly the tasty fried *rabanada*, akin to French toast.

Spiritus Pizza 190 Commercial St ☎508/487-2808. Combination pizza place and coffee bar with an especially lively after-hours scene.

Drinking, nightlife, and entertainment

On summer weekends, boatloads of revelers come to P-town in search of its notoriously wild **nightlife**, which is heavily geared towards a **gay** clientele. Some establishments have terrific waterfront locations, making them ideal spots to sit out with a drink at sunset. Cover charges will generally fall in the $5–10 range. You'll also find that many of Provincetown's restaurants have a lively bar scene. In terms of **entertainment**, check out the **Art House**, 214 Commercial St

(☎508/487-9222, ☻www.ptownarthouse.com), which contains a **theater** and **cinema**; shows generally comprise drag acts, vaudeville, campy thrillers, and comedy, while the cinema tends to feature independent films. You'll find a range of musicals and plays to suit all tastes at the **Provincetown Theater**, 288 Bradford St (☎508/487-7487, ☻www.provincetowntheater.org).

Atlantic House 6 Masonic Place, behind Commercial St ☎508/487-3821, ☻www.ahouse .com. The "A-House" – a dark drinking hole that was a favorite of Tennessee Williams and Eugene O'Neill – is now a trendy (and still dark) gay dance club and bar.

Boatslip 161 Commercial St ☎508/487-1669, ☻www.boatslipresort.com. The Sunday tea dances (4–7pm) at this resort are legendary; you can either dance away on a long wooden deck overlooking the water, or cruise inside under a disco ball and flashing lights.

Crown and Anchor 247 Commercial St ☎508/487-1430, ☻www.onlyatthecrown.com. A massive complex housing several bars, including *The Vault*, P-town's only leather bar (Thurs–Sun), *Wave*, a video-karaoke bar (Thurs–Sat), and

Paramount, a cabaret with nightly act; all venues open daily in the summer.

Good Times Pub 293 Commercial St ☎508/487-2890. This subterranean bar is the place to play pool or catch the latest sports event. Fri–Mon from 1pm.

Grotta Bar *Enzo Hotel*, 186 Commercial St ☎508/487-7555. One the newer bars in Provincetown, with campy live entertainment, bands, DJs, a 46-inch plasma TV, and zesty martinis. Live piano Tues, Fri & Sun.

Pied Bar 193 Commercial St ☎508/487-1527, ☻www.piedbar.com. Though largely a lesbian club (it's the oldest in the country), the outdoor deck and inside dancefloor at this trendy waterfront space attract a good dose of men, too, for their long-standing "After Tea T-Dance" (daily 6.30pm).

Martha's Vineyard

The largest offshore island in New England, twenty-mile-long **MARTHA'S VINEYARD** encompasses a good deal of physical and architectural variety: hills and pasturelands provide scenic counterpoints to beaches and windswept moors, while clapboards and gray shingles are supplemented by an array of Victorian homes and colorful wooden cottages. The most genteel town on the island is **Edgartown**, with its freshly painted Colonial homes and manicured gardens. The main port, **Vineyard Haven**, has a more commercial atmosphere, while **Oak Bluffs**, between the two, is best known for its gingerbread cottages. Remarkably, major development has been kept to a minimum, and though traffic can be heavy on the island in summer (when the population swells to 100,000), the island's size means it's not too hard to escape the crowds. Indeed, it's so large that traveling by bus or car is essentially a necessity.

Some history

Wampanoag Indians have been calling the island home for at least ten thousand years (a small community of around three hundred remains at **Aquinnah**). Wampanoag legend claims that in order to separate his tribe from enemies on the mainland, the Indian chief **Moshup** placed his cape on the ground and created Vineyard Sound. The island gained its English name in 1602, when explorer **Bartholomew Gosnold** named it after his daughter; the "vineyard" part was for its fertile store of vines – back then the island was virtually covered with wild grapes.

In 1642, one **Thomas Mayhew** bought the island from the Earl of Stirling for forty pounds and a beaver hat, paving the way for other Puritan farmers to settle here. They learned the **whaling industry** from the natives, and the economy flourished; the Vineyard never ousted Nantucket or New Bedford as whaling capital of the East, but many of its captains did very nicely, evidenced

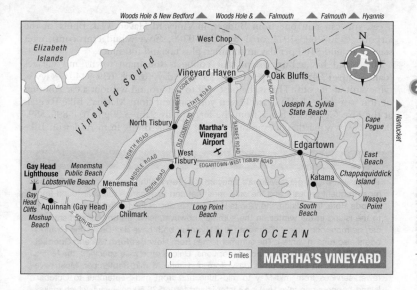

by the gracious houses that remain in Edgartown and Vineyard Haven. By the time of the Civil War, however, the whaling industry was in serious decline.

It was thanks to the **Methodist camp meetings** that took place here in the 1820s that the island's tourist industry took root. Methodist families from all over the nation started gathering in tents at **Oak Bluffs** for two weeks of preaching and recreation – by 1859 over 12,000 people were attending. As the movement grew, small cottages with extraordinarily fancy facades were constructed, now known as "**gingerbread**" style. In 1867, recognizing the island's potential as a resort, developers constructed a separate secular community next to the original campground, and large hotels were soon built around the harbor.

In 1974, the seminal movie *Jaws* was filmed on Martha's Vineyard. Don't worry – shark attacks are extremely rare in these waters (though Great Whites do occasionally prowl the beaches), and, ironically, the movie actually boosted tourism on the island.

Arrival and information

Most people come to Martha's Vineyard by **ferry**, arriving at either Oak Bluffs or Vineyard Haven, usually from Falmouth or Woods Hole (see box, p.194, for schedules and fares). For visitors arriving by plane, the **airport** (☏508/693-7022) is in West Tisbury. **Taxis** greet ferries and flights; all companies use the same fare sheets, and some share phone numbers. Try Martha's Vineyard Taxi (☏508/693-8660), A Big Cab Company (☏508/693-0037), or All Island Taxi (☏508/693-2929).

Tourist **information** is available in Vineyard Haven, Oak Bluffs, and Edgartown (see relevant sections). To check the **internet** for free, visit any of the island's public libraries.

Island transport

Bringing a **car** over on the ferry is expensive, and often impossible on summer weekends without reserving months in advance. If you just can't do without a car, you can rent one from Budget, in Vineyard Haven, Oak Bluffs, or the airport (☎508/693-1911 or 1-800/527-0700, ⓦwww.budgetmv.com); rates start at around $100 per day in summer, plus tax and insurance.

The island has a **bus** system that connects the main towns and villages (daily 7am–12.45am; $2 per ride, $6 per day; ☎508/639-9440, ⓦwww .vineyardtransit.com). This is the best way to get around without a car. Another option is to **bike**. In Vineyard Haven you can rent from Martha's Bike Rentals at the Five Corners, a block from the ferry (daily 9am–5.30pm; ☎1-800/559-0312, ⓦwww.marthasvineyardbikes.com); in Oak Bluffs from Anderson Bike

Travel to Martha's Vineyard

The easiest way to get to Martha's Vineyard is by **ferry**, although you can also **fly**. The most frequent ferries – and the only ones that can take cars – run year-round from **Woods Hole**. In addition, the Woods Hole ferry is one of the few reliable ways to get to the island in the **winter**. In the summer, however, leaving from somewhere else can be more convenient. **Falmouth** and **Hyannis** both have day-boats (the Hyannis boats also runs in winter). The summer ferries from **New Bedford, MA** and **Quonset Point, RI** have also become popular options. Unless otherwise specified, the ferries listed below run several times daily from mid-June to mid-September. Most have fewer services from mid-May to mid-June and from mid-September to October. Island-hoppers can take Hy-Line's inter-island ferry ($28.50 one-way), which makes one round-trip daily June–September between Oak Bluffs and Nantucket. **Parking** at the ferries is usually $10–15 per day, and most charge extra for bikes (up to $6 one-way). **Prices** listed below are for a round-trip.

Ferries from Cape Cod

Falmouth to Oak Bluffs (about 35min). The *Island Queen* ($16; ☎508/548-4800, ⓦwww.islandqueen.com). Passengers only.

Falmouth to Edgartown (1hr). Falmouth Ferry Service ($50; ☎508/548-9400, ⓦwww .falmouthferry.com). Passengers only; call ahead for reservations Fri–Sun.

Hyannis to Oak Bluffs. Hy-Line (☎508/778-2600 or 1-888/778-1132, ⓦwww .hy-linecruises.com). High-speed ferry (55min; $63) or traditional (1hr 35min; $39), both passengers only.

Woods Hole to both Vineyard Haven and Oak Bluffs (45min). Steamship Authority ($135 high season or $85 low season per car, not including passengers, who must pay $7.50 each way; ☎508/477-8600, ⓦwww.steamshipauthority.com). Car ferry, year-round. Reservations required to bring a car on summer weekends and holidays – you can bring a car stand-by all other times, though the wait can be long.

Ferries from elsewhere in Massachusetts and Rhode Island

New Bedford to Vineyard Haven or Oak Bluffs (1hr). New England Fast Ferry ($72; ☎1-866/453-6800, ⓦwww.nefastferry.com). Passengers only.

Quonset Point, Rhode Island, to Oak Bluffs (1hr 30min). Vineyard Fast Ferry ($75; ☎401/295-4040, ⓦwww.vineyardfastferry.com). Passengers only. Good for those traveling from Connecticut or New York; Quonset is south of Providence and Warwick. The ride can get rough on windy days – ask ahead – the staff is honest about what sea conditions are like. Shuttles are provided to Kingston Amtrak station ($18) and Providence airport ($15).

Flights

You can **fly** to Martha's Vineyard via Cape Air (☎508/771-6944 or 1-800/352-0714, ⓦwww.flycapeair.com) from Boston, Hyannis, Nantucket, New Bedford, or Providence, RI.

Rentals on Circuit Ave (April–Oct daily 8am–6pm; ☎508/693-9346); and in Edgartown from R.W. Cutler Bikes at 1 Main St (☎1-800/627-2763, ⓦwww .edgartownbikerentals.com). A basic bike generally starts at $25 per day.

There are also two hour thirty minute narrated **tours** run by Martha's Vineyard Sightseeing ($26; ☎508/627-TOUR, ⓦwww.mvtour.com); the trolleys run from spring to fall from all ferry arrival points.

Accommodation

There's plenty of **accommodation** on the island – everything from resort hotels to B&Bs oozing with charm and personality, as well as rental cottages, usually booked on a weekly basis and better deals for groups or families. Try ⓦwww.islandrealestatemv.com or www.mvvacationrentals.com, which offer a range of properties starting at around $1000 for two bedrooms (per week). You need to reserve well in advance for summer visits. Prices fall dramatically in the fall and spring, though even then weekends may be booked for weddings. Unless otherwise noted, the hotels listed below close in winter (Jan & Feb). If you want to save money, check out the Martha's Vineyard Family **Campground** in Edgartown, 569 Edgartown Rd (May–Oct; ☎508/693-3772, ⓦwww.campmv .com; $48 for two).

Edgartown

Edgartown Inn 56 N Water St ☎508/627-4794, ⓦwww.edgartowninn.com. This eighteenth-century home is a quintessential New England inn with colorful rooms that try to evoke another era (read: none of them have a TV). The Garden House and Barn out back have the least expensive rooms. ❽

Hob knob Inn 128 Main St ☎508/627-9510 or 1-800/696-2723, ⓦwww.hobknob.com. The place for unabashed luxury, with antique-laden rooms looking out over the town, and plenty of extras: flat-screen TVs, wi-fi, sauna, filling breakfasts, lavish afternoon teas, and more. ❾

🏃 **Jonathan Munroe House** 100 Main St ☎877/468-6763 or 508/627-5536, ⓦwww.jonathanmunroe.com. Gorgeous eighteenth-century house with just six enticing rooms, a great wrap-around porch and plenty of nooks and crannies to explore; the carafes of sherry in each room, and evening wine and cheese, are nice touches. ❾

Winnetu Inn & Resort South Beach ☎508/627-4747, ⓦwww.winnetu.com. This resort hotel is just a short walk from a private stretch of South Beach. Rooms come with kitch-enettes, and it's not all that much more expensive than the in-town options, though you really need a car to stay here. In high season expect two- to three-night minimum stays. ❾

Oak Bluffs

Attleboro House 11 Lake Ave ☎508/693-4346, ⓦwww.rentalsmv.com/attleborohouse. This old-fashioned Victorian guesthouse is a good budget option – it may have shared bathrooms and sloping ceilings, but the rooms are cozy and have access to a harbor-view front porch. Open May–Sept. ❺

Nashua House Hotel 30 Kennebec Ave ☎508/693-0043, ⓦwww.nashuahouse.com. Small rooms, some with shared baths, but this friendly, central hotel is an easy walk from the ferry, and with rates starting at $69 in low season, it's one of the less expensive choices on the island. It can get loud at night. ❸–❼

🏃 **Oak Bluffs Inn** 64 Circuit Ave ☎508/693-7171, ⓦwww.oakbluffsinn.com. One of the most inviting hotels on the island, with a convenient location, cozy, clean Victorian-style rooms, wi-fi, a wide porch, free cookies, and a great host. ❽–❾

🏃 **The Oak House** 79 Seaview Ave ☎866/693-5805, ⓦwww.vineyardinns .com. Another wonderful Victorian B&B, dating from 1872, with stupendous sea views and beachside location. Many of the rooms look like luxurious ships' cabins, and afternoon tea is served on the porch. ❾

Pequot Hotel 19 Pequot Ave ☎1-800/947-8704, ⓦwww.pequothotel.com. Friendly, mid-sized hotel in the gingerbread cottage neighborhood with rocking chairs on the porch, fresh cookies in the afternoon, and a quick walk to town – rooms are a bit small and showing their age, though. ❻

Elsewhere on the island

HI-Martha's Vineyard 525 Edgartown–West Tisbury Rd ☎508/693-2665 or 1-800/901-2087, ⓦwww.usahostels.org. Pleasant setting and a very neat (both clean and funky) place to stay, with 78 beds in dormitory accommodation, shared baths, and a full kitchen. It is a bit off the beaten track, so they try to make it easy for people to stay, with bike rental deals and free bike delivery. April to mid-Nov only; non-members $32–35 per night.

🏃 Menemsha Inn & Cottages and Beach Plum Inn North Rd, Menemsha ☏508/645-2521 and 508/645-9454,

www.menemshainn.com and www .beachpluminn.com. These adjacent properties are both beautifully maintained. Within walking distance of the Menemsha beach, they also include access to private town beaches on the south shore. The *Beach Plum Inn* is better for young adults, while the cottages at Menemsha are better for families. Open May–Nov; book early. ➒

The Island

The Vineyard is basically divided into two sections, the far busier of which is "**Down-Island**," which includes the ferry terminals of **Vineyard Haven** and **Oak Bluffs**, and smart **Edgartown**. The largely undeveloped western half of the island, known as "**Up-Island**," comprises woods, agricultural land, nature reserves, and a smattering of tiny villages, including **West Tisbury**, **Chilmark**, and **Aquinnah** (Gay Head). Much of the land in these areas belongs to private estates; check the Martha's Vineyard Land Bank website (www.mvlandbank .com) to see what is open for public exploration.

Vineyard Haven

Most visitors arriving by boat come into **Vineyard Haven** (officially part of **Tisbury**), at the northern tip of the island. Founded by islanders from Edgartown disillusioned with the iron-fist rule of the Mayhew family, Vineyard Haven supplanted Edgartown as the island's main commercial center in the mid-1800s because ferries preferred the shorter run to the mainland; today the town retains a business-like ambience, and the main draw for visitors is the selection of high-end antique, clothes, jewelry, and gift **shops**.

The **bus terminal**, visible as you get off the ferry, is also home to a small **visitors' kiosk** (May–Oct daily 8am–8pm), but for more information and help finding accommodation, walk up Beach Street to the **Chamber of Commerce**, no. 24 (Mon–Fri 9am–5pm, Sat 10am–4pm; ☏508/693-0085, www.mvy.com). Along the way you'll pass the **Black Dog Tavern**, as famous for its souvenirs as for its comestibles (see p.201).

From here, it's just a few yards to **Main Street**, many of whose original buildings were destroyed in the Great Fire of 1883, though it's rebuilt and thriving now. One building that escaped the blaze is the 1829 **Mayhew Schoolhouse**, at no. 110, the town's first school (and now the Seafarer's Center); the **liberty pole** out front honors three island girls who blew up the town's original liberty pole in 1776 to keep it from being used by a British warship.

Oak Bluffs

Oak Bluffs, just across Lagoon Pond from Vineyard Haven, is the newest of the island's six towns; it was a quiet farming community until the Methodists established their campground here in the nineteenth century. This section of Oak Bluffs, centered on the Trinity Park Circle, remains filled with the brightly colored "carpenter Gothic" or "**gingerbread**" cottages they built. During the summer, family-oriented events, Sunday-morning church services, and secular Saturday-evening concerts are still held in the **Tabernacle** in the center. The best-known event that takes place here is **Illumination Night** (third Wed in Aug; free), when all the cottages put up Japanese lanterns. At one end of the circle, the 1867 **Cottage Museum**, 1 Trinity Park (mid-June to Sept Mon–Sat 10am–4pm; $2 donation), offers a charming collection of photographs, old Bibles, and other artifacts from the campground's history.

▲ Gingerbread cottages, Oak Bluffs

After the Civil War, speculators built up the area near the waterfront with dance halls, a skating rink, a railroad linking the town to Edgartown, and resort hotels, of which only the 1879 **Wesley Hotel**, on Lake Avenue, survives. Most of the current action focuses on **Circuit Avenue**, where shops and bars attract a predominantly young crowd. The restored **Flying Horses Carousel**, indoors on Oak Bluffs Avenue near Circuit Avenue (mid-April to mid-Oct daily 10am– 10pm; $1.50 per ride), is the oldest operating carousel in the US; hand-carved in 1876, the 22 horses have real horsehair manes. Local maps are available nearby at the **information kiosk** (daily 9am–5pm) at Lake and Circuit avenues.

Oak Bluffs also has a few beaches worth checking out, though the **town beach**, on Sea View Avenue, can get very noisy and crowded in season. Farther south, the **Joseph A. Sylvia State Beach**, a six-mile stretch of sand, is more appealing, and it parallels an undemanding pedestrian/cycle path that leads all the way to Edgartown.

Edgartown

Six miles southeast of Oak Bluffs, **Edgartown**, originally known as Great Harbor, is the oldest and swankiest settlement on the island, its elegant Colonial residences glistening white and surrounded by exquisitely maintained gardens. The pageantry doesn't end there: the town brims with upmarket boutiques, smart restaurants, and art galleries.

Once you've got your bearings at the seasonal **visitors' center** on Church Street next to the bus stop (late May to early Sept Mon–Sat 8.30am–10pm, Sun 9am–9pm), which is basically just a gift and snack shop with restrooms and brochures, it's a short walk to the **Vineyard Museum**, at the corner of Cooke and School streets (mid-June to mid-Oct Mon–Sat 10am–5pm; rest of year Mon–Sat 10am–4pm; $7, $10 with lighthouse, $15 with lighthouse, church, and Vincent House Museum; ☎508/627-4441, ⓦ www.marthasvineyardhistory.org), a complex of buildings maintained by the Martha's Vineyard Historical Society. Buy tickets in the 1740 **Thomas Cooke House**, decorated in the Colonial style and full of absorbing displays relating to island history. Nearby, the **Carriage Shed** serves as a hodgepodge storeroom for, among other things, a peddler's cart and a whaleboat, while the **Ross Fresnel Lens Building** preserves the original lantern from Gay Head Lighthouse, made in France in 1854. The 1845 **Captain Frances Pease House** contains the gift shop and best of all, an Oral History Center, which traces the history of the island through more than 250 recorded narratives of locals. Don't miss the small collection of **Wampanoag** artifacts here, including the Burt Pot, made circa 1300.

A couple of blocks to the east, just behind the church on Main Street, the 1672 **Vincent House Museum** (May to mid-Oct Mon–Sat 10.30am–3pm; $5) is the oldest house on the island, and has the furniture to prove it. **Tours** of the museum (11am, noon, 1pm, 2pm; 45min; $10) also include the 1840 **Dr. Daniel Fisher House** and the **Old Whaling Church**, whose 92-foot-high clock tower is visible for miles around. Built in 1843 and more formally known as the United Methodist Church, it's also used as a performing arts center. The interior can only be visited as part of the tour, though you can take a peek inside for free on Sundays, when it opens for services.

At the other end of town, a short walk along North Water Street leads past more sea captains' homes to the **Edgartown Lighthouse** (Fri–Mon 11am–5pm, Thurs 11am–sunset; $5) – it's a replacement of the 1828 original, destroyed in the hurricane of 1938. Take the bus (route #8) from the visitors' center to **South Beach** in Katama, three miles south of town, for some of the island's best public access to the Atlantic.

Chappaquiddick

Chappaquiddick (aka "Chappy") is a strikingly beautiful and sparsely populated little island, an easy five-minute jaunt from Edgartown via the **ferry** ($3 per person, $10 for a car and one driver; ☎508/627-9427) which departs frequently from a ramp at the corner of Dock and Daggett streets. There are no stores, restaurants, or hotels, just private residences and hundreds of acres of dunes, salt marshes, ponds, and scrubland. The island is too large to walk comfortably, though easy to get around on a bike. The Trustees of Reservations' small Japanese garden **Mytoi**, on Dike Road (open dawn–dusk; free), is worth stopping by – it's unusual to see the typical rounded bridges and groomed trees in a pine forest. The Trustees are also the caretakers of **Wasque**, a windswept beach that is a continuation of South Beach in Edgartown, but much less crowded. In fact, you can walk between Edgartown and Chappy along this stretch of sand. On Chappy's far east side is the five-hundred acre **Cape Pogue Wildlife Refuge** ($3 entry; May–Oct), an important habitat for thousands of birds. Half the state's scallops are harvested here, too. The best way to see it is to take various **natural history tours** run by the Trustees, involving walking and kayaking; most run weekends May–October (1.5–2.5hr; $25–40 ☎508/627-3599, ⊛www.thetrustees.org).

West Tisbury

West Tisbury, the largest of the up-island communities, also has some of the best culture on the island. The locally grown produce at the **Farmers' Market**, held at the 1859 **Grange Hall** on State Road every Saturday (9am–noon) and also Wednesday mornings July and August, attracts buyers from all over Martha's Vineyard. Across the street from the hall is the **Field Gallery**, 1050 State Rd (Mon–Sat 10am–5pm, Sun 11am–4pm; free; ☎508/693-5595), locally famous for Tom Maley's larger-than-life sculptures of ladies dancing on the grass. Also on State Road, across from the Field Gallery, is **Alley's General Store** (Mon–Sat 7am–7pm, Sun 7am–6pm; ☎508/693-0088), an island institution since 1858, selling everything from canned goods to mini ouija boards, and with a wide front porch where locals often gather. You can get good sandwiches at *Garcia's Deli & Bakery*, behind the store. A short drive away at 636 Old County Rd is the picturesque **Granary Gallery** (Mon–Sat 10am–5pm, Sun 11am–4pm; free; ☎508/693-0455), which showcases works by notable local and regional artists.

West Tisbury has a bountiful supply of conservation areas, including the 216-acre **Cedar Tree Neck Wildlife Sanctuary**, Indian Hill Road (daily sunrise–sunset; free). Three main trails lead to a pretty but stony beach and a bluff with views to Gay Head and the Elizabeth Islands. Meanwhile, the **Sepiessa Point Reservation**, on New Lane off West Tisbury Road (daily dawn–dusk; free), surrounds West Tisbury Pond with trails ideal for birdwatching.

Chilmark

Five miles west of Tisbury, unspoiled **Chilmark** is the land that time almost forgot, full of pastures, dense woodlands, and rugged roads. That's not to say that the twenty-first century hasn't arrived: **Beetlebung Corner**, where Middle, State, South, and Menemsha Cross roads meet, and which is named for the wooden mallets (aka "beetles") and stoppers ("bungs") once made from local tupelo trees, is the village's center, heralded by the *Chilmark Store* (see p.202) and some other modern commercial concerns. Don't miss **Chilmark Chocolates** (closed Mon; ☎508/645 3013), halfway to Aquinnah at 19 State Rd, with a mouthwatering selection of sweets.

On South Road the tranquil **Chilmark Cemetery** is the final resting place of writer Lillian Hellman and funnyman John Belushi, who claimed that the island was the only place he could get a good night's sleep. Near the entrance, a boulder engraved with the comedian's name, a decoy to prevent fans from finding his actual unmarked grave, is where legions leave their rather unceremonious "offerings," like beer cans and condoms. Nearby, a dirt track leads to **Lucy Vincent Beach**, named after the town's librarian, who saw it as her mission to protect Chilmark residents from corruption by cutting out from the library books all pictures she deemed to be immoral. Rather ironically, the beach, which is open only to residents and their guests in the summer, doubles as a **nudist** spot in its less crowded areas. Off North Road, study the painted map at the trailhead of **Waskosim's Rock Reservation** for a three-mile hike through a variety of habitats.

Menemsha

A few miles north of Chilmark, another tiny village, **Menemsha**, is a picturesque collection of gray-shingled fishing shacks fronting a man-made harbor, which serves as an important commercial and sports-fishing port. Stroll past the fish markets of **Dutcher's Dock** for a real sense of the island's maritime heritage (see p.202), or bring a picnic to pebbly **Menemsha Beach** to enjoy the spectacular sunsets. The **Menemsha Hills Reservation**, off North Road a couple of miles towards West Tisbury, is also well worth a visit, its rocky shoreline and sand bluffs peaking at **Prospect Hill**, the highest point on the Vineyard, with views of the Elizabeth Islands.

Hikers and cyclists can take the tiny **ferry** (daily 9am–5pm; $5) across the Menemsha Pond inlet from the end of North Road, and continue along tranquil Lobsterville Road for five miles to Aquinnah – even on summer weekends this part of the island hardly sees any traffic.

Aquinnah (Gay Head)

In 1997, the people of Gay Head voted to change the town's name back to its original Wampanoag – **Aquinnah** – the culmination of a court battle in which the Wampanoags won guardianship of 420 acres of land, now known as the

Gay Head Native American Reservation. Most people come to this part of the island (its westernmost point), to see the **Gay Head Cliffs**, whose brilliant hues are the result of millions of years of geological work. When the Vineyard was underwater, small creatures died and left their shells behind to form the white layers. At other times, the area was a rainforest and vegetation compressed to form the darker colors. Glaciers thrust the layers of stone up to create the cliffs, dubbed "Gay Head" by English sailors in the seventeenth century on account of their brightness. The clay was once the main source of paint for the island's houses, but now its removal merits a fine; in any case, the cliffs are eroding so fast that it's not safe to approach them too closely.

A short path runs from the parking lot beyond the *Aquinnah* restaurant, ice cream shacks, and craft stalls to the **overlook**, which affords stunning views as far as the Elizabeth Islands, and, on a clear day, the entrance to Rhode Island's Narragansett Bay. Nearby, the imposing red-brick **Gay Head Lighthouse** (mid–June to mid–Sept Fri–Sun evenings; $5), built in 1854 to replace a wooden structure that dated from 1799, is well situated for sunset views. Below the lighthouse a **public beach** provides an equally impressive view of the cliffs. To reach it, take the wooden boardwalk from the **Moshup Beach** parking lot to the shore, then walk round towards the lighthouse.

Martha's Vineyard beaches

The island's **beaches** vary from calm, shallow waters, predominantly on the northern and eastern sides, to long stretches of pounding surf on the southern side, where the water also tends to be a bit warmer. Unfortunately, many of the best beaches are private, or are only open in the summer to residents, but there are some notable exceptions. All of the beaches listed below have lifeguards in at least some areas during summer days.

Aquinnah (Gay Head)
Lobsterville Beach Lobsterville Road. Two miles of prime Vineyard Sound beach backed by dunes. Parking on Lobsterville Road is prohibited, so bike or walk here via the ferry from Menemsha.

Moshup Beach (Gay Head Public Beach) State Road/Moshup Drive. Gorgeous setting at the foot of Gay Head Cliffs, best reached by bicycle, shuttle bus, or taxi. Parking costs $15 a day in season.

Chappaquidick
Cape Pogue Wildlife Refuge At the end of Dike Road. This sandy beach is less crowded than Wasque. $3 per person.

Wasque At the end of Wasque Rd south of School Road. Wide-open South Shore beach. $3 per person and $3 per vehicle.

Chilmark
Lucy Vincent Beach Off South Road. Sandy beach with access to some of the island's clay cliffs (note that bathing in the clay puddles is restricted) through the end of September to residents and visitors with passes.

Menemsha Public Beach Next to Menemsha Harbor. The only Chilmark beach open to the public, with sparkling waters and a picturesque setting. It becomes very crowded around sunset, since it is one of the few places to see the sun set over a beach on the East Coast.

Squibnocket Off State Road at the end of Squibnocket Road. This narrow, rocky beach is less attractive than the other Chilmark beaches, but the waves break farther

Eating

Eating is one of the principal pleasures of Martha's Vineyard; fresh lobster, quahogs (large clams), and fresh fish are particularly abundant. The ports have rows of restaurants to tempt tourists who've just disembarked the ferries, but head up–island for the best bargains. Four of the island's six towns are **dry**, meaning you can only purchase alcohol in Oak Bluffs and Edgartown. Note, though, that you can bring wine or beer purchased there to restaurants in the other towns.

Vineyard Haven

Artcliff Diner 39 Beach Rd ☎ 508/693-1224. Best diner on the island since the 1940s, with all the usual fry-ups supplemented by specials such as the "Bayou Bundle" (tortillas, sausage). Open 7am–2pm; closed Wed.

The Black Dog Bakery and Tavern 11 Water St ☎ 508/693-4786. Though you'll see their T-shirts all over the island and the mainland (never a good sign), the original restaurant and bakery serve fare as tasty as the spot is touristy. The (dry) waterfront tavern serves full and "light" (less expensive) seafood dinners, while you can stock up on muffins or bagels at the next-door bakery for the return ferry ride.

Oak Bluffs

Back Door Donuts Kennebec Ave, behind *Martha's Vineyard Gourmet Café and Bakery* ☎ 508/693-3688. Local

---

offshore, making it the best island spot for **surfing**. It's a town beach, which means it's off-limits during summer days, but anyone can show up after 5pm and in September – one of the best times to catch the waves.

Vineyard Haven

Lake Tashmoo Town Beach Herring Creek Road. Swim in the warm, brackish water of the lake, or in the cooler Vineyard Sound.

Owen Park Beach Off Main Street. A harbor beach close to the center of town, though it's not much of a swimming hole, or a beach.

Oak Bluffs

Joseph A. Sylvia State Beach Along Beach Road between Oak Bluffs and Edgartown. A narrow six-mile strand of sandy beach with clear, gentle waters and plenty of roadside parking.

Oak Bluffs Town Beach Between the Steamship Authority Dock and the State Beach. Narrow sliver of beach on Vineyard Sound that gets very crowded in season.

Edgartown

Bend-in-the-Road Beach Beach Road. Really an extension of the Joseph A. Sylvia State Beach, with similar facilities and access.

Katama Beach (South Beach) End of Katama Road. Beautiful barrier beach backed by a protected salt pond. Strong surf and currents.

Lighthouse Beach Starbuck's Neck, off North Water Street. Close to town, this harbor beach can get a bit mucked with seaweed.

West Tisbury

Lambert's Cove Beach Lambert's Cove Road. One of the island's prettiest beaches, but open only to residents during high season.

Long Point Wildlife Refuge Beach Off South Road. The perfect Vineyard beach: long and wide, with a freshwater pond just behind. Get there early for a parking space, on the south side of the street near the airport.

institution knocking out crispy doughnuts in honey-dipped, Boston cream, cinnamon and sugar, and apple fritter varieties; they'll be warm and delicious (and cost a dollar or less each). Daily 8.30pm–12.30am.

Giordano's 107 Circuit Ave ☎508/693-0184. Popular and fairly priced Italian family restaurant since 1930. Their chicken cacciatore is particularly good, and the adjoining clam bar has the best fried clams in town.

Slice of Life 50 Circuit Ave ☎508/693-3838. Casual café/bakery serving breakfast, lunch, and dinner. Relax on the sunny porch and enjoy a stack of buttermilk pancakes with Vermont maple syrup, or try the house speciality, a fried-green tomato BLT.

Edgartown

Détente Nevin Square, off Winter St (between N Water St and N Summer St) ☎508/627-8810. Of the fancier restaurants on the island, this one's your best bet for a great meal. Seasonal menus utilize local ingredients, ranging from halibut to lamb shank – it also has a fabulous wine list. Dinner only, entrees from $29.

Lure 31 Dunes Rd, *Winnetu Inn* ☎508/310-1733. This fabulous restaurant is one of the best on the island, but remains off the beaten track. Expect creations such as Vineyard swordfish "au poivre" and seared Long Island duck breast. Dinner entrees from $24.

Main Street Diner 65 Main St ☎508/627-9337. Best place for traditional diner breakfast in town, with plenty of 1950s nostalgia on display. Tucked away behind a store on Main St.

West Tisbury and Chilmark

Chilmark Store 7 State Rd, Chilmark ☎866/904-0819. Another island institution, but not for seafood; lines form here for the perfectly fired slices of pizza ($4), which come in four flavors with freshly made olive oil and pesto bases – try the whole-wheat.

Eileen Blake's Pies and Otherwise State Rd, West Tisbury ☎508/693-0528. Eileen (who passed away in 2008), sold her sumptuous home-made fruit pies from a shack outside her house. Her family is expected to continue the tradition. Open Thurs–Sat 10am–5pm; more days in summer.

Humphrey's Bakery 455 State Rd, Woodland Center, West Tisbury ☎508/693-6518. Fresh sandwiches on fresh bread, home-made cookies, and doughnuts are great to bring to the beach. Locals claim, with some justification, that the turkey sandwiches ($6) are the best in the world.

Menemsha

The Bite 29 Basin Rd ☎508/645-9239. Classic New England clam shack with a few outdoor tables and some of the juiciest fried belly clams you'll ever taste (from $14) – they also do mussels, fish and chips, squid and quahog chowder ($4).

Larsen's Fish Market 56 Basin Rd ☎508/645-2680. Primarily selling fresh fish and lobster to take away (great for picnics), this much-loved shack knocks out the best lobster rolls on the East Coast – freshly caught, boiled, and crammed into a hot-dog bun ($11).

Drinking, nightlife, and entertainment

Much of the Vineyard's evening **entertainment** comes in the form of private dinner parties, but that doesn't mean there's nothing to do if you're not invited to one. **Oak Bluffs** has the best nightlife, with a string of bars along the Dockside Marketplace. For current **listings** information, check the *Vineyard Gazette* (Ⓦwww.mvgazette.com), good for cultural events, and the weekly *Martha's Vineyard Times* (Ⓦwww.mvtimes.com), better for nightlife listings.

Bars and clubs

Coop de Ville Dockside Marketplace, Oak Bluffs ☎508/693-3420. Very hip hangout, with a lobster fest (Tues), Red Hook ales on tap, and the house speciality – eight flavors of chicken wings ($7) – to wash down the booze. *Bubba's Hot Dog* stand is next door.

David Ryan's 11 N Water St, Edgartown ☎508/627-4100. Loud two-story bar with a chi-chi martini lounge upstairs and raucous dancing – usually on the tables – to rock 'n' roll downstairs.

Lola's Southern Seafood At the *Island Inn*, Beach Rd, Oak Bluffs ☎508/693-5007, Ⓦwww.lolassouthernseafood.com. Trendy thirty-something disco with a Top 40 dancefloor. Live acts nightly during the summer, on the weekends the rest of the year.

The Newes from America 23 Kelley St, Edgartown ☎508/627-4397. Swill 500 beers in this atmospheric pub (not necessarily all in the same night) and they'll name a stool after you; New England favorites Harpoon, Smuttynose, and

Otter Creek are all here ($6). Decent and affordable pub grub, too.

🏃 **Offshore Ale Company** 30 Kennebec Ave, Oak Bluffs ☎508/693-2626. Friendly local brewpub with wooden booths, toss-on-the-floor peanuts, and live shows almost nightly in season. They also have great entrees and pizzas (lunch and dinner).

Outerland 17 Airport Rd, Edgartown ☎508/693-1137, ⓦwww.outerlandmv.com. The biggest nightclub and live music venue on the Vineyard, blending Top 40 and reggae hits on the dancefloor with almost nightly live entertainment during the summer. Cover typically $10–25.

Ritz Café 1 Circuit Ave, Oak Bluffs ☎508/693-9851. This cupboard-sized bar is anything but ritzy, with pool tables and live music acts (nightly in summer; weekends only rest of the year) that make a nice escape from the island scene.

Sugar Shack Dockside Marketplace, Oak Bluffs ☎508/696-8900. The Caribbean theme here works pretty well, with spicy Caribbean food complementing the laid-back bar and its mind-numbing rum cocktails: BVI "painkillers," Bermuda's "dark and stormy," and Florida's own "bushwhacker."

Cinema

Capawok Theatre Main St, Vineyard Haven ☎508/696-9200. First-run movies can be seen at this Art Deco theater for $9.

Entertainment Cinemas 65 Main St, Edgartown ☎508/627-8008, ⓦwww.entertainmentcinemas .com. Shows all the latest movies for $8.50.

Live music and dance

Vineyard Playhouse 24 Church St, Vineyard Haven ☎508/693-6450, ⓦwww.vineyardplayhouse .org. Weekend cabaret and musical productions are staged in this former Masonic lodge dating from 1833.

The Yard Off Middle Rd near Beetlebung Corner, Chilmark ☎508/645-9662, ⓦwww.dancetheyard .org. Specializes in modern dance performances (May–Sept) by a resident troupe.

Nantucket

The thirty-mile sea crossing to **NANTUCKET** from Cape Cod may not be an oceangoing odyssey, but it does give the "Little Gray Lady" a special, set-apart feel. The island's smaller size also adds to its unique identity, as does its architecture: the "gray" epithet refers not only to the island's frequent fogs, but to the gray clapboard and weathered shingle sidewall that are uniformly applied to buildings. Unlike the Vineyard, life on the island revolves around just one settlement, cobbled **Nantucket Town**. Frozen in time 150 years ago, its fine museums and restored mansions are monuments to the vast profits made in the era of *Moby Dick*. Beyond the town, Nantucket is easily navigated by bike, with a fantastic network of **paths** the best way to appreciate its natural beauty, including heaths, moorlands, and mile after mile of public **beaches**. The best route follows Polpis Road east to the rose-covered cottages of **Siasconset** (always called "Sconset").

Some history

Long before the arrival of Europeans, Nantucket was inhabited by the **Wamponoag** Indians. English settlement on the island dates from 1659, when **Thomas Mayhew**, who had been granted rights over the island, sold them on the cheap to shareholders eager to escape the repressive policies of the Massachusetts Bay Colony. The settlers, who landed at **Madaket**, were only able to survive their first winter thanks to assistance from the Wampanoag natives. In time, the number of settlers began to rival that of the natives, who were decimated by disease, and **whaling** became the business of the day. Though islanders had initially learned from the Indians to spear whales from the shore, they soon began to sail the ocean to pursue their prey. This paid off in 1712, when one of the ships was blown far out to sea and managed to harpoon a sperm whale, whose oil fetched very high prices.

For the next 150 years, the whaling trade flourished, as did the island; the population grew to more than 10,000, and at its peak the harbor was base

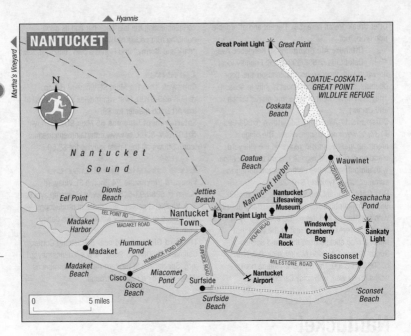

to some one hundred whaling boats. The beginning of the end came when larger ships became necessary for longer periods at sea, and Nantucket's harbor began silting in, quickly getting shallow. Whaling activity transferred to the deep-water harbors at New Bedford and Edgartown. Then, in 1846, a major **fire**, which started on Main Street, spread to the harbor, where it set light to barrels of whale oil. The harbor was almost completely destroyed, along with a third of Nantucket Town. The final blow to Nantucket's whaling business was the replacement of whale oil by kerosene as the fuel of choice.

Nantucket floundered for the next century, until a local entrepreneur revamped the **waterfront** in the 1950s; suddenly people began work to preserve the old buildings that still stood. Now the population jumps from 10,000 in winter to well over 60,000 in the summer, and property prices are more akin to Manhattan than other Massachusetts shore towns.

Arrival and information

Most likely you'll arrive in Nantucket by **ferry** from Hyannis (see box, p.177), with Hy-Line boats pulling in at Straight Wharf and the Steamship Authority ferries docking at Steamboat Wharf. It is much quicker, however, to **fly**: Island Airlines (☏1-800/248-7779, ⓦwww.nantucket.net/trans/islandair) and Nantucket Airlines (☏1-800/352-0714, ⓦwww.nantucketairlines.com) run year-round daily services from Hyannis to Nantucket (hourly in the summer); Cape Air (☏1-800/352-0714, ⓦwww.flycapeair.com) also offers daily services to and from Boston, Providence, and Martha's Vineyard. Jet Blue (☏1-800/538-2583, ⓦwww.jetblue.com) provides convenient flights from New York. The **airport** (☏508/325-5300, ⓦwww.nantucketairport.com) is about three miles southeast of Nantucket Town.

Visitor information is available from the **Chamber of Commerce**, Zero Main St, 2/F (Mon–Fri 9am–5pm; ☏508/228-1700, ⊛www.nantucketchamber .org), or from the helpful **Nantucket Information Bureau**, 25 Federal St (April–Dec 9am–6pm; rest of year Mon–Sat 9am–5pm; ☏508/228-0925, ⊛www .nantucket.net). Another useful resource is ⊛www.ack.net, the website for the island's main newspaper, the *Inquirer & Mirror*, with links to restaurant and shopping guides, and other practical information.

The **Nantucket Historical Association** (☏508/228-1894, ⊛www.nha.org), offers a $6 Historic Sites Pass for entry to the six of its buildings open to the public, as well as an $18 **combined ticket** which includes the whaling museum (tickets available at any of these sites). The properties are generally open from late May to mid-October Monday to Saturday 10am to 5pm and Sunday noon to 5pm.

Island transport

Once you've arrived, **getting around** should pose no problem. As island streets are extremely tiny, driving a **car** makes little sense, especially in peak season. A far better idea is to rent a 4WD **jeep** so that you can drive on the beach (up to Great Point, for example); rentals usually include permits. Try Nantucket Island Rent-A-Car at the airport (April–Oct only; ☏508/228-9989 ⊛www .nantucketislandrentacar.com) or Young's Bicycle Shop at 6 Broad St (Mon–Sat 8.30am–6pm, Sun 9am–5pm; ☏508/228-1151, ⊛www.youngsbicycleshop.com). Rates are very expensive; from $100 per day off season to around $200 per day in June and July (including beach permits, which are $125 in peak season).

Cars aside, you're best off renting a **bike** so you can explore the island's wonderful paths. From the moment you get off the ferry you're besieged by rental places. Try Young's Bicycle Shop (see above), just up Steamboat Wharf from the Steamship Authority dock; it should cost $25 per day for a standard mountain bike.

There is also an island **bus** system, with five shuttle routes operated by the Nantucket Regional Transit Authority (May–Sept 7.30am–11.30pm; $1 per in-town journey, $2 to Madaket, Sconset, and the airport; ☏508/228-7025 ⊛www .shuttlenantucket.com); you can get unlimited travel for one day ($7), three days ($12), a week ($20), or a month ($50). You can hop on and off at any of the red and gray signposts along the routes. The buses have bike racks, so you can stick yours on the front if you get tired of pedaling. Barrett's Tours (☏508/228-0174 or 1-800/773-0174) also runs ninety-minute narrated bus tours ($25) around the island.

You might also consider taking to the water, as several beaches are best approached from the sea. Nantucket Community Sailing (mid-June to early Sept; ☏508/228-5358; ⊛www.nantucketcommunitysailing.org) rents **kayaks** ($25 per hr) **windsurfers** ($35 per hr) and **sailboats** (from $40/hr) from Jetties Beach, just north of Nantucket Town. The less energetic can consider renting a powerboat from Nantucket Boat Rental at Straight Wharf (☏508/325-1001), though this will set you back at least $450 per day.

You probably won't need the aid of **taxis** while here, but they are usually available at the airport or by the ferry terminal; A-1 (☏508/228-3330) and All Point (☏508/228-5779) are both reliable.

Accommodation

There's a wide range of **accommodation** in Nantucket Town, from good-sized, sophisticated resorts to cozy inns and B&Bs; further afield, you can rent private homes by the week. One thing you won't find, however, is price diversity – it's not easy to find a room for under $200 in high season. For free, easy booking help contact **Martha's Vineyard and Nantucket Reservations** (☎508/693-7200 or 1-800/649-5671, ⓦwww.mvreservations.com). If you're stuck at the last minute with nowhere to stay, try the **Nantucket Information Bureau** (see p.205) which maintains a list of vacancies during the season. Unless otherwise indicated, all of the places listed below are in **Nantucket Town**.

Century House 10 Cliff Rd ☎508/228-0530, ⓦwww.centuryhouse.com. Elegant rooms with private baths and country-house ambience in this 1833 late Federal home. ❼–❾

Cliff Lodge 9 Cliff Rd ☎508/228-9480, ⓦwww .clifflodgenantucket.com. Quiet B&B in a 1771 whaling master's home, set in a residential area. They have some low-priced singles in the off season. ❽

Hawthorn House 2 Chestnut St ☎508/228-1468, ⓦwww.hawthornhouse.com. Central, well-appointed classic gray-clapboard guesthouse with handsome rooms outfitted with tapestries, quilts, and antique furnishings. ❽

HI-Nantucket Surfside Beach ☎508/228-0433, ⓦwww.usahostels.org. Dorm beds a stone's throw from Surfside Beach in an 1873 lifesaving station, just over three miles south of Nantucket Town. $32–35 per night. Open mid-May to Sept.

Martin House Inn 61 Centre St ☎508/228-0678, ⓦwww.martinhouseinn.com. Thirteen lovely rooms offer good value in this 1803 seaman's house, with inviting common areas and spacious veranda – local art and antiques feature throughout. Great single rates. ❽

Ship's Inn 13 Fair St ☎508/228-0040 or 1-800/564-2760, ⓦwww.shipsinnnantucket.com. Three-story whaling captain's home dating from 1831, with eleven biggish rooms, all with private bath. ❽

🏃 **Union Street Inn** 7 Union St ☎888/517-0707, ⓦwww.unioninn.com. This luxurious B&B boasts a central location, hearty breakfasts, and gorgeous rooms, with thick rugs, drapes, and period wallpaper – it's pricey, so much better value off season. ❾

🏃 **Veranda House** 3 Step Lane ☎508/228-0695, ⓦwww.theverandahouse.com. The theme at this boutique hotel is "retro chic", adding a refreshingly contemporary take on the island's traditional Victorian-style B&Bs; rooms are stylishly designed, most with harbor views, and come with free wi-fi. ❾

The Wauwinet Wauwinet Rd, Wauwinet ☎508/228-0145 or 1-800/426-8718, ⓦwww.wauwinet.com. For the super-rich, this is *the* place to stay on the island. A bit out from the main town, the luxury historic resort hotel offers a full range of leisure facilities, beautifully appointed rooms, excellent dining, and great views – and extortionate rates. ❾

Nantucket Town

Very much the center of activity on the island, **NANTUCKET TOWN** boasts cobbled streets and a delightful array of eighteenth- and nineteenth-century homes, most of them concentrated around **Main Street**. Before you hit there, though, you can get the salty feel of the harbor when arriving on the ferries, which dock at **Steamboat Wharf** or lively **Straight Wharf**, just to the south, dating from 1723 and lined with souvenir shops and restaurants.

Nantucket Whaling Museum and Brant Point

Steamboat Wharf leads directly to Broad Street, where the island's top sight, the newly refurbished **Nantucket Whaling Museum** (late May to mid-Oct daily 10am–5pm; every first and third Wed until 9pm; $15; ☎508/228-1894, ⓦwww .nha.org/sites/index.html), is housed in a candle-making factory built just before the 1846 fire. Its intriguing exhibits include scrimshaw artifacts – look out for the set of 21 whale types carved from whales' teeth – harpoons, and a gigantic sperm whale skeleton washed ashore in 1998. Before you leave, check out the phenomenal view over the town and harbor from the museum roof.

From the museum it's a pleasant stroll along South Beach and Easton streets up to Brant Point and the 26-foot **Brant Point Lighthouse**, guarding the entrance to the harbor. Completed in 1901 (the first version was erected in 1746), the whole site is a working Coast Guard station, but the grounds are open to the public.

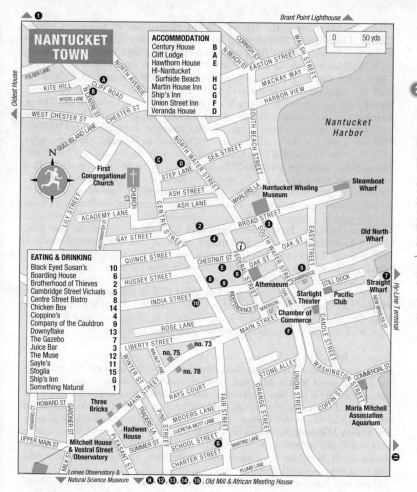

NANTUCKET TOWN

0   50 yds

ACCOMMODATION
Century House   B
Cliff Lodge   A
Hawthorn House   E
HI-Nantucket
  Surfside Beach   H
Martin House Inn   C
Ship's Inn   G
Union Street Inn   F
Veranda House   D

Oldest House

Folger Lane
KITE HILL
WYERS LANE
N CENTRE ST
CLIFF ROAD
NORTH AVENUE
CHESTER ST
WEST CHESTER ST
GULL ISLAND LANE

N BEACH ST
CORNISH STREET
EASTON STREET
WALSH STREET
MACKAY WAY
HARBOR VIEW
SOUTH BEACH STREET

Nantucket Harbor

First Congregational Church
CHURCH CT
LILY STREET
ACADEMY LANE
WESTMINSTER ST
NORTH WATER STREET
SEA STREET
STEP LANE HOUSE
ASH STREET
ASH LANE
CENTRE STREET
GAY STREET
QUINCE STREET
HUSSEY STREET
INDIA STREET
CHESTNUT STREET
WHALERS LA
BROAD STREET
SOUTH WATER STREET
OAK ST
EASY STREET
FEDERAL STREET

Nantucket Whaling Museum
Steamboat Wharf
Old North Wharf
Straight Wharf
Hy-Line Terminal

EATING & DRINKING
Black Eyed Susan's   10
Boarding House   6
Brotherhood of Thieves   5
Cambridge Street Victuals 2
Centre Street Bistro   8
Chicken Box   14
Cioppino's   4
Company of the Cauldron   9
Downyflake   13
The Gazebo   7
Juice Bar   3
The Muse   12
Sayle's   11
Sfoglia   15
Ship's Inn   G
Something Natural   1

Athenaeum
Starlight Theater
Pacific Club
Chamber of Commerce
CAMBRIDGE ST
STILL DOCK
COVE LANE
MADISON ST
MAIN STREET
CANDLE STREET
WASHINGTON STREET
COMMERCIAL ST
COFFIN ST
NEW WHALER ST

ROSE LANE
LIBERTY STREET
no. 73
no. 75
no. 78
WINTER ST
WALNUT LANE
STONE ALLEY
UNION STREET
ORANGE STREET
RAYS COURT
MAIN STREET
TRADERS LA
PINE STREET
FAIR STREET
MOOERS LANE
LUCRETIA MOTT LANE
MARTINS LANE

Three Bricks
Hadwen House
HOWARD ST
GARDNER ST
UPPER MAIN ST
MILL ST
PLEASANT ST
SUMMER ST
SCHOOL STREET
CHARTER STREET
PLUMB LANE

Maria Mitchell Association Aquarium

Mitchell House & Vestral Street Observatory
Loines Observatory & Natural Science Museum
▼ **H**, ⑫, ⑬, ⑭, ⑮ : Old Mill & African Meeting House

Downtown

Straight Wharf becomes **Main Street**, where, at its junction with South Water Street, you'll see the **Pacific Club**, a three-story Georgian edifice built for William Rotch, owner of two of the three ships involved in the Boston Tea Party. It once served as a customs house, but has been used since 1861 as an elite private club for retired whaling captains.

A short detour south to 28 Washington St takes you to the **Maria Mitchell Association Aquarium** (Mon–Sat 10am–4pm; $6; ☎508/228-5387), where you can learn about Nantucket's underwater ecology via twenty small salt-water tanks and two large "touch tanks," featuring scallops, whelks, and baby squid.

Return to Main Street, then walk north along Federal Street to the graceful **Athenaeum**, 1 Lower India St (summer Mon, Wed, Fri & Sat 9.30am–5pm, Tues & Thurs 9.30am–8pm; winter Wed, Fri & Sat 9.30am–5pm, Tues & Thurs 9.30am–8pm; free; ☎508/228-1110, ⓦwww.nantucketatheneum.org), the town library, archives, cultural center, and repository for various antiques and scrimshaw – its elegant interior is well worth a peek.

Back on Main Street, the **Henry Coffin House**, no. 75, and the **Charles Coffin House**, no. 78, belonged to two whale merchant brothers. Their handsome houses, two of the earliest red-brick buildings on the island, were built opposite each other in the early 1830s, both designed by master mason Christopher Capen. Further up Main Street, identical numbers 93, 95, and 97, built in a transitional Federal-Greek Revival style in 1837 and 1838 by Capen for whaling tycoon Joseph Starbuck and his three sons, are known as the **Three Bricks**, and are iconic symbols of Nantucket's boom years. The Starbucks had quite an impact on the street: Joseph's daughter Eunice married William Hadwen (owner of the candle factory that is now the Whaling Museum), who built the two flamboyant Greek Revival houses at no. 94 and no. 96 in the 1840s, while daughter Eliza built the ornate Victorian at no. 73 in 1871. The only one of these grand houses you can visit is the 1845 **Hadwen House**, 96 Main St (late May to mid-Oct Mon–Sat 10am–5pm, Sun noon–5pm; $6), which contains gas chandeliers, colossal pilasters, and silver doorknobs, and has a lovely period garden out back.

Built in 1834, the **First Congregational Church**, 62 Centre St (mid-June to Sept Mon–Sat 10am–4pm; $3 donation to climb tower; ☎508/228-0950), is famous for its 120-foot steeple, from which you can get a spectacular view of the island. The inside is worth a peek, too, for its trompe l'oeil ceiling, six-hundred-pound brass chandelier, and rows of old box pews. From here you can follow Centre and West Chester streets past Lily Pond Park to the aptly named **Oldest House** (aka the Jethro Coffin House), on Sunset Hill Road (late May to mid-Oct Mon–Sat 10am–5pm, Sun noon–5pm; $6). Built in 1686, the house is sparsely decorated, with an antique loom the most prominent feature inside.

Maria Mitchell sights

For a break from all things nautical, spend half a day exploring the legacy of local astronomer **Maria Mitchell** (1818–89), who discovered "Miss Mitchell's Comet" in 1847. The first professional woman astronomer in the US, she went on to reveal the cause of sunspots and later became the first female member of the American Academy of Arts and Sciences. Today her memory is kept alive by the **Maria Mitchell Association**, 4 Vestal St, which manages several attractions in town (June to mid-Oct; combined ticket $10; ☎508/228-9198, Ⓦwww .mmo.org). Check the Association website for their program of summer talks and field trips, especially good for kids.

Maria was born at the 1790 **Mitchell House**, 1 Vestal St (Mon–Sat 10am–4pm; $5; ☎508/228-2896), decorated in austere nineteenth-century Quaker style and embellished with displays covering the history of women and Quakers on Nantucket. The house contains many Mitchell family artifacts, including some of Maria's personal belongings, such as her telescope, beer mugs, and opera glasses. On the same grounds, the **Vestal Street Observatory** (Mon–Sat guided tours at 11am; $5; ☎508/228-927) features an outdoor scale-model of the solar system, a planar sundial, sunspot observations (when clear), and a permanent astronomy exhibit.

The **Natural Science Museum at Hinchman House**, nearby at 7 Milk St (Mon–Sat 10am–4pm; $5; ☎508/228-0898), boasts an extensive display of local flora and fauna, though the hands-on activities (shell and wildflower identification games, touch tables), live snakes, and turtles will mostly appeal to kids. Finally, at the **Loines Observatory**, 59 Milk St Ext (Mon, Wed & Fri 9–10.30pm weather permitting; $10; ☎508/228-9273), you can climb up to an aging telescope and peek into space, as well as admire the association's much newer 24-inch research telescope.

Old Mill and African Meeting House

A few blocks south of the Mitchell House, at Prospect and York streets, the **Old Mill** (late May to mid-Oct Mon–Sat 10am–5pm, Sun noon–5pm; $6) is the oldest operating windmill in the US, built around 1746. Weather permitting, millers grind corn daily and offer tours every 30 minutes till 4.30pm.

Walk down York Street and you'll come to the **African Meeting House**, 29 York St (July & Aug Tues–Sat 11am–3pm, Sun 1–3pm; free; ☎508/228-9833), a small post-and-beam shack in an area of the island once known as New Guinea. Built in 1827 by the African Baptist Society, the house is now managed by Boston's Museum of African-American History. As the only reminder of what was once a vibrant but segregated community, the house has special significance: it acted as a church, a school, and a meeting house for the African-American community on Nantucket well into the twentieth century. Today it hosts cultural programs and exhibits on the history of African-Americans on Nantucket. You can also pick up information here about the **Black Heritage Trail**, featuring nine stops in downtown and the old New Guinea area.

The rest of the island

Beyond the town, Nantucket remains surprisingly wild, a mixture of moors and marshes. Though the main draw remains the **beaches**, those with more time should check out the interior. Much of it is protected by the **Nantucket Conservation Foundation;** check the website for details (ⓦwww.nantucketconservation.com).

Polpis Road

Polpis Road, an indirect and arcing track from Nantucket Town to Sconset, holds a number of natural attractions both on and off its main course, all easily accessed from the **bike path** that shadows the road. Your first stop should be the **Nantucket Life Saving Museum**, off the northern side of the road at no. 158 (mid-June to mid-Oct daily 9.30am–4pm; $5; ⓦwww.nantucketlifesavingmuseum.com), which is packed to the gills with lifesaving rescue equipment, photographs, and artifacts from the *Andrea Doria*, which sunk off Nantucket forty years ago. Further on, an unmarked track leads south to **Altar Rock**, the island's highest point, which you'll want to walk around for views of the surrounding bogs. One of these, the two-hundred-acre **Windswept Cranberry Bog**, east on Polpis Road, is colorful at most times of the year, but especially in mid-October, when the berries, loosened from the plants by machines, float to the top of the water.

Siasconset, Great Point, and Coatue

Seven miles east of Nantucket Town, the village of **Siasconset**, or Sconset as it's universally known, is filled with cottages encrusted with salt and covered over with roses. Once solely a fishing village, it began to attract wealthy visitors eager to get away from Nantucket Town's foul-smelling whale-oil refineries, and in the late 1800s, enough writers and actors came from big cities to give Sconset some modicum of artistic renown.

There's not too much to see, other than the picturesque houses along Broadway and Center streets; the year-round population of 150 only supports a few commercial establishments, all close to one another in the center of town. A few miles north of town, the red-and-white striped **Sankaty Light**, an 1849 lighthouse, stands on a ninety-foot bluff, though it seems only a matter of time until it falls victim to the crashing waves below. North of here, and also accessible heading east on Polpis Road from Nantucket Town, **Wauwinet** is largely notable for holding the inn of choice on the island, *The Wauwinet* (see p.206).

Further north still, **Coatue–Coskata–Great Point**, a five-mile-long, razor-thin slice of sand, takes in three separate wildlife refuges, and is accessible by 4WD (see p.205; ℡ 508/228-5646, Ⓦ www.thetrustees.org) or on foot. In the Coskata section, the wider beaches are backed by salt marshes and some trees: with binoculars, you may catch sight of plovers, egrets, oystercatchers, terns, and even osprey. The beach narrows again as you approach the **Great Point Light**, at the end of the spit, put up in 1986 after an earlier light was destroyed during a 1984 storm; the new one is said to be able to withstand 240mph winds and twenty-foot waves. Unsurprisingly, this is not the safest place to swim, even on a calm day. Coatue, the last leg of the journey, is the narrow stretch that separates Nantucket Harbor from the ocean; so narrow, in fact, that stormy seas frequently crash over it, turning Great Point into an island.

Madaket and the South Shore

At the western tip of Nantucket, rural **Madaket** is a small settlement located on the spot where Thomas Macy landed in 1659. There's nothing in the way of visitor attractions, but the area's peacefulness and natural beauty make up for that. Unspoiled **Eel Point**, a couple of miles north, sits on a spit of sand covered

---

Nantucket beaches

With the majority of its fifty miles of **beaches** open to the public, Nantucket is a great place for ocean enthusiasts. The island's southern and eastern flanks, where the water tends to have rougher waves, are ideal for surfers, while the more sheltered northern beaches are good for swimming. With extremely limited, albeit free, **parking**, it makes sense to walk or cycle to all but the most far-flung beaches. See p.205 for **watersports rentals**.

Nantucket Town

Brant Point Off Easton Street. Very strong currents at the harbor entrance mean this beach is better for tanning and watching the comings and goings of boats than swimming.

Dionis Beach Eel Point Road. A quiet beach with high dunes and calm waters.

Jetties Beach Off Bathing Beach Road. Catch the shuttle bus that runs along North Water and South Beach streets in the centre of town, or leg it to this popular and kid-friendly beach whose facilities include lifeguards, changing rooms, and a snack bar. The real highlight is the fabulous sandbar at low tide.

East of Town

Sconset Beach (known also as Codfish Park) Off Polpis Road. Sandy beach with moderate surf and a full range of facilities. Just a short walk to several eating places.

South Shore

Cisco Beach Hummock Point Road. Long, sandy beach, ideal for surfing; note, however, that the main public access points were closed in 2008 due to massive erosion.

Madaket Beach At the end of Madaket Road. Another long beach with strong surf and gorgeous sunsets over the water. Like Cisco, the main beach area was closed in 2008 due to erosion (check with the information offices); you can continue on bike and foot to Smith's Point instead, one of the island's most beautiful corners.

Surfside Beach Off Surfside Road. Wide sands attract a youthful crowd of surfers; there's a large parking lot, but you'd do better to take the shuttle bus or bike from town.

with all manner of plants and flowers, including wild roses and bayberries, which attract an array of birds, including graceful egrets.

Eating

Nantucket abounds in first-rate dining establishments. If you're having dinner at a restaurant, though, be prepared for the bill: prices are often comparable to those in Manhattan. You'll find a bevy of cheaper takeout options on Broad Street near the ferry dock. **Picnics** are always an attractive option in summer; *Provisions* (on Straight Wharf) and *Something Natural* (see below) are best for sandwiches and fresh bread.

Nantucket Town: downtown

Aunt Leah's Fudge Straight Wharf ☎508/228-1183. Indulge your sweet tooth with slabs of creamy cranberry, walnut, peanut butter, and M&M-topped home-made fudge.

Black Eyed Susan's 10 India St ☎508/325-0308. Popular Southern-influenced breakfast and brunch place (and also dinner Mon–Sat in summer), serving big delicious omelets and grits with cheese for $9–10. Dinner entrees from $27.

Boarding House 12 Federal St ☎508/228-9622. The romantic downstairs dining room here serves a range of contemporary Euro-Asian-style meat and fish dishes; the lively bar upstairs offers lighter, cheaper bistro fare.

Cambridge Street Victuals 12 Cambridge St ☎508/228-7109. This smart restaurant morphs into a popular nightspot after dinner, with a selection of bottled beers and the local Cisco draft ($5); it's worth coming earlier for the seasonal menu, barbecue plates, and spicy grilled chicken wings (from $12). Dinner only.

Centre Street Bistro 29 Centre St ☎508/228-8470. Intimate (seven-table) café specializing in light seafood fare – the seared salmon with lemon aioli is gorgeously fresh – with wonderful home-made desserts to top it off. Serves a mean weekend brunch, too.

Cioppino's 20 Broad St ☎508/228-4622. Stylish Mediterranean and New American cuisine in the center of town. Try their grilled lobster tails and fresh shrimp on a bed of pesto pasta.

Company of the Cauldron 5 India St ☎508/228-4016. A romantic, vine-covered, candlelit haven with live harp music thrice weekly. Both evening seatings of the shifting *prix fixe* menu ($58) sell out quickly, so make reservations.

Juice Bar 12 Broad St ☎508/228-5799. The fresh juices are the healthiest options on offer at this small take-out shop near the ferry, but in summer expect long lines for the luscious home-made ice cream (try the "Crantucket"), served in cups or giant waffle cones ($3.30–4.50).

Ships Inn 13 Fair St ☎508/228-0040. Choose from artfully presented California-French style dishes, such as sautéed halibut, served in an intimate underground space dating from the 1830s. Closed Nov–April.

Nantucket Town: outskirts

Downyflake 18 Sparks Ave ☎508/228-4533. The island's best diner, a bit out of the way on the edge of town, but worth a visit for the reasonably priced plates of comfort food, and especially the fresh doughnuts (get them to go). Open Mon–Sat 6am–2pm, Sun 6am–noon.

Sayle's 99 Washington St Ext ☎508/228-4599. The closest thing in town to a classic clam shack, serving chowder ($3.25), fresh lobster, and fried clams (at market prices) – take out for a picnic or munch on the veranda.

Sfoglia 130 Pleasant St ☎508/325-4500. Classy Italian place with a carefully selected menu, porcelain-topped tables, and fresh, rustic interior; the Renaissance-influenced dishes change bimonthly with pastas from $13 and *secondis* from $26. Dinner only, closed Sun.

Something Natural 50 Cliff Rd ☎508/228-0504. Handy stopoff on the way to Madaket, serving high-quality, deli-style sandwiches, salads, and freshly baked breads, muffins, and cakes.

Siasconset

Sconset Café 8 Main St, facing the rotary ☎508/257-6365. Best place for a sit-down lunch or dinner in Sconset, with a varied menu which features not only clams and chowder ($10), but also various grills, salads, and sandwiches ($8–12).

Siasconset Market 4 Main St ☎508/257-9915. The village general store is the place to stock up on picnic fare and decent sandwiches to take away, munch on the beach, or eat in the square outside – also does excellent ice cream in summer. Daily 8am–10pm.

Drinking, nightlife, and entertainment

In terms of tried-and-true **nightlife**, Nantucket is quieter than the Vineyard, but Nantucket Town still has some good options to keep you out until after midnight (though not much later). There's certainly no shortage of live music, especially jazz and folk, to help you kick up your heels, but if you're after a big-city nightclub, you won't find it here. Current **listings** can be found in the weekly *Yesterday's Island* (ⓦ www.yesterdaysisland.com) and the daily *Inquirer and Mirror* (ⓦ www.ack.net).

Bars and clubs

Brotherhood of Thieves 23 Broad St ☎508/228-2551. This bar is a Nantucket institution and the place to go for live folk music, year-round; huddle in the dimly lit pub, or pose at the smarter bar upstairs – it also serves as a decent restaurant with outdoor deck.

Chicken Box 6 Dave St ☎508/228-9717. Literally a wooden box-like shack on the outskirts of town, this local dive bar is the place to escape the tourists and see great live bands – covers usually range $7–10.

The Gazebo 1 Harbor Square, Straight Wharf ☎508/228-1266. Easy to find on summer nights, when the crowds pile around this sociable bar (literally a gazebo), right on the wharf, for potent cocktails and beers.

The Muse 44 Surfside Drive ☎508/228-1471. A mix of rock, reggae, and just about anything else you can dance to, as well as a few pool tables, keep this venue popular.

Cinema

Starlight Theater and Café 1 N Union St ☎508/228-4435, ⓦ www.starlightnantucket.com. For the latest Hollywood movies, check out this small local theater ($10).

Theater

Theater Workshop of Nantucket Methodist Church, 2 Centre St ☎508/228-4305, ⓦ www.theatreworkshop.com. Local theater troupe, putting on plays and musicals throughout much of the year at the Methodist Church, and at Bennett Hall, 62 Centre St. Tickets rarely top $25.

Central and Western Massachusetts

CHAPTER 3 **Highlights**

✳ **Basketball Hall of Fame**
A real treat for hoops fans, the Hall of Fame resides in Springfield, the birthplace of the sport. See p.222

✳ **Five College Consortium**
The college towns of Northampton, Amherst, and South Hadley offer plenty in the way of arts, culture, and entertainment. See p.223

✳ **Historic Deerfield**
Magnificently preserved colonial town, offering a hazy window into seventeenth-century life on the harsh New England frontier. See p.232

✳ **Berkshires festivals** Music, dance, and drama junkies can get their summertime fix in the Berkshires, with many performances taking place at open-air venues in the countryside. See p.237

✳ **Naumkeag** Boasting the best of the Newport-style summer "cottages" to be found in the area. See p.238

✳ **MASS MoCA** This fine contemporary art museum is the centerpiece of North Adams, transformed from a post-industrial eyesore to the hippest place in the Berkshires. See p.247

▲ Naumkeag

Central and Western Massachusetts

The strip malls, franchises, and faded industrial towns of Central Massachusetts shouldn't detain you for too long, though it does have a few things worth checking out: the city of **Worcester** has one of the state's best collections of art, and **Springfield**, the largest city in the western part of the state, is home to the Basketball Hall of Fame. The **Pioneer Valley** stretches north from here, as small-town charisma and New England gentility begin to reassert themselves. Home to four separate colleges and a major university, the "Valley" supports a year-round population of academics, artists, and community activists who, in turn, patronize a bevy of restaurants, cafés, and bookstores – giving the area a continuous, if low-key, buzz. You can base yourself in any one of three or four locations to explore this region, but **Northampton** is probably the liveliest, with a good range of places to stay and most of the area's nightlife. **Amherst**, Northampton's eastern neighbor, is home to a museum honoring poet **Emily Dickinson**, who lived and died there.

From the Pioneer Valley, most roads lead west to the **Berkshires**, as the smattering of tiny towns nestled in among the Berkshire Mountains, dividing Massachusetts from New York, are collectively known. With its spas, pricey inns, and sophisticated cultural happenings, it's a lovely spot for a weekend break if you can afford it; stay in the slightly precious small towns of **Lenox** or **Stockbridge**

Outdoor activities in Central Massachusetts

Though Central Massachusetts has little in the way of traditional sights, there's plenty of outdoor activities on offer. The northern strip of Central Massachusetts is good scenic driving country, with Rte-2 dubbed the **Johnny Appleseed Trail** (ⓦwww .appleseed.org) as it heads west from Concord. This was the stomping ground of Johnny Appleseed (actually John Chapman, born in 1774 in Leominster, MA); he dedicated his life to planting apple trees and spreading the word of God. This section of Rte-2 takes in 25 towns, numerous orchards, wineries, rolling hills, and **Wachusett Mountain** (ⓣ978/464-2300 or 1-800/SKI-1234, ⓦwww.wachusett.com), a popular spot for skiing and snowboarding. For hiking, as well as cross-country skiing and snowshoeing, head deeper into the **Leominster State Forest** (ⓣ978/874-2303), part of the Wachusett Mountain State Reservation (ⓣ978/464-2987), where trails abound.

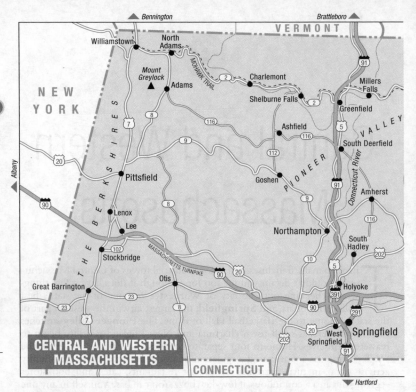

in the southern Berkshires, or **Williamstown** in the north, which has a good selection of museums and galleries. There's also the outstanding Massachusetts Museum of Contemporary Art (MASS MoCA) in nearby **North Adams**.

Worcester

Roughly forty miles west of Boston on I-90, **WORCESTER** is Massachusetts' second largest city. Incorporated in 1722, it enjoyed a century and a half of unbridled prosperity as a thriving town of textile mills and close-knit Greek, Yiddish, and Italian immigrant communities, before it lapsed into recession during the 1970s and 1980s. Notable (sort of) for birthing a mixed bag of American icons – including Abbie Hoffman and the Valentine's Day card – the town is only beginning to pick itself up again, so for the moment it doesn't have much to offer beyond its impressive art museum.

Arrival and information

Worcester is spread out and can be difficult to navigate **by car**. I-290 cuts across the eastern edge of downtown; the easiest way to Main Street is via Exit 16. There's a large multistory **parking lot** ($2 per hr) on Elm Street, just off Main Street, convenient for downtown, though if you've come solely for the art museum (Exit 18) simply park there and skip the city center altogether.

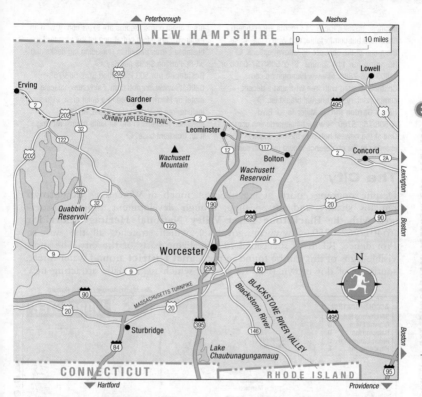

Union Station, 2 Washington Square, serves as both the **train** and **bus station**. Amtrak and MBTA run frequent services from Boston (around 1hr on Amtrak, 1hr 50min on MBTA), though the latter is around a third of the Amtrak fare (just $7.75). Peter Pan Bus Lines runs to Boston ($8) and Springfield ($22); Greyhound also serves the city. A comprehensive **local bus** service is provided by the RTA (℡508/791-9782, Ⓦwww.therta.com).

The **Worcester Regional Chamber of Commerce**, 446 Main St, inside the Sovereign Bank Building, 2/F (Mon–Fri 8.30am–5pm; ℡508/753-2924, Ⓦwww .worcesterchamber.org), has basic information on the city, while the friendly and well-equipped **Central Massachusetts Convention and Visitors Bureau** is located on the second floor of the historical museum at 30 Elm St (Mon–Fri 9am–5pm; ℡508/755-7400 or 866/755-7439, Ⓦwww.centralmass.org).

Accommodation

Worcester works best as a day-trip from Boston or Northampton, though if you want to stay the night you'll find plenty of reliable **hotels** and cheaper motel chains in and around the city.

Beechwood Hotel 363 Plantation St ℡508/754-5789 or 1-800/344-2589, Ⓦwww.beechwoodhotel.com. Even the smallest rooms at this glitzy hotel are spacious. HBO and internet are in each one, and there are complimentary newspapers and Continental breakfast to start your day, as well as free transportation anywhere within five miles of the hotel. ❻

Crowne Plaza 10 Lincoln Square ℡508/791-1600, Ⓦwww.cpworcester.com. Designed for the

business traveler, these 243 rooms are standard chain fare but comfortable, and web deals make them one of the cheaper downtown options. ⑥
Hampton Inn 110 Summer St ☎508/757-0400 or 1-800/426-7866, ⓦwww.hamptoninn.com. Centrally located with free wi-fi and a decent complimentary, Continental breakfast. ⑥
Hilton Garden Inn 35 Major Taylor Blvd ☎508/753-5700, ⓦwww.hiltongardeninn.com. One of the newest hotels in the city, mostly catering to the conference crowd but with some great deals online. Rooms are extra-comfy, with an expansive breakfast buffet and all the standard business extras thrown in (including big desks and wi-fi). Parking $8.95 per day. ⑦
Residence Inn 503 Plantation St ☎508/753-6300, ⓦwww.marriott.com. Fairly new, upscale motel by Marriott, located in a quiet area; extras include free lemonade, breakfast, and fully equipped kitchens in the all-suite rooms, making it an excellent base. ⑧

The City

Despite ongoing efforts at regeneration, much of Worcester's **downtown** remains shabby and unappealing, though development projects associated with the **Blackstone River Valley National Heritage Corridor** (☎401/762-0250, ⓦwww.nps.gov/blac), which stretches all the way to Providence, RI, have succeeded in revitalizing parts of the city. The most visible signs of this can be found in the **Canal District** around Water Street, southeast of downtown (I-290 Exit 14), which is gradually attracting new

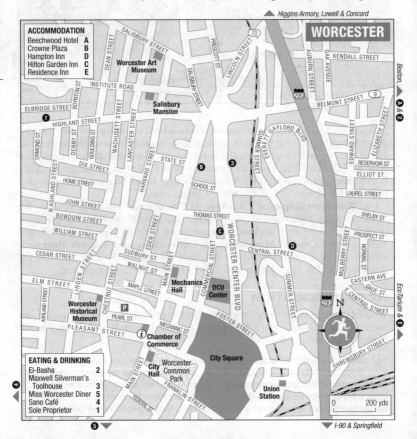

shops and restaurants. The most impressive building downtown is the 1857 **Mechanics Hall**, 321 Main St (℡508/752-5608, ⓦwww.mechanicshall.org), home to the annual Worcester Music Festival. You can usually have a peek inside, and tours are available if you call in advance.

Worcester's other historic districts are best experienced on a **guided tour** organized by Preservation Worcester (℡508/754-8760, ⓦwww .preservationworcester.org); walking tours cost $5–10 and usually run every day in summer. One of the most attractive neighborhoods runs along Elm Street, west of downtown, where you'll also find the engaging **Worcester Historical Museum**, 30 Elm St (Tues, Wed, Fri & Sat 10am–4pm, Thurs 10am–8.30pm; $5; ℡508/753-8278, ⓦwww.worcesterhistory.org). Worcester's industrial heritage is brought to life here through artifacts and oral histories; among other items, the city has been the birthplace of the space suit, the monkey wrench, barbed wire, the birth control pill, and the yellow "smiley face," designed by Harvey Ball in 1963.

Your museum ticket also includes admission to the elegant **Salisbury Mansion**, 40 Highland St, about a half mile north (Thurs 1–8.30pm, Fri & Sat 1–4pm; $5), built in 1772 for one of the city's wealthiest families. The interior has been restored in 1830s style, and houses changing exhibits on the history of the mansion and the Salisbury family.

Worcester Art Museum

A couple of blocks north of Salisbury Mansion, **Worcester Art Museum**, 55 Salisbury St (Wed, Thurs, Fri & Sun 11am–5pm, third Thurs of the month 11am–8pm, Sat 10am–5pm; $10, free Sat 10am–noon; ℡508/799-4406, ⓦwww .worcesterart.org) is an absolute gem. Its vast holdings include a Romanesque chapter house from the twelfth century, shipped from Europe and reassembled here; a permanent gallery of American portrait miniatures; and an impressive collection of mosaics from Antioch. In addition, there are lesser-known paintings by Braque, Cézanne, Gainsborough, Gauguin, Goya, Kandinsky, Matisse, Turner, and Renoir, and the museum is blessed with an extensive photography collection, with works from the Civil War to the present day, including recognizable images from Cartier-Bresson, Stieglitz, and Weston.

The EcoTarium and Higgins Armory Museum

Two and a half miles east of downtown is the **EcoTarium**, 222 Harrington Way (Tues–Sat 10am–5pm, Sun noon–5pm; $10; ℡508/929-2703, ⓦwww.ecotarium .org), the second oldest natural history society in the US. It's geared toward families with young ones: children can get their hands dirty with numerous interactive exhibits, outdoor nature walks, and train rides past animals.

To visit the remarkable castle-like **Higgins Armory Museum**, 100 Barber Ave (Tues–Sat 10am–4pm, Sun noon–4pm; $9; ℡508/853-6015, ⓦwww.higgins .org), follow I-290 toward Shrewsbury and take Exit 20. The museum is testament to years of collecting by John Woodman Higgins, the founder of the Worcester Pressed Steel Company, and is chock-full of armor and weapons from ancient Greece and Rome, medieval and Renaissance Europe, and feudal Japan.

Eating and drinking

El-Basha 424 Belmont St ℡508/797-0884. Near the UMass Medical Center, this popular, no-frills Lebanese spot offers zesty shawarma, falafel, and more. Everything on the menu is less than $10 or so. Closed Sun.

Maxwell Silverman's Toolhouse 25 Union St ℡508/755-1200. One of the more atmospheric places in town: the spacious dining room is a restored factory building, and the weekday surf-and-turf buffets are usually excellent value ($7). Note that it can get extremely busy.

Miss Worcester Diner 300 Southbridge St ☎508/753-5600. The city's most famous old-style diner, and the alleged model for the celebrated Worcester dining cars, once made across the street. Fabulous breakfasts.

The Salem Cross Inn On Rte-9 in West Brookfield ☎508/867-2345, ⓦwww.salemcrossinn.com. About twenty miles west of Worcester, but worth the detour, this rambling restaurant in a restored 1705 farmhouse on six hundred rolling acres serves consistently high-quality Yankee cooking – expect pot pies and lots of seafood. April–Dec only, closed Mon.

Sano Café 232 Chandler St ☎508/754-3663. Munch on bison and ostrich burgers at this friendly health-food store with an attached café – a welcome oasis in an impersonal area.

Sole Proprietor 118 Highland St ☎508/798-3474. Reliable seafood restaurant that's not especially cheap but well worth the price. The inflatable lobster on the roof belies the joint's sophisticated atmosphere.

Sturbridge

About fifteen miles southwest of Worcester, on US-20 near the junction of I-90 and I-84, the small town of **STURBRIDGE** holds only one point of interest, **Old Sturbridge Village** (April to late Oct daily 9.30am–5pm; late Oct to March Tues–Sun 9.30am–4pm; $20; ☎508/347-3362 or 1-800/SEE-1830, ⓦwww.osv .org). Made up of preserved buildings brought from all over the region, the village presents a somewhat idealized but engaging portrait of a small New England town of the 1830s. It's the usual heritage hokum, with lots of costumed actors working in blacksmiths' shops, planting vegetables, tending cows, and the like, but they pull it off with some style. The two-hundred-acre site, nicely landscaped and with footpaths, is also very pretty, making it a pleasant place to spend a few hours. There is an **information center** just opposite the entrance to the Village at 380 Main St (daily 10am–5pm; ☎800/628-8379, ⓦwww.sturbridge.org).

You'll find plenty of cheap **motels** in the area, while the *Sturbridge Host Hotel*, at 366 Main St, Rte-20 (☎508/347-7993, ⓦwww.sturbridgehosthotel .com; ⓪), is a smarter option, situated on nine acres with an indoor heated swimming pool and access to beautiful Cedar Lake. For a bit of character, stay at the *Publick House Historic Inn*, 277 W Main St, Rte-131 (☎508/347-3313, ⓦwww.publickhouse.com; ❹), a gorgeous 1771 inn with seventeen cozy rooms overlooking the common. For something to **eat**, try *Annie's Country Kitchen*, 140 Main St (☎508/347-2320), known for their skillet breakfasts with home fries and apple-walnut French toast.

Springfield

SPRINGFIELD, at the southern end of the Pioneer Valley, sprang up along the banks of the Connecticut River in the early 1600s, and went on to become the industrial hub of Central Massachusetts. America's first frozen foods were made here, and it was the home of the Springfield rifle and the late children's author **Dr Seuss**, né Theodor Geisel. More importantly, Springfield is the birthplace of **basketball**. But, like so many places in this part of the state, the city was hit by recession and became rapidly depopulated. The town is slowly restoring its fortunes, though the center remains eerily devoid of people outside workday hours.

Arrival and information

I-91 cuts right through downtown Springfield, with exits 6 and 7 providing easy access to the center. You should have no problems **parking**; one of the

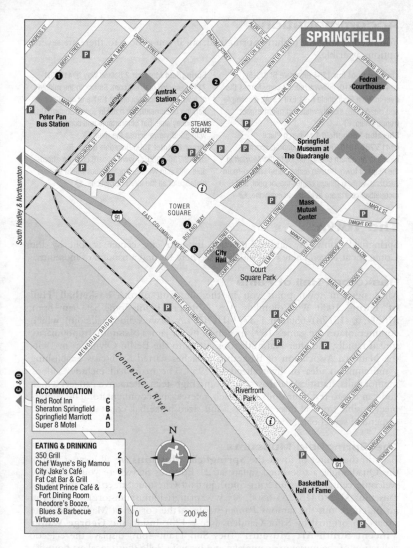

SPRINGFIELD

South Hadley & Northampton

G & D

Amtrak Station

Peter Pan Bus Station

STEAMS SQUARE

Springfield Museum at The Quadrangle

Fedral Courthouse

TOWER SQUARE

City Hall

Court Square Park

Mass Mutual Center

Riverfront Park

Connecticut River

Memorial Bridge

Basketball Hall of Fame

ACCOMMODATION
Red Roof Inn	C
Sheraton Springfield	B
Springfield Marriott	A
Super 8 Motel	D

EATING & DRINKING
350 Grill	2
Chef Wayne's Big Mamou	1
City Jake's Café	6
Fat Cat Bar & Grill	4
Student Prince Café & Fort Dining Room	7
Theodore's Booze, Blues & Barbecue	5
Virtuoso	3

N

0   200 yds

easiest lots to locate is Tower Square on Boland Way (Exit 7). Amtrak **trains** stop regularly at Springfield's downtown station at 66 Lyman St, a few blocks north of The Quadrangle. Peter Pan Bus Lines, which provides a daily **bus** service from Boston, New York, the Pioneer Valley, and the Berkshires, operates out of the nearby bus station at 1776 Main St (☎413/781-3320). The **Greater Springfield Convention & Visitors Bureau** (Ⓦwww.valleyvisitor.com) has two information centers: one opposite Tower Square at 1441 Main St (Mon–Fri 9am–5pm; ☎413/787-1548 or 1-800/723-1548) and the other by the river near the Basketball Hall of Fame, at 1200 W Columbus Ave (daily 8am–6pm; ☎413/750-2980).

Accommodation

You needn't **stay** the night in Springfield, but if you choose to, there are several options available.

The Red Roof Inn 1254 Riverdale St (US-5) ☎413/731-1010, ⓦ www.redroof.com. Across the river in West Springfield (I-91 Exit 13-A), it's simple and clean here, exactly what you might expect from a chain. ❸

Sheraton Springfield 1 Monarch Place ☎413/781-1010. Over three hundred spacious rooms in an atrium setting, opposite the *Marriott* in the heart of town. Sixteen suites come with in-room Jacuzzis, while a fitness center, indoor pool, and racquetball courts are available to everyone. ❼

Springfield Marriott 2 Boland Way ☎413/781-7111, ⓦ www.marriott.com. Smack in the middle of town, with easy access to I-91 and on-site parking underneath the hotel in Tower Square. On the pricey side, but comfortable and convenient with great views across the river. ❽

Super 8 Motel 1500 Riverdale St (US-5) ☎413/736-8080, ⓦ www.super8.com. An affordable option in West Springfield, but within striking distance of all the city's attractions. ❸

The Town

Springfield's unwieldy and unattractive modern city center is split by the Connecticut River. There's not much to see here beyond a handful of museums.

Basketball Hall of Fame

Most signs in town point you in the direction of the **Basketball Hall of Fame**, 1000 W Columbus Ave (Sun–Fri 10am–5pm, Sat 9am–5pm; $16.99; ☎413/781-6500 or 1-877/4HOOPLA, ⓦ www.hoophall.com), which commemorates the game's 1891 invention by Dr James Naismith. Its popularity spread rapidly, and after Naismith took a trip to the Berlin Olympics in 1936, the National Association of Basketball Coaches started to discuss establishing a museum, an idea finally realized in 1959. The main hall includes videos, memorabilia, statistical databases, and some high-tech interactive gadgets which you can use to test your skills as a coach, referee, and commentator. The centerpiece, visible from all three floors, is a full-sized basketball court complete with suspended scoreboard.

The Springfield Museums

Back in the center of town, the **Springfield Museums** are all located within the Quadrangle, a tree-lined square at 21 Edwards St (where you'll find the welcome center, Tues–Sun 9am–5pm), just off Chestnut Street (entrance to all museums $10; ☎413/263-6800, ⓦ www.springfieldmuseums.org). Before you go in, check out the famous *Puritan* statue at the corner of Maple and State streets, an original by Saint-Gaudens (see p.420). Inside, the **George Walter Vincent Smith Art Museum** (Tues–Sun 11am–4pm) displays the eclectic collection of the museum's namesake and his wife Belle (both local art hounds). The holdings focus on Asian decorative arts, including the largest collection of Chinese cloisonné pottery outside of Asia, though it also takes in nineteenth-century American painting and Middle Eastern rugs. **The Museum of Fine Arts** (Tues–Sun 11am–4pm) is slightly more coherent, proudly displaying Winslow Homer's *The New Novel* and Frederic Church's *New England Scenery* alongside lesser-known pieces by Monet, Picasso, Calder, and Georgia O'Keeffe. Also of local interest, the **Connecticut Valley Historical Museum** (Tues–Sun 11am–4pm) has the "Seuss on the Loose" exhibit commemorating the life and work of Springfield-born Theodor Geisel, as well as displays on the history of the region from 1636, enhanced with furniture, toys, paintings, games, and artifacts belonging to local settlers. This museum houses a **Genealogy and Local History Library** (Wed–Sat noon–4pm), with a large collection of French-Canadian records, and indexes to the Ellis Island passenger registers. Finally, the **Springfield Science Museum** (Tues–Sat 10am–5pm, Sun 11am–5pm) has a life-sized replica of a *Tyrannosaurus rex*, exhibits on animal life in the Connecticut River, and the **Seymour Planetarium** (daily shows $3). In the middle of the Quadrangle, the **Dr Seuss National Memorial Sculpture Garden** (spring & summer 9am–8pm; fall & winter 9am–5pm) contains metallic sculptures of characters and scenes created and inspired by Geisel. Finally, a new **Museum of Springfield History** is scheduled to open in 2009, and feature all sorts of famous city "firsts", including an Indian motorcycle collection. Note that all the Quadrangle museums tend to open on Mondays through July and August.

Eating and drinking

350 Grill 350 Worthington St ☎413/439-0666. Plush new restaurant set in an historic red-brick building with an outdoor patio. Specializes in eclectic "tapas" (rice balls, eggplant towers, and lobster ravioli), as well as pastas, sandwiches, grills, and fine seafood.

Chef Wayne's Big Mamou 53 Liberty St ☎413/732-1011. Take a break from New England fare with authentic Louisiana home-cooking: pots of simmering gumbo, catfish po'boys, and addictive bread pudding. Lunches cost $10 or less.

City Jake's Café 1573 Main St ☎413/731-5077. Best place in Springfield for a hearty diner-style breakfast for under $5. Open Mon–Fri 7.30am–2pm.

Fat Cat Bar & Grill 232 Worthington St ☎413/734-0554. No-nonsense rockers' pub, especially packed when bikers hit the state in the summer, with live (mostly hard) rock Fri–Sun and open-mic nights on Wed. Also serves excellent wings and other snack food.

Student Prince Café & Fort Dining Room 8 Fort St ☎413/734-7475. For over sixty years, this establishment has been a local favorite for German Wiener schnitzel, goulash, and sauerbraten.

Theodore's Booze, Blues and Barbecue 201 Worthington St ☎413/736-6000. Straight-ahead offerings of barbecued ribs, chicken, and salmon, with a solid beer selection and live blues most nights.

Virtuoso 272 Worthington St ☎413/731-0667. Hip contemporary cuisine such as prosciutto-wrapped monkfish, a sparkling list of cocktails, and carefully crafted desserts – the young and trendy atmosphere hits high gear when it morphs into the *Ultra Lounge* at night.

The Pioneer Valley

The Pioneer Valley, a verdant corridor shaped by the Connecticut River and centuries of glacial activity, is the epicenter of recreational and cultural activity in Central Massachusetts. The towns of **Northampton**, **South Hadley**, and **Amherst** share between them five colleges: Smith (in Northampton), Mount Holyoke (in South Hadley), and Amherst, Hampshire, and the University of Massachusetts (all in Amherst) – schools that have formalized their relationship through the cooperative "Five College Consortium." Just one and a half hours from Boston, the Valley is an enticing and less expensive alternative to Cape Cod or the Berkshires – an excellent choice for those who like to hike, bike, hang out in cafés, and browse bookstores.

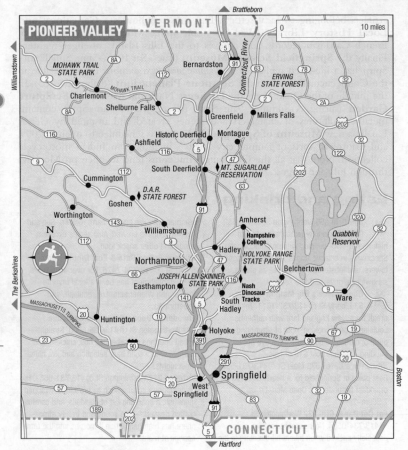

Northampton

In 1653, settlers from Springfield purchased some of the most fertile farmland in Central Massachusetts from the local Native American community, christening it **NORTHAMPTON**. These holdings became a liability after the Revolutionary War, however, when farmers here started losing their property to creditors looking to recover war debts. Rising to meet this injustice in 1786 was Daniel Shays, who led hundreds of his compatriots to the county courthouse in Northampton before attacking the federal arsenal in Springfield in what would later be known as **Shays' Rebellion.** In the nineteenth century Northampton blossomed as an industrial center, though in retrospect, the town's saving grace has been its investment in education and the intellectual environment it has fostered. **Smith College**, founded in 1871 by Sophia Smith and financed with her personal inheritance, survives as a prestigious women's college.

Today, liberal, progressive, and content to march to its own tune, Northampton, fondly nicknamed "NoHo," has settled into its role as a tolerant town of artists, writers, students, teachers, and activists. Oddly enough, it was cited in

Parents' Magazine as one of the best small towns in America to raise a family and in *Newsweek* as the "lesbian capital of the Northeast" – both distinctions it has accepted with pride.

Arrival and information

Northampton is just off I-91, approximately thirteen miles north of I-90; all exits marked "Northampton" lead to the center of town, where several parking lots are signposted – aim for the **garage** off Hampton Avenue, where the first hour is free ($0.50 per hr thereafter). Greyhound and Peter Pan buses pull in at 1 Roundhouse Plaza (T413/586-1030). The **Greater Northampton Chamber of Commerce**, 99 Pleasant St (Mon–Fri 9am–5pm, May–Oct also weekends 10am–2pm; T413/ 584-1900, Wwww.northamptonuncommon.com), offers an array of maps and advice, as well as copies of the *Pink Pages* for gay and lesbian travelers.

Accommodation

You shouldn't have a hard time finding somewhere to **stay** in Northampton, though many places tend to be of the stylish inn variety.

Autumn Inn 259 Elm St T413/584-7660, Wwww.hampshirehospitality.com. A Colonial-style inn boasting an attractive outdoor swimming pool and barbecue area surrounded by trees. Clean, comfortable, and close to the action. ❹

Clarion Hotel and Conference Center 1 Atwood Drive T413/586-1211, Wwww .hampshirehospitality.com. Sprawling but classy chain hotel; wood paneling, a roaring fireplace, and friendly staff in the lobby set the tone, and an indoor pool completes the scene. ❻

Hotel Northampton 36 King St T413/ 584-3100 or 1-800/547-3529, Wwww .hotelnorthhampton.com. Copious flower arrange-

ments in the entryway of this historic 1927 hotel give an immediate sense of its inflated – though entirely deserved – self-importance. The attention to detail and charm make up for the smallish rooms. ❾

North King Motel 504 N King St T413/584-8847. Eighteen clean and basic rooms in a well-worn 1950s-style roadside motel. The chatty owners give the place a comfortable, lived-in feel. ❸

Quality Inn & Suites 117 Conz St T413/586-1500, Wwww.qualityinn.com. A comfortable and reliable chain that's within walking distance of everything in town. Complimentary Continental breakfasts, wi-fi, indoor pool, exercise facility, and friendly service. ❹–❺

The Town

Northampton doesn't have much in the way of tourist attractions per se, but the town is an easy, livable place – judging by the wealth of shops, restaurants, cafés, and the diversity of the population, you could be in a major city, rather than a small college town. To learn about the town's history, walk or drive up to the **Historic Northampton Museum**, 46 Bridge St (Mon–Sat 10am–5pm, Sun noon–5pm; $3; T413/584-6011, Wwww.historic-northampton.org), a small but enlightening exhibition of artifacts and displays beginning with the area's

Pioneer Valley information and transportation

The **Pioneer Valley Transit Authority** (PVTA; T413/586-5806 or 1-877/779-PVTA, Wwww.pvta.com) runs shuttle buses ($1 per ride) between Northampton, Amherst, and South Hadley. Generally, buses begin circulating at 6am and head home at around midnight (later on Thurs, Fri & Sat), passing each stop every thirty minutes or so. Schedules are available on each bus and posted at the sidewalk stops. If you'd rather get around the area under your own power, the paved **Norwottuck Trail Bike Path** weaves its way for around 8.5 miles between Northampton and Amherst in the track of a former railroad bed.

Native American inhabitants. You'll learn about colorful residents such as Mary Parsons, accused of witchcraft, and President **Calvin Coolidge**, who spent much of his life here.

Northhampton's real highlight, the **Smith College Museum of Art** (Tues–Sat 10am–4pm, Sun noon–4pm; $5; ☎413/585-2760), lies in the grounds of the town's defining institution. Don't miss the bathrooms, which local artists helped overhaul. The collection focuses on nineteenth- and twentieth-century art, with works by Monet (*Field of Poppies*), Georgia O'Keeffe (*Squash Flowers, no. 1*), Jean Arp (*Torso*), and Frank Stella, who is represented by the enormous *Damascus Gate* (*Variation III*). The museum also boasts an eight-thousand-strong print collection, including a large number of works by Daumier, Delacroix, Dürer, Munch, Picasso, and Toulouse-Lautrec.

Before you leave the Smith campus, take a peek inside the **Mortimer Rare Book Room** (Mon–Fri 9am–noon & 1–5pm), tucked away on the third floor of the Neilson Library. This contains the precious **Sylvia Plath Collection**, four thousand pages of original manuscripts left by the poet and former student, including drafts of *Ariel* and the *Bell Jar* – a few pieces are always on display. You might also see the letters of **Virginia Woolf** here. The nearby modern **Campus Center** contains a shop selling Smith memorabilia and books (Mon–Fri 9am–4pm).

Eating and drinking

Northampton is *the* place in the Pioneer Valley to **eat** and **drink**. You're in college country: be prepared to have your ID checked every time you enter a bar.

Caminito 7 Old South St ☎413/387-6387. This Argentine steakhouse specializes in wood-fired Angus beef (steaks from $19), but also blends flavors from Italy, France, and Spain: try the lobster ravioli ($21) or the spinach, provolone, and mozzarella crêpes ($17). Dinner only.

Eastside Grill 19 Strong Ave ☎413/586-3347. Well-established steakhouse serving steaks, chicken, and seafood with a Cajun bite. Extensive menu and attentive service, but often crowded. Dinner only.

FitzWilly's 23 Main St ☎413/584-8666. Smack in the middle of it all, this local bar is a relaxing place to knock back a few and soak up the atmosphere.

Haymarket Café & Juice Joint 185 Main St ☎413/586-9969. Popular hangout for people looking for a cheap, healthy snack or light meal. Soups, salads, and sandwiches go for around $5. Drinks are served in the street-level café, food in the dimly lit basement. Free wi-fi.

Herrell's Ice Cream 8 Old South St ☎413/586-9700. Home base for a small but illustrious regional chain of ice-cream stores; original owner Steve Herrell was apparently the first to grind up candy bars and add them to his concoctions.

La Veracruzana 31 Main St ☎413/586-7181. Bright, cheerful, and informal, the folks at *La Veracruzana* are credited with bringing the take-out burrito to the Valley. There's another branch in Amherst.

Northampton Brewery 11 Brewster Court, behind Thorne's Marketplace ☎413/584-9903. With a solid selection of high-quality microbrews on tap, an extensive munchies menu, and a relaxing outdoor patio, this is a great place to while away a happy hour.

Paul and Elizabeth's 150 Main St, in Thorne's Marketplace ☎413/584-4832. Vegetarian and seafood entrees, home-made breads, and desserts served in a serenely airy dining room.

Pizzeria Paradiso 12 Crafts Ave ☎413/586-1468. A cozy pizza place kept warm with wood-fired ovens imported from Italy. The extensive choice of toppings, drinks, and desserts make this much more than just your average pizza joint.

Sylvester's 111 Pleasant St ☎413/586-5343. Housed in the former home of Sylvester Graham, inventor of the graham cracker, *Sylvester's* serves up tasty fare, including delightful treats such as banana-bread French toast and waffles. Breakfast and lunch only. Staff are child-friendly.

Tunnel Bar Beneath *Union Station Restaurant*, 125A Pleasant St, where Pearl St meets Strong Ave ☎413/586-5366. This old underground pedestrian walkway has been renovated into a dark martini bar – a good spot for the sophisticated urbanite, or those who want to feign as such.

Viva Fresh Pasta 249 Main St ☎ 413/586-5875. They make their own pasta here, and the special raviolis (like sweet potato) and sauces, such as fresh pesto and romesco, are mouthwatering. Portions are big but reasonably priced ($10 lunch, $15 dinner), and the cannoli ($4) is irresistible.

Entertainment

Due to its relative proximity to New York and Boston, as well as the efforts of energetic local promoters Iron Horse Entertainment Group, Northampton attracts some of the biggest names in **performing arts**. You can reserve tickets for many shows at the **Northampton Box Office**, 76 Main St (Mon–Sat 9am–6pm, Sun noon–5pm; ☎ 413/586-8686 or 1-800/THE-TICK, Ⓦ www .nbotickets.com). During summer check out the **New Century Theater** (Ⓦ www.newcenturytheatre.org), which produces new works, classic dramas, and comedies at the college.

Calvin Theater 19 King St ☎ 413/584-1444, Ⓦ www.iheg.com. The folks responsible for the Iron Horse (see below) have lovingly transformed this 75-year-old movie house into a beacon of the performing arts. Live theater, music, and dance performance for all ages and tastes.
Iron Horse Music Hall 20 Center St ☎ 413/585-0479, Ⓦ www.iheg.com. An institution in the world of folk music, this small, coffeehouse-style venue

has been cheering on emerging artists for twenty years as well as pulling in the big names of folk, bluegrass, jazz, and blues.
Pleasant Street Theater 27 Pleasant St ☎ 413/586-0935, Ⓦ www.amherstcinema.org. Though mainstream Hollywood movies increasingly show here, independent, classic, and foreign films are also screened in this worthy leftover from the pre-multiplex era (tickets $8.50).

Amherst and around

Settled in 1727, **AMHERST** has almost always been a college town. In 1821, its citizens opened the Collegiate Charitable Institution to educate their young men; just four years later this was incorporated as prestigious **Amherst College**. In the mid-nineteenth century, the Massachusetts Agricultural College opened to teach military, agricultural, and technical skills; today, as the **University of Massachusetts at Amherst**, it is the main cog in the state's public university system. Meanwhile, **Hampshire College**, just outside of town on the road to South Hadley, opened in 1970 as an experiment in true liberal arts study. Though the town maintains the feel of a small community, in fact it is a bit larger than Northampton, with a mix of students, hippies, families, and professionals – all in all a good place to relax for a day or two and explore the surrounding countryside.

Arrival and information

Amherst is easily accessible by **car** from I-91, roughly twenty miles north of I-90. Amtrak's Vermonter **train** service between Montréal, New York, and Washington, DC pulls into town at 13 Railroad St, while Peter Pan buses drop off at 8 Main St. For maps and further information, visit the **Amherst Area Chamber of Commerce**, 1B Amity St (Mon–Fri 8.30am–4.30pm; ☎ 413/253-0770, Ⓦ www.amherstarea.com).

Accommodation

Amherst's **accommodation** options range from expensive inns to B&Bs with an ecological bent to branches of national chains. Your best bet for finding inexpensive lodging is to drive along Rte-9 and check out some of the smaller, slightly rumpled-looking **motels** along the way.

Black Walnut Inn 1184 North Pleasant St
🏃 413/549-5649, Ⓦ www.blackwalnutinn
.com. This attractive 1821 Federal-style B&B is
shaded by tall black walnut trees, its gorgeous rooms
decorated with period antiques and super-comfy
beds. It's the whopping, scrumptious breakfasts,
though, that really win five stars. ⑤–⑥

Delta Organic Farm 352 E Hadley Rd
🕾 413/253-1893, Ⓦ www.deltaorganicfarm
.com. Nirvana for health-conscious travelers,
with special needs and requests welcomed by
the accommodating owners (it's constructed with
environmentally safe materials, and uses 100
percent cotton linens). The plain but comfortable
one- or two-bedroom private suites come with

kitchenette, and air- and water-filtration systems.
Organic breakfast available on request. ⑤

Econo Lodge 329 Russell St (Rte-9), Hadley
🕾 413/582-7077, Ⓦ www.econolodge.com. A
stone's throw from the Hampshire Mall, between
Amherst and Northampton, this chain motel is
clean, comfortable, and friendly, with a pool and
wi-fi available. ④

Lord Jeffery Inn 30 Boltwood Ave 🕾 413/253-
2576 or 1-800/742-0358, Ⓦ www.lordjefferyinn
.com. Situated on Amherst Common, this is a
quintessential rambling and richly decorated New
England inn – it's so picturesque that it's often
used for weddings. The rooms are a luxurious
treat. ④–⑧

The Town

Downtown Amherst serves as a fairly unremarkable service center for the college
and surrounding community. Just about everybody who comes here makes
straight for the **Emily Dickinson Museum**, 280 Main St (June–Aug Wed–Sun
10am–6pm, March–May & Sept–Dec Wed–Sun 10am–5pm; 🕾 413/542-8161,
Ⓦ www.emilydickinsonmuseum.org). The museum comprises **The Homestead**,
the birthplace and home of celebrated poet Emily Dickinson (see box opposite),
and **The Evergreens** next door, home to her brother Austin's family.

Begin your visit in the **Tour Center**, which houses the "My Verse is Alive"
exhibit, highlighting the publication of Dickinson's most popular poems. The
two houses can only be visited on **guided tours**: full tours (1hr 30min; $8)
depart on the hour, but there are also tours of just the Homestead (every 30min;
40min; $6). Much of the latter contains original furnishings, including an array
of Dickinson's personal effects and the desk where her poems were found after
her death. It's a pretty low-key display, but the enthusiastic tour guides enhance

▲ Emily Dickinson Museum

Born in Amherst in 1830, **Emily Dickinson** attended nearby Mount Holyoke College, but loneliness drove her back home without finishing her studies, and she shortly afterwards began a life of self-imposed exile in the family home on Main Street. Dickinson read voraciously, wrote incessantly, corresponded with friends, and over the course of her life penned some 1800 poems, most of which mirrored her lifelong struggle between isolation and an intense search for inspiration. Despite this literary hyperactivity, she published fewer than a dozen poems during her life, and was completely unknown when she died in 1886. Her work was collected and published in 1890 by her sister, and she has since been recognized as influential in giving American poetry its own resounding voice.

the experience with quotes, poems, and anecdotes about Emily's reclusive existence here. The grander, Italianate Evergreens is literally frozen in time and far more evocative of the 1890s. Here you'll learn about Emily's close relationship with Austin's wife, Susan, and the efforts of niece Martha to secure the poet's legacy in later years. Fans should also visit **Dickinson's grave** in the nearby West Cemetery, behind Pleasant Street.

Also of notable literary interest is the original copy of *Stopping by Woods on a Snowy Evening*, written by Robert Frost, who was a professor at Amherst College for thirty years. It sits under glass in the Special Collections Room (Tues–Fri 10am–5pm, Mon & Sat 2–5pm; free; ☎413/259-3097) at the town's **Jones Library**, 43 Amity St. Call in advance to make sure it's open.

The town's cultural attractions are rounded out by the **Mead Art Museum** (Tues–Sun 10am–4.30pm, first Thurs of each month 10am–8pm; free; ☎413/542-2335, ⓦwww.amherst.edu/~mead), on the lovely campus of **Amherst College**. Works by Frederic Church, Thomas Cole, John Singleton Copley, Thomas Eakins, and Winslow Homer dominate a collection strong on early twentieth-century American art. There's also a sprinkling of Renaissance European works, notably a seductive *Salome* by Robert Henri and a gory *Still Life with Dead Game* by Frans Snyders.

Eating and drinking

Amherst doesn't have as many **restaurants** as Northampton (the large student population has fostered a multitude of casual eateries), but you surely won't go hungry. A stroll along either Main Street or North Pleasant Street pretty much sums up your choices.

Amherst Brewing Company 24 N Pleasant St ☎413/253-4400. The brass bar and exposed brick add a touch of upscale yearning to this prime drinking spot. Live music – mostly jazz – and a street terrace are added attractions. Freshly brewed beers on tap (from $4.25).

🏃 **Amherst Chinese Food** 62 Main St ☎413/253-7835. The owners of this restaurant grow the organic vegetables they use in their dishes, adding nothing artificial as they pick, steam, sauté, fry, and deliver them to your table piping hot.

Antonio's 31 N Pleasant St ☎413/253-0808. There are just a few benches and stools to eat at,

but this is the pizza place in town. The good slices are always just out of the oven.

Bart's Homemade 103 N Pleasant St ☎413/253-9371. The street terrace is as inviting as the sundaes, smoothies, and ice creams on warm days; they also do mean burgers ($5) and breakfast bagels ($3), and potent coffee.

🏃 **Bistro 63 at The Monkey Bar** 63 N Pleasant St ☎413/259-1600. The lobster corn chowder, seafood Portuguese, and steak mignonette here are so good that they even offer classes on how to make them. Entrees $14–24.

The Black Sheep 79 Main St ☎413/253-3442. Stacked sandwiches, pastries, coffee, and desserts served in a down-to-earth café. Open late for coffee and occasional music, including open-mic nights.

Boltwood Tavern 30 Boltwood Ave ☎413/253-2576. Part of the *Lord Jeffery Inn*, this is a popular spot for good beers and pub grub, with breakfast, lunch, and dinner served daily; the menu includes standard American fare such as sandwiches and burgers (from $8.75), but also pastas (from $14) and German specialities like sauerbraten (pot roast) for $15.

🎿 **Bub's BBQ** 676 Amherst Rd (Rte-116), Sunderland ☎413/548-9630. Only minutes by car from Amherst center: from Rte-9, take Rte-116 (N) and look for the fluorescent pink porker on the right inviting you to "pig out in style" on delicious barbecue and home-style sides. Closed Mon.

La Veracruzana 63 S Pleasant St ☎413/253-6900. Sister restaurant of the Northampton burrito joint of the same name. Sip zesty margaritas for $5.45.

Lone Wolf 63 Main St ☎413/256-4643. A good place for breakfast, with dishes like challah French toast, lox and eggs, and vegan omelettes with coconut milk. Open daily until 2pm.

Around Amherst

There are several worthwhile attractions in the vicinity of Amherst. Two miles south of town, just off the main road (Rte-116) at the Hampshire College entrance, the **Eric Carle Museum of Picture Book Art**, 125 West Bay Rd (Tues–Fri 10am–4pm, Sat 10am–5pm, Sun noon–4pm; $7; ☎413/658-1100, ⓦ www.picturebookart .org), is the first museum in America devoted to children's book illustrations. Founded in part by Eric Carle, author of the classic *The Very Hungry Caterpillar*, exhibits change seasonally but have included work from Dorothy Kunhardt's *Pat the Bunny* and Tony DiTerlizzi and Holly Black's *The Spiderwick Chronicles*.

Inside the Hampshire campus itself you'll find the **National Yiddish Book Center**, 1021 West St (Mon–Fri 10am–4pm, Sun 11am–4pm; closed Jewish holidays; free; ☎413/256-4900, ⓦ www.yiddishbookcenter.org), which houses one of the world's largest collections of Yiddish books in a sprawling building designed to emulate an Eastern European *shtetl*.

Farther along Rte-116, four miles south of Amherst, is the entrance to **Holyoke Range State Park**, a densely wooded park laced with hiking trails ranging from the easy 0.75-mile Laurel Loop to the harder 1.6-mile hike up Mount Norwottuck (1106ft). The Notch Visitors Center, at the entrance (daily 8am–4pm; free; ☎413/253-2883), can provide hiking maps and information. On the other side of Rte-116, trails lead into the east side of the Joseph Allen Skinner State Park (see opposite), where you can hike to the top of **Mount Holyoke** (940ft) via the Metacomet-Monadnock Trail (around 5 miles; 2–3hr).

Finally, 6.5 miles south of Amherst (on Aldrich Rd, off Rte-116), the **Nash Dinosaur Tracks** (late May to early Sept Mon–Sat 10am–4pm, Sun noon–4pm, call to verify; $3; ☎413/467-9566) are a collection of locally excavated dinosaur bones and giant footprints in situ. Somewhat controversially, you can even buy assorted fossils ($50–900) here.

South Hadley and around

Located ten miles south of Amherst at the intersection of routes 116 and 47, **SOUTH HADLEY**, the home of **Mount Holyoke College**, completes the circle of towns in the Five College Consortium. Founded in 1836 by education pioneer Mary Lyon, Mount Holyoke is the oldest college for women in America and, like its neighbor Smith, is one of the most prestigious of the "Seven Sisters," a group of seven originally women-only colleges in the Northeast.

Though the smallest of the area's towns, South Hadley adds an exclamation point to the Pioneer Valley, mainly due to the presence of the **Mount Holyoke**

College Art Museum, adjacent to the greenhouse on Lower Lake Road (Tues–Fri 11am–5pm, Sat–Sun 1–5pm; free; ☎413/538-2000), which has an impressive permanent collection of Asian, Egyptian, and Mediterranean paintings, drawings, and sculpture, and regularly mounts high-quality special exhibitions.

Practicalities

Peter Pan buses stop at Crazy Moon Fashion, 21 College St (☎413/534-1190). The town doesn't have much in the way of lodging, so you're better off staying in Amherst or Northampton. For **something to eat**, your only sure choices for several miles are in the Village Commons shopping center, a faux clapboard village with plenty of **parking**, across the street from the college. The best bet here is *Tailgate Picnic*, 7 College St (☎413/532-7597), which has a large selection of bagels, sandwiches, pasta salads, and an ice cream shack attached, though the *Main Moon Chinese Restaurant* (☎413/533-8839), 11 College St, has $4.25 lunch specials, and *Johnny's Bar & Grill* (☎413/534-8222) at no. 23 is also worth trying for the half-price appetizers (Mon–Thurs).

Joseph Allen Skinner State Park

Just off Rte-47, about three miles north of South Hadley, a side road leads into the **Joseph Allen Skinner State Park** (☎413/586-0350), which blankets the slopes of Mount Holyoke. You can drive up to the aptly named **Summit House** (late May to mid-Oct weekends 10am–5pm; free), where the park's visitors' center has wide and stunning views of the river valley, particularly the bend referred to as the "Ox Bow" – immortalized in Thomas Cole's painting of the same name. From here trails lead to the Holyoke Range State Park (see opposite).

Deerfield

Despite the sedate appearance of present-day **DEERFIELD**, its history has been punctuated by episodes of unusual violence. In September 1675, the English suffered one of their biggest defeats of **King Philip's War** (see p.529) here, when an attack by local Nipmuck tribes culminated in the death of 64 settlers and soldiers. The town saw more bloodshed in February 1704, when, in a five-hour raid, hundreds of French-led Abenaki, Huron, and Mohawk warriors killed around fifty settlers and set fire to the town. Over a hundred prisoners were marched three hundred miles to Canada; more than twenty perished en route, and even though the remainder were eventually freed, many chose to stay with their captors. By the nineteenth century, this raid had become a crucial pillar of the myth-making Colonial Revival, with its simplistic emphasis on "savages" and "pilgrims." Today, the town's museums offer a more balanced interpretation of the events.

The chief town in the area is **South Deerfield**, though the main attractions lie along routes 5 and 10 (which here follow the same road), ending with **Historic Deerfield** five miles to the north. This area, known as the Upper Pioneer Valley, is best explored by car.

Accommodation

The only **place to stay** in Historic Deerfield is the *Deerfield Inn*, 81 Main St (☎413/774-5587 or 1-800/926-3865, ⊛www.deerfieldinn.com; ❼), a commodious country inn that also offers fine dining options. Cheaper **motels** can be found along Rte-5 further south. The *Red Roof Inn*, 9 Greenfield Rd,

Rte-5, off I-91 at Exit 24, (☏413/665-7161, ⓦwww.redroof.com; ❹), is completely lacking in rustic charm, but offers clean rooms, friendly service, and reasonable rates.

The Town

From I-91 Exit 24, the first point of interest is the sprawling **Yankee Candle Company** store on Rte-5/10 (daily 10am–6pm; ☏1-877/636-7707), which primarily attracts hordes of shoppers for its candles, toys, and home goods, but is worth a brief stop for its regular demonstrations of traditional candle-making techniques (head to the candle-making museum at the back).

Another 2.5 miles north along Rte-5/10 is **Magic Wings Butterfly Conservatory & Gardens** (daily: June–Aug 9am–6pm; Sept–May 9am–5pm; $12; ☏413/665-2805, ⓦwww.magicwings.com), a spacious greenhouse complex of tropical gardens and swarms of thousands of butterflies. The Enya-inspired soundtrack might wear you down after a while, but this remains an entrancing experience – kids will love it.

Historic Deerfield

With beautifully preserved old houses girdled by one thousand acres of lush meadows and farmland, **Historic Deerfield** appears frozen in time. The town has been milking this "Olde New England" appeal since the 1890s, when Alice Baker purchased the Frary House, restored it, and opened it to the public. These days the site tries to take a sophisticated approach to Colonial history, attempting to tell the Native American side of the story, though the emphasis, inevitably, remains on the early English settlers. The village includes 65 or so eighteenth- and nineteenth-century structures on either side of **The Street** (the main drag, running parallel to Rte-5), with eleven houses open to the public, in addition to a couple of museums.

The best way to orient yourself is to check in at the **Hall Tavern Visitor Center**, across from the *Deerfield Inn* (April–Dec daily 9.30am–4.30pm; limited hours Jan–March; $7 single house, $14 unlimited, good for two consecutive days; ☏413/775-7214, ⓦwww.historic-deerfield.org). Here you'll be able to watch an introductory film and see which of the historic properties are open for guided, or self-guided tours – other houses are open by appointment only.

The houses themselves are filled with over 20,000 objects, from furniture and fabrics to silver and glass, either made or used in America between 1650 and 1850. If you don't have the patience for guided tours – and unless you have an intense interest in antique home decor – you probably need not visit more than one or two. The best are the **Sheldon House** (self-guided), which illustrates the life of a middle-class farming family from 1755 to 1802, and the **Frary House** (guided).

The Montague Mill

Lovers of books will feel right at home at the **Book Mill**, 440 Greenfield Rd, off Rte-63 in Montague (daily 10am–6pm; ☏413/367-9206, ⓦwww.montaguebookmill.com). With 40,000 used and discount books, well-seasoned armchairs, and large windows overlooking the river, the mill is a magical place to spend a couple of lazy hours. Next door, in the same enchanting premises, the 🍴 **Lady Killigrew** pub and café (daily 8am–11pm; ☏413/367-9666) has plenty of space to kick back with a coffee, cake, and book (it also has free wi-fi and a big menu of more potent drinks). You should also consider having a meal (dinners and Sunday brunch only) next door at the romantic *Night Kitchen* (closed Mon–Wed; ☏413/367-9580).

Some of the most precious period pieces are displayed in the **Flynt Center of Early New England Life**, a modern timber building with a beautifully presented but otherwise dry ensemble of furniture, textiles, dresses, and powder horns.

Whichever houses you choose to visit, be sure to check out the absorbing **Memorial Hall Museum**, technically separate but included on the joint ticket (May–Oct daily 9.30am–4.30pm; $6 single entry; ☏413/774-3768 ext 10, ⓦwww .deerfield-ma.org). Inside you'll find exhibits depicting the history of the village, including the remnants of a wooden door from the "Indian House," which survived the 1704 attack. The most fascinating section is the Memorial Tablet, erected in 1882 to commemorate the victims, now overlain with a more sensitive translation of lines like "Mary Field, who married a savage and became one."

Eating and drinking

As you exit I-91 and turn north onto Rte-5/10, you will pass the Sugarloaf Shoppes and the *Red Roof Inn* before arriving at a stoplight. Take a right from here onto Elm Street and cross the railroad tracks – the small business district you see represents the extent of South Deerfield's **eating** and **drinking** options. It's easy to miss *Sienna*, 6 Elm St (dinner only; closed Mon & Tues; ☏413/665-0215), near the center of town, but this is one of the area's best-kept secrets, where you can dine on sumptuous dishes such as cornmeal-fried oysters and free-range duck breast with a tamarind demi-glace (entrees $16–21). *Wolfie's*, 52 S Main St (closed Sun; ☏413/665-7068), just around the corner, offers cheap lunch and dinner specials, excellent burgers, soups, and pies – and free popcorn.

Shelburne Falls

Nestled in the Berkshire foothills and straddling the Deerfield River is the tiny town of **SHELBURNE FALLS**, a community whose buzz of artistic activity and scenic surroundings give a taste of modern New England small-town life. The most prominent thing to see here is the **Bridge of Flowers**, an old 400ft trolley bridge that is festooned with foliage each spring through late fall – it's rather underwhelming from the riverbank, but more impressive once you walk across. The town's other main attraction is a series of fifty **glacial potholes** (ranging six inches to 39ft across), east of Bridge Street in an area known as Salmon Falls. Worth a quick look from the viewing area on the nearby riverbank, they resemble an enormous mass of once-molten stone that has now been whittled into a svelte sculpture along the riverbed. On the way you'll pass **North River Glass** (Thurs–Sun), a functioning glass workshop where you can watch skilled craftsmen turning bottles; buy their products next door at the **Young & Constantin Gallery** (☏866/625-6422).

Practicalities

Shelburne Falls is approximately two miles south of Rte-2 and ten miles west of the intersection of Rte-2 and I-91 at Greenfield. You'll find the **Village Information Center** at 75 Bridge St (May–Oct Mon–Sat 10am–4pm, Sun noon–3pm; ☏413/625-2544).

Accommodation options are spread out, but the *Dancing Bear Guest House*, 22 Mechanic St (☏413/625-9281, ⓦwww.dancingbearguesthouse.com; ⑤), is a cozy 1852 home with antique-filled rooms. Further west, on Rte-2 in Charlemont, the charming and comfortable *Charlemont Inn* (☏413/339-5796, ⓦwww.charlemontinn.com; ④) has entertained guests since 1787.

The Mohawk Trail

The best-known scenic route in the Berkshires is the 63-mile **Mohawk Trail**, otherwise known as Rte-2, from the town of Millers Falls to the Massachusetts–New York border. Working from east to west, the **Bridge of Flowers** and bizarre glacial potholes at **Shelburne Falls** (see p.233) are worth a look as the route leaves the Pioneer Valley. Just before Charlemont, you'll pass the **"Hail to the Sunrise"** monument, a huge statue of a Native American with outstretched arms. Nearby you can access the **Mohawk Trail State Forest** (T413/339-5504), a scenic woodland with hiking trails and a 56-place campsite (mid-April to mid-Oct; $14 per site). The route ends at the culturally rich towns of **Williamstown** and **North Adams** (see p.247), as well as Massachusetts' highest peak, **Mount Greylock**. In North Adams, New England's only **natural bridge**, a white marble arch formed by melting glaciers, is worth a visit. For more info on the trail, contact the **Mohawk Trail Association** (T413/743-8127, Wwww.mohawktrail.com).

It is hard to go wrong stopping for a **bite to eat** in Shelburne Falls; the town's culinary offerings are surprisingly good for a place so small. *Café Martin*, 24 Bridge St (closed Mon; T413/625-2795), serves international dishes with trendy ingredients, wooing patrons with home-made soups and lunch-time sandwiches (from $7). *Mocha Maya's Coffee House*, 47 Bridge St (T413/625-6292), offers a great range of coffees, cakes, and pastries as well as live music and free wi-fi. Finally, *The West End Pub*, 16 State St, across the Bridge of Flowers (closed Tues, lunch summer only; T413/625-6216), has an outdoor deck overlooking the river, and pub fare such as meatloaf, burgers, and fish and chips – it also serves Berkshire Brewing Co draft beer ($4).

The Berkshires

A rich cultural history, world-class arts festivals, and a verdant landscape make the **Berkshires**, at the extreme western edge of Massachusetts, an unusually civilized region. The area has been attracting moneyed visitors since the nineteenth century, the most visible manifestations of which are sumptuous summer "cottages" hidden in the woods around the sedate villages of **Stockbridge** and **Lenox**. The latter is also home to **Tanglewood**, summer quarters of the Boston Symphony Orchestra and symbol of putative East Coast cultural superiority. But venture beyond these bastions of gentility and the more typical aspects of New England quickly re-emerge, from the economically battered old mill town of **Pittsfield** to dignified **Williamstown**, along with time-warped hill towns as remote as any in Vermont or New Hampshire.

Note that tourism in the Berkshires is highly **seasonal**: virtually all the big cultural events happen in summer, and in the off season most of the museums either close or operate on skeleton schedules. Perhaps the best times to visit are late May or in September, when the foliage is changing but the "leaf peepers" have yet to arrive in force.

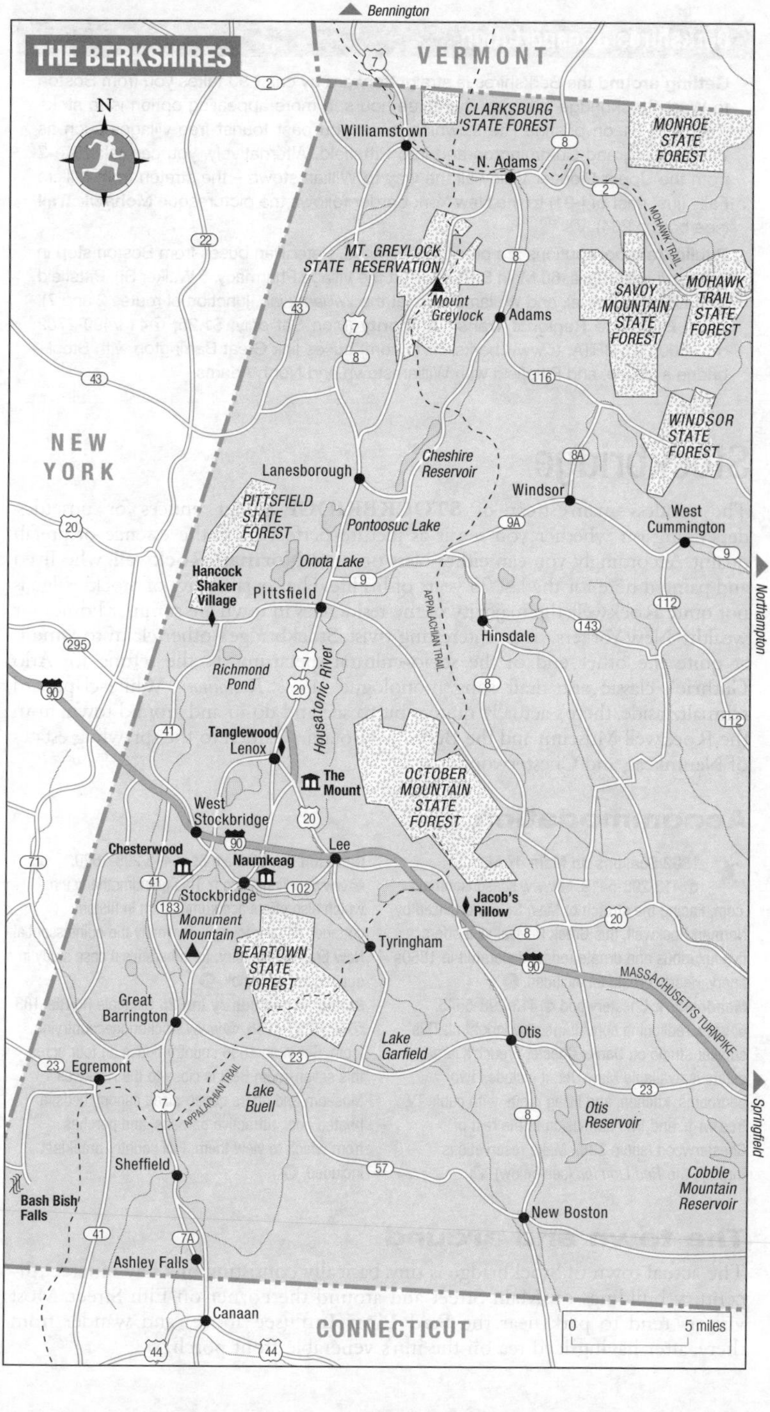

THE BERKSHIRES

N

VERMONT

Bennington

Williamstown

CLARKSBURG STATE FOREST

N. Adams

MONROE STATE FOREST

MT. GREYLOCK STATE RESERVATION

Mount Greylock

Adams

MOHAWK TRAIL

SAVOY MOUNTAIN STATE FOREST

MOHAWK TRAIL STATE FOREST

NEW YORK

WINDSOR STATE FOREST

Lanesborough

Cheshire Reservoir

PITTSFIELD STATE FOREST

Windsor

West Cummington

Pontoosuc Lake

Onota Lake

Hancock Shaker Village

Pittsfield

APPALACHIAN TRAIL

Northampton

Hinsdale

Richmond Pond

Housatonic River

Tanglewood

Lenox

The Mount

OCTOBER MOUNTAIN STATE FOREST

West Stockbridge

Chesterwood

Naumkeag

Lee

Stockbridge

Monument Mountain

BEARTOWN STATE FOREST

Jacob's Pillow

Tyringham

MASSACHUSETTS TURNPIKE

Great Barrington

Lake Garfield

Otis

Egremont

Lake Buell

APPALACHIAN TRAIL

Springfield

Sheffield

Otis Reservoir

Cobble Mountain Reservoir

Bash Bish Falls

Ashley Falls

New Boston

Canaan

CONNECTICUT

0   5 miles

Berkshires transportation

Getting around the Berkshires is straightforward by car. I-90 takes you from Boston to West Stockbridge in a very dull three hours; a more appealing option is to strike west off I-91 on pristine Rte-9, which takes you past tourist-free villages such as Williamsburg and Cummington and into Pittsfield. Alternatively, you can take Rte-2 from the Upper Pioneer Valley all the way to Williamstown – the stretch from Millers Falls (just east of I-91) to the New York border follows the picturesque **Mohawk Trail** (see box, p.234).

Public transport options are predictably limited. Peter Pan buses from Boston stop in Lee (at *Juice N Java*, 60 Main St), Lenox (at the Village Pharmacy, 5 Walker St), Pittsfield (at 1 Columbus Ave), and Williamstown (at the *Williams Inn*, junction of routes 2 and 7). Local **Berkshire Regional Transit Authority** (Mon–Sat only; $1.25; ☎413/499-2782 or 1-800/292-BRTA, ⓦwww.berkshirerta.com) buses link Great Barrington with Stockbridge and Lee, and Pittsfield with Williamstown and North Adams.

Stockbridge

The spotless main street of **STOCKBRIDGE** either entices or unsettles, depending on whether you see it as picture-perfect or as the essence of prefab quaint. Accordingly, you can either bless or curse **Norman Rockwell**, who lived and painted here for the last 25 years of his life. The social reality of Stockbridge is not quite Rockwell: the majority of the residences in town are summer homes for wealthy New Yorkers. In an interesting twist, Stockbridge's other claim to fame is at quite the other end of the socio-cultural spectrum: it's the setting for Arlo Guthrie's classic anti-draft song/monologue *Alice's Restaurant*. White-clapboard schmaltz aside, there's actually quite a bit to see and do in and around town, from the Rockwell Museum and the Berkshire Botanic Garden to the sprawling estates of Naumkeag and Chesterwood.

Accommodation

1862 Seasons on Main 47 Main St ☎413/298-5419, ⓦwww.seasonsonmain .com. Facing the stretch of Main St immortalized by Norman Rockwell, this Greek Revival villa offers five luxurious and ornate rooms decorated in 1860s finery. Hearty breakfast included. ❽

Meadowlark Chesterwood ☎413/298-5545, ⓦwww.redlioninn.com/rli/meadowlark.html. This smaller studio on Daniel Chester French's large estate is available May–Oct; it includes two bedrooms, kitchen, and living room, with cable TV, free wi-fi, and free admission to the rest of Chesterwood (see p.238). Make reservations through the *Red Lion Inn* (see below). ❾

Red Lion Inn 30 Main St ☎413/298-1690, ⓦwww.redlioninn.com. This grandmotherly inn, which also offers accommodation in historic cottages all over town, is for many the quintessential New England hostelry; for others it's a case study in quaintness run amok. ❺

Stockbridge Country Inn 26 Glendale Rd/Rte-183 ☎413/298-4015, ⓦwww.stockbridgecountryinn .com. Set in an 1856 country house on four acres, this seven-room B&B is close to the Rockwell Museum and offers queen-sized canopy beds, a heated pool, attractive gardens, and porches from which to view them. Full country breakfast included. ❽

The town and around

The actual town of Stockbridge is tiny, basically consisting of a few nineteenth-century buildings on Main Street and around the corner on Elm Street. Most visitors tend to park near the **Red Lion Inn** (see above) and wander from there, after having iced tea on the inn's venerable front porch.

There are few specific sights in the town center. The Historical Museum of the **Stockbridge Library**, at the corner of Main and Elm streets (Tues–Fri 9am–5pm, Sat 9am–2pm, ☏413/298-5501), contains artifacts made by the Mohicans who once lived in the area, while the **Mission House & Indian Museum**, 19 Main St, at the corner of Sergeant Street, just west of the center (late May to mid-Oct daily 10am–5pm; guided tours 7 times daily, last tour 4pm; $6, gardens and Indian Museum free; ☏413/298-3239), is where the Reverend John Sergeant planned his missionary work. Built in 1739, it was relocated here in 1927. The exterior has a pretty, arched Connecticut River Valley-style doorway, while the inside is noteworthy mainly for its eighteenth-century chairs. A grape arbor in the gardens behind the house leads to a small exhibition about the Mohicans he tried to convert.

Culture in the Berkshires

There are several **summer cultural festivals** in the Berkshires, but none so prominent as Tanglewood, Jacob's Pillow, and the Williamstown Theatre Festival. Tickets for the more popular events sell out far in advance, so plan accordingly. For a current calendar that includes all of the festivals, contact the **Berkshire Visitors Bureau** (☏413/743-4500 or 1-800/237-5747, ⊛www.berkshires.org).

Aston Magna Festival (☏413/528-3595 or 1-800/875-7156, ⊛www.astonmagna.org). The country's oldest annual summer festival, devoted to performances of Baroque music played on period instruments; concerts normally take place Saturdays (at Simon's Rock College, Great Barrington) throughout July, with a few Sunday shows at the Clark in Williamstown.

Berkshire Theatre Festival Main Street, Stockbridge (late June to Aug Mon–Sat; ☏413/298-5576, ⊛www.berkshiretheatre.org). Best known for its summer productions at the Berkshire Playhouse Mainstage, but also noteworthy for Unicorn Theater readings of plays in progress.

Jacob's Pillow Rte-20 between Becket and Lee (mid-June to Aug Wed–Sun; ☏413/243-0745, ⊛www.jacobspillow.org). The most famous contemporary dance festival in the country, improbably located in the middle of nowhere. Artists-in-residence give free performances of works in progress before the main programs.

Shakespeare & Company 70 Kemble St, Lenox (May–Nov; ☏413/637-1199, ⊛www.shakespeare.org). One of the country's biggest Shakespeare companies is based within a lovely garden property close to the center of town, currently with two stages and another slated for 2009. Productions are not limited to Shakespeare, and include new plays, dance, and dramatizations of stories by Edith Wharton, Henry James, and the like.

Tanglewood West Street/Rte-183, Lenox (July to late Aug; for advance tickets Sept–May, call ☏617/266-1492; otherwise ☏413/637-1600, ⊛www.bso.org). The Boston Symphony Orchestra gives concerts here, perhaps the most celebrated outdoor cultural venue in the country. Full orchestral concerts take place weekends at the Shed, while the newer Ozawa Hall is used on other days, mainly for chamber music concerts. Further musical options include open rehearsals for the BSO on Saturday mornings, plus jazz and pop performances. Tickets for the Shed and Ozawa Hall run anywhere from $32 to $105; it's cheaper (general admission $17) and arguably more enjoyable to sit on the grass – though if you do, bring a towel or lawn chair.

Williamstown Theatre Festival '62 Center for Theatre and Dance, Williams College, 1000 Main St, Rte-2, Williamstown (mid-June to late Aug Tues–Sun; ☏413/597-3400, ⊛www.wtfestival.org). Every summer some of the most accomplished actors from American stage and screen converge on this stately college town for a series of nearly a dozen productions, both time-tested and experimental.

Norman Rockwell Museum

Most people skip the town's minor sights in favor of the **Norman Rockwell Museum** (May–Oct daily 10am–5pm; Nov–April Mon–Fri 10am–4pm, Sat & Sun 10am–5pm; $15; Ⓣ413/298-4100, Ⓦwww.nrm.org), three miles from the town center off Rte-183. Several galleries of revolving Rockwell originals (usually including the provocative *Four Freedoms*, nostalgic *Stockbridge Main Street at Christmas*, and undeniably witty *Triple Self-Portrait*), and the work of vaguely related illustrators, are well displayed and annotated. Despite Rockwell's penchant for advertising endorsements, and the idealism that infused much of his work, it's hard not be sucked in by the artist's obsessive attention to detail, and his simple but clever ideas – see *Girl Reading the Post*. Take the tourists out of the scene, and the facility and grounds – which include the little red building that was Rockwell's **studio** (May–Oct 10am–4.45pm) – are rather tranquil, though you'd be forgiven for mistaking it for a nursing home.

Chesterwood

There's another, rather overrated, attraction just down the road in the form of **Chesterwood**, 4 Williamsville Rd (mid-May to mid-Oct daily 10am–5pm; $12; Ⓣ413/298-3579; Ⓦwww.chesterwood.org), the former summer home of sculptor Daniel Chester French, best known for his rendition of Abraham Lincoln at the Lincoln Memorial in Washington, DC. The plaster models in the artist's studio betray the fact that he had no formal training, though his 130-acre estate is idyllic. Hourly guided tours are the only way to visit the studio and residence, but you can peruse the exhibits in the visitors' center and wander the attractive gardens at will.

Naumkeag

With its spectacular views of the Stockbridge hills, distinctive gardens, and aesthetically balanced interiors, the Gilded Age estate of **Naumkeag**, on Prospect Hill Road, Rte-7 (late May to mid-Oct daily 10am–5pm; $12;

(T)413/298-3239, ext 3000), is like a Newport mansion without the forced opulence. It was built by Stanford White in 1886 as a family home for the prosperous attorney Joseph Hodges Choate, later the US ambassador to Britain (the estate's name, pronounced "Nómkeg," derives from the Native American word for Salem, Choate's birthplace). The master architect's touch is evident everywhere, from the American-style shingle roof to the European-style brick and stone towers to the understated interior flourishes, including a combination of cherry, oak, and mahogany paneling and a three-story hand-carved staircase. Original furnishings and domestic accoutrements from all over the world give the impression that the Choates have just slipped out for a minute; indeed, there are even coats left hanging in the closet. Although you can only visit the inside on a 45-minute guided tour, this is one of the few houses in the Berkshires where taking a tour is truly worthwhile.

As impressive as the house is, the real attraction is the eight acres of meticulously planned and tended **gardens**, subtly studded with contemporary sculpture. The first greenspace of note, more like an adjunct to the house, is the Afternoon Garden, a 1928 addition remarkable for its vividly painted Venetian-style posts. The Perugino View, named for a sixteenth-century painter, adjoins the Top Lawn and affords intoxicating views over the grounds and across to Monument Mountain. From here it's a short walk to the Blue Steps, named for its blue-colored fountains. The atmospheric Linden Walk ends with a statue of the Roman goddess Diana.

Eating and drinking

Glendale River Grille Rte-183 (T)413/298-4711. Elegant, spacious grill and tavern, about one mile south of the Rockwell Museum. Some adventurous entrees – such as roast duckling Cantonese with hoisin sauce – in addition to standard steaks and swordfish. Closed Mon.

Lion's Den At the *Red Lion Inn*, Main St (T)413/298-1654. Repair to the inn's atmospheric cellar tavern to get down with the rest of the town. Live music most nights, plus standard pub fare.

Main Street Café 40 Main St (T)413/298-3060. The most central option and best breakfast in town; half-pound burgers and deli-style sandwiches take the stage from lunch onwards.

Michael's Restaurant 5 Elm St (T)413/298-3530. Surf, turf, and pasta with a late-night menu and suds to suit every taste. Great place to watch games or shoot some pool. Karaoke on Fri.

Once Upon a Table 36 Main St (T)413/298-3870. Quietly tucked in the Mews off Main St, the decor here is romantic with a worldly menu (entrees $17–24). Popular among locals.

Lenox

From Stockbridge, a slight detour off Rte-7 takes you to Rte-7A and the genteel village of **LENOX**, the cultural nucleus of the Berkshires by virtue of its proximity to Tanglewood, the summer home of the Boston Symphony Orchestra. It's a quiet place for most of the year, but on summer weekends traffic jams are not uncommon. Summering in Lenox has been a New York (and not Boston) tradition since the mid-nineteenth century, and, not surprisingly, shops and restaurants display prices and attitude that's more Manhattan than New England.

Accommodation

The **Lenox Chamber of Commerce**, 5 Walker St, Rte-7A (June–Aug daily 10am–6pm; Sept–May Wed–Sat 10am–4pm; (T)413/637-3646, (W)www.lenox .org), will help you to find a place to stay, although in summer don't expect to stroll into town and find a room.

Blantyre 16 Blantyre Rd ☏ 413/637-3556, ⓦ www.blantyre.com. A former summer "cottage," this roomy Scottish Tudor mansion with Gothic flourishes has been refurbished as one of the country's most luxurious resorts, and as such is almost a destination in itself. ❾

Brook Farm Inn 15 Hawthorne St ☏ 413/637-3013 or 1-800/285-7638, ⓦ www.brookfarm.com. The innkeepers at this twelve-room 1870 Victorian B&B are poetry aficionados, and hold readings and other entertainments in the library, often at teatime, with home-made scones and strawberry jam; in winter curl up with a book of verse in front of a fireplace, either in the common area or in your room. ❽

The Village Inn 16 Church St ☏ 413/637-0020 or 1-800/253-0917, ⓦ www.villageinn-lenox.com. A 1771 country inn-style hotel with 32 rooms with antiques, bountiful breakfasts, and afternoon English tea in the center of Lenox. Good-value rooms if you visit during spring. ❽

Walker House 64 Walker St ☏ 413/637-1271, ⓦ www.walkerhouse.com. This informal eight-room B&B, an attractive 1804 Federal-style mansion, offers eight spacious doubles, each named after a composer with antique beds and wooden floors. Extras include afternoon tea and films screened nightly on a giant twelve-foot screen. ❺

Wheatleigh Hawthorne Rd ☏ 413/637-0610, ⓦ www.wheatleigh.com. Built by a New York financier in 1893 as a wedding present for his daughter, today this Florentine palazzo-style estate-cum-resort combines antique and contemporary decor to sumptuous, successful effect. The lush grounds were landscaped by Frederick Law Olmsted, designer of Boston's Emerald Necklace, and to stay any closer to Tanglewood you'd have to camp on its lawn. ❾

Whistler's Inn 5 Greenwood St ☏ 866/637-0975, ⓦ www.whistlersinnlenox.com. Three of the fourteen rooms at this 1820 English Tudor-style manor are said to be haunted, which both attracts and repels guests. Rooms vary in decor, from low, angled ceilings above a queen bed in the "Artist's Loft" to the romantic space of the "African Room." ❻–❾

The town and around

Even if you're visiting after late August, it's well worth making a stop off West Street (Rte-183), about a mile outside town, to walk around **Tanglewood** (visitors' center 10am–4pm: July–Aug daily, June & Sept–Oct Sat & Sun only). Though its lush grounds (daily 8am–dusk) were formerly part of the estate of a Boston banker, it was Nathaniel Hawthorne who coined the name. Today

▲ Downtown Lenox

the musicians practice in a reconstruction of the red farmhouse where he lived with his wife Sophia in 1850 and 1851, penning *The House of the Seven Gables* on the premises. On summer weekends, concerts are given in the aptly named Shed, a bare-bones, indoor/outdoor hall, as well as the newer Ozawa Hall (see box, p.237, for details).

Fans of **Edith Wharton** will want to visit **The Mount**, at the corner of Plunkett Street and Rte-7 (May–Aug daily 9am–5pm; Sept & Oct daily 10am–4pm; guided tours hourly mid-June to Aug; $16, tours $2 extra; ☎413/637-1899, ⊛www.edithwharton.org), the novelist's summer home from 1902 until 1911. Restorations are ongoing, but the grounds are relatively close to what Wharton intended when she designed the home at the turn of the century. The guided tour is especially revealing, illustrating how the order, scale, and harmony of the place are a reflection of the principles Wharton promoted in her first successful book, *The Decoration of Houses*, published a few years before she moved here. The knowledgeable guides are also a mine of information on Wharton's life, providing a biography of the author as you tour the house. Though her years at The Mount were productive – she wrote *Ethan Frome* here – they were not entirely happy; boredom with her husband and an unapologetic disgust for the turpitude of American culture ultimately sent her to France, where she lived until her death. Take time to appreciate the collection of Wharton's books in the **library**; the Mount was virtually bankrupted by their purchase from a private collector in 2006, and narrowly avoided foreclosure in 2008. Live **readings** of Wharton's work take place every Wednesday at 5pm in July and August.

Eating and drinking

🏃 **Berkshire Bagel** 18 Franklin St, just off Rte-7A ☎413/637-1500. Rare budget option in the center of town, where locals mingle with New Yorkers desperate for a bagel fix: great range of bagels and schmears ($2–5), with a few tables and a small parking lot on site. Mon–Sat closes at 2pm, Sun at 1pm.

🏃 **Bistro Zinc** 56 Church St ☎413/637-8800. Power-lunch spot filled with diners on cell phones gobbling up flavorful French fare at reasonable prices – dinner is considerably more expensive (entrees $18–29).

Church Street Café 65 Church St ☎413/637-2745. The tasty New England fare, from sautéed Maine crab cakes to maple- and cider-glazed pork chops, wins accolades for this eatery – more restaurant than

café – in the center of Lenox. Closed Sun & Mon Sept–May.

Firefly 71 Church St ☎413/637-2700. Ask the locals where they go for a night out, and they'll tell you about *Firefly*: the tavern, tapas, and dinner menus have something for every hour, like pan-seared scallops, edamame, and honey-glazed salmon, while the intimate bar makes it easy to chat with strangers. Entrees $25–26.

Wheatleigh Hawthorne Rd ☎413/637-0610. Very high prices, but you get what you pay for – outstanding flavors of contemporary Continental cuisine, including low-fat and vegetarian menus, artfully prepared desserts, and impeccable service. The decor, from crystal chandeliers to Italianate paintings, is undeniably soothing.

Lee and Tyringham

During the busy summer cultural season, many last-minute travelers to Lenox end up staying in nearby **LEE**, which is just as well, for there is a genuine quality to the place altogether lacking in its ritzier neighbor. If you need help finding a place to sleep, contact the **Lee Chamber of Commerce**, which runs an information booth on Main Street in front of the church (June–Oct Mon–Sat 10am–4pm; ☎413/243-0852, ⊛www.leechamber.org).

One of the better-kept secrets in Massachusetts is the scenic Tyringham Valley, practically hidden between routes 102 and 23 and accessible from Tyringham Road, off Rte-102 south of Lee. **TYRINGHAM** itself, which basically consists of a post office and a church, was settled in the eighteenth century and hasn't really changed since. The only tangible sight is the "Gingerbread" dwelling called **Santarella**, 75 Main Rd (℡413/243-2819, ⓦwww.santarella.us), designed and built by Englishman Sir Henry Hudson Kitson – sculptor of the *Minute Man* in Lexington – as his studio in the 1930s. Its signature feature is the eighty-ton roof, a sculpted simulation of thatching that succeeds in conveying the image of the undulating Berkshire Hills. The house is closed to the public, though you are free to wander up the garden path.

Just south of Santarella, Tyringham Road opens onto the **Tyringham Valley** and the **Tyringham Cobble**, a 400-foot forest-covered outcropping: to hike it, make a right on Jerusalem Road after the village and proceed for a quarter of a mile. The reward for your two-mile endeavor will be breathtaking views. A right turn on Art School Road, the next street down, takes you to **Joyous Spring Pottery** (July & Aug daily 10am–5pm; ℡413/528-4115), where you can view pieces made using Japanese techniques and fired in a *nobori gama* (an enormous kiln). It's worth continuing another mile to the end of Art School Road and the **Bidwell House Museum** (late May to mid-Oct Thurs–Mon 11am–4pm; $10; ℡413/528-6888, ⓦwww.bidwellhousemuseum.org), a Georgian saltbox built in 1750. The restored interior is rarely busy, and the gardens are full of hiking trails.

Accommodation

Applegate 279 W Park St, Lee ℡413/243-4451 or 1-800/691-9012, ⓦwww.applegateinn.com. A calm, ship-shape B&B in a Southern-style Georgian colonial home. The six guestrooms have old-fashioned character but a contemporary feel; fresh-baked goods contribute to great breakfasts. ❽–❾

Chambéry Inn 199 Main St, Lee ℡413/243-2221 or 1-800/537-4321, ⓦwww.chamberyinn.com. This 1885 French country house, built as the Berkshire's first parochial school, has nine meticulously refurbished suites with high ceilings, big windows, and modern touches such as cable TV (there are also two standard double rooms). ❾

Historic Merrell Inn 1565 Pleasant St/Rte-102, South Lee ℡413/243-1794 or 1-800/243-1794, ⓦwww.merrell-inn.com. Just south of town, between Stockbridge and Lee, this atmospheric inn has ten enticing rooms, warmly decorated with Victorian wallpaper and furnishings – four have a working fireplace in winter. Look for the vintage birdcage bar in the room where breakfast is served, a relic from its days as a stagecoach stop. ❽

Sunset Farm Bed & Breakfast 74 Tyringham Rd, Tyringham ℡413/243-3229, ⓦwww.sunsetfarminn .com. Old New England lives on at this blissfully isolated 1704 farmhouse on a hillock in the gorgeous Tyringham Valley. Five rooms, three of which have private baths, are a bit frayed at the edges, but the feel is very authentic without being twee. The owners are warm, the food good, and there's a nice place to hike out back. ❹

Eating

Cakewalk Bakery and Café 56 Main St, Lee ℡413/243-2806. Offers an affordable but tasty menu of soups, sandwiches, salads, quiches, and, oh yes, delicious pastries. Closed Mon.

Joe's Diner 85 Center St, Lee ℡413/243-9756. The best place to eat in Lee, whether you want a weighty corned-beef sandwich, tuna salad on rye, or scrambled eggs and waffles. Extremely popular, and with very low prices (superb sausages and eggs from $5).

Phó Saigon 5 Railroad St, Lee ℡413/243-6288. Authentic Vietnamese food in an old but spotless shack just off Main St, with $8.50 lunch specials, exquisite beef noodle soup ($10), and crispy spring rolls ($6). Closed Tues.

Salmon Run Fish House 78 Main St, Lee ℡413/243-3900. Boasts an informal atmosphere in which to eat a variety of reasonably priced seafood and pasta dishes – salmon is cooked all ways, from the simple (char-grilled;

$12), to the fancy (stuffed with lobster; $19). Closed Tues.

Sullivan Station 109 Railroad St, Lee ☎413/243-2082. Converted railroad station (you can sit in the old ticket office or caboose), serving great sandwiches and salads for lunch, and hearty steaks, ribs, and chops for dinner. May–Oct open daily; Nov–April closed Mon & Tues.

Great Barrington

South of Stockbridge, the landscape takes on a more rustic flavor, one that definitely colors the only town of any size, **GREAT BARRINGTON**. What buzz there is here centers on Main Street near Railroad and Castle streets, where upmarket home decor shops sit among a number of good eateries. The old-fashioned **Mahaiwe Performing Arts Center**, on Castle Street (☎413/528-0100, 🌐www.mahaiwe.org), was restored in 2005, and is the place to go for music, dance, theater, opera, and classic films. If it's the season (mid-Aug to mid-Oct), you may want to pick apples at Windy Hill Farm, 686 Stockbridge Rd (☎413/298-3217), or pumpkins at Taft Farms, Rte-183 (☎413/528-1515 or 1-800/528-1015, 🌐www.taftfarms.com).

Practicalities

The **Southern Berkshire Chamber of Commerce** runs a visitors' center at 62 Main St (Mon & Wed 11am–5pm, Tues & Thurs–Sun 9am–5pm; ☎413/528-1510), and can arrange accommodation via their lodging hotline (☎800/269-4825). Several chain **motels** sit along Rte-7 north of town. For more character, the *Wainwright Inn*, 518 S Main St (☎413/528-2062, 🌐www .wainwrightinn.com; ❻–❽), occupies a huge 1766 mansion right outside the center of town, while the *Windflower Inn*, 684 South Egremont Rd/Rte-23 (☎413/528-2720 or 1-800/992-1993, 🌐www.windflowerinn.com; ❾–❽), is a relaxed country inn with thirteen rooms, most with fireplaces. For something to eat and drink, *Barrington Brewery*, 424 Stockbridge Rd, Rte-7 (☎413/528-8282) is a family-friendly place, especially noted for its crab cakes ($16), stout chocolate cakes, and pints of well-crafted ales ($4.50), while *Babalouie's*, 286 Main St (☎413/528-8100), does excellent wood-fired sourdough pizzas made with local organic produce. If it's sushi you crave, visit *Bizen*, 17 Railroad St (☎413/528-4343), which has Japanese chefs and an energetic atmosphere; reservations are recommended for lunch and dinner.

Pittsfield and around

Once a prosperous center for paper milling and the home of GE's plastics division, working-class **PITTSFIELD** is one of the least attractive towns in the Berkshires, though it does boast a couple of worthy attractions. It's also become an unlikely claimant to the title of **birthplace of baseball**. In 2004, historian John Thorn went public with a controversial discovery: he had uncovered a 1791 Pittsfield town ordinance that outlawed baseball nearly half a century before its "invention" in 1839 by Abner Doubleday in Cooperstown, NY. You can view a copy of the "Broken Window Bylaw" at the public library, the **Berkshire Athenaeum**, 1 Wendell Ave (Mon–Thurs 9am–9pm, Fri 9am–5pm, Sat 10am–5pm; ☎413/499-9480, ⓦwww.pittsfieldlibrary.org) – the original is locked away in the library vault. Nearby, at 39 South St (Rte-7), the slick **Berkshire Museum** (Mon–Sat 10am–5pm, Sun noon–5pm; $10, children $5; ☎413/443-7171, ⓦwww.berkshiremuseum.org) has something for everyone, though its fine art exhibits, aquarium with touch-tank, and hands-on "innovation" hall will primarily appeal to kids; the dinosaurs and mummies probably will, too.

The only other sight that might keep you in Pittsfield is **Arrowhead**, just south of the town center on Holmes Road (late May to Oct daily 9.30am–4pm; $12; ☎413/442-1793, ⓦwww.mobydick.org), the eighteenth-century farmhouse where Herman Melville lived for thirteen years and wrote *Moby Dick*. The house is gradually being restored in 1850s period style, and can only be visited via 45-minute guided tours, which also shed light on Melville's often chaotic family life in the Berkshires.

Practicalities

Pick up maps and information at the **Pittsfield Visitors Center**, 111 South St, Rte-7 (May–Oct daily 9am–5pm, Nov–April Mon–Sat 10am–4pm; ☎413/443-9186). The most obvious **place to stay** in Pittsfield is the *Crowne Plaza*, 1 West St (☎413/499-2000, ⓦwww.berkshirecrowne.com;ⓞ), which dominates downtown and has comfortable rooms. If you're looking for a more personal experience, head about three miles out of town along Barker Road to *Hollyhock House* (☎413/443-6901, ⓦwww.hollyhockbb.com; ④–⑤), a friendly and spotlessly clean B&B with three rooms that are good value for money. For something to **eat**, *Dakota Steak House*, 1035 South St/Rte-7 (☎413/499-7900), is a capacious place with updated hunting lodge decor. Big portions of American staples such as Maine lobster and mesquite-grilled chicken are the draws, as is the large salad bar (entrees under $20). It's open daily, but serves lunch Sundays only. Meanwhile, the *Court Square Breakfast & Deli*, 95 East St (☎413/442-9896), across from the courthouse, is one of the brighter, more pleasant places in town to eat straightforward breakfasts and lunches (closes at 2pm). *Patrick's Pub*, 26 Bank Row (☎413/499-1994) right in the center, is the best place for a drink.

Hancock Shaker Village

From 1790 until 1960, the **Hancock Shaker Village**, at the junction of routes 20 and 41, five miles west of Pittsfield (daily: mid-April to late May 10am–4pm; late May to late Oct 10am–5pm; rest of year by guided tour only, Mon–Fri 1pm, Sat & Sun 11am & 1pm; summer and fall $15, rest of year $12.50; ☎413/443-0188 or 1-800/817-1137, ⓦwww.hancockshakervillage .org), was an active Shaker community; believers in a branch of the Quaker faith, Shakers were named for the convulsive fits of glee they experienced when worshipping. The pacifist sect, which was renowned for its vegetable seeds and simple but elegant furniture, all but disappeared during the twentieth century, largely due to its members' vows of celibacy (see box, p.411). Hancock was the third Shaker village ever established, and retains one of the biggest collections of furniture and objects. Its twenty preserved buildings, located in fairly close proximity amid 1200 acres, are worth poking about. The most interesting is the **Round Stone Barn**, built in 1826 and the only one of its kind. Its circular shape allowed a single man to feed 54 cows at the same time from the center.

▲ Round Stone Barn, Hancock Shaker Village

Much of the fun to be had at the Hancock Shaker Village is of the pastoral variety. In the Barn Complex you can try your hand at a spinning wheel or model Shaker fashions, while all over the village artisans demonstrate Shaker crafts, gardeners tend the land, and farmers discuss livestock management. You can also grab lunch or a snack in the on-site *Village Café*, which serves inexpensive and tasty Shaker-inspired dishes, such as cider-baked ham and savory baked goods.

Williamstown

Pretty **WILLIAMSTOWN**, at the northwesternmost corner of the state, may seem a bit remote to be one of the region's premier art destinations, but the presence of the **Clark**, with its excellent Impressionist collections, as well as the **Williams College Museum of Art**, has put it on the map. These, plus the tranquil Williams College campus – which essentially forms the center of the town – and the town's prime location at the terminus of the Mohawk Trail, make Williamstown a choice spot to spend a few days. Most of the action, of which there is actually little, save for during the summertime **Williamstown Theatre Festival** (see box, p.237) – centers on block-long Spring Street, with the requisite range of shops and restaurants, most infused with an unmistakable upscale collegiate atmosphere.

Accommodation

The 1896 House 910 Cold Spring Rd/ Rte-7 ☏413/458-1896 or 1-888/999-1896, Ⓦwww.1896house.com. Close to the center of Williamstown, this hostelry proffers spotless "brookside," "pondside," and "barnside" accommodations and a good restaurant. ❻

The Guest House at Field Farm 554 Sloan Rd
Ⓣ413/458-3135, Ⓦguesthouseatfieldfarm
.thetrustees.org. Six stylish bedrooms, each with
private bath, in a 1948 Bauhaus-inspired country
house littered with modern art and surrounded by
more than three hundred acres of meadows and
woodlands. ⑧–⑨
Maple Terrace Motel 555 Main St/Rte-2
Ⓣ413/458-9677, Ⓦwww.mapleterrace.com.
Reliable motel set off from the street, with worldly
wise Swedish owners, within easy walking distance
of the Williamstown Theatre Festival. ④–⑥
The Orchards 222 Adams Rd Ⓣ 413/458-9611 or
1-800/225-1517, Ⓦwww.orchardshotel.com.
Modern hotel with a country-inn theme, English

antiques, afternoon tea, and several rooms with
fireplaces. The spacious rooms were designed for
indulgence. ⑧
Steep Acres Farm B&B 520 White Oaks Rd
Ⓣ413/458-3774. Four rooms with shared baths in
a 1900 cottage on fifty very scenic acres with an
orchard and spring-fed pond; the breakfast is as
filling as the environs are relaxing, and it's just two
miles from the center of town. ④–⑦
🏃 The Williams Inn 1090 Main St, at the
junction of routes 7 and 2 Ⓣ413/458-9371,
Ⓦwww.williamsinn.com. Located on campus at
Williams College, two blocks from the center. All
125 rooms have modern amenities, and there's a
good restaurant and large bar. ⑧

The Town

Williamstown is an essential ingredient of a Berkshires tour not because of the
college itself – attractive as it is – but because of the town's two superb
museums, one of which, the **Sterling and Francine Clark Art Institute**, (or
just "The Clark") 225 South St (July & Aug daily 10am–5pm; Sept–June Tues–
Sun 10am–5pm; $12.50 June–Oct, free Nov–May, Ⓣ413/458-2303 Ⓦwww
.clarkart.edu), is known for its extensive collection of French Impressionist
paintings, including thirty by Renoir. The highlight is *At the Concert* (1880),
which established Renoir's niche of beautiful women in fashionable clothing.
There are also paintings by Constable, Fragonard, Géricault, Rembrandt, Turner
and Alma-Tadema, as well as a sizeable collection of American works by Homer,
Sargent, and Remington, whose *The Scout: Friends or Foes* details the anxiety and
loneliness of looking into the future. Allow two hours or so to take it all in,
longer if you have a snack or light lunch at the excellent museum café.

Meanwhile, on the Williams campus, the **Williams College Museum of Art**,
15 Lawrence Hall Drive (Tues–Sat 10am–5pm, Sun 1–5pm; free; Ⓣ413/597-2429,
Ⓦwww.wcma.org) is ravishing for both its facility and its collections. Part of the
museum is housed in an 1846 two-story brick octagon, capped by a Neoclassical
rotunda; a three-story entrance atrium connects it to a contemporary addition. The
thrust of the exceedingly well-curated collection is American visual art from the
late eighteenth century to the present day, and some of the best exhibits are those
by contemporary artists.

Eating and drinking

Hobson's Choice 159 Water St Ⓣ413/458-9101.
This country manor with beamed ceilings is a
local favorite, known for steaks, prime rib, various
chicken dishes, Cajun shrimp, blackened Norwegian
salmon, and Alaskan king crab. Dinner only.
Lickety Split 69 Spring St Ⓣ413/458-1818. Line
up here for fabulous ice cream, sourced from
Herrell's in Northampton.
🏃 Mezze 16 Water St Ⓣ413/458-0123.
Urban contemporary meets rural gentility.
Mediterranean, Moroccan, and American-
influenced dishes, like braised rabbit and home-
made pasta, sesame-seared organic tofu, and

lamb with thyme, jump off the seasonal menu.
Dinner only; entrees $17–27.
Pappa Charlie's Deli 28 Spring St Ⓣ413/458-
5969. From chicken cordon bleu to the "Bo Derek"
– a sandwich with peppers, onions, mushrooms,
melted provolone, sprouts, and tomatoes – they do
hot, cold, and vegetarian light fare with flare. Best
place for breakfast.
Spice Root 23 Spring St Ⓣ413/458-5200. Fairly
authentic Indian restaurant, and a welcome dose of
spice in this part of the world, with a liberal hodgepodge of North and South Indian favorites; the $9
lunch buffet is a bargain.

Sushi Thai Garden 27 Spring St ☎413/458-0004. The beige and green ambience makes for a Zen eating experience, with exotic choices like steamed ginger salmon or the fiery seafood *gra prow* – try the sushi combos from $12 and hefty lunchboxes from $9.50.

The Water Street Grill 123 Water St ☎413/458-2175. From blackened catfish to grilled sirloin, this is a safe choice for American and Tex-Mex dining. Nothing too exciting, but it's all done well.

North Adams and around

Settled in the 1730s and, during the nineteenth century, a fairly prosperous mill town, **NORTH ADAMS**, five miles east of Williamstown, might have been just another post-industrial eyesore if it weren't for the **Massachusetts Museum of Contemporary Art**, 87 Marshall St (aka MASS MoCA; July–Aug daily 10am–6pm; Sept–June Mon & Wed–Sun 11am–5pm; $15; ☎413/662-2111, Ⓦwww.massmoca.org). This huge arts center is housed in a resurrected old mill, and mounts an extensive range of exhibits in its 27 refurbished buildings, linked by a web of bridges, passageways, viaducts, and courtyards. Most of the work is installation-oriented, and although much of the content may provoke even the most open-minded to wonder aloud, "Can you really call this *art*?" there's an undeniable neo-funhouse pleasure in wandering through the configurations of materials, collages, video monitors, found objects, oversized photographs, and flashing lights.

Practicalities

Just across the street from MASS MoCA, 🏛 *The Porches Inn*, 231 River St (☎413/664-0400, Ⓦwww.porches.com; ➑–➒), an ultramodern **hotel** with DVD players, high-speed internet, and nary an antique in sight, occupies a row of houses formerly lived in by mill-workers. A more affordable option is the *Holiday Inn*, just minutes from the action at 40 Main St (☎1-800/664-9491; ➎).

As for a **meal**, you can dine at *Café Latino*, in Building 11 at MASS MoCA (Wed–Sat; ☎413/662-2004), on delectable citrus-braised pork shoulder or salmon with pineapple-rum salsa, or sip *caipirinhas* while facing the hip backlit bar. A similarly fun – but not as chic – vibe can be found at *Freghtyard Pub*, 9 Furnace St, Building 4 (☎413/663-6547), the town's best late-night **drinking** spot, which specializes in great live music (Fri & Sat) and excellent pub fare (try the chili).

Mount Greylock

To many visitors **Mount Greylock** will be pretty underwhelming, but Massachusetts citizens take great pride in the peak, the tallest in the state at 3491 feet. Though somewhat short of spectacular, it does make for a scenic hike, drive, or bike ride, especially in the fall. The ninety-foot-tall **War Memorial Tower**, erected to honor the Massachusetts casualties of all wars, stands near the top.

Access to Mount Greylock is easy enough: from North Adams, Notch Road leads straight into the reserve from Rte-2, just west of the town center; you'll find trail maps at the **visitors' center** (daily: mid-May to early Sept 9am–9pm; early Sept to late Oct 9am–7pm; rest of year 9am–4pm; ☎413/499-4262), eight miles south of the summit, or 1.5 miles north of Lanesborough on Rockwell Road. Note that the summit road was closed at the time of writing for extensive repairs, but is scheduled to re-open in 2009; the summit will thereafter be accessible by vehicles only from May through October. If you want to **eat** a cheap, bountiful diner-style breakfast or lunch before heading out on a hike, *Bob's Country Kitchen* (☎413/499-3934) in Lanesborough is a convenient place to stop.

Rhode Island

CHAPTER 4

Highlights

✳ **Federal Hill, Providence**
This firmly established Italian community in the state capital has (almost) as much charm as Naples itself. See p.258

✳ **Blackstone River boat tour** Get off the road and experience Rhode Island as the early settlers did: slowly, along the Blackstone River. See p.260

✳ **Blithewold Mansion and Gardens** In the midst of Bristol's patriotic passion, Blithewold is an oasis of blooming gardens and exotic trees. See p.261

✳ **Newport** With its phenomenal mansions, fine beaches, fancy yachts, and world-class summer music concerts, this coastal town has real appeal. See p.261

✳ **South County** Welcome to endless shores, sandy dunes, and lighthouses jutting out on rocky promontories. See p.272

✳ **Mohegan Bluffs, Block Island** Experience pure desolation at 200 feet up, peering down on the Atlantic below. See p.279

▲ Blithewold Mansion and Gardens

Rhode Island

4

RHODE ISLAND

ust 48 miles north to south by 37 miles east to west, **Rhode Island** may be the smallest state in the Union, but its influence on national life has been disproportionately large: on May 18, 1652, the territory enacted the first law against slavery in North America; just over one hundred years later, it was the first of the thirteen original colonies to declare independence from Great Britain. In addition to this fruitful cultural history, the state is also surprisingly land-rich, with more than four hundred miles of spectacular coastline and thousands of acres of pristine woodlands. These physical assets, especially, make the state a favorite destination within the region.

In addition to the mainland, the state is made up of over thirty tiny islands in the surrounding **Narragansett Bay**, including Hope, Despair, and Rhode Island (also known by its Native American title, "Aquidneck"), which gives the state its name – lore has it that in 1524 Italian explorer Giovanni da Verrazano spotted this island from the sea, and named it for its resemblance to the Greek isle of Rhodes (one can only surmise it was foggy, or there was rum involved). The bay itself has long been a determining factor in Rhode Island's economic development, with the **"Ocean State"** prospering through sea trade, whaling, and smuggling until the nineteenth century, when the focus shifted inland, and to manufacturing. Today, the state's principal destinations are its two original ports: **Providence**, home of Brown University and alleged birthplace of the US Navy (a claim contested by several other New England towns), and **Newport**, home to some outrageously extravagant mansions that once belonged to America's most prominent families, and still a major yachting center. Further west, lining the coast along US-1 are the lively small towns and fishing ports of the state's **South County**, most notably **Watch Hill** and **Galilee**; ferries run from the latter to **Block Island**, a tiny, undeveloped bump of land with sandy beaches and endless ocean views. Inland, northeastern Rhode Island boasts the woodsy **Blackstone River Valley**, an important player in the Industrial Revolution, and now home to a number of old mills and some wonderful hiking.

Rhode Island's compact size is one of its most endearing features – you are rarely more than an hour's drive or bus ride away from any other point in the state. Providence is well served by **bus** lines such as Bonanza and Greyhound, and by trains (both the MBTA **commuter rail** and **Amtrak**, which also stops at Westerly). Outside of the major cities, though, travelling by **car** is your best bet, though the public **buses** provided by **RIPTA** (Rhode Island Public Transit Authority) are another option.

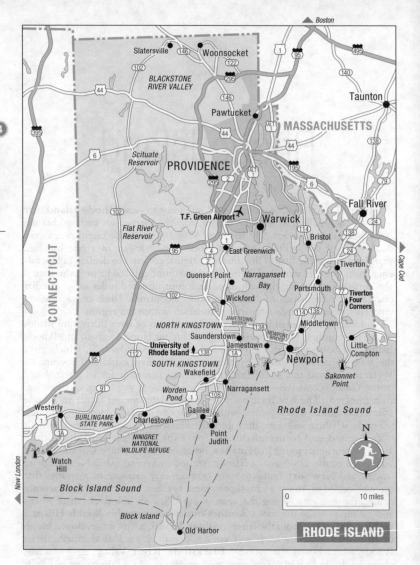

Boston

Slatersville · 146 · Woonsocket · 122 · 1 · 95 · 495

102 · BLACKSTONE RIVER VALLEY · 140

44 · 146 · Taunton

Pawtucket · ALT 1

44 · MASSACHUSETTS · 138

395 · 6 · Scituate Reservoir · PROVIDENCE · 295 · 2 · ALT 1 · 44 · 195 · 6 · 79

Fall River

Flat River Reservoir · T.F. Green Airport · Warwick · 114 · 24

102 · Bristol · 138

95 · 4 · 1 · East Greenwich · 2 · 24 · Tiverton

Quonset Point · Narragansett Bay · Portsmouth · 77 · Tiverton Four Corners

102 · Wickford · 114 · 138

JAMESTOWN BRIDGE · Middletown

NORTH KINGSTOWN · 138 · NEWPORT BRIDGE

Saunderstown · Little Compton

University of Rhode Island · 138 · Jamestown · 1A

112 · SOUTH KINGSTOWN · Wakefield · Newport · Sakonnet Point

Worden Pond · 1 · 108 · Narragansett

91 · Galilee · Rhode Island Sound

Westerly · 1 · BURLINGAME STATE PARK · Charlestown · Point Judith

1A · NINIGRET NATIONAL WILDLIFE REFUGE

Watch Hill

New London · Block Island Sound · N

0 · 10 miles

Block Island

Old Harbor · RHODE ISLAND

CONNECTICUT · Cape Cod

Some history

In 1636, the **Reverend Roger Williams** was exiled from the Massachusetts Bay Colony for espousing such radical ideas as the separation of church and state and Indians' rights. Moving south, he established the colony of Providence, on the Narragansett Bay, as a "lively experiment" in religious freedom. Rhode Island's tolerant basis did not ensure peace, however: relations with local Native Americans soured in 1675, when Wampanoag chief King Philip (Metacomet) clashed with colonists to protect tribal lands, resulting in the bloody conflict that became known as **King Philip's War** (see p.529). Despite the hostilities, Rhode Island flourished thanks to its growing maritime commerce, with Providence becoming one of the most important ports of call in the "**triangle trade**," in which New England rum was first exchanged for African slaves, who were exchanged in turn for West Indian molasses. Later, Rhode Island became the first colony to prohibit slave importation; it was also the first to declare independence from Britain, in May 1776, but the last to ratify the US Constitution, in May 1790.

Between the Revolution and the Civil War, the state's economic focus shifted from maritime trade to manufacturing, with the Blackstone Valley region playing a large role in the **Industrial Revolution**. In 1793, Pawtucket became the site of the nation's first water-powered **textile mill**, the brainchild of entrepreneur Samuel Slater. The textile industry lured thousands of immigrant workers to Rhode Island, contributing to the ethnic mix that exists today; manufacturing also continues to play an important role. In recent decades, the state's economic fortunes have fluctuated. Confidence took a major nosedive in 1990, when a disastrous **banking crisis** closed many state credit unions. Tightened regulations helped the state establish more secure financial footing for a period of time, prompting infrastructure improvements and urban renewal programs, but at the time of writing the state was facing yet another record deficit. Though the small state's future remains uncertain, a tough spirit has come to define it over the years, and visitors won't fail to notice the hospitality, quirkiness, and sense of community that have always been hallmarks of the Ocean State.

Providence and around

Stretching across seven hills on the Providence and Seekonk rivers, **PROVIDENCE** was Rhode Island's first settlement, established "in commemoration of God's Providence" on land given to **Roger Williams** by the Narragansett Indians. The state's **capital** since 1901, today Providence is one of the three largest cities in New England, with a vibrant arts scene, excellent restaurants, and lots of young people, drawn by the city's prestigious higher-education institutions. The aggressive urban renewal that took place all over Rhode Island in the late 1990s was especially effective here, utterly transforming the once bleak industrial landscape – while some grim pockets remain, the downtown area, known as **Downcity**, now gleams with new buildings and the Providence Place Shopping Mall. Perhaps more attractive, though, are the city's historic districts: west of Downcity, the vibrant Italian community on **Federal Hill** boasts some excellent restaurants, while east of the river lies **College Hill**, the oldest part of town, home to the campuses of **Brown University** and the **Rhode Island School of Design**, one of the nation's top art schools. In this area, **Benefit Street** is particularly atmospheric, with many historic buildings – in fact, the city holds one of the finest collections of Colonial and early Federal buildings in the nation.

Arrival and information

The state's major airport, **T.F. Green** (☎1-888/268-7222) is on Post Road, at Exit 13 off I-95 in Warwick, nine miles south of downtown Providence. An airport **shuttle** (daily 5am–11pm; $11) runs to select downtown Providence hotels and to the Amtrak **train station**, 100 Gaspee St (☎1-800/USA-RAIL), which is also served by the MBTA **commuter rail** from Boston (around 1hr; $7.75; ☎617/222-3200, ⊛www.mbta.com). Greyhound (☎401/454-0790) and Peter Pan (☎1-800/343-9999) **buses** stop downtown at the city's transportation center, Kennedy Plaza, as do local **RIPTA** buses (ticket window Mon–Fri

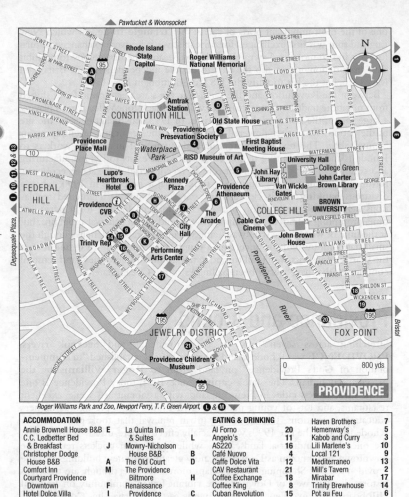

▲ Pawtucket & Woonsocket

Depasquale Plaza ◄

Bristol ►

Roger Williams Park and Zoo, Newport Ferry, T. F. Green Airport, ◐ & ◉ ▼

PROVIDENCE

0 _____ 800 yds

ACCOMMODATION		EATING & DRINKING		Haven Brothers	7
Annie Brownell House B&B **E**	La Quinta Inn	Al Forno	20	Hemenway's	5
C.C. Ledbetter Bed	& Suites **L**	Angelo's	11	Kabob and Curry	3
& Breakfast **J**	Mowry-Nicholson	AS220	16	Lili Marlene's	10
Christopher Dodge	House B&B **B**	Café Nuovo	4	Local 121	9
House B&B **A**	The Old Court **D**	Caffe Dolce Vita	12	Mediterraneo	13
Comfort Inn **M**	The Providence	CAV Restaurant	21	Mill's Tavern	2
Courtyard Providence	Biltmore **H**	Coffee Exchange	18	Mirabar	17
Downtown **F**	Renaissance	Coffee King	8	Trinity Brewhouse	14
Hotel Dolce Villa **I**	Providence **C**	Cuban Revolution	15	Pot au Feu	6
Hotel Providence **K**	The Westin **G**	Haruki East	1	Z Bar and Grille	19

7am–6pm, Sat 9am–noon & 1–5pm; $1.75 per trip, $5 for 24hr pass; ☏401/781-9400, ⓦwww.ripta.com).

The well-stocked **Visitors' Center**, in the rotunda lobby of the Rhode Island Convention Center, 1 Sabin St (Mon–Sat 9am–5pm; ☏401/751-1177 or 1-800/233-1636), provides maps and brochures, as does a small **kiosk** in the concourse of the Providence Place Mall, 1 Providence Place (Mon–Sat 11am–4pm), and another **information center** in the Roger Williams National Memorial Park, 282 N Main St (daily 9am–4.30pm; ☏401/521-7266). The **Rhode Island Historical Society**, 110 Benevolent St (☏401/273-7507, ⓦwww.rihs.org), leads a variety of tours and maintains a Library of Rhode Island History at 121 Hope St (☏401/273-8107). Self-guided tour info and pamphlets can be had at the **Providence Preservation Society**, 21 Meeting St (Mon–Fri 8.30am–5pm; ☏401/831-7440, ⓦwww.ppsri.org). If you're in for a splurge or romantic getaway, **La Gondola** (☏401/421-8877, ⓦwww.gondolari.com) offers gentle rides on two authentic Venetian gondolas down the Woonasquatucket and Providence rivers, from where you have beautiful evening views of the city (30–40min; $79–139 for two, $15 each for up to four additional passengers).

City transport

You don't really need a car to explore, but just in case, all the major **car rental** outfits are represented at the airport, including Hertz (☏401/738-3550) and Budget (☏401/739-8986); Enterprise has a location downtown at 90 Weybosset St (☏401/861-4408). **Taxis**, which aren't always readily available on the street, can be arranged by calling Providence Taxis (☏401/521-4200) or Yellow Cab (☏401/941-1122).

Particularly useful for getting around town are **RIPTA**'s Gold Line, which runs north–south across the central area, and its Green Line, running east–west. Also from Kennedy Plaza, a trolley (marked "Ferry") runs to the **ferry** docks at Providence Piers, 180 Allens Ave, from where you can catch ferries to Newport (May–Oct up to 6 daily; 1hr; $12; ☏866/683-3779, ⊛www.providencefastferry.com).

Accommodation

Providence has a several large downtown **hotels**, as well as a limited number of B&Bs and inns scattered around the city. There are fairly few **budget** options, though motorists will find a swath of mid-priced **motels** along I-95 towards Pawtucket, north of the city, and to the south near the airport.

Annie Brownell House B&B 400 Angell St ☏401/454-2934, ⊛www.anniebrownellhouse.com. Four rooms in a lovely 1899 Colonial Revival house near Thayer St. Full hot breakfasts. ⑤

C.C. Ledbetter Bed & Breakfast 326 Benefit St ☏401/351-4699, ⊛www.ccledbetter.com. A handful of rooms in a compact, 200-year-old house on historic Benefit St, close to Brown, RISD, and Downcity. ⑤

Christopher Dodge House B&B 11 W Park St ☏401/351-6111, ⊛www.providence-hotel.com. One of two properties making up the State House Inns (see *Mowry Nicholson House*, below), this small boutique hotel boasts 11-foot ceilings, marble fireplaces, and full breakfasts. ⑧

Comfort Inn 1940 Post Rd, Warwick ☏401/732-0470, ⊛www.choicehotels.com. Adequate chain lodging right by the airport. There's another branch at 2 George St in Pawtucket (see p.260; ☏401/723-6700). ⑤

Courtyard Providence Downtown 32 Exchange Terrace, at Memorial Blvd ☏401/272-1191 or 1-888/887-7955, ⊛www.marriott.com. Large, standard chain hotel with an indoor pool and gym in the heart of Downcity. ⑦

Hotel Dolce Villa 63 DePasquale Square ☏401/383-7031, ⊛www.dolcevillari.com. Fourteen elegant white suites in Federal Hill's choice boutique hotel, each with kitchenette, lounge, and Jacuzzi. ⑧

Hotel Providence 311 Westminster St ☏401/861-8000 or 1-800/861-8990, ⊛www.thehotelprovidence.com. New hotel with eighty plush and colorful rooms, and a trendy restaurant downstairs. ⑧

La Quinta Inn & Suites 36 Jefferson Blvd, Warwick ☏401/941-6600, ⊛www.marriott.com. Remodeled former Marriott close to I-95, with "continental plus" breakfast (hard-boiled eggs; make-your-own waffles). ⑤

Mowry Nicholson House B&B 57 Brownell St ☏401/351-6111, ⊛www.providence-suites.com. Sister inn of the *Christopher Dodge House*, with pleasant rooms in an 1865 mansion. ⑦

The Old Court 144 Benefit St ☏401/751-2002, ⊛www.oldcourt.com. Charming B&B in an old red-brick rectory near RISD, featuring ten rooms with Victorian decoration, all with private bath and TV. ⑦

The Providence Biltmore 11 Dorrance St ☏401/421-0700 or 1-800/294-7709, ⊛www .providencebiltmore.com. A Providence landmark since 1922, with impeccable refurbished rooms boasting enormous beds and flat-screen TVs. ⑥

Renaissance Providence 5 Ave of the Arts ☏401/919-5000, ⊛www.marriott.com. Luxurious new downtown hotel on the site of a former Masonic temple, with 272 comfortable, well-appointed rooms. ⑧

The Westin 1 W Exchange St ☏401/598-8000 or 1-800/937-8461, ⊛www.westin.com. Deluxe modern rooms in a palatial, 564-room tower, with indoor pool and two in-house restaurants, all conveniently connected to the Providence Place Mall. ⑧

The City

Providence's downtown, or **Downcity**, centers on **Kennedy Plaza**, a large public square that houses the city's transportation center. At the southwestern corner of the plaza, **City Hall** was completed in 1878, designed in the Second Empire style of the Louvre and the Tuileries palaces in Paris. Nearby, the Beaux Arts **Union Station** was built as a rail terminal in 1898 but today houses offices and restaurants. To the south of the Plaza, in Westminster Mall, is the 1828 **Arcade**, the sole survivor of many such "temples of trade" built in America during the Greek Revival period, and America's oldest indoor shopping mall. It's still a marketplace, with plenty of places to eat and drink, and small speciality shops to explore.

The state's only National Park Service property, the **Roger Williams National Memorial**, at the corner of North Main and Smith streets, was the site of the original settlement of Providence in 1636, and is now a four-acre greenspace; its small visitors' center (daily 9am–4.30pm; ☏401/521-7266) includes replicas of Williams' compass, an Indian Bible, and papers documenting the reverend's efforts. West from here, at the top of Constitution Hill, the **State Capitol** (Mon–Fri 8.30am–4.30pm; free; call ahead for guided tours ☏401/222-2357) dominates the city skyline with a vast dome, purportedly the fourth-largest self-supported marble dome in the world. Inside, you can view the original Rhode Island Charter of 1663 and a portrait of George Washington by Rhode Island artist Gilbert Stuart.

College Hill and around

Much of Providence's historic legacy can be found across the river from Downcity in the **College Hill** area, an attractive tree-lined district of Colonial buildings that is home to the historic 133-acre campus of **Brown University**. The third oldest college in New England, and seventh oldest in the nation, Brown was founded in 1764 in Warren as Rhode Island College; six years later it was moved to Providence, where it was renamed after graduate and donor Nicholas Brown, Jr. For **free tours** or self-guided maps of the university campus, contact the admissions office, 45 Prospect St (Mon–Fri 8am–4pm; ☏401/863-2378, ⓦwww.brown.edu).

On Prospect Street, the huge wrought-iron **Van Wickle Gates** – opened only for incoming students in the fall and graduates in the spring (you can get in through side entrances the rest of the year) – lead onto the core of the university, the pleasant **College Green**, which is skirted by a collection of Colonial and Greek Revival buildings. Among them are the 1904 Beaux Arts **John Carter Brown Library**, which holds a rich trove of early historical materials on the Americas, and nearby **University Hall**, the institution's oldest building. Dating to 1770, it was used as barracks for Continental troops during the Revolutionary War. Across the street, the English Renaissance-style **John Hay Library**, 20 Prospect St (term-time open to the public Mon–Fri 10am–6pm & Sun 1–5pm, summer Mon–Fri 9am–5pm; call ahead for tours ☏401/863-3723), houses a vast collection of rare books and special collections.

Behind College Hill, happening **Thayer Street** and neighboring lanes are home to bookstores, tattoo parlors, and funky thrift stores, while at the eastern end of the hill, **Wickenden Street** buzzes with cafés, galleries, and restaurants. Farther towards Gano Street lies the increasingly gentrified **Fox Point** district, once Providence's main Portuguese neighborhood, and still home to many bakeries selling Portuguese delicacies.

Benefit Street and around

Lined with beautifully restored residences that once belonged to merchants and sea captains, **Benefit Street** was a simple dirt track until it was improved in the eighteenth century "for the benefit of the people of Providence" – hence its name. This is Providence's "mile of history," with one of the most impressive collections of original Colonial and Federal homes in America, most of which remain privately owned. The Providence Preservation Society (see p.254) has a self-guided tour pamphlet with detailed information, while the Rhode Island Historical Society (see p.254) leads **walking tours** of the area (June–Oct Sat 11am; 1hr 30min; $12, combined museum and tour $16), beginning at the elegant **John Brown House**, 52 Power St (April–Dec tours Tues–Fri 1.30am & 3pm, Sat 10.30am–3pm every 1hr 30min; Jan–March Fri & Sat 10.30am–3pm every 1hr 30min; $8; ☎401/273-7507). A three-story residence constructed in 1786, it was home to one of the city's most aggressive merchants. There's a lovely central hall and many original furnishings, as well as displays on the formidable Brown family and Rhode Island history.

Farther up Benefit Street, the **RISD Museum**, no. 224 (Tues–Sun 10am–5pm; $8, free Sun mornings & last Sat of the month; ☎401/454-6500, Ⓦwww.risd.edu/museum.cfm), associated with the prestigious art school, houses over 80,000 works of art in 45 galleries. Highlights include the European and American decorative arts collections, a superb Asian collection with more than six hundred Japanese woodblock prints and a Heian Buddha, and multimedia contemporary art exhibits. Across the street at no. 251, the intimate **Providence Athenaeum** (Mon–Thurs 9am–7pm, Fri & Sat 9am–5pm, Sun 1–5pm; closed Sat afternoon & Sun in summer; free; ☎401/421-6970, Ⓦwww.providenceathenaeum.org), is one of America's oldest libraries. A few blocks north, the plain but dignified 1762 **Old State House**, no. 150 (Mon–Fri 8.30am–4.30pm; free; ☎410/222-2678), current home of the Rhode Island Historical Preservation & Heritage Commission, is of note for the courtroom where the Rhode Island General Assembly renounced allegiance to Britain on May 4, 1776, while down on the hill, the white clapboard 1775 **First Baptist Meeting House**, at 75 N Main St, is the third Baptist church of its kind in America.

▲ Providence Athenaeum

Federal Hill

Back west of Downcity, **Federal Hill** – informally considered Providence's **Little Italy** – can be entered through an arch topped with a bronze pine cone, the Italian symbol for hospitality, at Atwells Avenue. Long a powerful Mafia stronghold, this area is one of the safest and friendliest in the city, where you can savor the nuances of Italian culture in dozens of restaurants and bakeries. For drinks, head to the bars and cafés around lively **DePasquale Square**, where there's a large Italianate fountain.

The rest of the city

Just south of Downcity, in the Jewelry District, is the excellent **Providence Children's Museum**, 100 South St (April–Aug daily 9am–6pm; Sept–March Tues–Sun 9am–6pm; $6.50, free select Fri during extended evening hours; ☏401/273-5437, ⓦwww.childrenmuseum.org), where the interactive displays include a fun look at teeth in a giant mouth, a walk-in kaleidoscope, and a time-travelling adventure through Rhode Island's history. Further south near the Cranston city line, the **Culinary Arts Museum**, 315 Harborside Blvd (Tues–Sun 10am–5pm; $7; ☏401/598-2805, ⓦwww.culinary.org), houses a wealth of food history, including ancient utensils, recipes, and menus, on the satellite campus of Johnson & Wales University, one of the country's premier culinary colleges.

About a mile west of the museum, at 1000 Elmwood Ave, the 430-acre **Roger Williams Park** spills with serpentine paths, rolling hills, and peaceful ponds. In addition to a carousel and a **Museum of Natural History**, there's the spectacular **Roger Williams Zoo** (daily: April–Sept 9am–5pm; Oct–March 9am–4pm; $12; ☏401/785-3510, ⓦwww.rogerwilliamsparkzoo.org), the third oldest zoo in the country with 130 species of animals, including giraffes, cheetahs, moon bears, gibbons, and snow leopards. Even if zoos aren't normally your thing, you can't help but admire the imaginative way this one has been laid out, with its close attention to culture and history alongside zoology.

Eating

As the hometown of culinary college Johnson & Wales, it's no surprise that Providence has more accredited chefs per capita than any other city in the US. This fact, along with the city's ethnic diversity, means that you're spoiled as far as **food** is concerned. **Thayer Street** is lined with inexpensive eateries catering to university crowds; nearby **Wickenden Street** is more mature but still eclectic; the family-run Italian restaurants on **Federal Hill** offer great value in a lively atmosphere; and **Downcity** is home to a burgeoning group of up-and-coming establishments.

Al Forno 577 S Main St ☏401/273-9760. One of the best restaurants around, *Al Forno*'s relatively casual decor and simple menu belie the quality of the food: delicious Italian dishes, wood grills, and roasts, with seasonal variations. Dinner only, closed Sun & Mon.

Angelo's 141 Atwells Ave ☏401/621-8171. A staple in Federal Hill since 1924, with homey, no-frills Italian fare, including pastas ($6–9) and daily specials such as braised beef ($7.75) and baked veal chops ($14).

Café Nuovo 1 Citizens Plaza ☏401/421-2525. Upmarket Continental cuisine with an Asian touch; dine on the outdoor patio during WaterFire (see box opposite) for a great view of the twinkling river.

Caffe Dolce Vita 59 DePasquale Square ☏401/331-8240. Traditional Italian desserts next to a lively piazza. Also paninis and salads.

CAV Restaurant 14 Imperial Place ☏401/751-9164. A bit out of the way in the Jewelry District, *CAV* serves a mid-priced, eclectic menu (everything from clam chowder to maki rolls) in an atmospheric setting. The antiques and tribal pieces adorning the place are all for sale.

Coffee Exchange 207 Wickenden St ☏401/273-1198. Fair Trade, organic coffees and a delectable assortment of pastries, sandwiches, and other light fare (including some veggie options).

Coffee King 66 Fountain St ☎401/274-1888. Cheap, huge sandwiches and smoothies in a wonderfully hospitable hole-in-the-wall spot.

Haruki East 172 Wayland Ave ☎401/223-0332. Known as one of the best Japanese places in the city, with assorted sushi entrees and unique dishes like Japanese-style crabmeat chili releno.

Haven Brothers Diner-on-wheels since 1893, with classic hot dogs, burgers, and fries. Parked outside City Hall nightly 4.30pm–5am.

Hemenway's 121 S Main St ☎401/351-8570. Pricey, first-rate New England seafood like clam chowder, oysters, and fried Maine clams.

Local 121 121 Washington St ☎401/274-2121. Elegant restaurant serving Continental dishes with a New England touch, such as bacon-wrapped quail and molasses-braised brisket. The menu focuses on fresh, local, and sustainable products.

Kabob and Curry 261 Thayer St ☎401/273-8844. Above-average Indian food on lively Thayer St, with plentiful veggie options and fun twists like "naninis" (naan sandwiches with stuffings like lamb and cottage cheese with chickpeas; $6.50–7.25).

Mediterraneo 134 Atwells Ave ☎401/331-7760. This excellent Italian restaurant is the place to see and be seen, with prices to match.

Mill's Tavern 101 N Main St ☎401/272-3331. Contemporary, upscale American cuisine, including good wood-fired dishes. Dinner only.

Pot au Feu 44 Custom House St ☎401/273-8953. Head upstairs for expensive salon dining or downstairs for the more modest bistro; you'll find a cozy, romantic atmosphere and excellent French dishes in both.

Z Bar and Grille 244 Wickenden St ☎401/831-1566. Organic-minded, moderately priced American menu in the former *Ringside Café*.

Drinking and nightlife

Providence's **nightlife** bustles around Empire and Washington streets, south of Kennedy Plaza, and along **Thayer Street** near Brown University.

AS220 115 Empire St ☎401/831-9327. Hip, lively, anti-establishment café/bar/gallery, with eclectic local art and diverse nightly performances.

Cuban Revolution 50 Aborn St ☎401/331-8829. Sangria, Cuban beer, and tropical cocktails in a laid-back atmosphere; you can also munch on an assorted menu of tapas, sushi, and "Che" fries.

Lili Marlene's 422 Atwells Ave ☎401/751-4996. Small, low-key bar with red-leather booths and a pool table tucked out of the way in Federal Hill; this locals' haunt draws its crowd by word of mouth.

Lupo's Heartbreak Hotel 79 Washington St ☎401/272-5876. This is *the* spot in town to see

nationally recognized bands rock out. Tickets generally around $12–20 in advance, $30+ for big-name acts.

Mirabar 35 Richmond St ☎401/331-6761. Lively gay bar and dance club attracting a mixed crowd, with DJs almost every night and karaoke Mon. 18+, cover $3.

Trinity Brewhouse 186 Fountain St ☎401/453-2337. Hang out here after a Providence Bruins (minor league hockey) or Friars (college basketball) game. Everything on tap is brewed in-house.

Entertainment

Providence has a rich and varied **performing arts** and **film** scene. Complete **listings** can be found in the free weekly *Providence Phoenix* and the *Providence Journal*'s Thursday edition. On "Gallery Night," the third Thursday of the month from March to November (5–9pm; ☎401/490-2042, ⓦ www.gallerynight.info), free "Art Buses" leave from the corner of Stillman and Canal streets behind

Summer events in Providence

In July, the city hosts the "genre-defying" **Sound Session** music festival, bringing eclectic ensembles to town (ⓦ www.providencesoundsession.com). Throughout the summer months, the unusual event known as **WaterFire** (select Sat evenings May–Oct; ⓦ www.waterfire.org) enthrals visitors and locals alike with one hundred bonfires set at sunset along the center of the Providence River starting at Waterplace Park. Tended by gondoliers and accompanied by music, the fires burn until just past midnight.

Citizens Plaza (near Waterplace Park) and stop at many of the city's galleries and museums, where admission is free for the evening.

Cinema

Avon Rep Cinema 260 Thayer St ☎ 401/421-3315, ⓦ www.avoncinema.com. A good spot for indie films, near Brown.

Cable Car Cinema 204 S Main St ☎ 401/272-3970, ⓦ www.cablecarcinema.com. The latest art flicks shown in a theater with love seats and a café serving drinks and wraps.

Live music and theater

Providence Performing Arts Center 220 Weybosset St ☎ 401/421-2787, ⓦ www.ppacri.org. A grand, restored Art Deco movie house hosting musicals and other lavish productions.

Trinity Rep 201 Washington St ☎ 401/351-4242, ⓦ www.trinityrep.com. This Tony Award-winning company, one of America's foremost regional theaters, puts on innovative productions of contemporary and classic plays.

Pawtucket, Woonsocket, and Bristol

Northwest of Providence, the gritty **Blackstone River Valley** has been given special status by the Department of the Interior for its role in America's development as the world's leading industrial power. You can start your exploration of this legacy in **PAWTUCKET**, just a few miles north of Providence on I-95, at the **Slater Mill Historic Site**, 67 Roosevelt Ave (March & April Sat & Sun 11am–3pm; May–June & Oct–Nov Tues–Sat 10am–3pm; July–Sept Tues–Sat 10am–5pm; $9; ☎ 401/725-8638, ⓦ www.slatermill.org), where the **Old Slater Mill** was built to house Samuel Slater's inventions (see box below). Today, the mill contains a copy of an original carding engine, a spinning frame and mule, and some rare textile machines dating from 1838. Also on site is the 1810 **Wilkinson Mill**, where a nineteenth-century machine shop, complete with belt-driven machine tools, still operates, and the 1758 **Sylvanus Brown House**, a worker's home furnished as it was in the early 1800s. If you're inspired by the Americana, head to Pawtucket's **McCoy Stadium** to enjoy the country's favorite pastime: baseball. The **PawSox**, a Boston minor-league affiliate, play here from April to September (tickets $6; ⓦ www.pawsox.com).

The birthplace of the Industrial Revolution

The **Blackstone River National Heritage Corridor**, stretching from Providence to Worcester, MA, encompasses two dozen original manufacturing communities. The area was a desolate wilderness when its first white settler, **Reverend William Blackstone**, arrived here in 1635 after fleeing Boston's Puritan regime. More settlers followed, including one Joseph Jencks, Jr, a blacksmith by trade, who realized that the vast forests near **Pawtucket** would provide a virtually inexhaustible supply of timber to fire a forge. His smithy boomed, prompting other blacksmiths to settle here as well. In 1790, the industrial expansion received a huge boost when **Samuel Slater**, a manufacturer's apprentice from England – with the help of entrepreneur Moses Brown, of the Providence Browns – used technology surreptitiously imported from his native land to produce cotton yarn. The resultant success fueled a century of prosperity, though companies eventually relocated south, leaving the machinery an artifact of a bygone era.

For an unusual perspective of the Blackstone River Valley, the Blackstone Valley Tourism Council runs 45-minute narrated **riverboat tours** on Sundays in the summer and fall ($10; ☎ 1-800/454-BVTC, ⓦ www.rivertourblackstone.com). One route, with boats leaving from 45 Madeira Ave, Central Falls (June to mid-Aug), passes by marsh and wildlife, while the other, leaving from Market Square in Woonsocket (late Aug to Oct), highlights historic mills.

Another major manufacturing center, **WOONSOCKET**, is about fifteen miles northwest of Pawtucket, off Rte-146. Here, at 42 S Main St, you'll find the fascinating **Museum of Work and Culture** (Mon–Fri 9.30am–4pm, Sat 10am–5pm, Sun 1–4pm; $7; ☏ 401/769-9675), which traces the story of mill-workers who came from Québec in the early nineteenth century to work in the shoe and textile factories here. A self-guided walk through their workaday world takes you from the floor of a textile mill to the porch of a tenement house, then lets you out on the city streets.

In the other direction, fifteen miles southeast of Providence on Ferry Road (Rte-114), the town of **BRISTOL** holds the oldest and perhaps most enthusiastic **Fourth of July** celebration in the nation, with a massive parade and fireworks spectacle. The most scenic way to get here from Providence is the **East Bay Bike Path** (daily sunrise–sunset), a gentle 14.5-mile ride along an abandoned rail line that passes by salt marshes and the Narragansett Bay. The main attraction in town is the **Blithewold Mansion, Gardens & Arboretum**, 101 Ferry Rd (grounds open daily May–Oct 10am–4pm; Nov–April 10am–5pm; mansion open mid-April to mid-Oct Wed–Sat 10am–4pm, Sun 10am–3pm; $10; ☏ 401/253-2707, ⓦ www.blithewold.org), one-time summer residence of Pennsylvania coal magnate Augustus Van Wickle and his wife Bessie. The 45-room house is filled with knick-knacks from her globe-trotting adventures, and the gardens are wonderful, spread out around the 10-acre Great Lawn overlooking Narragansett Bay, with 3000 trees and shrubs.

Newport

With its lovely seaside location, fleets of polished yachts, rose-colored sunsets, and long-standing association with America's fine and fabulous, **NEWPORT**, nicknamed "America's First Resort," is straight out of a fairy tale. The Kennedys were married here (Jackie was a local girl), and Eisenhower spent time here at the Naval War College, which continues to introduce a uniformed presence to the lively town. Today it is best known for its opulent *fin-de-siècle* mansions – these huge estates and ornate palaces, former summer homes of the likes of the Astors and Vanderbilts, stand testimony to the town's enduring status as a desirable destination.

Newport has much more to offer than just a stroll past these extravagant facades, though – the streets are laden with history, and sights commemorate everything from the town's pioneering role in religious freedom in America to the landing of French forces here in support of the Continental troops during the Revolutionary War. Along the waterfront in the historic **Point** district, Colonial houses still stand with their rooftop "widow's walks," railed platforms where many a captain's wife watched for her husband's return. The views today are not as unobstructed as they were back then, though just a short drive from downtown takes you to unrivalled **shores**, with endless stretches of sand and grassy promontory.

Some history

Newport was first settled in 1639 by refugees from Massachusetts who sought **religious freedom**. The earliest settlers were Quakers, who were a dominant presence throughout the seventeenth century. Baptists came later, as did Jews, whose oldest existing burial ground in the country lies to this day behind Touro Synagogue downtown.

In the eighteenth century, Newport grew into a bustling port, with the local fleet heavily involved in the **slave trade**. Prosperity was brought to a halt when

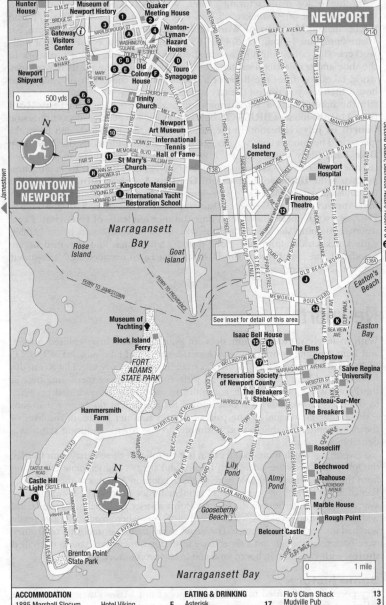

Portsmouth & Green Animals Topiary Garden ▲

NEWPORT

DOWNTOWN NEWPORT

Hunter House
Museum of Newport History
Quaker Meeting House
Gateway Visitors Center
Wanton-Lyman-Hazard House
Newport Shipyard
Old Colony House
Touro Synagogue
Trinity Church
Newport Art Museum
International Tennis Hall of Fame
St Mary's Church
Kingscote Mansion
International Yacht Restoration School

ELM ST
BRIDGE ST
MARSH ST
MARLBOROUGH ST
WASHINGTON SQUARE
CLARK STREET
TOURO ST
MARY STREET
AMERICA'S CUP AVE
CHURCH ST
BELLEVUE AVE
MILL ST
SPRING STREET
JOHN ST
MEMORIAL BLVD
WILLIAM ST
FAIR ST
ANN ST
BREWER ST
DENNISON ST
YOUNG ST
HOWARD ST

0   500 yds

Narragansett Bay

Rose Island

Goat Island

FERRY TO JAMESTOWN
FERRY TO PROVIDENCE

Museum of Yachting
Block Island Ferry

FORT ADAMS STATE PARK

Hammersmith Farm

Isaac Bell House
The Elms
Chepstow
Salve Regina University

Preservation Society of Newport County
The Breakers Stable
Chateau-Sur-Mer
The Breakers

Rosecliff

Beechwood
Teahouse

Marble House

Rough Point

Belcourt Castle

Island Cemetery
Newport Hospital
Firehouse Theatre

See inset for detail of this area

Easton's Beach

Easton Bay

Castle Hill Light
CASTLE HILL ROAD
CASTLE HILL AVE

Lily Pond

Almy Pond

Gooseberry Beach

Brenton Point State Park

Narragansett Bay

0   1 mile

RIDGE ROAD
HARRISON AVENUE
BEACON HILL RD
BRENTON ROAD
HAZARD ROAD
WICKHAM RD
OLD FORT RD
CARROLL AVENUE
COGGESHALL AVENUE
BELLEVUE AVENUE
OCEAN AVENUE
WINANS AVE
COMMONWEALTH AVE
ATLANTIC AVE
HARRISON AVE
RUGGLES AVENUE
NARRAGANSETT AVENUE
WEBSTER ST
LEROY AVE
WELLINGTON AVE
ANNANDALE RD
SEA VIEW AVE
CLIFF WALK
OVERSKY AVENUE

McKLINDOR AVENUE
GIRARD AVENUE
HILLSIDE AVENUE
WEST MAIN RD
MAPLE AVENUE
114
214
O'CONNELL HIGHWAY
ADMIRAL KALBFUS RD
138
MIANTONMI AVENUE
BLISS ROAD
BROADWAY
THIRD STREET
MALBONE ROAD
VAN ZANDT AVE
WARNER STREET
FAREWELL STREET
WASHINGTON STREET
AMERICA'S CUP AVENUE
THAMES STREET
SPRING STREET
KAY STREET
TOURO ST
OLD BEACH ROAD
RHODE ISLAND AVENUE
EUSTIS AVENUE
KAY STREET
MEMORIAL BOULEVARD
138A

N

RHODE ISLAND

4

Jamestown

Second Beach, Sachuest Nature Reserve & ⑬

ACCOMMODATION

1885 Marshall Slocum Guest House	D	Hotel Viking	F
Admiral Farragut Inn	E	Jailhouse Inn	A
Admiral Fitzroy Inn	H	Melville House	C
The Almondy	G	The Old Beach Inn	J
Castle Hill Inn & Resort	L	William Gyles Guesthouse	I
Chart House Inn	B		
Cliffside Inn	K		

EATING & DRINKING

Asterisk	17
Billy Goode's	2
The Black Pearl	6
Brick Alley Pub & Restaurant	5
Café Zelda	16
Coffee Grinder	7
Empire Tea and Coffee	4
Firehouse Pizza	17

Flo's Clam Shack	13
Mudville Pub	3
Newport Blues Café	10
Puerini's	14
The Red Parrot	11
Salvation Café	12
Scales & Shells	15
Smokehouse Café	9
The Wharf Pub & Restaurant	8
White Horse Tavern	1

262

British and Hessian troops occupied Newport in 1776: they blockaded the harbour, and forced the city's residents to burn the wharves as firewood during the brutal winter. During the next three years, many locals fled, and the city grew so impoverished that townsfolk could not afford to rebuild their homes, leaving the fine **Colonial buildings** still seen today.

While Newport's reputation as resort town dates as far back as the 1700s, it was in the latter half of the nineteenth century that it amassed its most extravagant estates. Wealthy Southern merchants, and later nouveau riche industrial magnates, flocked to Newport's spectacular coastline to build the summer "cottages" for which the town is now known. At the same time, the town acquired a deserved reputation as a playpen for the **yachting** set – from 1930 until 1983 Newport hosted the America's Cup Race. As well, the town benefited from the presence of the US Navy and at one point was home to a large fleet of warships, whose departure in the 1970s was accompanied by a period of economic decline. Today, though, Newport is doing as well as ever, owing in no small part to the **tourism** economy.

Arrival, information, and local transport

Newport is on **Aquidneck**, also known formally as Rhode Island. The island is connected to the mainland by I-95 and Rte-138, which crosses the impressive Newport Bridge ($2 toll). The nearest **Amtrak** station is on Rte-138 at Kingston, nineteen miles away; theoretically you can take RIPTA bus #64 (Mon–Sat; $1.75; ☏401/781-9400) from the Kingston station to Newport, but services tend to be infrequent – it's easier to get off the train in Providence and take a bus from there. The nicest way to arrive, though, is the Providence–Newport **ferry** (1hr; $12 one-way; ☏866-683-3779, ⓦwww.providencefastferry.com), which runs daily during the summer between 180 Allens Ave, Providence, and Perrotti Park in Newport, near the **Gateway Visitor's Center**, 23 America's Cup Ave. This last operation has plenty of maps, brochures, and advice to keep you busy (daily 9am–5pm; ☏401/845-9123 or 1-800/976-5122, ⓦwww.gonewport.com), and serves as the terminal for **Bonanza** (☏401/846-1820 or 1-888/751-8800) and **RIPTA** buses, as well as a **shuttle** to T.F. Green (Mon–Fri 6.30am–7.30pm, Sat 8am–5pm). For **taxis**, try Cozy Cab (☏800/846-1502), which also runs an airport shuttle ($25).

Tours of Newport

The Newport Historical Society and Newport Restoration Foundation organize a number of walking tours through downtown, departing from the **Brick Market Museum**, 127 Thames St (☏401/841-8770, ⓦwww.newportrestoration.com/histours). Easily the best way of getting a good overview of the mansions, however, is on a **boat tour**: you can take the beautiful 72-foot schooner *Madeleine* (5 times daily in summer; 1hr 30min; $27) or the motor yacht *Rum Runner* (5 times daily in summer; 1hr 15min; $18), both of which are organized by Classic Cruises of Newport (☏401/847-0298; boats leave from Bannister's Wharf). Gansett Cruises offers sunset excursions (5pm & 7pm daily, leaving from Bowen's Wharf; 1hr 30min; $25; ☏401/787-4438). For another sort of trip, Save the Bay organizes **seal watches** between November and April, leaving from Bowen's Wharf (1hr; $20; ☏401/324-6020). Easily the cheapest way to get on the water, though, is to hop on a **water taxi** from Bannister's Wharf ($3); routes aren't narrated, but you should get glimpses of some gorgeous yachts. Finally, if you're up for a splurge, the **Newport Dinner Train** makes for a very special ride: dine in authentic Pullman cars, as the 2hr 30min ride takes you along scenic Narragansett Bay (trains leave from 19 America's Cup Ave; reserve well in advance; ☏401/841-8700, ⓦwww.newportdinnertrain.com).

Bringing your **car** to Newport is an option, but parking downtown is atrocious. RIPTA buses, leaving from the Gateway Center, conveniently connect the major sights. **Bikes** are also a great way to get around, especially if you're heading to the beaches. For bike rental, try Ten Speed Spokes, 18 Elm St ($6 per hr, $30 per day; ☎ 401/847-5609). **Scooters** are also available; try Scooters of Newport, 476 Thames St ($39 per hr; ☎ 401/619-0573).

Accommodation

Accommodation in Newport is never cheap, and prices skyrocket even further during the summer. In town, there are many fine inns and B&Bs, while cheaper chain motels can be found a few miles north in Middletown. If you're stuck, try Bed & Breakfast Newport (☎ 401/846-5408 or 1-800/800-8765, ⊛ www .bbnewport.com), who can help find something affordable. You can also **camp** in Middletown and Portsmouth (see p.270).

1855 Marshall Slocum Guest House 29 Kay St ☎ 401/841-5120 or 1-800/372-5120, ⊛ www .marshallslocuminn.com. Five comfortable rooms in historic B&B near Bellevue Ave, with gardens and gourmet breakfasts. ❽

Admiral Farragut Inn 31 Clarke St ☎ 800/524-1386. Bright, spacious rooms, some with working fireplaces, in a centrally located 1702 house. ❽

Admiral Fitzroy Inn 398 Thames St ☎ 401/848-8000 or 1-866/848-8780, ⊛ www .admiralfitzroy.com. Cheerfully decorated B&B in the heart of town, with seventeen hand-stenciled rooms and a roof deck. ❽

The Almondy 25 Pelham St ☎ 401/848-7202 or 1-800/478-6155, ⊛ www.almondyinn.com. 1890s B&B with harbour views, Jacuzzis, gourmet breakfasts, and afternoon wine and cheese. ❽

Castle Hill Inn & Resort 590 Ocean Ave ☎ 401/849-3800, ⊛ www.castlehillinn.com. A Newport landmark overlooking Narragansett Bay from atop its own peninsula, with nine magnificent rooms in the main mansion and additional accommo-dation in the beach cottages nearby. Non-guests can come to Sunday brunch, a much more affordable way to enjoy the views. ❾

Chart House Inn 16 Clarke St ☎ 401/207-6418, ⊛ www.charthouseinn.com. Eight sunlit, airy rooms in centrally located B&B. All rooms have private baths, but some are in the hallway. ❻

Cliffside Inn 2 Seaview Ave ☎ 401/847-1811 or 1-800/845-1811, ⊛ www.cliffsideinn .com. 1880 Victorian manor house, with thirteen luxurious rooms in the main house and three in the adjacent cottage. Once the summer home of eccentric local artist Beatrice Turner, today it's decorated with more than one hundred of her works. ❾

Hotel Viking 1 Bellevue Ave ☎ 401/847-3300, ⊛ www.hotelviking.com. 222-room hotel built in 1926 to accommodate spill-over Bellevue mansion guests; it still lures jet-setters with Egyptian cotton duvets, antique furnishings, and coddling at on-site Spa Terre. ❾

Jailhouse Inn 13 Marlborough St ☎ 401/847-4638 or 1-800/427-9444, ⊛ www.jailhouse.com. Few vestiges of the former Newport County jail remain in this restored B&B, with compact modern rooms and occasional jailhouse trimmings. ❻

Melville House 39 Clarke St ☎ 401/847-0640 or 1-800/711-7184, ⊛ www.melvillehouse.com. Centrally located colonial B&B with seven cozy rooms; both private and shared baths available. ❻

The Old Beach Inn 19 Old Beach Rd ☎ 401/849-3479 or 1-888/303-5033, ⊛ www .oldbeachinn.com. Secluded, old-fashioned B&B with six cozy rooms, down the street from the Newport Art Museum, with garden and porch. ❻

William Gyles Guesthouse 16 Howard St ☎ 401/369-0243, ⊛ www.newporthostel.com. Newport's only hostel, *William Gyles* is welcoming and comfortable, and the hostess leads wonderful nightly tours of the town. In season, the handful of dorm beds run $35–39 per night weekdays, $59 per night weekends; winter rates are lower. Private accommodation also available.

The Town

While Newport is best known today for its palatial nineteenth-century summer "cottages," it boasts a remarkably rich architectural landscape, thanks in part to the city's preservation efforts. Along the water, the views may just remind you why you're here, and there is no lack of things to do, from swimming and biking to beautiful-people-spotting on the harbour. During summer weekends, downtown brims with weekenders from New York and Boston, helping to propel a thriving bar and restaurant scene.

Downtown Newport

Newport is eminently walkable, with Thames Street being the main drag downtown. Colonial Newport's commercial center, **Washington Square**, starts just southeast of the Gateway Center, where Thames Street meets the **Brick Market**. The 1762 market, off **Long Wharf**, has been reconstructed to include a mixture of galleries and pricey souvenir shops. Among them, the **Brick Market Museum**, also known as the **Museum of Newport History** (Mon–Thurs 10am–6pm, Fri & Sat 10am–8pm, Sun 10am–5pm; $4 donation; ☏401/841-8770), gives a good overview of the town's past through exhibits, photographs, and pithy oral histories. Across the square stands the **Old Colony House**, a pre-Revolutionary brick building and the state's seat of government from 1739 to 1900.

Just up from Washington Square, at 17 Broadway, the **Wanton–Lyman–Hazard House** (call for hours; ☏401/841-8770) is the oldest surviving house in Newport, dating to the mid-seventeenth century. The central chimney and pitched roof are typical of early settlers' homes, while inside the surviving original plasterwork is made from ground shells and molasses. Nearby, at the corner of Farewell and Marlborough streets, the 1699 **Quaker Friends Meeting House** (tours by appointment; ☏401/846-0813) is the oldest religious building in town, restored to its nineteenth-century state and completely free of adornment. The state's penchant for religious tolerance is further revealed by the elegant **Touro Synagogue**, 85 Touro St, the oldest house of Jewish worship in America, founded by descendants of Jews fleeing the Spanish Inquisition. The 1763 building is preserved intact, and houses a deerskin Torah which predates the synagogue by two hundred years (call for hours; $5 tours; ☏401/847-4794, ⓦ www.tourosynagogue.org).

The town boasts a number of other historic places of worship, notably the Anglican 1726 **Trinity Church** on Queen Anne Square (☏401/846-0660), based on Old North Church in Boston and the designs of Sir Christopher Wren. Notice the bleach-white 150-foot tower, which acted as a beacon for ships as well as worshippers; inside, the only triple-decked, freestanding pulpit left in America stands in its original position in front of the altar. South near downtown, the Roman Catholic **St Mary's Church**, Spring Street and Memorial Boulevard (☏401/847-0475), completed in 1852, witnessed the union of Jacqueline Bouvier and John Kennedy on September 12, 1953. Perhaps most enigmatic of all is the **Viking Tower** in Touro Park, a stone structure with mysterious, arguably Norse, origins.

At the northern end of Thames Street, **Easton's Point** (locally known as "the Point") is a charming waterfront area with many of the town's oldest houses, now converted into upmarket B&Bs; you can also sneak a peek at some of the world's most beautiful boats in the **Newport Shipyard** at 1 Washington St. In the other direction, **Lower Thames** leads to the former Irish neigborhood, the **Fifth Ward**. Nearby, the **International Yacht Restoration School**, 449 Thames St (daily 10am–5pm; free; ☏401/848-5777, ⓦ www.iyrs.org), is a fine place to learn about maritime history, with the 1831 Aquidneck Mill Building and the 1885 schooner yacht *Coroner* under restoration on campus at the time of writing. You can find out more about boats at the affiliated **Museum of Yachting** at **Fort Adams State Park** (June–Oct Mon & Wed–Sun 10am–6pm; $8; ☏401/847-1018), which hosts nautical exhibits and regattas. A **water taxi** connects IYRS and the museum (June–Sept every 30min daily noon–6pm; $3).

If fancy boats don't suite your taste, check out two noteworthy museums on Bellevue Avenue. The **Newport Art Museum**, no. 76 (late May to mid-Oct Mon–Sat 10am–5pm, Sun noon–5pm; rest of year Mon–Sat 10am–4pm, Sun noon–4pm; $8; T 401/848-8200, W www.newportartmuseum.org), exhibits New England art from the last two centuries in the 1864 mock-medieval Griswold House. The grand **Newport Casino**, no. 194, an early country club, held the nation's first tennis championships in 1881 – the tournament now known as the US Open. The casino currently houses the **International Tennis Hall of Fame** (daily 9.30am–5pm; $10; T 401/849-3990 or 1-800/457-1144, W www.tennisfame.com), and still keeps its grass courts open to the public (mid-May to Sept; reserve ahead at T 401/846-0642). Exhibits at the museum include the original patent for the game granted by Queen Victoria in 1874, and a vast, comprehensive collection of tennis-related memorabilia.

The mansions

Beginning in the 1870s, Newport was the summer playground of the New York elite, with industrial magnates and their families competing to outdo each other with a string of lavish estates. The gilded excess lasted only a few decades, though, and many of the mansions fell to bleak fates in the decades after the 1929 stock market crash. Today, a number of former homes have been converted into university buildings on **Salve Regina University**'s 75-acre campus on Ochre Point Avenue (T 401/847-6650), while the **Preservation Society of Newport County**, 424 Bellevue Ave (T 401/847-1000, W www.newportmansions.org) maintains the bulk of the dozen or so houses open for public viewing.

You need to visit the mansions to get a true impression of their size, but after herding into and rushing through more than one or two, the opulence rapidly begins to pall. The earlier, smaller houses are often more interesting (and tasteful)

▲ Cliff Walk

than the larger chateaus. Note that many houses are open by tour only (beginning on the hour or half-hour), with the last tour an hour before closing. With the exception of Beechwood, Belcourt Castle, and Hammersmith Farm, the houses listed below are all Preservation Society properties. A combined ticket to any five Society mansions (excluding Hunter House) is $31; the Breakers plus one other property is $23.

Perhaps the most pleasant (and cheapest) way to get a glimpse of nearly all the mansions' exteriors, however, is to follow the 3.5-mile oceanside **Cliff Walk**, which winds past their immense gardens, framed on the other side by the shoreline. The trail begins on Memorial Boulevard where it meets First (Easton's) Beach, and continues past some patches of jasmine and wild roses to concrete underpasses and unpaved rocky stretches along the southern part of the trail, ending at Bailey's Beach.

The Breakers

The capstone of Newport extravagance is Cornelius Vanderbilt's four-story Italian Renaissance-style palace **The Breakers**, on Ochre Point Avenue (daily: April to mid-Oct 9am–6pm; mid-Oct to Jan 9am–5pm; $16.50). Built for Vanderbilt, the president and chairman of the New York Central Railroad, by architect Richard Morris Hunt, the mansion sits on a thirteen-acre oceanfront estate – the waves crashing on the rocks below lend the house its name. The imposing "cottage," completed in 1895, includes a 45-foot-high central Great Hall and seventy other rooms, many of which were constructed in Europe and shipped to Newport. Also on the grounds, the **Breakers Stable and Carriage House** houses a variety of family memorabilia and the coach *Venture*.

Marble House, Rosecliff, Chateau-sur-Mer, and the Elms

Spread out along Bellevue Avenue are many other grand chateaus, each showcasing its own version of Gilded Age excess. **Marble House** (daily: April to mid-Oct 10am–6pm; mid-Oct to Jan 10am–5pm; $11), another Vanderbilt property built in 1892, boasts a golden ballroom bedecked by Greek and Roman figures and a Chinese teahouse. Nearby **Rosecliff** (daily: April to mid-Oct 10am–6pm; mid-Oct to Nov 10am–5pm; $11), built in 1902 for Nevada silver heiress "Tessie" Fair Oelrichs, was designed by Stanford White after the Grand Trianon at Versailles, complete with rose garden, heart-shaped staircase, and the largest ballroom of all the mansions; the house was later used as the film set for *The Great Gatsby*. Just north on Bellevue Avenue, the slightly more modest **Chateau-sur-Mer** (same hours as Rosecliff; $11), a stone villa built in 1852, is full of Victorian furnishings, Italian woodwork, and Oriental objects.

A long block north, the ornate French *maison* **The Elms** (daily April to mid-Oct 10am–6pm; mid-Oct to Jan 10am–5pm; $11) has marble stairways, Venetian paintings, and gardens fit for a king. Completed in 1901, it was modelled after the Parisian Château d'Asnières for Pennsylvania coal magnate E.J. Berwind. Come in season to wander among the majestic drooping trees for which the mansion is named; with reservations, you can also take an after-hours tour (June–Aug Fri 6–7pm), or rooftop and behind-the-scenes tour (daily on the hour; call ☎401/847-0478).

Kingscote, Isaac Bell House, Chepstow, and Hunter House

Kingscote, at the northern end of Bellevue Avenue (late May to Oct daily 10am–6pm; $11), is a quirky Gothic Revival cottage. Built in 1841 and expanded in 1876, it was the first of Newport's "cottages." The house's medieval exteriors are complemented by a lovely interior, with mahogany paneling and touches both exotic and Colonial; there is a Tiffany glass wall in the living room. You can combine your visit on a single ticket to the nearby, shingle-style **Isaac Bell House**, 70 Perry St (June–Sept daily 10am–6pm; $11), a living work in restoration, with a Japanese-inspired open floor plan and Old English influences. Almost as interesting is the 1860 Italianate **Chepstow**, 120 Narragansett Ave (same hours as Isaac Bell House; $11; reservation required for tours T401/847-1000 ext 165), home to a fine collection of nineteenth-century American landscape paintings.

Apart from all the other houses, at 54 Washington St, **Hunter House** (late June to Sept daily 10am–5pm; $25) marks the era when Newport was a mercantile capital and seaport. The house was built between 1748 and 1754 for a prosperous local merchant, and had a series of owners, including US senator William Hunter of the Jackson era; at one point during the American Revolution it was also the headquarters for the French naval forces.

Beechwood and Belcourt Castle

Privately owned **Beechwood**, 580 Bellevue Ave (Feb to mid-May Fri–Sun 10am–4pm; mid-May to Dec daily 10am–4pm; $15; T401/846-3772, Wwww.astors-beechwood.com), was built in 1851 and purchased by the Astors in 1881. Inside the house, costumed actors welcome visitors on behalf of Mrs Caroline Astor, the self-proclaimed queen of American society, known for her attempts to stave off advances made by the nouveau riche to penetrate the town's inner circle. Anecdotes and snarky asides make a visit great fun. Come for the murder mystery tour (summer Thurs 7pm; $30) or a number of other themed tours.

Still inhabited by its owners, **Belcourt Castle**, 657 Bellevue Ave (summer and fall daily 10am–4pm, other months times vary; $12; T401/846-0669, Wwww.belcourtcastle.com), was built to echo Oliver Belmont's love for equines and armor; in fact, his horses slept in white linen sheets in a special stable. Various themed tours are available, including champagne candlelight tours (Fri, Sun & Mon at 6pm) and ghost tours (Thurs 5pm).

Rough Point and Hammersmith Farm

At the southernmost end of Bellevue Avenue stands **Rough Point** (mid-April to mid-May Thurs–Sat 9.45am–1.45pm; mid-May to Oct Tues–Sat 9.45am–3.45pm; $25; T401/845-9130, Wwww.newportrestoration.org), the former home of Doris Duke, founder of the Newport Restoration Foundation and only child of electric and tobacco magnate James B. Duke. Rumors run that Ms Duke fell in love with her butler (who was then mysteriously murdered); it's not hard to see why, in such a romantic setting – the house is just steps away from the sea cliff, leading to a rocky beach.

Where the Cliff Walk ends, Ocean Avenue continues west, eventually running past shingle-sided **Hammersmith Farm**, John and Jackie Kennedy's 28-room summer home. Though not open to the public, Camelot junkies may still want a glimpse at the outside: the Kennedys' wedding reception was held here in 1953, and the couple were such frequent visitors that it came to be known as the "summer White House."

The beaches

The indubitable attraction of Newport's shoreline is slightly marred by the fact that several stretches are private; still, some of the best strands remain open to the public. From the end of Bellevue Avenue, **Ocean Drive** winds west along several miles of vast, spectacular shoreline to **Brenton Point State Park** (open daily sunrise–sunset; free), where panoramic views of Narragansett

Bay are shadowed only by the spray from the surf below. Along the way, the calm waters of **Gooseberry Beach**, nestled in an inlet, appeal to families. The town beach, also known as **First** or **Easton's Beach**, is a wide stretch at the east end of Memorial Boulevard with plentiful amenities, including surfboard rentals. The most attractive beach of all, though, is a couple miles east in Middletown: **Second (Sachuest) Beach** stretches a mile and a half, with soft sand and good surf. You can even **camp** nearby at *Second Beach Campground*, 474 Sachuest Point Rd (T 401/847-1500). **Third Beach** lies further east on the inner side of Narragansett Bay. The calmer waters and tidal pools here are good for children.

Combine a few hours on the beach with a visit to the **Norman Bird Sanctuary**, 583 Third Beach Rd (daily 9am–5pm; $5; T 401/846-2577, W www .normanbirdsanctuary.org), spanning three hundred acres, with seven miles of trails and a nature museum. South on Sachuest Point Road, at no. 769, the **Sachuest Point National Wildlife Refuge** (daily sunrise–sunset; T 401/847-5511), is another wonderful place to glimpse migratory birds, on 242 acres of diverse habitats. It's also a splendid spot to watch the sun set.

Eating

While many of Newport's **restaurants** are geared to tourists, with a little hunting you'll find plenty of marvellous exceptions. In general, the seafood here is worth the blowout if you can handle the cost. If you're coming in winter, be sure to check ahead, as many places close for the season.

Asterisk 599 Thames St T 401/841-8833. Upscale French bistro in a former car garage, with mouth-watering breakfasts, desserts, and entrees like sole meunière and chicken scallopini.

Belle's Cafe Newport Shipyard T 401/846-6000. At this well-kept secret, tucked away from the downtown bustle, you can grab delicious chowder and paninis in the company of the world's finest yachts.

The Black Pearl Bannister's Wharf T 401/846-5264. Harborside institution famous for its clam chowder and more – formal options (*escargots bourguignon*) and less formal ones (*escargots* with garlic butter) are both available.

Brick Alley Pub & Restaurant 140 Thames St T 401/849-6334. Attracts locals and tourists alike, with moderately priced ($20–26) American fare and a popular Sunday brunch.

Café Zelda 528 Thames St T 401/849-4002. Casual yachtie hangout with dressed-up standards like nori-wrapped tuna and *bouillabaise*.

Coffee Grinder Bannister's Wharf T 401/841-4325. A quiet spot amidst the harbour's bustle; sip coffee or a home-made granita and watch the world go by on the waterfront porch.

Empire Tea & Coffee 22 Broadway T 401/619-1388. Choose from bubble teas, lassis, coffees, or over 60 teas in a relaxed cafe setting. Free wi-fi.

Firehouse Pizza 595 Thames St T 401/846-1199. An old firehouse with kooky hand-painted booths and fair-valued twelve-inch pan pizzas.

Flo's Clam Shack 4 Wave Ave T 401/847-8141. Hugely popular joint across from First Beach. At $5.50 for a cup of clam chowder, three clam cakes, and a beer, it's worth the wait.

Puerini's 24 Memorial Blvd W T 401/847-5506. Classic Italian fare at reasonable prices make this a firm local favorite. Dinner only.

The Red Parrot 348 Thames St T 401/847-3800. An assorted menu of seafood, chicken, and steaks with a Caribbean flare, and speciality frozen and hot drinks like the "butterscotch belly warmer."

Salvation Café 140 Broadway T 401/847-2620. Funky spot off the main drag, with exotic concoctions like Moroccan chicken ($18), Thai shrimp cakes ($6), and hibiscus flower cocktail ($9). Dinner only; bar open till midnight daily.

Scales & Shells 527 Thames St T 401/846-FISH. Casual "only fish" restaurant serving high-quality seafare – raw, broiled, or mesquite-grilled. Dinner only.

Smokehouse Café America's Cup Ave and Scott's Wharf T 401/848-9800. Giant BBQ combos ($29) and baby back ribs ($16 half rack) in a lively atmosphere.

White Horse Tavern Marlborough and Farewell sts T 401/849-3600. Dine by candlelight at one of the oldest taverns in America, open since 1687. Continental cuisine with a New England touch; entrees $29–48.

Newport is world-famous for the plethora of prominent annual music festivals that take place here in the summer months, among them the **Newport Folk Festival** (ⓦwww.newportfolk.com) and the **JVC Jazz Festival** (ⓦjazz.jvc.com), held at the International Tennis Hall of Fame and Fort Adams State Park in August. Both feature big-name performers in their respective fields; call ⓣ877/655-4849 for more info. Over Labor Day weekend in early September, the **Waterfront Irish Festival**, among the country's largest Irish events, is held at the Newport Yachting Center. In a different vein, the **Newport Music Festival** (ⓣ401/846-1133, ⓦwww.newportmusic.org) takes place during July in a number of Newport's mansions, featuring world-class artists performing everything from chamber and orchestral music to sea shanties.

Drinking and nightlife

Newport has a reputation for being a lively party town, especially in the summer. You'll find no lack of **nightlife**, with happening **bars** and **clubs** lining the wharfs and Thames Street.

Billy Goode's 23 Marlborough St ⓣ401/848-5013. Get a feel for Newport's speakeasy days at this boisterous joint in the former sailors' district. Live country music Wed nights at 9.30pm.

The Boom-Boom Room Downstairs at the *Clarke Cooke House*, Bannister's Wharf ⓣ401/849-2900. Popular disco attracting a mixed crowd with standards, oldies, and Top-40. Cover $5–10 in summer.

Mudville Pub 8 W Marlborough St ⓣ401/849-1408. Irish pub and sports bar perched over Cardines field, where you can sneak a seat atop the stadium where Babe Ruth used to play. Extensive beer list.

Newport Blues Café 286 Thames St ⓣ401/841-5510. Come watch the legends and future acts in an old bank building by the harbor; live blues and jazz from 9.45pm nightly. Cover $5–10.

One Pelham East Thames and Pelham sts ⓣ401/847-9460. Popular venue that's hosted live bands since 1975; dance club upstairs.

The Wharf Pub & Restaurant 37 Bowen's Wharf ⓣ401/846-9233. The least expensive spot in the lively Bowen's Wharf area, serving a varied selection of microbrews. Live bands on summer weekends.

Around Newport

There are some worthwhile detours near Newport, including the town of **Portsmouth**, also on Aquidneck Island, and the towns of **Tiverton** and **Little Compton** on the **Sakonnet Peninsula**, a largely rural, agricultural area. Just west of Newport across the Newport Bridge, the island of **Jamestown** is also worth a stop. The pleasant nine-mile strip, lined with trees, old houses, and a few farms, is great for walking and cycling. At its southern tip, rocky **Beavertail State Park** affords spectacular ocean views, and boasts the site of the third oldest **lighthouse** on this side of the Atlantic coast (museum open daily June–Sept 10am–4pm; free; ⓣ401/423-3270).

Portsmouth

Founded in 1638 by Anne Hutchinson, another refugee from Massachusetts, **PORTSMOUTH** is today a pleasant, tree-lined suburb about ten miles north of Newport on Rte-114. Based in the Christian Union Church at 870 E Main Rd, the **Portsmouth Historical Society** (late May to mid-Oct Sun 2–4pm; free; ⓣ401/683-9178) comprises several old buildings, including what may be the oldest one-room schoolhouse in the country, completed in 1725, and the original Portsmouth Town Hall. The prime attraction in town, though, is the **Green Animals Topiary Garden**, on Cory's Lane off Rte-114 (mid-April to mid-Oct daily 10am–5pm; $11; ☎401/847-1000, ☖www.newportmansions.org), which has eighty animal-shaped trees and shrubs set on an idyllic lawn that slopes down to Narragansett Bay. Also on the property is a vintage toy exhibit, housed in a white clapboard building.

To **stay** in Portsmouth – not a bad option, as it's only a few miles from downtown Newport – try *Founder's Brook Motel*, 314 Boyd Lane (☎401/683-1244, ☖www .foundersbrookmotelandsuites.com; ❺–❻), featuring 32 units, many furnished with kitchenettes. You can also **camp** at *Melville Ponds Campground*, 181 Bradford Ave (April–Oct; ☎401/682-2424), with over one hundred acres of coastal woodland with opportunities for hiking, birdwatching and fresh-water fishing.

Tiverton

The rather nondescript northern section of **TIVERTON** that you first encounter when driving from Newport along Rte-77 is redeemed by occasional views of the **Sakonnet River**, which parallels the route. Heading south, the first spot of interest is **Fort Barton**, on Highland Street, an original redoubt built during the American Revolution and named after Colonel William Barton, who captured Newport's British commander during the war. Climb to the top of the observation tower for spectacular views of neighboring Aquidneck Island. Two miles south, Seapowet Avenue leads to the **Emile Ruecker Wildlife Refuge**, fifty acres of marshes and upland wood lots donated to the Rhode Island Audubon Society in 1965. Trails are well marked, and all kinds of birdlife can be seen, including ospreys, egrets, catbirds, and cardinals (daily dawn–dusk; free; ☎401/949-5454).

Farther south, **Tiverton Four Corners** is a motley collection of speciality stores, art galleries, and historic homes, several of which date from the eighteenth century. Among them is the 1730 gambrel-roofed **Chase Cory House**, 3908 Main Rd (☎401/624-2096), home to the Tiverton Historical Society. A mile south of Four Corners, **Fogland Road**, a pretty country lane bordered by lush hedges and rugged stone walls, traverses gentle farmland to reach **Fogland Beach** (parking Mon–Fri $5, Sat & Sun $10), Tiverton's shingly town beach, which skirts the southern edge of a comma-shaped peninsula jutting out into the Sakonnet River. There are splendid views downriver, with the Sakonnet Lighthouse looming in the distance.

Little Compton

The four thousand or so year-round residents of tiny **LITTLE COMPTON**, ten miles from Tiverton, owe their place on the map to a bird – the Rhode Island Red chicken was developed here. Fowl history notwithstanding, residents are ultra-protective of their environment, as evidenced by car stickers that bluntly demand "Keep Little Compton Little."

Today the square is dominated by the lofty, brilliant-white spire of the 1832 **Congregational Church**, with an adjacent burial ground that predates the building by 150 years. It contains the grave of one Benjamin Church, a colonist who took part in the execution of King Philip back in the 1600s. Opposite the church, the meandering maze that is **Wilbur's Store**, established more than two hundred years ago, is a Lilliputian department store, selling everything from food to hardware. The biggest draw in these parts, though, may just be the **Sakonnet Vineyards**, 162 W Main Rd (daily: late May to Sept 10am–6pm; Oct–May 11am–5pm; ☎1-800/91-WINES, ☖www.sakonnetwine.com), founded in 1975 and producing many Vinifera varietals. Continuing along West Main, the

Wilbor House, no. 548 (June–Sept Thurs–Sun 1–5pm; Sept to mid-Oct Sat & Sun 1–5pm; $5; ℡401/635-4035), spans the four centuries that members of the Wilbor family lived here, and includes excellent examples of period furnishings.

Main Road bends south toward the Atlantic to **Sakonnet Point**, where a broad vista is framed on one side by a newly restored **lighthouse** and on the other by the rocky Middletown shoreline. The waters are much more welcoming on the other side of the peninsula; park at **South Shore Beach** (Mon–Fri $7, Sat & Sun $12; ℡401/635-9974) at the end of South Shore Road, and walk to **Goosewing Beach Preserve**, a quiet, sandy nesting site for plovers and terns.

Tiverton and Little Compton practicalities

There is virtually no public transport on Sakonnet; to get here from Newport you'll need to drive north to Rte-24 and connect to Rte-77, which runs south the length of the peninsula. **Accommodation** in the two towns is limited, but should you choose to stay, you can try *Ferol Bink B&B*, 993 Neck Rd, Tiverton (℡401/624-6384; ⑤), a Victorian house on a working farm, with a suite (private bath) and four bedrooms (shared bath). In Little Compton, the *Edith Pearl B&B*, 250 W Main Rd (℡401/592-0053, ⓦwww.edithpearl.com; ⑧), features a handful of rooms in a Colonial farmhouse, set on two-hundred picturesque acres of farmland. For **food**, try *Evelyn's Drive-in*, 2335 Main Rd in Tiverton (℡401/624-3100), a waterfront, family-run diner famed for seafood, or *The Provender*, 3883 Main Rd, Tiverton Four Corners (℡401/624-8096), a delightful gourmet food store where you can choose from an array of sandwiches and desserts. In Little Compton, the roadside *Walker's Farm Stand*, 261 W Main Rd (℡401/635-4719; open daily June–Nov), is a veritable kaleidoscope of colorful produce, especially in the late summer and fall, when pumpkins and apples bask in the golden autumnal glow; there's also a deli next door.

South County: Rhode Island's southern coast

The term "**South County**" is used to describe Rhode Island's southernmost towns, mainly the coastal stretch that begins with **North Kingstown**, twenty miles south of Providence, and winds south past gently rolling hills and sandy beaches to **Westerly**, at the border with Connecticut. **Watch Hill** and **Narragansett** are lively resort towns, while the busy fishing port of **Galilee** is the departure point for ferries to unspoilt **Block Island**.

North Kingstown

NORTH KINGSTOWN, known as "plantation country" for its many long-standing farms, is less a town than a collection of rural communities straddling Rte-1A on the eastern shore of Narragansett Bay. The harborside village of **Wickford**, with its shady lanes and handsomely preserved eighteenth- and nineteenth-century homes, is home to the oldest Episcopal church north of Virginia, the 1707 **Old Narragansett Church**, on Church Lane (℡401/294-4357). Among its treasures are a Queen Anne Communion set and reputedly the oldest church organ in America, dating back to 1680; the austere box pews and slave gallery are reminders of a grim past. At the end of Main Street, quahog skiffs rub shoulders with posh yachts at the **Wickford Town Dock**, once a bustling trading port.

South County beaches

Many of Rhode Island's best **saltwater beaches** are in South County, though note that ocean temperatures here peak at 70–75 degrees, in August. State beaches charge a summer parking fee of $12 weekdays and $14 weekends, while town beaches fees are $10–15.

Charlestown Town Beach Charlestown Beach Road, Charlestown. Relatively strong surf and fine sand; a popular spot, with concessions.

East Beach Ninigret State Conservation Area, off E Beach Road, Charlestown. A three-mile long barrier beach with sugar-fine sand and aquamarine waters. Campsites available, but limited parking and no concessions.

East Matunuck State Beach Succotash Road, South Kingstown. Watch the boats at the port of Galilee from here. The waves are good for surfing and there's a gradual drop-off good for surf-casting.

Misquamicut State Beach Atlantic Avenue, Westerly. Rhode Island's largest state beach, this seven-mile stretch can get very crowded. Amusements, fast food, amenities are close at hand.

Napatree Point Watch Hill. Gorgeous, fragile barrier beach, with windswept dunes and views of Watch Hill Light. Great hiking and birding spot. Park downtown and walk here (10min); free.

Narragansett Town Beach Rte-1A, Narragansett. A half-mile-long beach popular with families and known for good surf.

Roger Wheeler State Beach Sand Hill Cove Road, Narragansett. A quarter-mile of gray sand with excellent facilities and expansive parking.

Scarborough State Beach Ocean Road, Narragansett. Busy beach near Point Judith, popular with students from nearby URI.

South Kingstown Town Beach South Kingstown. Beautiful beach backed by dunes, popular with families and picnickers.

Just north of town is **Smith's Castle**, 55 Richard Smith Drive (May & Sept–Oct Fri–Sun noon–4pm; June–Aug Thurs–Mon noon–4pm; other times by appointment; house tour $5, gardens free; ☏401/294-3521, ⓦwww.smithscastle .org), a seventeenth-century house whose origins trace back to a possibly fortified trading post (hence the "castle" in the name) established around the time of Roger William's arrival in the area in 1637. Burned down during the Great Swamp War by the Narrangansett Indians, the house was rebuilt and later overlooked one of the area's great plantations; today it houses educational exhibits on town life in the last four centuries. A few miles east, the only brick air hangar on the East Coast houses the **Quonset Air Museum**, 488 Eccleston Ave, Quonset Naval Air Base (April–Sept daily 10am–3pm; Oct–Mar Sat & Sun only; $7; ☏401/294-9540, ⓦwww.theqam.com), which displays vintage aircraft such as a Russian MIG-17 and an A-4 Skyhawk. Farther south in **Saunderstown**, the **Gilbert Stuart Birthplace and Museum**, 815 Gilbert Stuart Rd (May to mid-Oct Thurs–Mon 11am–4pm; $6; ☏401/294-3001, ⓦwww.gilbertstuartmuseum.com), displays the childhood home of the celebrated eighteenth-century portraitist, with a grist mill and herb gardens.

Narragansett

Ten miles along Rte-1A from Wickford, **NARRAGANSETT**, meaning "little spit of land" in Algonquin, is just that, with a rocky coastline interspersed by broad expanses of sand – a major attraction for swimmers, surfers, bird-watchers, and fishermen. The town center, known as **Narragansett Pier**, had its heyday during the Victorian era, when the town competed with Newport as a major resort destination. To some extent it succeeded, luring visitors to the **Narragansett Casino Resort**, designed in 1884. Hopes of fame and prosperity came to an abrupt end in 1900, however, when a fire swept through the casino, destroying all but its turreted towers, which today are the most striking feature of the town center, and which house the **visitor information center**, 35 Ocean Rd (Mon–Sat 9am–5pm; ☎401/783-7121). For more about the town's history, visit the **South County Museum**, Rte-1A at Canonchet Farm, opposite the Narragansett Beach Pavilion (May–June & Sept–Oct Fri–Sat 10am–4pm, Sun noon–4pm; July–Aug Wed–Sat 10am–4pm, Sun noon–4pm; $5; ☎401/783-5400, ⊛www.southcountymuseum.org), which holds thousands of local artifacts, a replicated print shop, smithy, textile arts center, carpentry shop, and farm exhibit with Rhode Island Red chickens.

Narragansett's long coastline boasts several outstanding **beaches** (see box, p.273) and the charmingly chaotic fishing port of **Galilee**, four miles south of the town center. The port's main drag is home to a large commercial fishing fleet (the smell can be overwhelming at times) and the **Block Island ferry** (see p.278 for details). If you want to go on a guided **whale-watching** tour, the boats of Francis Fleet (late May to early Sept Tues & Thurs–Sun 1pm; $40; ☎401/783-4988) depart for four hour thirty minute trips from a point just behind *Port of Call* restaurant on State Street. A mile east, the **Point Judith Lighthouse**, at the end of Ocean Road, has been warning ships away from the rocky coast since the early 1800s. The present structure, built in 1857, is closed to the public, but the view from the car park is breathtaking, especially on a stormy day.

Practicalities

Narragansett is a pleasant place to **stay**, but book well in advance in the summer. In Galilee, smack opposite the Block Island ferry, the *Lighthouse Inn* (☎401/789-9341 or 1-800/336-6662, ⊛www.lighthouse-inn-ri.com; ❽) is a modern, hundred-room hotel near all the activity. More atmospheric digs are found in the Narragansett Pier area, including the *1900 House*, 59 Kingstown Rd (☎401/789-7971, ⊛www.1900houseri.com; ❻) with elegant rooms on a quiet street, and the *Village Inn*, 1 Beach St (☎401/783-6767, ⊛www.v-inn.com; ❽), a newly renovated 62-room hotel near the center of town.

The Narragansett Pier area boasts several upmarket **restaurants**, including *Basil's*, 22 Kingstown Rd (☎401/789-3743), which has established a strong local following for its fine French cuisine. The Mediterranean restaurant *Amalfi*, 1 Beach St (☎401/792-3999) is a great seafood place with an outdoor patio. In Galilee, try the fresh catch at moderately priced *George's*, 250 Sand Hill Cove Rd (☎401/783-2306), or *Champlin's*, 256 Great Island Rd (☎401/783-3152), which has nice views of the fishing boats from an upstairs covered deck. A mile or so away, 🍴 *Aunt Carrie's*, 1240 Ocean Rd (☎401/783-7930), is a local institution, the place for traditional shore dinners in an unpretentious, relaxed atmosphere.

South Kingstown

Rhode Island's largest town by area, **SOUTH KINGSTOWN** takes in fourteen separate villages on both sides of Rte-1. Inland, dense woods hide well-preserved colonial villages, potato farms, and wildlife refuges. Rural **Kingston**, founded in 1674 and a former seat of Rhode Island government, is the unlikely location of the 1200-acre campus of **University of Rhode Island**, on Rte-138. South of Rte-1, several laid-back coastal communities are separated by a series of saltwater ponds protected by fragile barrier beaches. **Jerusalem** and **Snug Harbor** are worth stopping by for their clutch of summer cottages and stately homes. Otherwise, the main reason for coming down here is to join the crowds at the **beaches** (see box, p.273), namely Green Hill and East Matunuck, a favorite with university students.

For **accommodation**, try the *Admiral Dewey Inn*, 668 Matunuck Beach Rd, South Kingstown (℡401/783-2090, Ⓦwww.admiraldeweyinn.com; Ⓞ), a beautiful Victorian mansion minutes from the windswept shores, with dark wooden interiors and a wraparound porch. Three miles west on Cards Pond Road, at no. 364, Matunuck's **Theater by the Sea** (℡401/782-TKTS) hosts summertime musicals and theatre in an intimate historic house.

Charlestown

Laid-back **CHARLESTOWN**, South Kingstown's western neighbor, is one of the fastest-growing communities in the state, its newcomers having been seduced by an attractive coastline – miles of barrier beach backed by pristine salt ponds. First settled by the Narragansett Indians, Charlestown received its charter from King Charles II in 1663. The Narragansetts, however, still own plenty of land in town, and maintain a significant cultural impact, best observed during their **Annual Pow-Wow**, held the second weekend of August on tribal lands just off Rte-2 (℡401/364-1100). This "Gathering of the Green Corn," as it's also known, has been held for more than 330 years. Also located on these lands is the **Narragansett Indian Church**, a reconstruction of an 1859 granite Greek Revival building.

Also in the area, the **Ninigret National Wildlife Refuge**, 3679 Old Post Rd (dawn–dusk; ℡401/364-9124), comprises four hundred acres of diverse upland and wetland habitats on the shoreline of the state's largest salt pond. Over 250 species of birds frequent the former naval landing station, with its remnants of runways, miles of trails, and a new visitor center.

To **stay**, try the *General Stanton Inn*, 4115 Old Post Rd (℡401/364-8888 or 1-800/364-8011, Ⓦwww.generalstantoninn.com; Ⓞ), a stopping-place for travelers on the Providence–New London route since Revolutionary times, with seventeen adequate rooms. An adjacent flea market keeps guests busy at weekends. Just off the main drag, the *Surfside Motel*, 334 Narrow Lane (℡401/364-1010, Ⓦwww .thesurfsidemotel.com; Ⓞ), has fifteen clean rooms, several with kitchenettes. **Camping** is available in nearby **Burlingame State Park** (℡401/322-7994; sites $20, cabins $35).

Westerly

WESTERLY, a charming resort town, occupies the westernmost point of Rhode Island, eleven miles west of Charlestown near the Pawcatuck River. Formerly a prosperous textiles and granite manufacturing center, today the town draws crowds for its proximity to the spectacular area beaches. If you find yourself downtown with an hour or two to spare, pop by the handsome gambrel-roofed **Babcock-Smith House**, 124 Granite St (June–Oct Sat 2–5pm; July–Aug also Fri 2–5pm; $5; ℡401/596-5704, Ⓦwww.babcock-smithhouse .com), built circa 1734 for Dr Joshua Babcock, Westerly's first physician, who moonlighted as the town's postmaster, the state's chief justice, and a major-general in the Revolutionary army.

Most visitors, however, forsake Westerly's downtown in lieu of the **Watch Hill** area a few miles south, which, after Newport, is Rhode Island's most select resort, with salty seaside shops and 1900s-era **cottages** overlooking the Atlantic. At the end of Bay Street, the antique **Flying Horse Carousel** (children only; $1–1.50) spins out rides with twenty horses suspended from a central frame. The other town highlight is the old granite **lighthouse** at 14 Lighthouse Rd, with a small **museum** in the adjacent oil house (July & Aug Tues & Thurs 1–3pm). The lighthouse itself is closed to the public, but you're free to meander on the grounds. To the west, accessible from Watch Hill Beach, the half-mile-long barrier beach of **Napatree Point** once supported a number of homes before they were destroyed by a devastating hurricane in 1938, and is today a peaceful conservation area affording birding opportunities and stunning ocean views.

Practicalities

Perhaps the most tourist-friendly of the South County towns, Westerly has a wide range of **accommodation**. In Watch Hill, the *Harbor House Inn*, 5 Bay St (☎401/596-7500, ⊛www.oceanviewinns.com; ❸) offers eleven compact rooms and apartments near the water. Several miles east in Westerly, the *Shelter Harbor Inn*, 10 Wagner Rd (☎401/322-8883, ⊛www.shelterharborinn.com; ❸), is a 24-room country inn done up with early American fittings, with an excellent restaurant. Alternatively, the *Winnepaug Inn*, 169 Shore Rd (☎401/348-8350 or 1-800/288-9906; ❼), is set on nicely maintained grounds overlooking a golf course and close to the water. For **food**, the *St Clair Annex*, 141 Bay St, in Watch Hill (☎401/348-8407), serves wonderful breakfasts, sandwiches, and home-made ice cream. Down the street, the *Olympia Tea Room*, 74 Bay St (☎401/348-8211; May–Oct), offers more pricey seafood dishes.

Entertainment in Westerly centers on the **Granite Theatre**, 1 Granite St (☎401/596-2341, ⊛www.granitetheatre.com), presenting Broadway plays and cabaret acts. There's also the Colonial Theatre's free Shakespeare in the Park productions in July in Wilcox Park (☎401/596-7909), which is also the venue for the renowned **Westerly Chorus**'s Summer Pops concert. Throughout the rest of the year the ensemble puts on classical concerts at the **Westerly Performance Hall**, 119 High St (☎401/596-8663, ⊛www.chorusofwesterly .org), one of the Northeast's best small concert venues, set in a former church blessed with excellent acoustic.

Block Island

BLOCK ISLAND, twelve miles off Rhode Island's southern coast, somehow continues to preserve its melancholy, seductive charm: inhabited by only nine hundred year-round residents, it's a small bump of gently rolling hills and broad expanses of moorland, surrounded by a sometimes angry sea. Like Martha's Vineyard and Nantucket, the island bustles with tourist activity in the summertime, but attracts little of the accompanying scene. The beaches (and parking) are blessedly free, and the water temperature stays relatively high through October, so the early fall is a great time to visit, as the crowds clear and the migratory birds start making their way south, while the quiet, open land is perhaps best taken in on bike, or on foot – the island has nearly thirty miles of walking trails.

Some history

Native Americans, who called it "Manisses" or "Island of the Little God," inhabited Block Island for centuries before Giovanni de Verrazano spotted it in 1524 and named it **Claudia**, after the mother of the French king, Francis I,

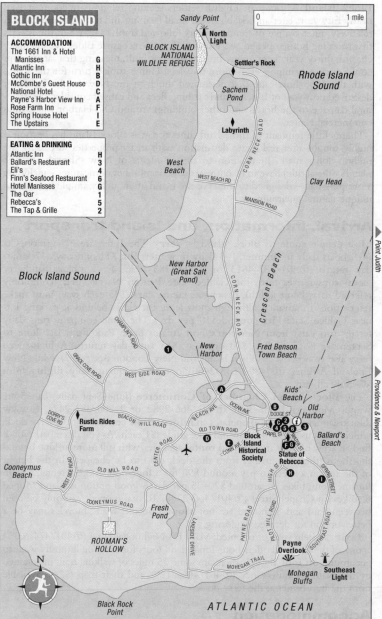

BLOCK ISLAND

ACCOMMODATION
The 1661 Inn & Hotel Manisses	G
Atlantic Inn	H
Gothic Inn	B
McCombe's Guest House	D
National Hotel	C
Payne's Harbor View Inn	A
Rose Farm Inn	F
Spring House Hotel	I
The Upstairs	E

EATING & DRINKING
Atlantic Inn	H
Ballard's Restaurant	3
Eli's	4
Finn's Seafood Restaurant	6
Hotel Manisses	G
The Oar	1
Rebecca's	5
The Tap & Grille	2

Sandy Point

North Light

BLOCK ISLAND NATIONAL WILDLIFE REFUGE

Settler's Rock

Rhode Island Sound

Sachem Pond

Labyrinth

West Beach

WEST BEACH RD

Clay Head

MANSION ROAD

CORN NECK ROAD

New Harbor (Great Salt Pond)

Block Island Sound

Crescent Beach

Fred Benson Town Beach

CHAMPLIN'S ROAD

New Harbor

GRACE COVE ROAD

WEST SIDE ROAD

BEACH AVE

OCEAN AVE

Kids' Beach

Old Harbor

DORRY'S COVE RD

BEACON HILL ROAD

Rustic Rides Farm

OLD TOWN ROAD

DODGE ST

CHAPEL ST

WATER ST

Ballard's Beach

Cooneymus Beach

CENTER ROAD

OLD MILL ROAD

Block Island Historical Society

CONN AVE

Statue of Rebecca

HIGH ST

Fresh Pond

COONEYMUS ROAD

LAKESIDE DRIVE

PAYNE ROAD

PLOT HILL ROAD

SPRING STREET

SOUTHEAST ROAD

RODMAN'S HOLLOW

WEST SIDE ROAD

Payne Overlook

MOHEGAN TRAIL

Mohegan Bluffs

Southeast Light

N

Black Rock Point

ATLANTIC OCEAN

0   1 mile

who had hired him. In 1614, Dutch explorer Adrian Block stopped on the island and gave it the name "**Adrian's Eyelandt**," which eventually became **Block Island**. A group of English settlers seeking religious freedom arrived nearly fifty years later and established a small farming and fishing community. A relatively quiet couple of hundred years followed until 1842, when the island's first rooming house opened and visitors began to recognize Block Island's many charms; thirty years later a new breakwater was built, meaning that larger ships could dock – bringing even more travelers. Things took a turn for the worse with the 1938 hurricane that devastated much of the New England coast: it destroyed nearly all of Block Island's fishing fleet and caused considerable structural damage to the hotels and other buildings around Old Harbor, the island's commercial center.

There's little remnant of those hard times today, as Block Island has become a highly sought-after real estate destination with many properties surpassing the million-dollar mark. In reaction to this, residents of **New Shoreham** (the island's official title) have in recent years passed a number of measures – including a camping ban – designed to preserve the island's tranquillity, simple beauty, and unique natural environment.

Arrival, information, and island transport

Most people come to Block Island by **ferry**. The Interstate Navigation Co. (4–9 boats daily in summer, 1–3 daily in winter; 1hr; $11 one-way, $17 same-day return; ☎401/783-4613 or 1-866/783-7996, ⓦwww.blockislandferry.com) runs ferries from the Galilee State Pier in Narragansett (commonly referred to as Point Judith). Passengers taking **cars** ($45 each way) must make reservations in advance, although most leave their cars behind at parking lots near Galilee State Pier (around $10 per day). The same company runs daily ferries (no cars) from Newport's Fort Adams State Park from late June to September (9.15am; 2hr; $10 one-way, $15 same-day return). A high-speed ferry also runs between Block Island and New London (see p.292), while New England Airlines (☎1-800/243-2460) operates frequent daily **flights** from Westerly all year.

The **Block Island Chamber of Commerce** (June–Sept daily 9am–5pm; winter Mon–Fri 10am–3pm; ☎401/466-2982 or 1-800/383-2474, ⓦwww.blockislandchamber.com) operates an **information center** near the ferry dock, which sells a useful island map and bike guide ($1 each). As you disembark, you'll find an array of **bike** and **moped rental** agencies, with still more lurking behind the shops (the ones further from the dock tend to be cheaper). In the height of the season, expect to pay around $90 for a four-hour moped rental, or $45 for one hour; bikes are around $20–25 per day. A good option is Island Moped & Bikes on Chapel Street (☎401/466-2700). Rental mopeds can only be used between 9am and 8pm, and are not allowed on dirt roads; bicycles may be a better option for detailed exploring.

Taxis can help you get oriented; Mary D's Nightingale Taxi (☎401/474-6377) is one of the best, and offers hour-long island tours for $55. You'll mostly want to get around **on foot**, though: there are some 25 miles of walking trails maintained by the Nature Conservancy (☎401/466-2129), and their map ($2) is available from the info center at the ferry dock.

Accommodation

In the summer tourist season, the island's limited **accommodation** fills up rapidly, so be sure to book well in advance if you plan on spending the night.

Accommodation is generally the fine inn variety, and while prices run upwards of $200 per night in season, there are also a number of smaller, more affordable guesthouses and cottages. The Chamber of Commerce (see opposite) is a good source of information. For longer-term stays and house rentals, Block Island Reservations maintains a number of rental properties (☎1-800/825-6254, ⓦwww.blockislandreservations.com), and the Block Island Tourism Council (☎1-800/383-BIRI, ⓦwww.blockislandinfo.com) also keeps a list of real estate agencies that handle rentals.

The 1661 Inn & Hotel Manisses Spring St, Old Harbor ☎401/466-2421 or 1-800/626-4773, ⓦwww.blockislandresorts.com. Luxurious island institution, with nine unique rooms in the *1661 Inn* and seventeen Victorian rooms in the *Hotel Manisses*. Inquire also about the other cottages and apartments on site, including the economical, contemporary guesthouse (**7**). **8**

Atlantic Inn High St, Old Harbor ☎401/466-5883 or 1-800/224-7422, ⓦwww.atlanticinn.com. Elegant, twenty-one-room Victorian inn set on six hilltop acres overlooking Old Harbor. **8**

The Gothic Inn Dodge St, Old Harbor ☎401/466-2918 or 1-800/944-8991, ⓦwww.thegothicinn.com. Family-run Victorian inn perched high above Crescent Beach, with gingerbread trimmings and a wide porch. **7–8**

🏃 **McCombe's Guest House** Old Town Rd ☎401/466-2684. One of the two dozen or so small guesthouses on the island, with two beautifully decorated rooms, each with private entrance. **8**

National Hotel Water St, Old Harbor ☎401/466-2901 or 1-800/225-2449, ⓦwww .blockislandhotels.com. Vast Victorian pile on Water St, with fair rooms, many with water views. The wraparound porch downstairs houses a popular restaurant. **8**

Payne's Harbor View Inn Beach Ave, New Harbor ☎401/466-5758, ⓦwww.paynesharborviewinn .com. Spacious rooms with whirlpool baths and sweeping harbor views; disabled accessible. **9**

Rose Farm Inn Roslyn Rd, Old Harbor ☎401/466-2034, ⓦwww.rosefarminn.com. Seventeen rooms in two properties on twenty idyllic acres close to the water. Adjacent bike rental shop. **7**

🏃 **Spring House Hotel** Spring St, Old Harbor ☎401/466-5844 or 1-800/234-9263, ⓦwww.springhousehotel.com. Stately 1852 waterfront hotel, the oldest on the island, with lovely rooms, many with ocean views; former guests include Ulysses S Grant and Billy Joel. **9**

The Upstairs Connecticut Ave, Old Harbor ☎401/466-2627, ⓦupstairsonbi.com. Secluded suite with private deck (**7**); also two-story cottage, which sleeps up to four, available for weekly rental ($1100).

The Island

Most visitors' first – and last – picture of Block Island is **Old Harbor**, developed after 1870 when the two breakwaters were built by the federal government. To encourage the fledgling tourist industry, huge Victorian hotels were built along **Water Street** as well, many boasting cupolas, porches, and gingerbread architecture. Remnants can still be found today amidst a touristy mix of boutiques and restaurants. At the southern end of Water Street, smack in the middle of the road, stands the **Statue of Rebecca**, an 1896 recasting of a biblical allegory erected by the Women's Christian Temperance Movement to remind folks of the dangers of alcohol. Ironically, restoration work uncovered that "Rebecca" is in fact more likely "Hebe", cupbearer to the gods. More local history can be found at the **Block Island Historical Society**, Old Town Road at Ocean Avenue (summer Thurs–Sun 11am–4pm; donation requested; ☎401/466-2481).

From Old Harbor, Spring Street trails to the southernmost tip of the island, where **Mohegan Bluffs**, spectacular 150-foot cliffs named for an Indian battle that occurred at their base, tower over the Atlantic. Positioned atop them is the red-brick **Southeast Light**, built in 1873 but not moved to its present position until 1993 after erosion threatened its survival. Laying claim to being the highest lighthouse in New England, the attraction here is the trip up the sixty-odd steps of the tower for the stunning **ocean views** (open daily July–Aug 10am–4pm, ℡401/466-5009). For a different perspective, head west to Payne Overlook, where a steep 150-step staircase descends down the cliffside to the beach and tidal pools below. Further west on the island's southern shore, **Black Rock Point** affords views of a dramatic seascape in which many ships have met their untimely end.

Also on this side of the island, the preserved sanctuary of **Rodman's Hollow** is accessible by a dirt track (Black Rock Road) from Cooneymus Road. The deep glacial depression is beautiful during the May shad bloom, while a nearby hill offers panoramic views of the Atlantic Ocean. On West Side Road, you can head out on a tranquil horse ride along the beaches or through the nature preserves from **Rustic Rides Farm** (rides daily year-round; $40 and up; ℡401/466-5060). At the farm, local Tim McCabe maintains the **Lost Manissean Indian Exhibit**, a collection of arrowheads, ax heads, and knives he's collected around the island, along with ancient mortars and pestles allegedly made by the natives.

A mile northwest of Old Harbor along Ocean Avenue, **New Harbor** boasts the only other would-be commercial area on the island: a handful of water-front restaurants, shacks, and sailing facilities on the shores of the **Great Salt Pond**. The pond was totally enclosed by land until a channel from the ocean was dredged; today a **ferry** runs from here to Montauk Point, Long Island (℡631/668-5700), docking at **Champlin's Marina**. Along the water, scenic

▲ Mohegan Bluffs

Block Island's beaches

Block Island has seventeen miles of great, often spectacular **beaches,** all of which are free. The island's eastern coast offers two and a half miles of flat sand, known as **Crescent Beach**, stretching from the Old Harbor to Clay Head. The main beach here is **Fred Benson Town Beach**, with lifeguards and full amenities, popular for swimming, kayaking, and surfing. At its sheltered southern tip, known as **Kid Beach**, children can play in relatively shallow water, while boisterous **Ballard's Beach** can be found just past the ferry dock. **West Beach** on the north-western coast is a better bet for some seclusion, bordered by a bird sanctuary to the south and dunes to the north, but the cobbly shores are more friendly to fishing than swimming.

Corn Neck Road leads north past an old **labyrinth** to **Settler's Rock**, commemorating where the settlers first landed, before the half-mile walk up to secluded **North Light**, at Block Island's isolated northern tip. The current incarnation is the fourth go-round for this lighthouse, a grim reminder of the power of nature. While it's closed to the public, a gaze from afar reveals a fine optical illusion – notice how close the lighthouse seems, yet how disproportionately large it is to the surroundings.

Eating

There are many great **places to eat** on the island, with **fresh seafood** topping the bill. Keep in mind that many of the places listed are open seasonally only.

Atlantic Inn High St, Old Harbor ☎401/466-54883. For a special night out, dine by candlelight and the sea; a contemporary American menu, with lots of seafare and a fine wine list, as well as a four-course *prix fixe* menu ($49).

Ballard's Restaurant Water St, Old Harbor ☎401/466-2231. Lively beachside stand-by with fried clams, lobster rolls, and the like.

Eli's Chapel St, Old Harbor ☎401/466-5883. Excellent, moderately priced bistro fare, like cedar plank salmon ($24).

Finn's Seafood Restaurant Water St, Old Harbor ☎401/466-2473. Moderately priced fresh catch, steaks, and hamburgers served overlooking the harbour, in a laid-back setting.

Hotel Manisses Spring St, Old Harbor ☎401/466-2421. Elegant evening dining in a Victorian inn, featuring tasty American cuisine, with fresh produce from the hotel's own backyard farm.

The Oar West Side Rd, New Harbor ☎401/466-8820. Famed for cheap, great seafood, with views of the Great Salt Pond from the deck.

Rebecca's Water St, Old Harbor ☎401/466-5411. Tasty chowder, clam cakes, and wraps, including a yummy grilled tuna sandwich.

The Tap & Grill Water St, Old Harbor ☎401/466-2901. Juicy steaks and standard saltwater fare ($17–26) served on a lively, harbour-side porch.

Drinking, nightlife, and entertainment

Although Block Island is usually so quiet you can hear the grass grow, the **nightlife** picks up in summer. Some **bars** are staid and courtly, while others are renowned for boisterous weekend parties. In recent years, the **Spring House Summer Concert Series** has even brought full-blown rock concerts to the island (call the *Spring House Hotel* for details; see p.279). More laid-back entertainment is provided by two **cinemas**: the Empire Theater on Water Street, Old Harbor (☎401/466-2555) and the Oceanwest Theater in New Harbor (☎401/466-2971). Pick up a copy of the local paper, the *Block Island Times*, for current listings and special events.

Albion Pub Ocean Ave, Old Harbor
⊕ 401/466-9990. Comfortable, dark, smoky pub on the main strip.
Captain Nick's Ocean Ave, Old Harbor
⊕ 401/466-5670. Live music throughout the summer, from national headliners to eager locals.
McGovern's Yellow Kittens Tavern Corn Neck Rd, Old Harbor ⊕ 401/466-5855. Popular

local hangout with outdoor deck; DJs play in summer.
Mohegan Café & Brewery 213 Water St, Old Harbor ⊕ 401/466-5911. Microbrews direct from an in-house brewery; open only till 10pm.
Mohogany Shoals Payne's Dock, New Harbor ⊕ 401/466-5572. Dockside bar featuring an Irish folk guitarist during the summer.

Connecticut

CHAPTER 5 # Highlights

✳ **Mystic** This coastal town is home to one of North America's premier aquariums, and the perennially popular Mystic Seaport. See p.288

✳ **Hammonasset Beach State Park** Camp next to two miles of sandy beach at the state's largest public shoreline park. See p.295

✳ **Yale University** Breathe in the erudite air in the magnificent libraries and Classical and Gothic buildings of the nation's second oldest Ivy League college. See p.301

✳ **Wadsworth Atheneum** Marvel at world-class art at the nation's oldest continuously operating public art museum. See p.314

✳ **White Memorial Foundation** Experience the gifts of nature at the 4000-acre wildlife refugee and conservation center. See p.323

✳ **Sloane-Stanley Museum** Discover a love for simplicity through an artist's personal, vast collection of wooden hand tools made before America's industrial age. See p.325

▲ Yale University

Connecticut

CONNECTICUT, New England's southernmost state, originally was named *Quinnehtukqut* ("great tidal river") by the Mohegan Indians, after the river that bisects it. Only ninety miles long by 55 miles wide, the little state nonetheless manages to be a land of contrasts: claiming both country and coast, it at once maintains rural estates and spectacular waterfront properties, and though it has no major cosmopolitan centers of its own, its position between New York City and Boston has helped to enliven and diversify the region in recent years. As a result, tourism here is of a sophisticated sort, with art galleries, vineyards, historical houses, and museums, and an increasingly eclectic cuisine, while the state's lesser known natural offerings make for pleasant surprises along the way.

The state was first settled in the 1630s by **English** refugees from Massachusetts seeking political and religious freedom. As one of the country's oldest settlements, it's been home to many of its firsts: in 1639, the colonial government produced the first written constitution in British North America, the "**Fundamental Orders**," which were used later as a model for the American Constitution; in 1784, Tapping Reeve established the country's first law school in Litchfield; and in 1806 the first American English dictionary was published in West Hartford by Noah Webster. During the Revolution, Connecticut's role in supplying the war effort earned it the nickname of the "**Provisions State**," though less officially the colony also came to be known for "**Yankee ingenuity**," principally the invention and marketing of many a useful household object. With steady industrialization helped along by Yale graduate **Eli Whitney**, who invented the cotton gin in 1794, Connecticut prospered during the late eighteenth and nineteenth centuries, producing some of the nation's great businessmen and activists, including writer **Harriet Beecher Stowe** and abolitionist **John Brown**.

Today, many of Connecticut's traditional industries have faded away, but the mark of previous generations is still evident in the scores of historic buildings open for tours. Though predominantly rural, the state is densely populated along the coast. The vibrant **southwestern** corner exudes the cosmopolitan air of neighboring New York City, and is home to industrial and intellectual **New Haven**, home of **Yale University**. Further east, the coast is dotted by charming small towns, while the US submarine fleet rests in Groton, near hip **New London**. Further inland, the old buildings scattered around **Hartford**, the state capital, tell many stories, though the city itself has fallen on rather hard times. More welcoming respite may be found in the state's northwestern section, around the **Litchfield Hills**, where roads wind down verdant hills into a picturesque landscape.

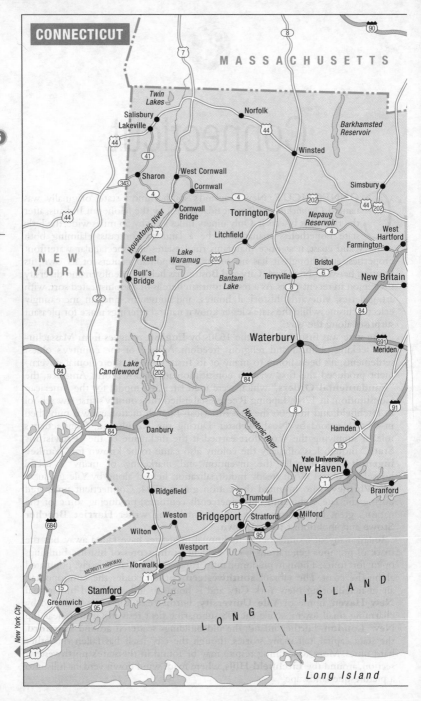

New York City

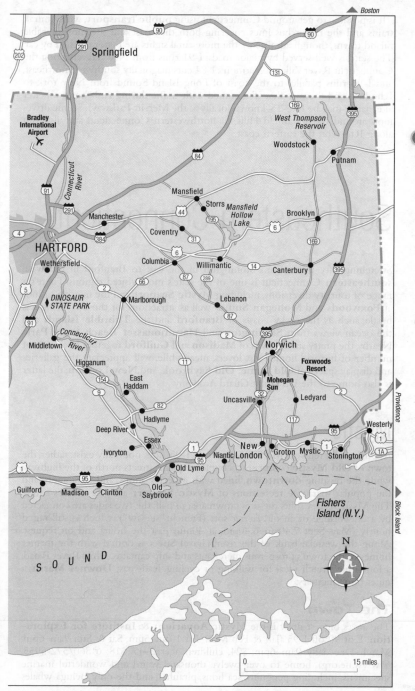

It is possible to get around Connecticut using **public transport**, with Amtrak trains and the major bus lines covering both the coast and the more sizeable inland towns, though admittedly, the more rural sights are better reached by car. The state is well served by major roads: I-91 runs from New Haven along the Connecticut River Valley to Vermont; I-84 cuts diagonally southwest–northeast; and I-95 runs parallel to the coast of Long Island Sound from New York to Rhode Island (beware that it's jammed with traffic during rush hour; a better alternative may be Rte-15, known locally as the Merritt Parkway). Scenic drives loop around the Litchfield Hills, in northwestern Connecticut, and also run along Rte-1 on the eastern coast.

Southeastern Connecticut

Stretching fifty miles, from Stonington in the east to Branford in the west, **southeastern** Connecticut is one of the state's most visited regions. There's a range of touristy diversions, including **Mystic Seaport** and the massive casinos at **Foxwoods** and **Mohegan Sun**, as well as attractions for those favoring less bustle, such as the rocky coasts of **Branford** and the **Thimble Islands** and the ocean views from **Stonington** and **Hammonasset Beach State Park**. Nearby, the pretty small towns of **Madison** and **Guilford** together boast a great number of historic homes. Art lovers, meanwhile, will appreciate the galleries and display spaces of **Old Lyme**, **Old Saybrook**, and **New London**; the latter is also home to the US Coast Guard Academy.

Mystic

As purists will tell you, **MYSTIC**, right on I-95, does not really exist; rather, the town of **Old Mystic** comprises a couple of quaint streets north of the highway, while the bustling **downtown**, lined with galleries, shops, and restaurants, and the popular maritime recreations of **Mystic Seaport** are a few miles south. The Mystic River splits the downtown area in half; the two sides are connected by a drawbridge of an old *bascule* sort (French: "seesaw"), which is still raised hourly (May–Sept 7.40am–6.40pm, at 40min past the hour) and on request. Along the western bank of the river, Gravel Street is dotted with the former homes of the town's prosperous merchants and ship captains, while River Road, a four-mile stretch ideal for walking or cycling, leads past **Downes Marsh**, a quiet bird sanctuary.

The Town

The area's biggest draw is the **Mystic Aquarium & Institute for Exploration**, Exit 90 off I-95 (Jan & Feb Mon–Fri 10am–5pm, Sat & Sun 9am–6pm; March–Dec daily 9am–6pm; $24, children ages 3–17 $18; ☎860/572-5955, ⓦwww.ife.org), home to over twelve thousand weird and wonderful marine specimens, including penguins, sea lions, piranhas, and the only Beluga whales

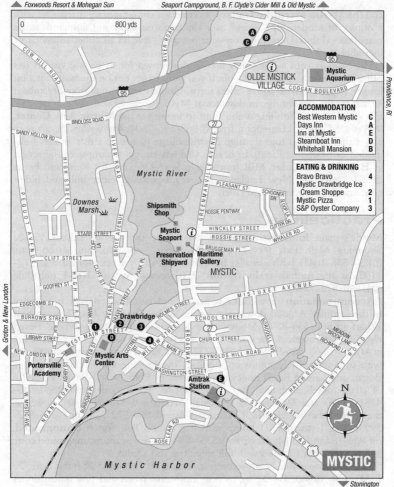

ACCOMMODATION
Best Western Mystic	C
Days Inn	A
Inn at Mystic	E
Steamboat Inn	D
Whitehall Mansion	B

EATING & DRINKING
Bravo Bravo	4
Mystic Drawbridge Ice Cream Shoppe	2
Mystic Pizza	1
S&P Oyster Company	3

in New England. With an advance reservation (℡860/572-5955 ext 520) and $159 you can even get in the water with the mammoth animals. Besides educational exhibits, the Institute also holds its own research and veterinary laboratories, and has a committed animal rescue program which has treated over three hundred marine mammals to date.

Mystic Seaport, or the Museum of America & the Sea, also at Exit 90 (daily: April–Oct 9am–5pm; Nov–March 10am–4pm; $18.50, children $13; ℡860/572-5315, ⒲www.mysticseaport.org), is the area's other big draw, with more than sixty buildings housing old-style workshops and stores reflecting life in a nineteenth-century seafaring village. The **Preservation Shipyard**, where you can watch the restoration and maintenance of a vast collection of wooden ships (including the 1841 *Charles W. Morgan*, the last wooden whaling ship in the world), is probably the most interesting of the attractions on the ground, though the Seaport also boasts the nation's most extensive maritime bookstore and the **Mystic Maritime Gallery**, a center for contemporary marine art with a display of model ships, as well as a children's museum and numerous other maritime exhibits. Depending on your point of view, it's all either authentic or incredibly tacky.

The Seaport runs a free water taxi to downtown for its paying visitors (it's otherwise about a 15min walk), but if you want to get out on the water for a bit longer, **Mystic River Tours** offers forty-minute harbor tours from Steamboat Wharf by the drawbridge in downtown Mystic (summer daily 11am–5pm; $5; ☎860/572-1421). You might also want to inquire at the **Mystic Arts Center**, 9 Water St (daily 11am–5pm; free; ☎860/536-7601, ⓦ www.mystic-art.org), about their walking tour through Mystic village past local artists' homes (self-guided or by appointment). In nearby Old Mystic, get a glimpse of the action at **B.F. Clyde's Cider Mill** (open daily Sept–Dec; call for tours and hours ☎860/536-3354), New England's last steam-powered cider mill and oldest continuous producer of hard cider.

Practicalities

Mystic's main **information office** lies in the tacky Olde Mistick Village Shopping Mall, Exit 90 off I-95 (Mon–Sat 9am–5pm, Sun 10am–5pm; ☎860/536-1641), with a smaller **branch office** (daily 10am–4pm; ☎860/572-1102) at the Amtrak **train station**, 2 Roosevelt Ave off Rte-1 (schedule ☎1-800/872-7245).

Accommodation in the area is pricey, and best booked well in advance in the summer. A good downtown option is the *Steamboat Inn*, 73 Steamboat Wharf (☎860/536-8300, ⓦ www.steamboatinnmystic.com; ❽), whose eleven elegant rooms overlook the water. At the intersection of routes 1 and 27 is the *Inn at Mystic* (☎860/536-9604 or 1-800/237-2415, ⓦ www.innatmystic.com; ❼–❾), with over sixty lovely rooms on a hillside overlooking the sound; Humphrey Bogart and Lauren Bacall honeymooned here in 1945. Near I-95 are a handful of chain motels, including *Best Western Mystic*, 9 Whitehall Ave (☎860/536-4281; ❹–❻), and *Days Inn*, 55 Whitehall Ave (☎860/572-0574; ❺), as well as the pretty *Whitehall Mansion*, 42 Whitehall Ave (☎860/572-7280 or 1-800/572-3993; ❺), a restored 1771 house with five rooms. The *Seaport* **campground**, off Rte-184 in Old Mystic (☎860/536-4044, ⓦ www.seaportcampground.com; $45 per site), has 130 sites with full amenities and a pool.

The downtown area boasts some fine restaurants, including ⌁ *Bravo Bravo*, 20 E Main St (☎860/536-3228), serving innovative pastas and fine Italian dishes like champagne risotto with lobster and asparagus, and *S&P Oyster Company*, 1 Holmes St (☎860/536-2674), serving fine seafood on the waterfront. The small, family-run *Mystic Pizza*, 56 W Main St (☎860/536-3700), makes huge pies ($10–16) and remains a pilgrimage site for movie fanatics (see "Films," p.539). For dessert, the perfect spot may just be the balcony outside *Mystic Drawbridge Ice Cream Shoppe*, 2 W. Main St (☎860/572-7978), where you can indulge in home-made sorbets while watching the drawbridge rise to let the boats go by.

Around Mystic

Around Mystic is a diverse range of attractions, from the picturesque town of **Stonington** by the sea to the naval centre of **Groton**. Just inland are the state's massive **gambling** operations, which draw millions annually to glitzy resorts tucked into the pine forests north of **New London**, the area's hub.

Gambling on Connecticut's Native American reservations

In 1988, Congress passed the Indian Gambling Regulatory Act, which recognized the rights of Native American tribes in the US to establish gambling and gaming facilities on their reservations. Despite objections from environmentalists, anti-gambling agencies, and concerned citizens, Connecticut has since become home to several major Native American casinos. **Foxwoods Resort and Casino**, Rte-2, Ledyard (☎1-800/FOXWOODS, ⍟www.foxwoods.com), operated by the Mashantucket-Pequot Indians, is among the largest casinos in the world, and just opened the adjacent **MGM Grand** after a $700 million expansion. Nearby, the **Mohegan Sun**, Rte-2A, Uncasville (☎1-888/226-7711, ⍟www.mohegansun.com), established by the Mohegan tribe, is now in the process of its own expansion, to be completed in 2010 and designed with tribal inspiration.

Stonington

STONINGTON, just south of I-95 near the state's eastern border, is a nice old fishing village. Originally settled in 1649, it's still very much "New England," with attractive whitewashed cottages and a peaceful waterfront. The main road, **Water Street**, is dotted with restaurants and shops. At no. 7, the **Old Lighthouse Museum** (May–Nov daily 10am–5pm; $8; ☎860/535-1440), relays fine textures of town life through the centuries in six small rooms of exhibits, including lots of fishing and whaling gear, a collection of local salt-glazed ceramics, and trinkets from the Orient brought back by the town's notable seafarers. An old cistern and well are also carefully displayed, while the view from the top, as from the entrance, is endless on sunny days. Museum admission also allows you access to the Italianate **Captain Nathaniel B. Palmer House**, 40 Palmer St (May–Nov Wed–Sun 10am–5pm; $8; ☎860/535-8445), at the north end of town. The house celebrates Stonington's premier seafarer, who was credited with one of the earliest sightings of Antarctica.

Practicalities

For **accommodation**, try the *Orchard Street Inn*, 41 Orchard St (☎860/535-2681, ⍟www.orchardstreetinn.com; ❻), with three rooms, each with garden patio, in a quiet cottage. In neighboring Pawcatuck, the *Cove Ledge Inn & Marina*, on Rte-1 at Whewell Circle (☎860/599-4130, ⍟www.coveledgeinn.com; ❹), offers twenty rooms close to the water. For **food**, try ⍟ *Noah's*, 113 Water St (☎860/535-3925; closed Mon), known for its fine home-style cooking and menu of eclectic dishes – everything from Korean pancakes to surprises conjured from the local catch. Alternatively, *Skipper's Dock*, 66 Water St (☎860/535-0111; closed Jan and Tues in winter), offers pricier seafood complemented by ocean views.

Groton

Seven miles west of Mystic Seaport, **GROTON** is the hometown of the **US Naval Submarine Base**. The headquarters for the North Atlantic Fleet are off Rte-12 on Crystal Lake Road, and have been a crucial fixture in the local economy since 1916. While the naval base is off-limits to the public, the **Submarine Force Museum** next door (mid-May to Oct Wed–Mon 9am–5pm, Tues 1–5pm; Nov to mid-May Wed–Mon 9am–4pm; free; ☎1-800/343-0079) welcomes visitors to trace the history of submersibles from as early as the Revolutionary era to the **USS Nautilus**, America's first nuclear-powered submarine, now docked at the museum for tours. For an above-ground perspective, **Project Oceanology** runs a series of **boat tours** from the University of Connecticut's Avery Point Campus,

I-95 Exit 87, including two hour thirty minute oceanographic research cruises and tours of **Ledge Lighthouse** (June–Sept; $19, children ages 6–12 $16; reservations ☎860/445-9007 between 9am–4pm, ⓦwww.oceanology.org), stuck out in the middle of the river and supposedly home to a resident ghost.

New London

NEW LONDON, with 26,000 residents, is the most populous city along this stretch of the coast. A wealthy whaling port in the nineteenth century, it relied heavily on military-base revenue in the twentieth century, then struggled in the 1990s due to spending cuts. Today the city is reviving, thanks largely to the presence of pharmaceutical giant Pfizer's R&D headquarters. This development has not come without controversy, however: in 2005 New London became the focus of national attention with the case of **Kelo v. City of New London**, in which the Supreme Court ruled to extend the privilege of eminent domain (which allows government seizure of private property for the public good), despite protests from homeowners.

The Town

One of New London's highlights, the **US Coast Guard Academy**, off I-95 at 31 Mohegan Ave, spreads out on an attractive campus overlooking the Thames. Visitors are welcome to take a self-guided tour (daily 9am–4.30pm; ID required; free), with maps available from Admissions in Waesche Hall on the north end of campus (☎860/444-8500). If you're lucky, you might catch a full-regalia cadet drill (fall and winter Fri 4pm, and special occasions). The **US Coast Guard Museum**, also on the campus (open daily, call for hours; free; ☎860/444-8511), explores two centuries of Coast Guard history and houses the figurehead from the USS *Eagle*, the only tall ship on active duty, now used as a training vessel and often docked at the Academy and open for tours (call ☎860/444-8595 for schedules).

Just opposite the Academy entrance, at the southern end of the **Connecticut College** campus, the **Lyman Allyn Art Museum**, 625 Williams St (Tues–Sat 10am–5pm, Sun 1–5pm; $8; ☎860/443-2545), contains all varieties of American arts and crafts, including a silver tankard made by Paul Revere, along with rotating exhibits of American and European art from the eighteenth century to today. On a clear day, Connecticut College itself sports a stunning view of Long Island Sound.

Downtown, be sure to walk along **Whale Oil Row**, a short strip of private 1830s Greek Revival homes once owned by leaders in the whaling industry, and **State Street**, the city's main thoroughfare, lined with a variety of shops and restaurants. Also downtown, the **Custom House Maritime Museum**, 150 Bank St (April–Dec Tues–Sun 1–5pm; Jan–March by appointment; free; ☎860/447-2501), hosts exhibits on New London history in the country's oldest continuously operating custom house. For a change of pace, visit the hip art space **Hygienic Galleries**, 79–83 Bank St (Thurs 11am–3pm, Fri & Sat 11am–6pm, Sun noon–3pm; ☎860/443-8001, ⓦwww.hygienic.org), which exudes a bohemian spirit and hosts a number of performances in the adjacent outdoor **Hygenic Art Park**.

A bit south, the **Shaw–Perkins Mansion**, 11 Blinman St (Wed–Fri 1–4pm, Sat 10am–4pm; $5; ☎860/443-1209), built in 1756 for wealthy merchant Nathaniel Shaw, has unusual paneled-cement fireplace walls and some period furnishings. Meanwhile, New London's oldest home, the 1678 **Joshua Hempsted House**, 11 Hempstead St (mid-May to mid-Oct Thurs–Sun noon–4pm; $5; ☎860/443-7949), is said to have been used as a safe haven on the Underground Railroad. Admission includes entrance to the adjacent **Nathaniel Hempsted House**, built by Joshua's grandson, with an outdoor stone beehive oven.

Continuing south, **Pequot Avenue** offers a gorgeous drive along the water, passing by the **Harbor Light** lighthouse and leading to **Ocean Beach Park**, 1225 Ocean Ave (open summer daily till late; parking $14–18, additional fees for activities; ☎860/447-3031), an extensive, if pricey, beach spot with arcade, carousel, mini-golf course, waterslide, and outdoor pool. Also on Pequot Avenue is the birthplace of playwright Eugene O'Neill, the **Monte Cristo Cottage**, at no. 325 (June–Sept Tues–Sat 10am–5pm, Sun 1–3pm; $7; ☎860/443-5378 ext 290). House tours include juicy details of his early life. The writer's spirit of genius seems to be hovering over the **Eugene O'Neill Theater Center**, at 305 Great Neck Rd in nearby Waterford, an acclaimed testing-ground for emerging playwrights and actors. Audiences can observe shows in rehearsal (June–Aug; ☎860/443-5378, ⓦ www.oneilltheatercenter.org).

Practicalities

Amtrak **trains** and Greyhound buses serve New London's **Union Station downtown**, at 27 Water St (☎1-800/872-7245, ☎860/447-3841). Close by, the **New London Ferry Dock**, 2 Ferry St, runs a number of ferries, including one to **Orient Point** on Long Island (Cross Sound Ferry; hourly; 1hr 20min; $14 one-way, $46 with vehicle; ☎860/443-5281) and one to **Block Island**, RI (Block Island Express; June–Sept up to 4 per day; 1hr 15min; $24 one-way, $43 same-day round-trip; ☎860/444-4624).

Information is available at the **Trolley Station**, on Eugene O'Neill Drive (May & Oct Fri–Sun 10am–4pm; June–Sept daily 10am–4pm; ☎860/444-7264), and the **Mystic Country CVB**, 32 Huntington St (Mon–Fri 8.30am–4.30pm; ☎860/444-2206). Both provide maps of downtown.

For a room with a view, a fine place to **stay** is the atmospheric *Lighthouse Inn Resort*, 6 Guthrie Place (☎860/443-8411; ⓦ www.lighthouseinn-ct.com; ⑤), with 51 elegant rooms in the former country mansion of steel magnate Charles S. Guthrie and the adjacent carriage house; there's also an outdoor pool and a beach nearby. Other options include the *Holiday Inn*, 269 N Frontage Rd (☎860/442-0631; ⑨), and the *Super 8*, 173 Rte-12 (☎860/448-2818; ⑨), among a number of motels scattered along I-95.

There are a few fine **restaurants** around town, including classy *Timothy's* at the *Lighthouse Inn* (see above), where you can sample a variety of seafood from your vantage point on Long Island Sound. A more rustic option is ⅍ *Mangetout,* 140 State St (Mon–Sat 8am–4pm, Sun 11am–4pm; ☎860/444-2066), serving fresh, organic breakfasts and lunches and yummy desserts like ginger pavlova and hummingbird cake ($4.50). For cheap drinks and a good time, try the old-fashioned *Dutch Tavern*, 23 Green St (☎860/442-3453), complete with the 100-year-old tables at which O'Neill once sat. Over the water in Noank, *Abbot's Lobster in the Rough*, 117 Pearl St (May–Sept daily noon–9pm; ☎860/536-7719), is the perfect spot for a lobster picnic, serving the delicious creatures and other seafood next to the water.

West to New Haven

Headed west towards New Haven, the coast is dotted by a number of small, picturesque towns, from the former artist colony of **Old Lyme** to lively **Madison** and historic **Old Saybrook** and **Guilford**. **Branford**, meanwhile, offers a stopover to the rocky **Thimble Islands**. I-95 connects all these towns, but Rte-1, locally known as the Boston Post Road, also weaves along the coast, and may be a more pleasant alternative if you're hopping from place to place.

Shore Line East (☎203/777-7433), a commuter rail service operated by the Connecticut Department of Transportation, connects New London and New Haven, while the Estuary Transit District (☎860/510-0429) provides local bus transport, with stops along Rte-1 between Old Saybrook and Madison, including the popular summer destination of **Hammonasset Beach State Park**.

Old Lyme

Fifteen miles west of New London along I-95, at the mouth of the Connecticut River, sits picturesque **OLD LYME**, the former site of a major American Impressionist art colony (and the namesake of the dangerous tick-borne disease). In 1899, resident Florence Griswold, an unmarried middle-aged woman saddled with a high mortgage, opened her home to boarders and began to attract a regular clientele of artists. The eleven-acre property of the **Florence Griswold Museum**, 96 Lyme St (Tues–Sat 10am–5pm, Sun 1–5pm; $8; ☎860/434-5542, ⓦwww.flogris.org), showcases her life and the Lyme Art Colony, with a 10,000-square-foot changing exhibition space next to the old boarding house. The house holds more than forty original panels painted directly onto the walls by the various artists who stayed here, including William Chadwick, whose studio is set up on site just as it was during his lifetime. A few doors away, contemporary creations can be found in the two galleries at **Lyme Academy College of Fine Arts**, 84 Lyme St (Mon–Sat 10am–4pm; donation requested; ☎860/434-5232).

Old Saybrook

Hugging both river and sea, the former shipbuilding center of **OLD SAYBROOK**, opposite **Old Lyme** on the western bank of the Connecticut River, is the oldest town on Connecticut's coast. Puritan settlers arrived here in 1635 and erected a fort to guard the town, though nothing of the battlements remain today. Instead, commercial activity bustles along Rte-1 and Main Street, the latter of which leads south from the town center to the churning waters of **Saybrook Point**. In 1707, the town became the home of the **Collegiate School**, which later moved to New Haven and renamed itself **Yale University**. With no must-see attractions, the town today is nevertheless a pleasant base from which to explore the state's southeastern coast, claiming a number of fine antique shops and historic houses. Among them is the 1767 **General William Hart House**, 350 Main St (July & Aug Fri–Sun 1–4pm; $5; ☎860/388-2622), the elegant residence of a prosperous merchant who served in the Revolutionary War.

Practicalities

Old Saybrook's **train** station, at 455 Boston Post Rd (☎860/388-3741), is served by Amtrak trains on the **Northeast Regional line** (Boston–New York–Washington, DC), and also by the Shore Line East commuter rail line (☎1-800/255-7433). The **Old Saybrook Chamber of Commerce** maintains an office at 146 Main St (Mon–Fri 9am–5pm; ☎860/388-3266, ⓦwww .oldsaybrookct.com).

There is a wide variety of **accommodation** in the area, ranging from historic B&Bs like the *Deacon Timothy Pratt House B&B*, 325 Main St (☎860/395-1229, ⓦpratthouse.net; ❸), with rooms furnished in period style, complete with canopy beds and Jacuzzi tubs, to the luxurious waterfront *Saybrook Point Inn & Spa*, 2 Bridge St (☎860/395-2000 or 1-800/243-0212, ⓦwww.saybrook .com; ❾). A number of motels are scattered along Boston Post Road, including

the friendly *Heritage Motor Inn*, at no. 1500, with wall murals in every room
(☎860/388-3743; ❹). For pricey, waterfront **dining**, try *Dock & Dine*, on College
Street, Saybrook Point (☎860/388-4665), where lovely views accompany classic
American steak and seafood dishes. At no. 910, *Johnny Ad's* (☎860/388-4032)
is a no-frills clam shack known for fresh fried clams and lobster rolls. For a
change, *Tissa's Market and Cafe*, at no. 855, serves delicious Moroccan food in an
unassuming shop setting, allowing you to savor the chef's concoctions next to
shelves of exotic speciality food items, also for sale.

Madison

Posh **MADISON** lies on the waterfront, just a few miles west of Old Saybrook
on Rte-1. It's a nice place to stop for a bit, with an attractive, shady town green
and broad main street lined with upmarket restaurants and shops, including
a superb independent bookstore, **R.J. Julia**, 768 Boston Post Rd (Mon–Sat
9am–9pm, Sun 10am–6pm; ☎203/245-3959). It's also home to some nice
historic buildings, among them the 1685 **Deacon John Grave House**, at
no. 581 (call for hours; ☎203/245-4798), the town's oldest residence, whose
functions over the years include schoolhouse, infirmary, weapons depot, tavern,
and courtroom. At no. 853, the 1785 white clapboard saltbox **Allias-Bushnell
House**, current home of the **Madison Historical Society** (Tues & Thurs
11am–4pm; ☎203/245-4567), contains some interesting artifacts, from costumes
and kitchenware to a Victorian hearing aid and working looms.

The area's biggest draw, however, is **Hammonasset Beach State Park** (daily
8am–sunset; summer parking $15), two miles east of downtown Madison off
Rte-1. Here, lush green meadows spread out next to two miles of sandy shoreline,
backed by dunes and a salt marsh. On stormy days, when the crowds are gone,
the view is truly endless. At the southernmost tip of the park, **Meigs Point**
offers a nature trail and **Nature Center** with small reptilian exhibits (Tues–Sun
10am–5pm). West of the park entrance, near **Camper's Beach**, the **camping**
area (May–Oct; $18; ☎203/245-2785) has bathhouses, a beach store, concession
stands, and 550 campsites.

Practicalities

There's plenty of good **accommodation**, including *The Inn at Lafayette*, 725
Boston Post Rd (☎203/245-7773 or 1-866/623-7498, ⓦwww.innatlafayette
.com; ❻–❼), an elegant establishment whose five rooms all boast marble
bathrooms and modern amenities; the *Dolly Madison Inn*, 73 West Wharf Rd
(☎203/245-7377; ❹), with seventeen compact rooms minutes from the water;
and the *Tidewater Inn*, 949 Boston Post Rd (☎203/245-8457, ⓦwww.thetidewater
.com; ❺), a pleasant woodsy retreat with charming rooms and hearty breakfasts.
For places to **eat**, try *Cafe Allegre*, 725 Boston Post Rd (☎203/245-7773), serving
fine Mediterranean dishes like sole fiorentina ($19) and veal casanova ($19), and
The Wharf, at the *Madison Beach Hotel*, 94 West Wharf Rd (☎203/245-0005; open
April–Nov), offering American cuisine in a waterfront setting.

Guilford

First settled by English vicar Reverend Henry Whitfield in 1639, **GUILFORD**,
just west of Madison, has one of the largest collections of seventeenth- and
eighteenth-century houses in New England. Among them is Whitfield's own
home at 248 Old Whitfield St, the oldest surviving stone house in New England,
built in 1639. The fortress-like dwelling, now the **Henry Whitfield State
Museum** (April to mid-Dec Wed–Sun 10am–4.30pm; $4; ☎203/453-2457,

▲ A house in Guilford

Ⓦwww.whitfieldmuseum.com), served as a meeting place for the village community and houses a variety of artifacts, including the first tower clock made in the colonies, dating from 1726. Nearby, at 84 Boston St, the **Hyland House** (June to early Sept Tues–Sun 10am–4.30pm; donations requested; Ⓦwww.hylandhouse.com) is a late seventeenth-century saltbox that belonged to esteemed clockmaker Ebenezer Parmelee. Little refurbishment has gone on since: the house is held together by the same old nails and bolts, and has its original casement windows and hand-hewn floorboards. The **Thomas Griswold House** (June–Sept Tues–Sun 11am–4pm; Oct Sat & Sun 11am–4pm; $3; ☎203/453-3176), another saltbox built in 1774, is distinguished by a working blacksmith's shop and Colonial-style garden. Guilford's spacious **village green** – purported to be the largest in New England – is the attractive location for summer concerts and recitals, lined on two sides with boutiques and restaurants.

Practicalities

For **accommodation** in Guilford, the *Guilford Suites Hotel*, 2300 Boston Post Rd (☎203/453-0123; ⑥), has 32 suites, all of which are equipped with lounge space and kitchenette. A short drive from town, the *B&B at Bartlett Farm*, 564 Great Hill Rd (☎203/457-1657, Ⓦwww.thebartlettfarm.com; ⑥; two-night minimum stay), offers three charming rooms on a working farm, complete with goats, donkey, and even a bison. There's no shortage of excellent **restaurants** in town, including the waterfront *Guilford Mooring*, 505 Whitfield St (☎203/458-2921), serving a variety of seafood and baked pasta dishes, and fun-filled *The Place*, 891 Boston Post Rd (☎203/453-9276; open late April to Oct), where seafood is grilled on a huge outdoor wood fire and tree stumps make for seats.

Branford and the Thimble Islands

You'll have little reason to stop in **BRANFORD**, eight miles west of Guilford, other than perhaps its surprisingly good collection of restaurants and its proximity to the **Thimble Islands**. If you do find yourself with an extra hour to kill, however, stop by the **Harrison House**, 124 Main St (June–Sept Sat 2–5pm; donations requested; ☎203/488-4828), built in 1724 and restored to its original condition in 1938, with an interesting display of farm implements in its barn.

The main attractions in the area are the **THIMBLE ISLANDS**, 365 tiny islets off the coast of nearby **Stony Creek**, best accessed by Exit 56 off I-95. The so-called chain of islands is in reality a cluster of granite rocks within a three-mile radius of shore, ranging from outcroppings that vanish at high tide to an island with 24 (mostly Victorian) homes. Years ago, the islands provided perfect hiding places for pirate ships waiting to attack boats in Long Island Sound; the infamous **Captain Kidd** is said to have hidden treasure here when being chased by the British (though it would have been hard to bury). You can hear colorful stories about the islands by taking a **tour** with one of several boats. The *Islander* ($10; ☎203/397-3921), the *Volsunga IV* ($10; ☎203/481-3345, ⓦthimbleislands .com), and the *Sea Mist* ($10; ☎203/488-8905, ⓦwww.thimbleislandcruise.com) offer daily 45-minute trips from mid-May until mid-October, departing from the Town Dock at the end of Thimble Island Road in Stony Creek, I-95 Exit 56. For a little more adventure, you can **kayak** around the islands with Coastal Kayaking (☎860/391-3837, ⓦctcoastalkayaking.com), whose three-hour tours start at $80 per person.

Practicalities

Most of Branford's fine **restaurants** are located around the town green. *Assaggio*, 168 Montowese St (☎203/483-5426), serves moderately priced contemporary Italian dishes and has a nice wine list, while *Le Petit Café*, 225 Montowese St (☎203/483-9791; dinner only, closed Mon & Tues; reservations required), one of the best restaurants around, offers French bistro cuisine (four-course *prix fixe* menu $44.50). Much more casual is *Lenny's*, 205 S Montowese St (☎203/488-1500), a reasonably priced seafood shack full of families. Near the dock in Stony Creek, the *Stony Creek Market*, 178 Thimble Island Rd (☎203/488-0145), sports a combined restaurant, bakery, deli, and (in the evenings) pizzeria, with stunning views of the Thimbles from its deck. Branford's absence of inns and B&Bs is compensated for by the abundance of inexpensive and generally basic **hotels** and **motels**, most of which are located on East Main Street, such as the newly renovated *Motel 6*, no. 320 (☎203/483-5828; ❸), and the *Branford Motel*, no. 470 (☎203/488-5442; ❸).

Southwestern Connecticut

Southwestern Connecticut, by far the state's most populated area, is an essential stop on any tour. Nicknamed "the gold coast" for its exceedingly wealthy towns like **Greenwich** and **Westport**, the region has long flourished from its proximity to New York City, simultaneously inheriting a certain cosmopolitan spirit and offering the moneyed sweetness of fresh country air. A world away, the state's largest city and former industrial centre **Bridgeport** is making valiant efforts to reverse the urban decline of the last decades, while **New Haven** is an intriguing mix of downbeat industrial hub and historic university town. Industrial vibes can be further felt in the former manufacturing town of **Norwalk**, near the bustling corporate hub of **Stamford**, and in **Danbury**, once the nation's "hat capital." Further inland lie the picturesque, hilly landscapes of the **Housatonic River Valley**.

New Haven

Don't be put off by the initial impression you get when you arrive in grubby **NEW HAVEN**: tucked away among the city's huge factories and architecturally nondescript office blocks are some of the best restaurants, most exciting nightspots, and diverting cultural activities in all of New England – not to mention, of course, the idyllic, leafy Ivy League campus of **Yale University**. The tensions between these two very different communities once made New Haven an uneasy place, though an active symbiosis has thrived since the 1990s, under the Yale presidency of Richard Levin. Residents are encouraged to take advantage of the university's cultural and public offerings, and over half of the student body volunteers in some sort of local outreach program. At the time of writing, the city was undergoing significant **development** in the downtown area, in spite of a December 2007 **fire** that destroyed several businesses on Chapel Street. Under the plan, vacant spaces around George Street will be transformed into new residential, cultural, and commercial spaces; the Long Wharf Theatre and Gateway Community College will also be relocated here.

Some history

Founded in 1638 by a group of wealthy **Puritans**, New Haven began life as an independent colony, the settlers living in relative harmony with the native Quinnipiac Indians. Very early on, the town was laid out in nine "**squares**," which can still be made out in the downtown area's grid pattern. The city formally became part of the Connecticut Colony in 1664, and the state's first university, the Collegiate School (later renamed Yale University after wealthy patron Elihu Yale), established its permanent home here in 1716.

While New Haven's shipping industry flourished thanks to its fine deepwater harbour, it was manufacturing that ultimately led the city forward. During the Revolutionary War, the city produced gunpowder and cannonballs, and soon enough, Yale-educated **Eli Whitney** started manufacturing mass-produced firearms at his factory just outside of town. New Haven also churned out Winchester rifles, musical instruments, tools, carriages, and corsets. In the late 1820s, local entrepreneurs decided to build an eighty-mile canal extending north as far as Northampton, Massachusetts; it later flopped with the advent of the railroad a decade later.

Nevertheless, New Haven continued to progress until the middle of the **twentieth century**, when the problems of unplanned urban growth and increasing economic competition from the suburbs began to take their toll. Millions of federal dollars were pumped into the city for urban renewal, but unemployment continued to grow and, today, with little manufacturing activity left, New Haven trades primarily on its Ivy League cachet.

Arrival, information, and city transport

New Haven lies at the junction of I-91 and I-95. Street **parking** downtown is atrocious, but parking lots are located conveniently around town – rates vary so you may want to look around. On Union Avenue six blocks southeast of the Yale downtown campus, **Union Station** is home to the Greyhound **bus** (☎203/772-2470), the Amtrak **train** terminal (☎1-800/872-7245) and the Metro North Commuter Railroad (☎1-800/638-7646); the latter also runs to the station at State Street. If you arrive at night, grab a **cab** to your hotel to avoid safety concerns. Metro Taxi (☎203/777-7777) has a good reputation. During the daytime, a **shuttle** ($1.25) runs between Union Station and Temple Plaza, across from the *Omni Hotel* (see p.300). **Local public transit** within New Haven and its outlying areas is provided by Connecticut Transit, 470 James St (℡203/624-0151), but on some routes the service deteriorates rapidly after 6pm.

There are two conveniently located **INFO New Haven** offices, one just off the Green at 1000 Chapel St (Mon–Thurs 10am–9pm, Fri & Sat 10am–10pm, Sun noon–5pm; ℡203/773-9494, ⓦ www.infonewhaven.com), and the other at 351 Long Wharf Drive, off I-95 Exit 46 (June–Oct Mon–Tues & Fri–Sun 11am–6pm; ℡203/752-9623). The **Greater New Haven CVB**,

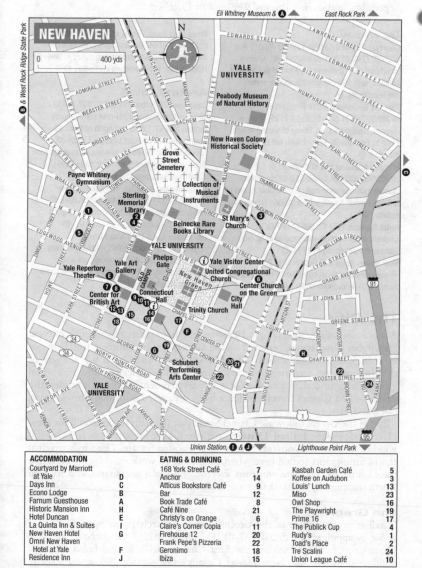

ACCOMMODATION		EATING & DRINKING			
Courtyard by Marriott		168 York Street Café	7	Kasbah Garden Café	5
at Yale	D	Anchor	14	Koffee on Audubon	3
Days Inn	C	Atticus Bookstore Café	9	Louis' Lunch	13
Econo Lodge	B	Bar	12	Miso	23
Farnum Guesthouse	A	Book Trade Café	8	Owl Shop	16
Historic Mansion Inn	H	Café Nine	21	Prime 16	17
Hotel Duncan	E	Christy's on Orange	6	The Playwright	19
La Quinta Inn & Suites	I	Claire's Corner Copia	11	The Publick Cup	4
New Haven Hotel	G	Firehouse 12	20	Rudy's	1
Omni New Haven		Frank Pepe's Pizzeria	22	Toad's Place	2
Hotel at Yale	F	Geronimo	18	Tre Scalini	24
Residence Inn	J	Ibiza	15	Union League Café	10

169 Orange St (Mon–Fri 8.30am–5pm; ℡1-800/332-7829 or 203/777-8550, ⓦwww.newhavencvb.org), also has a helpful staff and publishes a comprehensive **visitors' guide**.

Accommodation

New Haven has surprisingly few **hotels** for a city of its size. Given the shortage of rooms downtown, make sure to book well in advance if you intend to visit around Yale graduation in June, before the beginning of the semester in September, and during Parents' Weekend in October.

Downtown

Courtyard by Marriott at Yale 30 Whalley Ave ℡203/777-6221 or 1-888/522-1186, ⓦwww.courtyard.com. Conveniently located just west of campus, with 168 comfortable rooms; some weekend deals. ⑦

Farnum Guesthouse 616 Prospect St ℡203/562-7121 or 1-888/562-7121, ⓦwww.farnamguesthouse.com. Seven charming rooms close to Yale Divinity School, with full breakfast included. ④

Historic Mansion Inn 600 Chapel St ℡203/865-8324 or 1-888-512-6278, ⓦwww.thehistoricmansioninn.com. Comfortable rooms in a Greek Revival house, with a historic fire sprinkler system. ⑦

Hotel Duncan 1151 Chapel St ℡203/787-1273. Centrally located, good-value rooms in an old-fashioned hotel dating to 1894. ④

New Haven Hotel 229 George St ℡203/498-3100, ⓦwww.newhavenhotel.com. Ninety-two adequate rooms, with renovations under way. ⑥

Omni New Haven Hotel at Yale 155 Temple St ℡203/772-6664, ⓦwww.omnihotels.com. Over three hundred deluxe rooms and suites in New Haven's plushest downtown institution. ⑨

Around town

Days Inn 270 Foxon Blvd ℡203/469-0343, ⓦwww.daysinn.com. Fifth-nine comfy rooms located off I-91, Exit 8, just north of town. ④

Econo Lodge 100 Pond Lily Ave, Exit 59 off Rte-15 ℡203/387-6651, ⓦwww.econolodge.com. Good-value standard rooms four miles from downtown, with seasonal pool. ③

La Quinta Inn & Suites 400 Sargent Drive ℡203/562-1111, ⓦwww.fairfieldinn.com. 152 newly renovated rooms, many overlooking the harbor, at the junction of I-95 and I-91. ⑥

Residence Inn 3 Long Wharf Drive ℡203/777-5337 or 1-800/331-3131, ⓦwww.residenceinn.com. Well-equipped, all-suites Marriott affiliate. Complimentary shuttle to some area attractions. ⑦

The City

A succession of remarkably ugly 1950s-era buildings rather blight much of New Haven, but **downtown**, centered on the **Green**, retains a historic feel. Laid out in 1638 and originally called "**The Marketplace**," the Green was the site of the city's original settlement and also functioned as a meeting area and burial ground. Surrounded by a number of stately government buildings, it borders the student-filled Chapel Street district, a lively area filled with bookstores, shops, cafés, and bars.

East of the Green, following Chapel Street past the train tracks, you'll hit New Haven's close-knit **Italian District**, with well-kept brownstones and colorful window boxes on **Wooster Street** and Wooster Square. The city's original Italian immigrants settled here when they came to work on the railway. While there's little to see, there are some incredibly popular restaurants, and it's well worth stopping by when there's a festival on.

The Green

Standing in the middle of the Green, **Center Church** (tours April–Oct Thurs & Sat by appointment; ℡203/787-0121), built in 1812, is the successor to New Haven's first religious building, the First Church of Christ, and holds a Tiffany window depicting the New Haven Colony's first service. Below the church, a fascinating **crypt** holds tombs dating back to 1687. Close by, fronting Temple Street, the 1816 Gothic Revival **Trinity Episcopal Church** holds more Tiffany windows; and the **United Church**, originally known as **North Church** when it was built in 1813, is based on a design copied from a French book on English architecture. At the northeast corner of the Green is the restored 1861 High-Victorian **City Hall**, overlooking the 1992 **Amistad Memorial**, a three-sided bronze sculpture on the former site of the New Haven jail. The monument was erected in 1992 in memory of the 1839 revolt on the slave ship *Amistad*, during which 53 Africans seized control of the vessel. Intending to sail home, they instead ended up off Long Island, where they were seized by the US Navy and tried as murderers; the ensuing Supreme Court case, during which former president John Quincy Adams acted for the defence, took place in Hartford and New Haven. The tribesmen were ultimately acquitted, and were able to return to Africa in 1842.

Yale University and around

At the opposite end of the Green, Yale University's **Connecticut Hall**, built in 1750 and based on Harvard University's Massachusetts Hall, is the oldest surviving building in New Haven and the only remaining structure from Yale's Old Brick Row. Just outside of Connecticut Hall stands a statue of Revolutionary War hero and Yale grad **Nathan Hale**. A short way down College Street, the 1895 **Phelps Gate**, known as "Yale's front door," allows access to the cobbled courtyards of Yale's **Old Campus**, whose elegant Gothic Revival buildings, many constructed in the late nineteenth century, today serve as freshmen dorms.

While you're free to wander the campus at will, you may want to consider the free hour-long student-led **tours** (Mon–Fri 10.30am & 2pm, Sat & Sun 1.30pm), which set off daily from the **Yale Visitor Information Center** at 149 Elm St, on the north side of the Green (Mon–Fri 9am–4.30pm, Sat & Sun 11am–4pm; ☎203/432-2300, Ⓦwww.yale.edu/visitor), as many of the key sights have restricted access. The tour will take you into the cathedral-like **Sterling Memorial Library**, 120 High St, built in modern Gothic style with leaded glass windows and a fifteenth-century Italian-style mural paying tribute to the exalted privilege of learning. In front of the Library, the **Women's Table**, an ovate granite fountain designed by alum Maya Lin, commemorates the enrollment of women at Yale. Nearby, at 121 Wall St, the **Beinecke Rare Book and Manuscript Library** (currently closed to the public) houses priceless ancient manuscripts, including a 1300-page Gutenberg Bible, behind its translucent Vermont marble walls.

Other buildings of interest include the modernist, Louis Kahn-designed **Yale Center for British Art**, 1080 Chapel St (Tues–Sat 10am–5pm, Sun noon–5pm; free), which prides itself on having the most comprehensive collection of British art outside of the UK, including. portraits by Van Dyck, Gainsborough, and Reynolds, and landscapes by Turner and John Constable. Just opposite, the **Yale University Art Gallery**, 1111 Chapel St (Tues–Sat 10am–5pm, Sun 1–6pm; free), holds the nation's most venerable university art collection. Founded in 1832 with John Trumbull's original donation of a hundred paintings, the collection now has more than 100,000 objects from around the world, dating from ancient Egyptian times to the present. Among the highlights are Vincent Van Gogh's 1888 *Night Café*, and masterpieces by Manet, Monet, Picasso, and Homer.

A short walk just north of the Green, **Hillhouse Avenue**, designed by James Hillhouse in the 1790s and completed by his son in 1837, is a lovely thoroughfare lined with trees and stately old buildings – Charles Dickens proclaimed it the most beautiful street in America. Once the domain of the city's wealthy, much of it is now occupied by Yale's administrative offices. A quirky, eight-hundred-strong

Collection of Musical Instruments, some dating to the sixteenth century, can be seen at no. 15 (Tues–Fri 1–4pm, Sun 1–5pm; closed July & Aug), while steps away stands the Gothic St Mary's Roman Catholic Church, the first such parish in town, where Friar Michael McGivney founded the Knights of Columbus in 1882.

Whitney Avenue

Whitney Avenue leads north from the Green, with several worthy stops along the way. Yale's Peabody Museum of Natural History, 170 Whitney Ave (Mon–Sat 10am–5pm, Sun noon–5pm; $7; ☏203/432-5050, ⓦwww.peabody.yale.edu), is one of the largest museums in New England, easily recognizable by the huge bronze statue of a *Torosaurus latus* out front, named by Yale's first professor of paleontology. Inside, the impressive collection includes a 67-foot Apatosaurus skeleton and some very ancient reptiles. On the same street, at no. 114, the New Haven Colony Historical Society (Tues–Fri 10am–5pm, Sat noon–5pm; $4; ☏203/562-4183, ⓦwww.newhavenmuseum.org), housed in a 1930s Colonial Revival building, traces local history through a series of art displays, industrial artifacts, maps, and genealogical records. One of the galleries is dedicated to the *Amistad* story; you can also see Eli Whitney's original cotton gin and Charles Goodyear's rubber inkwell.

More Whitney-related exhibits can be seen at the Eli Whitney Museum, two miles north at no. 915 (Wed–Fri & Sun noon–5pm, Sat 10am–3pm; $3; ☏203/777-1833, ⓦwww.eliwhitney.org), located in the original gun factory where mass production originated. The museum includes artifacts from the era and an 1816 barn that was once part of Whitney's factory town.

The city outskirts

When you've had enough traipsing around museums and galleries, head for East Rock Park, at the corner of Orange and Cold Springs streets (daily sunrise–sunset; summit drive open April–Nov daily 8am–sunset, Nov–March Fri–Sun 8am–4pm; free; ☏203/946-6086), a 425-acre park named for the huge outcrop of reddish rock that dominates the skyline for miles around. From the rock's 350-foot summit there are spectacular views of New Haven, Long Island Sound, and beyond.

At the extreme southeastern tip of the city, follow Lighthouse Road at Exit 50 off I-95 to Lighthouse Point Park (daily 7am–sunset; parking in summer $10; ☏203/946-8790), an eighty-acre park with a public beach, nature trails, and a restored antique carousel. Nearby, at the end of Woodward Avenue, are the remains of Fort Nathan Hale and Black Rock Fort (summer daily 10am–4pm; free), from the Revolutionary and Civil Wars; both offer spectacular views of New Haven Harbor, though there's not enough left of either to warrant anything more than a quick poke around.

Eating

New Haven offers a rich and eclectic range of restaurants, many of which are located around the Green and on Chapel and College streets, but don't leave without trying the pizza, available at the family-run Italian restaurants in Wooster Square. The intellectual atmosphere of the city also lends itself to a fine downtown café culture.

Cafés

Atticus Bookstore Café 1082 Chapel St ☏203/776-4040. Artisan breads, sandwiches,

scones, and great coffee in a relaxed bookshop.
Book Trader Café 1140 Chapel St ☏203/787-6147. Salads, smoothies, and literary-inspired

sandwiches like "Vonnegut's Veggie" in a gently used bookstore with outdoor courtyard.

Kasbah Garden Café 105 Howe St ☎203/777-5053. Moderately priced Moroccan tagines ($10–12) and couscous dinners ($9–13) in an outdoor garden setting.

Koffee on Audubon 104 Audubon St ☎203/562-5454. Casual hangout favored by the student crowd, serving sandwiches, soups, and espresso drinks of varying potencies.

The Publick Cup 276 York St ☎203/787-9929. Favorite Yalie hangout, offering rightly public-minded Fair Trade coffee and pastries.

Restaurants

Claire's Corner Copia 1000 Chapel St ☎203/562-3888. The local vegetarian enclave for thirty years, with a wide selection of salads and sandwiches, as well as flatbread pizzas, veggie burgers, and a fine breakfast menu.

Frank Pepe's Pizzeria 157 Wooster St ☎203/865-5762. A Wooster St institution since 1925, drawing crowds with its coal-fired pies.

🏃 **Geronimo** 271 Crown St ☎203/777-7700. Inspired Southwestern fare and a range of speciality cocktails and tequilas. Entrees include oven-roasted sea bass and bouillabaisse de Santa Fe ($19).

Ibiza 39 High St ☎203/865-1933. Upscale Spanish restaurant serving traditional specialities accompanied by a fine list of Spanish wines.

Louis' Lunch 261–263 Crown St ☎203/562-5507. Small, dark, ancient burger institution which allegedly served America's first hamburger, c.1900. No ketchup; lunch only.

Miso 15 Orange St ☎203/848-6472. Upscale Japanese place, famed for its sushi.

Tre Scalini 100 Wooster St ☎203/777-3373. Fine Italian dining in an elegant setting. Mon–Fri lunch and dinner, Sat & Sun dinner only.

Union League Café 1032 Chapel St ☎203/562-4299. Expensive French bistro known as one of the finest restaurants around.

Drinking, nightlife, and entertainment

New Haven's rich **cultural scene** is especially strong in **theater**. The Yale Repertory Theater, 1120 Chapel St (☎203/432-1234, ⓦwww.yalerep.org), which boasts many luminaries among its alumni, turns out consistently good shows during term-time. The Shubert Performing Arts Center, 247 College St (☎203/562-5666, ⓦwww.shubert.com), is known for musicals, and offers tours revealing its role in the history of American theater (☎203/624-1825).

As you'd expect with such a large student population, there are plenty of excellent **bars** and **clubs**, mostly concentrated around Chapel and College streets. The *New Haven Advocate*, a free weekly news and arts paper, has detailed **listings** of what's on in and around the city.

168 York Street Café 168 York St ☎203/789-1915. New Haven's oldest gay joint, also serving home-style dinners. Imported beers $2.50.

Anchor 272 College St ☎203/865-1512. Authentic 1950s bar with snug plastic booths, dim lighting, frosted windows, and a jukebox. Cash only.

Bar 254 Crown St ☎203/495-8924. A simple name for a not-so-simple spot that's a combination pizzeria, brewery, bar, and nightclub.

Cafe Nine 250 State St ☎203/789-8281. Intimate club with live music every night, from punk to jazz to R&B. Cover $5–10.

Christy's on Orange 261 Orange St ☎203/777-5454. Authentic Irish pub where the Guinness is always poured right. Also has gourmet dining.

Firehouse 12 45 Crown St ☎203/785-0468. Full-service bar with speciality beers. Also part of a premier recording studio.

Owl Shop 268 College St ☎203/498-2484. Old-world bar and smoke shop, with an extensive list of imported cigars.

The Playwright 144 Temple St ☎203/752-0450. Four bars, ranging from boisterous pub to dance club, in a massive space with reassembled church interiors from Ireland. Live music and DJs Fri & Sat.

Prime 16 172 Temple St ☎203/782-1616. New Temple St hotspot with inventive gourmet burgers and two dozen beers on tap.

Rudy's 372 Elm St ☎203/865-1242. A favorite local dive bar with worn tables, great jukebox, and legendary *frites*. Cash only.

Toad's Place 300 York St ☎203/562-5589, ⓦwww.toadsplace.com. Mid-sized live music venue where Bruce Springsteen and the Stones used to "pop in" to play impromptu gigs. Some shows 21 and over.

Bridgeport

Long the state's leading industrial center, **BRIDGEPORT**, not quite twenty miles southwest from New Haven, suffered greatly during the 1960s and 1970s, a decline still evident in the abandoned factories and boarded-up stores littered throughout the city. In recent years, though, serious efforts have been made to revamp the place, and it merits a visit for the state's only zoo, the wonderful children's **Discovery Museum**, and the **Barnum Museum**, showcasing memorabilia from the life of showman and former Bridgeport mayor P.T. Barnum. A short drive from downtown, **Black Rock** is an affluent residential neighborhood dotted with artists' lofts.

The City

Bridgeport is home to the unique **Barnum Museum**, 820 Main St (Tues–Sat 10am–4.30pm, Sun noon–4.30pm; $7, children ages 4–17 $4; ☎203/331-1104, Ⓦwww.barnum-museum.org), named after the man who changed showbiz forever with his displays of the exotic and the bizarre. The museum houses exhibits on Barnum's life and props from his circus days, including an impressive scale model of a five-ring big top. Also on display are personal objects of the midget General Tom Thumb and the Swedish singer ("Nightingale") Jenny Lind, who helped make Barnum's fortune. A block away on the grounds of Housatonic Community College, the **Housatonic Museum of Art**, 900 Lafayette Blvd (Jan–April & Oct–Dec Mon–Wed & Fri 8.30am–5.30pm, Thurs 8.30am–7pm; Sept–May also Sat 9am–3pm, Sun noon–4pm; free; ☎203/332-5203), has a superb collection of works by a dozen major twentieth-century artists, including Picasso and Matisse, as well as new local creations.

A little way out of the city center, the **Discovery Museum**, 4450 Park Ave (Tues–Sat 10am–5pm, Sun noon–5pm; $8.50, children $7; ☎203/372-3521, Ⓦwww.discoverymuseum.org), is an interactive science and technology museum with a planetarium and more than a hundred engaging exhibits on topics like electricity, nuclear energy, and the science of color. Best of all, perhaps, is the Challenger Learning Center, honoring the memory of the ill-fated *Challenger* space shuttle crew. Another top-drawer destination for kids, the 52-acre **Beardsley Zoological Gardens**, 1875 Noble Ave (daily 9am–4pm; $11, children ages 3–11 $9; Ⓦwww.beardsleyzoo.org), is home to everything from North American mammals (the Canadian lynx, bison) to exotic species from South America. There's also a farmyard-like children's zoo and a splendid working carousel (open seasonally) on the grounds.

Practicalities

Bridgeport is served by both Amtrak and Metro-North **trains**, which run to the station at 525 Water St (☎1-800/872-7245). The Greater Bridgeport Transit Authority (GBTA) operates buses in Bridgeport as well as neighboring Stratford (☎203/333-3031). Leaving from the ferry dock at 330 Water St is a **car ferry** service to Port Jefferson, NY (hourly 6am–9pm; 1hr 15min; $17 one-way, $51 with car; ☎631/473-0286 or 1-888/443-3779, Ⓦwww.bpjferry.com).

Bridgeport area **accommodation** is rather minimal. The *Holiday Inn*, 1070 Main St (☎203/334-1234, Ⓦwww.hibridgeport.com; Ⓞ) is the only major downtown hotel, while the *Ramada Inn* at 225 Lordship Blvd in nearby Stratford (☎203/375-8866; Ⓞ) has an indoor pool. There's no shortage of **places to eat** in the area, however. *Ralph 'n' Rich's*, 121 Wall St (☎203/366-3597; closed Sun), is a downtown institution serving upscale Italian food, while *Tuscany*, 1084 Madison Ave (T 203/366-3597), is another excellent Mediterranean option set in a rather depressed neighborhood. In Black Rock, the *Bloodroot*, 85 Ferris St (T 203/576-9168), is a legendary feminist vegetarian restaurant founded in the 1970s. Over in Stratford, try the prime rib at the pricey *Augustyn's Blue Goose*, 326 Ferry Blvd (T 203/375-9130; closed Mon), or seafood at the more relaxed *Off the Wall*, 14 Beach Drive (T 203/375-7805), in a pleasant setting overlooking Long Island Sound.

Westport and around

Roughly halfway between the urban sprawls of Stamford and Bridgeport, **WESTPORT** is an entirely different world: the country refuge of the New York art circle in the early decades of the last century, the town continues to exude both sophistication and rustic charm. Downtown, Main Street is lined with designer boutiques and upscale galleries, while the prestigious **Westport Country Playhouse**, 25 Powers Court (T 203/227-4177, W www.westportplayhouse.org), is one of the oldest repertory theaters in the country. When stars like Gene Kelly and Henry Fonda first strutted their stuff here, the playhouse was little more than a rural barn, but in 2005 it reopened after a massive renovation and is now more than comfortable while retaining its rustic charm. For mementos of town history, visit the 1795 **Wheeler House**, home of the **Westport Historical Society**, 25 Avery Place (Mon–Fri 10am–4pm, Sat–Sun noon–4pm; T 203/222-1424), which has several beautifully restored Victorian rooms and an octagonal cobblestone barn. Two miles south, historic **Compo Beach** – where the local militia valiantly fired at encroaching British troops during the Revolutionary War – and **Sherwood Island State Park**, Sherwood Connector Road, I-95 Exit 18 (sunrise–sunset; May–Sept $10–15; T 203/226-6983), offer a different sort of respite along generous stretches of grass, sky, and sandy shoreline.

Practicalities

If you fancy a splurge, *The Inn at National Hall*, 2 Post Rd W (T 1-800/628-4255, W www.innatnationalhall.com; ⑨), steps away from downtown, offer luxurious rooms and suites overlooking the Saugatuck River. A less pricey alternative is the *Westport Inn*, 1595 Post Rd E (T 203/259-5236 or 1-800/446-8997, W www .westportinn.com; ⑦), a bit further out, with 105 agreeable units, lounge, gym, and indoor pool. There are some fine **restaurants** in downtown Westport, among them *Sakura*, 680 Post Rd E (T 203/222-0802), serving relatively inexpensive sushi and made-in-front-of-you hibachi meals, and the Mediterranean restaurant *Acqua*, 43 Main St (T 203/222-8899), where excellent seafood is the speciality and the soufflés are superb (entrees $16–38).

Weston and Wilton

A few miles inland from Westport, in the town of **WESTON**, the 1800-acre **Devil's Den Preserve**, 33 Pent Rd (dawn–dusk; free; T 203/226-4991), is so named for the strange hoof-like rock formations that charcoal-makers who once worked here believed were the footprints of the Devil. A favourite haunt of hikers and cross-country skiers, the nature conservancy also sports rare plant species such as the hog peanut and Indian cucumber root.

In nearby **WILTON**, don't miss the **Weir Farm National Historic Site**, 735 Nod Hill Rd (grounds open daily dawn–dusk; visitors' center May–Oct

Wed–Sun 9am–5pm; Nov–April Thurs–Sun 10am–4pm; free; ℗203/834–1896, ⓦwww.nps.gov/wefa), once home of prominent Impressionist **J. Alden Weir**, who acquired the 153-acre site in 1882 in exchange for a painting (not one of his own) and a measly $6; the wooded hills and meandering paths have also drawn the likes of John Singer Sargent and the informal art colony known as the "Ten American Painters." **Weir House** and the adjacent studios are accessible to the public through tours, while the adjacent **Weir Preserve**, with trails on 110 acres of woodland, makes for some nice day hikes. Combine a visit to Weir Farm with a tour around the **Wilton Heritage Museum**, 224 Danbury Rd (Mon–Thurs 10am–4.30pm, Sun 1–4pm; $5 donation; ℗203/762–7257), showcasing fourteen period rooms and a red-ware collection in two eighteenth-century center-chimney farmhouses, along with a working blacksmith's shop and an enchanting attic full of dollhouses and period toys.

Norwalk

A few miles west of Wesport, salt-water cool meets beat charm in **NORWALK**, whose maritime connections trace back to the eighteenth century, when it was home to a flourishing oyster-fishing industry and the prolific Silvermine River mills. Later a commercial town thriving on the manufacture of shoes, earthenware, candles, and ships, Norwalk retains a quaint charm in its brick factory buildings and waterfront railroad tracks. With its superb restaurants, bars, galleries, and museums, and with a growing number of company headquarters and the recent revamping of downtown **South Norwalk**, affectionately known as "**SoNo**," Norwalk ranks among the most happening towns along this stretch of the coast.

The Town

SoNo's chief attraction is its **Maritime Aquarium**, 10 N Water St (daily: July & Aug 10am–6pm; Sept–June 10am–5pm; $11.75; ℗203/852–0700, ⓦwww .maritimeaquarium.org), which presents the varied marine life of Long Island Sound. Residents include harbor seals, river otters, loggerhead sea turtles, and more than a hundred other species of indigenous marine life – watch out for the 110,000-gallon shark tank. You can even take a 2.5-hour boat study **cruise** ($20.50) out into the Sound to get a firsthand look at the catch of the day (reservations ℗203/852–0700 ext 2206). A boat ride of a different sort is available from the adjacent Seaport Dock out to the 1868 **Sheffield Island Lighthouse**, which warned boats off the Norwalk Islands until 1902. On a clear day, the New York City skyline is visible from the island (June to early Sept; $20; call for schedule ℗203/838–9444).

Back on land, head to the Second Empire-style **Lockwood-Mathews Mansion Museum**, 295 West Ave (mid-March to Dec Wed–Sun noon–4pm; $10; ℗203/838–9799, ⓦwww.lockwoodmathewsmansion.org), the 1864 home of insurance and railway giant LeGrand Lockwood. While the impressive house predates more opulent creations of the Gilded Age, technologically it was ahead of its time, with telephones, modern baths, and even a burglar alarm system, observable through the staff-like lines threading the mansion floor. Down the street, the **Stepping Stones Museum for Children**, 303 West Ave (Tues 1–5pm, Wed–Sun 10am–5pm; $9; ℗203/899–0606), with kinetic sculptures and a hands-on water gallery, is a must-visit for families. History buffs can opt for the **Norwalk Museum**, 41 N Main St (Wed–Sun 1–5pm; free; ℗203/866–0202), where the city's retail and manufacturing history is presented via rotating exhibits and a series of mock storefronts, or **Norwalk City Hall**, 125 East Ave (Mon–Fri 8.30am–4.30pm), displaying a rare collection of brightly colored WPA murals commissioned during the mid-1930s.

Practicalities

Norwalk is served by Metro-North **trains**, which stop at both the South Norwalk station, 1 Chestnut St, and the East Norwalk station, 1 Winfield St.

Pleasant **accommodation**, of a refined Yankee sort, is available at the *Silvermine Tavern*, 194 Perry Ave (℡203/847-4558 or 1-888/693-9967, ⓦwww .silverminetavern.com; ◔), which boasts ten delightful rooms and one suite in a nineteenth-century Colonial-style building next to a waterfall, along with a restaurant famous for its Sunday brunch buffet and honey buns. On weekend nights, it also hosts live jazz. Budget options abound on Westport Avenue, including the *Garden Park Motel*, no. 351 (℡203/847-7303; ◔), though for comfort and convenience you might consider the *Norwalk Inn*, 99 East Ave (℡203/838-2000, ⓦwww .norwalkinn.com, ◔), with 71 rooms and outdoor pool. You can **camp** on two of the Norwalk Islands, accessible by kayak or canoe – the Norwalk Recreation & Parks Department (℡203/854-7806) can provide more information.

SoNo features a variety of good **dining** and **nightlife** options along Main and Washington streets. *Habana*, 70 N Main St (℡203/852-9790; dinner only), serves unique Cuban dishes with decor and laid-back attitude to match. *The Brewhouse*, 18 Marshall St (℡203/853-9110), boasts gourmet burgers and more than fifty beers. Across the river, *Harbor Lights*, 82 Seaview Ave (℡203/866-3364), offers good-value waterfront dining, serving seafood with a Greek touch (entrees $22–32). Norwalk is also home to one of three Stew Leonard's, 100 Westport Ave (℡203/847-7213, ⓦwww.stewleonards.com), a marvel of a supermarket with not only fresh food (and free samples), but also animatronic displays and a tiny zoo. For more options, the **Coastal Fairfield County Convention & Visitors Bureau**, 297 West Ave (daily 9am–5pm; ℡203/853-7770 or 1-800/866-7925, ⓦwww.coastalct.com), is a great source of information.

Stamford

STAMFORD, with a population of over 110,000 and some massive downtown office buildings, has a definite corporate vibe. The upswing in the local economy in the last few years – several Fortune 500 companies have set up here, attracted by taxes lower than in nearby New York City – has contributed to a refurbished downtown, near I-95, though the city's gems are arguably further out.

The 1958 **First Presbyterian Church**, 1101 Bedford St (Mon–Fri 9am–5pm; free; ℡203/324-9522), designed by architect Wallace K. Harrison, is worth a visit for its fish-shaped sanctuary (a symbolic reference to Christianity) faceted with 20,000 pieces of stained glass; the modern carillon tower looms close by. In North Stamford, the **Stamford Museum & Nature Center**, 39 Scofieldtown Rd (Mon–Sat 9am–5pm, Sun 11am–5pm; $8; ℡203/322-1646, ⓦwww .stamfordmuseum.org), once the home of New York clothier Henri Bendel, now houses a farm, observatory, and museum. Nearby, the **Bartlett Arboretum & Gardens**, 151 Brookdale Rd (grounds open daily 8.30am–sunset; visitors' center open Mon–Fri 8.30am–4.30pm; $6, Wed free; ℡203/322-6971, ⓦwww .bartlettarboretum.org), is known for its formal gardens and collection of trees, and maintains walking trails on 91 acres of woodland, wetland, and meadow. On the border with Greenwich, **Mianus River State Park**, Merriebrook Lane (open daily dawn–dusk; ☎203/977-4688), has more varied terrain for hiking and biking. A ten-minute drive south from downtown, **Cove Island Park**, on Cove Road (open daily sunrise–sunset; parking for city residents only), is a grassy expanse overlooking Long Island Sound, with two small beaches and a salt marsh.

Downtown, the **Avon Theater**, 272 Bedford St (☎203/967-3660, ⓦwww .avontheater.org), in a renovated 1939 Neo-Colonial building, specializes in independent films, while the **Stamford Center for the Arts** (☎203/325-4466, ⓦscalive.org) maintains two fine theaters on Atlantic Street (the Palace Theatre, at no. 61, and the Rich Forum, at no. 307), both of which regularly host big names in entertainment.

Practicalities

Stamford is served by both Amtrak and Metro-North **trains**, as well as by Greyhound buses (☎203/327-7622), which all run to the terminal at Washington Boulevard and South State Street. CT Transit runs a network of **local buses** in the area, many of which leave from the train station.

Geared primarily to business travelers, Stamford's large chain **hotels** offer significant weekend discounts. Good choices are the *Courtyard by Marriott*, 275 Summer St (☎203/358-8822, ⓦwww.marriott.com; ❸), with spa and indoor pool, and the *Holiday Inn*, 700 E Main St (☎203/358-8400, ⓦwww.holidayinn .com; ❸). In nearby New Canaan, the *Roger Sherman Inn*, 195 Oenoke Ridge (☎203/966-4541, ⓦwww.rogershermaninn.com; ❼), offers well-appointed rooms in a more idyllic setting.

Stamford has a number of excellent **restaurants**, among them the organic-minded *Napa & Co*, 75 Broad St (☎203/353-3319), serving an eclectic new American menu with an outstanding wine selection in a classy setting. More casual *Brasitas*, 954 E Main St (☎203/353-3319), is famed for inspired Latin dishes like grilled monkfish in mango curry sauce. North on High Ridge Road, at no. 926, modest *Layla's Falafel* (☎203/461-8004) serves inexpensive, surprisingly authentic Lebanese fare.

Greenwich

GREENWICH, south of Stamford on Rte-1, has a much more well-heeled feel. Indeed, once a sleepy farming community, today Greenwich counts a host of media celebrities and CEOs among its residents and is ranked among the wealthiest towns in the nation. The main thoroughfare, walkable **Greenwich Avenue**, is lined with fine shops, boutiques, and restaurants, while the town's prized shoreline along Long Island Sound is home to private estates and luxurious marinas, which you can appreciate from the water via a number of ferries and boat tours.

Best known for its affluence, Greenwich also has a few cultural attractions, including the **Bruce Museum**, 1 Museum Drive (Tues–Sat 10am–5pm, Sun 1–5pm; $7, Tues free; ☎203/869-0376, ⓦwww.brucemuseum.org), set in the 1853 home of New York textile merchant Robert Bruce. The museum houses small, well-curated exhibits about everything from art to science, along with a permanent earth science wing that will delight both kids and taxidermists. Further from downtown, the shingle-sided 1690 **Putnam Cottage**, 243 E

Putnam Ave (Jan–March by appointment only; April–Dec Sun 1–4pm and by appointment; $6; ☎203/869-9697, ⓦwww.putnamcottage.org), has a bit of romantic history to it: legend has it that one day in 1779, local patriot General Israel Putnam, a regular at the tavern, was busy shaving when he noticed advancing British troops in his mirror. He jumped on a horse and managed to escape down a steep cliff, returning later with reinforcements to rout the enemy. The cottage contains original fieldstone fireplaces and some fine antique furniture. Also worth a visit is the **Bush-Holley Historic Site**, 39 Strickland Rd (Jan & Feb Sat & Sun noon–4pm; March–Dec Tues–Sun noon–4pm; $6, Tues free; ☎203/869-6899, ⓦwww.hstg.org), a two-story ivory clapboard building turned into a boarding house by the Holley family in the late 1800s. Like the Griswold home in Old Lyme (see p.294), the Holley residence attracted many artists, among them Childe Hassam and J. Alden Weir, some of whose original works hang today in the house.

In the laid-back neighbourhood of Old Greenwich, a mile or two east of downtown on the other side of Cos Cob Harbor, restaurants and shops form a lively stretch along **Sound Beach Avenue**, leading to Shore Road, where, at its very tip, the grassy peninsula at **Greenwich Point Park** (open daily 6am–sunset; parking for residents only) offers unparalleled views of Long Island Sound. In the summer, **ferries** depart from Roger Sherman Baldwin Park in central Greenwich (☎203/622-7814) to neighboring Great Captain's Island and Island Beach ($3), as well as around the harbor ($7). For something fancier, Fjord Fisheries, 143 River Rd (☎203/622-4020), offers weekend dinner cruises.

Practicalities

The closest Amtrak station is in Stamford, but you can easily catch a connection to Greenwich on Metro-North trains. In Greenwich, the main station is near downtown between Arch Street and Greenwich Avenue, at 1 Railroad Ave.

Accommodation in Greenwich tends to be of a refined sort. At the high end is the *Homestead Inn*, 420 Field Point Rd (☎203/869-7500, ⓦwww.homesteadinn .com; ❾), with eighteen elegant rooms in a 1799 mansion and an excellent restaurant overlooking the grounds. Close to the water in Old Greenwich, the more modest *Harbor House Inn B&B*, 165 Shore Rd (☎203/637-0145, ⓦwww .hhinn.com; ❽), offers twenty-three rooms and options for longer-term stays. The *Cos Cob Inn*, 50 River Rd (☎203/661-5845, ⓦwww.coscobinn.com; ❻), also on the water but with a view somewhat dominated by the I-95 bridge, has twelve rooms in a 1870s Federal-style house, with access to the Greenwich Water Club.

You're spoiled for choice in Greenwich as far as **eating** is concerned – though, not surprisingly in such an affluent place, restaurants can be pricey. French cuisine seems to dominate the scene; if you're up for a splurge, try *Thomas Henkelmann* at the *Homestead Inn*, 420 Field Point Rd (☎203/869-7500), where you can savor entrees like grenadin of veal with a Maine lobster risotto and port wine sauce in a charming setting overlooking the garden. At *L'Escale*, 500 Steamboat Rd, in the luxury hotel *Delamar Greenwich Harbor* (☎203/661-9800; ❾), dine in style while gazing at the posh yachts in Greenwich Harbor. Less expensive options include *Thataway*, 409 Greenwich Ave (☎203/622-0947), serving excellent burgers, pastas, and sandwiches as well as some heavier fare, in a laid-back, pubby atmosphere. *Meli-Melo*, 362 Greenwich Ave (☎203/422-5001), is a cozy café serving savory crêpes. For dessert, try *Versailles*, 315 Greenwich Ave (☎203/661-6634), something of a local institution, known for its heavenly cakes and tarts.

Danbury and the Housatonic Valley

The manufacturing town of **DANBURY**, 25 miles north of Norwalk on Rte-7, was once famous as the "hat capital" of America, with more than three dozen factories engaged in hat-making at one point. When that industry declined in the 1960s and 1970s, Danbury's savior became **Union Carbide**, whose headquarters are still located here. There's not much of interest in the city, but for a break from all the historic houses, the **Military Museum of Southern New England**, 125 Park Ave, I-84 Exit 3 (Tues–Sat 10am–5pm, Sun 1–5pm; $6; ☎203/790-9277, Ⓦwww.usmilitarymuseum.org), contains enough life-size dioramas of World War II scenes to sate any military buff. There's also a 1917 Renault, the first tank ever made in the US, and an original self-propelled howitzer. Danbury's other main visitor attraction is the **Railway Museum**, 120 White St (Nov–March Wed–Sat 10am–4pm, Sun noon–4pm; April–Oct Tues–Sat 10am–5pm, Sun noon–5pm; $6; ☎203/778-8337), with a station and a six-acre railroad yard where you can take a ride on a number of vintage trains ($3–10).

Picturesque **RIDGEFIELD**, about ten miles south of Danbury, seems like an extension of the Litchfield Hills (see p.321), with a main street lined by charming historic houses. If you make it here, check out the **Keeler Tavern Museum**, 132 Main St (Feb–Dec Wed, Sat & Sun 1–4pm; $5; ☎203/438-5485), open to the public through 45-minute tours led by guides in period costume. A popular watering hole even before the Revolutionary War, the tavern was a hotbed of patriotic fervor after it was hit by British artillery fervor. The offending cannonball is still embedded in the building. Down the street, the **Aldrich Contemporary Art Museum**, 258 Main St (Tues–Sun noon–5pm; $7, free Tues; ☎203/438-4519, Ⓦwww.aldrichart.org), opened in 1964, was one of the first museums in America devoted to contemporary art. Its twelve galleries feature superb rotating exhibitions; there's also a lovely sculpture garden out back.

Outside Danbury and Ridgefield, the **Housatonic Valley** offers a few natural attractions. The **Saugatuck Reservoir**, near Redding, bordering Devil's Den Preserve (see p.305), is so peaceful and undeveloped you'd swear you were in northern Maine, while **Huntington State Park** (☎203/938-2285) is prime mountain-biking territory, with well-maintained trails by ponds and woodland. For avid hikers, in Newtown, east of Danbury, you can walk along the banks of the Housatonic River in the **Paugussett State Forest**.

Practicalities

Danbury is served by **trains** on the Metro-North Danbury line, which runs between Danbury and New York City, with connections in Stamford. The station is downtown at 1 Patriot Drive. The Housatonic Area Regional Transit operates **local buses** in the greater Danbury area (☎203/744-4070).

Danbury's *Ethan Allen Hotel*, Exit 4 off I-84, 21 Lake Ave Extension (☎203/744-1776 or 1-800/742-1776, Ⓦwww.ethanallenhotel.com; ❻), is a large, modern hotel with spacious rooms full of authentic Ethan Allen furniture. Slightly more idyllic is Ridgefield's *Stonehenge Inn*, Rte-7, Stonehenge Road (☎203/438-6511, Ⓦwww.stonehengeinn-ct.com; ❻), an 1827 Colonial inn by garden and pond. Also in Ridgefield, the *West Lane Inn*, 22 West Lane (☎203/438-7323, Ⓦwww.westlaneinn.com; ❼), has eighteen antique-stuffed rooms.

For something to **eat**, try *Ondine,* 69 Pembroke Rd, Danbury (☎203/746-4900; Wed–Sat dinner, Sun brunch & dinner), for superb contemporary French cuisine, similarly found at pricier *Bernard's*, 20 West Lane (☎203/438-8282), in Ridgefield. By contrast, *Rosy Tomorrows*, in Danbury at 15 Old Mill Plain Rd

(☎ 203/743-5845), is a local institution serving generous portions of American staples like barbecued ribs; there are also good veggie options.

The Connecticut River Valley

The **Connecticut River**, New England's largest, starts in the mountains of New Hampshire close to the Canadian border and runs all the way down to Long Island Sound. In the state of Connecticut it's lined for the most part with peaceful towns, the main exception being **Hartford**, the depressed state capital. A mile west of the city, Nook Farm was home to Mark Twain and Harriet Beecher Stowe, while Noah Webster published the first American English dictionary in 1806 in the now suburban town of **West Hartford**. Farther west, gentle country-side leads to the pleasant town of **Farmington** and the less idyllic but stimulating industrial city of **New Britain**, known for its hardware companies, art museum, and minor league baseball.

South of Hartford, the Connecticut River wends its way past **Wethersfield**, where Washington planned the final stages of the Revolutionary War; **Rocky Hill**, whose 185-million-year-old dinosaur tracks can be seen in Dinosaur State Park; and **East Haddam**, site of the Goodspeed Opera House and the unusual hilltop Gillette Castle, one of the state's leading peculiarities. **Ivoryton**, famed for its summer theater, and quaint **Essex**, with a range of old-fashioned diversions, complete the picture near the river delta.

Hartford

Among the nation's oldest cities, **HARTFORD** is today a place of contrasts, with some beautiful old architecture lying amid urban neighborhoods that are often grim. Indeed, the city that Mark Twain once described as "the best built and handsomest … I have ever seen" is today hardly recognizable as such, better known instead as the insurance center of America and home to a hodgepodge of nondescript office buildings and multistory parking garages. Despite being the capital of Connecticut, the city will probably not take you more than a day or so to explore – though the longer you stay, the more unexpected charms you are likely to find. Among the landmarks here are the 1878 **State Capitol**, with its golden dome and verdant grounds overlooking Bushnell Park; the historic, leafy greens of **Elizabeth Park** and **Trinity College**; and the **Wadsworth Atheneum**, which boasts the nation's oldest continuously operating public museum.

Some history
Originally known by the Indian name of *Suckiaug* ("black earth"), Hartford was dubbed "House of Good Hope" by Dutch merchants who established a trading post here in 1633. The Hartford colony was established a few years later by Puritan settlers from Massachusetts, who called it Newtown, then renamed it Hartford after the town of Hertford, England. The colonists' leader, the Reverend Thomas Hooker, declared that governmental authority lay "in the free consent

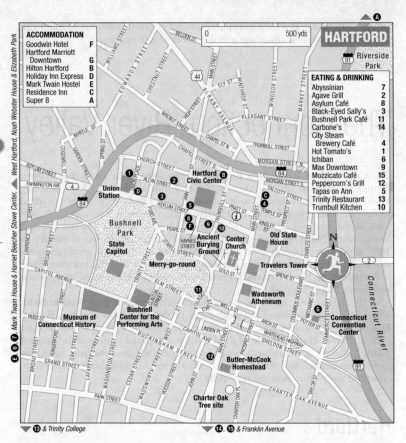

ACCOMMODATION
Goodwin Hotel	F
Hartford Marriott	
Downtown	G
Hilton Hartford	B
Holiday Inn Express	D
Mark Twain Hostel	E
Residence Inn	C
Super 8	A

EATING & DRINKING
Abyssinian	7
Agave Grill	2
Asylum Café	8
Black-Eyed Sally's	3
Bushnell Park Café	11
Carbone's	14
City Steam	
Brewery Café	4
Hot Tomato's	1
Ichiban	6
Max Downtown	9
Mozzicato Café	15
Peppercorn's Grill	12
Tapas on Ann	5
Trinity Restaurant	13
Trumbull Kitchen	10

▼ ⑬ & Trinity College   ▼ ⑭, ⑮ & Franklin Avenue

of the people," and helped to establish the Fundamental Orders of Connecticut in 1639. The first written constitution in the country, this would later serve as inspiration for the US Constitution.

Hartford became a **manufacturing** hub in the next centuries, with the Hartford Woolen Company being the first in the country to devote itself to producing woolen cloth; other goods made locally included Colt revolvers, Sharps rifles, and the Pope motor car. The pioneering city was also the first in the nation to be lit by **electricity**. With the formation of the Hartford Fire Insurance Company in 1810, Hartford gradually established itself as the nation's **insurance** capital, and some fifty companies had set up shop here by the mid-twentieth century. In the last decades, though, the city has taken a downturn, particularly after September 11, 2001, and today it struggles to balance a host of urban problems with some major development, such as the brand new **Connecticut Convention Center** downtown, and the $150 million Connecticut Science Center, due to open in spring 2009.

Arrival, information, and city transport

Hartford lies at the junction of I-91 and I-84, and so is easily accessible by **car**. The city is also well served by Amtrak **trains** (☎1-800/USA-RAIL) and long-distance buses like Greyhound (☎860/231-2222) and Peter Pan (☎860/237-8747) – all pull into the **Union Station terminal** (☎860/247-5329) downtown. Connecticut Transit (☎860/525-9181, ⓦwww.cttransit.com; $1.25) maintains an extensive bus route serving the greater Hartford area. Just twelve miles north of town lies Connecticut's main **airport**, Bradley International Airport (☎860/292-2000, ⓦwww.bradleyairport.com), served by a CT Transit **shuttle** to the Old State House in downtown Hartford. **Taxis** are available outside; otherwise, reliable companies include Yellow Cabs (☎860/666-6666).

Downtown Hartford is "patrolled" by the **Hartford Guides** (☎860/522-0855), who can help with directions and information, while the Hartford Star shuttle loops around major tourist destinations, with frequent services and stops (Mon–Fri 7am–11pm, Sat 3–11pm; free; ⓦwww.ctconventions.com/visitors/star_shuttle .php). For more local info, the **Greater Hartford Welcome Center**, 45 Pratt St (Mon–Fri 9am–5pm; ☎860/244-0253, ⓦwww.hartford.com), has a helpful staff.

Accommodation

Hartford has a limited range of **accommodation** options, with only a handful of downtown hotels catering mainly to business travelers. For more charming stays, you might consider the nearby towns of Farmington (see p.317) or Wethersfield (see p.318), both within ten miles of the city.

Goodwin Hotel Goodwin Square, 1 Haynes St ☎860/246-7500 or 1-800/922-5006, ⓦwww.goodwinhotel.com. Luxurious downtown hotel opposite the Civic Center, with 124 plush rooms. ⑧

Hartford Marriott Downtown 200 Columbus Blvd ☎860/249-8000 or 1-800/228-9290, ⓦwww .marriott.com. Connected to the new Convention Center, with 401 rooms, gym, and spa. ⑨

Hilton Hartford 315 Trumbull St ☎860/728-5151 or 1-800/HILTONS, ⓦwww.hilton.com. A swanky spot connected to the Civic Center, with 24hr gym, indoor pool, and sauna. ⑧

Holiday Inn Express 440 Asylum St ☎860/246-9900, ⓦwww.hiexpress.com.

Ninety-six good-value rooms conveniently located across from Bushnell Park and close to the train station. ⑥–⑧

Mark Twain Hostel 131 Tremont St ☎860/523-7255. 30 or so beds in an old house near West Hartford, just off Farmington Ave. Dorm beds $28; private rooms with shared bath $45–60. HI member hostel.

Residence Inn 942 Main St ☎860/524-5550, ⓦwww.residenceinn.com. 120 well-furnished, spacious downtown suites. ⑧

Super 8 I-91 Exit 33 ☎860/246-8888 or 1-800/800-8000, ⓦwww.super8.com. Budget motel with inexpensive, clean rooms, conveniently located a half-mile from downtown. ⑨

The City

Bleak insurance towers dominate downtown Hartford's skyline, but it's otherwise a surprisingly open city. The lawns and plantings of **Bushnell Park**, designed in 1861 by Swiss-born architect Jacob Weidenmann, surround the golden-domed **State Capitol** (tours hourly Mon–Fri 9.15am–1.15pm, July & Aug additional tour at 2.15pm; also April–Oct Sat 10.15am–2.15pm; 1hr; free), an 1878 mixture of Gothic, Classical, and Second Empire styles. Its ornate exterior, stained-glass windows, and lofty ceilings make it look more like a church than a place of politics. Besides the usual bits of history, the tour takes you past the public galleries of the General Assembly, from where you can view the state legislative bodies when they're in session. After you've had a look around, take a ride on the 1914 antique wooden **carousel** in the park (mid-May to Oct Tues–Sun 11am–5pm; $1). Across the road in the Connecticut State Library, 231 Capitol Ave, the **Museum of Connecticut History** (Mon–Fri 9am–4pm, Sat 9am–3pm; free; ☎860/757-6535) holds an impressive collection of Colt firearms, a selection of early American coins of early American coins, and the original 1662 Connecticut Royal Charter.

Main Street

Many of Hartford's most important buildings are on **Main Street**, starting with the yellow clapboard **Butler-McCook House & Garden**, no. 396 (Wed–Sat 10am–4pm, Sun 1–4pm; $7 tours only; ℗860/522-1806), which was home to the same family for 189 years. A small gallery documents the city's history from 1750 on through their eyes; other highlights include a collection of Japanese armor acquired by a globetrotting family member, and behind the house, one of the oldest domestic gardens in the US.

Hartford's pride and joy is the Greek Revival **Wadsworth Atheneum Museum of Art**, 600 Main St (Wed–Fri 11am–5pm, Sat & Sun 10am–5pm; $10; ℗860/278-2670, Ⓦwww.wadsworthatheneum.org), founded by Daniel Wadsworth in 1842 and the nation's oldest continuously operating public art museum. The world-class collection includes a distinguished assembly of American paintings and sculpture; Renaissance and Baroque masterpieces; an extensive array of costumes, furniture, and decorative items; and a number of significant contemporary pieces.

A few hundred yards north at 1 Tower Square, the 527-foot-high **Travelers Tower**, home of the Travelers Insurance Company since 1919, can be ascended for spectacular views of the city and beyond from an open-air **observation deck**; it'll take some effort, though – after the 24-floor elevator ride, you'll need to climb seventy steps up a spiral staircase (weekdays May–Oct; free; reservations requested ℗860/277-4208). Across Main Street at no. 675, the elegant **Center Church** was established by the Reverend Thomas Hooker and modeled after London's St Martin-in-the-Fields in Trafalgar Square, with no fewer than five Tiffany windows and a barrel-vaulted ceiling. It overlooks the tranquil 1640 **Ancient Burying Ground** (April–Dec Mon–Fri 8.30am–4.30pm, Sat 9am–5pm; free; ℗860/228-1717), Hartford's oldest historical landmark and the final resting-place for many of the city's first settlers.

At no. 800, the 1796 Federal-style **Old State House** (Tues–Fri 11am–5pm, Sat 10am–5pm; $6; ℗860/522-6766, Ⓦwww.ctosh.org) was the first public commission of architect Charles Bulfinch (see box, p.90). The restored early nineteenth-century ornamental iron fencing and gaslights make it particularly atmospheric against the surrounding office buildings. Inside, the Court Room, which witnessed the *Amistad* trials, among others, has been restored to its 1920 appearance, while the **Museum of Natural and Other Curiosities**, on the second floor, has a collection of exotic and bizarre items, including a two-headed calf.

Trinity College

South of downtown, at 300 Summit St, the beautiful campus of **Trinity College** is located on a hundred acres at the highest point in the city. Founded in 1823, the college boasts a stunning array of Victorian Gothic architecture, particularly on the main square, known as the Long Walk. The most striking building is the college **chapel**, claimed by some to be the best example of Victorian Gothic in the nation. Regular organ and chamber concerts are held here, while across the green, the college's Cinestudio (℗860/297-CINE) hosts nightly public showings of independent and classic movies. For details on events at the college, call ℗860/297-2001.

Mark Twain House and Harriet Beecher Stowe Center

A mile west of downtown on Rte-4, a hilltop community known as Nook Farm was home in the 1880s to next-door neighbors **Mark Twain** and

▲ Mark Twain House

Harriet Beecher Stowe. Today, their Victorian homes, furnished much as they were then, are open for guided tours. The bizarrely ornate **Mark Twain House and Museum**, 351 Farmington Ave (April–Dec Mon–Sat 9.30am–5.30pm, Sun noon–5.30pm; rest of year same hours, closed Tues; $14; ☎860/247-0998, Ⓦwww.marktwainhouse.org), which the author (real name: Samuel Clemens) built in 1874 and inhabited till 1891, was where he wrote many of his classic works, including *Huckleberry Finn*. It's easy to see how the author spent his royalties: the place is decked with black-and-orange brickwork, elaborate woodwork, and the only domestic Tiffany interior open to the public. Next door, the much less flamboyant **Harriet Beecher Stowe Center**, 77 Forest St (May–Oct Mon–Sat 9.30am–4.30pm, Sun noon–4.30pm; rest of year same hours, closed Mon; $8; ☎860/522-9258, Ⓦwww.harrietbeecherstowecenter .org), celebrates the author of *Uncle Tom's Cabin*, one of the most important American literary works of the nineteenth century for its staunch anti-slavery perspective. The white Victorian Gothic home is a fine example of the nineteenth-century "cottage" style with a hint of the romantic villa, and you can see Stowe's writing table and some of her paintings inside the house.

West Hartford

Farmington Avenue, a long strip of diners, restaurants, and shops, heads out of the capital to **WEST HARTFORD** and the **Noah Webster House**, 227 S Main St (Thurs–Mon 1–4pm; $6; ☎860/521-5362), an eighteenth-century farmhouse that was home to the compiler of the pioneering *American Dictionary*, first published in 1828. Closer to town, north of Farmington Avenue, Prospect Avenue is lined with stately historic mansions still owned by the city's well-to-do, and leads up to the verdant grounds of **Elizabeth Park**, at Asylum Avenue (daily dawn–dusk; free; Ⓦwww.elizabethpark.org), the first municipal rose garden in the nation. June is the best time to visit to see the more than eight hundred varieties of roses in bloom, but in addition there are rock gardens, greenhouses (Mon–Fri 8am–3pm), and tranquil walking paths. The park is also home of a free summer concert series; the info center (☎860/231-9443) has information on thematic walking tours and events.

Eating

To take advantage of Hartford's surprisingly good **eating** options, you'll need to visit a few different neighborhoods. **Farmington Avenue**, near West Hartford, offers some eclectic selections, while a growing number of ethnic restaurants have popped up on **Franklin Avenue**, in an old Italian district. Along Main and Asylum streets downtown are more sophisticated, expensive French and American options.

Abyssinian 535 Farmington Ave ☎860/218-2231. Authentic Ethiopian stews, salads, fish dishes, and breads, with plentiful vegetarian options (entrees $8–16).

Bushnell Park Cafe 60 Elm St ☎860/728-6730. Burgers, salads, pizzas, and the like ($9–12) served on a patio overlooking the green, next to a funky gallery.

Carbone's 588 Franklin Ave ☎860/296-9646. Superb, upscale Italian restaurant since 1938; leave room for dessert, flambéed tableside.

Hot Tomato's 1 Union Place ☎860/249-5100. Energetic Italian restaurant near the train station, popular for its huge garlicky portions and fair prices.

Ichiban 530 Farmington Ave ☎860/236-5599. Korean and Japanese restaurant serving tasty sushi, stews, hot-pot, and *bibimbap*.

Max Downtown 185 Asylum St ☎860/522-2530. Upscale nouveau-American restaurant, serving

entrees like basil-crusted lamb loin ($28), with a fine wine list.

Mozzicato Caffe 329 Franklin Ave ☎860/296-0426. Historic Franklin Ave café, with delicious pastries from the bakery next door.

Peppercorn's Grill 357 Main St ☎860/547-1714. Minimalist, stand-out trattoria, known for its creative contemporary Italian dishes like roasted, porcini-crusted chicken breast ($18) and sautéed osso buco braised with white wine ($23).

Tapas on Ann 126–130 Ann St ☎860/525-5988. Moderately priced downtown favorite, with Basque, Cajun, and veggie tapas creations ($9–13).

Trinity Restaurant 243 Zion St ☎860/728-9822. Trinity College hangout, with home-style dishes like lamb shank with goat cheese polenta ($19).

Trumbull Kitchen 150 Trumbull St ☎860/493-7417. Trendy eatery with an eclectic menu, from dim sum and tapas to tacos and meatloaf.

Drinking, nightlife, and entertainment

There's no shortage of **nightlife** in Hartford, whether you want to see a play, listen to a symphony concert, or bop till the wee hours. The main music venues are: the **Bushnell Center for the Performing Arts**, 166 Capitol Ave (☎860/987-5900, ⓦwww.bushnell.org), home to the Hartford Symphony Orchestra, the Hartford Ballet, and the Connecticut Opera; the **New England Dodge Music Center**, 61 Savitt Way (☎860/548-7370, ⓦwww .dodgemusiccenter.com), the venue for rock, pop, country, blues, and jazz acts; and the **Hartford Civic Center Coliseum**, Trumbull and Asylum streets (☎860/727-8010), home of the American Hockey League (minor league NHL) Wolfpack hockey team and host to a variety of sports competitions and rock and pop concerts. The award-winning **Hartford Stage Company**, 50 Church St (☎860/527-5151), stages classic plays and bold experimental productions, while **TheaterWorks**, 233 Pearl St (☎860/527-7838), is a local company presenting contemporary pieces.

Hartford's **bars** and **nightclubs** are mainly confined to the downtown area, particularly around Allyn and Asylum streets. For current listings, check out the free arts and entertainment weekly the *Hartford Advocate* or the city's daily newspaper, the *Courant*.

Agave Grill 100 Allyn St ☏ 860/882-1557. Trendy corner bar with 60+ tequilas; also dinner fare and live mariachi bands.

Asylum Cafe 253 Asylum St ☏ 860/524-8651. A lively local hangout, with martinis ($8), cocktails ($7), and famed pizza pies ($15+).

Black-Eyed Sally's 350 Asylum St ☏ 860/278-7427. This atmospheric restaurant and club hosts live blues bands Wed–Sat and offers hearty Cajun cooking.

City Steam Brewery Cafe 942 Main St ☏ 860/525-1600. Hand-crafted and speciality beers in a 15-barrel brew-house and seven-level space, also home of the *Brew Ha Ha Comedy Club* (Fri–Sat 7 & 10pm).

Around Hartford

Within ten miles of Hartford are a cluster of towns that have somehow managed to retain much of their traditional charm, with a number of historic houses and museums that make for pleasant afternoon excursions.

Farmington

Ten miles west of Hartford, lush **FARMINGTON** saw its heyday in the 1830s and 1840s, when the Farmington Canal operated between New Haven and Northampton, Massachusetts. Though today a more mundane suburb, it still merits a visit for the **Hill-Stead Museum**, 35 Mountain Rd (May–Oct Tues–Sun 10am–5pm; Nov–April Tues–Sun 11am–4pm; $9; ☏ 860/677-4787, ⓦ www.hillstead.org), a Colonial Revival mansion dating to the turn of the last century, set on an idyllic 152 acres. The former home of industrial magnate Alfred A. Pope, the house was designed by his daughter Theodate, one of the nation's first female architects, and holds in its original setting the family's outstanding collection of Impressionist paintings, including works by Monet, Manet, Degas, and Whistler. Guided tours run just under an hour. Also in Farmington, the **Stanley-Whitman House**, 37 High St (Wed–Sun noon–4pm; $5; ☏ 860/677-9222, ⓦ www.stanleywhitman.org), is a 1720 Colonial homestead, complete with antique furnishings and period gardens.

Practicalities

From downtown Hartford, CT Transit's E line runs along Farmington Avenue, with stops in West Hartford and Farmington, including the Hill-Stead Museum. Farmington has some nicer (and cheaper) **accommodation** than downtown Hartford. Try the *Farmington Inn*, 827 Farmington Ave (☏ 860/677-2821 or 1-800/648-9804, ⓦ www.farmingtoninn.com; ⑥), which offers spacious, elegant rooms with paintings by local artists. For something to **eat**, *Apricots*, 1593 Farmington Ave (☏ 860/673-5405), is a true gem set in a former trolley barn with an English-style pub downstairs and more formal Continental cuisine upstairs. The *Connecticut Culinary Institute*, 230 Farmington Ave (☏ 860/677-7869; Mon–Fri 11am–2pm), a culinary training school, offers a varied menu at its public cafeteria.

New Britain

A couple miles southwest of Hartford on I-84, industrial **NEW BRITAIN**, once one of the country's leading producers of hardware items, is the unlikely location for one of the Northeast's best collections of American art. The **New Britain Museum of American Art**, 56 Lexington St (Tues, Wed & Fri 11am–5pm, Thurs 11am–8pm, Sat 10am–5pm, Sun noon–5pm; $9, free Sat 10am–noon; ☏ 860/229-0257, ⓦ www.nbmaa.org), boasts some five thousand works spanning the colonial era to the present, including pieces by Sargent, Homer, and several twentieth-century artists. For a different sort of aesthetic, the **New Britain Industrial Museum**, 185 Main St (Mon–Tues & Thurs–Fri 2–5pm, Wed noon–5pm; free; ☎860/832-8654, ⓦwww.nbim.org), hosts exhibits devoted to the city's manufacturing history, with everything from tools to Art Deco kitchenware.

Near Exit 24 on Rte-9, in Willow Brook Park, the **New Britain Stadium**, 230 John Karbonic Way (☎860/224-8383), is home to popular minor league baseball team the New Britain Rock Cats, an affiliate of the Minnesota Twins. Fans fill up the stadium during weekend games (season April–Aug; tickets $5–12).

Wethersfield and around

Just south of Hartford on I-91, **WETHERSFIELD** is allegedly Connecticut's oldest town, and maintains a certain colonial aura with its numerous well-preserved historic houses. Founded around 1634, the town's highlights include the **Webb-Deane-Stevens Museum**, made up of three eighteenth-century houses at 211 Main St (May–Oct Mon & Wed–Sat 10am–4pm, Sun 1–4pm; April & Nov Sat 10am–4pm, Sun 1–4pm; $8 for three-house tour; ☎860/529-0612, ⓦwww.webb-deane-stevens.org), which each tell a different story about local society. The **Webb House**, built in 1752 by a prosperous merchant, contains a bedroom designed especially for George Washington, who came here to plan the Yorktown campaign in 1781. The 1766 **Silas Deane House** was home to lawyer-diplomat Silas Deane, who played an important role in the First Continental Congress and travelled to France to seek assistance for the Revolution. Deane was later accused of treason for dubious businesses abroad; although never convicted, he spent much of the rest of his life unsuccessfully attempting to clear his name. The more modest **Stevens House** was built in 1788 by a local leatherworker for his bride; it's charming for its simple decor. The museum also maintains the 1720 **Buttolph-Williams House**, one of the oldest houses in town, down the road at 249 Broad St ($4). At once medieval and romantic, it has dark clapboards, small windows, and a massive open hearth.

Back on Main Street, at no. 200, the Wethersfield Historical Society maintains the **Wethersfield Museum and Visitor Center** (Mon–Sat 10am–4pm, Sun 1–4pm; museum $5; ☎860/529-7161), which hosts rotating exhibits on town history, and an archive at the **Old Academy** (☎860/529-656) at no. 150, a handsome brick building which has served a variety of public functions since 1804. The Historical Society also runs tours of the Georgian-style **Hurlbut Dunham House**, at no. 212, adjacent to the museum, and the **Historic Cove Warehouse**, at the north end of Main Street, the lone survivor of a 1692 flood that destroyed the town's harbour.

Practicalities

Wethersfield's fine **dining** options include the atmospheric *J Michaels Tavern*, set in a historic house at 222 Main St (☎860/257-0700), with a moderately priced Italian menu, and the *Carmen Anthony Fishhouse*, 1770 Berlin Turnpike (☎860/529-7557), at the other side of town, serving award-winning seafood. **Accommodation** can be found at the *Chester Bulkley House*, at 184 Main St (☎860/563-4236, ⓦwww.chesterbulkleyhouse.com; ❺–❻), with five Victorian-style rooms, and the *Silas Robbins House B&B*, 185 Broad St (☎860/571-8733, ⓦwww.silaswrobbins.com; ❽–❾), set in the luxurious 1873 Second Empire mansion of entrepreneur Silas Robbins.

Dinosaur State Park

In 1966, the discovery of thousands of dinosaur tracks at **Rocky Hill**, south of Wethersfield, led to the foundation of the bizarre attraction that is **Dinosaur State Park**, a mile east of Exit 23 off I-91 (grounds open daily 9am–4pm, exhibition center open Tues–Sun 9am–4.30pm; $5, children ages 6–12 $2; ℗860/529-8423, ⓦwww.dinosaurstatepark.org), where you can view the largest on-site display of dinosaur tracks in North America. The garishly lit display pit, housed under a gigantic geodesic dome with some 500 prints, feels like something out of Hitchcock, but kids will enjoy the break from historic houses. Behind the exhibition center, you can make your own dinosaur prints at the outdoor studio, and find prehistoric echoes along two miles of trails winding past a basalt ridge and woodland swamp.

Middletown and Higganum

The suburbs end and the valley starts again with **MIDDLETOWN**, once the busiest port on the Connecticut River. A number of graceful nineteenth-century merchants' homes still stand here, including several on the campus of **Wesleyan University**. Of these, the most prominent is the 1810 **General Mansfield House**, 151 Main St (Wed 1–5pm, Thurs & Fri 11am–5pm; $5; ℗860/346-0746, ⓦwww.middlesexhistory.org), home to the Middlesex County Historical Society, which showcases rotating exhibits and a permanent display on the Civil War. Also on the campus, the **Zilkha Gallery**, Washington Terrace/Wyllys Avenue (Tues–Sat & Sun noon–4pm, Fri noon–8pm; free; ℗860/685-2695), displays interesting modern works.

South of Middletown on Rte-154, **HIGGANUM** merits a visit for the **Thankful Arnold House**, at the corner of Hayden Hill and Walkley Hill roads (Wed 9am–3pm, Thurs 2–8pm, Fri noon–3pm; also late May to early Oct Sun 1–4pm; $4; ℗860/345-2400, ⓦwww.haddamhistory.org), a three-story gambrel-roofed home built around the turn of the nineteenth century, with a magnificent **herb and vegetable garden**, carefully researched to reflect period plantings. Another horticultural treat is the nearby **Sundial Herb Garden**, Brault Hill Road Extension (mid-May to mid-Oct Sat & Sun 10am–5pm; $2 donation; ℗860/345-4290, ⓦwww.sundialgardens.com), which comprise a series of formal gardens based on seventeenth- and eighteenth-century principles, with topiary, avenues, knots, statuary, and sundials. A tea shop (weekends year-round 10am–5pm) specializes in rare and exotic teas from around the world.

East Haddam

About seven miles south, on the opposite side of the river, the village of **EAST HADDAM** is the unlikely location for the magnificent **Goodspeed Opera House**, 6 Main St off Rte-82 (tours June–Oct Sat 10.30am–1pm; $5; performances April–Jan; ℗860/873-8668), rising above the shore like a giant wedding cake. Built in 1876 by shipping and banking magnate William Goodspeed, the Opera House later served as a military base and as a storage depot for the Connecticut Highway Department, until local preservationists initiated its renovation in the late 1950s. East Haddam's other notable feature is the **Nathan Hale Schoolhouse**, behind St Stephen's Church at 29 Main St (May–Oct Wed–Sun noon–4pm; $2; ℗860/873-3399), a one-room schoolhouse where the Revolutionary War hero taught in 1773–74.

A further four miles south, also on the east bank of the river, is the **Gillette Castle**, 67 River Rd (grounds daily 8am–sunset, castle late May to early Oct daily 10am–4.30pm; grounds free, castle $5; ℗860/526-2336), the centerpiece of **Gillette Castle State Park**. This 24-room stone fortress was built between 1914 and 1919 by actor/playwright William Hooker Gillette (known for his portrayal of such characters as Sherlock Homes), and houses such grand features as a dining table on tracks, an enormous hall with balconies on three sides, and a replica of Sherlock Holmes' fictional London home, 221B Baker St, complete with violin, chemistry set, and pipe.

Practicalities

Among the **places to stay** in East Haddam are the *Bishopsgate Inn*, Rte-82 (℡860/873-1677, ⊛www.bishopsgate.com; ❺–❼), a charming 1818 Colonial house with five cozy rooms, and *Gelston House*, adjacent to the Opera House at 8 Main St (℡860/873-1411, ⊛www.gelstonhouse.com; ❺–❽), with seven elegant rooms. *Gelston House* is also known for its **restaurant**, a pre-theater favorite serving moderately priced fine American cuisine in the main dining room and a less formal outdoor patio, with spectacular river views.

Ivoryton and Essex

Back across the river on Rte-9, the village of **IVORYTON**, together with the nearby town of Deep River, is said to have handled more than three-quarters of all the ivory exported from Zanzibar in 1884. Phineas Pratt first manufactured ivory combs here in 1789, and the industry grew to include items like piano keys, crochet needles, brushes, and organ stops. These days, though, the hamlet is best known for its theater, the **Ivoryton Playhouse**, 103 Main St (℡860/767-7318, ⊛www.ivorytonplayhouse.com). Many a career has been launched from this fairly insignificant-looking wooden structure, including that of local girl Katharine Hepburn. For more pomp and circumstance, head to the **Museum of Fife and Drum**, 62 N Main St (July–Sept Sat & Sun 1–5pm; $3; ℡860/767-2237, ⊛www.companyoffifeanddrum.org), where the history of military music is traced through costumes, photographs, and instruments. The museum sponsors free Tuesday evening concerts in the summer.

The river widens noticeably as you head further south towards **ESSEX**, a quaint New England town with some lovely Colonial homes and a riverfront marina. Just south of downtown, the 1701 **Pratt House**, 19 West Ave (June–Sept Sat & Sun 1–4pm; donation requested; ℡860/767-0681), is one of the oldest houses in the area, once belonging to the town founders. At the end of Main Street, in an 1878 waterfront dockhouse, the **Connecticut River Museum** (Tues–Sun 10am–5pm; $8; ℡860/77-8269, ⊛www.ctrivermuseum.org) traces local maritime history, and contains a full-sized reproduction of the *American Turtle*, the world's first submarine, powered by hand cranks. Meanwhile, the **waterfront park** outside is a great place to watch the boats coming and going; Connecticut River Expeditions also offers **cruises** on the lower Connecticut River, leaving from the dock outside the museum (summer daily, spring and fall weekends; $15–20; ℡860/662-0577, ⊛www.ctriverexpeditions.org). For something completely different, the **Essex Steam Train & Riverboat** (summer daily; fall, spring, and Dec weekends; train only $17, children $9; train and boat $26, $13 children; ℡860/767-0103, ⊛www.essexsteamtrain.com), offers narrated excursions into the valley on a restored steam train and riverboat.

Practicalities

In these parts, fine dining and accommodation come together. In **Essex**, the 1776 *Griswold Inn*, 36 Main St (℡860/767-1776, ⊛www.griswoldinn.com; ❻), is as well known for its luxurious suites as for its sumptuous Sunday brunch (reserve ahead). In Ivoryton, the *Copper Beech Inn*, 46 Main St (℡860/767-0330 or 1-888/809-2056, Ⓦwww.copperbeechinn.com; Ⓑ), has thirteen rooms in the main house and adjacent carriage house, many with vaulted ceilings; the **restaurant** on the premises serves elegant French cuisine, matched by a superior wine list. Far more casual is *Crow's Nest*, 35 Pratt St, Essex (Ⓣ860/767-3288), serving fresh breakfast treats, excellent coffee, and soups and sandwiches.

The Litchfield Hills

The rolling, tree-clad **LITCHFIELD HILLS**, tucked away in Connecticut's tranquil northwestern corner, provide a vivid contrast to the hustle and bustle of the state's coast. Here, long, winding country roads lead past meadows and rushing brooks to picture-perfect colonial villages deep in pine-scented forests. The small town of **Litchfield**, with its maple-dotted green and elegant clapboard homes, serves as a fine base for exploring the area's numerous natural and cultural offerings. Near Litchfield is picturesque **Washington**, antique-laden **Woodbury**, and handsome **New Preston**, perched above the lush green banks of **Lake Waramaug**. Due west, **Kent** touches the **Appalachian Trail**, and remains a relaxed country town even as it was "discovered" by artists

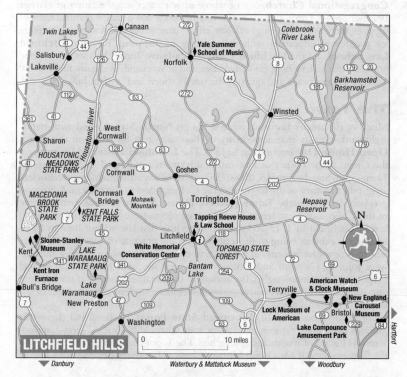

LITCHFIELD HILLS

0   10 miles

▼ *Danbury*   *Waterbury & Mattatuck Museum* ▼   ▼ *Woodbury*

Hartford

from New York in the 1980s. Nearby **West Cornwall** boasts one of the area's two historic covered bridges (the other one is on Rte-7 near Kent). North of **Sharon**, in the far northwestern corner, a cluster of tiny villages nestle close by the **Twin Lakes** and Connecticut's tallest peaks, Bear Mountain and Bald Peak, and scenic drives loop along routes 4, 7, 41, and 44. Close to the border of Massachusetts, **Norfolk** is home of the Yale Summer School of Music, while **Falls Village** hosts the annual Music Mountain chamber music festival. A world apart are the region's commercial centres at **Torrington** and **Waterbury**, south on Rte-8; both are relatively insignificant for visitors save a handful of industrial museums and some interesting architecture.

Public transportation in the area is scarce. While Waterbury is served by a few CT Transit **buses** and by Metro-North **trains** from New York City (2hr), outside of these, your best bet for getting around is by car. A helpful source of **information** for the area is the *Unwind* guide, published yearly by the Northwest Connecticut CVB (☎860/567-4506, ⓦwww.northwestct.com), and its *Touring* guide, highlighting the area's outdoor offerings, with detailed itineraries for self-guided tours by car, foot, bike, and boat. Pick up both guides at the Litchfield **visitors' kiosk**, right on the **Litchfield Green** (May–Oct, daily 11am–4pm).

Litchfield

First settled in 1720, the town of **LITCHFIELD** spreads out around an exceptionally long and pretty village green, overlooked by the white steeple of the 1828 **Congregational Church**, one of whose early pastors was the father of Harriet Beecher Stowe. During the Revolution, the town was a major manufacturer of supplies for George Washington's war effort; later, it became known as a centre for progressive education with the opening of **Tapping Reeve's Litchfield Law School** and the **Litchfield Female Academy**. Today, the area has become popular with gallery hoppers and cyclists, and at weekends is usually full of New Yorkers seeking peace and quiet in the town's streets and verdant hills.

The Town

Much of the town's historical interest lies on **North Street**, lined with stately eighteenth-century mansions; many of these are open for tours on the annual **Open House Day** (second Sat in July). The **Litchfield History Museum**, on the Green at the corner of East and South streets (mid-April to Nov Tues–Sat 11am–5pm, Sun 1–5pm; $5; ☎860/567-4501, ⓦwww.litchfieldhistoricalsociety .org), tells the story of the town from the Colonial days to the present. Admission gets you into the nearby **Tapping Reeve House & Law School**, former home of the College of New Jersey (now Princeton) graduate who began practicing law in Litchfield in 1773 and opened America's first law school here in 1774. Interactive exhibits bring to life a time when the practice of law was intimately tied to progressive reforms in politics and civil society; among Reeve's students were John C. Calhoun and Horace Mann, and the man himself was an avid proponent of women's rights. Pay tribute to the notable educator at the adjacent one-room **schoolhouse**, where you will feel like a student again in front of the authentic Colonial desks.

East of town on Rte-118, **Topsmead State Forest**, on Buell Rd (June–Oct grounds open daily 8am–sunset, call for tour schedule ☎860/567-5694), spreads across 411 acres of woods and rolling hills. The Tudor mansion on the property is the former estate of Miss Edith Morton Chase, a Waterbury heiress with a love of all things English, and indeed the well-kept grounds, with trails and unpaved roads perfect for romantic long walks, is surreally evocative of the English countryside. Also east on Rte-118 is the **Lourdes in Litchfield Shrine**. Founded by the Montfort Missionaries in 1958, the shrine re-creates the famous shrine of Our Lady of Lourdes, France, by means of a grotto built with local fieldstone. Services are still held regularly, and in the surrounding hills, the twelve stations of the cross spread out across a mile-long path. A fun time to come is the annual **Blessing of the Motorcycles**, when motorists trail here from all around the state.

For a complete contrast, visit the **White Memorial Foundation** (daily dawn–dusk; ☎860/567-0857, ⓦwww.whitememorialcc.org), on Rte-202 West, which encompasses three-quarters of the Bantam Lake shoreline and maintains over 35 miles of well-marked trails on varied terrain. There are also ample opportunities for cycling, horseriding, birdwatching, and fishing, and between May and October you can **camp** at one of 47 campgrounds on a peninsula in Bantam Lake. The **Nature Museum** (Mon–Sat 9am–5pm, Sun noon–5pm; $5) offers educational exhibits on the sanctuary's ecology and conservation.

Six miles north on Rte-63, Goshen hosts the annual **Litchfield Jazz Festival** in August, drawing legends near and far to the Goshen Fairgrounds (ⓦwww .litchfieldjazzfest.com).

Practicalities

There is no lack of charming **places to stay** in Litchfield; try the *Abel Darling B&B*, 102 West St (☎860/567-0384, ⓦwww.abeldarling.com; ❼), a 1782 Colonial building steps from the village green. West on Rte-202, *The Litchfield Inn* (☎1-800/499-3444, ⓦwww.litchfieldinnct.com; ❼) is a modern hotel built in the Colonial style, with thirty bright, elegant rooms, while the *Tollgate Hill Inn*, also on Rte-202 (☎860/567-1233 or 1-800/567-1233, ⓦwww.tollgatehill.com; ❺), offers twenty gracious rooms in a 1745 main house and adjacent, newer building. In Goshen, the *Mary Stuart House B&B*, 160 Sharon Turnpike/Rte-4 (☎860/491-2260, ❹), has six pretty rooms.

Many of Litchfield's **restaurants** line the green along West Street; reservations are recommended on the weekends. The *West Street Grill* (☎860/567-3885), at no. 43, has a small but fabulous international menu, while the more moderately priced *The Village*, at no. 25 (☎860/567-8307), offers home-style cooking. The *Tollgate Hill Inn* (see above) serves fine American cuisine in its historic tavern. More casual options include *The Blue Bakery*, near the green at 3 South St (☎860/567-1742), offering yummy sandwiches and desserts, and *Wood's Pit BBQ & Mexican Cafe*, 123 Bantam Lake Rd (☎860/567-9869), famed for its barbecued ribs. The *Dutch Epicure Shop*, 491 Bantam Rd (☎860/567-5586), has tasty Teutonic treats like veal goulash, spaetzle, and German potato salad.

New Preston, Washington, and Milford

About ten miles southwest of Litchfield on Rte-202 lies tiny **NEW PRESTON**, best known as the home of Lake Waramaug, the second-largest natural lake in Connecticut, and the attendant **Lake Waramaug State Park** (daily 8am–sunset; weekday parking free, summer weekends $10; camping $13; park office ☎860/927-3238 or reservations 1-877/668-2267). The tree-lined shores of the rippled expanse are especially beloved during the fall foliage season. Between late May and October you can rent canoes and kayaks ($10 per hr), and camp alongside the lake, with advance reservations.

More than a dozen wineries dot Connecticut's idyllic farmland and hills, particularly in the western part of the state. The Farm Winery Act, passed in 1978, opened up the soil, and Litchfield's **Haight Vineyard**, Chestnut Hill Road (☎203/567-4045) was soon growing Chardonnay and Riesling grapes behind its handsome English Tudor building in Litchfield. In New Preston, **Hopkins Vineyard**, 25 Hopkins Rd (☎860/868-7954), is the only Connecticut grape farm to benefit from a microclimate (yielding a longer season) from its stunning location overlooking Lake Waramaug. Some interesting choices are produced by the large **DiGrazia Vineyards**, 131 Tower Rd, Brookfield (☎203/775-1616), which add blueberries, pears, or honey (eliminating the need for sulfites) to the formula. In the eastern part of the state, picturesque Rte-169 leads to Lisbon's **Heritage Trail Vineyard**, 291 North Burnham Highway (☎860/376-0659), while **Stonington Vineyards**, 523 Taugwonk Rd, Stonington (☎860-535-1222), offer premium wines close to its coastal attractions. **Tastings** and **tours** are offered at many of these and other vineyards along Connecticut's **Wine Trail**; visit ⑩www .ctwine.com or call ☎860/267-1399 for more info.

Neighboring **WASHINGTON** is purportedly the first town in the nation to have been named for the country's first president, who traveled through the area several times during the Revolutionary War. Built in 1908, the **Gunn Memorial Library**, 5 Wykeham Rd (open daily except Wed & Sun; ⑩www .gunnlibrary.org), is a fine example of American Renaissance architecture, with classical inspirations and an intricate ceiling mural painted by Henry Siddons Mowbray in 1914. Just off Rte-199, **The Institute for American Indian Studies**, 38 Curtis Rd (Mon–Sat 10am–5pm, Sun noon–5pm; $5; ☎860/868-0518, ⑩www.birdstone.org), opened in 1975 as the premier archeological research center on New England's native peoples. In addition to research, the institute houses three galleries, a recreated longhouse room, and a replica of a traditional Algonkian village.

West on Rte-7, **NEW MILFORD** is home to the **Henderson Cultural Center**, 44 Upland Rd (Mon & Wed–Sun 10am–5pm; donation requested; ☎860/355-0300, ⑩www.hunthillfarmtrust.org), located on historic Hunt Hill farm and co-founded by the late Skitch Henderson, former director of the New York Pops. The on-site **Skitch Henderson Museum** houses an American music archive containing over 450 magnetic and film tape recordings. Also on the property is a converted hay barn and gallery, and **The Silo**, a two-in-one culinary school and gourmet food store, with regular tastings and events.

Practicalities

Lodging in these parts is luxurious, and expensive. Overlooking Lake Waramaug, *Boulders Inn*, East Shore Rd, New Preston (☎860/868-0541 or 1-800/455-1565, ⑩www.bouldersinn.com; ⑨), offers twenty gorgeous rooms and suites. A less pricey alternative is the lakeside *Hopkins Inn*, 22 Hopkins Rd, New Preston (☎860/868-7295, ⑩www.thehopkinsinn.com; ⑥), with eleven guestrooms, some with shared bath, and two apartments; there is an Austrian restaurant and vineyard nearby. The exclusive *Mayflower Inn*, on Rte-47 in Washington (☎860/868-9466, ⑩www.mayflowerinn.com; ⑨), is an elegant Relais & Chateaux property with manicured gardens and spa. **Dining** options include *Doc's*, Rte-45, Lake Waramaug (☎860/868-9415), a reasonably priced pizzeria; and the outstanding Mediterranean eatery ✻ *Oliva*, E Shore Road, New Preston (☎860/868-1787), where flavours come together wonderfully, even in basic sides like lentil soup.

The scenic northwest corner

Connecticut's **northwest corner** boasts some of the most striking scenery in the state: verdant hills abound with weathered barns, sleeping cows, and grazing horses; farms are lined with beautifully maintained split-rail wooden fences; and fields burst with corn in the summer and glisten with snow in the winter. The area has become a hotspot for New Yorkers looking for a quiet retreat, and as a result the small country towns here – including **Kent**, **West Cornwall**, and **Norfolk** – offer upscale galleries and superb restaurants alongside local coffee-shops and fruit stands.

Kent

It's hard to imagine the scene witnessed in 1694 by English traveler Benjamin Wadsworth when he described **KENT**, nestled on a flat alluvial plain among the hills bordering the Housatonic Valley, as a "howling wilderness." By the early nineteenth century, Kent was a bustling industrial town, with production at the **Kent Iron Furnace** beginning in 1826 and ceasing some seventy years later. Today, though, hardly an industrial trace can be found in the town's shady hills, except perhaps for the furnace ruins on Rte-7, and Kent has evolved into a refined country town. Following the opening of contemporary art gallery **Paris–New York–Kent** in 1984, an influx of boutiques and galleries have sprung up along Main Street, while the town itself remains low-key, welcoming antique-shoppers and backpackers alike to this part of Connecticut's Appalachian Trail.

The town and around

Among the town's top attractions, the **Sloane-Stanley Museum**, Rte-7, one mile north of downtown (mid-May to Oct Wed–Sun 10am–4pm; $4; ☏860/927-3849), showcases the love for all things pre-industrial of Connecticut writer and artist Eric Sloane. A vast assortment of early American handtools is meticulously nailed to the wall by the man himself, who found in them a uniquely American aesthetic. Along with the collection, Sloane's studio is recreated, intact with his last painting. Next door, perhaps not without irony, the **Connecticut Antique Machinery Association** (May–Oct Wed–Sun 10am–4pm; donation; ☏860/927-0050) maintains Kent's industrial legacy, with a sprawling collection of gigantic combustion engines, steam and diesel engines, vintage tractors, and the reassembled nineteenth-century Cream Hill Agricultural School, one of the country's first. Don't forget to peek into the tiny **Museum of Mining and Mineral Science** (also on site), an earth science teacher's dream come true, with a display of fluorescent minerals, mine shaft, collection of Connecticut bricks, and educative exhibits on the history of mining in the state.

For venturing into the great outdoors, **Kent Falls State Park**, about four miles north of downtown on Rte-7 (daily 8am–sunset; weekend parking $10; ☏860/927-3238), is known for its namesake 250-foot falls. The most dramatic drop is a seventy-foot cascade that's visible from the road, not far from the parking lot; from there, a quarter-mile trail winds up along the water. Nearby, off Rte-341, the 2,300-acre **Macedonia Brook State Park**, 159 Macedonia Brook Rd (☏860/927-3238), boasts deep gorges, falls, and the 1350-foot summit of Cobble Mountain, which commands views as far as the Catskills in New York State; you can also camp here ($11) between mid-April and October, though it's fairly primitive and alcohol is not allowed.

Four miles south of town on Rte-7, a right turn at Bulls Bridge Road leads to **Bulls Bridge**, one of only two original covered bridges in the state open to vehicular traffic (the other one is in West Cornwall, see below). Rebuilt and restored over the years, it's certainly in better condition today than when George Washington crossed it on horseback: his expense reports for March 3, 1781 read: "getting a horse out of Bull's Bridge Falls, $215.00." White blazes at the parking area mark an entrance to the Appalachian Trail.

Back in town, **Backcountry Outfitters**, 5 Bridge St (☎1-888/549-3377), is a good stop for maps of local hikes and gear. Next door, the **Bicycle Tour Company**, 9 Bridge St (☎1-888/711-KENT), offers bike rentals.

Practicalities

There are several nice **places to stay** in Kent. An upscale option is *The Inn at Kent Falls*, 107 Kent Cornwall Rd (☎860/927-3197, ⓦwww.theinnatkentfalls .com; ❽) – but don't be fooled by the name: the falls are more than three miles up the road. Located at the top end of Kent's shopping district is the *Starbuck Inn*, 88 N Main St (☎860/927-1788, ⓦwww.starbuckinn.com; ❽), where highlights include a hearty breakfast and afternoon high tea and sherry.

Kent makes for a great rest-stop for anyone with a **sweet tooth**. The classy patisserie *Belgique*, 1 Bridge St (☎860/927-3681) boasts handmade Belgian truffles and other fine European confections, while the *Kent Coffee and Chocolate Company*, 8 Main St (☎860/927-1445), the chocolates are delicious, and the prices easier to digest. For fine meals like roast duck flambéed tableside, try the *Fife 'N Drum Restaurant & Inn*, 53 N Main St (☎860/927-3509), whose pub-style bar features nightly piano music by proprietor Dolph Traymon, who's played with the likes of Sinatra.

West Cornwall, Cornwall, and Cornwall Bridge

East of Kent on Rte-4, the tiny village of **CORNWALL** was home to the **Cornwall Foreign Mission School** from 1817 to 1827. Despite its place in local history, though, it's primarily a residential town with few actual attractions. You may find more to do in **WEST CORNWALL**, a separate town three miles west on Rte-7, whose tiny main street is lined with a few lively craft shops and

▲ West Cornwall covered bridge

restaurants. At the foot of the street, the Housatonic River streams giddily under the 172-foot bright-red, much photographed **covered bridge**, built in 1864 of native oak and later restored.

The third namesake in the area is **CORNWALL BRIDGE** (not, in fact, where the bridge is located), four miles south of West Cornwall on Rte-7, known for nearby **Housatonic Meadows State Park** (open daily 8am–sunset; seasonal camping $13; ℡860/927-3238), a densely forested two-mile stretch along the Housatonic River that's popular with picnickers and fly-fishers. **Clarke Outdoors**, 163 Rte-7 (℡860/672-6365, ⓦwww.clarkeoutdoors.com), rents kayaks, canoes, and rafts, and also offers guided river trips. In the winter, a better bet is the **Mohawk Mountain Ski Area**, Great Hollow Road (℡860/672-6100 or 1-800/895-5222, ⓦwww.mohawkmtn.com), the largest in the state with five lifts and 24 trails good for all levels; a full day-pass costs $50.

Practicalities

There's little in the way of **lodging** in the immediate vicinity, but you could try the *Breadloaf Mountain Lodge & Cottages*, 13 Rte-7, Cornwall Bridge (℡860/672-6064, ⓦwww.breadloafmountainlodge.com; ⑨), with five fully furnished "cottages" and one five-bedroom unit. The *Cornwall Inn*, 270 Kent Rd, Cornwall Bridge (℡860/672-6884, ⓦwww.cornwallinn.com; ⑦), is conveniently located on Rte-7, offering thirteen guestrooms. For **food**, try *The Wandering Moose Cafe*, next to the covered bridge in West Cornwall (℡860/672-0178), serving pizzas and heavy meat dishes like steak au poivre ($26) and beef tenderloin ($27). Down the street, the more casual *Smokin' BB*, 9 Railroad Square (℡860/248-3127), offers generous, good-value portions of beef briskets and country-style ribs.

Sharon, Falls Village, Limerock, and Salisbury

Due west of West Cornwall on Rte-41, **SHARON** is yet another quintessential New England village with a long, narrow green, some pristine nineteenth-century homes, and a white-steepled church. On Rte-4, at the **Sharon Audubon Center**, 325 Cornwall Bridge Rd (trails daily dawn–dusk, center Tues–Sat 9am–5pm, Sun 1–5pm; $3; ℡860/364-0520), you can explore 1200 acres and eleven miles of nature trails, along with an interpretive center, sugarhouse, and raptor aviaries housing a dozen species of resident birds of prey. The **Sharon Playhouse**, 49 Amenia Rd (℡860/364-SHOW, ⓦwww.triarts.net), is known for its excellent summer theater and also offers readings of new works throughout the year.

Further north, a cluster of quaint villages lies amid some of the state's most attractive scenery. On Rte-126, tiny **FALLS VILLAGE** is home to the prestigious **Music Mountain** chamber music festival (℡860/824-7126, ⓦwww.musicmountain.org), held every summer, while **Lime Rock Park**, routes 7 and 112 (℡860/435-5000), in nearby **LIMEROCK**, hosts some of New England's premier car racing events. Further north near the state's border, **SALISBURY** lies close to the clear blue waters of the **Twin Lakes**, where you can rent boats and buy tackle at **O'Hara's Landing Marina**, 254 Twin Lakes Rd (℡860/824-7583), or simply sit by the shore and observe the ripples on a calm day.

Norfolk

Rte-44 leads east from Salisbury through dairy farming country to **NORFOLK**, a quaint little town whose tall church steeple stands sentinel over a lush **village green**, today best known as home to the **Yale Summer School of Music** and the **Norfolk Chamber Music Festival**. During the months of July and

August, you may just find legendary maestros and virtuosos strolling down the town's peaceful streets, though you're more likely to run into lively crowds of young music students.

Norfolk began as a cultural center with the 1889 opening of the **Norfolk Library**, a still functioning pretty red-stone building with vaulted ceilings (Mon & Tues 10am–8pm, Wed–Fri 10am–5pm, Sat 10am–2pm, Sun 1–4pm; ☎860/542-5075). Up the street, the **Norfolk Historical Museum** (late May to Oct Sat & Sun noon–4pm; donation requested; ☎860/542-5761), housed in the former Norfolk Academy, hosts changing exhibits on town history. Across the street on the green, the graceful **Eldridge Fountain**, designed by Stanford White in 1889, was once a drinking fountain for both men and their horses. Also on the green, the so-called **Whitehouse** was once part of the **Ellen Battell Stoeckel Estate**, routes 44 and 72, owned until 1939 by a music-loving local resident who entertained such luminaries as Rachmaninov and Sibelius. Today, the estate is home to the Yale Summer School of Music and accessible to the public during the summer concerts, held in the 947-seat wood-paneled "Music Shed" (☎860/542-3000, ⓦwww.yale.edu/norfolk).

Practicalities

Accommodation options in the Norfolk area include the *Blackberry River Inn*, 538 Greenwoods Rd, Rte-44 W (☎860/542-5100 or 1-800/414-3636, ⓦwww .blackberryriverinn.com; ➐), which offers four suites in an eighteenth-century Colonial house and twenty rooms in the adjacent carriage house, and the romantic *Manor House*, 69 Maple Ave (☎860/542-5690 or 1-866/542-5690, ⓦwww.manorhouse-norfolk.com; ➏), a Victorian Tudor mansion that features Tiffany windows and gardens just outside. Another nice choice is the *Mountain View Inn*, 67 Litchfield Rd (☎860/542-6991, ⓦwww.mvinn.com; ➏), a beautifully restored 1875 yellow house on a hill. For something to **eat**, the *Speckled Hen*, Rte-44 (☎860/542-5716), with English pub decor, offers good-value American fare, along with an extensive selection of domestic and imported beers.

Torrington

TORRINGTON, the birthplace of abolitionist **John Brown** in 1800, is today the largest town in northwest Connecticut. It's a good base to explore the surrounding areas, with some budget **accommodation**, like the *Super 8 Motel*, 492 E Main St (☎860/496-0811 or 1-800/800-8000; ➍). More expensive, but full of character, is the *Yankee Pedlar Inn*, opposite the Art Deco Warner Theatre at 93 Main St (☎860/489-9226, ⓦwww.pedlarinn.com; ➍), with sixty rooms complete with Hitchcock furnishings, famous for their elaborate stencil work. For something to **eat**, *Marino's*, 12 Pinewoods Rd (☎860/482-6864; closed Sun), serves Italian-American cuisine in a casual, laid-back atmosphere, while the classic *Venetian Restaurant*, 52 E Main St (☎860/489-8592; closed Tues), is one of the best Italian restaurants around; you can also buy their home-made pastas and bottled dressings to stock away for a later meal.

Terryville and Bristol

An unusual opportunity is on offer in the village of **TERRYVILLE**, once an important manufacturing town, about twelve miles southeast of Torrington on Rte-6: the **Lock Museum of America**, 230 Main St (May–Oct Tues–Sun 1.30–4.30pm; $3; ☎860/589-6359, ⓦwww.lockmuseum.com), which stands on the site of the old Eagle Lock company factory and holds the largest collection of locks, keys, and ornate Victorian hardware in the US. Key items, so to speak, include an 1846 combination padlock, a 4000–year-old Egyptian-made pin tumbler lock, and the original patent model of the mortise cylinder pin lock designed by Linus Yale, Jr, in 1865.

In neighboring **BRISTOL**, part of the region once known as the "Switzerland of America," make time for the **American Clock & Watch Museum**, 100 Maple St (April–Nov daily 10am–5pm; $5; ☎860/583-6070), reputed to be the finest collection of American clocks in existence. The more than 1500 clocks include "Dewey," one of a series of six clocks introduced in 1899 to commemorate the Spanish–American War, with a likeness of Admiral Dewey at the top. Be prepared to cover your ears on the hour, when hundreds of chimes resonate around the museum house. Equally unique, the **New England Carousel Museum**, 95 Riverside Ave (April–Nov Mon–Sat 10am–5pm, Sun noon–5pm; Dec–March Thurs–Sat 10am–5pm, Sun noon–5pm; $5; ☎860-585-5411, ⓦwww .thecarouselmuseum.org), houses an enormous collection of antique carousel art and memorabilia, while a restoration department repairs old carousel pieces.

Also in Bristol, **Lake Compounce Family Theme Park**, Exit 31 off I-84 (open May–Sept; $34; ☎860/583-3300, ⓦwww.lakecompounce.com) makes for another sort of diversion if you're into watery fun; most famous is its wooden roller coaster, winding through the woods, and its miniature-Corvette rides. For the budget-conscious, further south in Middlebury, the old-fashioned **Quassy Amusement Park**, on Rte 64 (☎203/958-2913), is a good alternative. Family-owned since 1937, the park offers waterslides, bumper cars, boat rides, and a lakeside theater; you can pay by ride ($3 per ticket).

Waterbury and Woodbury

At the very southern edge of the Litchfield Hills, and certainly no part of it in spirit, **WATERBURY** – known to the Indians as "the place where no trees will grow" because of persistent flooding – valiantly celebrates its glorious past of brass- and copper-making. That's not necessarily a reason to come, though if you do, you'll find the requisite history in the **Mattatuck Museum**, 144 W Main St (Tues–Sat 10am–5pm, Sun noon–5pm; $4; ☎203/753-0381, ⓦwww .mattatuckmuseum.org), a haven of local art and memorabilia devoted to telling the story of the state. Highlights include a 10,000 button collection and a $2 interactive exhibit detailing the history of Waterbury. The rest of downtown is pleasing enough, with red-brick and white marble municipal buildings, including the Chase Building and the former Waterbury National Bank, both designed by **Cass Gilbert**, architect of the Woolworth Building and the George Washington Bridge in New York. Look, too, at 389 Meadow St, the town's former main **railroad station** modeled on the City Hall in Siena, Italy, with a tall campanile-style tower that is the city's most notable landmark. Like nearby Bristol, Waterbury has a history of clock-making; the Waterbury Clock company was renamed Timex in the 1970s, and its progression through the years is recounted in the **Timex Museum**, 175 Union St (Tues–Sat 10am–5pm; $6; ☎203/755-TIME, ⓦwww.timexpo.com).

West on Rte-6 is **WOODBURY**, touted as the antiques capital of New England, with a main street lined by eighteenth- and nineteenth-century houses that have nearly all been converted into shops. Of particular note is **Mill House Antiques**, which has an extensive array of French and English furniture and collectibles. Also of note is the **Glebe House Museum & Gertrude Jekyll Garden**, 49 Hollow Rd (May–Oct Wed–Sun 1–4pm, Nov Sat & Sun 1–4pm; $5; ☎203/263-2855, ⓦwww.theglebehouse.org), where the nation's first Episcopal bishop was elected in 1783. The charming farmhouse provides a fine glimpse into life of the period, and also boasts an English-style garden.

Practicalities

If you want to **stay** in Waterbury, the *Courtyard by Marriott*, 63 Grand St (T 203/596-1000; ⑤) is right downtown and has a gym and indoor pool. On the less expensive side, Woodbury lays claim to the oldest inn in the state, the *Curtis House*, 506 Main St S (T 203/263-2101, W www.thecurtishouse.com; shared bath ③, private ④). For **food**, try *Drescher's*, 25 Leavenworth St, Waterbury (T 203/573-1743), open since 1868, offering a variety of moderately priced German and American dishes. The *Carmen Anthony Steakhouse*, 495 Chase Ave (T 203/757-3040), is known for its Angus steaks, while its sister restaurant *Carmen Anthony Fishhouse*, 757 Main St South, Woodbury, has a seafood focus. Also in Woodbury, the smart *John's Cafe*, 693 Main St South (T 203/263-0188), serves inspired American cuisine, while the *Good News Café*, 694 Main St S (T 203/266-4663; closed Tues), is a vibrant spot with unusual dishes like pecan-crusted oysters with jicama and cherries ($16).

Northeastern Connecticut

Northeastern Connecticut, north of Norwich, stretching from Coventry in the west to the Rhode Island border in the east, comprises the majority of the corridor also known as "the Last Green Valley." Dispersed among the area's 695,000 acres are seven state forests, five state parks, and sixteen state wildlife management areas. Highlights include the **Pachaug State Forest**, on Rte-49, the state's largest at 24,000 acres (T 860/376-4075), and the **Airline Trail** in Windham County, stretching nearly fifty miles to the border of Massachusetts, with panoramic views. The Last Green Valley office, 107 Providence St (Mon–Thurs 8am–4pm; T 866/363-7226, W www.thelastgreenvalley.org), publishes a comprehensive 96-page **visitors' guide** available at forty locations throughout the region, and is an excellent resource for trails and accommodations. The Connecticut Department of Environmental Protection (T 860/424-3000, W www.ct.gov/dep) has more info.

Besides its natural endowments, the region also boasts a number of historic sites, scattered among the few dozen villages and towns that dot the rural landscape, although nothing of specific interest: simply drive – or bike – and you'll find surprises along the way. Notable excursions include antique-laden **Putnam**, named after the Revolutionary War general who allegedly made the famous "whites of their eyes" command at the Battle of Bunker Hill; **Lebanon**, whose historic village green stretches on for a mile along Rte-87; and **Coventry**, home to Revolutionary War hero Nathan Hale, hanged by the British for spying. Nearby **Storrs** is home to the campus of the **University of Connecticut**, attractive for its greenhouses and art museum. Especially scenic is the 32-mile stretch of **Route 169** running from Canterbury to Woodstock. The region is best accessed by car; Bonanza **buses** (T 888/751-8800), run through the region, with stops at Willimantic and Storrs, but local transportation is virtually non-existent.

Vermont

CHAPTER 6

Highlights

✴ **Grafton** The iconic New England village, with white clapboard houses, steepled church, and a fast-flowing stream shaded by maples. See p.339

✴ **Skiing** The state abounds with challenging mountains and excellent facilities. See p.347, p.349, p.351, p.353, p.367, p.387 & p.388

✴ **Long Trail** Walking the length of the entire state wins serious bragging rights for competitive hikers; for others, the magnificent vistas from Vermont's highest peaks will more than justify the effort. See p.348

✴ **Ben and Jerry's Factory Tour** Who can resist a scoop of cold calories served in a cone? See p.364

✴ **Montpelier** Relaxed, friendly, genuine, and relatively tourist-free, the only state capital without a *McDonald's* is bounded by rivers and a forest of tall trees. See p.369

✴ **Burlington** In a complete contrast to Vermont's profusion of perfect villages, this is a genuine city, with a waterfront, a vibrant downtown, and the state's best restaurants and nightlife. See p.374

✴ **Shelburne Museum** Two centuries of American life stuffed into fifty acres of northern Vermont. See p.381

▲ Walking the Long Trail

6

Vermont

With its white churches and red barns, covered bridges and clapboard houses, snowy woods and maple syrup, **Vermont** comes closer than any other New England state to fulfilling the quintessential image of small-town Yankee America. True, in certain areas, the bucolic image can seem a bit packaged, but exploring the state's minor roads is captivating nonetheless, as you'll discover myriad little villages, alluring country inns, and splendid lakes and mountains; indeed, much of the state's landscape is smothered by verdant, mountainous forests (the name Vermont supposedly comes from the French *vert mont*, or green mountain).

With the occasional exception, such as the extraordinary assortment of Americana at the **Shelburne Museum** near **Burlington** (a lively city worth visiting in any case), there are few specific sights as such to seek out. Indeed, tourism here is more activity-oriented, and though the state's rural charms can be enjoyed year-round, most visitors come during two well-defined seasons: to see the **fall foliage** in the first two weeks of October, and to **ski** in the depths of winter, when resorts such as **Killington** and **Stowe** spring to life.

Some history

Settled early in the eighteenth century, Vermont is the youngest of New England's states. As colonists moved north, the governors of New Hampshire and New York began issuing land grants, creating antipathy between settlers from those two states. In 1770, **Ethan Allen** established the Green Mountain Boys to protect the interests of the original New Hampshire-ites. When the Revolutionary War broke out, this all-but-autonomous force captured Fort Ticonderoga from the British and helped to win the decisive **Battle of Bennington**. For fourteen years, Vermont existed as an independent republic (it was not one of the original thirteen states), with the first constitution in the world to forbid slavery and grant universal (male) suffrage; it joined the Union only in 1791. It has always been a bucolic place, with agriculture (particularly butter- and cheese-manufacturing) dominating the economy into the twentieth century, though since the late 1800s, when the state began to be branded as a rural paradise, the tourism industry has also played a large role in its prosperity.

Today, Vermont remains fairly liberal when it comes to politics: the state has been attracting a mix of hippies, environmentalists, and professionals escaping the rat-race since the 1960s, most aspiring to an eco-friendly philosophy best epitomized by **Ben & Jerry's** additive free, locally produced ice cream. Though the environment does tend to unite residents, many issues have alienated the state's still vocal conservatives; in 2000, when Democratic Governor **Howard**

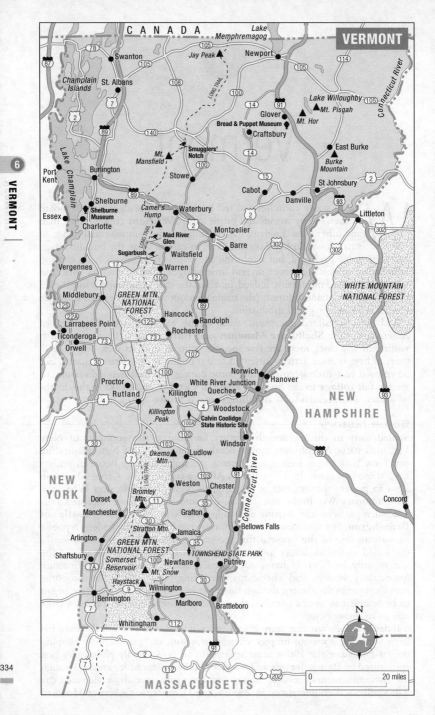

Dean made Vermont the first state in the US to sanction same-sex marriage, it prompted a backlash of "take back Vermont" road signs in many areas, and Republican Jim Douglas won the Governorship in 2003.

Southern Vermont

North of Western Massachusetts, the Berkshires roll into the much higher Green Mountains of **Southern Vermont**, the state's forested backbone. Most visitors begin their explorations of the area at **Brattleboro**, a lively college town with plenty of enticing stores and bars but little in the way of sights, or **Bennington**, forty miles on the other side of the hills and home to a smattering of historic attractions. From either town routes lead north through a hinterland of traditional Vermont villages such as **Grafton**, while in between, Hwy-100 cuts a more central course through the **Green Mountain National Forest** to **Weston** and the **Okemo Valley**.

Brattleboro

Home to yoga studios, vintage record shops, and bookstores catering to the town's youthful and vaguely "alternative" population, **BRATTLEBORO** has little in common with the clapboard villages that dominate much of Vermont. Despite boasting one of the liveliest arts scenes in the state, however, it's essentially a red-brick college town with little in the way of conventional sights – the real draws lie in the countryside nearby.

Sitting beside the Connecticut River, the city lies near the site of **Fort Dummer**, the first English settlement in the state, which was built in 1724 to protect Massachusetts from Indian raids (the site was flooded when the Vernon Dam was built in 1908). Gradually businesses and farms sprang up alongside the river and the fort, and in the 1800s Brattleboro enjoyed a modest reputation as a railroad and mill town. **Rudyard Kipling** penned his two *Jungle Books* here in the 1890s, giving the town its lone claim to fame, though one you can't really experience fully unless you stay at his former home **Naulakha**, now restored as a posh rental property (see p.337 for review).

Arrival, information, and city transport

Driving into Brattleboro is straightforward enough, and you can park in the lots on High Street or in the Transportation Center on Elliot Street ($0.25 per hr). The city lies on the *Vermonter* Amtrak train route, connecting it to Washington, DC and New York, though there's only one train in each direction daily; the "station" on Vernon Street is just a stop on the tracks (office open daily 11am–1pm & 4–6pm). The Greyhound **bus** terminal (☎802/254-6066) is a couple of miles north of downtown near the junction of US-5 (Putney Rd) and I-91, behind the Citgo gas station. There are services to White River Junction, Hanover (New Hampshire), and Boston and Northampton (Massachusetts). Brattleboro's **town bus**, The

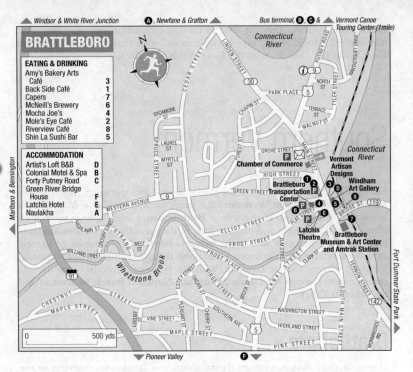

Brattleboro BeeLine (☎802/251-8137; $0.75), can get you to the bus terminal, as well as various other points in and around town.

The **Chamber of Commerce**, 180 Main St (Mon–Fri 9am–5pm; ☎802/254-4565, ⓦwww.brattleborochamber.org), has a wide selection of brochures on area attractions, and operates an information **kiosk** (Sat & Sun 9am–5pm) on the Brattleboro Town Common, just north of the center on Putney Road. The **Southeast Vermont Welcome Center**, on I-91 south of Brattleboro (daily 7am–11pm, lobby open 24hr; ☎802/254-4593), is probably the most elaborate visitors' center in the whole state, and has plenty of information about the various attractions in the Brattleboro area.

If you're interested in seeing the town from the **Connecticut River**, visit the **Vermont Canoe Touring Center** (May–Oct daily 10am–7pm; ☎802/257-5008) at 451 Putney Rd (US-5), under the bridge north of the center, which rents kayaks ($20 for 2hr, $40 per day; cash only). Kipling's former home **Naulakha** (see opposite) is usually off-limits to casual visitors, but the **Landmark Trust** (☎802/254-6868) occasionally arranges guided tours.

Accommodation

A number of chain and independently owned **motels** line Putney Road (US-5) north of town; the independent ones are cheaper and have a bit more character. For **camping**, the *Brattleboro North KOA* park is at 1238 Rte-5 in East Dummerston (☎802/254-5908; pitches $39).

Artist's Loft B&B and Gallery 103 Main St ☎802/257-5181, ⓦwww.theartistsloft.com. This tiny B&B above an art gallery offers only one suite, but it's a luxurious two rooms overlooking the Connecticut River. Private entrance, and video and book libraries available. **G**

Colonial Motel & Spa Putney Rd (US-5/Rte-9)
☎802/257-7733 or 1-800/239-0032, ⓦwww
.colonialmotelspa.com. This family-owned lodge
has an indoor pool, sauna, and health club, though
the rooms are starting to show their age. Still a
good deal, considering the low rates. ❸

Forty Putney Road 192 Putney Rd ☎802/254-
6268 or 1-800/941-2413, ⓦwww.fortyputneyroad
.com. B&B in a French Provincial-style house
decorated with antiques 1 mile from the town
center. ❼–❽

Green River Bridge House 2435 Stage Rd
☎802/257-5771 or 1-800/528-1868, ⓦwww
.greenriverbridgehouse.com. This former 1830s
post office was totally gutted and restored to house
high-end comfort. The three colorful rooms are
tastefully decorated and overlook a quiet lawn and
a covered bridge. Geared more toward couples
than families. ❼–❽

Latchis Hotel 50 Main St ☎802/254-6300,
ⓦwww.latchis.com. Thirty-room restored Art Deco
hotel in a good location. The centrally controlled a/c
may leave you a bit chilly, though. The four-person
suites are good value ($150). ❹

🏃 Naulakha 481 Kipling Rd, Dummerston
☎802/254-6868, ⓦwww.landmarktrustusa
.org. Rudyard Kipling designed this four-bedroom
house in 1892, and today it's owned and rented
by the Landmark Trust. Staying here is a magical
experience for fans: you can meditate in Kipling's
study, play pool in his attic, or relax in his original
tub. The house comes with all mod cons and is
available for stays of 3 days to 3 weeks. ❾

The Town

Main Street spans the length of Brattleboro's diminutive downtown, and is lined
with hip coffee houses, art galleries, holistic apothecaries, and used-CD shops.
You could spend time browsing in any of them, including **Vermont Artisan
Designs**, 106 Main St (Mon–Sat 10am–6pm, Sun 11am–5pm; ☎802/257-7044,
ⓦwww.vtartisans.com), with its blown glass, intricate jewelry, and woodblock
prints, or funky **Windham Art Gallery**, 69 Main St (Thurs–Sun noon–5pm;
☎802/257-1881, ⓦwww.windhamartgallery.com), an artists' cooperative exhib-
iting an eclectic array of fine arts. The town is rich in artistic tradition and
sponsors a **Gallery Walk** (ⓦwww.gallerywalk.org) every first Friday of the
month (5.30–8.30pm), when local and regional artists are spotlighted in over
forty of the town's galleries, inns, and cafés.

Elliot Street, which runs west off Main Street, also has an enticing line-up
of shops, including a couple of excellent **bookstores**. Brattleboro Books at
no. 36 (Mon–Sat 10am–6pm, Sun 11am–5pm), purveys a staggering array of
used volumes at incredibly low prices, while Everyone's Books, no. 25 (Mon–
Thurs 9.30am–6pm, Fri 9.30am–8pm, Sat 9.30am–7pm, Sun 9.30am–5pm)
is part leftist bookstore, with special sections for indie 'zines and anarchic
political tracts, and part community center.

At the foot of Main Street, just before it intersects with Bridge Street, the
1930s Art Deco **Latchis Theatre** is worth a look for its sleek style and interior
trimmings, including a series of faux Greek friezes. Across the bridge at 10
Vernon St, the **Brattleboro Museum and Art Center** (Wed–Mon 11am–5pm;
closed end March to end April; $4; ☎802/257-0124, ⓦwww.brattleboromuseum
.org) occupies the old railroad station building. It features changing – and sometimes
rather nondescript – exhibits of contemporary art and regional history.

Eating, drinking, and entertainment

Brattleboro's **restaurants** cater to the youthful counterculture with a variety of
cuisines. Ranging from cosmopolitan and sophisticated to low-budget and
health-conscious, most of the best options are on or just off Main Street; the
same goes for **bars** in town. A good place to stock up for a camping trip is the
Brattleboro Food Co-op, 2 Main St (Mon–Sat 8am–9pm, Sun 9am–9pm;
☎802/257-0236), in the Brookside Plaza at the intersection of Canal and Main
streets. The local **music scene** bops with talented local acts on a near-nightly

basis; pick up a Thursday edition of the *Brattleboro Reformer* for listings of the week's events. The Latchis Theatre's meticulously restored **cinema** shows both studio and indie flicks (Ⓦwww.latchis.com).

Amy's Bakery Arts Café 113 Main St Ⓣ802/251-1071. Simple but tasty pastries, breads, and some basic sandwiches. Good views from the outside tables out back. Open until 6pm.

Back Side Café 24 High St Ⓣ802/257-5056. One of the town's older cafés, at the back of the Midtown Mall. Good breakfasts, omelettes, burgers, soups, and desserts, all at bargain prices. Closed Mon.

Capers 51 Main St Ⓣ802/251-0151. Cozy upscale restaurant with Scandinavian-like blond wood furnishings. The menu features dishes such as seared duck breast, and sweet pea and chive risotto (entrees $17–25). Dinner only; closed Sun & Mon.

McNeill's Brewery 90 Elliot St Ⓣ802/254-2553. Rough-hewn bar where you can sample eleven of their own microbrews, including Big Nose Blond, Old Ringworm, and Slopbucket Brown.

Mocha Joe's 82 Main St Ⓣ802/257-7794. Good caffeine-filled beverages in a stylish basement below Main St. A dark and dingy alternative to the comfy chairs and soothing music found at *Starbucks* and the like.

Mole's Eye Café 4 High St Ⓣ802/257-0771, Ⓦwww.themoleseyecafe.com. Brattleboro's most happening nightspot, bar, and dancefloor, with a wide range of live music most nights – blues, Latin, R&B, jazz, calypso – for a $5 cover. Talented locals enjoy the jam night every Tues, with live bands on Thurs. Usual menu of burgers and sandwiches. Closed Sun.

Riverview Café 36 Bridge St Ⓣ802/254-9841. The good seafood and comfort-food favorites make for an ample (and reasonably priced) meal, but the real treat is the outdoor dining on the deck, accompanied by great views of the Connecticut River.

Shin La Sushi Bar 57 Main St Ⓣ802/257-5226. Pretty much your only sushi option for miles. Chinese standards, too. Most dishes under $10. Closed Sun.

North from Brattleboro

Driving north from Brattleboro, highways 30 and 35 provide quieter and far more appealing routes into central Vermont than I-91, passing through some of the state's best small towns.

Newfane

Thirteen miles from Brattleboro, **NEWFANE** is a beautifully restored village, with white churches and clapboard inns. There's nothing of real note to see, though it does boast a nice town green flanked by three steepled buildings: the union hall, the Congregational church, and the county courthouse. On Sundays, the **Newfane Flea Market** (May–Oct 7am–5pm) is the largest in the state, attracting up to two hundred dealers of antiques, crafts, and books.

The village makes for a more rustic overnight alternative to Brattleboro. **Accommodation** includes the *West River Lodge & Stables*, 117 Hill Rd (Ⓣ802/365-7745, Ⓦwww.westriverlodge.com; shared bath ❹, private bath ❺), a nineteenth-century farmhouse where you can eat hearty breakfasts around an open fireplace before hitting the nearby hiking trails. In Newfane itself, smack on the green, the ⚞ *Four Columns Inn*, 21 West St (Ⓣ1-800/787-6633, Ⓦwww.fourcolumnsinn .com; ❻), has comfortable rooms, many with Jacuzzis, as well as a gourmet **restaurant** serving carefully prepared New American, Asian, and French cuisine. Also on the green, the *Old Newfane Inn* (Ⓣ802/365-4427, Ⓦwww.oldnewfaneinn.com) serves hearty, tasty capon and venison dinners.

Hikers should make for **Townshend State Park** (mid-May to mid-Oct; $3; Ⓣ802/365-7500), just a few miles north of Newfane. Trails include the steep, rocky, 1.7-mile climb to the summit of Bald Mountain (1680ft), as well as plenty of less challenging walks along the valley.

Grafton

Few villages come closer to the stereotypical image of rural Vermont than **GRAFTON**, a truly gorgeous ensemble of white clapboard buildings, shady trees, and a bubbling brook, the Saxtons River. Though the village center was restored by the Windham Foundation (see below), this is no theme park: with 650 permanent inhabitants and regular town hall meetings, Grafton is a vibrant, genuine community. For local maps and **information**, visit Hunter Artworks gift shop (daily 11am–4pm; ☎802/843-1440; ⓦwww.graftonvermont.org), which acts as the local visitors' center from next to *Daniels House Café* in the heart of the village.

You'll pass Grafton's biggest attraction, the **Grafton Village Cheese Company** (Mon–Fri 8am–5pm, Sat & Sun 10am–5pm; ☎802/843-2221 or 1-800/472-3866, ⓦwww.graftonvillagecheese.com), a half-mile before the village center on Rte-35 (Townshend Rd). Here you can buy (and sample) the main types of cheddar produced, and witness the cheese-making process (Mon–Fri 8am–noon).

In the village itself, kids will enjoy the **Nature Museum**, 186 Townshend Rd (summer Sat & Sun 10am–4pm, other times call for appointment; $4, kids 3–12 $2; ☎802/843-2111, ⓦwww.nature-museum.org), a somewhat haphazard taxidermic and geological collection crammed into two floors of a creaky old house, with plenty of activities year-round. The **Windham Foundation** (ⓦwww.windham -foundation.org) is based opposite the Nature Museum; a small exhibit behind the building explains its work in preserving the local sheep industry. If you've an interest in local history, the **Grafton Historical Society Museum**, 147 Main St (mid-May to mid-Oct Fri–Mon & holidays 10am–4pm; open daily last week of Sept to first week Oct; $3 donation; ☎802/843-2584, ⓦwww.graftonhistory .org), is a collection of annually changing exhibits from Grafton homesteads, such as soapstones from local quarries, textiles, and Civil War artifacts. For more activity, visit the **Grafton Ponds Nordic Ski & Mountain Bike Center** (☎802/843-2400, ⓦwww.graftonponds.com), south of the village on Townshend Road (next to Grafton Cheese), open daily for Nordic cross-country skiing in winter and biking in the summer (standard bikes $30 per day).

Otherwise, make for the ⅍ *Old Tavern*, 92 Main St (☎1-800/843-1801, ⓦwww.old-tavern.com; ◉), an upmarket **inn** and **restaurant** at the heart of the village. Around since 1801, it has accommodated everyone from Rudyard Kipling to Teddy Roosevelt. The old carriage house is now a cozy bar, *Phelps Barn*. For something lighter (and cheaper), try *David's House Café* (☎802/843-2255) next door, which serves soups, sandwiches, and salads. In summer you can also check out the free Sunday concerts on the common (5.30pm) given by the **Grafton Cornet Band** (ⓦwww.graftonband.org).

Chester

Seven miles north of Grafton, at the junction of routes 103, 11, and 35, is the tiny village of **CHESTER**, whose houses – a blend of typical Vermont clapboard and more ornate Victorian styles – are laid out charmingly along a narrow green. Drop by the **Chester Historical Society Museum** (July & Aug Sat & Sun 1–4pm; free; ☎802/875-3767, ⓦwww.chesterhs.avenet.net) on Main Street, housed in the old Academy Building next to leafy Brookside Cemetery. Inside you'll find a quirky collection of curios such as a rare *carte de visite* (photographic visiting card) of John Wilkes Booth. The local inn association stocks a usually unmanned but useful **information booth** (summer only) next door, but if that's closed, visit Misty Valley Books (Mon–Fri 10am–6pm, Sat 10am–5pm, Sun 11am–4pm; ☎802/875-3400) across the road for maps and advice.

Besides wandering through the village, you can jump aboard the **Green Mountain Flyer** (July & Aug Sat–Sun 12.30pm; mid-Sept to mid-Oct daily same time; 2hr round-trip; $19; ☎802/463-3069, ⓦwww.rails-vt.com), a sightseeing train that runs from Chester Depot down to Bellows Falls. The engine chugs across rivers and past covered bridges at a leisurely pace, leaving lots of time to take in the scenery, which is spectacular in the fall.

There is a good range of enticing historic **accommodation** in Chester, much of it around the village green. The *Inn Victoria*, 321 Main St (☎802/875-4288 or 1-800/732-4288, ⓦwww.innvictoria.com; ⑤–⑨), goes to town on the Victorian theme with its ornate and comfortable rooms. You could also try the *Chester House Inn*, 166 Main St (☎1-888/875-2205, ⓦwww.chesterhouseinn .com; ⑥), which has seven rooms with private baths, each decorated in a different style and color. Just off the main road at 55 School St, *Rose Arbour* (☎802/875-4766, ⓦwww.rosearbour.com; ⑦) is a pretty B&B with an attached tearoom; the top floor is a five-room suite, complete with kitchen. About one mile west of town, the *Motel-in-the-Meadow*, 936 Rte-11 (☎802/875-2626, ⓦwww.motelinthemeadow.com; ③), is a friendly "mom and pop" motel with cheap, comfortable, well-kept rooms. To **eat**, try *Williams River Café*, 90 Main St (Wed–Sun; ☎802/875-4486), serving bistro-type steaks and grilled meats (and hot cider) from $17, or *Moon Dog Café*, 295 Main St (☎802/875-4486), with fresh salads and sandwiches from $7.

Bennington

Little has happened in **BENNINGTON** to match the excitement of the days when Ethan Allen's Green Mountain Boys were based here – two hundred years ago. Settled in 1761 on a rise by the Walloomsac River, overlooking the valley between the Green and Taconic mountains, the town became a leading nineteenth-century industrial outpost for paper mills, potteries, gristmills, and the largest cotton-batting mill in the US. Today, it's most notable for its Revolutionary history, covered bridges, and fine, hand-crafted pottery, though the exclusive, arts-oriented **Bennington College** has seen the likes of authors Bret Easton Ellis and Donna Tartt pass through its halls (Tartt set her *Secret History* in a fictional version of the town).

Arrival and information

Bennington straddles the intersection of US-7 and Rte-9, a junction known locally as the "Four Corners." In town, Rte-9 is referred to as Main Street, while the local stretches of US-7 above and below the Corners are called North and South streets. You'll find a **free parking lot** on Main Street, east of the Four Corners.

Getting here by public transit is tough; there are no trains and no long-distance buses, though the Green Mountain Express (☎802/447-0477; $2), runs four times daily between Bennington and Manchester, with stops along Historic Rte-7A. The Bennington stop is at the Bank North parking lot, on Main Street one block east of Four Corners.

The **Bennington Area Chamber of Commerce**, north of Four Corners, US-7 (Mon–Fri 9am–5pm, Sat 10am–4pm; May–Oct also Sun 10am–4pm; ☎802/447-3311 or 1-800/229-0252, ⓦwww.bennington.com), provides information on surrounding attractions and has clean public restrooms. The **Downtown Welcome Center**, on South Street near the Four Corners (daily 10am–5pm; ☎802/442-5758), offers a similar array of information.

EATING & DRINKING

Alldays and Onions	8
Blue Benn Diner	4
Hunter's	1
Izabella's Eatery	6
Kevin's	2
Madison Brewing Co.	7
Pangaea	3
Rattlesnake Café	5

ACCOMMODATION

Alexandra Inn	B
Bennington Motor Inn	E
Catamount Motel	G
Four Chimneys Inn	C
Harwood Hill Motel	A
Paradise Motor Inn	D
Samuel Safford Inne	F

A, B, 1, 2, 3, Bennington College, North Bennington & Shaftsbury

BENNINGTON

Albany, NY, Center for the Arts & Covered Bridge Museum

Walloomsac River

Bennington Battle Monument

Chamber of Commerce

Old First Church

OLD BENNINGTON

Old Cemetery

Bennington Museum

Bennington Potters

Four Corners

Downtown Welcome Center

0   500 yds

& Williamstown

& Brattleboro

Accommodation

Budget motels line South and West Main streets, and there are a few other options scattered about. Those who prefer "name brand" chain motels will be disappointed in what the area has to offer (namely just a *Best Western* on Northside Drive), but its independent motels and hotels are generally clean and reasonably priced. Several miles away in Woodford, the *Greenwood Lodge Hostel and Campsites*, Prospect Mountain off Rte-9 (☎802/442-2547, ⓦwww.campvermont.com /greenwood), an HI/AYH-affiliated property, has dorm beds with kitchen and recreation access, available for $28 ($25 for members; sheets $3) and wooded campsites for $23 (open mid-May to late Oct).

Alexandra Inn 916 Orchard Rd, just off Rte-7A ☎802/442-5619 or 1-888/207-9386, ⓦwww.alexandrainn.com. Restored Colonial with twelve luxurious rooms featuring jet tubs, fireplaces, hearty gourmet breakfasts, and a garden and beautiful views of its two green acres. ⑤–⑧

Bennington Motor Inn 143 Main St ☎802/442-5479 or 1-800/359-9900, ⓦwww.coolcruisers.net.

Family-run inn with sixteen comfortable rooms with the standard conveniences, plus microwaves and data ports for the internet. ④–⑤

Catamount Motel 500 South St ☎802/442-5977, ⓦwww.catamountmotel.com. Large, slightly worn rooms, with a pool and a picnic area. Worth considering for its low rates out of season. Within walking distance of downtown. ③–⑤

Four Chimneys Inn 21 West Rd (Rte-9)
ⓣ 802/447-3500, ⓦ www.fourchimneys.com.
Eleven comfortable, country rooms, most with a
fireplace and sofa, in an elegant white manor
on eleven acres. Full breakfast included; the
restaurant is open for sumptuous dinners
Wed–Sun. ⑥–⑧

🎿 **Harwood Hill Motel** 864 Harwood Hill Rd
(Rte-7A) ⓣ 802/442-6278, ⓦ www
.harwoodhillmotel.com. If you don't mind staying
out of town, this friendly motel is a superb deal,
with spacious and immaculate rooms equipped
with free wi-fi and microwaves. See website for
directions. ④

Paradise Motor Inn 141 Main St
ⓣ 802/442-8351, ⓦ www.theparadisemotorinn
.com. Perfectly satisfactory accommodation a few
blocks from the Four Corners. Heated outdoor pool
and tennis courts, and some of the 76 rooms are
equipped with saunas. A relatively large hotel,
so a good place to try if there are no vacancies
elsewhere. ④–⑤

Samuel Safford Inne 722 Main St,
ⓣ 802/442-5934, ⓦ www.samuelsaffordinne.com.
Gorgeous B&B with just two rooms right in the
center, perfect for couples; hearty breakfast
included. Reserve months in advance. ④–⑥

The town and around

The best place to begin your exploration of Bennington is the section of town known as **Old Bennington**, one mile west of the Four Corners. This area is home to the town's most prominent icon, the **Bennington Battle Monument**, 15 Monument Circle (daily: mid-April to late Oct 9am–5pm; $2), a 306-foot limestone obelisk that commemorates the August 1777 Battle of Bennington. This pivotal conflict pitted the New Hampshire militia, led by John Stark, and the Green Mountain Boys, under Seth Warner (Ethan Allen was an English prisoner at the time), against the forces of General Burgoyne, who wanted to capture Bennington's arsenal. The unexpected victory of the Revolutionaries denied Burgoyne's troops of crucial supplies, contributing to their defeat at the subsequent Battle of Saratoga, the war's major turning point. The monument stands on what was Burgoyne's objective (the battle actually took place just over the Walloomsac River, in New York State). You can reach the 200-foot observation deck via elevator – the views of Bennington and its surroundings are magnificent.

Just down Monument Avenue on Main Street (Rte-9) is the **Old First Church**, erected in 1805. The abutting cemetery is the resting place of poet **Robert Frost**, buried here in 1963. Signs point the way to his tombstone, which reads simply, "I had a lover's quarrel with the world," an epitaph that never ceases to amuse the church's many visitors. East of here, the **Bennington Museum**, 75 Main St (Mon–Tues & Thurs–Sun 10am–5pm; $9; ⓣ 802/447-1571, ⓦ www.benningtonmuseum.org), contains a fine array of Americana: several Tiffany lamps; an American flag that may be the oldest in existence (though some historians claim it was actually made in the nineteenth century); tiny sewing machines; nineteenth-century furniture made by local craftsmen; and a Martin-Wasp luxury touring car, built in Bennington in 1925 and the only surviving example of its kind. The highlight of the collection, however, is its exhibit on American folk artist Anna Mary Robertson Moses (1860–1961), more familiarly known as **Grandma Moses**. The artist, who first started painting her simple representations of rural life at the age of 73, experienced a meteoric rise to fame in the 1940s, and by the time she reached her hundredth birthday in 1960 she enjoyed national adulation. In addition to the largest public collection of her work, the museum moved the **schoolhouse** she attended as a youngster to their grounds in 1972; inside are displays of many of her personal belongings, photographs, painting equipment, and awards.

Downtown Bennington has little in the way of sights, though **Bennington Potters**, 324 County St (Mon–Sat 9.30am–6pm, Sun 10am–5pm;

ⓣ 800/205-8033, ⓦ www.benningtonpotters.com) remains a popular attraction for its robust, handmade New England-style pottery. You can tour the workshop, open for over sixty years, before browsing the store.

If you have time, it's worth driving out to the **Bennington Center for the Arts** (Wed–Mon 10am–5pm; $9; ⓣ 802/442-7158, ⓦ www.bennington centerforthearts.org), around two miles west of the center of town on Rte-9. Here you'll find several galleries showing the work of local artists and an engaging room of Native American (Hopi) artifacts, collected by a Colorado

▲ Bennington Battle Monument

miner in the 1890s and discovered in a local house in 1929. The real highlight, though, is the **Covered Bridge Museum**, a small but enlightening exhibition covering just about everything connected with the iconic New England structure – there are around three hundred bridges remaining, a third of which are in Vermont.

North Bennington and Shaftsbury

Rte-7A splits off from US-7 north of the center and continues on for five miles to **NORTH BENNINGTON**, passing three **covered bridges** – the Silk Road, Paper Mill Village, and the Burt Henry – spanning the Walloomsac River. In the center of the village, the elaborate Italianate and Second Empire-style **Park-McCullough House**, Park and West streets (daily: mid-May to late Oct 10am–4pm, tours hourly; $8; ☎802/442-5441, ⓦwww.parkmccullough.org), a sumptuous 1864 mansion, is filled with most of its original period furnishings, including children's toys.

In the nearby village of **SHAFTSBURY**, the **Robert Frost Stone House Museum**, 121 Rte-7A (May–Nov Tues–Sun 10am–5pm; $5; ☎802/447-6200, ⓦwww.frostfriends.org), is a memorial to one of New England's favorite poets. The house should appeal to Frost enthusiasts, as you can see the rooms in which poems such as *Stopping by Woods on a Snowy Evening* were crafted. The surrounding scenery no doubt provided Frost with valuable inspiration when he lived here (1920–29).

Eating, drinking, and entertainment

There's not an overwhelming variety when it comes to types of cuisine served in Bennington, though there are plenty of **restaurants** that knock out decent American staples, as well as a few high-end places. Nights are fairly quiet, as the college population rarely gets too rowdy. In the summer, the **Oldcastle Theater Company** (ⓦwww.oldcastletheatreco.org) holds court at the Bennington Center for the Arts (see p.343).

Alldays and Onions 519 Main St ☎802/447-0043. Creative meat and fish dishes at reasonable prices, served with bread from the in-house bakery. Essentially a lunch place, though it's also open for dinner Tues–Sat and breakfasts Sat–Sun.

Blue Benn Diner 314 North St (US-7) ☎802/442-5140. This authentic, 1940s-era diner is a local institution that draws a diverse crowd of hard-boiled locals and artsy students. In addition to the usual diner favorites, vegetarian dishes also feature on the menu. Open from 6am daily.

Hunter's 782 Harwood Hill Rd (Rte-7A), near the US-7 intersection ☎802/442-7500. Remodeled barn turned gourmet restaurant perched on a hill with excellent views of New York, New Hampshire, and Massachusetts and serving high-quality but reasonably priced steaks and seafood (entrees $14–23).

Izabella's Eatery 351 Main St ☎802/447-4949. Creative and tasty selection of sandwiches and paninis (from $6) for breakfast and lunch, featuring plenty of Cabot cheddars, peanut butter, and fresh honey-apple chutney. Open Tues–Sat till 3pm.

Kevin's 27 Main St, N Bennington ☎802/442-0122. Locals flock to this sports bar and restaurant (with 9 TVs and prime rib specials, wings, burgers, and seafood on the menu) that doubles as a casual venue for live bands or karaoke on the weekends. Entrees $9–15.

Madison Brewing Co 428 Main St ☎802/442-7397. Fun, stylish brewpub with hearty burgers ($7) and six varieties of in-house beer ($3.25–5). Live blues most nights of the week. Open daily until 2am.

Pangaea 1–3 Prospect St, N Bennington ☎802/442-7171. Fine dining with an eclectic menu featuring such dishes as Thai curry, maple-glazed pork loin, and spring rolls (entrees $19–23); the lounge menu is simpler and a bit cheaper (burgers for $9). Almost forty beer and 75 wine options from all over the world. Open Tues–Sat 5–9pm (lounge open daily).

Rattlesnake Café 230 North St ☎802/447-7018. A popular no-frills Mexican joint with a great selection of microbrews on tap. Tacos start at $6, quesadillas at $14. Closed Mon.

North along Historic Rte-7A

US-7 and **Historic Rte-7A** parallel each other as they run from Bennington north to Manchester, though the latter is the preferable road to take – not only is it a more picturesque drive, but there are a few notable stop-offs along the way. The great spine of the Green Mountains rises up to the east, with the Taconics somewhat more irregularly splayed out along the west, putting the route smack in the so-called "Valley of Vermont."

Arlington

About halfway up Rte-7A, the small town of **ARLINGTON** is the former home of illustrator Norman Rockwell (see box, p.238), who created some of his most memorable *Saturday Evening Post* covers while living here between 1939 and 1954. By far the most interesting aspect of the otherwise modest **Norman Rockwell Exhibition** (May–Oct daily 9am–5pm; Nov–April Mon–Fri 10am–4pm, Sat & Sun 10am–5pm; $3; T 802/375-6423) at 3772 Rte-7A, are the volunteers on duty, invariably locals that Rockwell used as his models; the best part of the gallery (which shows mostly copies of his work) pairs his images with photos of some of these characters.

Practicalities
There is a self-service **visitors' booth** with maps and brochures (daily 9am–5pm; T 802/362-2100) in Arlington on Rte-7A next to Stewart's store. The Green Mountain Express (see p.340) also stops at Stewart's.

There is **accommodation** both in Arlington and along Rte-7A. Rockwell fans should opt for the *Inn on Covered Bridge Green*, 3587 River Rd off Rte-313 (T 802/375-9489, W www.coveredbridgegreen.com; ❼–❽), his attractive former home. The lovely landscaped grounds and pet llamas at the *West Mountain Inn*, about half a mile west of Arlington at 144 West Mountain Inn Rd, at the intersection of River Road and Rte-313 (T 802/375-6516, W www.westmountaininn .com; ❽–❾), are the trade-off for telephone- and TV-free rooms and a hefty price tag. The *Arlington Inn*, Rte-7A (T 802/375-6532 or 1-800/443-9442, W www .arlingtoninn.com; ❺), is another very comfortable option, this time in the middle of town. Cheaper lodgings can be found north of Arlington on Rte-7A at *Cut Leaf Maples Motel* (T 802/375-2725, E cutleaf@verizon.net; ❸). You can **camp** at *Camping on the Battenkill*, Rte-7A, less than one mile west of Arlington (April–Oct; T 802/375-6663 or 1-800/830-6663), which has over a hundred sites starting at $26. The **restaurant** at the *West Mountain Inn* serves five-course dinners for $42, while romantic candlelit meals (try the hazelnut-crusted chicken) are served at the *Arlington Inn* (Tues–Sun from 5.30pm).

Manchester and around

The last town on Rte-7A before it merges with US-7 is **MANCHESTER**, which has been a resort town for some two hundred years, a fact evidenced by its transformation into little more than a giant outlet mall – when locals grumble about "*faux* Vermont," this is what they mean. Still, **Hildene** is one of the most impressive mansions in the state, and the surrounding area is well situated for outdoor pursuits, especially **skiing** on nearby **Bromley** and **Stratton** mountains, and **fly-fishing** in its many trout streams. It's no coincidence that **Charles Orvis**, founder of fly-rod manufacturer Orvis Company, is a Manchester native. A visit to the company's flagship store is a worthwhile excursion, even if you have no intention of making a purchase.

Arrival and information

The **Green Mountain Express** (☎802/442-9458) runs four buses daily from Arlington and Bennington ($2), while Marble Valley Regional Transit runs **Commuter Connection**, a similar service, north to Rutland (five times daily; $2; ☎802/773-3244, ⊛www.thebus.com). You'll find plenty of information at the **Manchester and the Mountains Chamber of Commerce**, 5046 Main St, Manchester Center (Mon–Fri 8.30am–5pm; ☎802/362-2100 or 1-800/362-4144, ⊛www.manchestervermont.net), or the information booth opposite (Sat 10am–5pm, Sun 10am–3pm).

Accommodation

Manchester's resort status weighs heavily on the rates at the town's most centrally located **inns and motels**. You'll find more reasonably priced places outside Manchester Center.

Aspen Motel 5669 Main St (Rte-7A), north of Manchester Center ☎802/362-2450, ⊛www .theaspenatmanchester.com. Family-run motel that's been a fixture for years, with comfortable rooms, a pool, and a two-bedroom cottage available for larger groups. ⑤

🎿 **Equinox Resort** 3567 Main St (Rte-7A), Manchester Village ☎802/362-4700 or 1-800/362-4747, ⊛www.equinoxresort.com. The swankiest place in town, the sprawling *Equinox* is full of restored Victorian-era quarters, upscale amenities, and old-world New England charm. Includes the *1811 House* and the *Charles Orvis Inn*, which provides access to a billiards room, honor bar with cigars, and other luxuries, in the former home of Orvis himself. ⑨

Four Winds Country Motel 7379 Main St (Rte-7A), north of Manchester Center ☎802/362-0905 or 1-877/456-7654, ⊛www.fourwindscountrymotel .com. Ceramic-tiled baths and understated decor figure prominently at this simple country inn. Cable TV, microwaves, and front patio for every room. ④

Ira Allen House 6311 Rte-7A, south of Manchester Village ☎877/362-2284, ⊛www .iraallenhouse.com. Warm, comfy rooms, all with

cable TV and some with wood-burning fireplaces and four-poster beds. Ethan Allen and cousin Ira are said to have built the house; you can even stay in Ethan's alleged room. ⑥

🎿 **Manchester View** Rte-7A, north of Manchester Center ☎802/362-2739 or 1-800/548-4141, ⊛www.manchesterview.com. Not much to look at from the road, but the *View* has an unbeatable vista of the Green Mountains. Each of the 35 relaxing, great-value rooms – including some extra spacious "speciality" rooms – comes with refrigerator and deck. Amenities include a heated pool, golf, and tennis. ⑥

Reluctant Panther Inn 17–39 West Rd, Manchester Village ☎802/362-2568 or 1-800/822-2331, ⊛www.reluctantpanther.com. Modern furnishings line the splendid Victorian-style suites here, with a full three-course Vermont breakfast included. Their excellent (and très expensive) gourmet restaurant is here too. ⑧–⑨

Stamford Motel 6458 Main St (Rte-7A), north of Manchester Center ☎802/362-2342, ⊛www .thestamfordmotel.com. Tastefully decorated budget motel, with views of the hills from most rooms. There's also a heated pool. ④–⑥

The Town

The first place of interest heading into Manchester on Rte-7A, five miles north of Arlington, is historic **Hildene** (daily 9.30am–4.30pm; $12.50, $5 for grounds only; ☎802/362-1788, ⊛www.hildene.org), a 24-room Georgian Revival mansion that belonged to longtime Manchester resident Robert Todd Lincoln, son of sixteenth US president Abraham Lincoln and a prominent diplomat and businessman in his own right. It's a magnificent four-hundred-acre estate, made more intimate with many of the family's personal effects. An exhibit dedicated to Abraham Lincoln displays one of his familiar black stovepipe hats – one of only three still in existence – along with presidential portraits. Free guided **tours** are offered at noon each day.

Another mile north along Rte-7A is **Manchester Village**, the pristine historical section of the town, anchored by its immaculate clapboard church, courthouse, and *Equinox Resort* (see above; park for free behind the Equinox

Village Shops). Somewhat less artificial, the **Southern Vermont Arts Center** (Tues–Sat 10am–5pm, Sun noon–5pm; $8; ☎802/362-1405, ⊛www.svac.org), on West Road off Rte-7A, is home to a fine ensemble of works, including the world's largest collection of Luigi Lucioni paintings.

The flagship **Orvis Store** (Mon–Sat 10am–6pm, Sun 10am–5pm; ☎802/362-3750), a short drive beyond Manchester Village on Rte-7A, was opened in 2002, and doubles as a shrine to the company's locally born founder. The extravagantly expensive fly-fishing rods are worth a look, as are the on-site trout pond used for casting demonstrations and the beautiful handcrafted hunting rifles, yours for $10,000 (or more). Just along the road is the **Orvis Outlet** (same hours), which offers last year's models for around fifty percent less.

Beyond here lies **Manchester Center**, essentially one huge open-air shopping mall, though **Northshire Bookstore** (Mon–Wed & Sun 10am–7pm, Thurs–Sat 10am–9pm; ☎802/362-2200), at the intersection of routes 7A and 11, ranks as one of the region's finest independent bookstores.

Eating, drinking, and entertainment

Places to eat in Manchester tend to be upscale and pricey – albeit rather good. Note that many hotels also run excellent restaurants, such as the *Marsh Tavern* in the *Equinox Resort*. The summer brings a variety of events to town, including Shakespeare and craft fairs at Hildene, and the **Manchester Music Festival** (☎802/362-1956, ⊛www.mmfvt.org), a series of Thursday concerts at the Southern Vermont Arts Center.

The Bean 4201 Main St, opposite Orvis ☎802/362-0110. Superb Mexican food; highlights include the crispy *chimichangas*, the platter of three giant tacos, and very potent margaritas. Vegetarian-friendly.

Manchester Pizza House Rte-11/30, in Manchester Shopping Center ☎802/362-3338. It's plain as can be, but the pizza's good. All the usual toppings, plus calzone and pastas.

Maxwell's Flat Road Grill 575 Depot St (Rte-11/30) ☎802/362-3721. Oldest tavern in town, with burgers and salads and pub grub. Live entertainment Wed and Fri, with karaoke on Sat nights.

The Perfect Wife 2594 Depot St (Rte-11/30), east of Manchester Center ☎802/362-2817. Creative fare (Peking duck with pancake starter, sesame-crusted tuna) on the expensive side (entrees $19–28), or a

more traditional menu in the tavern room for the budget-conscious (entrees from $9).

Spiral Press Café 15 Bonnet St ☎802/362-9944. The destination for excellent caffeinated drinks and wi-fi, alongside some muffins, bagels, and sandwich specials. It's connected to Northshire Books (see above).

Up for Breakfast 4935 Main St ☎802/362-4204. If you crave interesting omelettes, French toast, or blueberry pancakes, this is the obvious choice. Fun and friendly, with decent portions. Closes Mon–Fri at 12.30pm, Sat & Sun at 1.30pm.

Ye Olde Tavern 5183 Main St ☎802/362-0611. This 1790 building is romantic and candlelit, and the perfect place for Yankee favorites like exceptional pot roast and chicken pot pie (entrees $17–29). Very extensive wine list.

Bromley Mountain Resort and Stratton Mountain Resort

Two **ski resorts** within striking distance of Manchester, both a short drive into the Green Mountains, offer quite different winter vacation experiences. **Bromley Mountain Resort**, six miles east of town on Rte-11 (one-day lift tickets $63 Sat & Sun, $39 Mon–Fri; ☎802/824-5522, ⊛www.bromley .com), is great for families. In summer, it's transformed into the **Sun Mountain Adventure Park**, complete with Alpine Slide, 24-foot climbing wall, 100-foot zipline, and bumper boats (mid-June to Aug daily 10.30am–5pm; mid-May to mid-June & Sept to mid-Oct weekends only; all-day package $39 Sat & Sun, $29 Mon–Fri).

Larger and slightly higher than Bromley, **Stratton Mountain Resort** (one-day tickets $78 Sat & Sun, $69 Mon–Fri; ☎802/297-4000 or 1-800/

STRATTON, (🌐www.stratton.com) ranks as one of Vermont's premier ski destinations. Although it's a better choice for serious skiers than Bromley, be aware that this far south you may be sliding on artificial snow. There is good **cross-country skiing** on the twenty-plus miles of trails at the Stratton Nordic Center; some of the routes weave through secluded forests and others cut across open countryside. Things are a bit more refined here in summer, with a focus on tennis and golf.

The Green Mountains and Hwy-100

Hwy-100 offers a third route into the heart of Vermont, running just to the east of the **Green Mountains**. The road is rarely busy, even in peak season, and offers unspoiled views of evergreen slopes as well as a few charming towns as it snakes north. Note that although the Green Mountains are not as harsh as New Hampshire's White Mountains, the hills are still buried in snow for most of the winter, and the higher roads are liable to be blocked for long periods.

Pick up the route in **Wilmington**, almost halfway between Brattleboro and Bennington, where the road leads up to the unassuming ski resort at **Mount Snow**. North of here, Hwy-100 weaves through the village of **Weston**, with its fun country stores, and on to more commercial **Ludlow** and **Okemo Mountain**, another of the state's top ski resorts. Beyond Ludlow, **Plymouth Notch** is one of the most absorbing presidential hometowns in the country, beautifully preserved as the **Calvin Coolidge State Historic Site**.

The Long Trail

Running along the ridge of Vermont's Green Mountains, 272 miles from the Massachusetts border to Québec, the **Long Trail** is one of America's premier **hiking trails**. The northern section is a more strenuous – and an ultimately more rewarding – hike, crossing some of the highest peaks in Vermont. **The Camel's Hump** (4083ft) and **Mount Mansfield** (4393ft) are both well-trod peaks from which you get some fine views, but not the sense of splendid isolation that kicks in farther north across the Jay Peak Range, as the trail nears its end. The Long Trail actually follows the same route as the **Appalachian Trail** for 97 miles before splitting near Rutland.

The presence of white blazes indicates that you're walking on the Long Trail. Intersections are usually marked with signs; double blazes signal important turns; and the almost one hundred side trails (totaling 175 miles) are blazed in blue and signposted. Those planning on hiking the entire length of the trail should count on it taking between twenty-five and thirty days. The most conventional way of accomplishing this feat is to hike from shelter to shelter (see below), although with good preparation (and some transport assistance from others) you could complete the trail by taking only day-hikes.

Accommodation on the Long Trail consists of about seventy shelters, maintained during summer and usually no more than a gentle day's hike apart. A moderate fee is charged at sites with caretakers, and availability is on a first-come, first-served basis. All shelters are on the primitive side (no electricity or running water), and can be fully enclosed wood cabins, three-sided lean-tos, or tent sites. All sites have a water source, although this doesn't necessarily mean that the water is drinkable without treatment. For further reading, get the *Long Trail Guide* ($19), published by the caretakers of the trail, the Green Mountain Club (☎802/244-7037, 🌐www .greenmountainclub.org).

Wilmington

Seventeen miles west of Brattleboro, at the intersection of Rte-9 and Hwy-100, you'll encounter **WILMINGTON**, a genial place situated along the North Branch Deerfield River and lined with stores full of knick-knacks, New England crafts, and more than enough Vermont maple syrup and cheddar. The only real stop of note is the **Young & Constantin Gallery** at 10 South Main St, not far from the junction of highways 9 and 100 in the center of town (July 4 to mid-Oct daily 11.30am–5pm; rest of year Thurs–Mon 11.30am–5pm; ⊤802/464-2515). Though they carry an assortment of expensive handmade items (which can include ceramics and metal pieces), they specialize in glasswork. The **Mount Snow Valley Chamber of Commerce**, a short walk from the intersection on West Main Street (Mon–Sat 10am–5pm, Sun 10am–4pm; ⊤802/464-8092 or 1-877/VTSOUTH, ⓦwww .visitvermont.com), can help with any questions you may have about the town and surrounding area. There are several worthy (and expensive) **restaurants** here too, like *The White House*, 178 Rte-9 (⊤802/464-2135), perched on a hilltop east of the center, where you can order Steak Diane or Veal Oscar. But even the ultra-casual and super-friendly *Dot's*, 3 Main St (⊤802/464-7284), a lunch-counter diner at the junction in the center of town (with parking), has award-winning chili (bowls for $5) and scrumptious "berry berry" pancakes and muffins, a blend of several berries and cream cheese (from $1.75).

Mount Snow

Traveling north from Wilmington, Hwy-100 ambles on to the resort of **Mount Snow** near the town of West Dover. Officially part of the **Green Mountain National Forest**, this is a perfectly fine place to ski, and without the crowds of other major snowbound havens such as Killington and Stowe. **Mount Snow Resort** (⊤802/464-2151, ⓦwww.mountsnow.com) offers some 130 trails (lift tickets $75 Sat & Sun, $69 Mon–Fri).

You'll also find plenty of outdoorsy stuff to occupy you here in the summer. Mount Snow has a sizeable **mountain-biking** fan base: the National Off-Road Bicycling Association has held championship events here since 1988. It's $30 for lift and trail day passes and $55 per day to rent a bike, but note that all trails accessed by lift are for advanced-level bikers only. Mount Snow ($44–75 per day) and the Haystack Golf Club, 70 Spyglass Drive, Wilmington ($49–79 per day; ⊤802/464-8301, ⓦwww.haystackgolf.com) cater to golfers with championship courses.

You can **stay** inside the resort at the extremely plush *Grand Summit Resort Hotel* (⊤800/498-0479; ❺–❽). If you wish to stay nearby, try the *Deer Hill Inn*, 14 Valley View Rd just off Hwy-100, West Dover (⊤802/464-3100, ⓦwww.deerhillinn .com; ❻–❽) which have fourteen cozy and colorful rooms, or the *Snow Goose*, 259 Hwy-100, West Dover (⊤802/464-3984, ⓦwww.snowgooseinn.com; ❼–❽), whose rooms have fireplaces and Jacuzzis. If you wish to camp, Molly Stark State Park, 705 Rte-9 East (⊤802/464-5460), has 23 tent sites (late May to mid-Oct; $14–21), but as this is on a popular travel route, you should reserve in advance. There are several **places to eat** at Mount Snow, including upmarket *Harriman's Restaurant* (⊤802/464-1100 ext 6032), and the cheaper *Grand Country Deli* (both in the *Grand Summit Resort*).

Weston

One of the prettier villages along Hwy-100, **WESTON** spreads beside a little river on an idyllic green. In town, Hwy-100 turns into Main Street, and is lined with stores selling antiques, toys, and fudge. The spell is slightly broken when you realize that the labyrinthine **Vermont Country Store** (daily 9am–5.30pm;

@ www.vermontcountrystore.com), for all its seeming quaintness, is actually part of a chain of superstores that packages and markets the state's bucolic image. The **Weston Village Store**, opposite at 660 Main St (daily 9am–5pm; @ www.westonvillagestore.com), contains a much more authentic – and cheaper – range of vaguely rural and domestic articles, such as locally produced maple syrup and cheeses.

On the other side of the town green is Weston's diminutive **Historic District**, a cul-de-sac of restored buildings managed by the Weston Historical Society (T832/824–5294). The 1795 **Farrar-Mansur House** (July to mid-Oct Wed & Sun 1–4pm, Sat 10am–4pm; $2), a former tavern that has been restored to depict lives of early Vermont settlers, presents an array of antique housewares and some decent American folk art. Next door, the **Old Mill Museum** (same times) occupies the site of a sawmill built in 1780, though the current building was restored in the 1930s. Inside you'll find the old gristmill and an impressive assortment of tinsmith, woodworking, farming, and dairy tools. You can also visit the **old firehouse**, now containing a vintage Concord carriage from 1880. Nearby and facing the green, the **Weston Playhouse** (Tues–Sun; T802/824–5288, @ www.westonplayhouse.org) is an elegant Neoclassical theater, which spawned the career of the late Lloyd Bridges. The building was rebuilt in 1962 after a fire destroyed the original. It puts on a mixture of standard summer-stock musicals, occasionally with more daring offerings, such as works by Brian Friel and Molière.

Practicalities

The best **accommodation** in town is the inviting, centrally located *Inn at Weston*, 630 Main St (T802/824–6789, @ www.innweston.com; ❽–❾), which also features a first-class restaurant serving divine rainbow trout ($32), and a snug pub. The *Darling Family Inn*, 815 Hwy-100 north of the green (T802/824–3223, @ home.att.net/~darlingfamilyinn; ❹–❻), is another nice B&B, set in a 170-year-old farmhouse. Decent alternatives away from the town center include the *Colonial House Inn & Motel*, south at 287 Hwy-100 (T802/824–6286 or 1-800/639-5033, @ www.cohoinn.com; ❹), and the *Brandmeyer's Mountainside Lodge*, north at 913 Hwy-100 (T802/824–5851, @ www.brandmeyerslodge.com; ❺–❻).

If you're looking to **eat**, a magnificent soda fountain dominates the 1885 mahogany bar of the *Bryant House* restaurant, on Main Street two doors down from the Vermont Country Store (open for lunch Mon–Sat, dinner Fri & Sat; T802/824–6287). The menu includes such classic New England fare as "johnnycakes" of cornbread with molasses ($3.25) and chicken pie ($10.25), as well as burgers and sandwiches (from $8). Another worthy option is *Café at the Falls* (T802/824–3358), inside the playhouse and overlooking the mill and waterfall. Bistro-style cuisine (entrees $16–24) is usually served before every evening performance. Lighter, cheaper fare (sandwiches, ice cream) is available at the Weston Village Store.

Ludlow and Okemo Mountain

Around ten miles north of Weston, Hwy-100 gets slightly more built up as it nears **LUDLOW**, the access point for the family-friendly ski area of **Okemo Mountain Resort** (lift tickets $77 Sat & Sun, $72 Mon–Fri; T802/228-4041 or 1-800/786-5366 for reservations, @ www.okemo.com). Intermediate skiers and snowboarders will find the 106 trails on Okemo Mountain and the seven trails on neighboring **Jackson Gore** (part of the resort) challenging enough, although the expert will probably get bored after a while. One thing that Okemo can guarantee at all times is snow (in season), no small thing this far south: its 95 percent snowmaking coverage is the largest of any resort in Vermont.

Practicalities

The **Okemo Valley Regional Chamber of Commerce** (Mon–Sat 9am–5pm; ☎802/228-5830, ⓦwww.okemovalleyvt.org), on Rte-103/100 in the Okemo Marketplace mall (opposite the turning to the resort), is an excellent source of information. Free **buses** (☎1-800/786-5366) connect Ludlow to Okemo Mountain in season (Dec–March). The resort has free wi-fi, or you can check the **internet** at *Java Baba's* (see below).

Okemo Mountain Resort has plenty of expensive **places to stay**, such as the *Jackson Gore Inn* (☎1-800/786-5366, ⓦwww.okemo.com; ⑨), and Ludlow has no shortage of cheaper inns and motels, but you should obviously plan ahead if you intend to arrive during the ski or fall foliage seasons. Antique-filled lodgings within a mile of the lifts include the *Andrie Rose Inn*, 13 Pleasant St (☎802/228-4846 or 1-800/223-4846, ⓦwww.andrieroseinn.com; ⑤–⑥), and the *Governor's Inn*, 86 Main St (☎802/228-8830 or 1-800/468-3766, ⓦwww.thegovernorsinn.com; ⑤–⑥). Further south along Rte-103, the *Best Western Ludlow Colonial Motel*, 93 Main St (☎802/228-8188, ⓦwww.bestwesternludlow.com; ⑤), has 48 comfortable rooms. The *Happy Trails Motel*, one mile south of town on Rte-103 (☎802/228-8888 or 1-800/228-9984, ⓦwww.happytrailsmotel.com; ④), has rooms with balconies and views of Okemo Mountain, as well as three self-catering suites and two cottages. There's nowhere to **camp** in town, but Coolidge State Park, a mile past the state historic site on Hwy-100A, does have facilities for tents (late May to mid-Oct; $14–25; ☎802/672-3612).

Finding a reasonable place to **eat** won't be too difficult. Try *Trappers*, 190 Main St (☎802/228-5477), for a hearty breakfast, and *Wicked Good Pizza*, 117 Main St (☎802/228-4131) for dinner: New York-style pizzas, calzones, sandwiches, and other stomach-fillers. Slightly more effort is required to eat at *Sam's Steakhouse*, heading south out of town on Rte-103 (dinner only; ☎802/228-2087), but the steaks and prime rib are worth it. For coffee, hot chocolate, soups, and the like, head for *Java Baba's*, Rte-103/100 in the Okemo Marketplace (☎802/228-2326), where the cozy atmosphere and comfy couches are welcome during the winter months.

Plymouth Notch

Eleven miles beyond Ludlow, the village of **PLYMOUTH NOTCH**, just off Hwy-100 on Hwy-100A, is essentially a museum dedicated to the thirtieth US president. One of the best of its kind, the **Calvin Coolidge State Historic Site** (daily late May to mid-Oct 9.30am–5pm; $7.50; ☎802/672-3773, ⓦwww.historicvermont.org/coolidge) goes one step farther than most other presidential historic sites by restoring not just a particular building connected to the president, but an entire village. Born here in 1872, and buried in the local cemetery in 1933, Coolidge never lost ties to the town, taking the presidential oath of office in the family home in 1923 after the unexpected death of Warren Harding (Coolidge was vice president at the time), and conducting "Summer White House" sessions here thereafter. All of the buildings in which Coolidge's life – and a good part of his presidency – played out have been kept more or less the way they were. Other structures, such as a cheese factory, a Congregational church, and a general store (where Coolidge's father was storekeeper), help fill in the details of everyday life in the late nineteenth century.

Central Vermont

While **central Vermont**'s eastern edge is made up mainly of villages and small farms, the rest is a region of great diversity, home to a refined college town, **Middlebury**, picturesque small burgs like cultured but unstuffy **Woodstock**, and the tiny but appealing state capital, **Montpelier**. Two notable ski resorts are also here: rowdy **Killington**, the state's most popular snowy destination, and **Stowe**, a highly regarded vacation spot with a history both as a center of cross-country skiing and as the home of the Von Trapp family (familiar from *The Sound of Music*). Central Vermont also holds the most visited attraction in the state: the **Ben and Jerry's Ice Cream Factory**, perhaps the purest embodiment of Vermont activism and "green" thinking.

Killington

Scenic Hwy-100 eventually winds its way to **KILLINGTON**, nine miles north of Plymouth Notch, a sprawling resort that has grown out of nothing since 1958 to become the most popular ski destination in the state. Killington's permanent population is roughly one thousand, but it's estimated that in season there are enough beds within twenty miles to accommodate some ten thousand people each and every night.

Arrival and information

Other than a small collection of stores and motels on US-4, you'll find most of the action along **Killington Road**, which starts just before the northern intersection of US-4 and Hwy-100. **Killington Resort** itself sits at the top of the road, which terminates at the K-1 Lodge. Your best bet via public transport is to travel on Amtrak to Rutland and take the Marble Valley Regional Transit **buses** here (daily; $2; ℡802/773-3244, ⓦ www.thebus.com).

The **Killington Chamber of Commerce** (Mon–Fri 10am–4pm; ℡802/773-4181 or 1-800/337-1928, ⓦ www.killingtonchamber.com) is on US-4, beyond the turning to Killington Road.

Accommodation

You're spoiled for choice in terms of **accommodation** around these parts, though you may wind up paying a pretty penny, especially during ski season. Accommodation within the resort itself is most prized (but expensive), for its proximity to the lifts. *Wise Vacations*, 405 Killington Rd (℡802/773-4202 or 1-800/639-4680, ⓦ www.wisevacations.com), rents private homes and condos in and around Killington; prices vary, but are only a bit higher than the average inn or B&B.

Cedarbrook Motor Inn On US-4, at the southern junction with Hwy-100, 6 miles south of Killington Rd ℡802/422-9666 or 1-800/446-1088. Good-value option outside the main ski area, with standard but adequate rooms. ❸
Happy Bear Motel 1784 Killington Rd ℡802/422-3305 or 1-800/518-4468,

ⓦ www.happybearmotel.com. Very convenient though basic digs, with refrigerators, wi-fi, and cable TV. Kids under 12 stay for free. ❸
Inn at Long Trail 709 US-4, Sherburne Pass ℡802/775-7181 or 1-800/325-2540, ⓦ www.innatlongtrail.com. After several nights spent in primitive shelters with no electricity or running

water, hikers on the Long Trail will appreciate the comfort of this family-run B&B with tree-trunk beams and a stone fireplace. ❹

Inn of the Six Mountains 2617 Killington Rd ☎802/422-4302 or 1-800/228-4676, ⓦwww.sixmountains.com. The designation "inn" is deceiving, as *Six Mountains* has almost 100 well-appointed quarters, with a spa, tennis court, and fitness and game rooms. Seasonal shuttle to Killington mountain. ❺–❻

Killington Grand Resort Hotel 228 E Mountain Rd, Killington Resort ☎1800/372-2007, ⓦwww.killington.com. The resort's premier hotel features luxury rooms, and a ski-bridge to the slopes. Extras include spa, health club, and outdoor-heated pool. ❾

 Mountain Meadows Lodge 285 Thundering Brook Rd ☎802/775-1010 or 1-800/370-4567, ⓦwww.mountainmeadowslodge.com. Just off US-4, near the turning to Killington Rd, you'll find this unspoiled lakeside farm; it also has an above-average restaurant. ❺

Summit Lodge & Resort 1253 Killington Rd ☎802/422-3535 or 1-800/635-6343, ⓦwww.summitlodgevermont.com. Long-standing area favorite, with free wi-fi and a casual lodge feel, enhanced by the owners' two friendly St Bernards guarding the lobby. ❺

Val Roc Motel On US-4, near the junction with Hwy-100, 6 miles south of Killington Rd ☎802/422-3881 or 1-800/238-8762, ⓦwww.valroc.com. Another quiet and cheap spot, a bit divorced from the main drag, with aging but clean standard motel rooms and plenty of activities for kids. ❹–❺

Skiing and other outdoor activities

Sometimes called the "Beast of the East," on account of its size – its two hundred trails sprawl over seven mountains – and its notoriously rowdy nightlife, **Killington Resort** (lift tickets $82 Sat & holidays, $77 Mon–Fri; ☎802/422-6200 or 1-800/621-6867, ⓦwww.killington.com) sports a freewheeling and wild attitude. Indeed, Killington is often considered to be the eastern equivalent of Vail, and the resort does provide the longest ski and snowboarding season in the eastern US. A less boisterous option is nearby **Pico Mountain**, along US-4 (lift tickets $49 per day; ☎802/422-6200, ⓦwww.picomountain.com;), which is officially part of Killington Resort but much tamer and smaller in style and scale. Its 48 trails are best for skiers of mid-range ability, and there's not as much hot-dogging as you'll find on the other peaks. Killington lift tickets are also valid here.

▲ Killington Resort in summer

Like many other New England mountains, the area has also opened itself up to all sorts of summer activities. At Killington, the focus is on **hiking** and **mountain-biking**, with 45 miles of trails (basic park access $15; with K-1 Gondola rides $35 per day). Rentals are $50 a day. Pico has an **Adventure Center** (10am–5pm: end June to Aug daily; Sept to mid-Oct Sat & Sun) with a climbing wall, alpine slide, mini-golf, and the Pico Power Jump (like a bungee jump). An all-day pass is $34 (the Alpine slide can also be purchased separately for $10).

You can also take the K-1 Gondola (10am–5pm: end June to Aug & first half Oct daily; Sept Sat & Sun; $10 one-way, $15 round-trip) from the K-1 Lodge to the summit of **Killington Peak** (4241ft) and hike down. Pick up trail maps beforehand at the Bike Shop at K-1 Lodge (☎802/422-6232).

Eating

Killington sports a large variety of **dining** establishments – many try to be ambitious, but the greater number aim for simple satisfaction. Look to restaurants attached to inns or hotels for finer fare. Almost everything is to be found on Killington Road.

Birch Ridge Inn 37 Butler Rd at Killington Rd ☎802/422-4293. The seasonal selections are frou-frou (risotto with duck confit, roasted apple and onion soup) and tasty. The Vermont maple crème brûlée dessert is outstanding.

Casey's Caboose 2841 Killington Rd ☎802/422-3795. This favorite train-themed family restaurant offers free chicken wings at its daily happy hour (3–6pm), and plenty of steaks, seafood, and pasta dishes.

The Garlic 1724 Killington Rd ☎802/422-5055. A tasty but not-very-Spanish version of tapas awaits in the *Olive Bar* (think hummus and fried sweet potato chips; $2–8), while in the restaurant, ravioli, chicken, and seafood are liberally spiked with the namesake seasoning. Entrees from $19.

Hemingway's 4988 US-4, three miles south of Killington Rd ☎802/422-3886. You'll be served by professional staff at one of Vermont's finest restaurants, with impeccable surroundings and presentation. The expensive and excellent nouvelle cuisine includes specials like scallops, crab cake, and decent vegetarian-friendly options (entrees $27–36).

Pizza Jerks 1307 Killington Rd ☎802/422-4111. Choose your camp: "Tree Hugger" (all veggie) or "Carcass" (all meat), both $18. Otherwise, choose your own toppings for the New York-style pizzas (from $7.50), washed down with draft beer or wine.

Sushi Yoshi 1915 Killington Rd ☎802/422-4241. Chinese staples and Japanese sushi rolls, all affordable. Hibachi meals ($23 and up), too, for those looking for something a bit different.

Drinking, nightlife, and entertainment

Killington does tend to attract a wild crowd, and accordingly, **drinking** is the most prevalent form of entertainment, though a few places manage to scare up some live music or give people a place to dance. Note that many places close over the summer.

Long Trail Brewing Co Bridgewater Corners (southern intersection of US-4 and Hwy-100) ☎802/672-5011. One of Vermont's best microbreweries offers self-guided tours and, more importantly, a bar where you can sample the freshly made suds. Pints $4; Vermont pints $5. Daily 10am–6pm.

McGrath's Irish Pub 709 US-4, at *Inn at Long Trail* ☎802/775-7181. Warm, inviting hangout, with live Irish music on the weekends, and a tavern menu of American and Irish standards. Rumor has it that they sell the most Guinness in the state.

Mogul's 2630 Killington Rd ☎802/422-4777. Basic sports bar with cheap drafts, pool tables, and 30 TVs, including one large screen.

Pickle Barrel 1741 Killington Rd ☎802/422-3035. A rowdy bar and nightclub that gets crazy on winter weekends (opposite *Garlic*, halfway up). Open Oct–April.

Skybox Grille 133 E Mountain Rd, Mountain Green Ski Resort (top of Killington Rd) ☎802/422-7499. Sports-themed hangout, with 24 big-screen satellite TVs to park yourself in front of, with a draft beer, of course. Open Nov–April.

Wobbly Barn Steakhouse 2229 Killington Rd ☎ 802/422-6171, ⓦ www.wobblybarn .com. Some sort of lively entertainment every weekend, but the draw since 1963 has really been the beef and prime rib (broiled, mesquite-grilled, and barbecued). Come for "Wild Game Night" on Tues (elk, venison, buffalo), or "Lynchburg Southern Barbecue Sundays" for a bit of non-regional amusement. Entrees from $25. Open Nov–April, daily from 4.30pm.

Woodstock and around

WOODSTOCK, a few miles west of the Connecticut River on US-4, has long been considered a bit more refined than its rural neighbors, with something of an artistic vibe. This can be attributed to the town's status as the home of a few minor artists and writers, such as sculptor Hiram Powers, novelist Sinclair Lewis, and painter Paul Cadmus. Adding to its appeal are the distinguished houses that surround its oval green, most of which have been taken over by antiques stores and tearooms, and the art galleries and upscale eateries populating its tiny downtown area. Don't confuse this town with the Woodstock of festival fame, though; that town is in upstate New York.

Arrival and information

Getting to Woodstock is tough without your own car; Amtrak and Greyhound serve White River Junction, 14 miles east, but you'll have to take a taxi from there (Big Yellow Taxi ☎ 802/281-8294). The **Woodstock Welcome Center** on Mechanic Street (daily 9am–5pm; ☎ 802/432-1100, ⓦ www.woodstockvt .com), just off the main street, has tons of visitor information, and also has parking nearby ($0.25 for 30min).

Accommodation

Places to stay in Woodstock are plentiful and luxurious, but usually expensive. Sites farther from town are cheaper; there are several cookie-cutter motor lodges along US-4 east of the center. The welcome center can organize accommodation in private houses ("overflow homes") during very busy periods such as fall foliage season.

1830 Shire Town Inn 31 South St (Rte-106) ☎ 802/457-1830 or 1-866/286-1830, ⓦ www.1830shiretowninn.com. In downtown Woodstock, this restored farmhouse offers three guestrooms with mammoth beds, clawfoot tubs, and hearty breakfasts, across the street from Vail Field park. ⑥

Applebutter Inn 7511 Happy Valley Rd (just off US-4) in Taftsville, 4 miles east of Woodstock ☎ 802/457-4158, ⓦ www.applebutterinn.com. Cozy B&B in an 1854 gabled house, with comfortable beds, personable proprietors, and breakfasts featuring home-made granola. ⑤–⑧

Ardmore Inn 23 Pleasant St ☎ 802/457-3887, ⓦ www.ardmoreinn.com. Charming Victorian/Greek Revival home with five airy, stylish rooms close to the center. Daily breakfasts are huge, and the friendly hosts provide guests with a treat or two to take home. ⑥

Braeside Motel 432 Woodstock Rd (US-4) ☎ 802/457-1366, ⓦ www.braesidemotel.com. Not quite a mile east of the village, you'll find clean and basic family-owned motel digs with very few extra amenities, save for a swimming pool. ⑤

Kedron Valley Inn Rte-106, South Woodstock ☎ 802/457-1473, ⓦ www.kedronvalleyinn.com. A private lake, nearby stables, home-made quilts, fireplaces, and Jacuzzis are welcome extras at this ultra-comfortable spot with twenty-odd country-style rooms. ⑦

Shire Riverview 46 Pleasant St ☎ 802/457-2211, ⓦ www.shiremotel.com. A good mid-range option on the eastern edge of town. The elegant, spacious rooms come with gas fireplaces and antique furnishings, and some overlook the Ottauquechee River. ⑤–⑥

Village Inn of Woodstock 41 Pleasant St ⊤802/457-1255 or 1-800/722-4571, ⊛www .villageinnofwoodstock.com. Quaint B&B, renovated in the Victorian style, with an inviting front porch and attractive gardens. The tavern room, for guests only, offers cocktails, beer, or espresso. ❼–❽

Woodstock Inn and Resort 14 The Green ⊤802/457-1100 or 1-800/448-7900,

⊛www.woodstockinn.com. The largest, fanciest, and best place to stay in the area, with sumptuous rooms, beautiful grounds, an 18-hole golf course, and four gourmet restaurants. It's also got a winter sports facility, and a health and fitness center with a spa for the ultimate in pampering. ❾

The Town

Woodstock's center is an oval green at the convergence of Elm, Central, and Church streets, which are lined with architecturally diverse houses that provide a genteel foreground to the landscape of rolling hills. The **Dana House Museum**, 26 Elm St (May–Oct Mon–Sat 10am–4pm, Sun noon–4pm; $5; ⊤802/457-1822, ⊛www.woodstockhistorical.org), is one of the best museums of its kind, with well-organized multimedia displays, including tape recordings of older residents' reminiscences and an admirably complete town archive. The multimedia center leads into the house itself, an 1807 gem with a varied collection of artifacts. Don't miss the assemblage of children's toys and the elegant Victorian parlor with a Carrera marble fireplace and reductions of *Greek Slave*, a statue by Hiram Powers. Another historical landmark, at 16 Elm St, is **F.H. Gillingham's** (Mon–Sat 8.30am–6.30pm, Sun 10am–6pm; ⊛www .gillinghams.com), an operating country store since 1886. Also near the green are the town's many galleries, the most notable of which is **Woodstock Folk Art Prints and Antiquities**, 6 Elm St (Mon–Sat 10am–5pm, Sun 10am–4pm; ⊤802/457-2012), which displays vivid local folk art.

The town's other attractions are located a little farther afield. The museum section of the **Billings Farm and Museum**, off Rte-12 north of town (May–Oct daily 10am–5pm; Nov–Dec Sat & Sun 10am–4pm; $11; ⊤802/457-2355, ⊛www.billingsfarm.org), puts on demonstrations of skills and exhibits that highlight the lives and culture of Vermont's rural families of yore, while the grounds are run as a modern dairy farm where you can pet cows and churn butter. Across the street from the Billings Farm, the **Marsh–Billings–Rockefeller National Historical Park** (daily: late May to Oct 10am–5pm; house and garden tours $8; ⊤802/457-3368, ⊛www .nps.gov/mabi) was originally the home of George Perkins Marsh, whose 1864 book *Man and Nature* is a seminal work of ecological thought, inspired by the author's distress at the deforestation of his native Vermont. The house was purchased in 1869 by Frederick Billings, who tried to counter this trend, reseeding and replanting tracts of land. Conservationist and philanthropist Laurence Rockefeller, who married Billings' daughter, Mary, took the ethos a step further by combining the ideals of preservation with the benefits of public access; the Rockefellers opened the Billings Farm in 1983, and donated the rest of the property to the National Park Service in 1992. Today the **Carriage Barn** acts as the park visitors' center, while the 1807 **Mansion** can only be visited on regular ranger-guided tours from here. You can also explore 553 acres of forest which contain a network of **hiking trails**, some leading to splendid vistas with Mount Tom in the distance.

Perhaps the most visited Woodstock attraction is **Sugarbush Farm**, 591 Sugarbush Farm Rd (Mon–Fri 8am–5pm, Sat & Sun 9am–5pm; ⊤802/ 457-1757 or 1-800/281-1757, ⊛www.sugarbushfarm.com), which somewhat dubiously claims to produce more "authentic" cheddar and maple syrup than other Vermont farms.

Eating and drinking

Woodstock's **restaurants**, expensive and undeniably good, cater for an upscale crowd. Many have somewhat cheaper tavern menus available for bar or outside dining. In any case, it's best to make reservations ahead of time. Restaurants attached to inns and B&Bs tend to be a little less expensive.

Bentley's 3 Elm St ☎802/457-3232. Upmarket versions of traditional bistro food (tequila and lime chicken, duck quesadillas, garlic and Guinness mussels) and a good range of microbrews. Casual and moderately priced (entrees $18–24).

Jackson House Inn and Restaurant US-4, 1.5 miles west of the village green ☎802/457-2065. Very upscale New American cuisine. Try to get a table with a view of the lovely four-acre garden. Extensive wine list and knowledgeable sommelier.

Kedron Valley Inn Rte-106, South Woodstock ☎802/457-1473. Eating in the tavern or on the formal front porch is more fun – and less expensive – than in the dining room, but the food, often from local sources, is superb throughout; the tender, juicy steaks and local vegetables are uniformly praised. Reservations recommended. Closed Tues & Wed Nov–July.

Mangowood US-4, 3 miles west of village green at the *Lincoln Inn* ☎802/457-3312. New American cuisine with Asian accents from the Singaporean chef/owner, such as pepper sesame tofu fries, and penne pasta with green curry. Expect to spend $100+ per head for a full dinner.

Mountain Creamery 33 Central St ☎802/457-1715. Filling country breakfasts and lunch fare served daily, as well as some fine home-made ice cream. Try the mile-high apple pie ($5.25).

Osteria Pan e Salute 61 Central St ☎802/457-4882. Italian fine dining and wine bar, with wood-fired pizza options. Open Thurs–Sun; dinner only.

The Prince and the Pauper 24 Elm St ☎802/457-1818. Continental cuisine – braised veal, filet mignon – in an incongruously casual dining room ($48 fixed-priced diner). There's less pricey bistro fare as well ($18–23). Open daily from 5pm.

Wasp's Snack Bar 57 Pleasant St ☎802/457-3334. This tiny roadside shack is a local institution, right on US-4 at the eastern end of town (near the motels), and specializing in home-cooked breakfasts. Open Tues–Sat 6–11am.

Woodstock Coffee & Tea 43 Central St ☎802/457-9268. Get your morning fuel-up and muffin at this laid-back, eco-friendly shop, where you can lounge at the wooden tables for as long as you like.

Quechee

Six miles east of Woodstock, **QUECHEE** (pronounced quee-chee) is a mixed bag. The **town** proper, off US-4, is a combination of quaint Vermont village and expensive housing developments where you'll find upmarket restaurants and B&Bs. Right on US-4 is **Quechee Gorge**, one of Vermont's greatest natural wonders, while the adjacent **Quechee Gorge Village shopping mall** is a mire of tourist kitsch, hard not to notice but easy to skip.

Even if you're just passing through, be sure to stop and ogle the Queechee Gorge, the so-called "Grand Canyon" of Vermont (free parking on either side). A delicate bridge spans the 165-foot chasm of the Ottauquechee River and hiking trails lead down through forests to its base. The **Quechee Gorge Visitor Center** (daily 9am–5pm; ☎802/295-6852) sits on the east side, and can provide local information and trail maps of the surrounding **Quechee Gorge State Park** (late May to late Oct).

Heading back to Woodstock on US-4, visit the Raptor Center at the **Vermont Institute of Natural Science** (May–Oct daily 10am–5pm; Nov–April Wed–Sun 10am–4pm; $9; ☎802/457-2779, ⊛www.vinsweb.org). Tours reveal how the staff rescues and treats injured birds of prey, and you can also view recovering falcons, owls, and hawks; some of these participate in thirty-minute programs (three times a day in summer, just once in winter), during which you can watch them in graceful, powerful action.

If you have more time, hit the town center of Quechee (take Waterman Hill Rd off US-4 and drive across the covered bridge), where a waterfall on the river turns the turbines of **Simon Pearce Glass** on Main Street (daily 9am–9pm; ☏802/295-2711, ⓦwww.simonpearce.com). Housed in a former wool mill, this is an unusual combination of glass-blowing center and restaurant (see review, below). There is a good path for **biking**, known locally as the River Road, which starts in Main Street, Quechee town, and leads west into Woodstock, following the Ottauquechee River and running parallel to US-4. **Wilderness Trails**, on Deweys Mills Road next to the *Quechee Inn at Marshland Farm* (☏802/295-7620), dispenses information on the challenging **hiking** and **cross-country skiing** trails behind Quechee town, and also provides rentals (bikes $18 per day, cross-country skis $15 per day). For those more water-oriented, they also run 4hr river float trips ($40 along Connecticut River, or $45 along the rougher White River), and rent kayaks on the North Hartland Reservoir ($28).

Practicalities

If you're equipped to **camp**, the best place to stay is in the **Quechee Gorge State Park**, just off US-4 (☏802/295-2990), which has 54 well-maintained sites ($14–25) in a forest of fir trees. The *Quality Inn*, on US-4 between the gorge and the mall (☏802/295-7600 or 1-800/732-4376, ⓦwww.qualityinnquechee .com; ⑤), offers the area's least expensive accommodation. If you're willing to shell out more, the town of Quechee has a few sumptuous **inns**: the *Quechee Inn at Marshland Farm*, 1119 Main St (☏802/295-3133 or 1-800/235-3133, ⓦwww.quecheeinn.com; ④–⑧) offers 24 comfy rooms with period furnishings and a fabulous setting, and has links with Wilderness Trails (see above), while the *Parker House Inn*, in a ravishing red-brick Victorian at 1792 Main St (☏802/ 295-6077, ⓦwww.theparkerhouseinn.com; ⑥–⑧), has seven guestrooms and a restaurant serving sophisticated meals utilizing local ingredients.

Most **restaurants** in the area are either chi-chi affairs or "family" establishments. One notable exception is *Firestone's* (☏802/295-1600), at Waterman Place along US-4 (at the turning to Quechee town), serving creative pasta dishes, flatbread pizzas, and traditional Vermont fare, which you can enjoy on their pleasant rooftop patio. Another is ⅍ *Shepherd's Pie on the Green*, 91 Village Green (☏802/295-2786), just off Main Street, which crafts mouthwatering home-made pies and sandwiches. The restaurant at ⅍ *Simon Pearce Glass*, Main Street (☏802/295-1470), serves inventive New American-type entrees starting at around $22, as well as occasional no-nonsense Irish dishes such as beef and Guinness stew and shepherd's pie. The best place for breakfast along US-4 is the 1947 Worcester diner car that houses the *Farmer's Diner*, Quechee Gorge Village (☏802/295-4600), where the food (supplied by local farmers) is filling and inexpensive (big plates $7–9).

Windsor

About fifteen miles south of Woodstock and Quechee, undistinguished **WINDSOR** sits right on the bank of the Connecticut River. The town does have an important past, though: the original constitution of the Republic of Vermont was drawn up here in 1777, an event which made Windsor the "birth-place of Vermont."

Today this distinction is preserved in one of its absorbing museums, the **Old Constitution House**, 16 Main St, at the north end of town (late May to mid-Oct Sat–Sun 11am–5pm; $2.50; ☏802/674-6628, ⓦwww.historicvermont.org /constitution). Housed in the original tavern where the delegates met and consti-tutional debates took place, it contains a well-done re-creation of the tavern's interior plus a fascinating series of history-related displays, featuring artifacts such as coins and newspapers from the brief republican period. In the center of town, take a peek inside graceful **Windsor House**, a former hotel built in 1836 and now home to shops, galleries, and displays by the local historical society. Further along, the **Cornish Colony Museum**, 147 Main St (May–Oct Tues–Sat 10am–5pm, Sun noon–5pm; ☎802/674-6008, ⓦwww.cornishcolonymuseum.org), in the old firehouse, showcases revolving exhibits of art created between 1885 and 1935 by Maxfield Parrish and other members of the nearby Cornish Colony (see p.420). Further south, the **American Precision Museum**, 196 Main St (daily late May to Oct 10am–5pm; $6; ☎802/674-5781, ⓦwww.americanprecision .org), focuses on mechanization – the construction, function, and historical significance of machinery. The small but impressive displays of items (many still in working condition, such as "Mississippi" rifles and sewing machines) incorporate antique machine tools to illustrate not only the importance of technology, but also the beauty of its precision.

Between the two museums, Bridge Street branches off Main Street to the east; at its terminus, you'll find the **Cornish–Windsor covered bridge**, which dates from 1866 and is open to traffic. At 460ft, it's the longest covered bridge in the US. Cross to New Hampshire for the best photo opportunities.

Beer drinkers should follow the scent of roasting hops to the **Harpoon Brewery**, one of the state's high-quality microbreweries, 2.5 miles north of Windsor on US-5 (May–Aug Mon–Wed & Sun 10am–6pm, Thurs–Sat 10am–8pm; Sept–Oct Tues–Sun 10am–6pm; Nov–April Tues–Sat 10am–6pm). You can grab a draft ($4.25) or sandwich (from $4.50) at the café, or take a free tour (Fri & Sat 3pm; first 30 people only).

Practicalities

For affordable **accommodation**, it's best to backtrack to Woodstock or Quechee. However, the *Juniper Hill Inn*, off US-5 at 153 Pembroke Rd (☎802/674-5273 or 1-800/359-2541, ⓦwww.juniperhillinn.com; ⑥–⑦), has thirty tidy rooms in a mansion overlooking the town. The best **diner** in the area – 🍴 *Stub's and Laura's*, around one mile north of the center on US-5 (closed Sun; ☎802/674-5715) – is a real gem. It might look like a rundown truckstop, but the burgers ($2.60) and desserts are some of the best anywhere – try the tapioca pudding ($2) or Boston cream pie ($3). *Dan's Windsor Diner* (☎802/674-5555), a traditional chrome-finished rail car at 135 Main St, comes a close second.

Rutland and around

When Vermonters describe downtown **RUTLAND**, west of Killington at the junction of US-4 and US-7, as "a little bit of New Hampshire in Vermont," it is not meant as a compliment. Rather, it's an indictment of a bland town dominated by a steady, modest, industrial base and afflicted by a strip-mall aesthetic. Unsurprisingly, the main attractions lie outside the center.

Two miles east of the town center along US-4 sits the worthwhile **Norman Rockwell Museum** (daily 9am–4pm; $5.50; ☎802/773-6095, ⓦwww .normanrockwellvt.com), which displays more than two thousand reproductions of Rockwell paintings, including all of his *Saturday Evening Post* covers. It's a well-contextualized retrospective of the artist's work, which can be irritatingly wholesome but is nevertheless an important contribution to American graphic art (see box, p.238).

The importance of marble to the development of the state is significant, and showcased at the **Vermont Marble Museum**, 62 Main St (daily: mid-May to Oct 9am–5.30pm; $7; ☎802/459-2300 or 1-800/427-1396, ⓦwww .vermont-marble.com), in the town of **Proctor**, six miles northeast of Rutland

and clearly signposted. Essentially a monument to the once mighty **Vermont Marble Company**, established here by Redfield Proctor in the 1880s, the museum provides a comprehensive history of the town and industry, while the final hall is like a vast kitchen showroom, with examples of virtually every type of marble on display. Unless you have an abiding interest in stones or local history, it's all rather dull.

A short drive southwest from Proctor, on West Proctor Road, the **Wilson Castle** (late May to Oct daily 9am–6pm; $9.50; ⓦwww.wilsoncastle.com) is an intriguing relic of an aristocrat's past glory. The castle was built in 1867 by Dr John Johnson, who married into English nobility and decided to take advantage of his wife's fortune by constructing a castle in a "blend of European styles." He spared no expense, recruiting the best craftsmen and materials from across Europe to fashion elements such as stained-glass ceilings. The Wilson family still owns it and has added to the already oversized manor. Upstairs in the bedrooms, the paint is peeling a bit, adding to the air of faded grandeur. Visits are by guided tour only (around 1hr).

Practicalities

Rutland is a regional transport hub, with Cape Air offering three daily **flights** from Boston to Southern Vermont Regional Airport (ⓦwww.flyrutlandvt .com), five miles south of the city. Amtrak **trains** arrive at the station in Rutland Plaza, Merchant's Row; the bus terminal is in the center of town at 102 West St (℡802/773-2774). Local **bus** company Marble Valley Regional Transit runs services ($2; ℡802/773-3244, ⓦwww.thebus.com) to Killington. The **Rutland Region Chamber of Commerce**, 256 N Main St (Mon–Fri 8am–5pm; ℡802/773-2747 or 1-800/756-8880, ⓦwww.rutlandvermont.com), open year-round, is your best bet for information.

Aside from the standard hotel chains, most of Rutland's **places to stay** are nondescript, independent motels, but they're generally cheap, clean, and close to major highways. Among the almost indistinguishable accommodations that line US-7 are the *Red Roof Inn* (℡1-800/733-7663 or 802/775-4303, ⓦwww .redroof.com; ❹), and the bargain *Roadway Inn* (℡802/775-2575, ⓦwww .rutlandvthotel.com; ❸). *Iröquois Land* (May to mid-Oct; $30–40; ℡802/773-2832, ⓦwww.irocamp.com), three miles south of Rutland in Clarendon, is an adequate **campground**, though it tends to be dominated by the RV crowd.

There's little point in driving in to the center **to eat**, but if you're passing through, the *Coffee Exchange*, 101 Merchant's Row at Center St (℡802/775-3337), is fine for a light snack, and is close to the bus station.

Mount Independence

From Rutland, a forty-minute drive northwest (US-7 to Rte-73) brings you to **Mount Independence**, outside **Orwell** on the very southeastern tip of Lake Champlain, the scene of a major American defeat in the Revolutionary War. The fort was established here in 1776 to repel a British attack from Canada, part of a defensive network that included the more famous Fort Ticonderoga on the opposite shore (which was completed in the 1750s). The two forts initially provided such an intimidating sight that British general Guy Carleton aborted his invasion in October 1776. However, the following winter was brutal, and most of the troops deserted; 2500 American soldiers who remained behind fell ill or froze to death. Springtime reinforcements were insufficient to withstand an attack from General Burgoyne, and the fort was abandoned on July 5, 1777. The British occupied the Mount until November of the same year, when they burned the fort in response to General Burgoyne's surrender across the water at Saratoga. Today, the **Mount Independence State Historic Site** (daily late May to mid-Oct 9.30am–5pm; $5; ☏802/948-2000) is a pleasingly low-key affair, with displays in the **Visitors Center Museum** telling the story of that dreadful winter, plus four hiking trails around the Mount and the remnants of the fort. It's a relaxing place, with few visitors and spectacular views of the lake.

Middlebury and around

Thirty-two miles north along US-7 from Rutland lies the town of **MIDDLE-BURY**, named for its central location between Salisbury and New Haven, two once-prominent Vermont towns whose stars have dimmed in the past two centuries. In 1800, a small group of local citizens banded together here to form a "town's college," primarily intended to train young men for the ministry. Today Middlebury College – one of the most endowed (and expensive) liberal arts colleges in the US – is at the heart of the town, one of Vermont's most charming villages.

Information

Information on Middlebury lodgings and activities can be found through the Addison County visitor website (⊛www.midvermont.com), or by stopping by their offices at 2 Court St (Mon 10.30am–5pm, Tues–Fri 9am–5pm; brochures and hiking information available at entrance Sat & Sun; ☏802/388-7951).

Accommodation

The village green boasts two lovely **inns**, and there are also a couple of **motels** two or three miles south of town along Rte-7.

Blue Spruce Motel 2428 Rte-7 South ☏802/388-4091 or 1-800/640-7671, ⊛www .bluesprucemotelmiddlebury.com. Best of the motels outside the center, with clean and well-equipped rooms; microwaves, fridges, and mountain views thrown in. ❹

Inn on the Green 71 S Pleasant St ☏802/388-7512 or 1-888/244-7512, ⊛www.innonthegreen .com. This aptly named hotel has eleven luxurious rooms in a light blue Federal-style landmark building, with Continental breakfast in bed included. ❽

Middlebury Inn 14 Court Square ☏802/388-4961 or 1-800/842-4666, ⊛www.middleburyinn.com. Open since 1827, with 75 rooms, a porch with rocking chairs, an operational 1926 elevator, and a fine restaurant. ❼

Waybury Inn 457 East Main St (Rte-125) ☏802/388-4015 or 1-800/348-1810, ⊛www .wayburyinn.com. Sitcom junkies will want to check out this small 1810 inn, whose exterior was used on the 1980s US TV show *Newhart*. The relationship with the show ends there, but there are fourteen comfortable, well-kept rooms. ❻

The Town

All roads converge at the **Middlebury Town Green**, an idyllic place with a pretty and ornate white **Congregational church** at its northern end and a more somber gray church on the green itself. Middlebury's small downtown has a fairly hip collection of shops, with a few bookstores, a record shop, and the **Vermont Craft Center at Frog Hollow**, 1 Mill St (Mon–Sat 10am–5.30pm, Sun noon–5pm; ☏802/388-3177, ⊛www.froghollow.org), a bright space showcasing high-quality crafts from all over the state. The **Henry Sheldon Museum of Vermont History**, 1 Park St (Mon–Sat 10am–5pm, May–Oct also Sun 1–5pm; $5; ☎802/388-2117, ⓦwww.henrysheldonmuseum.org), is an endearingly quirky collection of tools, household objects, and "one-of-a-kind oddities," such as the remains of the "Petrified Indian Boy," actually a mid-nineteenth-century hoax.

Catch Rte-125 west to the **Middlebury College Museum of Art**, off Rte-30 (Tues–Fri 10am–5pm, Sat–Sun noon–5pm; free; ☎802/443-5007, ⓦmuseum.middlebury.edu), for a look at the small permanent collection of nineteenth-century European and American sculpture and modern prints; the campus spreads out around it, with no other individually compelling sights, though it makes for a pleasant wander.

Eating and drinking

The **restaurant** scene in Middlebury is pretty good for a town of this size, owing largely to the college.

Fire and Ice 26 Seymour St ☎802/388-7166. Cavernous steak and seafood restaurant, with a massive salad bar and enough memorabilia to fill a museum. The centerpiece is a 22ft motorboat from the 1920s.

Green Peppers 10 Washington St ☎802/388-3164. Serves cheap pasta (from $5.75) and the best brick-oven pizza in town; slices are $3.50, special 10-inch pizzas $9.75 and up.

Morgan's Tavern At the *Middlebury Inn*, 14 Court Square ☎802/388-4961. If you're in the mood for a hearty meal, check out this posh restaurant, where grilled buffalo and

pan-fried monkfish grace the menu (entrees $17–25).

Sama's Café 54 College St ☎802/388-6408. Offers wholesome wraps ($6.50), wood-fired pizzas (from $13), and spicy falafel ($6).

The Taste of India 1 Bakery Lane ☎802/388-4856. Heaps of curry and rice dishes for a very reasonable $12 or so, with the bonus of picturesque views over Otter Creek.

Tully & Marie's 7 Bakery Lane ☎802/388-4182. This is more of a chic urban bistro, with sleek interior, extensive menu of salads, burgers, and sandwiches, and views of the creek.

Hwy-125: Robert Frost country

Robert Frost spent 23 summers in Vermont on land that has since been overrun by **Hwy-125** (also called the **Robert Frost Memorial Highway**). The road cuts right across the Green Mountains National Forest from Rte-7 in East Middlebury to Hancock.

Just under six miles along you'll pass the **Robert Frost Trail**, a 1.2-mile loop walk punctuated by placards quoting his work. Although it may not sound like much, it is actually quite evocative – an affecting environment in which to read his deceptively simple, old-fashioned words. Around 500 yards further on is the **Robert Frost Wayside**, a peaceful picnic area amidst red pines, right by the highway. Adjacent to this is **Frost Road**, a dirt track that leads half a mile to a white, wood-frame house known as **Homer Noble Farm**. Frost actually lived in a nearby log cabin, still visible about a hundred yards beyond the farmhouse up a wide, grassy lane; walk until you see an opening on your left that leads into a mountain dell where the cabin is situated. Now a National Historic Landmark and owned by Middlebury College, it's okay to take a look, even if no one is around.

Less than a mile west along Hwy-125 is the **Bread Loaf Mountain Campus**, home of a highly regarded summer writers' conference initiated at Frost's suggestion while he was a professor at Middlebury. Though there's nothing much to see, budding writers may want to stroll here and commune with the spirits of notables, such as Frost, Willa Cather, and John Gardner, who have taught or studied here. Hwy-125 ends a few miles on at Hwy-100 and Hancock, where you can continue north into the Mad River Valley.

Mad River Valley

From the intersection with Hwy-125, Hwy-100 runs 33 miles north to Waterbury and I-89 via the untrammeled ski resorts of the **Mad River Valley**. A couple of miles beyond the town of **Warren** is the turning to **Sugarbush Resort** (℡802/583-6300 or 1-800/53-SUGAR, Ⓦwww.sugarbush.com), comprising two hills, Lincoln Peak and Mount Ellen, with 115 trails (lift tickets $72–75) and year-round activities. Continue north and you'll pass the moving local **memorial to US soldiers** killed in Iraq – a field of white flags, one for each soldier. At **Irasville**, Rte-17 leads five miles west to **Mad River Glen** (lift tickets $60 Sat & Sun, $39 Mon–Fri; ℡802/496-3551, Ⓦwww.madriverglen .com), one of the most unadulterated resorts in North America, with narrow, unforgiving trails which look pretty much as they did when they were cut fifty years ago. In keeping with tradition, no snowboards are allowed here, although **Telemark skiing** is promoted aggressively. There are 44 trails, of which nearly half are considered suitable for expert skiers.

Irasville blurs into **Waitsfield**, a good base for the area, with plenty of accommodation, stores, and places to eat; it's also just 12 miles off the interstate. You can go **horseriding** at the **Vermont Icelandic Horse Farm** ($50 for 1hr; ℡802/496-7141, Ⓦwww.icelandichorses.com), in an extremely tranquil location on North Fayston Road off Rte-100 a few miles north of Waitsfield. As well as day-rides, they offer two- to five-day treks stopping at country inns (May–Nov; rates start at $600).

Practicalities

You really need a car to get to the Mad River Valley. A taxi from Waterbury to Waitsfield is a possibility, albeit an expensive one (around $45; try Mad Cab, ℡802/793-2320). Once at Waitsfield, however, during ski season Mad River Valley Transit (℡802/496-7433) has a free **shuttle** service to Warren and the ski resorts, and buses to Montpelier ($2). The **Mad River Valley Visitor Center**, on Hwy-100 at the north end of Waitsfield's Main Street (Mon–Fri 8.30am–6pm; ℡802/496-3409 or 1-800/828-4748, Ⓦwww.madrivervalley.com), can provide all sorts of information, and tell you about the annual Vermont Festival of the Arts (Ⓦwww.vermontartfest.com), a three-week-long series of summer events that includes art showings, concerts, cheese-making, pottery and glass-blowing demos, and sometimes, sheepdog competitions.

Visitors will find ample **lodging** in the area. Perhaps most notable is the *1824 House*, 2150 Main St in Waitsfield (℡802/496-7555, Ⓦwww.1824house .com; ⑥), a country inn with three-course breakfasts. Other comfortable places within easy reach of the slopes include the *Mountain View Inn*, three miles from Mad River Glen on Rte-17 (℡802/496-2426, Ⓦwww.vtmountainviewinn .com; ⑥), with seven guestrooms in a restored farmhouse, and the yellow *Mad River Inn* on Tremblay Road off Hwy-100 north of Waitsfield (℡802/496-7900, Ⓦwww.madriverinn.com; ⑥). Cheaper rooms (some with shared bath) can be had at the *Slide Brook Lodge*, 3180 German Flats Rd in Warren (℡802/583-2202, Ⓦwww.slidebrooklodge.com; ③, with bath ⑤).

While these quiet communities are not known for their **restaurants**, there are a few worth mentioning. At the junction of routes 17 and 100 in Irasville, *John Egan's Big World Pub & Grill* (℡802/496-3033) has an eclectic menu (rotisserie chicken, pad thai, lamb, Hungarian goulash), which is nonetheless well executed in a friendly ski-lodge atmosphere. More refined palates will be happier with *Chez Henri* in the Sugarbush Village (℡802/583-2600), where dishes like *filet* *au poivre* or *bouillabaisse* are served in a Parisian-style café. For lighter fare and sandwiches try *La Patisserie Bakery* (T 802/496-2144) at 5197 Main St in Waitsfield. There is no **nightlife** to speak of, especially in summer, when you'll only have the crickets for entertainment.

Waterbury

Few people gave much notice to **WATERBURY** before 1986, but ever since aging hippies Ben Cohen and Jerry Greenfield opened **Ben and Jerry's Ice Cream Factory** here in that year, the city has been home to the number-one tourist destination in Vermont. The ice cream empire, which began in 1978 as a stand at the front of a Burlington gas station, is nestled one mile north of I-89 in the village of Waterbury Center, on the way up to Stowe. The brand's rabid fans includes not only those with a sweet tooth, but believers in its earth-friendly philosophy: the company has a three-part mission statement, which gives social, environmental, and financial benefits equal importance. The two founders are long retired from day-to-day involvement, and corporate giant Unilever bought the company in 2000, but to its credit has maintained the philosophy and family-like ethos. Half-hour tours run by friendly locals (every 30min daily: July to mid-Aug 9am–8pm; mid-Aug to late Oct 9am–6pm; late Oct to June 10am–5pm; store and "scoop shop" close 1hr later; $3, kids under 12 free; T 1-866/BJ-TOURS, W www.benjerry.com) feature a short film on the collaborators' early days, then head into the production factory where (weekdays) machines turn cream, sugar, and other natural ingredients into over fifty flavors. Afterwards, you get a free mini-scoop of the stuff – you can buy more at the gift shop and ice-cream counter outside ($3–4). Every summer, free movie showings on Saturdays bring in visitors and locals alike.

There's not really much else to see in Waterbury; your best bet is to trawl the **culinary outlet shops** clustered along Hwy-100, which each offer free samples of their wares. The pick of the bunch is probably the **Cabot Annex Store** (daily 9am–6pm; T 802/244-6334), where you can taste several varieties of the well-known cheddar cheese (see p.386), though **Cold Hollow Cider Mill** (daily 8am–6pm; T 802/244-8771, W www.coldhollow.com), where you can see how cider is made (weekdays only), comes close, if only for the heavenly aroma of apples and cider donuts (foreign visitors should note that in North America "cider" denotes non-alcoholic, unfermented apple juice).

Practicalities

Amtrak's *Vermonter* **trains** pull into downtown Waterbury, once in the morning heading south and once in the evening heading north. For general information, check the **Waterbury Tourism Council** website (W www.waterbury.org).

There are several top-notch **accommodation** options in and around town. The Teutonic-themed ⚜ *Grunberg Haus* 94 Pine St/Hwy-100 (T 802/244-7726 or 1-800/800-7760, W www.grunberghaus.com; ⑤) is a woodsy A-frame with great breakfasts and reasonable rates. Other quality establishments along Hwy-100 include the *Birds Nest Inn*, five miles north of I-89 (two-night minimum; closed April & Nov; T 802/244-7490 or 1-800/366-5592, W www.birdsnestinn .com; ⑥), which features cozy rooms finished with floral Waverly wallpaper, and the *Old Stagecoach Inn* at 18 N Main St (T 802/244-5056 or 1-800/262-2206, W www.oldstagecoach.com; ④), which dates from 1826 and features eleven individually styled rooms.

One of the better places to **eat** is ⚘ *The Alchemist*, 23 S Main St (☎802/244-4120), which serves its own brews along with panini, pizzas, and somewhat upscale pub food. *Arvad's*, 3 S Main St (☎802/244-8973), also serves up fresh grill fare with pints of good ale. *Coffee Bean Cafe*, in the *Best Western Hotel*, Hwy-100 just north of I-89 (☎802/244-1740), has satisfying diner fare, and also super desserts, coffee, and cocktails.

Stowe

Unlike most of Vermont's other resort towns, there is still a beautiful nineteenth-century village at the heart of **STOWE**, with its white-spired meeting house and town green. Though it has been a popular summer destination since before the Civil War, what really put the town on the map was the arrival of the **Von Trapp family**, of *The Sound of Music* fame, in 1941. After fleeing Nazi-occupied Austria, they established a lodge here – since burned down – where Maria Von Trapp held singing camps; a complex composed of a rebuilt lodge, restaurant, and theme park devoted to the celebration of alpine culture has taken its place. Today, the approach road to the main ski area is swamped with malls, equipment stores, and condominium complexes – extremely at odds with the village below. Nonetheless, the setting remains spectacular, at the foot of Vermont's highest mountain, the 4393-foot **Mount Mansfield**.

Arrival and information

Mountain Road (Rte-108) is Stowe's primary thoroughfare, stretching from the main village on Hwy-100 up to the ski areas, and on through the mountain gap known as "Smugglers' Notch," so named because of the illegal trading that happened here after Jefferson's 1807 Embargo Act banned exports to Canada. The road narrows considerably at the pass itself, which is generally closed in winter.

If you're not driving, the only way to get here is by **bus**. Green Mountain Transit Agency (☎802/223-7287 or 1-866/864-0211, ⓦwww.gmtaride.org) provides services year-round from Montpelier and Burlington to Waterbury, from where you can take connecting buses up to Stowe ($2). Once here, the free **Mountain Road Shuttle** runs up and down Mountain Road, between the Town Hall in Stowe Village and the base of the ski areas (ski season only). The staff at the **visitors' center**, 51 Main St, at Depot Road (summer: Mon–Sat 9am–8pm, Sun 9am–5pm; other months hours vary; ☎802/253-7321 or 1-877/GOSTOWE, ⓦwww.gostowe.com) are very helpful. Watch out for the variety of **events** held throughout the year, like the ice-carving and snow golf competitions at the amusing Winter Carnival (third week in Jan), and the Antique & Classic Car Show (second weekend in Aug).

Accommodation

Multiple **accommodation** options line Mountain Road, ranging from luxury hotels to modest B&Bs; as always, the most convenient (and sought-after) lie inside the resort itself. Make sure you reserve ahead in winter. The closest **campground** is *Gold Brook Campground* (year-round; ☎802/253-7683), two miles south on Hwy-100, with the usual amenities and sites from $23, but you can stake yourself out in Smugglers' Notch State Park for just $14 (May–Oct; ☎1-888/409-7579).

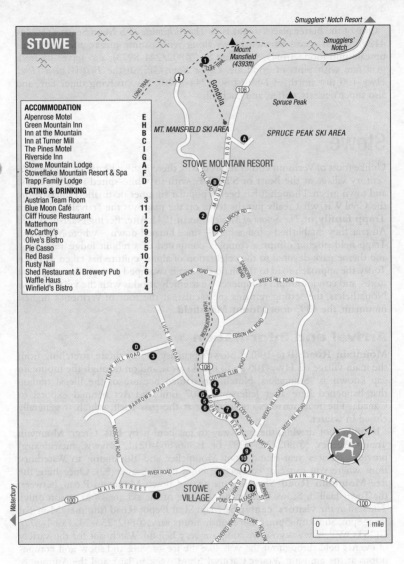

STOWE

Mount Mansfield (4393ft)

Smugglers' Notch

Spruce Peak

MT. MANSFIELD SKI AREA

SPRUCE PEAK SKI AREA

STOWE MOUNTAIN RESORT

ACCOMMODATION

Alpenrose Motel	E
Green Mountain Inn	H
Inn at the Mountain	B
Inn at Turner Mill	C
The Pines Motel	I
Riverside Inn	G
Stowe Mountain Lodge	A
Stoweflake Mountain Resort & Spa	F
Trapp Family Lodge	D

EATING & DRINKING

Austrian Team Room	3
Blue Moon Café	11
Cliff House Restaurant	1
Matterhorn	2
McCarthy's	9
Olive's Bistro	8
Pie Casso	5
Red Basil	10
Rusty Nail	7
Shed Restaurant & Brewery Pub	6
Waffle Haus	1
Winfield's Bistro	4

TRAPP HILL ROAD

LUCE HILL ROAD

RECREATION PATH

EDSON HILL ROAD

BROOK ROAD

SANBORN ROAD

WEEKS HILL ROAD

COTTAGE CLUB ROAD

CAPE COD ROAD

BARROWS ROAD

MOSCOW ROAD

WEST HILL ROAD

MAYO RD

RIVER ROAD

MAIN STREET

STOWE VILLAGE

DEPOT ST
POND ST
PARK ST
PLEASANT ST
SUNSET ST
STOWE HOLLOW RD
COVERED BRIDGE RD

MAIN STREET

Waterbury

0   1 mile

Alpenrose Motel 2619 Mountain Rd ☎802/253-7277 or 1-800/962-7002. Small hotel halfway between the ski slopes and Stowe Village, just off the Recreation Path. Rooms and efficiencies with private baths, cable TVs, and refrigerators. German spoken. **4**

Green Mountain Inn 1 Main St ☎802/253-7301 or 1-800/253-7302, ⊛www.greenmountaininn.com. Stately hotel built in 1833, centrally located in the village (at a busy intersection) and amply outfitted. Offers not one, but two good restaurants,

complimentary health club, pool, and afternoon tea and cookies. **7**

Inn at the Mountain 5781 Mountain Rd ☎802/253-3656 or 1-800/253-4754, ⊛www.stowe.com. The cheaper of the two main accommodation options within Stowe Resort. The slopeside rooms are certainly comfortable, but only good value as part of "ski and stay specials," which combine two nights at the inn with a discounted two-day ski pass. **5–8**

Inn at Turner Mill 56 Turner Mill Lane (5.2 miles up Mountain Rd) ☎802/253-2062 or

1-800/992-0016, ⓦwww.turnermill.com. Quaint streamside quarters with handcrafted furnishings at the foot of Mount Mansfield. Swimming pool and excellent home-made breakfasts. ⑤

The Pines Motel 1203 Waterbury Rd (Hwy-100) Ⓣ802/253-4828. Cheap, fairly clean, basic motel rooms, one step above your average hostel. ③

Riverside Inn 1965 Mountain Rd Ⓣ802/253-4217 or 1-800/966-4217, ⓦwww.rivinn.com. Modest, basic rooms in converted farmhouse with all the essentials, though not much more, and slightly better motel rooms with cable TV, DVD, fridge, and microwave. ④

🏃 **Stowe Mountain Lodge** 7412 Mountain Rd Ⓣ802/253-3560 or 888/478-6938, ⓦwww.stowemountainlodge.com. The pride of Stowe Mountain Resort opened in 2008 right next to the Spruce Peak ski area, offering the latest in luxury; floor-to-ceiling windows make the most of the scenery, while rooms are tricked out in designer furnishings and contemporary art. LCD TVs, iPod docks, and stone-frame fireplaces are standard. ⑨

Stoweflake Mountain Resort & Spa 1746 Mountain Rd Ⓣ802/253-7355 or 1-800/253-2232, ⓦwww.stoweflake.com. Sumptuous rooms filled with tasteful antiques and home-made quilts, coffee and snacks throughout the day, well-informed and courteous staff, all set in sweeping grounds with pool, spa, and sports club. ⑨

🏃 **Trapp Family Lodge** 42 Trapp Hill Rd Ⓣ802/253-8511 or 1-800/826-7000, ⓦwww.trappfamily.com. Twenty-seven hundred acres of Austrian-themed ski resort (as fancy as it is expensive) on the site of the original Trapp family house, also the first cross-country ski center in America. Nightly entertainment can include concerts in the Trapp Meadow. Rates include cross-country ski passes and access to skiing and hiking trails. ⑨

Skiing and other outdoor activities

Alpine experts hotly debate whether the **Stowe Mountain Resort** (lift tickets $79–84 per day; Ⓣ802/253-3000, ⓦwww.stowe.com) is still the "ski capital of the east," a distinction it clearly held until Killington and other eastern ski centers began to challenge its supremacy a decade or so ago. Regardless, it's an excellent mountain, and its popularity remains intact, as anyone who has driven through Stowe Village on winter weekends can attest. There are 48 well-kept trails spread over two ski areas, **Mount Mansfield** and **Spruce Peak**, with excellent options for skiers of every level. A less crowded option is the family-oriented **Smugglers' Notch Resort** (lift tickets $62 per day; Ⓣ802/664-8851 or 1-800/451-8752, ⓦwww.smuggs.com), on the other side of the mountain, which actually has more trails than Stowe (78, with about twenty "expert" runs).

Stowe offers almost as much to do in the **summer**, when the crowds thin out considerably. The area's cross-country skiing trails double as **mountain-bike routes**, and the Stowe Mountain Bike Club (Ⓣ802/253-1947, ⓦwww.stowemtnbike.com), a grassroots organization promoting responsible biking, sponsors group rides several times a week. They also supply a list of rental outfits, including AJ's Ski & Sports, 350 Mountain Rd (bikes from $38 per day; Ⓣ802/253-4593 or 1-800/226-6257, ⓦwww.ajssports.com). Nearby streams and small rivers offer ample opportunity for **canoeing** and **kayaking**: Umiak Outdoor Outfitters, 849 S Main St (Ⓣ802/253-2317, ⓦwww.umiak.com), gives tours on the gentle Lamoille River (from $39) and rents full sets of equipment ($30 for 2hr) at Waterbury Reservoir.

Mount Mansfield

Ascending to the peak of **Mount Mansfield** is a challenge no matter how you do it, but the rewards are spectacular views all the way to Canada. Weather permitting, the easiest approach is the **Toll Road**, a winding 4.5-mile ascent of mostly dirt track that begins seven miles up from the village on Mountain Road (late May to mid-Oct daily 9am–4pm; $23 per car). Originally built in the 1850s as a carriage road, the track ends at a tiny **visitors' center** (3850ft) manned by Green Mountain Club volunteers. From here it's a short scramble to the ridge that runs along the mountain top, and around 1.5 miles to the peak, known as "the Chin" (4393ft), following the Long Trail. Alternatively, you can take the **Gondola Skyride** (mid-June to mid-Oct daily 10am–5pm; $16, $22 round-trip; ☎802/253-7311), which affords jaw-dropping views and ends at **Cliff House** (3660ft). Hikers can continue from here along a short but extremely strenuous 0.7-mile path up to the Chin.

If you've got the stamina, the most rewarding approach is to **hike** the full way to the summit; you can simply follow the Toll Road or take the steep, steady, 4.7-mile section of the Long Trail from Rte-108, halfway through Smugglers' Notch. Serious hikers should visit the new **GMC Hiking Center** on Cabin Lane, off Hwy-100 back towards Waterbury (late May to early Oct Mon–Sat 9am–5pm; rest of year Mon–Fri 9am–5pm; ☎802/244-7037, ⓦwww.greenmountainclub .org) – it's around one mile north of Cold Hollow Cider Mill (see p.364).

Those who would rather keep to lower elevations should check out the **Stowe Recreation Path**, a 5.3-mile paved trail that starts in the village behind the Community Church and ends at Brook Road, halfway up Mountain Road. It never feels too crowded, and it offers scenic views of the West Branch River and Mount Mansfield.

Eating and drinking

There are many places to **eat** in and around Stowe, ranging from low-budget delis, bakeries, and pizza joints to expensive restaurants, frequently run by an inn or resort. The **drinking** scene brings together resting skiers, hard-boiled locals, and well-heeled yuppies in various watering holes.

Restaurants

Austrian Tea Room 42 Trapp Hill Rd ☎802/253-5705. The high prices are more for the kitschy, Germanic atmosphere than the food, but the cuisine's still authentic enough and the setting fun (in season, try to get seated on the flower-lined balcony). *Wursts* go for $12, pastries for $6.

Blue Moon Cafe 35 School St, Stowe Village ☎802/253-7006. Inventive, expensive New American fare featuring local game (braised venison and the like) and seafood; probably Stowe's best all-round dining choice. Good wine list. Dinner only, daily 6–9pm.

Cliff House Restaurant On Mount Mansfield, at the Gondola Summit ☎802/253-3665. Fine dining near the highest point in the state, featuring regional cuisine – open for lunch when the Gondola is in operation, and occasionally dinners.

McCarthy's 2043 Mountain Rd ☎802/253-8626. Irish-themed joint, especially noted for its great heaping breakfasts.

Olive's Bistro 1036 Mountain Rd ☎802/253-2033. Great tapas bar in addition to French-, Greek-, and North African-inspired Mediterranean specialities. Enticing selection of martinis, single malt scotches, and assorted cocktails at the bar. Closed Sun.

Pie Casso 1899 Mountain Rd ☎802/253-4411. New York-style pizzas from $13, as well as plenty of pastas and zesty wings, served up in a trendy dining room – more lounge bar than *Pizza Hut*.

Red Basil 294 Mountain Rd ☎802/253-4478. Fresh herbs bring *Red Basil*'s Thai dishes (and your palate) to life, with decent staples like green curry and pad thai ($15).

Waffle Haus On Mount Mansfield, at the Gondola Summit ☎no phone. The perfect antidote to a morning of chilly winter activity: Belgian waffles and hot cider or cocoa for refueling. Open Wed–Sun 10am–3pm in ski season only.

Winfield's Bistro 1746 Mountain Rd ☎802/253-7355. The liberal use of ingredients like "pecan dust" and "tawny port syrup" on the menu here tips this as a creative New American bistro (and also as "expensive"). Open Wed–Sun only, reservations recommended.

Bars

Matterhorn 4969 Mountain Rd ☎802/253-8198, ⓦwww.matterhornbar.com. The region's best bands have been coming here for years – you can enjoy the live music in the nightclub on weekends most of the year, or listen from the downstairs wood-paneled dining room (specializing in, oddly, pizzas and sushi).

Rusty Nail 1190 Mountain Rd ☎802/253-6245, ⓦrustynailbar.com. Rotating DJs and live jazz on Thursdays fill the bill, but the *Nail* is also a sports

New England food and drink

In the popular perception, New England cuisine equals pot roast, baked beans, and boiled dinner (corned beef and cabbage, to be precise), yet seafood is the real staple of the day, appearing in everything from creamy clam chowder to messy fried platters to the ultimate, if utterly simple, meal of boiled lobster. The region's distinctive produce includes tart cranberries, rich maple syrup, and crunchy apples, while its fine speciality products, such as cheddar cheese, microbrewed beer, and iconic ice cream, have received international acclaim.

Seafood

New England's coastline is the source of its tastiest treats. **Lobsters** are generally eaten two ways: as a **lobster roll** and as a boiled entree. Lobster rolls consist of lobster meat, mayonnaise, salt, and pepper, all stuffed inside a toasted bun. Eating **boiled lobster** is fun but laborious: the hard-shelled claws must be cracked open, the body and tail snapped apart, and the meat dug out with fingers or tiny forks. **Clams** are another staple. The plump and tender bellies are generally breaded and fried, or simply steamed and eaten from the shell. Clams are also the key ingredients in **clam chowder**, a cream-based soup with chunks of clam and potato. Other shellfish specialities include raw **oysters**, splayed on the half-shell and served on a bed of ice with lemon juice, horseradish, and hot sauce – keep an eye out for the Damariscotta, Cuttyhunk, Wellfleet, and Pemaquid varieties. As for fish, **cod** and **scrod** (young cod and haddock) are ubiquitous, traditionally broiled with butter and spices.

Maine lobsters for sale ▲

Fried clam platter ▼

Oysters at a raw bar ▼

Clambakes

Clambakes are local traditions older than New England itself. First a deep pit is dug in the sand, and lined with rocks. Wood is added and ignited; its ashes are eventually swept away, with the rocks left hot enough to cook on. Seaweed is piled on these rocks, followed by layers of potatoes, onions, corn, and clams. Then comes another layer of seaweed, and finally a wet canvas, which traps the steam. The result is an unforgettable meal. Clambakes are usually organized by churches and other similar non-profit groups. Your best bet if you want to participate is to search out **local papers** for advertisements.

Produce

Thanks to its unique four-season climate, New England features a wide variety of excellent **produce**. The most unusual is **maple syrup**: sap drawn from maple trees that is boiled down until it reaches a sweet, thick consistency. The industry is centered in Vermont, where up to 5.5 million pounds of the stuff are made annually. To see how syrup is made (and to have a taste), seek out one of the hundreds of **sugarhouses** across the state.

Local fruits include the indigenous **cranberry**, a distinctive New England crop mainly because its tricky growing conditions (sandy, acidic bogs) make it difficult to transplant elsewhere. While their intensely sour flavor prevents them from being eaten raw, cranberries are frequently found in baked goods or as a relish for meats. Although **blueberries** don't require such an exacting environment, much of the nation's crop comes from northern Maine. Apples are of course easy to find most anywhere, but **apple-picking** in the fall – when the cider is hot and the leaves ablaze with color – is a memorable New England experience. Western Massachusetts and New Hampshire's ten-mile "Apple Way" are both great orchard areas.

Fresh, sweet **corn** is another treat, found in summer at farm stands throughout the region and served alongside lobster and barbecued meats. Native Americans introduced the Pilgrims to the benefits of planting corn, and it is believed that knowledge of this crop is what preserved them through their first harsh New England winters. In celebration of their survival, the Pilgrims held the first **Thanksgiving** dinner, with corn as a cornerstone of the meal.

▲ Harvested blueberries

▼ Maple syrup advertisement

PURE MAPLE SYRUP

▼ Apple orchard

Ben & Jerry's ice cream truck ▲

Cabot Creamery store ▼

HOME OF THE BEST CHEDDAR IN THE U.S.A.

AND NOW HOME OF THE BEST CHEDDAR & THE BEST FLAVORED CHEESE IN THE WORLD

Sam Adams beer tap ▼

Cheese, chocolate, and ice cream

New England's dairy herds once produced much of the nation's milk, and today they supply a host of creamy speciality products. Vermont in particular pioneered the creation of fine American **cheddar cheese**, and today its farms knock out award-winning brands such as Cabot Cheddar and Grafton Village Cheese.

Ben & Jerry's, also Vermont-based, has become one of the best loved **ice cream** brands in the world, and just as famously committed to its local dairy farmers and drug-free cows. Wickedly tempting home-made ice cream is made all over the region. Gourmet **chocolate** is another milk-based sweet treat; Vermont's Lake Champlain Chocolates, New Hampshire's Burdick Chocolates, and Chilmark Chocolates on Martha's Vineyard are the most sought-after varieties.

Microbreweries

New England is credited with jump-starting the **microbrew industry** (whereby beer is crafted and sold on a small scale) in the US. Boston-based Sam Adams began in 1985, when fifth-generation brewer Jim Koch deemed the nation ready for "better beer." The success of Sam Adams served as a catalyst for other small-time New England brewers, and the region now boasts a variety of tasty beers. While only a select number of these (such as Harpoon and Portsmouth) are consistently available, excellent smaller-time options can be found at any decent New England bar. Most notable are Vermont-brewed Magic Hat, Otter Creek, and Rock Art; Smuttynose of New Hampshire; Shipyard and Geary's in Maine; and Connecticut's Ten Penny Ale.

bar with a 20ft TV screen. Check out the website for the entertaining story of the place's history. **Shed Restaurant and Brewery Pub** 1859 Mountain Rd ℡802/253-4364. Hearty American fare – the speciality is the ample "Mighty Shed Burger." The attached bar has daily specials on pints and bar chow (which includes surprisingly, a number of vegetarian choices). Open 'til late.

Montpelier and around

With fewer than ten thousand residents, **MONTPELIER** (mont-PEEL-yer), in a beautiful valley on the Winooski and North Branch rivers, is the smallest state capital in the country. Around the **Vermont State House** building – urban in style but not in scale – the vital downtown area is lined exclusively with nineteenth-century buildings and boasts a number of fine restaurants, museums, and theaters. Despite its considerable charms, the city still bears a low tourist profile, and it is this lack of commercialism that makes Montpelier a refreshing counterpoint to the cultivated rural quaintness that pervades the rest of the state.

Arrival, information, and local transport

Montpelier is thirteen miles east of Waterbury via I-89. You should have no problem parking; try the lot behind the Visitors Center (free; see p.370) or Blanchard Court, behind City Hall on Main Street ($0.35 per hr). Montpelier

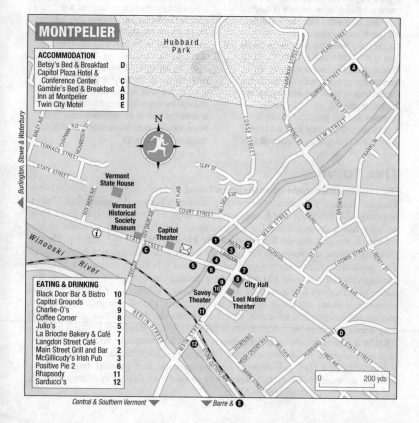

MONTPELIER

ACCOMMODATION
Betsy's Bed & Breakfast	D
Capitol Plaza Hotel & Conference Center	C
Gamble's Bed & Breakfast	A
Inn at Montpelier	B
Twin City Motel	E

EATING & DRINKING
Black Door Bar & Bistro	10
Capitol Grounds	4
Charlie-O's	9
Coffee Corner	8
Julio's	5
La Brioche Bakery & Café	7
Langdon Street Café	1
Main Street Grill and Bar	2
McGillicudy's Irish Pub	3
Positive Pie 2	6
Rhapsody	11
Sarducci's	12

Hubbard Park

Vermont State House

Vermont Historical Society Museum

Capitol Theater

City Hall

Savoy Theater

Lost Nation Theater

Winooski River

Burlington, Stowe & Waterbury

Central & Southern Vermont ▼   ▼ Barre & Ⓔ

0   200 yds

shares a stop on Amtrak's *Vermonter* line with its neighbor Barre; the station lies two miles west of downtown near I-89. The **bus** terminal (☎802/229-9220) is next to the river on Taylor Street, a block from State Street, one of the town's main thoroughfares. Green Mountain Transit Agency runs **buses** (☎802/223-7BUS) to Waterbury ($2) and Burlington ($4).

The **Capitol Region Visitors Center**, opposite the State House at 134 State St (Mon–Fri 6am–6pm, Sat & Sun 10am–6pm; ☎802/828-5981 or 1-800/VERMONT, ⊛www.vermontvacation.com), offers plenty of information on local and statewide attractions. Check out the daily *Times-Argus* for arts and entertainment schedules and listings.

Accommodation

Montpelier boasts a decent range of affordable **places to stay**, with some of the best options being B&Bs. The riverside *Green Valley Campground*, northeast of town at the intersection of Rte-2 and Rte-302, four miles from Exit 7 or 8 off I-89 (May–Oct; ☎802/223-6217), offers 35 **campgrounds** from $19, with showers, convenience store, and laundry room.

Betsy's Bed & Breakfast 74 E State St ☎802/229-0466, ⊛www.betsysbnb.com. Twelve-room B&B in two Victorian homes on a quiet, leafy street a few-minutes' walk from downtown. Rooms are attractively (if busily) decorated, each with a bathroom – a rarity for this type of accommodation. ❻

Capitol Plaza Hotel and Conference Center 100 State St ☎802/274-5252 or 1-800/274-5252, ⊛www.capitolplaza.com. Comfortable and spacious digs across from the Art Deco Capitol Theater. Friendly, family-run, and aimed at the business traveler. ❽

Gamble's Bed and Breakfast 16 Vine St ☎802/229-4810. The three large and colorful rooms in this 1895 building, a 5min walk from

downtown, show a little wear and tear, but you can't beat the price. No in-room phones or TV, and shared bathrooms. ❸

Inn at Montpelier 147 Main St ☎802/223-2727, ⊛www.innatmontpelier.com. Spacious, well-appointed rooms in a pair of Federal-style buildings. The Continental breakfast is simple and healthy, and access to both common areas and a pleasant wrap-around porch is welcome. ❻

Twin City Motel 1537 Barre–Montpelier Rd (Rte-302), just off I-89 Exit 7 ☎802/476-3104 or 1-877/476-3104, ⊛www.twincitymotel.com. Probably the pick of the several motels located southeast of town on the Barre–Montpelier Road. Rooms have usual motel amenities, like cable TV, fridge, and telephone. ❸

The Town

Diminutive **downtown Montpelier** is home to four college campuses – New England Culinary Institute, Woodbury College, Vermont College of Union Institute & University, and Community College of Vermont – though it feels nothing like a college town (or a state capital, for that matter). Its most visible landmark, the gilt-domed **Vermont State House** (Mon–Fri 7.45am–4.15pm), rises high above the town center on State Street. Most visitors just stroll around the impeccably kept exterior gardens, particularly brilliant during the fall, and photograph the statue of **Ethan Allen** guarding the front doors – though the statue of Vermont's first governor **Thomas Chittenden**, to the left of the main entrance, is more attractive. It's well worth taking a stroll through the vaulted marble hallways inside, however, especially up to the second floor where you'll find a vast painting by Julian Scott representing the Battle of Cedar Creek, a Civil War skirmish in which Vermonters played a pivotal role. You can normally also have a peek inside the elegant Governor's Office, Senate Chamber, and Representative's Hall. Informative and enthusiastic free **guided tours** of the interior are available every half-hour (July to mid-Oct Mon–Fri 10am–3.30pm, Sat 11am–2.30pm; ☎802/828-2228).

▲ Vermont State House

The entirety of Vermont's history from the 1600s on is outlined in the **Vermont Historical Society Museum**, in the distinctive Pavilion Building at 109 State St (Tues–Sat 10am–4pm, also May–Oct Sun noon–4pm; $5; ☎802/828-2291, Ⓦwww.vermonthistory.org). The "Freedom and Unity" exhibition highlights the evolution of Vermont's unique character, from early settlement to the present day, with some thoughtful displays on the influence of Native Americans, the independence efforts of the Green Mountain Boys, and videos dramatizing local debates on the historically explosive issues of slavery, women's suffrage, and gay civil unions.

East of downtown, in the Vermont College campus, lies the small but distinguished **T.W. Wood Gallery**, 36 College St (Tues–Sun noon–4pm; free; ☎802/828-8743, Ⓦwww.twwoodgallery.org), showcasing local painter T.W. Wood's fascinating depictions of everyday New England life in the nineteenth century, plus experimental American folk art and photos created for the Work Projects Administration between 1936 and 1943. It's also worth checking out **Morse Farm Maple Sugarworks** 1168 County Rd, 2.7 miles from downtown (May–Oct daily 8am–8pm; Nov–April 9am–5pm; ☎1-800/242-2740, Ⓦwww.morsefarm.com), one of the most traditional maple syrup farms in the state. Free tours and tastings provide an illuminating introduction to their products, best experienced in the early spring, when maple sugaring takes place.

Though the muddy, unpredictable, and seemingly endless weeks of March in New England have few virtues, you can count on two constants: the proximity of spring and **maple syrup**. Vermont is the largest producer of maple syrup in the US, boasting small, traditional sugarhouses deep in the forest as well as large farms using the latest technology. Surrounded by ancient maples and using time-honored methods, these low-key, often family-owned producers generally welcome visitors, give tours, and sell everything from maple-coated nuts to maple lollipops and jelly, in addition to high-quality maple syrup – Morse Farm (see p.371) and Sugarbush Farm (see p.356) are two of the best for visits. The season starts as early as February in southern Vermont and lasts into April in the northern part of the state, but many sugarhouses are open year-round. For a full list of over forty producers, contact the Vermont Maple Sugar Makers' Association (☎802/763-7435; ⊛www.vermontmaple.org), which also organizes the annual **Vermont Maple Open House Weekend** each March.

Eating

Students from the New England Culinary Institute (NECI) have lent their expertise to Montpelier's dining scene, resulting in a number of alluring, experimental **restaurants**. The area is blissfully resistant to fast food – it's the only state capital without a *McDonald's*, though a *Subway* and a *Quizno's* have found their way to Main Street.

Capitol Grounds 45 State St ☎802/223-7800. The wooden interior of this former bank invites casual lounging over your morning coffee, which you can order from the genuinely friendly staff in four sizes: Conservative, Moderate, Liberal, and Radical (20oz; $2). Good tea selection as well.

Coffee Corner 83 Main St at State St ☎802/229-9060. A Montpelier standard for over sixty years, where you can scarf down cheap diner food at Formica tables or rub elbows with Vermont's political potentates at the lunch counter. Daily 6.30am–3pm.

Julio's 54 State St ☎802/229-9348. Pretty good Tex-Mex for this area of New England, including cheap, filling burrito and enchilada dishes and zippy margaritas ($6).

La Brioche Bakery & Cafe 89 Main St ☎802/229-0443. Cheerful, well-designed bakery run by NECI. The "1/2 Bag Lunch" ($6) will

get you half a sandwich, a small but interesting salad or soup, and a cookie (try the "Vermont Crunchy": a peanut butter oatmeal cookie with chocolate chips and nuts). Closed Sun.

Main Street Grill and Bar 118 Main St ☎802/223-3188. The delectable, inventive specialities from NECI alums range $13–20 for dinner; American grill fare and shellfish are stand-outs. Closed Mon.

Rhapsody 28 Main St ☎802/229-6112. Hippy-friendly, multinational restaurant where you can wolf down curried tofu and vegan chocolate cake from the organic buffet ($7.49/lb). Also has wi-fi. Open from 11.30am; closed Sun.

Sarducci's 3 Main St ☎802/223-0229. Long-established, Tuscan-inspired trattoria next to the river. Pasta dishes will set you back around $8.50, or you could opt for a house speciality such as wood-roasted salmon in a white wine sauce ($17).

Drinking and entertainment

The town's main drama venue is the **Lost Nation Theater** in the City Hall Arts Center on Main Street (☎802/229-0492, ⊛www.lostnationtheater.org), where the resident company performs everything from Shakespearean epics to popular musicals to experimental contemporary plays. Across the street at 26 Main St, the tiny **Savoy Theater** (☎802/229-0598, ⊛www.savoytheater.com) shows first-rate foreign, classic, and independent films. More current ones are screened at the **Capitol** (☎802/229-0343) on State Street. During the summer, the City Band holds evening concerts on the State House lawn, and the Vermont Philharmonic takes a turn in July. Other than that, there are a handful of decent **bars**; there are also all sorts of places that feature **live music** at least several nights a week.

Black Door Bar & Bistro 44 Main St ☎802/223-7070, ⓦwww.blackdoorvt.com. Along with its trendy, moderately expensive bistro fare (mains $17–19), live music (ranging from funky jazz to zydeco) is on offer Wed–Sat. Sometimes a $5 cover. Closed Sun.

Charlie-O's 70 Main St ☎802/223-6820. Just a tad scruffy in this pleasant city, *Charlie-O's* is simple: a pool table, wood floors, and a bar. You can easily get your rock or blues fix here most weekends. Open from 2pm daily.

Langdon Street Café 4 Langdon St ☎802/223-8667, ⓦwww.langdonstreetcafe.com. Music every night in a wood-paneled community space with the feel of a friend's living room.

Expect anything from poetry and games nights to folk-punk, jazz, and reggae. And it's family-friendly, with free wi-fi, beer, wine, and coffee drinks available, but no hard stuff.

McGillicuddy's Irish Pub 14 Langdon St ☎802/223-2721. Standard bar fare, most notable for its spicy hot wings and a wide selection of microbrews. Draws a lively, younger crowd and gets loud and busy on weekends.

Positive Pie 2 22 State St ☎802/229-0453, ⓦwww.positivepie.com. Live hip-hop or groove on weekends make the New York-style pizzas and Sicilian pastas available here that much better. Sometimes a $5 cover.

Rock of Ages

Seven miles southeast of Montpelier, the humdrum town of **Barre** has little to recommend it, despite being at the center of the state's booming **granite** industry. Instead, make for the **Rock of Ages Quarry**, I-89 Exit 6 (May–Oct Mon–Sat 8.30am–5pm, Sun 10am–5pm; $3.50 for tours, otherwise free; ☎802/476-3119, ⓦwww.rockofages.com), which is actually southeast of town on Hwy-63 in the municipality of **Graniteville**. This is the world's largest deep-hole (600ft) granite quarry, as you'll almost certainly be told by the fleet of enthusiastic guides. You can check out the **visitors' center** (which shows videos about the site and has small displays), and have a look inside the cavernous hangar-like workshop, where stone is cut, ground, and polished, all for free. If you've come all this way, though, it's worth shelling out a few bucks for the narrated shuttle-bus tour that takes you to the far more impressive fifty-acre working quarries, and through the manufacturing centers where artisans busy themselves making fleets of **tombstones**. If this piques your interest, check out **Hope Cemetery**, just north of Barre town center on Hwy-14. While the city's stonecutters lived modestly, they knew how to die in grand style, commemorating themselves and their families with massive, elaborately wrought granite tombstones up to ten feet in height.

Lake Champlain

Forming the boundary between Vermont and New York, 150-mile-long **Lake Champlain** never exceeds twelve miles across at its widest point, though its area of about 490 square miles makes it the sixth largest freshwater lake in the US. The first non-native to see the lake was French explorer **Samuel de Champlain** in 1609, who humbly named it in his own honor. Today the life and soul of the valley is the French Canadian-influenced city of **Burlington**, whose long-standing trade links with Montréal have filled it with elegant nineteenth-century architecture. Within just a few miles of the center, US-2 leads north onto the supremely rural **Champlain Islands**, covered in meadows and farmlands, while to the south, the **Shelburne Museum** is a sprawling village of historic homes and artifacts, and the **Lake Champlain Maritime Museum** offers the best insights into the history and ecology of the lake itself.

Burlington and around

With a population of around forty thousand, lakeside **BURLINGTON** is the closest Vermont gets to a city. It's also notable as one of New England's most purely enjoyable destinations – a hip, relaxed fusion of Montréal, eighty miles to the north, and Boston, over two hundred miles southeast. In fact, from its earliest days, Burlington has looked as much to Canada as to the south – shipping connections with the St Lawrence River were far easier than the land routes across the mountains, and the harbor became a major supply center. Burlington today is the definitive youthful university town. From its waterfront walkways to its lively brewpubs, the city is at once cosmopolitan and pleasantly manageable in scale. It's one of the few American cities to offer something approaching a café society, with a downtown – especially around the Church Street Marketplace – you can stroll around on foot, and plenty of open-air terraces.

Arrival, information, and city transport

Amtrak's *Vermonter* **trains** arrive at Essex Junction, an inconvenient five miles northeast of town (connecting buses $1.25). Note that the station only opens twice a day (for the two trains) and there is no ticket office. Greyhound **buses** stop at the bus station at 345 Pine St, four blocks south of Main Street (daily 7am–7.30pm; ☎802/864-6811). **Burlington International Airport** (☎802/863-1889) is a few miles east of town along US-2 (buses to downtown run every 30min 6.30am–10pm; $1.25), with connections from Boston, Chicago, New York City, Washington, DC, and several other cities.

Practical information is available from the **Lake Champlain Regional Chamber of Commerce**, 60 Main St (July–Sept Mon–Fri 8.30am–5pm, Sat–Sun 9am–5pm; Oct–June Mon–Fri 8.30am–5pm; ☎802/863-3489 or 1-877/686-5253, ⓦwww.vermont.org). The chamber also has an **information center** at the **airport** (daily 9am–midnight), while the Information Gallery runs **information booths** in the middle of Church Street between Cherry and Bank streets (Mon–Sat 11am–5pm, Sun noon–5pm; ☎802/865-4636), and at the waterfront on College Street (same hours), which have a range of maps and brochures.

Burlington is a great place for **walking**, as the main downtown shopping area is fairly compact. For those who choose to drive, **parking** remains a bit of a problem: the numerous public garages are often full during the day, and most streetside meters only allow a maximum of two hours. The local **CCTA** bus ($1.25; ☎802/864-0211, ⓦwww.cctaride.org) connects points all over the downtown area, and travels to the nearby towns of Winooski, Essex, and Shelburne. You can get route maps and schedules at the main downtown terminal on the corner of Cherry and Church streets. CCTA also operates a very convenient (free) shuttle along College Street between the University of Vermont and the waterfront, with stops at the Fleming Museum and the Church Street Marketplace (every 15–30min: Mon–Fri 6.30am–7pm; late May to June &

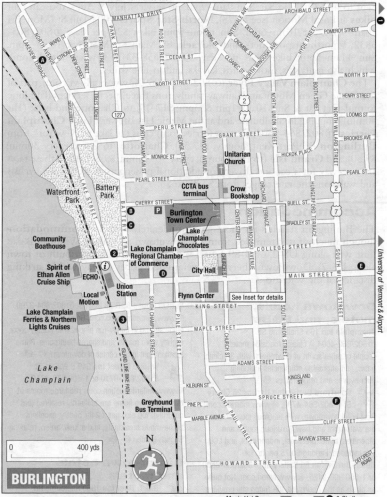

Ethan Allen Homestead

ARCHIBALD STREET
POMEROY STREET
MANHATTAN DRIVE
INTERVALE AVE
DECATUR ST
SPRING ST
CROMBIE ST
CLOAREC ST
NORTH WINOOSKI AVE
HYDE STREET
NORTH AVENUE
WARD ST
STRONG ST
BLODGETT STREET
DROW STREET
PITKIN STREET
PARK STREET
ROSE STREET
CEDAR ST
NORTH ST
BOOTH STREET
HENRY STREET
LOOMIS ST
NORTH STREET
LAKEVIEW TERRACE
A
2
7
PERU STREET
NORTH CHAMPLAIN ST
GEORGE STREET
ELMWOOD AVENUE
GRANT STREET
NORTH UNION STREET
HICKOK PLACE
BROOKES AVE
NORTH WILLARD STREET
127
MONROE ST
Unitarian Church
PEARL STREET
ORCHARD TERRACE
HUNGERFORD TERRACE
PEARL STREET
2
7
CCTA bus terminal
Crow Bookshop
BUELL ST
BRADLEY ST
CHERRY STREET
B
C
P
Burlington Town Center
Lake Champlain Chocolates
CENTER STREET
SOUTH WINOOSKI AVENUE
COLLEGE STREET
Community Boathouse
Lake Champlain Regional Chamber of Commerce
2
BATTERY STREET
LAKE STREET
Spirit of Ethan Allen Cruise Ship
ECHO
i
D
City Hall
CHURCH STREET
MAIN STREET
E
SOUTH WILLARD STREET
Local Motion
Union Station
Flynn Center
See Inset for details
Lake Champlain Ferries & Northern Lights Cruises
3
SOUTH CHAMPLAIN STREET
KING STREET
PINE STREET
MAPLE STREET
CHURCH ST
SOUTH UNION STREET
Lake Champlain
ISLAND LINE BIKE PATH
ADAMS STREET
KILBURN ST
KINGSLAND ST
F
PINE PL
SPRUCE STREET
Greyhound Bus Terminal
SAINT PAUL STREET
MARBLE AVENUE
CLIFF STREET
BAYVIEW STREET
DEFOREST ROAD
0   400 yds
N
HOWARD STREET

BURLINGTON

Magic Hat Brewery   G & Shelburne

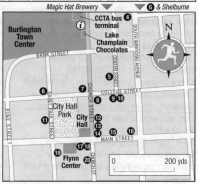

Burlington Town Center
CCTA bus terminal
4
i
Lake Champlain Chocolates
BANK STREET
SOUTH WINOOSKI AVENUE
N
6
5
CENTER STREET
COLLEGE STREET
SAINT PAUL STREET
7
CHURCH STREET
8
9 10
PINE STREET
City Hall Park
City Hall
11
12
13
14
MAIN STREET
15
16
17 18
0   200 yds
19
Flynn Center
20

EATING & DRINKING	
American Flatbread	11
Club Metronome	16
Daily Planet	5
Leunig's Bistro	7
Muddy Waters	15
Nectar's	16
Penny Cluse Café	4
Rasputin's	18
Red Onion	13
Red Square	12
Ruben James	17
Second Floor	20
Shanty on the Shore	3
Skinny Pancake	2
Smokejack's	14
Sneakers	1
Sweetwaters	8
Three Needs	9
Trattoria Delia	19
Vermonty Pub & Brewery	6
Zabby & Elf's Stone Soup	10

ACCOMMODATION	
Champlain Inn	G
Courtyard Burlington Harbor	B
Hilton Burlington	C
Lang House on Main Street	E
One of a Kind B&B	A
Sunset House B&B	D
Willard Street Inn	F

Sept to mid–Oct also Sat–Sun 9am–9pm; no services July & Aug). You can rent **bikes** at Local Motion (see p.378), **North Star Sports**, 100 Main St (Mon–Fri 10am–7pm, Sat 10am–6pm, Sun noon–5pm; bikes $28 per day; ☎802/863-3832, ⓦnorthstarsports.net), and **Skirack**, 85 Main St (Mon–Sat 10am–7pm, Sun 11am–5pm; bikes $28 per day; ☎802/658-3313, ⓦwww.skirack.com), which also rents skis, snowboards, kayaks, and in-line skates.

The **Champlain Valley Flyer** (☎802/463-3069, ⓦwww.rails-vt.com), part of the scenic Green Mountain Railway family, runs three special services (late June to mid–Oct Sat & Sun 10am, 1pm & 3pm; $17–19) to Charlotte and back (1hr 40min), stopping in Shelburne and at the Magic Hat Brewery. **Lake Champlain Ferries** (☎802/864-9804, ⓦwww.ferries.com) cross the lake to New York from **Burlington** (to Port Kent; hourly; $17.50), **Charlotte** (to Essex; every 30min; $9.50), and **Grand Isle** (to Plattsburgh; every 10–15min; $9.50). All of these rates are one-way for a car and driver; for additional passengers as well as for cyclists and walk-ons the rate ranges from $3.75 to $6.

Accommodation

The Burlington area has no shortage of moderately priced **accommodation**, though much of it is removed from the downtown area, along Williston Road (just west along US-2, off I-89 Exit 14) and Shelburne Road (south of town along US-7). Downtown, there are several good places to stay within striking distance of the waterfront.

Downtown hotels, motels, and B&Bs

Champlain Inn 165 Shelburne St ☎802/862-4004. A classic roadside motel a couple of miles south of downtown, with 33 clean, basic, and affordable efficiencies including microwaves and refrigerators. ❸

Courtyard Burlington Harbor 25 Cherry St ☎802/864-4700, ⓦwww.marriott.com. Best hotel downtown, with fabulous location near the waterfront and new, luxurious rooms and amenities; buffet breakfast, indoor pool, and LCD TVs included. Parking $0.75 per hr. ❽

Hilton Burlington 60 Battery St ☎802/658-6500 or 1-800/996-3426, ⓦwww.hilton.com. Not quite as plush as the *Courtyard*, the *Hilton* still provides all the standard upscale amenities, with a few extras (check out the Herman Miller chairs), right on the lake; it's also much cheaper (book on the website). ❼

Lang House on Main Street 360 Main St ☎802/652-2500 or 1-877/919-9799, ⓦwww.langhouse.com. Handsome 1881 Victorian conveniently located between UVM campus and downtown, offering nine rooms with fireplaces, many with views of Lake Champlain. ❼–❽

One of a Kind B&B 53 Lakeview Terrace ☎1-877/479-2736, ⓦwww.oneofakindbnb.com. Two cozy rooms, with extensive Continental breakfast, right on the lake in a quiet area of town. Free wi-fi. ❻–❽

Sunset House B&B 78 Main St ☎802/864-3790, ⓦwww.sunsethousebb.com. Good choice if you enjoy staying in family-run places with homey decor, slightly worn rooms, and shared bathrooms. Prime location right in the center of downtown. ❺–❻

Willard Street Inn 349 S Willard St ☎802/651-8710 or 1-800/577-8712, ⓦwww.willardstreetinn.com. The large rooms at this distinctive home are brilliantly restored (but not frilly). You also get a 24hr pantry, excellent home-made breakfasts, and a lush, green, relaxing English garden. ❼–❾

Out-of-town hotels and motels

G.G.T. Tibet Inn 1860 Shelburne Rd, South Burlington ☎802/863-7110, ⓦwww.ggttibetinn.com. Popular motel run by amiable Tibetan emigrés; the rooms, though small and simple, are good value (cable TV, fridge, microwave), but it's the touches added by Kalsang and his family (arts and crafts, Tibetan library, prayer flags) that make it so memorable. ❹

Heart of the Village Inn 5347 Shelburne Rd, Shelburne ☎802/985-2800 or 1-877/808-1834, ⓦwww.heartofthevillage.com. Nine beautifully decorated rooms in a pair of Victorian houses with period antiques and delectable breakfast. Cable TV available on request. ❽

Ho-Hum Motel 1660 Williston Rd, South Burlington ☎802/863-4551. This motel is basic and a little worn around the edges, but reasonably priced, three miles east of downtown. Four adjacent restaurants and a bike path nearby help liven it up. ❹

Inn at Essex 70 Essex Way, Essex Junction ☏802/878-1100 or 1-800/727-4295, ⓦvtculinaryresort.com. Country inn meets business hotel at this classy establishment about eight miles from Burlington, which has a golf course, a pool, comfortable rooms, and two excellent restaurants run by the NECI. Complimentary shuttle to nearby transportation. ❽

Inn at Shelburne Farms 1611 Harbor Rd, Shelburne ☏802/985-8498, ⓦwww .shelburnefarms.org/comevisitus/inn. Wide range of posh digs, perhaps the nicest around, in a mansion on the lovely Shelburne Farms. May–Oct. ❼–❾

La Quinta Inn & Suites 1285 Williston Rd, South Burlington ☏802/865-3400, ⓦwww.lqm.com.

One of the better chain motels around the city, with clean, newly renovated rooms, pool, spa, coffee round the clock, and free Continental breakfast and local calls. ❺

Camping

Lone Pine Campsite 52 Sunset View Rd, Colchester ☏802/878-5447, ⓦwww.lonepinecampsites.com. About eight miles north of town, with two hundred sites starting at $32 a night. No beach, though two swimming pools should be adequate compensation. In any case, Lake Champlain is not too far away. May to mid-Oct.

North Beach Campground 60 Institute Rd ☏802/862-0942 or 1-800/571-1198. Less than two miles north of town on the shores of Lake Champlain. A total of 137 sites ranging from $24 to $33, various other facilities (including plenty for the kids), and access to a sandy beach. Open May to mid-Oct.

The city and around

Most visitors' first stop in Burlington is the **waterfront**; indeed, kayaks seem to be strapped to the roof of every third car. The aptly named **Waterfront Park** stretches a couple of miles along Lake Champlain, with ample green spaces, gorgeous swing benches, and a popular dog run. At its northern end, **Battery Park** makes a particularly good place to watch the sun go down over the Adirondacks – especially when there's a band playing, as there usually is on summer weekends. Note, though, there is no boardwalk south of the park, and walking between piers involves following the road or the twelve-mile **Island Line bike path**, which traces a former railroad bed and is a good way to see the waterfront and some of the city beaches. Starting a couple of miles south of Burlington's downtown, it winds along the shoreline all the way north to Colchester, before

▲ Burlington waterfront

ending abruptly past the end of Mills Point in Mallets Bay. **Local Motion** (T802/652-BIKE, W www.localmotion.org), the cycling advocacy group here, is pushing for the trail to connect to the Champlain Islands and on to Canada. It also rents bikes (mid-May to mid-Oct daily 10am–6pm; $28 per day, $48 for two days) from its home on the path behind Union Station.

If you're looking to actually get on the water, the convivial *Spirit of Ethan Allen III* (May–Oct; 1hr narrated cruises from $10.75; T802/862-8300, W www .soea.com) sets out from the Community Boathouse at the end of College Street, while *Northern Lights* (1.5hr for $12; T802/864-9669, W www .lakechamplaincruises.com) offers a similar service from the adjacent King Street dock. You can rent sailboats at **Winds of Ireland** (from $430 per day; T802/863-5090, W www.windsofireland.net), also in the Community Boathouse. At the end of College Street is **ECHO Lake Aquarium and Science Center** (daily 10am–5pm; $9.50, children $7; T802/864-1848, W www.echovermont.org), which affords opportunities to handle all sorts of lake-dwelling creatures and offers exhibits on area marine life; it's more for kids than parents.

Church Street Marketplace

The **Church Street Marketplace**, a pedestrian mall a few blocks from the waterfront, holds Burlington's remaining old buildings (the area in between is crammed with nondescript modern blocks), including the stately City Hall, a red-brick Victorian. The street is at its busiest at night and on weekend days, both good people-watching times. Although locals complain that the marketplace has become inundated with chain stores, it still supports a number of unique businesses. Check out the excellent **Art Market** (May–Oct Sat 9am–2.30pm), held in City Hall Park (also featuring great snack food), and leaf through the **Crow Bookshop**, 14 Church St (T802/862-0848), one of the better independent bookstores downtown. Another spot with local flavor is **Lake Champlain Chocolates**, 63 Church St (Mon–Thurs 10am–9pm, Fri & Sat 10am–10pm, Sun 11am–6pm; T802/862-5185), a gourmet chocolate shop and café that tempts passersby with hot chocolate and espresso, ice cream, fudge, and, of course, chocolates. You can view the candy-making process at their **factory store**, a short drive south at 750 Pine St (Mon–Fri on the hour 9am–2pm; free; T802/864-1807), and, of course, snag some free samples.

Robert Hull Fleming Museum

College Street leads east from the marketplace to the sleepy campus of the **University of Vermont**, founded in 1791 by Ethan Allen's brother Ira. The university's **Robert Hull Fleming Museum** (May to early Sept Tues–Fri noon–4pm, Sat–Sun 1–5pm; early Sept to April Tues, Thurs & Fri 9am–4pm, Wed 9am–8pm, Sat–Sun 1–5pm; $5; T802/656-2090, W www.flemingmuseum .org), at 61 Colchester Ave, holds some European Baroque paintings and pre-Columbian artifacts. To catch more art, arrive on the first Friday of each month, when Burlington City Arts sponsors the free **First Friday Artwalk**, which traverses over fifteen downtown galleries (April–Oct; 5–8pm; T802/865-7166).

Magic Hat Brewing Company

More raucous entertainment can be had at the **Magic Hat Brewing Company**, five minutes' drive south of downtown off Rte-7 at 5 Bartlett Bay Rd, South Burlington (store open Mon–Sat 10am–6pm, Sun noon–5pm; tours every hour Thurs–Fri at 3pm, 4pm & 5pm, Sat noon, 1pm, 2pm & 3pm; T802/658-BREW, W www.magichat.net). The tours make the science of beer-making look fun, and the free samples enhance the experience even further.

Ethan Allen and his Green Mountain Boys

Flamboyant and controversial, folk hero **Ethan Allen** (1738–89) typifies the independent ethos Vermont has long been known for, even if he did start out a Connecticut farmer.

In the 1740s, Benning Wentworth, the royal governor of New Hampshire, began issuing land grants for the area now known as Vermont, but in 1764, King George III decided that New York's governor wielded the rightful authority over the same territory, and the original settlers and their townships were subjected to burdensome New York fees or, worse, had their lands confiscated. The settlers responded by forming a citizens' militia, the **Green Mountain Boys**, to protect their rights, electing Ethan Allen as their colonel. Shortly thereafter, Allen and other family members formed the Onion River Land Company to speculate on the contested Wentworth land grants; eventually, the Allens were selling grants purchased at ten cents an acre for five dollars an acre, a pretty profit indeed. In the meantime, Allen and his fellow settlers were developing the area, building roads and establishing a population center on Burlington Bay.

Allen and (future traitor) Colonel Benedict Arnold were behind the capture of Fort Ticonderoga, but Allen was captured by the Brits in Canada in 1775 and took little part in the remainder of the Revolutionary War. After his release in 1778 he returned to Vermont, where his energies were directed more towards ending the old land disputes than the struggle with England – after failing to get Congress recognition for an independent Vermont, he even began secret negotiations with the British to rejoin the Empire. These negotiations became considerably less attractive after the Treaty of Paris in 1783, which ended the war.

With the coming of peace, Ethan Allen began to put together an impressive farm on the Winooski (Onion) River at Burlington, now known as the Ethan Allen Homestead (see below), where he settled down to become a philosopher and writer. Allen died in 1789, with Vermont yet to join the Union.

Ethan Allen Homestead

North of Burlington along Rte-127 in **Winooski**, the **Ethan Allen Homestead** (June–Oct Mon–Sat 10am–4pm, Sun 1–4pm; $5; guided tours Fri–Sun; rest of year call ☎802/865-4556, ⓦ www.ethanallenhomestead.org) is the 1787 farmhouse in which the Revolutionary War hero spent the last two years of his life. The attached museum occupies a re-created eighteenth-century tavern where you can hear about colonial life and pastimes as you sit on uncomfortable, true-to-period furniture. The 1400-acre farmland, which is owned by the Winooski Park District, is open to the public, meaning you can picnic on the grounds or even kayak your way here from Burlington.

Eating

Burlington's best **restaurants** are on Main and Church streets. American cuisine dominates the menus, but a few ethnic eateries provide alternatives. The presence of ten thousand students ensures that there are plenty of inexpensive spots, while the academic tone brings a certain sophistication to the café culture.

American Flatbread 115 St Paul St ☎802/861-2999. Wildly popular pizza place, especially on weekends, for its organic wheat dough and all-natural toppings, including locally made cheeses and sausage. Closed between lunch and dinner.
Daily Planet 15 Center St, behind the Church Street Marketplace ☎802/862-9647. This brightly

colored spot offers an eclectic menu melding Asian, Mediterranean, and Southwestern cooking with old-fashioned American comfort food, à la Thai Peanut noodles ($7) and peppered ribs ($12). Open from 5pm daily.
Leunig's Bistro 115 Church St ☎802/863-3759 or 1-800/491-1281. Sleek, modern bistro serving

contemporary Continental cuisine; dinner entrees range $18–28, but the lunch plates are better value ($10–15). Outdoor dining when weather permits, and live jazz Tues–Thurs.

Penny Cluse Café 169 Cherry St ☎802/651-8834. Omelettes, pancakes, sandwiches, salads, and good vegetarian lunches for under $10. Only open for breakfast and lunch – expect long lines at the weekends.

Red Onion 140 Church St ☎802/865-2563. The best sandwiches in town are made to order in this small shop with a mouthwatering menu, which includes breakfast and some good vegetarian options. The "red onion" sandwich is a standout, and one can easily feed two people. Closes 8pm and Sun.

Shanty on the Shore 181 Battery St ☎802/864-0238. Fresh seafood in a laid-back setting with views of Lake Champlain. Burlington's best – if not only – raw bar.

🏃 **Skinny Pancake** 60 Lake St ☎802/540-0188. Facing the waterfront with outdoor seating (but not much view), this is the place for a crêpe fix (from $6.50). The innovative combos – using mostly local ingredients – include the "Green Mountain" (apples and Cabot cheddar cheese) and the "Love Maker" (warm Nutella, strawberries, and Vermont whipped cream).

🏃 **Smokejack's** 156 Church St ☎802/658-1119. Innovative American cuisine as well as standard steak and seafood, all smoked over an oak-wood grill. Their Angus burgers are recognized as some of the best in the country ($13). Liquid refreshment comes in the form of punchy Bloody Marys, intriguing original cocktails, and a multitude of beer options. Choose from the many wines to help wash down the regional cheese plate.

Sneakers 36 Main St, Winooski ☎802/655-9081. This is the place for breakfast, and you should arrive early for it on weekends. Delicious waffles, home-made granola, eggs Benedict (try the smoked-turkey version) and fresh juices served in a diner-like setting with Art Deco mirrors. Good weekday lunches, too.

Sweetwaters 120 Church St ☎802/864-9800. American grill standards in a converted bank with sidewalk dining, most notable for its bison burgers ($9) and extensive Sunday brunch. Attractive raised street terrace – open in good weather.

Trattoria Delia 152 St Paul St ☎802/864-5253. Traditional regional Italian fare that goes beyond the usual pasta dishes – try the wild boar served over soft polenta – and a great wine list, at reasonable prices (pastas from $13.50, *secondis* from $19.50).

Zabby and Elf's Stone Soup 211 College St ☎802/862-7616. Excellent "mostly vegetarian" café, featuring a wide variety of sandwiches, home-made soups, cakes, and the like.

Drinking, nightlife, and entertainment

The **drinking** scene here is at its most active when school is in session, but Burlington's cafés and bars come to life during the summer as well. Though there are a handful of dance clubs, **nightlife** revolves mostly around live music. Pick up a copy of the free newspaper *Seven Days* (ⓦwww.7dvt.com), which has listings of music and stage shows. Several of Burlington's concert venues are big enough to draw indie bands from New York and around New England, but the local band scene is a formidable presence in its own right. Downtown's Art Deco-style **Flynn Center**, 153 Main St, across from City Hall and the Church Street Marketplace (☎802/863-5966, ⓦwww.flynncenter.org), plays host to a wide array of talent. Also, during the school year, UVM presents the **Lane Series** (☎802/656-4455, ⓦwww.uvm.edu/laneseries), a collection of musical performances during which you can hear everything from folk to jazz to the occasional opera. Beware that bars and clubs are quite strict about checking IDs, as this is a college town.

Club Metronome 188 Main St ☎802/865-4563, ⓦwww.clubmetronome.com. This very hip club above *Nectar's* (see below) hosts some live acts, but is mainly a funked-out dance venue featuring house and techno music. Eighties music dominates the dancefloor during Sat night's "Retronome" ($5).

Muddy Waters 184 Main St ☎802/658-0466. Colorful, crunchy clientele adorn this popular coffee house with a crazy interior lined with used furniture, thrift-store rejects, plants, and rough-hewn paneled walls. Extremely potent caffeinated beverages. Open late.

Nectar's 188 Main St ☎802/658-4771, ⓦwww.liveatnectars.com. Follow the rotating neon sign to this retro lounge lined with vinyl booths and Formica tables. This was the inspiration for

Phish's 1992 album title *A Picture of Nectar*, as the club hosted many of their earliest shows. Cover charge on weekends or for bigger local acts (usually $5).

Rasputin's 163 Church St ☎802/864-9324, ⓦwww.rasputinsvt.com. Popular UVM hangout with a raucous drinking scene that carries on until late in the evening. Good DJs pump up the energy level to new heights on weekends.

Red Square 136 Church St ☎802/859-8909, ⓦwww.redsquarevt.com. For those in the mood for a cosmopolitan experience, *Red Square* is the place to sip cocktails amidst a highbrow clientele. The food menu is also quite inviting and worth further investigation. Live music every night, often jazz, played outside when the weather permits. Cover on weekends.

Ruben James 153 Main St ☎802/864-0744. This joint brings in a slightly older crowd for satisfying microbrews, loud live music, pool tournaments, and football on the TV.

Second Floor 165 Church St ☎802/660-2088, ⓦwww.secondfloorvt.com. *Second Floor* serves as the site for some serious dancing, usually to hip-hop and techno, with the occasional theme night thrown in for variety.

Three Needs 207 College St ☎802/658-0889. This bar does a fine job of taking care of its customers' three most important needs: great beer, cheap pool, and Sun night *Simpsons* parties with excellent drink specials. Like a small private taproom; all microbrews, their own as well as guest beers.

Vermont Pub and Brewery 144 College St ☎802/865-0500, ⓦwww.vermontbrewery.com. Roomy and convivial brewpub, offering free tastes of its various beers – Dogbite Bitter is the best – plus an appetizing inexpensive menu (until midnight) with live music on some weekends.

The Shelburne Museum

It takes a whole day, if not more, to take in the fabulous fifty-acre collection of unalloyed Americana gathered at the **Shelburne Museum**, seven miles south of Burlington on US-7 in Shelburne (daily May–Oct 10am–5pm; $18, children $9; tickets good for two days; ☎802/985-3346, ⓦwww.shelburnemuseum.org). The brainchild of heiress Electra Havemeyer Webb (1888–1960), who aimed to create a distinctly American "collection of collections," the museum is probably the nation's finest celebration of its inventive past. The grounds themselves are also a joy to browse; paths lead over covered bridges and past lilac gardens in spring and stunning foliage in the fall.

More than thirty buildings dot the grounds. Besides seven fully furnished historic houses that were moved intact from elsewhere in the region, there's a smithy, a schoolhouse, a jail, a railroad station, and a general store, all of which aim to re-create aspects of everyday life over the past two centuries. Get oriented at the striking 80-foot diameter **Round Barn**, built in 1901 and now serving as the museum visitors' center, just inside the main entrance. One of the most popular structures, the horseshoe-shaped **Circus Building**, lies nearby. A homage to spectacle, American-style, the interior features the hand-carved miniature Arnold Circus Parade, as well as the Edgar Kirk Brothers Toy Circus, a tableau of the big top carved over a fifty-year period and made up of over 3,500 wooden spectators, vendors, animal acts, and trapeze artists. An operating vintage **carousel** operates daily (weather permitting) just outside the building.

From here you can stroll up through the old railroad buildings to the museum's enormous, 892-ton steam **paddlewheeler**, the *SS Ticonderoga*, which once plied the lake between Burlington and Plattsburgh, NY before being retired in 1953. Its tiny quarters have been restored to its 1923 elegance, complete with concession stand and deck chairs. A lighthouse built in 1871 on Lake Champlain's Colchester Reef now stands opposite.

The exhibits at Shelburne go beyond Americana as well. One of the best sections of the museum is the Greek Revival **Electra Havemeyer Webb Memorial Building**, just next door to the lighthouse, constructed between 1960 and 1967, complete with towering Ionic columns. Inside, six rooms are a meticulous reconstruction of Webb's luxurious 1930s Manhattan apartment.

The highlight is the artwork, including pieces by Rembrandt and many French Impressionists. This theme continues at the nearby **Webb Gallery**, which focuses on nineteenth-century American art. Much of its rotating collection consists of naturalist work, such as James Audubon's bird prints; there is also an intriguing portrait of Seneca Indian leader Sagayewatha, and one of Anna Mary Robertson Moses' (aka Grandma Moses) few cityscapes, *Cambridge, ca. 1944*. The gallery is most notable, however, for its assemblage of folk art, including decoys, weather vanes, tools, quilts, carriages, and circus memorabilia.

Another must-see is the 1783 **Stagecoach Inn** at the northern end of the museum grounds, which holds a wonderfully nostalgic assemblage of trade and tavern signs, most notably cigar-store figures, and a giant copper tooth forged in 1900.

Shelburne Farms

Next to the Shelburne Museum, **Shelburne Farms**, 1611 Harbor Rd (mid-May to mid-Oct 9am–5pm; $6 grounds only, with guided tour $9; ☎802/985-8686, Ⓦwww.shelburnefarms.org), is a working farm reborn as a non-profit environmental education center. A guided tour of railroad mogul Dr Seward Webb's estate reveals his descendants' commitment to sustainable farming. The undulating landscape is punctuated by three massive buildings: the main house, which overlooks Lake Champlain and the Adirondacks, a coach barn, and a horseshoe-shaped farm barn. You can get some exercise by walking the 4.5-mile Farm Trail, which circles the property, or the half-mile Lone Tree Hill trail and numerous side paths diverging from the roadways. The farm's hotel is the *Inn at Shelburne Farms*, with 26 deluxe guestrooms (see p.377 for review). The dining room serves breakfast, dinner, and Sunday brunch.

Lake Champlain Maritime Museum

Vermont is one of the few states with designated **Underwater Historic Preserves**, where divers can see wrecks on the lake floor. There are several of these underwater "state parks," and the best place to find out about them is at the **Lake Champlain Maritime Museum** in Basin Harbor (daily mid-May to mid-Oct 10am–5pm; $10; ☎802/475-2022, Ⓦwww.lcmm.org), thirty miles southwest of Burlington. The museum boasts a life-sized replica of the 1776 gunboat *Philadelphia II*, displays about Lake Champlain shipwrecks and the technology used to research them, and details of the horse-powered ferry that plied the lake a century ago. The museum is on the grounds of the Basin Harbor Club, where the *Red Mill Restaurant* serves three meals a day in summer, breakfast-only at other times.

Champlain Islands

Curling southward into Lake Champlain from Canada, the sparsely populated **Champlain Islands** comprise four narrow, oblong land masses – **NORTH HERO**, **GRAND ISLE**, **ALBURG**, and **ISLE LA MOTTE** – that never really caught on development-wise, despite being the site of the first settlement in Vermont, way back in 1666. After the Revolutionary War, Vermonters Ira and Ethan Allen staked claims to much of the islands' area, modestly naming them North and South Hero (the latter was later changed to Grand Isle). Today, though, the islands' only real industry is farming, evidenced by the silo-dotted hayfields and ubiquitous bovine odor.

French explorer Pierre de St-Paul's short-lived encampment is now occupied by **St Anne's Shrine** (mid-May to mid-Oct; ☎802/928-3362, ⓦwww.saintannesshrine.org) on West Shore Road, Isle La Motte. Groups of devoted Catholics and amateur miracle purveyors surround a statue of a prayerful St Anne during the summer; the shrine is right near a popular beach. Also on the island is a massive granite statue of **Samuel de Champlain**, who first landed here in 1609. Grand Isle's claim to historical fame is the **Hyde Log Cabin**, US-2 (July to mid-Oct Sat & Sun 11am–5pm; $2; ☎802/828-3051), built in 1783. Its modest museum is notable for its collection of old household artifacts such as makeshift ovens from Vermont's earliest days.

There is surprisingly little outdoor activity in these parts save for hunting and fishing, though some good opportunities exist for swimming during the summer. The area's best beach is the nearly half-mile strand at **Sand Bar State Park** (☎802/893-2825), actually on the mainland just below the US-2 bridge to Grand Isle. If that one's too crowded (as it often is in summer), head to **Knight Point State Park**, North Hero (☎802/372-8389), a placid, sandy shoreline enclosing a bay.

Practicalities

The Champlain Islands are accessible by road along US-2, which is linked to Grand Isle, North Hero, and Alburg by a network of bridges. Isle La Motte lies at the end of Rte-129. For a **place to stay** on the islands, the *Thomas Mott Homestead*, Blue Rock Road off Rte-78, Alburg (☎802/796-4402 or 1-800/348-0843, ⓦwww.thomas-mott-bb.com; ❺), is the superior choice, with large rooms, fantastic breakfasts, comfortable beds, and modern furniture. Less expensive is *Charlie's Northland Lodge*, along US-2 in North Hero (☎802/372-8822, ⓦwww.charliesnorthlandlodge.com; ❺), a cozy hostelry with shared baths. The Champlain Islands do offer some of Vermont's best **camping**. Knight Island State Park (late May to early Sept; ☎802/524-6353) is secluded, with a multitude of unspoiled nature trails, though you should reserve early to get one of the seven primitive campgrounds ($14-21). Grand Isle State Park, 36 E Shore Rd S, Grand Isle (May to mid-Oct; ☎802/372-4300), provides a suitable alternative, with 156 highly developed campgrounds ($16–25) and cabins ($46) complete with restrooms, hot showers, and RVs galore.

The islands offer nothing special in the way of **eating**. The *Ruthcliffe Lodge and Restaurant*, 1002 Quarry Rd, Isle La Motte (☎802/928-3200 or 1-800/769-8162), serves decent Italian-American fare for daily dinner, and scrumptious home-made desserts (try the blueberry bread pudding).

For information on attractions and accommodation, contact the **Lake Champlain Islands Chamber of Commerce**, US-2, North Hero (Mon–Fri 9am–4pm; ☎802/372-8400 or 1-800/262-5226, ⓦwww.champlainislands.com).

St Albans and around

Sleepy **ST ALBANS**, about halfway between Burlington and the Canadian border along I-89, is a town only by Vermont's standards, which means you can cover it by foot in less than an hour. Although there's some ugly mall sprawl to the north, St Albans' center has a large town green on the slope of a hill, lined with churches at the top and small, mostly local, shops at the bottom. The town has the curious distinction as the site of the northernmost engagement of the Civil War: the "**St Albans Raid**" took place on October 22, 1864, when disguised Confederate soldiers entered the town from Canada, robbed its three banks of over $200,000, took some hostages, and decamped to Québec, where they were arrested and tried but never extradited back to the US. The town makes much of this event, particularly during the Civil War Days festival in late October, when history buffs descend here to re-create the event. Meanwhile, the **St Albans Historical Museum**, Church Street, at Bishop (May to mid-Oct Tues–Sat 1–4pm; $4; ☎802/527-7933, ⓦwww.stamuseum.com), also has displays on the raid, as well as military memorabilia, a re-created railroad station, and antique medical devices recovered from local apothecaries. St Albans is also, as seat of the largest maple-producing county in the US, home to Vermont's Annual **Maple Festival**, held in April (ⓦwww.vtmaplefestival.org).

Practicalities

The **St Albans Area Chamber of Commerce**, 2 N Main St (Mon–Fri 8.30am–5pm; ☎802/524-2444, ⓦwww.stalbanschamber.com), is your best bet for tourist information. The town is the last stop on Amtrak's *Vermonter* service; the station is at 40 Federal St (Rte-36), a couple of blocks from Main Street. **Accommodation** in and around the town is reasonable compared to the rest of the state. Least expensive is the *Cadillac Motel*, 213 S Main St (☎802/524-2191, ⓦwww.motel-cadillac.com; ❸), which is low on amenities, but very clean and set in pleasant grounds. The area's best B&B is *Back Inn Time*, 68 Fairfield St (☎802/527-5116, ⓦwww.backinntime.net; ❺), featuring antique-filled rooms in a restored Victorian house. Special events include Murder Mystery dinners ($49) and cooking lessons.

Eating options won't dazzle or disappoint. Hearty and inventive Italian fare can be had at *Chow! Bella*, 24 N Main St, (closed Mon–Tues; ☎802/524-1405). *Bayside Pavilion*, 10 Georgia Shore Rd, St Albans Bay (☎802/524-0909), offers waterside dining (seafood, Tex-Mex favorites, and the like), with an outdoor deck on Lake Champlain, while true to its name, *Always 80s*, 139 Lake St (☎802/524-9807; closed Sun), is decked out in kitsch but fun 1980s memorabilia.

Northeast Kingdom

Remote and rural, Vermont's **Northeast Kingdom** takes its name from a remark made by Vermont senator George Aiken in 1949, referring to the several counties that bulge out eastward in the state's uppermost corner. You can drive for hours, passing through vast expanses of green, garnished by cows, barns, and other bucolic accessories. The only locales approaching town status in the area are **St Johnsbury** and **Newport**, at the region's southern and northern boundaries, each of which still has less than nine thousand inhabitants. Aside from its idyllic character, the region offers little in the way of formal sights, with a few notable exceptions, such as the **Cabot Creamery**, though opportunities for recreation abound; indeed, two of the state's least crowded and most challenging ski areas, **Jay Peak** and **Burke Mountain**, are in this region.

St Johnsbury and around

The town of **ST JOHNSBURY**, estimated population 7560, imagines itself a thriving center in the midst of Vermont's sparsely populated northeast; however, its abundance of elaborate architecture, all turrets and marble and stained glass, seems terribly out of proportion to its size.

St J, as it's referred to by locals, grew from a frontier outpost to its current size thanks to the ingenuity of resident **Thaddeus Fairbanks**, the "scale king," who earned his fortune and a minor place in history by inventing the platform scale in the 1830s. Much of his wealth was showered on the city in the form of funding for new municipal buildings and elaborate churches. One place that celebrates his legacy, the Romanesque **Fairbanks Museum and Planetarium**, 1302 Main St (Tues–Sat 9am–5pm, Sun 1–5pm, also open Mon 9am–5pm Oct–May; planetarium shows July–Aug Mon–Fri 11am & 1.30pm, Sat & Sun 1.30pm; rest of year Sat & Sun 1.30pm; museum $6, planetarium $5; ☎802/748-2372, ⓦwww.fairbanksmuseum.org), has the predictable range of platform scales, but also contains a collection of historical artifacts, from Civil War pieces to Zulu war shields, Japanese handicrafts, antique dolls, and in the first floor's natural science exhibit, over one hundred stuffed hummingbirds. Just down Main Street, the **St Johnsbury Athenaeum** (Mon & Wed 10am–8pm, Tues, Thurs & Fri 10am–5.30pm, Sat 9.30am–4pm; free; ☎802/748-8291, ⓦwww.stjathenaeum.org) houses a number of paintings from the Hudson River school, including Albert Bierstadt's gargantuan *Domes of Yosemite*.

Practicalities

The Northeast Kingdom Chamber of Commerce has a **Welcome Center** at 51 Depot Square in the old train station (May–Oct: Mon–Sat 9am–8pm, Sun 11am–4pm; Nov–April: Mon–Fri 8.30am–5pm, Sat 10am–5pm; ☎802/748-3678 or 1-800/639-6379, ⓦwww.nekchamber.com), which dispenses information on the whole region.

Accommodation is limited mostly to relatively cheap, independent motels. One of the better-equipped ones is the *Fairbanks Inn*, 401 Western Ave (☎802/748-5666, ⓦwww.stjay.com; ❹), which has a heated pool, putting green, and cable TV. There's also the *Yankee Traveler Motel*, 342 Portland St (☎802/748-3156; ❸), a 42-room hotel with a pool, cable TV, and cheerful staff. Cheaper and closer to the town center, the *Holiday Motel*, 222 Hastings Hill (☎802/748-2393 or 742-8192; ❺), has comfortable rooms with all the basics.

There is not as much choice as far as **eating** goes. Try *Elements*, 98 Mill St (☎802/748-8400; closed Sun), which serves what they call "creative comfort food" in a familiar, brick-walled space. *Anthony's Diner*, at 321 Railroad St, opposite the welcome center (☎802/748-3613) is good for a quick grilled-cheese sandwich or meatloaf platter. Nearby, a simple wrap or pastry with some strong coffee can be found at the *Boxcar Bookshop & Caboose Café*, 394 Railroad St (☎802/748-3551), which also carries a quirky collection of books.

Cabot

Vermont is justifiably proud of its cheese (see box, p.386), and the small town of **CABOT**, around 20 miles west of St Johnsbury, is the epicenter of the state's cheese production. The **Cabot Creamery** (visitors' center: daily June–Oct 9am–5pm; Nov–Dec & Feb–May Mon–Sat 9am–4pm; Jan Mon–Sat 10am–4pm; ☎1-800/837-4261, ⓦwww.cabotcheese.com) churns out around

Vermont's cheeses

Something of an economic lightweight, Vermont does do a few things very well: ice cream, maple syrup, and **cheese**. Nostalgic cheese historians will look back to the turn of the last century, when eighty percent of Vermont's milk was being churned into butter and cheese, and lament that things aren't what they once were, but the state still produces a very respectable seventy million pounds of cheese a year, with a significant amount coming from family farms using traditional methods. Predictably, the tourist industry has cashed in on the reputation of Vermont cheese, and refrigerators containing the most sought-after brands hum and rattle in gift shops statewide. If it's cheddar you're after, the best known is probably Cabot Cheddar, which comes in a variety of sharp flavors. Crowley Cheese (made in Healdville) is less acidic and moister than the English-style cheddars made elsewhere in Vermont (it's officially designated a colby cheese); Grafton Village Cheese is known for its older cheddars with an earthy, creamy taste; and Neighborly Farms (Randolph Center) carries the flag of organic cheddar. Cheeses made with sheep's milk, such as feta, camembert, and brie, are produced by Peaked Mountain Farm (Townsend) and Vermont Shepherd (Putney), among others. Lazy Lady Farm (Westfield) and Vermont Butter and Cheese Company (Websterville) are the top names in goat's-milk cheese. Such is the pull of cheese in this state, that several of the above-mentioned producers – and others not mentioned here – have formed the **Vermont Cheese Trail**, opening their doors to the paying public to reveal cheese-making methods and give away pound upon pound of free samples. For more information, contact the Vermont Cheese Council (T866/261-8595, W www.vtcheese.com).

fifteen million pounds of cheese a year, or approximately twenty percent of the total state production. Tours leave every thirty minutes ($2), starting with a ten-minute video explaining how Cabot got to where it is today, then take you through the plant itself, and end with the opportunity to gorge yourself on several different varieties of cheddar.

Craftsbury Common

CRAFTSBURY COMMON, farther north and two miles off slow, bumpy Rte-14, is just about in the middle of nowhere – which is exactly its appeal. This is one of the most enchanting villages in the state. Ignore the separate village of Craftsbury and drive two miles up the hill to the vast common, ringed by a white fence, a post office, church, and the white clapboard buildings of **Sterling College**, founded in 1958 and the smallest accredited four-year college in the country. The common hosts a small **farmers' market** every Saturday (May–Oct 10am–1pm). While the main recreation here is getting away from activity, the surrounding hills are crisscrossed with a web of **trails** popular for mountain-biking and skiing. For rentals and more information, contact the **Craftsbury Outdoor Center** (T1-800/729-7751, Wwww.craftsbury.com).

There are a couple of gorgeous **places to stay** here: the very upmarket *Inn on the Common* (T802/586-9619 or 1-800/521-2233, Wwww.innonthecommon.com; **7**), whose dining room, *Trellis*, serves excellent traditional American fare (call ahead), and the homey *Whetstone Brook B&B*, 1037 S Craftsbury Rd (T802/586-6916; **6**). For a coffee and muffin, pop into *Stardust Books and Café*, overlooking the common (Mon–Tues & Thurs–Fri 7.30–9.30am, Wed 7.30–9.30am & 3–6pm, Sat 10am–1pm).

North to Canada

From St Johnsbury, I-91 runs north up to Canada; everything east of the highway is fairly mountainous, and there are a few good diversions not too far off the main road. This part of the Kingdom is home to pristine lakes and abundant wildlife, including some ten thousand moose (watch carefully for the enormous creatures while driving – collisions are frequent, and most often fatal).

Burke Mountain and Lake Willoughby

The top young downhill skiers in the US train at **Burke Mountain Resort** (lift tickets $57; ☎802/626-3322, ⓦwww.skiburke.com), Mountain Road, East Burke, best approached from I-91 Exit 23 onto US-5, then north on Rte-114. Because of the mountain's isolation, Burke's 43 trails are virtually deserted compared to places such as Killington and Stowe, but they're all tough; three-quarters of the trails are intermediate and higher. East Burke is also the home of **Kingdom Trails Welcome Center** (Sun–Thurs 8am–5pm, Fri & Sat 8am–6pm; ☎802/626-0737 or 802/535-5662, ⓦwww.kingdomtrails.org), which maintains over a hundred miles of publicly and privately owned land where you can **mountain-bike**, **hike**, or **cross-country ski** (trail passes $10 a day).

Venture up US-5 to its intersection with Rte-5A and continue north for several miles to be rewarded with views of **Lake Willoughby**, which is flanked on either side by **mounts Hor** and **Pisgah**. Few people **stay** here, but the *Willough Vale Inn* (☎802/525-4123 or 1-800/594-9102, ⓦwww.willoughvale.com; ❼), just off Rte-5A, offers both rooms and lakefront cottages in a wonderfully secluded setting; there's also a first-rate restaurant. In season, you can also **camp** at Burke Mountain (May–Oct, $20 tent site or $25 for a lean-to).

Glover and Newport

The only reason to hit **GLOVER**, fifteen miles north of St Johnsbury (take Rte-122 north and turn right on Rte-16) is to stop by the **Bread and Puppet Museum** (daily 10am–6pm; free; ☎802/525-3031, ⓦwww.breadandpuppet.org). The Bread and Puppet Theater was established by Peter Schumann in 1962 in New York, moving to Vermont in 1970 and performing anti-Vietnam War puppet shows. The oversized puppets – they can be as big as five feet and require up to four people to operate – are on view in a peaceful barn setting, a far cry from the group's more volatile protest days. There are free performances every Sunday.

The final stop on I-91 before the Québec border, unassuming **NEWPORT**, seems more French-Canadian than New England in character. Its main draw is **Lake Memphremagog**, which spans the border and was once a choice resort area. The lake area is no longer quite so upscale, but is still popular with vacationing Québecois, who flock here to boat, jet-ski, and swim. The town's drag, Main Street, is lined with quaint brick buildings, many of which are restored relics from the Victorian era. The best **dining** here is at *Eastside Restaurant*, 47 Landing St (☎802/334-2340), with grilled steaks and chicken and a wonderful view of the lake, but running a close second is *Lago Trattoria*, 95 Main St (☎802/334-8222), with a menu of Italian favorites and hand-crafted pizzas. Serving breakfast and lunch, *Brown Cow*, 350 E Main St (☎802/334-7887), offers omelettes and excellent soups, but closes by early afternoon. Should you need to **stay** in Newport, the *Newport City Motel*, 444 E Main St (☎802/334-6558 or 1-800/338-6558; ❸), is a decent, if bland, option.

Jay Peak

The four-thousand-foot summit of the **Jay Peak Resort**, on Rte-242 (lift tickets $65; ☎802/988-2611 or 1-800/451-4449, ⓌWww.jaypeakresort.com), looms just south of the Canadian border, about fifteen miles west of I-91. Jay's 75 trails are some of New England's toughest, and typically only serious skiers venture this far out. Jay Peak consistently receives more snow than any other New England resort, an average of 351 inches a year, something which makes deep-powder skiing a distinct possibility through late April. The most popular **accommodation** is *Hotel Jay* (make reservations through the resort at ☎1-800/451-4449; ⑤–⑨), a snazzy ski lodge at the base of the peak; the hotel has deals on lift tickets, a hot tub, and the *Golden Eagle Lounge*, which hosts the area's best après-ski scene (ski season only). In the summer, rates are lower, and there's an outdoor pool, golf course, and country club. The nearby *Jay Village Inn*, Jay Village (☎802/988-2306, ⓌWww.stayatjay.com; ④), offers good-sized rooms overlooking the slopes, with billiards, hot tub, and a huge stone fireplace in the lobby. For a good meal, venture a few miles from Jay, where *The Belfry*, on Rte-242 in Montgomery Center (daily from 4pm; ☎802/326-4400), has a relaxed pub atmosphere and meaty specials.

7

New Hampshire

CHAPTER 7

Highlights

✳ **Portsmouth** That rare commodity: a seaside town with culture and class, displayed in historic buildings, gourmet restaurants, and highbrow shows. See p.394

✳ **Canterbury Shaker Village** Tours reveal the crafts and gadgets of an eighteenth-century religious community that died out only in 1992. See p.410

✳ **Lake Winnipesaukee** Whether from its eastern or western shores, this grand expanse of blue offers a multitude of watery activities. See p.422

✳ **Grand resort hotels** If you can afford it, hit the luxury of the *Mount Washington* or *Balsams* up in the White Mountains – a far cry from a spartan campground. See p.441 & p.449

✳ **Cross-country skiing, Jackson** For all its mountainous terrain, New Hampshire still has some excellent places for cross-country skiing, none finer than the pristine and varied trails at Jackson. See p.446

✳ **Mount Washington** So what if there's a road leading up to the summit of the highest mountain in the northeastern US – it's still one of the most remote, awe-inspiring, and unpredictably exciting places in New England. See p.448

▲ Lake Winnipesaukee

7

New Hampshire

New Hampshire, the sixth smallest state in the US, is a narrow wedge of land with a surprisingly varied terrain. The short Atlantic coastline is a stretch of mellow, sun-drenched beaches capped by **Portsmouth**, a well-preserved Colonial town with a crop of excellent restaurants and stylish inns. Farther inland, there are over 1300 lakes; the largest, **Lake Winnipesaukee**, is ringed with both tourist resorts and quiet villages. The splendid **White Mountains** spread across northern New Hampshire, culminating in the highest peak in New England, formidable **Mount Washington**. Quaint communities are scattered across the southern part of the state, connected by shaded, winding roads and the enduring small-town pride of their residents.

Thanks to its geographic diversity, New Hampshire is probably the premier state in the region for outdoor activities. In the summer months you can kayak, canoe, swim, fish, hike, climb, or bike, while during the winter you can cross-country ski at tiny **Jackson** or downhill ski in the **Franconia Notch** area or at a dozen other resorts. As with much of the rest of New England, fall is also a popular time to visit, as the trees turn vibrant shades and the air temperature drops refreshingly.

Some history

The first European settlement in New Hampshire was established in 1623, when David Thomson brought a small group to **Odiorne Point**, at the mouth of the Piscataqua River. The colony was primarily a fishing venture, funded by **John Mason** (the second governor of Newfoundland), who had been ceded the area in 1622. Without ever laying eyes on the land, Mason named the region New Hampshire, for his home county in England. After he died in 1635, a small group of settlers stayed along the coast, while the interior remained the preserve of the Abenaki and Pennacook tribes, both **Algonquin** peoples. Relations with the Native Americans soured as settlers moved inland, prompting Abenaki involvement in **King Philip's War** in 1676 (see p.529). Sporadic Abenaki and French raids plagued the state for the next fifty years until the **French and Indian War** (1754–63) finally removed the French from North America. By 1700, the state's Indian population had been reduced to less than a thousand, and by 1730, had just about vanished. By this time, **Portsmouth** was a thriving port, thanks mostly to the timber and shipbuilding industries. In January 1776, New Hampshire became the first state to declare independence.

Following the Revolutionary War, life remained a struggle for many settlers until the Industrial Revolution, when towns in the Merrimack Valley, such as Nashua, Concord, and Manchester, became major manufacturing centers – by 1915 the enormous brick **Amoskeag Mills** in Manchester produced more cloth than any

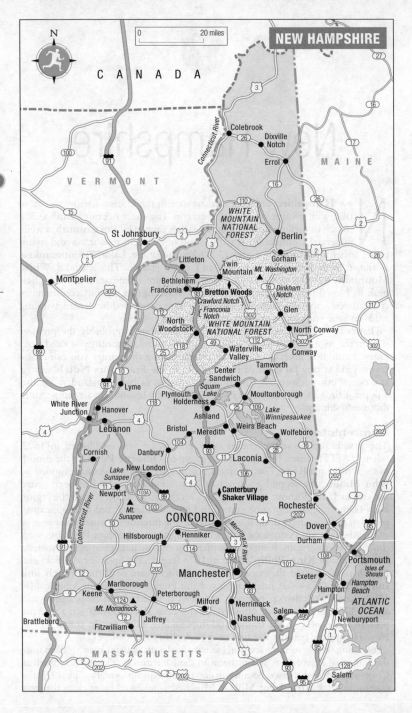

Several major airlines fly in and out of the state's main **airport**, Manchester-Boston Regional (℡603/624-6556, ⊛www.flymanchester.com), which is conveniently located just off I-93 on I-293 (via Exit 2). That's about all that is convenient as far as public transport in New Hampshire is concerned. **Train** services are limited to the tourist trains which run in the mountain areas and Amtrak's *Downeaster* (⊛www.amtrakdowneaster .com), which connects Boston and Portland, and only stops at the towns of Exeter, Durham, and Dover. You can get to a few more places by **bus**, but don't bank on seeing much of the northern part of the state if you don't have your own car. Bus companies serving New Hampshire include Concord Coach Lines (℡1-800/639-3317, ⊛www .concordcoachlines.com), C&J Trailways (℡603/430-1100 or 1-800/258-7111, ⊛www .ridecj.com), and Greyhound (℡1-800/231-2222, ⊛www.greyhound.com).

other textile facility in the world. Meanwhile, large-scale summer tourism began in the latter half of the nineteenth century, when city folk checked into several dozen grand resort hotels (the *Mount Washington* in Bretton Woods and the *Balsams* in Dixville Notch are the only two that remain). With the collapse of manufacturing after World War II, **tourism** is now the state's top money earner.

New Hampshire today remains a bastion of rugged individualism. Big government is frowned upon, and there is no sales or even personal income tax, in fulfillment of the state motto, "Live Free or Die;" New Hampshire's nickname of "the Granite State" alludes to this stoicism as much as to its geology and once mighty granite industry. The state has also earned a degree of notoriety as the venue of the **first state primary of every presidential election**. Since 1952, the state has picked the candidates eventually nominated by both the Democrats and the Republicans about 85 percent of the time. Once safe Republican territory, New Hampshire has been something of a **swing state** since the 1990s, giving its small size some political clout.

The coastline region

New Hampshire's **coastline** stretches for just eighteen miles, making it the shortest of any US state with ocean access. Though only a short distance apart, the two main coastal towns couldn't be less similar: **Portsmouth**, New Hampshire's resurgent cultural center, is bursting with well-preserved Colonial architecture, gourmet restaurants, and historic attractions, while **Hampton Beach** is a sprawling arc of sand packed in summer with giggling teenagers and lined with a corresponding collection of video arcades, ice-cream parlors, and waterslides. In between, sleepy towns blend into each other, spilling into laid-back beaches, such as **Jenness State Beach** and **Wallis Sands State Beach**. Overall, the whole coastline is well developed, but it's not difficult to find sparsely populated stretches of sand.

West of I-95 – something of a commuter corridor for Boston, fifty miles south – the density of people and attractions drops off sharply. The only town of real interest is handsome **Exeter**, home to one of the country's premier private schools, Phillips Exeter Academy.

North Hampton and around

It's difficult to understand why the resort town of Hampton is so popular when the beaches of **NORTH HAMPTON**, a few miles north along Rte-1A, are far more pleasant. **North Beach** and **North Hampton State Beach** are usually pretty quiet, with abundant metered parking ($1.50 per hr), though they still catch a bit of the slough from their brash neighbor. **Hampton Beach** itself is a mess of bad restaurants, crowded sands, and ugly condominiums; unless you have kids (who may enjoy the arcades), it's best avoided.

If you tire of the beach, stop by the colorful **Fuller Gardens** (daily mid-May to mid-Oct 10am–5.30pm; $6.50; ☏603/964-5414, ⓦfullergardens.org), at the junction of routes 1A and 111. Designed in 1939 for Massachusetts governor Alvin Fuller, the gardens include over two thousand rose bushes and a Japanese section complete with bonsai trees. You might also head inland to **Hampton Airfield** (ⓦwww.hamptonairfield.com), just off Rte-1 in the center of North Hampton town, three miles from the beach. Here you can stuff yourself for less than $7 at the ⚇ *Airfield Café* (daily 7am–2pm; ☏603/964-1654), an enticing diner; try the grilled smoked sausage with eggs for breakfast ($5.50) or juicy burgers for lunch (from $5). Watch planes take off and land as you eat, or inquire about exhilarating **aerial tours** of the coast in an open-cockpit biplane (2-person minimum, 4-person maximum; $65 each; ☏603/964-6749). You'll see small signs to the airfield just south of the Rte-111 intersection (on your right heading north).

Continuing north along the shore, Rte-1A winds between several lovely, picturesque beaches, where many stately homes greet the ocean from enormous bay windows – this whole stretch of coast is known as "Millionaires' Row." If you decide you'd like to take in the mansions at a more leisurely pace, there's a paved **walking path** along the water; the best stretch is the three miles or so between North Hampton State Beach (where you can park) and the Rye Beach Club.

Popular with families, **Jenness State Beach**, a long, curving stretch of sand with a smallish parking lot ($1.50 per hr), is a few miles north of North Hampton. Surfers tend to congregate just to the south at Sawyer Beach, also known as Surfers' Beach thanks to its year-round supply of decent waves. In **RYE HARBOR**, just beyond here, you can go **whale-watching** with Atlantic Fleet at the State Marina (late June to early Sept daily 1pm; Sept–Oct Sat & Sun 1pm; $29, children $22; ☏603/964-5220 or 1-800/WHALE-NH, ⓦwww.atlanticwhalewatch.com). You can also take a ferry (May–Sept; $19–27; ☏603/964-6446, ⓦwww.uncleoscar.com) to tranquil **Star Island** (ⓦwww.starisland.org), one of the Isles of Shoals (see p.398). North of Rye Harbor and even more serene than Jenness is **Wallis Sands State Beach** ($15 per car), the best place in the area for swimming and sunning.

Portsmouth

Surprisingly attractive **PORTSMOUTH**, just off I-95 at the mouth of the Piscataqua River, blends small-town accessibility with the enthusiasm of a rejuvenated city. Having endured the cycles of prosperity and hardship typical of most New England towns, Portsmouth has found its most recent triumphs in the cultural arena, attracting artists, musicians, writers, and, notably, gourmet chefs. In addition to a wealth of tantalizing restaurants, Portsmouth's unusual abundance of well-preserved Colonial buildings makes for an absorbing couple of days.

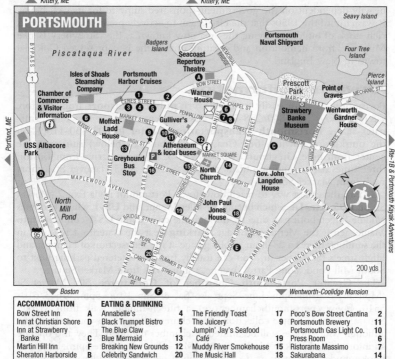

ACCOMMODATION		EATING & DRINKING					
Bow Street Inn	A	Annabelle's	4	The Friendly Toast	17	Poco's Bow Street Cantina	2
Inn at Christian Shore	D	Black Trumpet Bistro	5	The Juicery	9	Portsmouth Brewery	11
Inn at Strawbery		The Blue Claw	1	Jumpin' Jay's Seafood		Portsmouth Gas Light Co.	10
Banke	C	Blue Mermaid	13	Café		Press Room	6
Martin Hill Inn	F	Breaking New Grounds	12	Muddy River Smokehouse	15	Ristorante Massimo	7
Sheraton Harborside	B	Celebrity Sandwich	20	The Music Hall	18	Sakurabana	14
Sise Inn	E	Ceres Bakery	8	The Oar House	3	Shalimar India	16

Some history

Founded in 1630 by English settlers led by Captain Walter Neal, Portsmouth was known as **Strawbery Banke** until 1653, after the abundance of wild strawberries in the area; as maritime trade expanded, however, taking the name of one of England's most important ports seemed far more appropriate. By then the town was one of America's leading ports. With an abundance of timber in the surrounding regions, Portsmouth's prosperous shipyards produced enormous masts, trading vessels, and warships, and its ships were soon carrying goods – and fighting wars – all over the world.

As industry flourished, so did a well-heeled class of merchants and ship captains, who constructed many of the fine mansions and commercial buildings that remain prominent in the town today. The city's golden age peaked in 1800, after which the combination of the 1807 Embargo Act, the War of 1812, and three devastating **fires** plunged the city into decline. The **Portsmouth Naval Shipyard**, which had been founded in 1800 by John Paul Jones, was the area's largest employer by 1900 (and is still active today, just across the Piscataqua River in Maine). In the nineteenth century, Portsmouth became notorious as a seedy port of call, complete with a busy **red-light district**, a skyrocketing crime rate, and a raucous assortment of grungy taverns. Portsmouth also became a major center for **beer and ale** production. Angry citizens eventually drove the revelers and prostitutes from the city in the early 1900s, and the beer industry collapsed after the onset of Prohibition in 1920, causing Portsmouth to settle into a long period of stagnation, heavily dependent on the government-sponsored shipyard for its well-being. It wasn't until the 1950s that the city began to actively preserve and restore its rich stock of buildings, saving the area now known as the "Strawbery Banke Museum" from demolition and creating one of the best-preserved Colonial towns in New England.

Arrival and information

Portsmouth is most easily accessible via **public transport** from Boston. C&J Trailways (℡1-800/258-7111) has frequent daily services but terminates at the **Portsmouth Transportation Center** (℡603/430-1100), on the outskirts of town; a free Coast Trolley bus (see below) runs into the center from here. Greyhound (℡603/433-3210) buses arrive from Boston three times daily, stopping outside *Mainly Gourmet* at 55 Hanover St, a short walk from Market Square.

By **car**, the easiest way to reach downtown Portsmouth is via Exit 7 (Market St) off **I-95**. **Rte-1A**, which becomes Miller Avenue, and **US-1**, which becomes Middle Street, both pass directly through the city center; US-1 continues into Maine, across the Memorial Bridge. **Parking** near the waterfront is scarce in the summer; there's a 24-hour public garage at the intersection of Hanover and High streets ($0.75 per hr). You can usually find non-metered parking next to South Mill Pond, along Parrot Avenue, a short walk from Market Square.

The **Greater Portsmouth Chamber of Commerce**, 500 Market St (Mon–Fri 8.30am–5pm, June–Sept also Sat & Sun 10am–5pm; ℡603/610-5510, Ⓦwww.portsmouthchamber.org), a fifteen-minute walk from Market Square, houses an ample collection of brochures and can help you find a room, although your choices will be limited to chamber members. They also operate an information **kiosk** in Market Square (May–Oct daily 10am–5pm). For travel books, guides, and maps, you can't do much better than Gulliver's (Mon–Sat 10am–5pm, Sun noon–5pm; ℡603/431-5556), downstairs at 7 Commercial Alley, off Market Street.

City transport

Portsmouth is compact and easily manageable on foot. However, the **Coast Trolley** (Mon–Sat 10.30am–5.30pm; ℡603/743-5777, Ⓦwww.coastbus.org) operates two routes around the city as well as the Downtown Loop (late June to Aug; every 30min; $0.50), stopping at most attractions. The **Seacoast Trolley** (mid-June to early Sept Sun–Wed 11am–4pm; $8 per day; ℡603/431-6975) links historic Portsmouth with several area beaches, shopping malls, and sights, and stops at Market Square hourly.

Several companies run **cruises** in Portsmouth Harbor and beyond. Portsmouth Harbor Cruises, at the Ceres Street Dock, features several trips, and has a full bar on every boat (90min harbor cruise $16, 1hr evening cruise $12; call ℡603/436-8084 or 1-800/776-0915 for departure times, Ⓦwww.portsmouthharbor.com). The Isles of Shoals Steamship Company, 315 Market St (℡603/431-5500 or 1-800/441-4620, Ⓦwww.islesofshoals.com), offers similar trips, including a $25 journey to the **Isles of Shoals**. With both companies, you need to buy your tickets in advance to guarantee a spot. If you'd rather see the coastline up close, daily **kayaking tours** (1hr 30min/2hr 30min; $40/59) and kayak rentals ($59 per day) are offered by Portsmouth Kayak Adventures, 185 Wentworth Rd (℡603/559-1000, Ⓦwww.portsmouthkayak.com), which originate at their store in Witch Cove Marina, south of the town center (Rte-1B).

Accommodation

Accommodation in and around Portsmouth's historic district can be expensive – in high season on weekends you'll likely pay $150 or more for a room in a B&B. A collection of slightly cheaper – and less pleasant – **motels** can be found at the traffic circle where I-95, the US-1 bypass, and routes 4 and 16 intersect. **Camping** in the area is limited to crowded RV-type parks, such as the *Shel-Al Campground*, US-1, North Hampton (☎603/964-5730, ⊛www.shel-al.com; $27), and the *Wakeda Campground*, Rte-88, Hampton Falls (☎603/772-5274, ⊛www.wakedacampground.com; $30).

In Town

🏊 **Bow Street Inn** 121 Bow St
☎603/431-7760, ⊛www.bowstreetinn.com. Portsmouth's only waterfront inn is centrally located and comfortable. The ten cozy rooms occupy a remodeled brick brewery; two rooms offer full harbor views. Continental breakfast included. **7**

🏊 **Inn at Christian Shore** 335 Maplewood Ave ☎603/431-6770, ⊛www.innatchristianshore.com. Early nineteenth-century Federal-style house with six rooms full of tasteful antique furnishings. Big, tasty gourmet breakfasts. **6**

Inn at Strawbery Banke 314 Court St ☎603/436-7242 or 1-800/428-3933, ⊛www.innatstrawberybanke.com. Seven bright, relaxing rooms in a sumptuous old Colonial home near the waterfront. Reservations strongly recommended. **7**

Martin Hill Inn 404 Islington St ☎603/436-2287, ⊛www.martinhillinn.com. Meticulously furnished house with seven guestrooms and a shaded garden within walking distance of the city center. Excellent full breakfast and helpful owners. **6–8**

Sheraton Harborside 250 Market St ☎603/431-2300 or 1-877/248-3794, ⊛www.sheratonportsmouth.com. Large hotel with conference facilities and a predominantly business clientele. Predictably comfortable and expensive, and in a central location. **9**

Sise Inn 40 Court St ☎603/433-1200, ⊛www.siseinn.com. One of the larger inns in Portsmouth, this Queen Anne-style home of 1880s shipping magnate John Sise has 34 elegant, luxurious rooms with phones and TVs. The breakfast is a delicious buffet. **8**

Near the traffic circle

Anchorage Inn 417 Woodbury Ave ☎1-800/370-8111, ⊛www.anchorageinns.com. A large and comfortable modern hotel with 93 rooms, an indoor pool, sauna, and whirlpool. **7**

Holiday Inn Portsmouth 300 Woodbury Ave ☎603/431-8000. Standard – yet comfortable and clean – rooms, outdoor pool, and game and exercise rooms at this business hotel. **6–7**

Port Inn 505 US-1 Bypass South ☎603/436-4378 or 1-800/282-PORT, ⊛www.theportinn.com. These good-value, comfortable rooms, some with microwaves and refrigerators, are (depending on the season and day) among the cheapest in Portsmouth. **5**

The Town

Market Square, where Daniel, Pleasant, Congress, and Market streets all converge, has been Portsmouth's commercial center since the mid-eighteenth century. Once a military training site, the brick-dominated square is now surrounded by bustling cafés and gift shops. Despite the upscale shopping, this part of town maintains an unpretentious, lived-in feel. Grab the informative **Portsmouth Harbor Trail** walking tour guide and map ($2) at the information kiosk (see opposite), detailing three walks that trace the city's history and originate in the square. In the summer you can also join guided tours here (Mon & Thurs–Sat 10.30am & 5.30pm, Sun 1.30pm; $8; ☎603/436-3988).

Start by admiring the 1817 **Athenaeum**, 9 Market Square (Tues & Thurs 1–4pm, Sat 10am–4pm; ☎603/431-2538), one of the oldest private libraries in the country. The 1854 **North Church** flanks the southwest side of the square, and its towering spire makes it the tallest building you'll see in town.

Market Street

Scanning the chic boutiques and fashionable restaurants that line **Market Street**, it's hard to believe the brick buildings that house them were once occupied by breweries. In the late nineteenth century, when Portsmouth's **beer and ale industry** was booming, Frank Jones, founder of the Portsmouth Brewery Company, created what was once considered to be the best beer in the nation – the aptly named "Frank Jones Ale." Jones and his competitors were shut down during Prohibition and never recovered. The company's old brick warehouse, at 125 Bow St, was transformed in 1979 into a theater, presenting mostly mainstream plays and musicals. The closest you can get to Portsmouth's storied brewing history today is a trip to the **Redhook Brewery**, 35 Corporate Drive, outside the center (call for tour schedule; $1; ⓣ603/430-8600, ⓦwww.redhook.com), though even this isn't native, as the company was founded in Seattle, Washington.

Of the grand old mansions in Portsmouth, the **Moffatt-Ladd House**, 154 Market St (mid-June to Oct Mon–Sat 11am–5pm, Sun 1–5pm; $6; ⓦwww.moffattladd.org), is one of the most impressive. Completed in 1763, the building is particularly notable for its Great Hall, which occupies more than a quarter of the first floor. Using inventories left by Captain John Moffatt, who designed the home and later monitored his shipping business from an office on the second floor, historians have transformed the Yellow Chamber (also on the second floor) into one of the best-documented eighteenth-century American rooms. Portraits of past occupants by artists such as Gilbert Stuart hang throughout the home, including a painting of William Whipple, who signed the Declaration of Independence and lived here in the late eighteenth century. For information on other historic homes open to the public, see the box opposite.

Farther up Market Street is the departure point for harbor cruises and for boats (see "City transport," p.396) that take you six miles off the coast to the **Isles of Shoals**, an archipelago of nine islands that were a summer meeting place for many well-known writers of the nineteenth century, including Nathaniel Hawthorne and Annie Fields. You can visit **Star Island** by ferry from Rye Harbor (see p.394).

▲ Market Street, Portsmouth

Beyond the walls of Strawbery Banke, Portsmouth is home to eight restored **Colonial homes**, which are open to the public during the summer. Hourly tours, led by scholars full of stories, can be fascinating, although after one or two, you will have probably had your fill. The presence of a blue flag outside a building indicates its status as a historic home open to visitors. When you purchase your ticket, ask for a "passport" entitling you to $1 off admission at the others (and Strawbery Banke).

Governor John Langdon House 143 Pleasant St (June 1–Oct 15 Fri–Sun tours on the hour 11am–4pm; $6; ☎603/436-3205, ⓦwww.historicnewengland.org). John Langdon – three-term governor, New Hampshire Senate president, and delegate to the 1787 Constitutional Convention – and his wife, Elizabeth, hosted many visitors here, including George Washington. The home, constructed in 1784, is in every way a tribute to his affluence and influence.

John Paul Jones House 43 Middle St (daily late May to mid-Oct 11am–5pm; $8, self-guided tours only; ☎603/436-8420). Home to the Portsmouth Historical Society's museum (ⓦwww.portsmouthhistory.org), this 1758 Georgian structure was where John Paul Jones, the US's first great naval commander, stayed in 1777 while his ships were outfitted in the Langdon shipyards. Inside the boxy yellow structure you can view some of his naval memorabilia and period-furnished rooms. The museum mounts changing exhibits on subjects such as the Portsmouth Peace Treaty (1905), which ended the Russo-Japanese War.

Warner House 150 Daniel St (mid-June to mid-Oct Mon–Tues & Thurs–Sat 11am–4pm, Sun noon–4pm; $5; ☎603/436-5909, ⓦwww.warnerhouse.org). Built for local merchant Captain Archibald MacPhaedris in 1716, this was the first brick house constructed in the state. It contains New Hampshire's oldest murals, painted on the staircase wall, which depict some of the earliest known images of Native Americans. Additionally, Benjamin Franklin is said to have installed the lightning rod on the west wall.

Wentworth-Coolidge Mansion 375 Little Harbor Rd, off of Rte-1A (late June to early Sept daily tours 10am, 11.30am, 12.45pm, 2pm & 3pm; Sept to mid-Oct tours Fri–Sun 1.30pm & 3pm; $7; ☎603/436-6607). Home to English governor Benning Wentworth from 1753 to 1770, this rambling 42-room, mustard-yellow mansion, which is beautifully situated on an isolated plot overlooking Little Harbor, hosts occasional concerts and classes during the summer. It's not furnished, but the wallpaper in several of the rooms is original, and there are several original Wentworth items on display.

Still farther along Market Street, at no. 600, you'll find the **USS Albacore Park and Port of Portsmouth Maritime Museum** (late May to mid-Oct daily 9.30am–5pm; rest of year Thurs–Mon 9.30am–4pm; $5; ☎603/436-3680, ⓦwww.ussalbacore.org), a worthwhile diversion highlighted by a 205-foot, 1200-ton **submarine**. Built in 1952, it was then the fastest electric/diesel submarine in the world. Tours of the underwater vessel offer glimpses of the cockpit, cramped living quarters, and the engine room.

Prescott Park

At the other end of the historic district, along the river on Marcy Street, is **Prescott Park** (☎603/431-8748), a welcoming expanse of grass and shrubbery that slopes gently toward the water's edge. Featuring free music and entertainment throughout the summer, the park is immaculately maintained, and is a great spot for a picnic or afternoon nap. You could also check out **Point of Graves cemetery**, a creepy plot of crumbling Colonial graves, opposite the park on the southeast corner of Mechanic Street (near the bridge to Pierce Island) – the oldest headstone dates from 1682.

Strawbery Banke Museum

Although historic buildings can be found all over Portsmouth, for a more concentrated look at American architecture over the last three centuries, pay a visit to the **Strawbery Banke Museum**, 64 Marcy St (May–Oct daily 10am–5pm; Nov guided walking tours offered on the hour Sat & Sun 10am–2pm; $15; tickets good for two days; ☎603/433-1100, ⓦ www.strawberybanke.org), a fenced-off ten-acre neighborhood that takes in a collection of forty meticulously restored and maintained old wooden buildings. This area began life as the home of wealthy shipbuilders and was successively the lair of privateers and a red-light district before turning into a respectable – and, in the 1950s, decaying – suburb. Restoration began in 1958, starting with the removal of all newer buildings, and the museum opened in 1965. A few people still live here, tucked away on the buildings' upper floors, but the complex really serves as a living museum that you can explore either on a guided tour or on your own; in either case, several of the houses have attendants.

Each building is shown in its most interesting former incarnation, whether that means it dates to 1695 or 1955. In the **Shapley Drisco House**, two eras collide: half of the house is outfitted as from the 1790s, the other half, the 1950s. The 1766 **Pitt Tavern** holds the most historic significance, having acted as a meeting place for patriots and loyalists during the Revolution. The museum also contains the boyhood home of novelist **Thomas Bailey Aldrich** (1836–1907), which he depicted in his semi-autobiographical novel, *The Story of a Bad Boy*. Even the gardens here are historically accurate, recreated from surviving plans from different time periods. Traditional crafts are studied and practiced on site; the **Lowd House** contains a display on New England craftsmen and the implements they used, and in the **Dinsmore Shop**, a cooper manufactures barrels with the tools and methods of 1800. After 5pm, the museum opens its gates, and you can wander around for free and observe the building's exteriors in the waning hours of the day (though it's hardly the same experience).

Eating

Portsmouth likes to bill itself as the "food capital of New England," and while this may be an exaggeration, there are plenty of good spots in town to grab an excellent meal. The city's **restaurants** include both expensive highbrow **bistros** and cheap, down-to-earth **cafés**. There is a particularly high concentration of places to eat along Ceres and Bow streets, and you should treat yourself to at least one waterfront meal at one of the outdoor patios or decks that line the Piscataqua River.

Annabelle's 49 Ceres St ☎603/436-3400. Highly caloric home-made ice cream, in ultra-delicious flavors like raspberry chocolate-chip and "Yellow Brick Road" (golden vanilla with roasted pecans and caramel). A city favorite since 1982.

Black Trumpet Bistro 29 Ceres St ☎603/431-0887. One of Portsmouth's smartest eateries boasts a romantic dining room on the first floor, and wine bar upstairs. The eclectic menu, which changes every six months, features flavors from all over the Mediterranean and the Americas in such dishes as eggplant tamales, paella, and steaks (entrees $17–33). Open from 5.30pm daily.

The Blue Claw 58 Ceres St ☎603/427-2529. Set right on the old wooden dock, with excellent views of the harbor. Justly popular for its freshly made lobster rolls and dinners; all crustaceans locally caught.

Blue Mermaid 409 The Hill, Hanover and High sts ☎603/427-2583. A carefully selected, though not particularly large, selection of mid- to high-priced grill food with Caribbean and Pacific Rim influences. Meals come with home-made fire-roasted "sunsplash" salsa. Live music Fri & Sat.

Celebrity Sandwich 171 Islington St ☎603/433-2277. Great, enormous deli sandwiches ($5.25; 125 choices, all named after celebrities,

though only a few, such as the "David Letterman ham sandwich," make much sense), with cheap daily specials and a handful of tables. Closed Sun.
Ceres Bakery 51 Penhallow St ⊤603/436-6518. Excellent fresh breads, good soups, and fine pastries in this down-to-earth café with a bright blue exterior. Open until 5pm, closed Sun.

The Friendly Toast 121 Congress St ⊤603/430-2154. Kitschy thrift-store decor with an interesting selection of sandwiches and omelettes ($7–10), a huge menu of mixed drinks, shakes, and coffees, and an equally eclectic crowd. The portions are enormous. Try "Matt's Sandwich" ($9), with black beans, avocado, and cheese. Open 24hr on weekends, 7am–11pm during the week.
The Juicery 51 Hanover St ⊤603/431-0693. The healthiest hole-in-the-wall in town. Order something fruity from the organic juice bar, or try one of several vegan wraps. Take-out only.

Jumpin' Jay's Seafood Café 150 Congress St, ⊤603/766-3474. Hands down the best seafood in Portsmouth (and probably the state), with a regular menu featuring dishes like baked haddock and fisherman's stew, and a "catch of the day" menu, which might offer Atlantic salmon and swordfish. Entrees from $21.
The Oar House 55 Ceres St ⊤603/436-4025. One of Portsmouth's several slightly old-fashioned gourmet stand-bys serves standard seafood and grilled meat entrees for $26 and up. You can do just as well with an appetizer and a salad for the same price.
Portsmouth Gas Light Co 64 Market St ⊤603/430-8582, Ⓦwww.portsmouthgaslight .com. Large, popular restaurant with four sections; dine on juicy burgers and steaks in the *Street Level* restaurant, take in live music on the *Deck*, or enjoy Portsmouth's favorite pizzas at *Downtown Pizza* (downstairs; all-you-can-eat $7.25, weekdays 11.30am–2pm). The *Third Floor* nightclub opens at 8pm Fri–Sat ($5).

Ristorante Massimo 59 Penhallow St ⊤603/436-4000. Cozy, upscale Italian restaurant, with fresh pastas ($12–14) and plenty of fish *secondis* ($22–33), such as tender halibut. Service is exceptional. Reservations essential. Closed Sun.
Sakurabana 40 Pleasant St ⊤603/431-2721. The best Japanese restaurant in the area, with fresh sushi, sashimi, tempura, and teriyaki. The combination sushi platter ($29) is enough for four or five. Lunch Tues–Fri, dinner Mon–Sat, closed Sun.
Shalimar India 80 Hanover St ⊤603/427-2959. For those looking for a little spice, the North Indian choices here are the best around (dishes $11–14). Vegetarian options, too. Dinner daily, lunch Sat & Sun only.

Drinking, nightlife, and entertainment

Despite its size, Portsmouth's **social scene** can be pretty stimulating. The city is home to several vibrant **cafés**, a host of well-attended **bars**, and several **live music** venues presenting a diverse range of bands. If theater is your thing, the **Seacoast Repertory Theatre**, 125 Bow St (⊤603/433-4472 or 1-800/639-7650, Ⓦwww .seacoastrep.org), housed in a converted brewery, is Portsmouth's major venue, presenting mainstream professional stage productions. For complete up-to-date listings, the *Portsmouth Herald* prints an exhaustive **entertainment** supplement (*Spotlight*) every Thursday.

Breaking New Grounds 14 Market St ⊤603/436-9555. This friendly coffeeshop is always bustling, from 6.30am to 11pm (midnight on weekends). Grab an excellent cup of coffee and relax with a book at an indoor table, or take it outside to watch the Market Square goings-on.
Muddy River Smokehouse 21 Congress St ⊤603/430-9582, Ⓦwww.muddyriver.com. Eclectic mix of DJs, reggae, acoustic, and rock Thurs–Sat. Decent BBQ upstairs. Usually $6 covers.
The Music Hall 28 Chestnut St ⊤603/436-2400, Ⓦwww.themusichall.org. Boasting some nine hundred seats, Portsmouth's largest performance space hosts well-known nationally touring folk, rock, jazz, and blues bands, classical concerts, plus dance, theater, and other performances throughout the year.
Poco's Bow Street Cantina 37 Bow St ⊤603/431-5967. The reasonable food here is typical Tex-Mex fare (entrees from $10), but the margaritas ($7) on the riverfront patio are great.
Portsmouth Brewery 56 Market St ⊤603/431-1115, Ⓦwww.portsmouthbrewery.com. Typical microbrew pub, with attractive wood paneling, extensive pizza and burger menu (from $8), visible beer tanks, towering ceilings, and a rowdy young crowd. The beer here is exceptional; don't miss the Old Brown Dog. Open until 1am nightly, with occasional live music.

Press Room 77 Daniel St ☎603/431-5186, ⓦwww.pressroomnh.com. Popular for its nightly live jazz, blues, folk, and bluegrass performances, which feature local and national talents. Also serves decent microbrews, inexpensive salads, sandwiches, and soups in a casual pub-style setting.

Around Portsmouth

Inland from Portsmouth, the area between I-95 and Rte-125 has a few historically notable towns, particularly **Exeter**, although aside from its colonial charm, there's really not much in the way of sights.

Exeter

Eight miles west of the Atlantic down Rte-101 from Portsmouth, friendly **EXETER** was settled in 1638 by a rebellious Bostonian preacher, the Reverend John Wheelwright. Sitting on the Squamscott River and an abundance of timber, Exeter thrived in the eighteenth century, selling masts and lumber to shipbuilders. It became the state capital in 1775 (Portsmouth, the previous capital, was too Loyalist), and remained so until Concord assumed the role fourteen years later. Today, Exeter's tree-shaded avenues and stately old neighborhoods make the attractive town center worth a quick look.

The Town

Phillips Exeter Academy (ⓦwww.exeter.edu), one of the top college preparatory schools in the US, occupies a large portion of the attractive town center, its regal brick buildings sprawling over well-manicured lawns. Founded in 1781 by Dr John Phillips, the school counts among its prominent alumni the great orator Daniel Webster (see box, p.408) and author Dan Brown, who also taught here before hitting the big-time with *The Da Vinci Code*. Along Front Street (Rte-111), near Elm Street south of the center of town, is the school's boxy brick **library**, designed by architect Louis Kahn in 1971. Begin your self-guided walking tour of the campus at the admissions office (☎603/777-3433) on Front Street across from the Phillips Church.

The well-preserved Art Deco **Ioka Theater** (☎603/772-2222, ⓦwww .iokaentertainment.com), in the center of town at 55 Water St, has been in operation since 1915. A hundred yards down the street, in the center of the traffic circle, is the **Swasey Pavilion**, a circular bandstand by Henry Bacon, the architect of the Lincoln Memorial. The Exeter Brass Band, founded in 1847, still gives summer concerts here. Exeter native Daniel Chester French, known for his Abe Lincoln inside the Lincoln Memorial, also created Exeter's **World War I Memorial**, in Gale Park on Front Street.

The **American Independence Museum**, in the Ladd-Gilman House at 1 Governors Lane, just north on Water Street (tours hourly May–Oct Wed–Sat 10am–4pm; $5; ☎603/772-2622, ⓦwww.independencemuseum.org), houses a slightly dull collection of artifacts documenting New Hampshire's role in the American Revolution, including a copy of the Declaration of Independence, drafts of the US Constitution, and a few oddities, such as a ring containing a piece of George Washington's hair. Exeter stages the **American Independence Festival** ($5; call the Independence Museum for details) the third weekend in July, when the grounds of the museum are transformed into a militia encampment, with arts and crafts, talks, parades, and fireworks.

For local information, contact the **Exeter Area Chamber of Commerce**, inside City Hall at 20 Water St (Mon–Fri 8.30am–4.30pm; ☎603/772-2411, Ⓦwww.exeterarea.org). There are several upscale **places to stay**, including the *Inn by the Bandstand*, 6 Front St (☎603/772-6352, Ⓦwww.innbythebandstand .com; ⑥), a restored 1809 Federal-style inn where many rooms have fireplaces, and the *Exeter Inn*, 90 Front St (☎603/772-5901 or 1-800/782-8444, Ⓦwww .theexeterinn.com; ⑥), which offers easy-going elegance and superior service in a three-story Georgian-style building. You can **camp** at the *Exeter Elms Family Riverside Campground*, 188 Court St, two miles south on Rte-108 (May–Oct; $29 per site; ☎603/778-7631 or 1-866/778-7631, Ⓦwww.exeterelms.com).

Exeter's **restaurants** are nothing special, but there are a few affordable options worth noting. The *Green Bean on Water*, 33 Water St (☎603/778-7585; closed Sun), serves fresh sandwiches on home-made bread, with outdoor seating in a leafy courtyard. The *Tavern at River's Edge*, 163 Water St (☎603/772-7393; closed Sun), has a good range of international cuisine in a cozy Victorian dining room along the river (entrees $16–26). *Penang and Tokyo*, 97 Water St (☎603/778-8388), is primarily a Chinese restaurant (mains $5–10), with additional Malaysian and Japanese dishes, something of a rarity in these parts. For pastries, fresh breads, light salads, and coffee, head to the *Baker's Peel*, at 231 Water St (Mon–Fri 6.30am–2pm, Sat & Sun 6.30am–1pm; ☎603/778-0910).

The Merrimack Valley

The financial and political heartland of New Hampshire is the **Merrimack Valley**, which – first via the Merrimack River and now via I-93 – has always been the main thoroughfare north to the lakes, the White Mountains, and Canada. First settled by the Penacook Indians, early pioneers established a trading post near Concord by 1660, and by the 1720s large groups of English settlers were calling the area home. In the nineteenth century, the valley boomed with industry, and Nashua, Manchester, and Concord were all major manufacturing centers. **Concord** became the state capital in 1784 and remains the center of New Hampshire's political life – particularly evident during the quadrennial presidential primaries – while **Manchester** is the most populous city in the state, with ample evidence of its gritty industrial past.

Manchester

Once a prosperous mill town, **MANCHESTER**, New Hampshire's largest city (population 107,000), has been in a perpetual state of recovery ever since the **Amoskeag Manufacturing Company** went belly-up in 1935. From 1838 to 1920, the company was the world's largest textile manufacturer; at its peak, it employed 17,000 people and spewed out over four million yards of cloth per week. The company – and the entire town, for that matter – was the brainchild of a group of Boston entrepreneurs, who purchased 15,000 acres of

Amoskeag Fishways ▲   Zimmerman House ▲

MANCHESTER

Amoskeag Dam
Scenic overlook
PSNH Energy Park
Currier Museum of Art

PENNACOOK ST
BLODGET ST
BLODGET ST
W BROOK STREET
BROOK STREET
LANGDON ST
HARRISON STREET
PROSPECT STREET
MYRTLE STREET
ORANGE STREET
W SALMON ST
DOW ST
ELM STREET
CHESTNUT STREET
HOLLIS ST
RIDDER ST
W BRIDGE ST
PEARL STREET
ARLINGTON STREET
BRIDGE ST
E HIGH ST
HIGH ST
Pulaski Park
LOWELL STREET
Victory Park
CONCORD ST
CONCORD ST
SPRING ST
Arms Park
AMORY STREET
MECHANIC ST
STARK ST
AMHERST STREET
HANOVER STREET
Bronstein Park
Intown Manchester & Chamber of Commerce
AMOSKEAG MILLYARD HISTORIC DISTRICT
MARKET ST
MIDDLE ST
Manchester Information Center
MANCHESTER STREET
MERRIMACK STREET
See Science Center
PLEASANT ST
LAUREL STREET
Millyard Museum
Veterans Park
CENTRAL STREET
CENTRAL STREET
Manchester Transportation Center
LAKE AVENUE
LAKE AVENUE
PHILLIPPE COTE STREET
SPRUCE STREET
CEDAR STREET
CONANT STREET
CANAL STREET
GRANITE STREET
AUBURN STREET
Sheridan Emmett Park
DOUGLAS STREET
GREEN ST
Merrimack River
GROVE STREET
BELL ST
Valley Cemetery
VALLEY STREET
MERRILL ST

N

ACCOMMODATION
Ash Street Inn   A
Comfort Inn   D
Fairfield Inn   E
Hilton Garden Inn   C
Radisson Manchester   B

0   500 yds

EATING & DRINKING
Café Momo   2
Chateau Restaurant   3
Fratello's   1
Jillian's   7
Lala's Hungarian Pastry   5
Merrimack Restaurant   6
Strange Brew Tavern   4

Nashua (NH), Massachusetts & ⓓ ▼   Merrimack & Airport ▼   Robert Frost Farm, ▼ America's Stonehenge & ⓔ

land around the Amoskeag Falls, acquired the rights to water power along the entire Merrimack River, built a dam, and constructed the enormous Amoskeag Mills. Today, although the city remains rather rough around the edges, new apartments are slowly gentrifying the downtown area and riverfront; renovated mills are pulling in businesses, restaurants, and artists; and its handful of attractions – including the Millyard Museum – provide a striking contrast to the state's rustic pleasures.

Arrival, information, and city transport

The only bus service to Manchester from Boston is run by Boston Express ($13; ☏603/521-6000, ⓦ www.bostonexpress.com), which drops off passengers at Canal Street. The nearest Concord Coach Lines and Greyhound stops are at Exit 5 on I-93 (where there is free parking, designed to entice Boston commuters), so you have to switch to Boston Express there. **Manchester-Boston Regional Airport**, off Rte-3A, is served by several major carriers; take a bus (see opposite) or taxi into the center ($20).

Downtown, at 889 Elm St, you'll find the offices of **Intown Manchester** (Mon–Fri 9am–5pm; ☏603/645-6285, ⓦ www.intownmanchester.com), and the **Manchester Chamber of Commerce** (Mon–Fri 8.30am–5pm; ☏603/666-6600, ⓦ www.manchester-chamber.org), both with maps and brochures, and there is also the helpful **Manchester Information Center** (☏603/624-6465) on Elm Street next to Veteran's Park; staffed by knowledgeable volunteers, it's

7

NEW HAMPSHIRE | Manchester

404

usually open daily 9am–3pm, but call to make sure. The **Manchester Transit Authority** (☎603/623-8801) runs an extensive network of buses all over town ($1.25), although apart from the service to the airport (Mon–Fri 5.25am–5.25pm, Sat 8.25am–4.25pm), you will not have much cause to use it, as most of the city's limited attractions are concentrated in the downtown area.

Accommodation

With little tourism to speak of, the city has only a few **hotels**, though there are plenty of chain **motels** along the nearby interstates.

Ash Street Inn 118 Ash St ☎603/668-9908, Ⓦwww.ashstreetinn.com. For a bit of character, try this homely Victorian B&B, built in 1885 and featuring original stained glass and bright, comfortable rooms with hardwood floors. **❼–❽**

Comfort Inn 298 Queen City Ave ☎603/668-2600, Ⓦwww.comfortinn.com. Best of the chain motels that ring the city, just off I-293 and a short drive across the Merrimack from downtown (3 miles from the airport). With smart rooms, decent breakfast, indoor pool, and free airport shuttle, it's an excellent budget alternative to the downtown hotels. **❺**

Fairfield Inn 860 S Porter St ☎603/625-2020, Ⓦwww.fairfieldinn.com. Marriott-run motel, halfway between downtown and the airport,

offering typical but clean and adequate rooms with all the usual extras (free wi-fi) and complimentary breakfast. **❺**

Hilton Garden Inn Manchester Downtown 101 South Commercial St ☎603/669-2222, Ⓦwww .hilton.com. Downtown's newest hotel, perfectly located in the Millyard district (overlooking a minor league baseball stadium) with all the amenities: microwaves, LCD TVs, indoor pool, 24hr business center, and free wi-fi. **❻**

Radisson Manchester 700 Elm St ☎603/625-1000 or 1-800/333-3333, Ⓦwww .radisson.com/manchesternh. Most of the politicos stay at this otherwise standard chain hotel, which becomes a media circus during the primary season. The location is second to none. **❻**

The City

Manchester's main commercial drag, **Elm Street**, runs north–south parallel to the Merrimack River (doubling as US-3), though there's little to see here. Instead, make for the **Amoskeag Millyard Historic District**, several blocks west along the banks of the river between Bridge and Granite streets.

Your first stop should be the Manchester Historic Association's illuminating **Millyard Museum**, at the intersection of Commercial and Pleasant streets (Tues–Sat 10am–4pm, Sun noon–4pm; $6; ☎603/622-7531, Ⓦwww .manchesterhistoric.org), which has exhibits chronicling the town's history, including looms from the mills and a re-creation of what Elm Street looked like when Manchester was an economic powerhouse. Kids will enjoy the **See Science Center** (Mon–Fri 10am–4pm, Sat & Sun 10am–5pm; $5; ☎603/ 666-3906, Ⓦwww.see-sciencecenter.org), around the corner on Bedford Street, with plenty of hands-on displays (robots, periscopes, and the like) and a scale model of the old mills, made out of LEGO. Alternatively, take a stroll along the **Riverwalk**, a pedestrian path on the river's east bank, which ends up at the PSNH Energy Park and the **Amoskeag Falls Scenic Overlook** (daily mid-April to Oct 8am–6.30pm; free), north of Bridge Street, with fine views of the mills, the **Amoskeag Dam**, and the city skyline. Just across the Amoskeag Bridge north of here (but best approached by car), the **Amoskeag Fishways Learning and Visitors Center** (Mon–Sat 9am–5pm; free; ☎603/626-3474, Ⓦwww.amoskeagfishways.org) offers an absorbing introduction to the history, flora, and wildlife of the Merrimack River. The highlight is the underwater viewing gallery at the 54-step fish ladder, which bubbles into life during May and June when migrating shad, herring, and sea lamprey power around the dam on their way upriver.

Currier Museum of Art

Featuring works by painters such as Monet, O'Keeffe, Hopper, and Wyeth, the **Currier Museum of Art**, 150 Ash St (Sun, Mon, Wed, & Fri 11am–5pm, Thurs 11am–8pm, Sat 10am–5pm; $10, free Sat 10am–noon; ☏603/669-6144, Ⓦwww.currier.org), is New Hampshire's best fine arts museum. Pride of place in the lower level goes to *Visit of the Gypsies*, a rare 1505 Flemish tapestry; look out also for works by Constable and Tiepolo. The main level is dedicated to Contemporary, Modern, and European painters, while the upper galleries focus on American art from 1680 to 1915. Much of the permanent collection is shown on a revolving basis, but you might see Picasso's colorful *Spanish Woman Seated in a Chair*, from 1941, and Winslow Homer's watercolor *American in the Woods*. Local paintings are also well represented, such as Jasper Francis Cropsey's glowing 1857 *American Indian Summer Morning in the White Mountains*. The *Winter Garden Café* inside makes for a pleasant pit-stop (free wi-fi). The museum also runs tours of the nearby **Zimmerman House** (April–Dec), a one-story wooden structure designed in 1950 by Frank Lloyd Wright that epitomizes his vision of form in harmony with landscape. One-hour introductory tours (Sun 1.30pm) are $15, while full two-hour tours (Mon, Thurs & Fri 2pm, Sat 10.30am & 12.30pm, Sun 11.30am) cost $16 – buy tickets at the museum (tours leave by shuttle from here).

Eating and drinking

Manchester tends to gets a bad rap when it comes to **eating** and **drinking**, but there are plenty of places for a decent meal or beer.

Café Momo 1065 Hanover St ☏603/623-3733. Cozy Nepalese restaurant giving some much needed color to the local dining scene; the lamb dumplings (*momos*; $8) are superb, and there's an excellent choice of vegetarian dishes. Entrees $13–18. Closed Mon.

Chateau Restaurant 201 Hanover St ☏603/627-2677. This local institution is an old-fashioned upscale eatery, but has also teamed up with local outfit *Checkmate Pizza* to offer 20-inch pies (from $15) and tasty calzones in a more relaxed family dining room.

Fratello's 155 Dow St ☏603/624-2022. Busy most nights for its solid menu of classic Italian dishes, pastas, and pizzas. Lunch is the cheapest meal, with pizzas and paninis going for under $10.

Jillian's 50 Phillippe Cote St ☏603/626-7636. The city's younger crowd drinks beer and listens to live music at this billiard and sports-themed bar right along the river, just off Commercial St.

Lala's Hungarian Pastry 836 Elm St ☏603/647-7100. Offers fabulous pastries, goulash, soups, and other Eastern European classics such as stuffed cabbage ($9.50–12). Closed Sun.

Merrimack Restaurant 786 Elm St ☏603/669-5222. This institution pays host to everyone from politicos and presidents to local seniors, all chowing down on the home-style cooking, breakfasts, and burgers. Mon–Tues 7am–2pm, Wed–Sat 7am–8pm, Sun 7am–noon.

Strange Brew Tavern 88 Market St ☏603/666-4292, Ⓦwww.strangebrewtavern .net. Live music six nights a week (blues, jazz, and rock) and 65 beers on tap (from $4) make this one of the best joints to kick back in the city, supplemented by an enticing menu of pub food.

South of Manchester

South of Manchester, alongside the Daniel Webster Highway (Rte-3) in **MERRIMACK**, the massive **Anheuser Busch Brewery** (daily: May & Sept–Dec 10am–4pm; June–Aug 10am–5pm; Jan–April Thurs–Mon 10am–4pm; ☏603/595-1202, Ⓦwww.budweisertours.com), offers free tours of its facility – one of thirteen it operates nationwide – including free tastings. Already America's biggest beer company, a 2008 merger with Belgium's InBev created the world's largest brewer.

The **Robert Frost Farm** (May–June & Sept to mid-Oct Wed–Sun 10am–5pm; July & Aug daily 10am–5pm; gardens free, farmhouse $7; ☎603/432-3091, ⓦrobertfrostfarm.org), just off of Rte-28 (take Exit 4 from I-93), north of Salem and south of Derry, is slightly difficult to find, but worth visiting for its small exhibit of Frost's handwritten poems and photos, an hour-long guided house tour filled with peeks into Frost's character, and a nature trail. Frost lived at the farm between 1900 and 1911, and composed or drew inspiration for many of his most famous poems here. Though looked upon locally as a failed farmer and a bit of an eccentric, he gave such a moving reading of his poem *Tuft of Flowers* to the local Derry Village Men's Club that the teachers in the group convinced him to take a position teaching English at the nearby Pinkerton Academy, where he worked for two years before turning to writing full-time. *MaryAnn's Diner*, 29 E Broadway in Derry (daily until 2pm; ☎603/434-5785), a popular 1950s-themed diner with a huge menu, makes a good stop for something to **eat** on the way to the Frost farm.

A rather unusual attraction, **America's Stonehenge**, is off of Rte-111 in **NORTH SALEM** (daily 9am–5pm; $9.50; ☎603/893-8300, ⓦwww .stonehengeusa.com). This grouping of stone slabs and tunnels purports to be a site of ancient and mysterious origins – perhaps some sort of sacrificial altar – built by Native Americans, or less credibly, Bronze Age Europeans. There is undoubtedly an enigmatic feel to the place, but note that all the experts featured in the portentous documentary shown to visitors are employed by the site, and many independent experts believe much of the area is a legacy of local farming in the eighteenth century.

Concord and around

Just twenty minutes north by car from Manchester along I-93, New Hampshire's state capital, **CONCORD** (pronounced "conquered"), is worth a brief look for the State House and the Museum of New Hampshire History, both easily seen in a morning or an afternoon. The Christa McAuliffe Planetarium should take up another couple of hours, while the nearby **Canterbury Shaker Village**, the area's outstanding attraction, will keep you busy for at least a day. Otherwise, despite its capital status, Concord itself is a fairly typical small town with little in the way of sights.

Arrival and information

Concord is readily accessible via **public transportation** and easily reached by **car** from I-93, which passes through the eastern side of the town. Metered **parking** is available on Main Street, and there's a convenient lot at School Street, in the middle of Main Street. Concord Coach Lines and Greyhound buses stop at the **bus terminal** (☎603/228-3300) at 30 Stickney Ave – it's a short walk or Concord Area Transit (CAT) **bus** ride into town (Mon–Fri 6.30am–5.30pm, 11 times daily; $1; ☎603/225-1989); note, however, that there are no buses to the nearby Canterbury Shaker Village.

The **Greater Concord Chamber of Commerce** (Mon–Fri 8.30am–5pm; ☎603/224-2508, ⓦwww.concordnhchamber.com) is about a mile north of the town center in the Grappone Conference Center (Commercial St and Constitution Ave, just off I-93 Exit 15) where you'll also find the main **visitors' center** (also open weekdays 8.30am–5pm). They also maintain an **information kiosk** in front of the State House (same hours), which distributes historical walking-tour brochures. The local newspaper, the *Concord Monitor*, is widely available and offers **entertainment listings**.

Accommodation

Concord is short on remarkable **accommodation**, although several chain motels are located outside of town near the interstate. Smaller area towns, such as Henniker, feature some first-rate B&Bs.

Centennial Inn 96 Pleasant St ☎603/225-7102, Ⓦwww.thecentennialhotel.com. Renovations have added contemporary style to this Victorian landmark, supplementing its original charm with designer furniture, LCD TVs, and free wi-fi. Ⓖ

Comfort Inn 71 Hall St ☎603/226-4100 Ⓦwww.comfortinn.com. Newest and thus smartest motel in town, with comfortable rooms, a tad more stylish than the chain's usual offerings. Extras include heated indoor pool, breakfast, free laundry, and wi-fi. Ⓖ

Concord Courtyard by Marriott 70 Constitution Ave ☎603/225-0303, Ⓦwww.marriott.com. Standard business hotel at the Grappone Conference Center, and convenient for sights in the north end of the city; airport shuttle ($15), and car rentals on site. Ⓖ

Holiday Inn 172 N Main St ☎603/224-9534, Ⓦwww.holidayinn.com. Popular with visiting politicians and business people due to its proximity to the State House. Predictably comfortable rooms and good facilities, including pool, sauna, and fitness center. Ⓖ

The Town

Government is the main focus in Concord, and the town seems to revolve, both physically and spiritually, around the gold-domed **State House** on Main Street (Mon–Fri 8am–5pm; ☎603/271-2154). Designed by Stuart J. Park, the original structure was completed in 1819, then expanded and twice remodeled later; the handsome stone facade was quarried from local granite. The state legislature – the largest in the country, with some four hundred members – has met continuously in the same chambers since June 2, 1819, the longest such tenure in the US. Both self-guided and guided tours are available from the **visitors' center** (Mon–Fri 8am–4.15pm) on the first floor, where you'll also find dioramas of Revolutionary War battles (including John Stark's victory at Bennington; see p.342). Portraits of over 150 legislators hang on all three floors. Outside, bronze statues of New Hampshire notables, including Stark, Daniel Webster (see box below), and President Franklin Pierce, strike dignified poses.

Birthplace of Daniel Webster

New Hampshire's best-known statesman, orator, and public figure, **Daniel Webster**, was born in 1782 in a two-room farmhouse on Flaghold Road off Rte-127 in **FRANKLIN**, eighteen miles north of Concord. Now known simply as the **Daniel Webster Birthplace** (late June to early Sept Sat & Sun 9am–5pm; $7; ☎603/934-5057), the restored home contains period furniture, antiques, and some Webster memorabilia, including books he read as a child. Webster attended Phillips Exeter Academy, graduated from Dartmouth College in 1801, and went on to build a successful law practice before serving in Congress from 1813 to 1817 and in the US Senate from 1827 to 1841. He loomed large on the political scene in his day, delivering persuasive speeches on topics as far-ranging as states' rights, slavery, the US–Canadian border, and Dartmouth College. As secretary of state under presidents William Henry Harrison, Tyler, and Fillmore, Webster remained a staunch defender of the Union. During a particularly heated discussion in 1850, in which Webster debunked the idea of states' rights, he coined the memorable phrase "Liberty and Union, now and forever, one and inseparable." In perhaps his most famous debate, the Dartmouth College Case of 1817, Webster defended his alma mater before the Supreme Court, which decided that states could not interfere with royal charters.

The compact but enlightening **Museum of New Hampshire History** (Tues–Sat 9.30am–5pm, Sun noon–5pm; July–Oct 15 & Dec also open Mon 9.30am–5pm; $5.50, children $3; ℡ 603/228-6688, ⓦ www.nhhistory.org) is tucked behind the brick buildings on Main Street across from the State House, in **Eagle Square**. In the gallery on the first floor, a well-presented collection of paintings, photographs, maps, and artifacts, including a restored 1855 Concord coach and a Native American canoe (used on Lake Ossipee sometime between 1430 and 1660), chronologically traces the state's history. Upstairs are rotating displays, a replica forest fire watchtower, and various hands-on exhibits for the kids.

At the north end of Main Street, at 14 Horseshoe Pond Lane, is the **Pierce Manse** (mid-June to early Sept Tues–Sat 11am–3pm, tours on the hr; $5; ℡ 603/225-4555, ⓦ www .piercemanse.org), where President Franklin Pierce lived with his family between 1842–1848. Known mainly as one of the US's least successful leaders (see box, p.414), Pierce had a flourishing private law practice here. The restored white two-story 1838 home is now a museum filled with his personal effects, such as a top hat and some period furniture, including the family's writing table. The man himself is buried in **Old North Cemetery**, near the intersection of North State Street and Keane Avenue, at the northern end of downtown.

Set within the campus of the New Hampshire Technical Institute, between I-93 and the river, the **Christa McAuliffe Planetarium**,

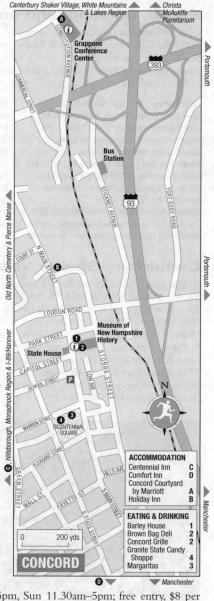

ACCOMMODATION

Centennial Inn	C
Comfort Inn	D
Concord Courtyard by Marriott	A
Holiday Inn	B

EATING & DRINKING

Barley House	1
Brown Bag Deli	2
Concord Grille	2
Granite State Candy Shoppe	4
Margaritas	3

CONCORD

2 Institute Drive (Mon–Sat 10am–5pm, Sun 11.30am–5pm; free entry, $8 per show; ℡ 603/271-7827, ⓦ www.starhop.com), was named for the Concord High School teacher who perished in the Space Shuttle *Challenger* disaster in 1986. The 92-seat theater stages impressive public astronomy shows and hosts free Skywatch events the first Friday of every month. McAuliffe was selected from a pool of 11,500 applicants to participate in the trip, which tragically ended her life, and the lives of her crewmates, just 73 seconds after lift-off.

Eating, drinking, and entertainment

Concord's **restaurants** can seem uninspired, especially when compared with those of Portsmouth. However, you can find some good-value lunches around the state house. Note that many of the town's eateries are closed on Sundays, if not the whole weekend. Other than a couple of basic bars, some with **live music**, there is really no nightlife to speak of here.

Barley House 132 N Main St ☎603/228-6363, ⓦwww.thebarleyhouse.com. Watering hole for state legislators on lunch breaks. Good, mostly inexpensive pub-style food and live music, especially jazz, throughout the week.

Brown Bag Deli 1 Eagle Square ☎603/225-9110. Wholesome salads ($3.25) and deli sandwiches ($4.50–5.25) across from the History Museum. Open Mon–Fri 7.30am–2.30pm.

Concord Grille 1 Eagle Square ☎603/228-6608. The restaurant serves sandwiches, steaks, pastas, and seafood dishes, but patrons come as much for

the karaoke on Sun, Tues, Wed & Thurs (9pm), and the live music or DJs on Thurs, Fri & Sat.

Granite State Candy Shoppe 13 Warren St ☎603/225-2591. Get your sweet fix in this venerable chocolate and candy store, open since 1927 and selling addictive ice cream in the summer. Try the almond butter crunch or chocolate nut bark.

Margaritas 1 Bicentennial Square ☎603/224-2821. Housed in a former police station, this popular chain serves some of the biggest Mexican dishes around. You can sit in a former jail cell while you sip your margarita – very atmospheric.

Canterbury Shaker Village

About twenty minutes north of Concord, in Canterbury Center, **Canterbury Shaker Village**, Exit 18 off I-93, 288 Shaker Rd (daily: mid-May to Oct 10am–5pm; Nov to early Dec Fri–Sun 10am–5pm; $15, good for two consecutive days; ☎603/783-9511, ⓦwww.shakers.org), is New England's premier museum of Shaker life (see box opposite), and perhaps the most fascinating tourist destination in New Hampshire. The tranquil village – a collection of simple buildings – is beautifully spread out over rolling hills, and the site's quiet isolation is soothing. In 1792, Canterbury became the sixth Shaker community in the US, and, at its zenith in the mid-nineteenth century, there were some three hundred people living on the grounds; the last Shaker living in Canterbury died in 1992 at age 96.

▲ Canterbury Shaker Village

The Shakers in America

The **Shaker** church – originally an offshoot of the Quaker movement – was founded in the US by **Mother Ann Lee**, who arrived from England with nine followers in 1774, seeking religious freedom. The "Shaking Quakers" (so named because of their tendency to dance in church, thereby shaking off sins) lived apart from the world in communities devoted to communal living, efficiency, equality, pacifism, and, perhaps most notoriously, celibacy – the sect relied upon conversion and adoption to expand. Also, believing that technology would create more time for worship, the Shakers were creative and industrious **inventors** and **craftsmen**; today the sect is probably best known for its legacy to the furniture, architecture, and agriculture industries.

The first formal Shaker community was set up in New Lebanon, NY in 1787, and during the next century eighteen other major communities were established across Massachusetts (including the Hancock Shaker Village; see p.244), New Hampshire, Maine, Connecticut, Kentucky, Ohio, and Indiana; smaller ventures were also attempted in Florida and Georgia. The sect flourished in the nineteenth century, with numbers peaking in the 1850s. Decline, when it came around the turn of the twentieth century, happened quickly, and was ultimately exacerbated by the denomination's self-imposed sexual chastity. Today only a handful of Shakers remain in the world, at the Sabbathday Lake community in New Gloucester, Maine.

After watching the excellent Ken Burns documentary in the Trustees Office, next to the visitors' center at the entrance, you can take several different engrossing one-hour **tours** of the site. Led by Shaker experts, these introduce the ideals, day-to-day life, and architecture (there are 25 perfectly restored buildings on the site) of these people as you wander from building to building – including the church, the schoolhouse, and the laundry room – and around the property. You are also free to wander around on your own, though only some of the buildings are open for self-guided tours; get a map at the visitors' center. It's worth a peek inside the **Carriage House** near the entrance, where precious examples of Shaker furniture are displayed. There is also an acclaimed **restaurant** on site, the *Shaker Table* (T603/783-4238; lunch daily, dinner Fri & Sat), which serves Shaker-inspired meals, such as "Sister Amelia's chicken pot pie," and cheaper snacks and drinks are available all day at *Shaker Box Lunch* – try the mouthwatering brownies and apple hand-pies.

The Monadnock region

Known as the "quiet corner" of New Hampshire, the **Monadnock region**, which occupies the southwestern portion of the state, encompasses deserted country roads and sleepy small towns, all centered around the 3165-foot peak of **Mount Monadnock**. Aside from the mountain itself, which attracts plenty of outdoor enthusiasts, the region boasts no real stand-out attractions, and, although the slow pace can be appealing, you may very well find yourself restless after a day or so of exploring.

The region is probably best known for being the inspiration behind *Our Town*, the perennially popular play by Thornton Wilder. You can get a feel for the playwright's small-town New England in any of the region's many picturesque villages, but several are worth highlighting. **Keene**, an amiable place with a provincial disposition, is the area's biggest town; **Peterborough**, along US-202, is the region's – perhaps the state's – artistic center; **Hillsborough** was the birthplace of New Hampshire's only US president, Franklin Pierce; and **Jaffrey** rests quietly at the base of Mount Monadnock.

Keene

With 23,000 residents, **KEENE** is the most populous community in the Monadnock region, though you could hardly call it cosmopolitan – it manages to maintain a friendly, if somewhat dull charm, but there's not much to do other than shop and eat along the unusually wide **Main Street** (allegedly the "widest Main Street in the US"), which culminates in the lovely **Keene Common**. Still standing at 399 Main St, the **Wyman Tavern** (June to early Sept Thurs–Sat 11am–4pm; $3; ☎603/352-5161) was built in 1762 by Isaac Wyman, a staunch patriot who later led a group of Minute Men to fight in the Revolutionary War. The tavern was also the site of the first official meeting of the trustees of Dartmouth College, which was founded in 1769. The restored taproom, living quarters, and ballroom are open to the public. While you're in that part of town, it's worth stopping in at the **Thorne –Sagendorph Art Gallery** (June–Aug Wed–Sun noon–4pm; Sept–May Sat–Wed noon–4pm, Thurs & Fri noon–7pm; free; ☎603/358-2720, ⓦwww .keene.edu/tsag), on the attractive campus of Keene State College. It only has two rooms, but the eclectic permanent collection ranges from African statues to Robert Mapplethorpe photographs to a Goya print. Take some time to peruse Peter Milton's print, *20th Century Limited*, which depicts last century's cultural achievements as a train wreck.

Practicalities

Greyhound **buses** going to and from Burlington and Brattleboro in Vermont and Springfield and Northampton in Massachusetts stop at *Corner News*, 67 Main St (☎603/352-1331). **Biking** is a pleasant way to explore the surrounding countryside, although the terrain can be a bit hilly. For bike rentals, the only place for miles is **Summers' Backcountry Outfitters**, 16 Ashuelot St (Mon–Wed 10am–6pm, Thurs & Fri 10am–8pm, Sat 9am–6pm, Sun 10am–5pm; ☎603/357-5107, ⓦwww.summersbc.com); bikes are $25 per day, and they'll also give you plenty of advice on routes.

For **information** and accommodation bookings, try the **Greater Keene Chamber of Commerce**, 48 Central Square (Mon–Fri 9am–5pm; ☎603/352-1303, ⓦwww.keenechamber.com). Apart from a few chain **hotels** on the outskirts

Burdick Chocolates

Northwest of Keene, off Rte-12 in the tiny town of **Walpole**, you can find one of New Hampshire's most delectable stores, **Burdick Chocolates** (Mon 7am–6pm, Tues–Sat 7am–9pm, Sun 7.30am–5pm; ☎603/756-2882 or 1-800/229-2419, ⓦwww .burdickchocolate.com). Situated in an unassuming storefront at 47 Main St, Swiss-trained Larry Burdick makes his home-made treats from French Valrhona chocolate. If the chocolate isn't enough, you can get coffee and pastries in the adjoining café.

of town, the best of which is the *Holiday Inn Express*, 175 Key Rd (℡866/464-2417, ⓦwww.keenehi.com; ❼), the *Carriage Barn Bed and Breakfast*, 358 Main St (℡603/357-3812, ⓦwww.carriagebarn.com; ❺), has four rooms with private bath in a cozy house just a few-minutes' walk from downtown.

If you're looking for a bite to **eat**, there are a few places worth noting. The popular *Blue Trout Grill*, at 176 Main St (℡603/357-0087), has a carefully prepared menu of seafood and grilled dishes such as crispy calamari and crab cakes, as well as a large selection of wines. For authentic Italian food in a warm setting, head to *Nicola's Trattoria*, 39 Central Square (dinner only, closed Sun & Mon; ℡603/355-5242). *Brewbakers*, 97 Main St (℡03/355-4844), is a hip coffee joint with comfy couches that also serves cheap soups, sandwiches, and salads. One of the top spots for **shopping** is the Colony Mill Marketplace, 222 West St (ⓦwww.colonymill.com), a converted brick wool mill with an interesting grouping of relatively upscale shops. The Marketplace also houses the best **place to drink** in town, the *Elm City Brewery and Pub* (℡603/355-3335), which serves hearty American meals in addition to its own microbrews.

Hillsborough

About 25 miles northeast of Keene on Rte-9, the tiny town of **HILLSBOROUGH** – actually a grouping of four small villages (Bridge Village, Hillsboro Center Historic District, Lower Village, and Upper Village) – is the birthplace of Franklin Pierce (see box, p.414), fourteenth president of the United States.

Bridge Village, just off Rte-9 on Rte-149, is home to the area's one-street downtown. The **Chamber of Commerce**, 25 School St, (Tues–Thurs 9am–3pm; ℡603/464-5858, ⓦwww.hillsboroughnhchamber.com), stocks local maps and information. A few miles west, just outside **Lower Village**, you can tour the restored home of Hillsborough's most famous son, the **Franklin Pierce Homestead**, on Rte-31 at the intersection with Rte-9 (July & Aug Mon–Sat 10am–4pm, Sun 1–4pm; June & Sept Sat 10am–4pm, Sun 1–4pm; $5; ℡603/478-3165). The docents downplay Pierce's shortcomings – alcoholism, ineffective leadership – to portray him as a misunderstood hero. The building is a fine example of the Federal-style homes common in the region, and though the rooms are relatively bare, there are a few nicely painted wallpapers, including one depicting the harbor at Naples. The house was built by Franklin's father, **Benjamin Pierce**, who first came to Hillsborough in 1786 after having served as a general in the Revolutionary War – he's buried in the cemetery up the road, just outside **Upper Village**.

Historic **Hillsboro Center**, four miles north of Bridge Village on Center Road, is also worth checking out. This is the oldest and prettiest part of town, a collection of clapboard buildings set around a leafy green. The **Well Sweep Art Gallery** (Wed–Sun 10am–5pm; ℡603/464-6585, ⓦwww.wellsweepgallery .com) sells antiques, rugs, and fine art, while **Gibson Pewter** (Mon–Sat 10am–4pm; ℡603/464-3410, ⓦwww.gibsonpewter.com) has been creating pewter products since 1966.

Once you've tired of the **shops**, head for the **Fox State Forest**, a state-maintained nature preserve off Center Road (between the Bridge and Center villages), which has over twenty miles of hiking and cross-country skiing trails, as well as some interesting wetland areas. You can get a trail map at the Fox Forest Headquarters (℡603/464-3453).

Not highly rated in history's annals, **Franklin Pierce** was born in Hillsborough, New Hampshire, on November 23, 1804. Though Ralph Waldo Emerson wrote that Pierce was "either the worst, or one of the weakest of all our Presidents," modern New Hampshire residents overlook his shortcomings in the White House and have in fact transformed him into something of a local hero.

Handsome, charming, and amiable, Pierce studied law at Bowdoin College in Maine before returning to New Hampshire to win his first election to public office. Only 25 at the time, he served in the state legislature, and later became speaker of the New Hampshire House. Pierce served five terms in the House of Representatives before being elected to the US Senate. His love of the law then led him to return to Concord, where he set up a successful practice. After serving in the Mexican War, he unexpectedly received the presidential nomination at the 1852 Democratic National Convention. Even more surprisingly, Pierce edged out Whig candidate Whitfield Scott in the general election.

Pierce's presidency began on a black note, when his son Bennie was killed in a train accident just before his inauguration. Pierce's wife, Jane, was rarely seen in public afterwards, and it was said that Pierce himself never recovered. At a time when the nation was severely divided over slavery, Pierce remained opposed to antislavery legislation, wrongly believing that his status as a Northerner with Southern values would strike an acceptable compromise with the nation. After he signed the 1854 Kansas–Nebraska Act, which allowed settlers to choose whether to allow slavery, conflict erupted in Kansas, and Pierce effectively lost his authority over the American people. By then he'd become an alcoholic – it is said that Pierce's parting words from the White House were, "Well, I guess there's nothing left to do but go get drunk." To this day, Pierce is the only US president not to have been nominated by his party for a second term.

Practicalities

Accommodation is limited in these parts, but if you're stuck, *1830 House Motel*, at 626 West Main St (℡603/478-3135; ❹) offers basic but adequate rooms, while *Serenehaven B&B*, 615 East Washington Rd (℡603/848-4506; Ⓦwww.serenehaven.com; ❼), north of Center Village, is more remote but far more appealing, a tranquil clapboard house with comfy, inviting rooms.

Bridge Village has a few must-try **places to eat**, chief among them ✳ *German John's Bakery*, 5 W Main St (℡603/464-5079; closed Mon, also Sun & Tues Jan–May), a fabulous German-style bakery offering fresh breads, pretzels, and scrumptious apple strudel. Next door, the *Central Square Ice Cream Shoppe* (daily noon–9pm; ℡603/464-3881) offers more sweet treats, while *Nonni's Italian Eatery*, 17 W Main St (℡603/224-0400; closed Mon), knocks out brick-oven pizzas (from $12.50) and family-style pastas ($17) for dinner.

Peterborough

The riverfront town of **PETERBOROUGH**, south of Hillsborough along Rte-202, has a youthful, artistic focus. Immortalized by Thornton Wilder in the play *Our Town* and now claiming to be "an entire community devoted to the arts," Peterborough is home to a wide range of cultural activities, but really centers on the **MacDowell Colony**, 100 High St (℡603/924-3886, Ⓦwww.macdowellcolony.org), which hosts over two hundred artists – including musicians, painters, filmmakers, and photographers – in its studios each year.

Dedicated to providing a distraction-free environment since 1907, the colony has hosted such notables as Alice Walker, Studs Terkel, Milton Avery, Thornton Wilder, Oscar Hijuelos, and Willa Cather. Artists open their studios to the public only once a year on Medal Day, usually in mid-August (call for exact date), when the Edward MacDowell Medal is awarded to "an American creative artist whose body of work has made an outstanding contribution to the national culture."

The tiny, brick-dominated downtown, centered around **Grove Street**, was largely the inspiration of architect Benjamin Russell, who designed the Town House, where the city still holds town meetings, as well as the Historical Society and the Guernsey Building office complex. Inside the **Peterborough Historical Society Museum**, 19 Grove St (Tues–Sat 10am–4pm; $3; ⊺603/924-3235, ⓦwww.peterboroughhistory.org), a dusty hodgepodge of old artifacts, including photographs and farming tools, describes the "story of a typical New Hampshire town." One of the finest **bookstores** in the state, the Toadstool Bookshop, 12 Depot Square (Mon–Fri 10am–6pm, Sat 10am–5pm, Sun 10am–4pm; ⊺603/924-3543), has a huge selection of fiction, nonfiction, and travel books.

Three miles east of Peterborough along Rte-101, **Miller State Park** (⊺603/ 924-3672; $4) has a few excellent hikes. Try the Wapack Trail, which takes you to the 2290-foot summit of Pack Monadnock Mountain (2.8 miles round-trip), from where you can sometimes see the Boston skyline and Mount Washington.

Practicalities

For local maps and information, visit the **Peterborough Chamber of Commerce**, at the junction of Rte-101 and US-202 (mid-June to mid-Oct Mon–Fri 9am–5pm, Sat 10am–3pm; ⊺603/924-7234, ⓦwww .peterboroughchamber.com), which also stocks an unmanned kiosk next door. The most convenient **place to stay** is the 泳 *Little River Bed & Breakfast*, 184 Union St (⊺603/924-3280, ⓦwww.littleriverbb.com; ⑤), an 1870s farmhouse close to the Nubanusit River with four homey rooms and free wi-fi. Otherwise, the *Apple Gate Bed and Breakfast*, 199 Upland Farm Rd, two miles from downtown (⊺603/924-6543; ④–⑤), offers pretty much the same level of comfort at similar prices. Of several **places to eat** in Peterborough, *Aqua Bistro*, Depot Square (⊺603/924-9905), is the most interesting, serving delicious and creative American bistro dinners and a wonderful Sunday brunch. *Harlow's Pub*, 3 School St (⊺603/924-6365; closed Sun), offers hearty sandwiches and Tex-Mex classics as well as a healthy dose of town gossip. For fancy sandwiches, head to *Twelve Pine*, Depot Square (⊺603/924-6140), which also serves espresso and fresh juice.

Each year in mid-July, Peterborough hosts the **Monadnock Festival for the Arts** (⊺603/924-7234), a weekend of dance, art, theater, and music. From late June through mid-September, the **Peterborough Players** (⊺603/924-7585, ⓦwww.peterboroughplayers.com) stage traditional and experimental theater performances in an eighteenth-century barn on Hadley Road off Hancock Middle Road, a few miles outside of town.

Jaffrey

The area commonly referred to as **JAFFREY** actually takes in the towns of Jaffrey and Jaffrey Center. Not much goes on in the former, and you're better off concentrating on picturesque **Jaffrey Center**, long the domain of novelist

Willa Cather, who came here every fall during the early twentieth century. In a studio in the woods, Cather wrote parts of *My Ántonia* (1918) and *One of Ours* (1922). Cather is buried beside her lover, Edith Lewis, in the **Old Town Burial Ground**, along Rte-124 in Jaffrey Center.

Beyond that, you really visit Jaffrey for **Mount Monadnock**, reputedly the second most-climbed mountain in the world (after Mount Fuji) and the center-piece of **Monadnock State Park** ($4; ☏603/532-8862), just west of town on Rte-124. The park is the most striking natural feature of the region, a rolling countryside carpeted with birch and pine trees. Although the mountain is only 3165ft high, its gently sloping peak seems dominant because it is so isolated. This was a popular spot with nineteenth-century writers and artists, including Henry David Thoreau, whose writings are featured at the **visitors' center** (daily 8am–sunset) near the parking lot, along with displays on the history of the park. They also have information about the park's forty miles of scenic hiking trails; the White Dot Trail is the most popular and direct route to the summit, taking about three and a half hours round-trip. If you reach the peak on a clear day, you'll be able to see all six New England states.

Practicalities

You can **camp** in the park at the base of Mount Monadnock all year round, with the 21 basic tent sites costing $23 (☏603/271-3628 for reservations). Closer to Jaffrey, the *Emerald Acres Campground*, 39 Ridgecrest Rd (May to mid-Oct; ☏603/532-8838), has 52 sites in a pine forest for $27.50.

The *Inn at Jaffrey Center*, 379 Main St (☏603/532-7800, ⊛www .theinnatjaffreycenter.com; ❺), enjoys, as its name suggests, a central location in Jaffrey Center, with eleven individually decorated rooms in a house with a shady garden. *The Currier's House*, 5 Harkness Rd (☏603/532-7670, ⊛www .thecurriershouse.com; ❹), also in town, has views of Mount Monadnock and a back porch from which to enjoy them. Just outside of town, the antique-filled *Benjamin Prescott Inn*, 433 Turnpike Rd, off Rte-124E (☏603/532-6637 or 1-888/950-6637, ⊛www.benjaminprescottinn.com; ❹–❺), offers ten quiet rooms and substantial gourmet New England breakfasts.

Western New Hampshire

The **Connecticut River** forms the entire western border of New Hampshire. Along its banks and further inland, serene stretches of green farmland and a smattering of tranquil villages form a wedge between the Monadnock region and the wilder landscapes of the White Mountains. At the region's heart, **Hanover** is New Hampshire's intellectual center, the home of **Dartmouth College**, which attracts some of the country's best students and maintains an active arts scene. To the south, tiny **Cornish** was once a popular artists' colony. As I-89 runs south from Hanover towards Concord, it grazes the northern tip of **Lake Sunapee**, a quieter alternative to the more developed lake areas further east (see p.422).

Hanover

Almost everyone in **HANOVER** has some connection to **Dartmouth College**. Indeed, the city and college are pretty much one and the same thing, and have been since 1769, when the college was founded. Dartmouth's reputation as one of the more conservative Ivy League schools is not unfounded, but stereotypes aside, it's an active place, with all the cultural benefits you expect from a college town: an engaging museum; regular performances by international musicians, dancers, and actors; inviting bookstores; and a decent choice of places to eat and drink.

Arrival, information, and local transport

Like the rest of New Hampshire, the upper Connecticut River Valley is most easily accessible by **car**. Amtrak's *Vermonter* **train** stops once a day across the river in White River Junction, less than five miles from Hanover; local buses (see p.418) can get you into town from there. One Greyhound **bus** a day between Boston and Montréal stops in Hanover at the *Hanover Inn*. There is a larger terminal in White River Junction (℡802/295-3011), with buses south to Boston and north to Montréal, via Burlington (VT). The Concord Coach Lines-affiliated Dartmouth Coach (℡1-800/637-0123) has seven daily services to and from Boston and Logan Airport from the *Hanover Inn*.

The **Hanover Area Chamber of Commerce**, 2/F Nugget Arcade, 48 South Main St (Mon–Fri 9am–4pm; ℡603/643-3115, ⓦ www.hanoverchamber.org), has a vast selection of brochures and tourist information, supplemented in summer by

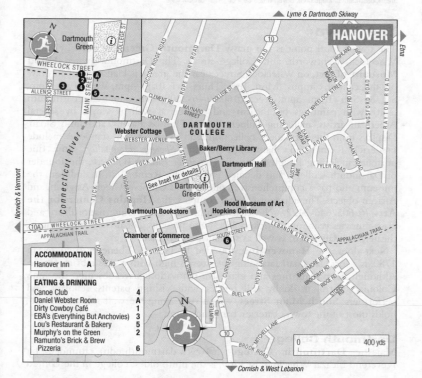

▲ Lyme & Dartmouth Skiway

HANOVER ▶ Etna

◀ Norwich & Vermont

ACCOMMODATION
Hanover Inn   A

EATING & DRINKING
Canoe Club	4
Daniel Webster Room	A
Dirty Cowboy Café	1
EBA's (Everything But Anchovies)	3
Lou's Restaurant & Bakery	5
Murphy's on the Green	2
Ramunto's Brick & Brew Pizzeria	6

0   400 yds

▼ Cornish & West Lebanon

an **information booth** on the green (May–Sept daily 9am–4pm; ☎603/643-3512), jointly maintained by Hanover and the College.

In and around Hanover, Advance Transit (☎802/295-1824, ⓦwww.advancetransit.com) provides a comprehensive free **local bus** service Monday to Friday – schedules and route maps are available at the Chamber of Commerce.

Accommodation

Accommodation in Hanover tends to be expensive and luxurious. Things are mellower (though usually just as expensive) in the surrounding countryside.

Chieftain Motor Inn 84 Lyme Rd, about 2.5 miles north of Hanover on Rte-10 ☎603/643-2550, ⓦwww.chieftaininn.com. The best of the few budget places in the area, with access to a guest kitchen and canoes for use in the nearby river ($20 per day). ❻

Hanover Inn corner of Main and Wheelock sts ☎603/643-4300 or 1-800/443-7024, ⓦwww.hanoverinn.com. The top end of Hanover's accommodation options, with dozens of spacious, elegantly furnished rooms overlooking Dartmouth Green. See also below. ❾

Moose Mountain Lodge end of Moose Mountain Rd, Etna ☎603/643-3529, ⓦwww.themoosemountainlodge.com. Seven miles east of

Hanover, in Etna, the *Lodge* is a marvelously remote option year-round, but is best as a base in winter for cross-country skiing. Meals available; no credit cards. Open Jan & Feb, June, and Sept to mid-Oct. ❼

Sunset Motor Inn Rte-10, 305 N Main St, West Lebanon (2 miles south of Hanover) ☎603/298-8721. This mom-and-pop place has eighteen rooms with cable TV and wi-fi overlooking the Connecticut River, and offers a filling Continental breakfast. ❸

Trumbull House Bed and Breakfast 40 Etna Rd ☎603/643-2370 or 1-800/651-5141, ⓦwww.trumbullhouse.com. Luxury accommodation in a quiet country setting four miles east of Dartmouth Green. ❻

The Town

The town's focal point is the grassy **Dartmouth Green**, bounded by Main, Wheelock, Wentworth, and College streets. The Dartmouth-owned **Hood Museum of Art**, on Wheelock Street near the green, is Hanover's main draw off the central campus (Mon, Tues, Thurs, Fri 10am–4pm, Wed 10am–9pm, Sat & Sun 10am–5pm; free; ☎603/646-2808, ⓦhoodmuseum.dartmouth.edu), with paintings by Picasso and Monet, as well as works by several American artists, including Gilbert Stuart, Thomas Eakins, and John Sloan. Displays from the permanent collection tend to change, but standouts include Frederick Remington's hauntingly realistic *Shotgun Hospitality*; some fine portraits, including Joseph Steward's *Portrait of Eleazar Wheelock*, the founder of Dartmouth College; and detailed etchings by Rembrandt. In addition, the museum also has a comprehensive collection of Chinese, Greek, Assyrian, and African objects. The adjacent cultural complex, the **Hopkins Center for the Arts** (☎603/646-2422, ⓦhop.dartmouth.edu), screens international art and classic movies year-round (tickets $8). It also presents globally acclaimed music, theater, and dance acts, as well as student performances.

Next door, the **Hanover Inn**, founded by General Ebenezer Brewster in 1780, is a local landmark, standing five stories high with a classic brick facade. Although devastating fires and extensive renovations have obscured the inn's Colonial charm, its lobby still bustles with visiting parents, scholars, and performers. **South Main Street**, which runs along the west side of the inn, holds most of the town's eateries, bars, and shops.

Dartmouth College

Majestic **Dartmouth College** (ⓦwww.dartmouth.edu), founded by Reverend Eleazar Wheelock in 1769, is the ninth oldest college in the United

States. The college was an outgrowth of a school for Native Americans that Wheelock had established in Connecticut, but few Native Americans ever studied here. Named for its initial financial backer, the Earl of Dartmouth, the Ivy League institution attracts some of the top students in the world, with particularly strong programs in medicine, engineering, and business.

The stately two-hundred-acre campus is spread out around the Dartmouth Green. Flanking the north end of the green, along Wentworth Street, the looming **Baker/Berry Library**, with its 207-foot belltower, is an imposing landmark. Inside, on the lower level, is the most arresting attraction on the campus, a series of **frescoes** by Mexican artist José Clemente Orozco. The politically rousing murals were painted between 1932 and 1934, while Orozco was an artist-in-residence and visiting professor. It's easy to see why conservative college officials and alumni viewed the violent depiction of the artist's theme, *An Epic of American Civilization*, as a direct insult: on one of the panels a skeleton gives birth upon a bed of dusty books as a group of arrogant, robed scholars look on, while on another a Jesus-like figure stands angrily next to a felled cross with an ax in his hand. Though college officials initially threatened to paint over the murals, they soon backed down, careful to avoid living up to Orozco's vision.

On the east side of the green stands **Dartmouth Row**, a collection of four impressive old buildings that look out over the grass from a slight hill. **Dartmouth Hall**, an imposing white structure with a large "1784" on its hulking pediment, was the college's first permanent building and remains a symbol of the school's academic prowess. Although it burned to the ground in 1904, the restored structure, which today houses Dartmouth's language departments, remains on its original foundation. The other three halls in the row are **Reed** (literature, Jewish Studies, and classics), **Thornton** (religion and philosophy), and **Wentworth** (undergraduate advising and research) – the latter two are the oldest original buildings on campus (1828–29).

Outdoor activities in the Dartmouth area

Dartmouth students and Hanover residents take their **outdoor** time seriously. Hiking, biking, rowing, and swimming are all popular, as are skiing (both cross-country and downhill) and skating.

Former resident Bill Bryson wrote *A Walk in the Woods* chronicling his adventures along the Appalachian Trail, which runs right through Hanover along Rte-10A – during the summer, grizzled hikers trudge into town with some regularity. The Dartmouth Outing Club, in Robinson Hall (☏603/646-2428), maintains hundreds of additional miles of **hiking trails** in the area and also leads group **bike rides**. You can take out posh demo **mountain bikes** for $45 per day from Omer and Bob's Sportshop, 7 Allen St (closed Sun; ☏603/643-3525). **Paddling** on the Connecticut River remains an extremely popular way to take in the scenery; the Ledyard Canoe Club (☏603/643-6709) rent **canoes** and **kayaks** (May–Oct; $20–30 per day). In the winter, Dartmouth's very own **alpine ski** area, the Dartmouth Skiway, ten miles north in Lyme (☏603/795-2143; $25 weekdays, $40 weekends), rents skis and snowboards ($30 per day). Dartmouth Outdoor Rentals (Mon–Fri 10am–5pm; ☏603/643-6534) rents skis, **ice skates**, and snowshoes, as well as mountaineering gear and tents – it also rents bikes for just $15 per day.

If you're in the mood for an Ivy League-flavored **workout**, Dartmouth's enormous athletic facility (☏603/646-3074, ⓦdartmouthsports.com), centered around the **Fitness Center**, along East Wheelock Street, has a modern gym, two pools, tennis courts, racquetball and squash courts, and a basketball court. Non-students can buy an all-day guest pass for $10.

Farther north along Main Street, the memory of the school's most celebrated graduate, Daniel Webster (see box, p.408), is preserved in **Webster Cottage**, 32 N Main St (late May to mid-Oct Wed, Sat & Sun 2.30–4.30pm; free; T603/643-6529), where he supposedly lived during his senior year in 1801.

Eating and drinking

Canoe Club 27 S Main St T603/643-9660, Wwww.canoeclub.us. The vibe here is more easy-going than the prices on this satisfying menu (pastas from $11, steaks $30), but it's a spirited place, with live music – jazz, blues, folk – 363 days a year.

Daniel Webster Room Inside the *Hanover Inn*, corner of Main and Wheelock sts T603/643-4300. The most elegant place for breakfast (from $6.25) and lunch in town ($15–17); For dinner, next door *Zins* bistro and wine bar serves fine tapas and grilled meats from $19.50.

Dirty Cowboy Café 7 S Main St T603/643-1323. Get your coffee drinks, as well as smoothies and fresh-squeezed juices here.

EBA's (Everything But Anchovies) 5 Allen St T603/643-6135. Families dine on salads and burgers here, but the real deal is the pizza (28 toppings and seventeen speciality pies). And yes, you can get anchovies if you want.

Lou's Restaurant & Bakery 30 S Main St T603/643-3321. Filling breakfasts of tasty hashbrowns, eggs, and sausage for under $10. Serves lunch also, but it's not as good. Closes at 3pm.

Murphy's on the Green 11 S Main St T603/643-4075. The best spot in town for a drink is also a popular restaurant serving an eclectic array of American cuisine. The good draft selection includes regional favorites Smuttynose and Magic Hat, along with Bass, Guinness, and Harp.

Ramunto's Brick 'n' Brew Pizzeria 9 East South St T603/643-9500. Delicious wood-fired pizzas ($7–10), including the notorious "Philly Cheese Steak Brick," as well as draft beers. Open daily till midnight.

Cornish

Other than a collection of scenic pastures and a few covered bridges, there's not much left in the town of **CORNISH**, twenty miles south of Hanover along Rte-120, which was a well-known artistic center in the late nineteenth century. Its most famous current inhabitant is **J.D. Salinger**, reclusive author of *Catcher in the Rye*, who hasn't given an interview since 1980.

The thing to see here is the **Saint-Gaudens National Historic Site**, 16 miles south of Hanover off Rte-12A (daily: late May to late Oct 9am–4.30pm; $5; T603/675-2175, Wwww.sgnhs.org), where sculptor Augustus Saint-Gaudens lived and worked from 1885 until his death in 1907. Saint-Gaudens is best known for his lifelike heroic bronze sculptures, including the Shaw Memorial in Boston and the General William T. Sherman Monument in New York City. Many well-known artists, writers, poets, and musicians, including Maxfield Parrish, Kenyon Cox, and Charles Platt, followed Saint-Gaudens to Cornish, establishing the **Cornish Colony**.

The visitors' center on site shows an enlightening video about the life and times of Saint-Gaudens, while the surrounding grounds and houses contain all his major works, replicas or castings of his Shaw Memorial, Lincoln statue, and New York's Farragut Monument among them. The New Gallery displays various bas-reliefs, and you can also visit Saint-Gaudens' "Little Studio," a soaring, sun-filled barn containing more of his work. To visit his actual house, **Aspet** (built in 1800 and retaining many of the original furnishings), you'll have to join a ranger-led tour (usually five times a day; 25min). Take the time to wander around the beautiful grounds, which feature well-cared-for gardens, two wooded nature trails, and a relaxing expanse of green grass. You can also check out works in progress by the artist-in-residence at the **Ravine Studio**, in the woods along the northern edge of the property.

A few minutes south of town off Rte-12A, the 460-foot long **Cornish–Windsor covered bridge**, connecting New Hampshire with Vermont, is the longest such bridge in the US, and quite stunning. It was constructed in 1866 and restored in 1989.

If you're looking for a comfortable **place to stay**, the best is the luxurious *Chase House Bed and Breakfast*, on Rte-12A (☎603/675-5391, ⓦwww.chasehouse.com; ➐). The well-decorated nineteenth-century mansion is also the birthplace and one-time residence of Salmon Portland Chase, Chief Justice of the US Supreme Court in the 1860s. Today the inn features seven exquisitely furnished rooms and delicious breakfasts.

Lake Sunapee

Lake Sunapee, the northern tip of which just brushes I-89, lies about twenty-five miles south of Hanover. The lake has been a popular summer escape since the beginning of the nineteenth century, though development has never been anything like the scale of its huge northeastern neighbor, Lake Winnipesaukee (see p.422). The region is still very low-key, and should be enjoyed while it can – recent heavy investment, especially in Mount Sunapee, while no doubt providing a new boom, may also sound the death knell for its secluded charm.

Sunapee Harbor and around

The action, such as it is, is all in **SUNAPEE HARBOR**. The only boats on the clear, clean waters are the occasional mail boat and regular **boat tours**, such as those run by Sunapee Cruises (daily: July to early Sept 2pm; late May to June & early Sept to mid-Oct weekends 2pm; $18; ☎603/763-4030, ⓦwww.sunapeecruises.com). The knowledgeable captain will share Sunapee lore and point out the sights, such as the lake's three lighthouses.

At the southern end of the lake, off Rte-103A, stands **The Fells** (grounds open year-round dawn to dusk; house tours: late May to late June weekends and holidays 10am–4pm; late June to late July Wed–Sun 10am–4pm; late July to early Sept daily 10am–4pm; $8; ☎603/763-4789, ⓦwww.thefells.org), the Hay family estate. John Milton Hay was an adviser and friend of Abraham Lincoln, and later became secretary of state under Teddy Roosevelt. He built the mansion here in the 1870s, then passed it on to his son, Cecil, who designed the grounds in a pleasing mix of Asian and European styles. These days, the mansion itself is empty, and the guided tours, while enjoyable, tend to make visitors feel as if they are being shown the house for prospective purchase. Far more interesting are the **gardens**, with the surrounding lake and forests adding to their charm. There are also **nature trails**, which provide opportunities for birdwatching.

Winter activities in the area take place at **Mount Sunapee** (☎603/763-2356, ⓦwww.mountsunapee.com; lift tickets $62–66), a family-oriented resort at the southern end of the lake on Rte-103. With millions of dollars invested since the owners of Vermont's Okemo Mountain (see p.350) took over operations here in 1998, vast improvements have been made to lifts, snowmaking facilities, and transportation to the mountain. The gentle slopes will suit learners and the mildly proficient more than expert skiers.

Practicalities

You'll find the helpful **Sunapee Welcome Center** (May–Oct daily 10am–5pm; ☎603/763-2201) on Rte-11 in Sunapee Harbor, at the intersection with

Rte-103B, while the **Lake Sunapee Chamber of Commerce** (☎1-877/526-6575, ⓦwww.lakesunapeenh.org) is based in **New London**, three miles from Lake Sunapee's eastern shore; the chamber is expected to open a new information center in the town in 2009. For **accommodation**, the *Best Western Sunapee Lake Lodge*, 1403 Rte-103 (☎603/763-2010 or 1-800/606-5253, ⓦwww.sunapeelakelodge.com; ⑤–⑧), at the entrance of the ski resort, has plenty of comfortable though impersonal rooms. More picturesque quarters with mountain views can be found in Sunapee at the *Blue Acorn Inn*, 21 Sleeper Rd, (☎603/863-1144, ⓦwww.blueacorninn.com; ④–⑤) or at *Twin Doors*, 49 High St in Sunapee Harbor (☎603/763-2236, ⓦwww.twindoors.com; ⑤), a snug 1900 Cape Cod-style house a short walk from the lake. Friendly and convenient places to eat nearby include *One Mile West*, 6 Brook Rd (Rte-103), literally one mile west of Sunapee rotary (☎603/863-7500), for solid American grills and diner-type fare, or *The Anchorage* 71 Main St in Sunapee Harbor (☎603/763-3334), a waterfront restaurant with live music weekends and a satisfying menu of sandwiches, steaks, pastas, and burgers.

The Lakes Region

The vacation-oriented **Lakes Region**, occupying the state's central corridor east of I-93, almost doubles its population between May and September, when visitors throng the area's restaurants, hotels, lakefront cottages, beaches, and crystal-clear waters. Luckily, there are literally hundreds of lakes here, created by the snowmelt from the White Mountains.

The biggest by far (some 72 square miles) is **Lake Winnipesaukee**, the definitive center of the region. Long segments of the shoreline, especially in the east, are carpeted with thick forests that sweep down from surrounding hills. The lake is dotted with 274 islands – most of which are privately owned – and its irregular shape, a seemingly endless continuum of inlets and peninsulas, resembles a giant paint splatter. The eastern and western shores of Lake Winnipesaukee are quite distinct: sophisticated **Wolfeboro** is the center of the sparsely populated and more upscale region to the east, while **Weirs Beach**, on the crowded western shore, is the epitome of summertime overkill, with enough arcades, ice-cream parlors, and roadside fun-parks to keep the kids happy for weeks. Farther north, the down-to-earth nineteenth-century towns around beautiful **Squam Lake** are some of the most inviting in the region.

Lake Winnipesaukee

The largest lake in New Hampshire and the third largest in New England, **Lake Winnipesaukee** has been a holiday hotspot since the 1850s, when the annual Harvard-Yale boat race first took place here (it now takes place in Connecticut). Today the lakeside towns offer plenty of variety, but it's difficult to appreciate the lake's size and beauty from the road – you really need to get on the water to make the most of a trip here.

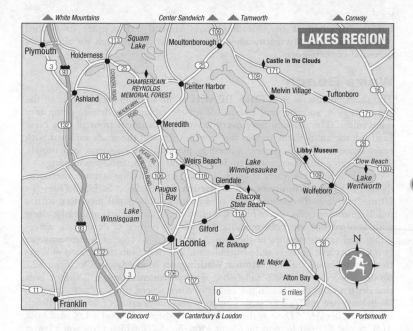

LAKES REGION

Plymouth

Holderness

Squam Lake

Moultonborough

Castle in the Clouds

Ashland

CHAMBERLAIN REYNOLDS MEMORIAL FOREST

Center Harbor

Melvin Village

Tuftonboro

Meredith

Libby Museum

Weirs Beach

Lake Winnipesaukee

Clow Beach

Glendale

Lake Wentworth

Paugus Bay

Ellacoya State Beach

Wolfeboro

Lake Winnisquam

Gilford

Mt. Belknap

Laconia

Mt. Major

Alton Bay

Franklin

N

0   5 miles

7 NEW HAMPSHIRE | Lake Winnipesaukee

Gilford

The pleasant village of **GILFORD**, just south of the lake along Rte-11A, is worth a quick detour if you're approaching the region from the south, though there is not a whole lot to actually see or do there. For excellent vistas of the lake and surrounding region, head for the top of **Mount Belknap**, which at 2384 feet is the highest peak in the Belknap Range, along the west side of the lake. The easiest and shortest route up the mountain begins along Belknap Mountain Carriage Road – turn off Rte-11A at the lights in the center of Gilford, drive through the village on Cherry Valley Road and follow the signs for the Fire Tower on Belknap. If you're feeling more sedentary, **Ellacoya State Beach**, along Rte-11 (mid-May to mid-Oct; $4; ☎603/293-7821), is one of the finer sandy beaches – and the only one that's state-maintained – on Lake Winnipesaukee, with six hundred feet of sand, and a **campground** that affords some great views of the lake from many of its 38 sites ($47).

Practicalities

There are some reasonable **places to stay** in Gilford. The *Belknap Point Motel*, 107 Belknap Point Rd (☎1-888/454-2537, ⓦwww.bpmotel.com; ⑤), offers somewhat characterless accommodation, but magical views of the lake and mountains. Some rooms have kitchens and can be rented by the week. *B Mae's Inn & Suites*, 17 Harris Shore Rd (☎603/293-7526 or 1-800/458-3877, ⓦwww.bmaesresort .com; ⑤), has two pools, a Jacuzzi, and an exercise room, all within walking distance of the beach. Just past Gilford on Rte-11A, the **Gunstock Mountain Resort** (☎603/293-4341 or 1-800/486-7862, ⓦwww.gunstock.com) acts as a ski area during the winter and a recreation area during the summer, offering **campsites** from $27 a night, and cabins, with electricity and water, for $70 per night.

For a drink or hearty snack, try *Patrick's Pub*, at the intersection of Rte-11 and Rte-11B (☎603/293-0841). If you're looking for **entertainment**, check out the program at the Meadowbrook Musical Arts Center in Gilford (☏603/293-4700, ⓦwww.meadowbrookfarm.net), with room for almost six thousand concert-goers.

Weirs Beach

The short boardwalk at **WEIRS BEACH** is the summer social center of the Lakes Region, and the very essence of seaside tackiness – despite being fifty miles inland. The wooden jetty overflows with vacationers from all over New England, the amusement arcades jingle with cash, and the roads are lined with neon signs, mini-golf courses, waterslide playland extravaganzas, and motels. There's even a little crescent of sandy beach, suitable for family swimming.

You'd best head elsewhere if you're looking for a relaxing lakeside afternoon, though the **Lake Winnipesaukee Museum**, 503 Endicott St/US-3 (Tues–Sat 10am–2pm; free; ☏603/366-5950) offers a more thoughtful diversion, with a mildly absorbing collection of historical photos, maps, and charts of the lake, along with assorted bits and bobs revealing the vibrant history of steamboats, water-skiing, and summer camps in the area. A great way to take in Winnipesaukee's beautiful expanse of inlets and peninsulas and get away from the ugliness of Weirs Beach is to board the **MS Mount Washington** (mid-May to Oct; from $22; ☏603/366-5531 or 1-888/843-6686, ⓦwww.cruisenh.com), a 230-foot boat that departs from the dock in the center of town several times a day to cruise to Wolfeboro (see p.427). The same company also offers cruises from Weirs Beach on the smaller *M/V Doris E* (late June to early Sept; $15) and a US mail boat, *M/V Sophie C* (mid-June to mid-Sept Mon–Sat; $22), which gives you a better opportunity to see some of the lake's many islands.

Another attraction here is the **Winnipesaukee Railroad** (late May to early June & Sept–Oct weekends; daily mid-June to Aug; $12 for 1hr, $13 for 2hr; ☏603/279-5253, ⓦwww.hoborr.com), which operates scenic trips along the lakeshore between Weirs Beach and Meredith.

Practicalities

If you want to find a **place to stay** within earshot of the amusement arcades, there are plenty of choices on Tower Street, up the hill behind the jetty. There is a real army barracks feel to the *Half Moon Motel & Cottages*, 12 Tower St (☏603/366-4494, ⓔhalfmoonmotel@weirsbeach.com; ❾), where a block of motel rooms and individual cottages (some with kitchens) are laid out around the austere pool. Slightly cozier is the *Bear Tree Lodge*, 2.5 miles up US-3 towards Meredith (☏603/279-9013, ⓦwww.beartreelodge.com; ❹), whose rooms include efficiency kitchens, and where off-season room rates are among the cheapest in the state. When it comes to **eating**, you're better off heading to nearby Meredith for anything beyond hot dogs and burgers.

Meredith

MEREDITH, four miles north of Weirs Beach, is more upscale than its neighbor. The pretty town center is up the hill from the busy intersection of US-3 and Rte-25, where you'll find a few places to eat and the quirky **Meredith Historical Society Museum**, 45 Main St (May–Oct Wed–Sat 11am–4pm; free; ☏603/279-1190, ⓦmhsweb.org), which displays old photos, documents, maps, muskets, bottles, and other odd bits and pieces. Most of the action takes place back on US-3, where the Mill Falls Shopping Center spills into the pleasant **Meredith Marina**, on the lake itself at 2 Bayshore Drive (☏603/279-7921, ⓦwww.meredithmarina.com); you can rent a motorboat here for $295 per day, or $200 per half-day. The sandy town **beach**, with mountain views, is located on Waukewan Street along the shores of tiny **Lake Waukewan**.

Practicalities

Concord Coach Lines (☎1-800/639-3317) buses from Boston call in at Meredith at the public parking lot on US-3, next to Aubuchon Hardware. Your best source for **information** in the area is the **Meredith Area Chamber of Commerce** (daily 9am–5pm; ☎603/279-6121, ⊛www.meredithcc.org), at 272 Daniel Webster Hwy (US-3), a half-mile south of the Rte-25 intersection. For those who wish to **camp**, try *Harbor Hill* (☎603/279-6910, ⊛www.hhcamp.com), 1.5 miles up Rte-25, with tent sites ($30) and camper cabins ($60), and a swimming pool and camp store on the premises. The **place to stay** in town is *The Inns at Mill Falls*, 312 Daniel Webster Hwy (☎603/279-7006 or 1-800/622-6455, ⊛www.millfalls .com), actually a set of four notable accommodations: the *Inn at Mills Falls* (◑) and *Chase House* (◑), which feature plush rooms overlooking the lake, the waterside *Inn at Bay Point* (◑), and the newer *Church Landing* (◑), with its polished rustic interior. Some cozy B&Bs are also strewn around: at Main and Waukewan streets, the *Meredith Inn*, a rose-colored Victorian (☎603/279-0000, ⊛www.meredithinn .com; ◑), and *Tuckernuck Inn*, 25 Red Gate Lane (☎603/279-5521, ⊛www .thetuckernuckinn.com; ◑), are both good-value choices.

As for **eating**, you could do worse than to end up in Meredith. For a quick bite of authentic Chinese, *Phu Jee*, 55 Main St (closed Mon; ☎603/279-1129), will do the trick for less than $15, while *Camp* (☎603/279-3003) is an entertaining trip back to summer camp, complete with log-cabin walls and casual comfort food like fried chicken, pan-fried trout, and s'mores. *Town Docks*, on US-3 just south of the intersection (☎603/279-3445), will give you a seafood fix, and *Lago* (☎603/279-2253), right on the US-3/25 intersection, does good Italian, with a busy terrace on the water. Perhaps the best dinner option in town is *Lakehouse Grill* at the *Church Landing* (☎603/279-5221), further down US-3. Creative starters, heaping main plates of pork, steak, or salmon (entrees $17–23), and a fairly happening bar scene await you just about every night.

Center Harbor

The relaxing village of **CENTER HARBOR**, five miles north of Meredith, is a good base from which to explore the Lakes Region, especially if you have a car. There isn't much here except for the usual diversions of canoeing, kayaking, and boat cruises (the *MS Mount Washington* stops here; see opposite for more details), but it's also close to the larger settlements of Lake Winnipesaukee if you're looking for some action. You can get to Center Harbor by **bus**; Concord Coach Lines stops at the Village Car Wash and Laundromat in the Dunkin' Donuts Plaza on Rte-25. If you're looking for a **place to stay**, the *Kona Mansion Inn*, Moultonboro Neck Road (☎603/253-4900; ◑), has tennis, golf, and swimming in a tranquil lakeside setting.

Moultonborough and around

Other than some remote B&Bs and quiet country roads, there's not much to the sprawling town of **MOULTONBOROUGH**, north of Lake Winnipesaukee on Rte-25 and five miles on from Center Harbor. If you're passing through, however, you might take a break in the **Old Country Store** (daily 9am–6pm) at the intersection of routes 25 and 109. One of the oldest of its kind (dating from 1781), it sells everything from home-made pickles and usual maple syrup to candles, dolls, and carved wooden ducks. The bizarre "museum" upstairs houses

▲ Old Country Store, Moltonborough

a dusty collection of artifacts, including axes, saws, and carved Indian sculptures. For some time in the sun, the **town beach** (make a right off of Rte-25 onto Moultonboro Neck Rd, and follow to near the end of Long Island Rd), is a particularly good spot for picnicking and swimming.

Two miles east of town on Rte-171, **Castle in the Clouds** (daily mid-May to mid-Oct 10am–4pm; $10; ☎603/476-2352 or 1-800/729-2468, Ⓦwww .castleintheclouds.org) is the 5200-acre mountain estate of eccentric millionaire Thomas Plant, which, in spite of its fancy name, is just a large house on a hill. What sets this place apart is the uniqueness of the building itself, an interesting amalgamation of architectural styles, betraying Spanish, Japanese, and Swiss influences. Completed in 1914 to reflect Plant's interest in the Arts and Crafts Movement, which emphasized living in harmony with nature, the massive mansion was somewhat advanced for its time, with a centralized vacuum system, intercom, and a self-cleaning oven – the interior has been preserved much as he left it. You can also eat at the *Carriage House Café* on site, and **hike** the 45 miles of trails that crisscross the 5,500-acre gorgeous reserve attached to the estate.

The Loon Preservation Committee maintains the small **Loon Center**, along quiet Lee's Mills Road off Blake Road (Mon–Sat 9am–5pm; July to mid-Oct also Sun 9am–5pm; free; ☎603/476-5666, Ⓦwww.loon.org), which houses a collection of exhibits about the endangered and much-loved birds, focusing on environmental awareness. You can view Lake Winnipesaukee from several points along the **Loon Nest Trail**, which begins at the center and winds through forests and marshes. You'll find Blake Road off Rte-25, south of Moultonborough (the center is signposted).

Practicalities

A good place to **stay** is the *Olde Orchard Inn*, 108 Lee Rd (☎603/476-5004 or 1-800/598-5845, Ⓦwww.oldeorchardinn.com; ⑥), a relaxing B&B in the middle of an apple orchard. Some of the nine rooms feature fireplaces and Jacuzzis. Meanwhile, the best place to **eat** in town is *The Woodshed*, 128 Lee Rd (☎603/476-2311; dinner only, closed Mon), an old barn turned restaurant where prime rib is the speciality, and lamb chops, lobster, and grilled fish are also on the menu (entrees $19–28). Ask for a table on the screened-in patio on warm summer evenings. Take the Old 109 Road from Rte-25 (first right after the Country Store, heading north), and you should see Lee Road on the right after a mile.

Wolfeboro

Because Governor John Wentworth built his summer home nearby in 1768, upscale **WOLFEBORO** claims to be "the oldest summer resort in America." Sandwiched between the eastern shore of Lake Winnipesaukee and smaller Lake Wentworth, at the intersection of routes 109 and 28, it's certainly the most attractive town in the region – access to the **waterfront** here, with wide, fine views of the lake, is one of the best reasons to stay.

Information and local transport

The best source for **information** on the eastern shore is the **Wolfeboro Chamber of Commerce**, in the old red station building on Central Avenue, just off Main Street in the center of town (Mon–Sat 10am–3pm, Sun 10am–noon; ☎603/569-2200 or 1-800/516-5324, @www.wolfeborochamber.com). You need a car to really see the area, though the **Wolfeboro Trolley Company** operates "Molly the Trolley" during the summer, which makes a short loop around Wolfeboro (July & Aug daily 10am–4pm; $5; ☎603/569-1080).

Accommodation

Lake Motel 280 S Main St ☎603/569-1100 or 1-888/569-1100, @www.thelakemotel.com. Modern accommodation, with tennis courts and private beach; some rooms have kitchens. Open May–Oct. ⑤

Lakeview Inn and Motorlodge 200 N Main St (Rte-109) ☎603/569-1335, @www.lakeviewinn.net. Nicely decorated rooms with modern amenities, in a restored inn and two-story hotel. ⑥

Tuc' Me Inn B&B 118 N Main St (Rte-109) ☎603/569-5702, @www.tucmeinn.com. Cozy, 1850 Federal/Colonial inn close to the lake and town. Rooms are tastefully furnished and full breakfast is included. ⑥

Willey Brook Campground Rte-28 ☎603/569-9493, @www.willeybrookcampground.com. Three miles north of Wolfeboro and only one mile from Wentworth State Beach. Open mid-May to mid-Oct; sites from $26.

Wolfeboro Inn 90 N Main St (Rte-109) ☎603/569-3016 or 1-800/451-2389, @www.wolfeboroinn.com. Built in 1812, this historic inn is on the waterfront with its own beach and some of the best restaurants in town (see p.429). It has 44 elegant rooms, ranging from plush, modern suites to vintage rooms dating back to the foundation of the inn – some have private balconies overlooking the lake. ⑧

The Town

Other than admiring the lake view, there's little to see downtown, though strolling the short, bustling Main Street (Rte-109) can be fun if you want to while away a few hours. Further east, the 4300-square-foot summer mansion of Governor John Wentworth, known as the **Wentworth House Plantation**, with its own sawmill, orchards, workers' village, and six-hundred-acre deer park, was, at one time, a sort of Hearst Castle of New Hampshire. It burned to the ground in 1820 and was never rebuilt, but the area once occupied by the plantation, on Rte-28 three miles southeast of Rte-28, is now the **Governor John Wentworth State Historic Site** (June to early Sept; $4; ☎603/436-1552), an undeveloped park and archeological site.

Another worthwhile stop, a few miles north of downtown Wolfeboro on Rte-109, is the eclectic **Libby Museum** (June to mid-Sept Tues–Sat 10am–4pm, Sun noon–4pm; $2; ☎603/569-1035), where an early twentieth-century dentist's obsession with evolution is manifested through some ineptly stuffed animals and skeletons of bears, orangutans, and humans. There's also a mastodon's tooth, a random assortment of fossils and insects, Native American artifacts, and a fingernail supposedly pulled out by its Chinese owner to demonstrate his newfound Christian faith. The setting of the museum, a 1912 Historic Landmark house with superb views of the lake and a grassy park, makes the detour even more rewarding.

The best way to take in Lake Winnipesaukee's subtle beauty is aboard *MS Mount Washington* (see p.424), which departs from the dock in the center of town and connects with Weirs Beach across the lake. From the same place you can also take two-hour trips on former mail boat *Blue Ghost* (☏603/569-1114), or take a quick spin in *Millie B*, a 1928-style mahogany speedboat (June–Sept daily 10am–4pm; spring & fall Sat & Sun 11am–2pm; $20; ☏603/569-1080).

Eating and drinking

Bailey's Bubble Railroad Ave ☏603/569-3612. Luscious ice cream in the center of town; try "Maine Black Bear" (raspberry, chocolate chips, and truffles), or "Moose Tracks" (vanilla, fudge, and peanut butter cups). Summer only.

The Cider Press 30 Middleton Rd, off Rte-28 ☏603/569-2028. Hearty American food – ribs, steak, grilled salmon ($16–20) – in a rustic, candlelit dining room.

Lydia's Café 33 N Main St ☏603/569-3991. Smoothies, espresso drinks, bagels, and excellent sandwiches are served in this cute café, just up from the dock on Rte-109. Daily 7am–2.30pm.

The Strawberry Patch 50 N Main St (Rte-109) ☏603/569-5523. Excellent, freshly prepared breakfasts and lunches in a cozy and unpretentious dining room. Daily 7.30am–2pm.

Eastern shore outdoor activities

The eastern shore of Lake Winnipesaukee has enough **outdoor activities** to keep even the most avid enthusiast busy. Hiking, boating, sailing, fishing, swimming, mountain-biking, and kayaking are all big in summer, while cross-country skiing and snowmobiling should sate any outdoor urges during the winter.

The best **beach** for swimming and picnicking in the Wolfeboro area is **Clow Beach** (mid-June to early Sept; $4; ☏603/569-3699) in Wentworth State Park on Lake Wentworth. **Brewster Beach** (mid-June to early Sept; free; ☏603/569-1532) on Lake Winnipesaukee at the end of Clark Road, south of Wolfeboro, is also good for sunbathing and swimming. Once you're done sunning, there are a couple of decent local **hiking routes**. The **Mount Major Trail**, north of Alton on Rte-11, offers excellent lake views and takes about an hour and a half to cover 1.75 miles. The trail to the top of **Bald Peak**, at the Moultonborough–Tuftonboro town line on Rte-171, is a mile long, while the Mount Flag Trail in Tuftonboro is a strenuous seven-mile route. For a shorter jaunt (half a mile), with rewarding panoramic views, try the **Abenaki Tower Trail**, off Rte-109 in Tuftonboro across from Wawbeek Road, featuring an eighty-foot tower overlooking Lake Winnipesaukee. **Snowmobiles** and **cross-country skiers** fill the trails during the winter; call the Wolfboro Cross Country Ski Association (☏603/569-3151, ⓦwww.wolfeboroxc.org) or the New Hampshire Snowmobile Association (☏603/224-8906, ⓦwww.nhsa.com) for information and guidance.

As for **watersports**, Wet Wolfe Rentals, 17 Bay St, Wolfeboro (☏603/569-3200), rents waverunners for a minimum of two hours ($150) or a sixteen-foot aluminum hull with 25hp motor ($225 per day). Goodhue Hawkins Navy Yard, 244 Sewall Rd in Wolfeboro (☏603/569-2371, ⓦwww.goodhueandhawkins.com), rents **boats** from $320 a day. You can take an all-inclusive light-tackle guided **fishing** trip with Angling Adventures, 79 Middleton Rd, Wolfeboro (☏603/569-6426, ⓦwww.gadaboutgolder.com), for $260 per person ($300 for two).

Wolfeboro Dockside Grill and Dairy Bar 11
Dockside ☏ 603/569-1910. Some of the best views
in town, with a menu of cheap, no-frills comfort
food (burgers $6), plus an ice cream take-out
counter at the back.

Wolfeboro House of Pizza 37 N Main St
(Rte-109) ☏ 603/569-8408. No-frills Greek-owned
place, serving tasty pizzas, pastas, and subs,
though no *souvlaki* or *baklava*.

🏃 **Wolfe's Tavern** 90 N Main St (Rte-109)
☏ 603/569-3016. Enticing restaurant
attached to the *Wolfeboro Inn*, offering four main
dining areas. The fancy *1812 Room* serves fine,

expensive, New England-style cuisine, while the
old tavern section is a dark pub-like eatery and
much better value of the two. The *Maple Room*
features a large gas fireplace and Colonial decor,
while the lakeside patio is the best option in
summer. Enjoy one of their 72 beers on tap (and
ask about the over 1900 pewter beer mugs on the
tavern room ceiling).

Wolfetrap Grill and Rawbar 19 Bay St
☏ 603/569-1047. Unpretentious restaurant just
outside of town. The range of seafood plates
includes lobster, clams, and softshell crab. Open
May to early Sept.

Squam Lake

Much smaller than its sprawling neighbor, but still the second largest body of
water in the state, beautiful **Squam Lake** actually holds more appeal than Lake
Winnipesaukee – the pace is slower, the roads less crowded, and, thanks to a conscientious group of residents, the land is less developed. However, it's difficult to access
the forested shore unless you're a resident, and the only way to really appreciate the
lake's tranquil charm is to take a boat ride.

As expected, most of the action in the area revolves around the **outdoors**: hiking,
boating, and swimming are all popular activities. It's easy to see why producers
chose Squam Lake as the setting for the 1981 film *On Golden Pond*, starring Henry
Fonda – the water is pristine and glassy, and the setting sun brings a quiet calm over
the lake and surrounding forests. With a population of 1700, **Holderness** is the
largest town in the area, although it's really nothing more than a gas station, a few
stately old inns, a couple of restaurants, and a dock, though there's a great beach
and some enjoyable hikes nearby. **Center Sandwich**, to the north of the lake, also
maintains its nineteenth-century quaintness.

Holderness

Named for the Earl of Holderness, a friend of Governor Wentworth's,
HOLDERNESS, at the intersection of US-3 and Rte-113, was granted its
original town charter in 1751. Although nothing of much historical significance
ever happened here, the Holderness School has remained a prestigious preparatory school since its founding in 1879. Today, the tiny village brings together a
loosely defined grouping of buildings along the shore next to a well-used public
dock. Note that the water here is **Little Squam Lake**; Squam Lake itself is just
to the north, connected via the Squam River but completely hidden from the
road (there are no public docks or towns on Squam Lake itself).

The Holderness General Store (daily 7am–9pm), at the intersection of US-3
and Rte-113 in town, is the place to come for supplies before you head out for a
day on the lake. The best public **beach** is accessible along a short trail through the
Chamberlain–Reynolds Memorial Forest, off College Road – follow US-3
south, take a left on College Road, and park in the first small lot. Walk up West
Fire Road for about twenty minutes to reach the beach (bring insect repellent).
The most popular **hike** in the area begins at the Rattlesnake Trailhead along
Rte-113 and follows the **Old Bridle Path** to the top of **Rattlesnake Mountain**,
providing spectacular views of Squam Lake and the surrounding hills, with only
half an hour of effort. Other trails to the top of Rattlesnake Mountain, such as

The Barnstormers

Founded in 1931 by Francis Cleveland (son of 22nd US president Grover Cleveland), his wife Alice, and Edward Goodnow, the **Barnstormers** (☎603/323-8661, ⓦwww .barnstormerstheatre.org) is the oldest professional summer theater group in the state. It is also perhaps the only theater company in the country in which the same actors perform a different play each week. Presenting a wide range of productions, the theater company plays to consistently large crowds. Housed in a refurbished old store in the center of **Tamworth Village** since 1935, the company typically produces eight plays per summer. Call ☎603/323-8500 from late May until the end of the season in August for schedule and ticket information.

the **Ramsey Trail**, begin along Pinehurst Road, also off Rte-113. The **Mount Morgan Trail** begins at the trailhead along Rte-113, 5.4 miles northeast of US-3, and ascends 1400 feet along a 2.1-mile trail. Additional hiking suggestions are available at the Squam Lakes Association headquarters (see below).

An introduction to the area's flora and fauna is provided by the **Squam Lake Natural Science Center**, near the intersection of routes 113 and 25 in the center of town (daily May–Oct 9.30am–4.30pm; $13; ☎603/968-7194, ⓦwww .nhnature.org), which features live animals – including bears, bobcats, owls, and otters – housed in settings that resemble their natural habitats along a quarter-mile nature walk. Compared to a typical zoo, it's refreshingly spacious, though numerous hands-on exhibits and educational presentations tend to attract large groups of schoolchildren.

Outdoor activities

The ninety-minute boat trips offered by **Science Center Lake Cruises** (May–Oct; depart from beside *Walter's Basin* restaurant on Rte-3 at 11am, 1pm & 3pm; $20, children $16; ☎603/968-7194) provide an absorbing tour of the lake, and include a look at **Thayer Cottage**, where the bulk of *On Golden Pond* was filmed; guides usually embellish the tour with plenty of trivia about the movie, and you may also see endangered loons and bald eagles which inhabit the lake. Special tours, more focused on observing the loons, are accompanied by the center's naturalist (July to mid-Oct Tues, Wed & Thurs 4–5.30pm; same prices). **Experience Squam** (☎603/968-3990, ⓦwww.experiencesquam.com) runs more personalized excursions across the lake in smaller powerboats ($95 per hr or $215 for 2hr).

If you'd rather steer your own vessel, you can rent five-person motorboats for $119 per day or three-person canoes for $49 per day from **Squam Lakeside Farm**, on US-3 (☎603/968-7227, ⓦwww.squamlakesresort.com). The **Squam Lakes Association** (SLA), with a helpful office on US-3 (☎603/968-7336, ⓦwww.squamlakes.org; rentals 9am–4.30pm: late May to early Sept daily, early Sept to mid-Oct Sat & Sun only), rents **canoes** and **kayaks** ($45 per day), and **sailboats** ($60 per day), and sells trail guides to the region ($6). They also run half-day kayak tours and give lessons ($50–80). The nearest place to rent a **bicycle** is seven miles away, off I-93 Exit 25 in Plymouth, at Rhino Bike Works, 1 Foster St ($25–30 per day; ☎603/536-3919), where you can also get advice on local trails.

Practicalities

By far the ritziest and most expensive **place to stay** in Holderness is the *Manor on Golden Pond*, on US-3 overlooking the lake (☎603/968-3348 or 1-800/545-2141, ⓦwww.manorongoldenpond.com; ❾), an elegant mansion with crystal chandeliers, sweeping vistas, and stone fireplaces. Their award-winning dining room offers gourmet New American cuisine. Less expensive and more down-to-earth, the welcoming *Inn on Golden Pond*, on US-3 along Little Squam Lake (℡603/968-7269, Ⓦwww.innongoldenpond.com; ❼), has eight large rooms, friendly hosts, full breakfasts, and a games room. Though its rooms are nothing special, the *White Oak Motel*, at the intersection of Rte-25 and US-3 (℡603/968-3673 or 1-888/965-1850, Ⓦwww.whiteoakmotel.com; ❹), is the cheapest place around. They also rent cottages per week ($649–999), as does *Cottage Place on Squam Lake* (℡603/968-7116, Ⓦwww.cottageplaceonsquam.com; ❸). The Squam Lakes Association maintains primitive **camping sites** on Moon Island, Bowman Island, and in the Chamberlain-Reynolds Memorial Forest ($50 per site weekends, $45 weekdays; reservations required; ℡603/968-7336; May–Oct).

The only waterfront **restaurant** in town, *Walter's Basin*, on US-3 (℡603/968-4412), serves decent rainbow trout and other fish dishes in a pleasant setting (entrees from $17) – the name alludes to the monster trout hunted by Henry Fonda in *On Golden Pond*. May to October, the *Squam Lake Inn Café* (Tues–Sat 11am–2pm; ℡603/968-4417), on Shepard Hill Road (off US-3 at the Citgo gas station), is renowned for its lobster rolls and ice cream.

Center Sandwich

Thirteen miles northeast of Holderness along Rte-113, at the base of the Sandwich Range, **CENTER SANDWICH** is the most alluring town in the region, comprising a string of enchanting white clapboard buildings. There's not much in the way of sights here, but you might visit the friendly folks at the **Sandwich Historical Society**, 4 Maple St (June–Oct Tues–Sat 10am–4pm; free; ℡603/284-6269; Ⓦwww.sandwichhistorical.org), who can give you local maps, and check out their museum of local period tools, house furnishings, textiles, and the work of early local painters.

The best **place to eat** in town is the *Corner House Inn*, 22 Main St (℡603/284-6219), an informal, historic (the structure's been around since 1849), and popular joint with both casual and upscale food – it's on the intersection of routes 113 and 109. To **stay** overnight, you could try the quiet *Strathaven Inn*, 576 North Sandwich Rd/Rte-113 (℡603/284-7785, Ⓦwww.strathaveninn.com; cash only; ❹), with four cozy rooms (two with shared bath).

The White Mountains

Thanks to their accessibility from both Montréal and Boston, the **WHITE MOUNTAINS** have become a year-round tourist destination, popular with summer hikers and winter skiers alike. It's a commercialized region, with quite a lot of development flanking the main highways, but the great granite massifs retain much of their majesty. **Mount Washington**, the highest peak in the entire Northeast, claims some of the severest weather in the world – conditions are harsh enough to produce a timberline at four thousand feet.

Vacationing in these mountains is not a new trend – the area has long been appreciated for its exquisite beauty. After railroads were built here during the mid-nineteenth century, lumber companies bought up much of the land and began to log the forest. However, quick to recognize the value of the mountains' beauty, residents formed conservationist groups such as the **Appalachian Mountain Club** (AMC), and eventually ensured the passage of the Weeks Act in 1911, which allowed the federal government to purchase the land to preserve it. The national forest area now encompasses almost 800,000 acres, covering much of the northern part of the state, and even spills over into Maine.

Piercing the range are only a few high passes – called "**notches**" – discovered by early pioneers during arduous crossings. The roads through these gaps, such as the **Kancamagus Highway** between **Lincoln** and **Conway**, make for predictably scenic routes. However, you won't really have made the most of the White Mountains unless you also set off on foot, bike, or skis, across the long expanses of thick evergreen forest that separate them. Some of the best hiking trails are in the state parks of **Franconia Notch**, straddling I-93, **Crawford Notch**, straddling

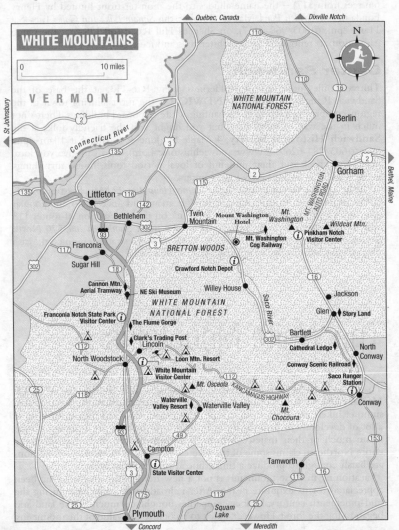

You will need a **parking pass** for your vehicle when you park and leave it unattended in the White Mountains National Forest, though not if you're just stopping briefly to take pictures or use restrooms, nor if you're staying in a National Forest campground. Passes cost $5 for seven consecutive days, and you can buy them from many local stores and at all Forest Service offices. If you decide on the spur of the moment to hike to the top of a mountain or spend the afternoon at a swimming hole, you can purchase a day-pass for $3 at self-pay kiosks in parking lots across the forest.

US-302, and **Pinkham Notch**, along the eastern base of Mount Washington. Downhill skiing is popular at resorts such as **Waterville Valley** and **Loon Mountain**, both a few miles east of I-93, while cross-country skiing is particularly good at **Jackson**, which, along with **North Conway** and **Glen**, makes up the region's most built-up area, the **Mount Washington Valley**. Even if you don't intend to stay, check out the grand resort hotels in **Bretton Woods** and **Dixville Notch** (the first town in New Hampshire – and therefore the nation – to announce the results of its primary elections).

It's best to have your own transport, but daily **bus services** to the White Mountains from Boston and the southern part of the state are provided by Concord Coach Lines, stopping at Conway, North Conway, Jackson, Pinkham Notch, Gorham, and Berlin; another route services Franconia, Lincoln, and Littleton.

Waterville Valley

East of I-93 along Rte-49, the sparkling **Waterville Valley Resort** (℡ 1-800/468-2553, ⓦ www.waterville.com) was the brainchild of developer Tom Corcoran, who bought the *Waterville Valley Inn* and its surrounding land in 1965 with the intent of creating a family-oriented outdoor center. Today, the many resort-goers enjoying all manner of summer and winter activities are evidence that he succeeded – not altogether surprising considering the stunning tree-covered setting.

At the center of the resort is the **Town Square**, a development of shops and restaurants alongside **Corcoran's Pond**, where you can lounge on the sand or rent a kayak, canoe, or paddleboat (all $10 per hr). If no one is around, ask at the nearby Nordic Center (daily 9am–5pm; ℡ 603/236-4666), which also rents **mountain bikes** ($32 per day) and has trail maps. You can also rent bikes and ride the chairlift to the top of the hill at nearby **Snow's Mountain** (June–Sept daily 10am–5pm; $42 including rental, non-bikers $9 one-way).

Though relatively active in summer, Waterville Valley really comes to life in the winter months, and the intermediate slopes of the **ski area** (lift tickets $65 per day; equipment rental $40 per day), a network of trails covering 2020 vertical feet on Mount Tecumseh and Snow's Mountain, are usually packed. The main ski area is three miles from the Town Square; free shuttles run in ski season. The Nordic Center at Waterville Valley has over forty miles of **cross-country trails** (℡ 603/236-4666; $18 trail fee; $19 equipment rental).

The rugged area surrounding Waterville Valley makes for excellent **hiking** and **camping**. Of several notable hikes that originate along Tripoli Road, the **Mount Osceola Trail** is the best, starting around 3.8 miles from the village. It's a strenuous 3.5-mile trek to the summit at 4326ft, from where you can continue for another two miles to the Greeley Ponds Trail and the Kancamagus Highway (see p.436).

The **Waterville Valley Region Chamber of Commerce**, 12 Vintner Rd in Campton, ten miles west at Exit 28 off I-93 (daily 9am–5pm; ☎603/726-3804 or 1-800/237-2307, ⓦwww.watervillevalleyregion.com), is your best bet for information on hiking, camping, and lodging in the area; it stocks the usual brochures and has helpful attendants and good maps.

Accommodation options in the immediate Waterville Valley area are geared to families and all-inclusive vacationers. During the summer, prices are surprisingly reasonable, and rates at all nine of the resort's lodges, inns, and condos include use of the athletic club, mountain-bike rental, golf, tennis courts, and kayak rental. One of the best value of these lodges is the *Best Western Silver Fox Inn* (☎1-888/236-3699, ⓦwww.silverfoxinn.com; ⑤), which is not your usual chain hotel: it's got attractive common areas, and the price includes unlimited tennis-court time and two hours' bike rental. At the *Black Bear Lodge*, 3 Village Rd (☎603/236-4501 or 1-800/349-2327, ⓦwww.black-bear-lodge.com; ⑧), the units can sleep up to six people, and the *Snowy Owl Inn*, 4 Village Rd (☎603/236-8383 or 1-800/766-9969, ⓦwww.snowyowlinn.com; ④), has 85 rooms with cozy fireplaces and attractive furnishings. Be aware, though, that prices go up by as much as fifty percent in winter. In Campton, which has a number of pleasant B&Bs, the *Osgood Inn*, 14 Osgood Rd (☎603/726-3543; cash only; ④), housed in a stately old home with a sun-drenched back porch, is one of the better ones.

You can camp at the *Waterville Campground*, with 25 wooded sites off Tripoli Road, ten miles east of I-93 (open year-round; ☎1-877/444-6777; $16), or the privately owned *Branch Brook Campground*, Rte-49, Campton (☎603/726-7001, ⓦwww.campnh.com; $25–30). There are thirteen tent sites at the *Osceola Vista Campground* (☎1-877/444-6777; $16), just outside of Waterville Valley on Tripoli Road, and undeveloped wilderness sites with no facilities between Waterville Valley and I-93 along Tripoli Road (get a parking/camping permit at the Fee Station, I-93 Exit 31).

Most of the places **to eat** in the Waterville Valley are just what you'd expect: slightly monotonous and not great value. There's a no-nonsense pizza joint, the *Olde Waterville Pizza Company* (☎603/236-FOOD), in the lower level of Town Square, and a more upscale restaurant serving creative American cuisine with a seasonally changing menu, the *Wild Coyote Grill*, above the White Mountain Athletic Club on Rte-49 (☎603/236-4919). The Jugtown Country Store, in Town Square (☎603/236-3669), with a full-service deli and wide selection of cheeses and breads, is good for picnic supplies. For better value, you're better off heading to nearby Campton, where you can stuff yourself with large portions of well-prepared pasta, seafood, chicken, steak, or, on Wednesday evenings, Mexican food at the *Mad River Tavern*, Rte-49, one mile from I-93 Exit 28 (Mon–Fri from 3pm, Sat & Sun from 11.30am; ☎603/726-4290). The ⤞ *William Tell*, Rte-49, two miles from I-93 on the way to Waterville (☎603/726-3618; closed Mon & Tues), is a bit more expensive and less relaxed, serving upscale New England fare (with lots of seafood), and a few German specialities such as *sauerbraten* (entrées $16–32).

Lincoln and North Woodstock

Straddling opposite sides of I-93 at the start of the Kancamagus Highway, the twin towns of Lincoln and North Woodstock maintain relatively distinctive personalities while catering to both skiers and hikers. **NORTH WOODSTOCK**, a small-town mountain retreat at the intersection of routes 3 and 112, is the nicer and more low-key of the two, with an attractive row of restaurants and shops and a few good places to stay. **LINCOLN**, a continuous strand of strip malls and condominium-style lodgings on Rte-112, is less appealing, though it makes a good base from which to explore the western White Mountains. Neither town offers much in the way of things to see – the real attraction lies in getting out of town and into the forest.

Information

The enormous **White Mountains Visitor Center**, in North Woodstock near I-93 (July–Sept 8.30am–6pm; Oct–June 8.30am–5.30pm; ☎603/745-8720 or 1-800/FIND-MTS, ⓦwww.visitwhitemountains.com), gives lodging advice and sells maps of the region, including the excellent *White Mountains Map Book* ($16.95), which gives 400 trail descriptions and is essential if you plan on embarking on any extended hiking expeditions.

Accommodation

The best place to look for cheap **motels** is along US-3, between North Woodstock and Franconia Notch. There are also many solid opportunities for **camping**, the closest being *Russell Pond Campground*, off Tripoli Road, 3.7 miles east off I-93 Exit 31 ($20; ☎603/726-7737). It's near a pond and has 86 well-maintained spots and hot showers. A bit farther away, *Lost River Valley Campground*, on Rte-112 four miles west of I-93 (☎1-800/370-5678, ⓦwww.lostriver.com), has over a hundred sites (from $25) and a playground. Five miles farther down Rte-112, *Wildwood Campground* ($16; see *Russell Pond* contacts for info) offers 26 wooded sites with picnic tables.

Econolodge Inn & Suites 381 US-3, just off I-93 Exit 33, Lincoln ☎603/745-3661 or 1-800/762-7275, ⓦwww.econolodgeloon.com. Slightly more luxurious than the *Franconia Notch Motel*, this is good value, with a pool, sauna, Jacuzzi, and exercise room. ❸

Franconia Notch Motel 572 US-3, 1 mile from I-93 Exit 33, Lincoln ☎1-800/323-7829, ⓦwww.franconianotch.com. Standard, clean lodging along a tacky strip of US-3. ❸

Indian Head Resort 664 US-3, Lincoln ☎1-800/343-8000, ⓦwww.indianheadresort.com. An unpretentious resort motel with plenty of facilities and outdoor activities. Its restaurant

serves fairly good comfort food, with some veggie selections, and is popular with coach tours. ❻

Wilderness Inn 57 Main St (US-3) at Courtney St, one block south of Rte-112, North Woodstock ☎603/745-3890 or 1-888/777-7813, ⓦwww.thewildernessinn.com. Guests in the seven antique-furnished rooms here enjoy sumptuous breakfasts. ❹

Woodstock Inn 135 Main St (US-3), North Woodstock ☎603/745-3951 or 1-800/321-3985, ⓦwww.woodstockinnnh.com. Comfortable rooms, an outdoor Jacuzzi, and reasonable ski/lodging packages in the center of town. ❺

Loon Mountain Resort

Lincoln and North Woodstock really come to life in the winter, when enthusiastic skiers and snowboarders come to hit the slopes at nearby **Loon Mountain Resort** (lift tickets $73 per day; ☎603/745-8111 or 1-800/229-LOON, ⓦwww.loonmtn.com), two miles east of I-93 on the Kancamagus Highway. The trails here, while good for intermediate skiers, might not be challenging enough for the expert. During the summer, Loon offers many of the activities you'd expect from a large full-service resort – swimming, tennis, aerobics, horseriding, mountain-biking – and if you'd like a nice view of the surrounding terrain without going through the trouble of hiking or biking up the mountain, you can ride the **gondola** to the top ($14). You can rent **mountain bikes** for $36 per day at the base of the mountain. In Lincoln, you can rent bikes at Rodger's Ski Outlet, on Main Street (☎603/745-8347); true to its name, you can rent winter equipment as well.

Clark's Trading Post

A mile north of North Woodstock along US-3, local landmark **Clark's Trading Post** (daily mid-June to Aug 9.30am–6pm; weekends only May to mid-June & Sept to mid-Oct 10am–5pm; $15; ☎603/745-8913, ⓦwww.clarkstradingpost .com) is a much-touted, family-friendly collection of tourist attractions, including a haunted house, an 1890s fire station, bumper boats, the "Old Man" climbing tower, and a thirty-minute black bear show, in which a group of bears do tricks – just the ticket if you're in the mood for some hokey tourist fodder, or have kids in tow.

Eating, drinking, and entertainment

There's ample selection of places to eat and drink in both Lincoln and North Woodstock. The **Papermill Theatre Company**, in the Mill at Loon Mountain just off Main Street, Lincoln (☎603/745-2141, ⓦwww.papermilltheatre.org), presents "Broadway blockbusters" and children's plays during the summer.

Clement Room 135 Main St (Rte-3), *Woodstock Inn*, North Woodstock ☎603/745-3951. Feast on duck, veal, seafood, or steak. Definitely North Woodstock's most elegant dining experience. Daily 5.30–9.30pm (entrees $17–28).
GH Pizza & Greek Restaurant 75 Main St (Rte-112), Lincoln ☎603/745-6885. *GH* has the best gyros and pizza in town – though the dining room's not particularly interesting.
Gordi's Fish and Steak House 260 Main St (Rte-112), in Depot Mall, Lincoln ☎603/745-6635. Catering to the jovial after-ski crowd, *Gordi's* is more upscale than other Lincoln restaurants, specializing in seafood and grilled meats ($12–17).

Kimber Lee's Deli Depot Mall, Main St (Rte-112), Lincoln ☎603/745-3354. Filling sandwiches ($6.50) and deli salads, as well as decent bagels for breakfast (from $4).
Truant's Taverne 98 Main St (US-3), North Woodstock ☎603/745-2239. A cozy, affordable restaurant serving well-cooked American grill fare. Entrees $14–17.
Woodstock Station 135 Main St (US-3), *Woodstock Inn*, North Woodstock ☎603/745-3951. A great place to go for drinks – the beer is brewed on the premises, there's an outdoor deck in summer, and nearly every night there's live entertainment. The range of hearty food includes pizza, pasta, steak, seafood, and burritos.

The Kancamagus Highway

Affording plenty of panoramic glimpses of tree-coated peaks and valleys, the **KANCAMAGUS HIGHWAY** (Rte-112), running 34 miles from Lincoln east to Conway, is one of only two National Scenic Byways in northern New England. The road is named for **Chief Kancamagus** ("Fearless One"), whose grandfather united seventeen Indian tribes into the Penacook Confederacy in 1627. Chief Kancamagus struggled to maintain peace between the Indians and pioneering whites, but bloodshed eventually forced the tribes to scatter to the north.

You can easily pass a pleasant afternoon driving the length of "the Kank," parking briefly at a couple of designated lookouts, but you'll gain a better appreciation of the area if you take a hike or have a swim in the Swift River, which runs parallel to the highway for twenty miles. Better still, plan to camp at one of the many well-maintained campgrounds along the road (see opposite). No motorist services are available, so don't forget to pick up your supplies and gas in Lincoln or Conway.

Hiking and camping along the Kancamagus

On the west side of the highway, the best place for information on hiking and camping is the **White Mountains Visitor Center** (see p.435). On the east side, it's the **Saco Ranger Station** (Mon 9am–4.30pm, Tues–Sun 8am–4.30pm; ☎603/447-5448), at the start of the highway at Rte-16 in Conway, which is staffed with friendly and knowledgeable rangers.

Among the particularly good **hikes** along the Kancamagus are the **Lincoln Woods Trail** (5 miles east of I-93), an easy 6.8-mile round-trip hike to the Franconia Falls, which are good for swimming and sunbathing; the **Greeley Ponds Trail** (9 miles east of I-93), a 4.5-mile round-trip to a dark aqua body of water; the **Sabbaday Falls Hike** (19 miles east of I-93), a half-mile walk to waterfalls, which, although stunning, are not suitable for swimming; and the **Mount Potash Hike** (20 miles east of I-93), a more difficult 3.8-mile round-trip to the summit of Mount Potash (2681ft). About ten miles outside of Conway lies **Mount Chocorua**, whose little curved granite notch on the top makes it one of the most distinctive mountains in the area. It's a strenuous climb (7.6-mile round-trip), and will take several hours to reach the summit via the **Champney Brook Trail** (8 miles return). The top – that notch you can see – is particularly dazzling, as you emerge from the forest to a stretch of pure rock. The views, including the "Presidential Range," are, of course, stunning.

The six **campgrounds** (☎603/447-5448, ⓦwww.campsnh.com) along the highway are usually populated with vacationing families, and most crowded in July and August. Traveling from west to east, you'll hit *Hancock* (5 miles east of Lincoln; open year-round) and *Big Rock* (also year-round, 2 miles farther). Fourteen miles east is *Passaconway*, near the historic Russell Colbath House, and another 1.5 miles on, *Jigger Johnson*. A stretch of 6.5 miles brings another pair: *Covered Bridge* and *Blackberry Crossing*, on opposite sides of the road near the Lower Falls, a jumble of boulders abutting small waterfalls. Just six miles from here is the terminus of the highway at Conway.

▲ Sabbaday Falls

The campgrounds are rather primitive affairs (many have vault toilets), and sites are allocated on a first-come-first-served basis. Fees are $16 per site (*Hancock* and *Jigger Johnson* are $20), and aside from the noted exceptions, are open mid-May to mid-October. Call ☎1-877/444-6777 to book ahead at *Covered Bridge*, the only campground that accepts reservations.

Franconia Notch and around

North on I-93, past Lincoln and North Woodstock, the White Mountains continue to rise dramatically above either side of the freeway, boldly announcing their presence with enormous tree-covered peaks. **Franconia Notch State Park** is the highlight of the area, with miles of hiking trails and several natural wonders. Past the White Mountains, farther north along I-93, the landscape flattens into an inviting valley dotted with former resort towns turned quiet mountainside retreats, such as pleasant **Franconia**, secluded **Sugar Hill**, sleepy **Bethlehem**, and the largest town in the area, **Littleton**.

Franconia Notch State Park

Headed towards Canada, I-93 and the more leisurely US-3 merge briefly as they pass through **Franconia Notch State Park** (☎603/823-8391). Though it's dwarfed by the surrounding national forest, and split in two by the noisy interstate, the park, which features excellent hiking and camping, has several sights that are well worth a visit.

From the **Flume Visitor Center**, I-93 Exit 33 (daily May to late Oct 10am–5pm; ☎603/745-8391), where there is a helpful information desk about the whole park, a cafeteria, and a gift shop, you can walk 1200 yards or ride the shuttle bus to the short trail that leads through the narrow riverbed gorge, otherwise known as the **Flume** (entry $12). Formed nearly 200 million years ago and discovered in 1808 by 93-year-old "Aunt" Jess Guernsey, the 800-foot-long gorge (with 70 to 90ft-high cliffs) has been fitted with a wooden walkway that weaves across cascading falls and between towering granite walls. With the rumbling water echoing through the misty crevice, it's more impressive than you might expect, though during high season the crush can be overwhelming. You can walk back to the bus stop from the top of the gorge, or return to the visitors' center on foot via a scenic trail (the whole loop is two miles). From the visitors' center parking lot, the 1.7-mile **Mount Pemigewasset Trail** leads up a moderate incline to the 2557-foot summit of Mount Pemigewasset, affording views of the Franconia Range.

The Old Man of the Mountain and Cannon Mountain

Two miles north on I-93, you can take the exit to the **Basin**, a curious 25,000-year-old, 20-foot-wide granite pothole that catches a cascading waterfall. From the Basin, a marked trail links with the **Cascade Brook Trail**, traversing 2.4 miles to **Lonesome Pond**.

Four miles north of the Basin on I-93, Exit 34B leads to the former viewing site of the **Old Man of the Mountain**, a natural rock formation known for its semblance to an old man's profile. Having inspired scores of photographs, appeared on New Hampshire's license plate, and served as the state emblem since 1945, it succumbed to gravity and slid off the mountain in 2003. A **museum** and elaborate **monument** of five giant granite stones are in the works to honor the "old man" – something may be open by late 2010 (see ⓦ www.oldmanofthemountainlegacyfund .org), but until then there's nothing to see.

Just to the north, state-owned **Cannon Mountain** offers rides to the top of its 4180-foot peak in an **Aerial Tramway** (daily late May to mid-Oct 9am–5pm; $12 round-trip, $10 one-way), displaying panoramic views of the mountains that are especially impressive – and popular – during the early fall foliage season. During the winter, Cannon Mountain (℡603/823-8800, ⓦwww.cannonmt .com; lift tickets $64) offers some of the more challenging **alpine skiing** terrain in the state. You can learn about the history of New England skiing, browse a collection of old ski equipment and photos, and watch a ski documentary at the **New England Ski Museum**, next to the tramway (daily 10am–5pm, closed April; free; ℡603/823-7177, ⓦwww.skimuseum.org). If you'd rather hike to the top of the mountain, take the slightly difficult, roughly two-mile **Kinsman Ridge Trail** from the southwest corner of the tramway parking lot. An equally rewarding, but shorter and less strenuous half-mile hike leads to **Artists Bluff** overlooking Echo Lake; the trail begins in the parking area on the north side of Rte-18, across from the Peabody Base Lodge (I-93 Exit 34C). At **Echo Lake** you can swim, rent a canoe ($10 per hr), or just enjoy the short stretch of sand (daily mid-June to early Sept 10am–5.30pm; $4).

Practicalities

As well as the Flume Visitor Center (see opposite), you can get advice about outdoor activities in the park from the *Lafayette Place Campground* off I-93 (mid-May to mid-Oct; ℡603/271-3628; $24), which, despite being a bit close to the interstate, is a good place to **camp**. The quieter sites are along the western edge of the grounds where car noise is minimal.

Franconia

FRANCONIA, a friendly village on I-93 just north of Franconia Notch and the White Mountains, began attracting summer vacationers, such as literary notables Nathaniel Hawthorne and Henry Wadsworth Longfellow, soon after railroad tracks made the town accessible in the mid-nineteenth century. Today, skiers and leaf-peepers come in droves to check out the area's fall foliage and snow-covered slopes. The **Franconia Notch Chamber of Commerce** (℡603/823-5661, ⓦwww.franconianotch.org) runs an information booth on Main Street (mid-May to mid-Oct Wed–Sun 10am–6pm), with 24-hour access to maps and pamphlets.

Accommodation

Horse & Hound Inn 205 Wells Rd, off Rte-18 south of Franconia ℡603/823-75501 or 1-800/450-5501, ⓦwww.horseandhoundnh.com. Beautifully renovated 1830 farmhouse with eight old-fashioned, cozy rooms and a pine-paneled dining room; all rooms come with private bath, but TV is shared in the lounge. ⑤

Franconia Inn 1300 Easton Valley Rd (Rte-116) ℡603/823-5542 or 1-800/473-5299, ⓦwww .franconiainn.com. A 31-bed inn two miles south of Franconia, with great views, a relaxing porch, and an excellent restaurant; it's a good cross-country ski base, too. ⑥

Fransted Campground Rte-18, Franconia ℡603/823-5675, ⓦwww.franstedcampground .com. This family-oriented campground is a developed site with private streamside tent sites. Open mid-May to mid-Oct; $31 for a standard tent site.

Gale River Motel 1 Main St, Franconia ℡603/823-5655 or 1-800/255-7989, ⓦwww.galerivermotel.com. Slightly cheaper lodgings than others nearby, this sweet little ten-room motel has a heated outdoor pool, hot tub, and home-made chocolate-chip cookies. Two cottages sleep four to six people. ④

Lovetts Inn Rte-18, Sugar Hill ℡603/823-7761 or 1-800/356-3802, ⓦwww.lovettsinn.com. *Lovett's*, peacefully set at the foot of Cannon Mountain, is a 1794 Cape Cod-style home complete with swimming pool, a comfortable common area, cozy rooms, an excellent restaurant, and charming staff. ⑥

Sugar Hill Inn 116 Rte-117, Sugar Hill
☎ 603/823-5621, ⓦwww.sugarhillinn.com.
This posh secluded inn is ideal for romantic
getaways, with antique-filled rooms, fireplaces, and
mountain views (and free wi-fi). ❽
Sunset Hill House 231 Sunset Hill Rd, Sugar
Hill ☎ 603/823-5522 or 1-800/786-4455,

ⓦwww.sunsethillhouse.com. This country inn
is in a fine location on a quiet hill, and all
the uniquely decorated rooms have mountain
views. The romantic dining room features
gourmet meals like maple-glazed salmon with
caviar. ❺–❾

The Town

Modest attractions in town include the tiny **Franconia Heritage Museum**,
553 Main St (May–Oct Thurs–Sat 1–4pm; free; ☎ 603/823-5000, ⓦwww
.franconiaheritage.org), proudly displaying tools, antiques, and various objects
scooped up locally in an 1880 farmhouse, while the even smaller **Iron Furnace
Interpretive Center** (always open) displays iron-making objects related to the
1840 brick furnace opposite, looming across the river like a medieval ruin (the
furnace itself is off-limits).

The town is best known, however, as the one-time home of poet **Robert
Frost**. After owning a small farm in Derry, and residing for a bit in England,
Frost settled here in 1915 at age 40. You can visit his old home, now known
as the **Frost Place**, at Ridge Road off Bickford Hill Road one mile south on
Rte-116 (July to mid-Oct Wed–Mon 1–5pm; June weekends only; free,
suggested donation $5; ☎ 603/823-5510, ⓦwww.frostplace.org). The poet
lived here with his wife and children for five years and wrote many of his
best-known poems, including *The Road Not Taken*. Memorable largely for the
inspiring panorama of mountains in its backdrop, the house is now a Center
for Poetry and the Arts, with a poet-in-residence, readings, workshops, and a
small display of Frost memorabilia, such as signed first editions and photographs. There's a short **nature trail** complete with placards displaying Frost's
poetry and signs that supposedly mark the exact spot certain poems were
composed. A longer and more rewarding hike begins 3.4 miles south of
Franconia on Coppermine Road off Rte-116, following the **Coppermine
Trail** to the beautiful **Bridalveil Falls** cascading eighty feet. The wooden
Coppermine Shelter, near the end of the 2.5-mile excursion, is a good spot
to camp, although there are no facilities. For advice on **bike routes** in the
area and to rent bikes ($19 per day), stop in at the Franconia Sport Shop, 334
Main St, Franconia (☎ 603/823-5241).

Eating

The Franconia region is not known for fine **dining**, although many of the inns
and B&Bs in the area serve excellent (if expensive) food in dining rooms that
welcome non-guests.

Dutch Treat 317 Main St, Franconia
☎ 603/823-8851. Purveyors of nutritious
home-made organic breads, muffins, and
croissants.
Franconia Inn 1300 Easton Valley Rd (Rte-116)
☎ 603/823-5542. The inn offers elegant first-class
service in its candlelit dining room, and features
well-prepared steak and seafood dishes. See also
accommodation review, p.439.
Lovetts Inn Rte-18, Sugar Hill
☎ 603/823-7761. Some of the best gourmet food
in the area, including well-prepared classics such

as grilled salmon and stuffed chicken breast.
Entrees go for about $25, and reservations
are a good idea. See also accommodation
review, p.439.
Polly's Pancake Parlor I-93 Exit 38,
Rte-117, Sugar Hill ☎ 603/823-5575.
Polly's might be in the middle of nowhere, but it's
well worth the trip if you love pancakes ($7 for 3).
The original menu – around since 1938 – has
since been supplemented by healthier options.
Open early May to Oct 7am–3pm.

Littleton

Northwest of Franconia along I-93, **LITTLETON**, straddling the Ammonoosuc River, has a compact Main Street that's lined with attractive old brick buildings and the largest population in the area (6000). Though there's really not much to see, the town is a good place to find reasonably priced accommodation, and strolling Main Street will while away an hour or so. Stop at **Chutter's**, 43 Main St (Mon–Thurs 9am–6pm, Fri & Sat 9am–8pm, Sun 10am–6pm; ☎603/444-5787), which holds the *Guinness Book of World Record* title for Longest Candy Counter (at 111ft), good for some goofy fun: grab a paper bag and start filling from the 600-odd jars of chocolate nuts, malted milk balls, fruit sours, and bubble gum.

Practicalities

The **Littleton Area Chamber of Commerce** (☎603/444-6561, ⓦwww .littletonareachamber.com) has an info booth (late May to mid-Oct Mon–Fri 9am–5pm) downtown across from *Thayer's Inn*. The Forest Service runs the **Ammonoosuc Ranger Station**, Trudeau Road, 1.2 miles off Rte-302, near Bethlehem (Mon–Fri 7.30am–4pm; ☎603/869-2626), particularly good for backcountry help.

As a general rule, nearby **Bethlehem** is the place to go for superior **accommodation**, while Littleton has a number of reasonably priced places to stay. *Thayer's Inn*, 111 Main St, Littleton (☎603/444-6469 or 1-800/634-8179, ⓦwww.thayersinn.com; ④) is a creaky but comfortable local landmark, having hosted the likes of Richard Nixon and Ulysses S. Grant, while the *Hampton Inn*, 580 Meadow St (Rte-302) at I-93 Exit 42 (☎603/444-2661 or 866/579-0037, ⓦwww.littletonhotel.com; ⑥), is the best of the motels outside town. In Bethlehem, rich wood floors and furnishings reflect the elegance of *Mulburn Inn*, an English Tudor at 2370 Main St (☎603/869-3389 or 1-800/457-9440, ⓦwww.mulburninn.com; ⑥), and the *Adair Country Inn*, 80 Guider Lane (☎603/444-2600 or 1-888/444-2600, ⓦwww.adairinn.com; ⑧) features deluxe antique-furnished rooms, sweeping views, and an impeccable staff.

Dining is usually a fairly casual affair in these parts, like at the *Littleton Diner*, 145 Main St in Littleton (☎603/444-3994), or at *Rosa Flamingo's*, 2312 Main St in Bethlehem (dinner daily, lunch Sat & Sun only; ☎603/869-3111), which has some decent Italian dishes to its credit and also serves as a lively place to grab a cocktail.

Crawford Notch and around

The ease with which US-302 now crosses the middle of the mountains belies the effort that went into cutting a road through **Crawford Notch**, a twisty and awe-inspiring pass halfway between the Franconia area and Conway. The main man-made attraction on the route is the magnificent **Mount Washington Hotel**, which stands in splendid isolation in the wide valley known as **Bretton Woods**. A few miles east lies the **Mount Washington Cog Railway**, probably the most romantic way of getting to the summit of Mount Washington.

Mount Washington Hotel

At the grand opening of the **Mount Washington Hotel**, US-302, Bretton Woods (☎603/278-1000 or 1-800/258-0330, ⓦwww.mountwashingtonresort .com; ⑨) in the summer of 1902, Joseph Stickney reputedly exclaimed, "Look at me gentlemen … for I am the poor fool who built all this!" Its glistening white

▲ Mount Washington Hotel

facade, capped by red cupolas and framed by Mount Washington rising behind it, has barely changed since then. In its heyday, a stream of horse-drawn carriages brought families up from the train station, deliberately located at a distance to increase the sense of grandeur. Displays in the lobby commemorate the **Bretton Woods Conference** of 1944, which laid the groundwork for the post-war financial structure of the capitalist world, by setting the gold standard at $35 an ounce (it was well over $900 in 2008), and creating the International Monetary Fund and the World Bank.

Restoration by a group of investors who purchased the decaying building and surrounding property in 1991 has ensured that the cruise-ship-sized hotel remains marvelously – if somewhat eerily – evocative of past splendor, with its quarter-mile terrace, white wicker furniture, grand dining room, and 24-carat views. None other than Babe Ruth reputedly got sauced in the former speakeasy downstairs – fittingly known as the "Cave" because of its faux-rocky walls – before sauntering to the indoor pool and taking a fully clothed dip; these days, the bar hosts more mellow live entertainment nightly, though the rock walls are still there. In the 1990s the resort opened its doors to the winter ski crowd for the first time, and in the summer there are weekend golfing, tennis, and spa packages, along with an equestrian center and miles of hiking trails. Also on the property, the 33-room *Bretton Arms Inn* (☎603/278-1000; ❽), has slightly more affordable rooms, while the *Lodge* (same phone; ❹), across US-302 from the *Mount Washington*, has even cheaper modern rooms.

Mount Washington Cog Railway

It took a hundred men three years to build the **Mount Washington Cog Railway**, off Mount Clinton Road at the base of Mount Washington. Completed in 1869, its rickety trains lumber up gradients as steep as 38 percent – the second steepest railway in the world – while consuming a ton of coal and a thousand gallons of water and spewing out clouds of smoke. It's a truly momentous experience, inching up the steep wooden trestles while avoiding descending showers of coal smut, though anyone who's not a train aficionado might find it not really worth the money. The three-hour round-trip (with a scant twenty minutes at the summit) costs $59, and trains leave hourly (late May to late Oct; call for other dates and times; ☎603/278-5404 or 1-800/922-8825, ⓦwww.thecog.com). The Cog also runs uphill in the winter season (Nov–March) to access one-mile-long groomed downhill ski trails ($31).

If you'd rather **hike** up Mount Washington, the **Ammonoosuc Ravine Trail** starts in the Cog parking lot, hooking up with the Crawford Path at the AMC's Lakes of the Clouds hut (see box, p.447). If you're in good physical shape, the 4.5-mile trip takes roughly four and a half hours one-way. This hike is not for the faint-hearted, however, due to the extremely unpredictable weather once you near the peak (for more, see p.448). Take warm clothing (temperatures above the treeline can be fifty degrees colder than at the base), plenty of water and food, and do not hesitate to turn back if the weather turns foul; several hikers die of exposure to the harsh weather atop the mountain every year. Another option, the **Jewell Trail**, also originating in the parking lot, zigzags up the north shoulder to the summit in 4.6 miles (roughly 4hr).

Crawford Notch State Park

Within White Mountain National Forest, **Crawford Notch State Park** is split in two by US-302, which winds through the dramatic gap formed by the steep slopes of Mount Field to the west and Mount Jackson to the east. Discovered in 1771 when hunter Timothy Nash was tracking a moose through the woods, the notch was soon recognized as a viable route through the White Mountains. A railroad was completed at great expense in 1857.

The old **Crawford Notch Depot** along US-302, three miles south of *Mount Washington Hotel* and across from tiny Saco Lake, is now a helpful AMC-maintained **information center** and store selling backcountry necessities (late May to mid-June Fri–Sun 9am–5pm; mid-June to mid-Oct daily 9am–5pm; ☎603/278-5170). Go to the nearby Highland Center if it's closed (see p.444). The Depot is also on the **Conway Scenic Railway** (see p.445). Recommended **hikes** in the area include the **Mount Willard Trail**, a 1.6-mile (1hr) jaunt up to dizzying views of Crawford Notch at Mount Willard (2865ft) starting at the Crawford Notch Depot.

Three miles south, in the shadow of Mount Willey (4285ft), the **Willey House Historic Site** is named for a family who lived here and died in a terrible landslide in 1826 – the ruins are still visible. Next door a shack serves as the tiny **park visitors' center** (mid-May to mid-Oct daily 10am–4pm; ☎603/374-2272), selling maps and trail guides and offering advice on camping; they also maintain a small café.

Another three miles south on US-302, the **Arethusa Falls Trail** is a steep 1.5-mile hike to the highest falls in the state (200ft). A half-mile back up US-302, the *Dry River Campground* (May to mid-Dec; ☎603/271-3628; $23)

Hiker shuttle service

The AMC runs a hiker **shuttle service** daily from June through mid-September (and weekends through mid-Oct) with vans that make stops at many of the trailheads and AMC lodges throughout the Mount Washington region (call ☎603/466-2727 for information, reservations strongly recommended). Stops include the Crawford Notch Depot (see above) and the Pinkham Notch Visitor Center (see p.447). Drivers will stop anywhere along the route if requested, and the trips cost $16, no matter how long you ride.

has 36 wooded sites, thirty of which are by reservation only; note that there is no water after mid-October. AMC's Highland Center at Crawford Notch (℡603/278-4453, ⊛www.outdoors.org), next to Crawford Notch Depot, is a great choice year-round: an environmental education center which also offers lodging in a shared room for $40–64 or double rooms (cheapest with shared bath) for $81–141. Hearty alpine breakfasts and family-style dinners are included, as are a full roster of activities like guided hikes and game nights, and free L.L. Bean gear for use in AMC programs (at a small fee for your private use).

The Mount Washington Valley

There are no clear boundaries to the **Mount Washington Valley**, though it is generally thought to center around the crowded town of **North Conway**, a once-beautiful mountainside hamlet now overwhelmed by outlet malls and other modern encroachments. In general, the region is more congested than the western White Mountains, but if you can avoid the crowds that cram their cars onto the mile-long strip of Rte-16/US-302 south of downtown North Conway, you'll find there's plenty to do around here. In the winter, there are numerous trails for **cross-country skiers**, while in the summer **rock climbers** test their skills on the highly popular **Cathedral Ledge**. North of North Conway, the pace slows and opportunities for solitary hiking and camping increase. Peaceful **Jackson** has excellent cross-country skiing trails and an unusual concentration of first-class lodging and eating, presenting a good opportunity to spoil yourself amid the quiet greenery.

North Conway

Surrounded on all sides by shopping malls, factory outlets, and fast-food chains, **NORTH CONWAY** is a major resort town and consequently fairly depressing, with the strip south towards Conway particularly over-developed. Fortunately, there is some relief in the center, a village core that manages to maintain a hint of rustic backcountry appeal – you'll also find plenty of budget accommodation and places to eat here.

The **Mount Washington Valley Chamber of Commerce** in North Conway (℡603/356-3171 or 1-800/367-3364, ⊛www.mtwashingtonvalley.org) on Rte-16, near the station, has a reservation service (Mon–Fri 9am–5pm) and information on local attractions (daily 9am–6pm).

Accommodation

If you can bear the traffic, crowds, and kitsch, North Conway offers plenty of bargains when it comes to places to stay, and all the major **motel** chains line Rte-16.

1785 Inn 3582 White Mountain Hwy (Rte-16) ℡603/356-9025 or 1-800/421-1785, ⊛www .the1785inn.com. Though it's right on the main road, the spacious rooms, gracious hosts, delicious food, and mountain views here make this a good base from which to explore (or to shop). Shared bath ❹, private bath ❺.

Albert B. Lester Memorial Hostel 36 Washington St, Conway ℡603/447-1001, ⊛www.conwayhostel .com). Nearby Conway boasts a great HI/AYH hostel,

which has particularly clean dorm lodging for $23 per night and private rooms for $48.

Nereledge Inn 94 River Rd, off Rte-16 ℡603/356-2831 or 1-888/356-2831, ⊛www .nereledgeinn.com. Friendly and informal Colonial inn with wood stoves and fireplaces near skiing, the Saco River, and rock climbing. ❺

North Conway Grand Hotel 72 Common Court, off Rte-16 in Settlers' Green Outlet Village ℡603/356-9300 or 1-800/648-4397,

@www.northconwaygrand.com. This vast, modern hotel has 200 rooms and is a good bet for late arrivals with no reservations. Rooms are spacious and equipped with microwave, cable, and fridge – you also get two pools, Jacuzzi, and all sorts of sports rentals on site. Reasonable rates online. ➎

Saco River Camping Area 1550 White Mountain Hwy (Rte-16) ☎603/356-3360, @www.sacorivercampingarea.com. Camping in the area (from $26) is available at this wooded and open site, nicely located along the Saco River, and well enough away from the highway. Open early May to mid-Oct.

School House Motel 2152 White Mountain Hwy (Rte-16), near the shopping outlets and Sunset Hill Rd ☎603/356-6829 or 1-800/638-6050, @www.schoolhousemotel.com. Probably the cheapest in town, with basic but adequate rooms, all with cable TV and free morning coffee. ➍–➏

Spruce Moose Lodge 207 Seavey St ☎1-800/600-6239, @www.sprucemooselodge.com. Another good base, this time for rock climbers and other outdoor types, occupying a quiet spot well off the main drag, with nine conservatively decorated rooms and five cottages. ➍

The Town

The centerpiece of downtown is the **North Conway Railroad Station**, a hulking brown and yellow 1874 Victorian structure that you can't miss along Main Street. From here, the **Conway Scenic Railway** (mid-April to late Dec, call for reservations and schedule; ☎603/356-5251 or 1-800/232-5251, @www .conwayscenic.com) runs antique steam trains to Bartlett (1hr 25min; $21 round-trip), Conway (55min; $13 round-trip), the Crawford Notch Depot (5hr; $44 round-trip), and the Fabyan Station in Bretton Woods (5hr 30min; $49 round-trip). The trains are especially worth the money in early fall, when the trees are at their peak – reservations are a must.

West of town along River Road, you can go for a swim at **Echo Lake** (not to be confused with the Echo Lake in Franconia Notch State Park) beneath the towering granite face of the White Horse Ledge (1470ft). Just north off West Side Road, scores of rock climbers test their skills on the wall of the steep, sheer faces of **Cathedral Ledge** (1150ft), the most popular spot for the sport in the state. Chauvin Guides in North Conway (☎603/356-8919, @www.chauvinguides .com) offer various **guided climbs** and lessons starting at $125. You might also check with **Eastern Mountain Sports** on Main Street in North Conway for guidance (☎603/356-5433). If you'd rather not spend hours (and lots of money) tethered to the cliff's sheer face, you can simply drive to the top, where you're presented with views of the entire area. Further north on West Side Road, you can hike to **Diana's Bath**, an easy half-mile walk to a mountain stream. For a longer and more challenging trek (elevation gain 2500ft), head to the top of **Mount Kearsarge** (3268ft) from the north side of Hurricane Mountain Road, one and a half miles east of Rte-16 at Intervale; it's a four- to five-hour round-trip (6 miles) that is rewarded with panoramic views.

Eating and drinking

1785 Inn 3582 White Mountain Hwy (Rte-16) ☎603/356-9025 or 1-800/421-1785, @www .the1785inn.com. Probably the best place to eat in North Conway, with its highly praised, expensive gourmet food, such as apple-wood smoked rabbit, and fine wines, with prices to match (entrees $18–30). Served in a dark, romantic dining room.

Bellini's 1857 Main St (Rte-16), Willow Place Mall ☎603/356-7000. You can get big portions of freshly prepared Italian dishes here, all served in an attractively decorated dining room. Dinner only, closed Tues.

Chef's Market 2724 Main St ☎603/356-4747. This cozy café has great sandwiches, pasta salads, and smoothies for lunch. Closed Tues.

Horsefeather's 2679 Main St (opposite the station on Rte-16) ☎603/356-6862. Top choice for a drink or entertainment, with live rock or Irish music at the weekends, in addition to what many consider to be the best burgers in town (from $7.55).

Shalimar 27 Seavey St ☎603/356-0123. For something a little spicier, check out this huge menu of reasonably priced authentic Indian dishes ($11–13), with a good selection of vegetarian specialities.

Jackson

With a high concentration of first-class lodgings and restaurants and hundreds of miles of trails within easy reach, **JACKSON** is one of the premier **cross-country ski** centers in the country. Indeed, the **Jackson Ski Touring Foundation**, 153 Main St (T603/383-9355 or 1-800/927-6697, Wwww.jacksonxc.org), with 158km of trails, has frequently been rated the number one cross-country ski area in the East. The trails run over rolling countryside, woodland terrain, mountain descents, and race-course areas, and are all perfectly maintained. In order to use them, you have to be a member of the Ski Touring Foundation. Day membership cost $19, and you can rent equipment for $16 a day (snowshoes for $12). On summer days, a great place to cool off is at **Jackson Falls**, which tumble down a stretch of boulders in the riverbed along Rte-16B.

If you're traveling with children, don't miss New Hampshire landmark **Story Land**, on Rte-16 south of Jackson (mid-June to early Sept daily 9am–6pm; early June & early Sept to mid-Oct Sat & Sun only 9am–5pm; $24; T603/383-9776), a colorful theme park, akin to a miniature Disneyland, with immaculately maintained grounds, rides such as the "Turtle Twirl" and "Bamboo Chutes," and lots of places for climbing. For any further information, contact the **Jackson Area Chamber of Commerce** (Mon–Fri 10am–4pm; T603/383-9356 or 1-800/866-3334, Wwww.jacksonnh.com) at the Jackson Falls Marketplace at the intersection of routes 16A and 16B.

Accommodation

Bernerhof Inn US-302, Glen T603/383-9132 or 1-800/548-8007, Wwww.bernerhofinn.com. Nine comfortable and elegant guestrooms, with conscientious service. There's also a pub and a gourmet restaurant on the first floor. ⑤–⑧
Inn at Thorn Hill Thorn Hill Rd, Jackson T603/383-4242 or 1-800/289-8990, Wwww.innatthornhill.com. A luxurious hillside inn with wraparound porch, designer furnishings, whirlpool tubs, and private cottages out back. Rates include breakfast, afternoon tea, and a three-course dinner at the inn's gourmet restaurant. ⑨
Village House 49 Main St (Rte-16A), Jackson T603/383-6666 or 1-800/972-8343,

Wwww.villagehouse.com. A pleasant B&B just beyond the covered bridge, with private baths and a great lap porch. ④
Wildcat Inn & Tavern 94 Main St (Rte-16A), Jackson T603/383-4245 or 1-800/228-4245, Wwww.wildcattavern.com. Cozy and unpretentious, the *Wildcat* is right in the center of town and has a comfortable ski-cabin feel. Especially popular in winter (as is the tavern). ⑥
Will's Inn US-302, Glen T603/383-6757 or 1-800/233-6780, Wwww.willsinn.com. Family-friendly, cheap, and perfectly satisfactory. Plus, there's a heated pool. ④

Eating, drinking, and nightlife

As You Like It Jackson Falls Marketplace, Jackson T603/383-6425. Great home-made coffee cake, cookies, pies, and bread, also deli sandwiches and panini ($3–7). Closed Mon & Tues.
Christmas Farm Inn 3 Blitzen Way, Rte-16B, Jackson T603/383-4313. A romantic, chi-chi restaurant, centrally located and good for special occasions. Dishes include honey soy-glazed salmon ($24) and herb-crusted rack of lamb ($31).
Red Parka Pub US-302, Glen T603/383-4949. A favorite place for a few drinks, some sports on the TV and excellent steaks, spare ribs (from $16) and

meatloaf ($14). The place hops especially during ski season and at weekends, when there's live music. Mon is open-mic night.
Shannon Door Intersection of routes 16 and 16A, Jackson T603/383-4211, Wwww.shannondoor.com. The town's long-standing Irish pub, with a suitably dark bar, plenty of Guinness, and live entertainment Thurs–Sun. Open from 4pm daily.
Wildcat Inn & Tavern 94 Main St (Rte-16A), Jackson T603/383-4245, Wwww.wildcattavern.com. Gourmet country cuisine in the dining room and garden, while cheaper sandwiches

and appetizers are served in the less-formal couch-filled tavern, which often hosts a lively après-ski scene.

Yesterday's Rte-16A (next to *Wildcat*), Jackson ☎603/383-4457. Big, cheap American breakfasts are the order of the day here. Daily 7am–3pm.

Pinkham Notch and Mount Washington

Roughly ten miles north of Jackson along Rte-16, **PINKHAM NOTCH**, along the eastern base of towering **MOUNT WASHINGTON**, is the most jaw-dropping mountain pass in the White Mountains, with a reputation for serious outdoor activity. The Appalachian Trail and a number of other remote wilderness trails converge here, making the Notch overrun with adventurers during the summer. Luckily, the crowds don't detract too much, and they're easy to forget once you've made your way into the forest.

The best place to get information on hiking, camping, and a whole range of other outdoor activities is at the AMC's **Pinkham Notch Visitor Center**, Rte-16 (daily 6.30am–10pm), where you can buy the indispensable and exhaustive *AMC White Mountain Guide* ($24.95), good hiking maps, supplies, and basic

AMC mountain huts

The Appalachian Mountain Club (AMC) operates eight delightfully remote mountain huts in New Hampshire along a 56-mile stretch of the Appalachian Trail, each about a day's hike apart. Generally offering full service in season (June to mid-Oct, exceptions noted below), including two hot meals per day, for $98 Saturdays and $89 other nights (Lonesome Lake is $79 Sun–Fri), they are a fairly popular choice – reservations are required (call ☎603/466-2727). All the huts except Lakes and Madison offer self-service lodging (without sheets, heat, or food) for $30, but only out of season (Carter Notch is the exception). For additional information, contact the Appalachian Mountain Club, 5 Joy St, Boston, MA 02108 (☎617/523-0655, ❂www.outdoors.org).

Carter Notch (full service June to mid-Sept; self-service all year). Accessible via the Nineteen Mile Brook Trail and the Wildcat Ridge Trail, both originating along Rte-16 north of Jackson.

Galehead. On the Garfield Range, this is the most remote hut in the chain. Accessible via the Gale River Trail and the Garfield Ridge Trail, both originating off US-3 south of Bethlehem.

Greenleaf. Accessible via the Greenleaf Trail and the Old Bridle Path Trail, off of I-93 in Franconia Notch State Park (see p.438).

Lakes of the Clouds (full service June to mid-Sept). On the southern shoulder of Mount Washington, this is the highest and most popular hut. Accessible via the Ammonoosuc Ravine Trail and Crawford Path, off Mount Clinton Road, just south of Bretton Woods.

Lonesome Lake. Good family destination, with daily hikes and activities. Accessible via the Cascade Brook Trail, Dodge Cutoff Trail, Fishin' Jimmy Trail, Lonesome Lake Trail, and the Whitehouse Trail, west of I-93 in Franconia Notch State Park.

Madison Spring (full service June to mid-Sept). Great sunsets from a perch above the Madison Gulf. Accessible via the Crawford Path, Gulfside Trail, Westside Trail, and the Valley Way Trail, southwest of Gorham off US-2.

Mizpah Spring. On Mount Clinton above Crawford Notch. Accessible via the Mount Clinton Trail and the Webster Cliff Trail near Crawford Notch State Park along US-302.

Zealand Falls. Open all year, near waterfalls and good backcountry skiing. Accessible via the Zealand Trail, off Zealand Road south of Twin Mountain.

camping/mountaineering equipment. The center organizes workshops, guided trips, and programs that cost anywhere from a couple of dollars to a couple hundred dollars. They also serve three hearty family-style **meals** per day in a huge, noisy dining room at the visitors' center; the fixed-price dinner ($17) includes salad, soup, vegetables, home-made breads and dessert, an entree, and plenty of conversation. As if that weren't enough, the club maintains the *Joe Dodge Lodge* (☏603/466-2727, ⊛www.outdoors.org), where you can get bunks or double rooms with shared bath and meals for $64 ($51 without meals). The *Dolly Copp Campground* (☏603/466-2713; $20) has 177 **campsites** and is open from mid-May through mid-October.

A half-mile up the road from the visitors' center, local favorite **Wildcat Mountain** (☏603/466-3326 or 1-800/255-6439, ⊛www.skiwildcat.com) offers some of the best and most challenging **skiing** (lift tickets $65 per day, with additional days $39 each) in the state during the winter, as well as **mountain-biking** and **gondola rides** to the 4062-foot summit of Wildcat Mountain (daily: mid-June to mid-Oct 10am–5pm; late May to mid-June weekends only; $15).

Mount Washington

The 6288-foot **MOUNT WASHINGTON**, the highest peak in the northeastern US, was named for George Washington before he even became president. Over the years, other mountains in this "Presidential Range" have taken the names of Madison, Jefferson, and even Eisenhower – though it should be noted that Mount Nancy was called that long before the Reagans were in the White House, and Mount Deception just happens to be close by.

Driving to the summit

On a clear day, you can see all the way to the Atlantic and into Canada from the top of Mount Washington, once called the "second greatest show on earth" by P.T. Barnum, but the real interest in making the ascent lies in the extraordinary severity of the weather up here. The wind exceeds hurricane strength on over a hundred days of the year, and in 1934 it reached the highest speed ever recorded anywhere in the world – 231mph.

On the way to the top, you pass through four distinct climate zones, with century-old fir and ash trees so stunted as to be below waist height, before emerging amid Arctic tundra. The drive up the **Mount Washington Auto Road** (three miles north of Pinkham Notch) ascending eight miles up the east side of the mountain from Rte-16 (early May to late Oct – weather permitting – 7.30am–6pm in peak season; call ☏603/356-0300 to check weather conditions), is not quite as hair-raising as you may expect, although the hairpin bends and lack of guard-rails certainly keep you alert. There's a $20 toll for private cars and driver (plus $7 for each additional adult and $5 for kids), which includes a "This car climbed Mt. Washington" bumper sticker and a short audio-tour cassette. Specially adapted minibuses, still known as "stages" in honor of the twelve-person horse-drawn carriages that first used the road, give narrated **tours** (daily 8.30am–5pm; $26, 90min round-trip; ☏603/466-3988, ⊛www.mtwashingtonautoroad.com) as they carry groups of tourists up the mountain. Driving takes thirty or forty minutes under normal conditions. The record for the annual running race up the mountain, held each June, currently stands at 56 minutes 41 seconds.

Hiking to the summit

Some fifteen **hiking trails** – in addition to the Appalachian Trail itself – lead to the summit of Mount Washington. The most direct route on the eastern side of the mountain is the **Tuckerman Ravine Trail**, which originates at the AMC

Pinkham Notch Visitor Center (see p.447) and traverses the often snow-filled Tuckerman Ravine, a popular place for backcountry skiing. If you're in good condition, the 4.1-mile trail can be completed in about four and a half hours, and it is possible to hike up and back in one day, but don't forget that the weather at the top of the mountain is unpredictable, and potentially dangerous. You should not hesitate to turn back should any signs of a storm become apparent.

For hikes to the summit that originate on the west side of the mountain, see p.443. You can also ride to the top on the coal-fired steam train of the **Mount Washington Cog Railway**, originating in Bretton Woods – detailed on p.442. Incidentally, unless otherwise posted, you can **camp** anywhere on Mount Washington below the treeline two hundred feet from the trail and water sources, and a quarter-mile from any road or facility.

The family-oriented **Great Glen Trails Outdoor Center** at the foot of the Auto Road (☎603/466-2333, ⓦwww.greatglentrails.com), can provide information about trails and conditions, as well as renting **bikes** ($30 for 4hr), and arranging whitewater trips ($65); it becomes a ski center in winter (trail pass $18 per day; ski rentals $20 per day).

The summit

Once on the summit, you'll see the remarkable spectacle of buildings actually held down with great chains. The utilitarian (but much stronger) **Sherman Adams Summit Building** (mid-May to mid-Oct 8am-6pm; ☎603/466-3347), serves as the headquarters of Mount Washington State Park, and contains a cafeteria, restrooms, and a gift shop, as well as the new **weather observatory** (☎603/356-2137, ⓦwww.mountwashington.org). Scientists here research the effects of wind, ice, and fog; their various findings, exhibits on the environment and history of the mountain, are displayed at the **Mount Washington Museum** downstairs (daily 9am–6pm; $3). You can climb the few remaining feet to the actual summit point, sadly surrounded with cement structures – including a large viewing platform – and smothered by photo-snapping tourists balancing themselves on lichen-covered rocks. The **Tip Top House**, once a hotel for wealthy travelers erected in 1853, has been turned into an unremarkable historic museum (June–Oct daily 10am–4pm; free), providing "a link between the mountain's past and present" through antique furniture and a restored interior.

Gorham and beyond

Spread out along the northern reaches of the White Mountain National Forest, working-class **GORHAM** can be used as an inexpensive base from which to visit Mount Washington and other nearby peaks. Basic **accommodation** can be found at the *Hikers Paradise Hostel*, 370 Main St (☎603/466-2732 or 1-800/470-4224, ⓦwww.hikersparadise.com), where you can get a bed, sheets, full kitchen, and full (shared) bath for $19 (you'll need to mail a check to make advance reservations). For **camping**, the *Moose Brook State Park*, Jimtown Road, off Rte-2 in Gorham (late May to mid-Oct; ☎603/466-3860; $23 per site), has 62 secluded tent sites. Reasonably priced home-made Italian **food** can be had at *La Bottega Saladino's* at 152 Main St (☎603/466-2520), while *Yokohama*, at 288 Main St (closed Mon; ☎603/466-2501), offers reasonably priced Asian (and American) specialities.

Up north on Rte-16, **DIXVILLE NOTCH** is a quiet hideaway centered on the sprawling turn-of-the-century *Balsams Hotel* (☎603/255-3400 or 1-800/255-0800 in NH or 1-800/255-0600 outside NH, ⓦwww.thebalsams.com; ⓸),

First-in-the-nation presidential primary

The mountains of the "Presidential Range" might have made the state's name in tourist guides, but New Hampshire and the tiny mountain village of **DIXVILLE NOTCH** are really famous for a quite different presidential connection: the primary election. Since 1952, New Hampshire has been the first state in the US to hold its presidential primary, which more or less marks the start of the winnowing process to see who each party's presidential candidates will be, and Dixville Notch has had the privilege of being the first town in the state – and therefore the nation – to report its results. Every four years, the tiny electorate of Dixville Notch (year-round population: 32) files into the ballroom at the *Balsams Hotel* (guestrooms: 202) just before midnight on election day, to cast votes at the stroke of midnight. Since 1968, Dixville Notch has never failed to predict the Republican nominee, and the state as a whole has a good record for picking the candidates eventually nominated by both Democrats and Republicans to run for president. Due to the high media profile of the primary, as well as the state's compact size, campaigning is based very much on knocking on doors and actually meeting the people.

another of the last grand White Mountains resort hotels. Built in the 1860s, the enormous palace has 202 guestrooms, its own lake, 15,000 acres of land, a golf course, and a ski area. Rates include all meals and use of facilities.

For detailed information on other lodging and eating options in these farthest reaches of the state, contact the **Androscoggin Valley Chamber of Commerce**, 961 Main St in Berlin (Mon–Fri 8.30am–4.30pm; ☎603/752-6060 or 1-800/992-7480, ⓦwww.androscogginvalleychamber.com). You'll find the chamber at the 1853 Brown Company House, site of the **Northern Forest Heritage Park** (Mon–Fri 9am–4pm; $6; ☎603/752-7202, ⓦwww.northernforestheritage.org), which features a logging museum, summer lectures, river tours (Tues–Sat 2pm & 5pm; $15), and other special events.

The **North Country Chamber of Commerce**, on US-3 north of Colebrook (daily 8am–6pm; ☎603/237-8939 or 1-800/698-8939, ⓦwww .northcountrychamber.org), is just across the Connecticut River from Vermont, at the end of Rte-26.

8

Maine

CHAPTER 8 # Highlights

* **Portland** As cosmopolitan as the state gets, coastal Portland has everything to offer, save big-city aggravation and high prices. See p.464

* **Rockland** With its incredible arts scene and working harbor, this hip little enclave is a great spot for viewing a Wyeth or sailing a windjammer. See p.488

* **Stonington harbor** Among Maine's most beautiful inlets, Stonington is filled with boats and offers exploratory kayaking, biking, and even puffin-sighting trips. See p.499

* **Acadia National Park** Bike, boat, hike, climb, or simply commune with nature in the state's recreational mecca. See p.505

* **Bethel** Close to the White Mountains, remote Bethel is the quintessential New England small town and a hub for winter and summer outdoor adventures. See p.515

* **Katahdin** In the deepest heart of Maine, the beginning of the Appalachian Trail sits atop this 5300-foot peak. See p.523

▲ Downtown Portland

Maine

M AINE more than lives up to its unofficial motto of being "the way life should be." Filled with lobster shacks, dense forests, scenic lakes, and seaside enclaves, the state offers ample opportunities for exploring, or just for lounging in Adirondack chairs and watching the leaves change color – there's a little something for everyone here.

As large as the other five New England states combined, Maine's year-round population barely equals that of Rhode Island. In theory, therefore, there's plenty of room for all the visitors who flood the state in summer; in practice, though, most people head straight for the **coast**. At the southern end of the coastline, the beach towns of **Ogunquit** and **Old Orchard Beach** quickly lead up to Maine's most cosmopolitan city, **Portland**. The **Mid-Coast**, between Brunswick and Bucksport, is characterized by its craggy shores, windswept peninsulas, and sheltered inlets, though the towns of **Boothbay Harbor** and **Camden** are certainly busy enough. Beyond the gorgeous Blue Hill Peninsula, **Down East** Maine is home to **Acadia National Park**, the state's most popular outdoor escape, in addition to the bustling summer retreat of **Bar Harbor**. Farther north, you'll find foggy weather and exhilarating, increasingly uninhabited scenery, capped by the candy-striped lighthouse at **Quoddy Head**, the easternmost point in the United States.

You can only really begin to appreciate the size and space of the state, however, farther north or inland, where vast tracts of mountainous forest are dotted with lakes and barely pierced by roads. This region is ideal territory for hiking and canoeing, particularly in **Baxter State Park**, site of the northern terminus of the Appalachian Trail. In the northwestern part of the state, closer to the New Hampshire border, a cluster of ski resorts are scattered about the mountains, including **Sugarloaf USA**, one of New England's finest ski areas.

Maine's climate is famously harsh. In **winter**, the state is covered in snow, and often ice. Officially, **summer** is spread between two long weekends – Memorial Day (the last Mon in May) and Labor Day (the first Mon in Sept) – though temperatures don't really start to rise until June or even July. This is nonetheless Maine's most popular season, with its start heralded by sweet-corn and bustling lobster shacks and its end marked by the wild blueberry harvest. Brilliant **fall colors** begin to spread from the north in late September, when, unlike elsewhere in New England, off-season prices apply, and the cool weather is great for apple-picking, leaf-peeping, or simply curling up with a blanket and a book.

Some history

Although in many ways inhospitable – the **Algonquin** called it the "Land of the Frozen Ground" – Maine has been in contact with Europe since around 1000 AD, when the **Vikings** first explored its shores. European fishermen began setting up summer camps here about five hundred years later.

North America's first agricultural **colonies** were also in Maine: Samuel de Champlain's **French** Protestants near Mount Desert Island in 1604, and an **English** group that survived one winter at the mouth of the Kennebec River three years later. In the face of the unwillingness of English settlers to let them farm in peace, local Indians formed alliances with the French and, until as late

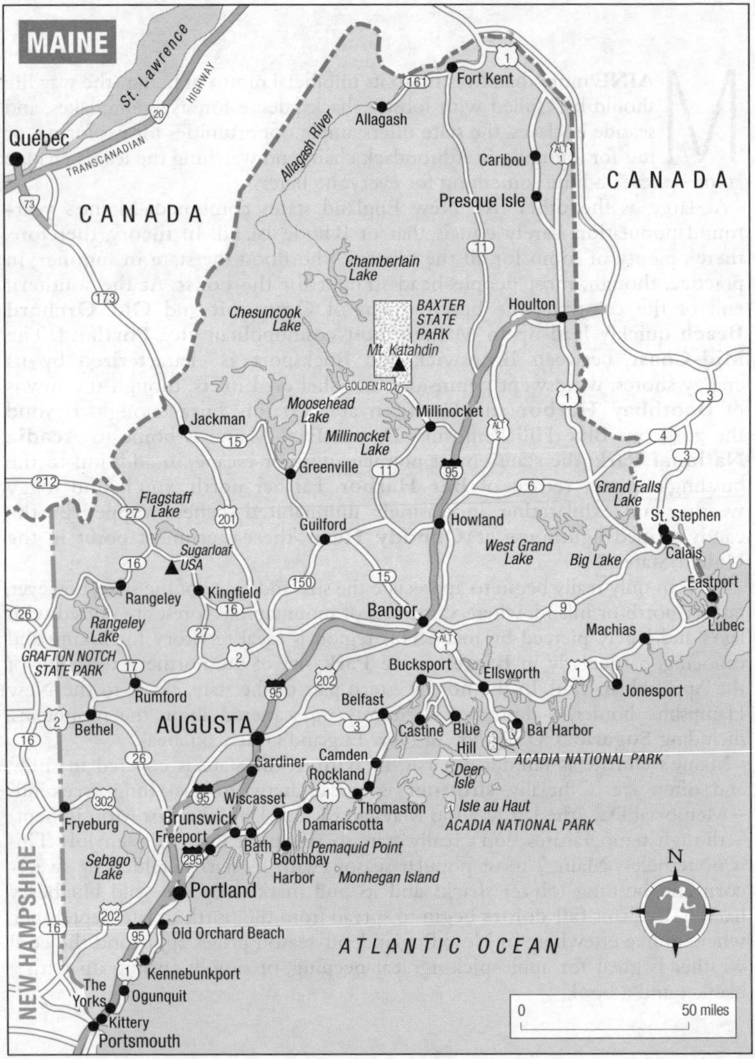

Finding your way in Maine

With public transport generally nonexistent, you'll most likely want to **drive** to Maine. The most enjoyable route to follow is **Rte-1**, which runs within a few miles of the coast all the way from the border with New Hampshire to Canada. In each town, Rte-1 usually becomes a named street; sometimes several names are used. All this may make your destination difficult to locate, but locals will inevitably be able to provide assistance. You should be prepared for traffic backups at the height of summer, particularly in Ogunquit, Camden, and Wiscasset. If you're in a hurry, **I-95** offers speedy (though tolled in parts) access to the Portland area and beyond. In the interior, roads are quiet and views spectacular; many of the northernmost routes are gravelled and belong to the lumber companies. At any time of year, bad weather can render these roads impassable; be sure to check before setting off.

Whatever your destination, be sure to pick up a **DeLorme Maine Atlas** (sold state-wide in bookstores, or online at ⊛ www.delorme.com) – this gazetteer is a lifesaver when trying to orient yourself along local byways. DeLorme's headquarters, in Yarmouth, are also worth a visit (see box, p.474).

as 1700, regularly drove out streams of impoverished English refugees. By 1764, however, the official census claimed that even Maine's black population was more numerous than its Native Americans.

At first considered part of Massachusetts, Maine became a separate entity only in 1820, when the Missouri Compromise made Maine a free, and Missouri a slave, state. In the nineteenth century, its people had a reputation for conservatism and resistance to immigration, manifested in anti-Irish riots. Today, the **economy** remains heavily based on the sea, although many of those who fish also farm. Lobster fishing in particular has defied gloomy predictions and continued to boom, as evidenced by the many thriving **lobster pounds**.

The southern coast

Stretching between the two shopping hubs of **Kittery** and **Freeport**, Maine's **southern coast** is the state's most settled region. Blessed with its best **beaches** – indeed, most of its beaches – this area was already a popular summer vacation spot by the mid-nineteenth century, when trains began bringing city-dwellers up from Boston and New York or down from Canada. The eleven-mile strip of sand at **Old Orchard Beach** is still one of the finest in the country, attracting huge crowds in July and August, while more attractive **Ogunquit**, the other popular resort town in the area, is only slightly less overrun in summer, with a long-established artistic community, a lively gay and lesbian scene, and a collection of excellent restaurants. Though commercial development has definitely had an impact on the region, you can still find attractive old towns with plenty of historical interest, such as **York**, the first chartered city in America, and beautiful **Kennebunkport**, best known as the summer residence of former presidents George Bush and George W. Bush. Further north, the coast becomes more varied and prone to peninsulas, harbors, inlets, and islands. At the mouth

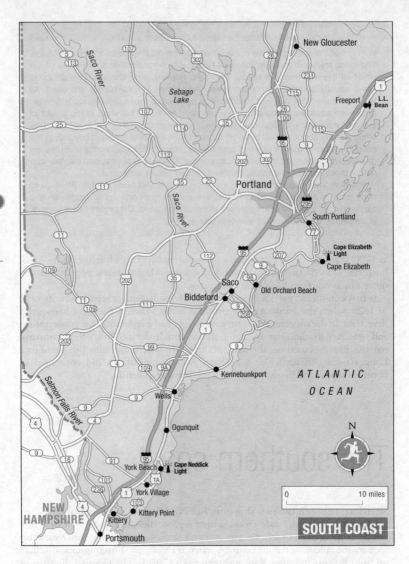

of the Fore River, Maine's largest city, **Portland**, has a hip, twenty-something population, innovative restaurants, and a dynamic arts scene.

Kittery

KITTERY is only just in Maine, right across the Piscataqua River from Portsmouth, NH, and it makes for an excellent place to get oriented, namely at its **information center** at the intersection of I-95 and Rte-1 (daily: summer 8am–6pm; rest of year 9am–5.30pm; ☎207/439-1319), which has brochures, weather information, and volunteers who can give insiders' tips and help make reservations. If you follow Rte-1 through Kittery, you'll pass a string of **outlet shops** (☎1-888/ KITTERY, ⓦwww.thekitteryoutlets.com), which offer good deals on clothing from companies like Banana Republic, and J. Crew, although the atmosphere lags behind that of rival outlet hotspot Freeport, about 75 minutes up the road.

The small bit of land south along Rte-103 called Kittery Point makes for a pleasant drive, taking you a few miles and a thousand cultural light years away from all the shopping. It also brings you past the 1714 First Congregational Church, Maine's oldest house of worship, to a rocky cliff overlooking the Portsmouth Naval Shipyard on Seavey Island, where the treaty ending the Russo-Japanese War of 1905 was signed. Kittery was a major shipbuilding center in the mid-eighteenth century, when the *Ranger* sailed out of a Kittery shipyard under the command of Revolutionary War hero John Paul Jones. For a detailed look at the city's maritime and cultural history, including a fourteen-foot model of the *Ranger*, stop off at the Kittery Historical and Naval Museum, on Rogers Road near the intersection of routes 1 and 236 (June to mid-Oct Tues–Sat 10am–4pm; $3; ☎207/439-3080).

Practicalities

Near the history museum is one of Kittery Point's best places to eat, *Chauncey Creek Lobster Pier*, 16 Chauncey Creek Rd (☎207/439-1030), whose fair-priced, BYOB seafood menu is served on a deck overlooking picturesque Pepperrell Cove. At 36 Walker St (Rte-103) lies newcomer *Loco Coco's Tacos*, (☎207/438-9322), while long-time local favorite *Bob's Clam Hut* (☎207/439-4233), a campy fish eatery open since 1956, is at 315 Rte-1 in Kittery. For dinner, swing by sleek *Anneke Jans*, 60 Wallingford Square (☎207/439-0001, ⓦwww.annekejans .net), which serves stylish bistro dishes such as seared sea scallops with potato purée ($27). The best places to stay in town are the inviting *Portsmouth Harbor Inn & Spa*, 6 Water St (☎207/439-4040, ⓦwww.innatportsmouth.com; ❼–❽), and the clean, adequate *Coachman Motor Inn*, right near the outlets at 380 Rte-1 (☎207/439-4434, ⓦwww.coachmaninn.net; ❻).

The Yorks

The pleasant **YORKS**, a few miles north of Kittery on routes 1 and 103, are actually five separate entities: York, York Village, Cape Neddick, scenic York Harbor, and lounge-worthy York Beach. This cumulative network of villages

---

Surfing Maine's southern coast

Every year a small number of hardy souls brave the North Atlantic to pursue the unlikely pastime of **surfing** off Maine's coast. If you're used to surfing anywhere else, beware: the water here in January can dip below 40°F, daunting even with the newest developments in wet-suit technology. Though wave and tide conditions are usually best in fall and winter, on certain warm summer days the waves come up and the crowds swell with the tides. The best spots are at **Higgins Beach**, south of Portland in Scarborough, **Fortune Rocks** in Biddeford, **Gooch's Beach** in Kennebunk, **Long Sands** in York, **Old Orchard Beach**, and **Wells Beach**. For equipment **rentals** and **lessons**, contact Aquaholics, 166 Port Rd (Rte-35) in Kennebunk (☎207/967-8650), or Liquid Dreams Surf, 731 Main St (Rte-1) in Ogunquit (☎207/641-2545).

– sometimes referred to as "York" – bears the distinction of being America's first chartered city, incorporated in 1642 (though it was demoted to the status of "town" in 1670). Its past is well preserved in the seven buildings that comprise the **Old York Historical Society** in York Village (mid-June to early Sept Mon–Sat 10am–5pm; $10 for all buildings, $5 for one; ☎207/363-4974). **Jefferd's Tavern**, 5 Lindsay St, offers a starting point for the tour of the old buildings, with a visitors' center where tickets are sold. Foremost among the structures is the **Old Gaol**, which really is old – it's the earliest British colonial public structure still standing on its original site, dating from 1653. It was used as Maine's primary prison until the Revolution, then continued to confine York County prisoners until the Civil War. Inside, a museum reconstructs the jailer's quarters and has displays on some of the prison's more colorful criminals. Old York also includes the **Old Schoolhouse**, which houses exhibits on education in the eighteenth century; the **John Hancock Warehouse and Wharf**, which has maritime displays in the original Customs House; and the **Old Burying Yard**, where it's rumored that a grave covered with a stone slab was thus protected to prevent its occupant, reputedly a witch, from escaping. In fact, the slab was actually placed there by her husband to prevent cattle from grazing on her grave.

As well as its historical attractions, the Yorks boast several fine beaches, a vintage arcade (the endearing Fun-O-Rama at York Beach), and a number of invigorating cliff walks. Head beyond Old York, for example, towards **Nubble Light**, at the end of Shore Road, off Rte-103, at York Beach, where you'll find one of Maine's most striking lighthouses, situated on an island of its own. If you have little ones in tow, or if you're interested in jumping up and down, be sure to visit the **Wiggly Bridge**, a local landmark just off Rte-1A on Lilac Lane (Rte-103) in York Harbor. This flexible bridge enables you to jump wildly while watching the tide go in or out beneath you.

Practicalities

All four villages have their points of interest linked by a trolley service ($1; ☎207/363-9600, ⓦwww.yorktrolley.com). The Yorks host some fine **accommodation**, best of which is the *York Harbor Inn*, on Rte-1A in York Harbor (☎207/363-5119 or 1-800/343-3869, ⓦwww.yorkharborinn.com; ⑦–⑨), which incorporates five beautiful properties, four of which are right across from the shore. It also has a sunlit fine-dining restaurant, as well as the *Ship's Cellar Pub*, for burger-and-beer cuisine. The *Morning Glory Inn, at* 120 Seabury Ave in York Harbor (☎207/363-2062, ⓦwww.morninggloryinnmaine.com; ⑧), has three lovely rooms, all with wi-fi and private porches, while the cheerful *Katahdin Inn*, 11 Ocean Ave Extension in York Beach (☎207/363-1824, ⓦwww.thekatahdin.com; ③–⑤), is right on Short Sands Beach and has inexpensive, shared-bath rooms. The new *Best Western York Inn*, 2 Brickyard Lane, just off Rte-1 in York (☎207/363-8903, ⓦwww.yorkinnmaine.com; ⑤), is a good, clean motel; there are also a number of cheap motels and B&Bs along Long Beach Avenue.

As for **food**, good seafood spots abound. Two tasty, casual eateries are the *Lobster Cove Restaurant*, 756 York St (Rte-1A) in York Harbor (☎207/351-1100), and the loveable *Cape Neddick Lobster Pound*, right on the water on Shore Road in Cape Neddick (☎207/363-5471). People love to line up for hot dogs at *Flo's*, 1359 Rte-1, also in Cape Neddick (closed Wed) – be sure to get the special sauce. In York Village's main square, *Rick's*, 240R York St (☎207/363-5584; closed Mon), opens early for big breakfasts and laid-back lunches. Up the hill from Nubble Light, *Brown's Ice Cream*, 232 Nubble Rd (☎207/363-1277), has been scooping some of the state's best flavors for over forty years (head straight for the cookie dough), while out by the Fun-O-Rama at York Beach local institution *The Goldenrod*, 2 Railroad Ave (☎207/363-2621), has been churning out saltwater taffy for more than a hundred years. It currently resembles the New York Stock Exchange of candy, replete with frenzied customers trying to get their order heard. The view is safer from the sidewalk, where you can quietly watch the hypnotizing taffy machine pull and wrap the "Goldenrod Kisses." Opposite *The Goldenrod* and yet light years away, quality-wise, is Boston chef Lydia Shire's *Blue Sky* (☎207/363-0050); if you don't feel like splurging on the stylish entrees, at least have a drink at the sleek marble bar. Also not to be missed is condiment purveyor Stonewall Kitchen's flagship store, 2 Stonewall Lane, just off Rte-1 (☎207/351-2712), which has fresh lobster BLTs and salads to take to the beach alongside its signature displays of mustards, jams, and chocolate sauces.

Ogunquit

Approaching **OGUNQUIT** from the south, it's easy to understand why Maine's Native Americans named the small oceanside town "beautiful place by the sea." In the nineteenth and twentieth centuries, Ogunquit enjoyed fame as the vacation spot of choice for such folks as Bette Davis and Tommy Dorsey; today it's also known for its gay and lesbian scene, arguably the best in New England outside of Provincetown, Massachusetts. The town also has a reputation as an artists' colony, and is home to a scenic art museum and handful of well-tailored galleries. Ogunquit has a little bit of a privileged attitude, but streets with names like "Whistling Oyster Lane" and "Ho Hum Hill" point to the playful character underneath.

Arrival, information, and local transport

The **Ogunquit Chamber of Commerce**, just south of Ogunquit Village on Rte-1 (daily 9am–5pm in summer; rest of the year Mon–Fri 9am–5pm, Sat 10am–3pm; ☎207/646-2939 or 1-800/639-2442, ⓦwww.ogunquit.org), has brochures and operates as a fully staffed **information center**. If you prefer a car-free vacation, **Amtrak's** *Downeaster* pulls into neighboring Wells five times daily from Boston's North Station (one-way $19; ☎1-800/USA-RAIL, ⓦwww.amtrakdowneaster.com); in summer, there is a **hotel shuttle** that can ferry you from the station to downtown ($10; 48hr advanced reservation required; ☎1-800/696-2463, ⓦwww.shorelineexplorer.com). Traffic can be terrible, so if you do drive it may be a good idea to use the **trolley** ($1.50), which connects with the York Trolley to the south as well as Perkins Cove, Ogunquit Square, and the beach, continuing north to connect with the Wells/Kennebunkport Trolley.

Wheels and Waves, in Wells, two miles north of Ogunquit Square on Rte-1 (☎207/646-5774), rents **bikes** and has maps of local cycling trails. If you're looking to get out on the water, a number of **sailing cruises** depart from Perkins Cove. Both *Finestkind* (☎207/646-5227) and *The Silverlining* (☎207/646-9800) run several cruises daily from May to October; the *Ugly Anne* ($45 half-day, $75 full day; ☎207/646-7202) and the *Bunny Clark* cater to deep-sea fishing enthusiasts ($45 half-day, $75 full day; ☎207/646-2214); and the *Deborah Ann* charters whale-watching expeditions from mid-May to October (☎207/361-9501).

Accommodation

The pier at the beach is home to some decent **hotels**, though they tend to be high-priced due to their proximity to the ocean. Shore Road has a number of good-quality **B&Bs** within walking distance of the beach, town square, and Marginal Way. The stretch of Rte-1 north of Ogunquit Square has cheap **motels**, and once you get to the town of **Moody**, a mile out, prices drop precipitously. The best **camping** in the area is at *Pinederosa Campground*, 128 N Village Rd in Wells (℡207/646-2492; $28), or *Dixon's Campground* (℡207/363-3626; $30), 1740 Rte-1 in Cape Neddick.

Beachmere Inn 62 Beachmere Place, off Shore Rd ℡207/646-2021 or 1-800/336-3983, ⓦwww .beachmereinn.com. Beautiful rooms in a turreted old wooden hotel overlooking the ocean. The inn also operates a few more modern, motel-style buildings nearby. **❼–❾**

Dunes on the Waterfront 518 Main St (Rte-1) ℡207/646-2612, ⓦwww.dunesonthewaterfront .com. Situated on twelve beautiful acres, this well-loved hotel has clean and basic rooms, many with water views, in addition to twelve two-bedroom cottages that sleep four or five ($270–295 in season). Open May–Oct only. **❺–❽**

Gazebo Inn 527 Main St (Rte-1) ℡207/646-3733, ⓦwww.gazeboinnogt.com. An Ogunquit favourite renowned for its friendly innkeepers, tasty breakfasts, beautiful rooms (many in a renovated barn), pool, Jacuzzi, gardens, and even a trolley stop at its doorstep. **❻–❽**

Meadowmere Resort 74 S Main St (Rte-1) ℡207/646-9661, ⓦwww.meadowmere.com. This spacious resort inn has appealing, eco-friendly rooms, three pools, a fitness center, spa, restaurant, and happy guests. **❽**

The Nellie Littlefield House 27 Shore Rd ℡207/646-1692. Individually designed, well-appointed B&B rooms in a pretty house just outside the square. **❽**

Seacoast Motel 40 Rte-1 N ℡207/646-2187. Basic, clean motel north of the square. **❻**

Terrace by the Sea 11 Wharf Lane ℡207/646-3232, ⓦwww.terracebythesea.com. The gorgeous garden will lure you into this pretty motel on the water's edge. Many rooms have spectacular ocean views. Open May–Oct only. **❻–❽**

Wells-Ogunquit Resort Motel 203 Rte-1 N ℡207/646-8588 or 1-800/556-4402. Impeccably kept modern motel rooms with cable TV and refrigerators, plus barbecue setups. Open May–Oct only. **❺–❽**

The Town

Ogunquit Square, along Main Street (Rte-1), is the center of town, home to most of the town's best restaurants, coffeehouses, and quirky shops. East of the square, Beach Street leads over the Ogunquit River to **Ogonquit Beach**, one of Maine's finest, with three miles of sugary white sand. The water is always freezing, but the sun is mellow and the sand great for sunbathing. Parking near the pier costs $5, but there's a better way to access the beach: take Rte-1 north of Ogunquit Square and go right on Ocean Street, which leads to a less populated area of the beach – and cheaper parking.

Perkins Cove, a pleasant knot of restaurants and shops a few miles south of Ogunquit Square, is best reached by walking along **Marginal Way**, a windy path that traces the crescent shoreline from Ogunquit Beach. The two-mile trail offers unspoilt views of the Atlantic coast, particularly stunning in fall when the ocean undulates alongside the fiery foliage. The folk art, pottery, and jewelry shops in and around the cove warrant an hour's browse, and there are a few places to indulge in an ice cream or some saltwater taffy. A half-mile south of Perkins Cove at 543 Shore Rd is the **Ogunquit Museum of American Art** (July–Oct Mon–Sat 10.30am–5pm, Sun 2–5pm; $7; ℡207/646-4909), whose tiny space is blessed with a strong collection of nineteenth- and twentieth-century American art, including sumptuous seascapes by Marsden Hartley and Rockwell Kent, enhanced by the museum's sweeping ocean views.

The grounds feature a diverse sculpture garden, where grinning animals mingle with serene marble women.

Eating, drinking, and entertainment

You'll find the standard profusion of **seafood shacks** and restaurants all over Ogunquit, but the best eateries are in the town square and around Perkins Cove. There are also a couple of **bars** and gay clubs in town, offering occasional live musical acts, karaoke, and friendly piano-bar singalongs. For more serious entertainment, the **Ogunquit Playhouse**, along Rte-1 south of town (May–Oct; tickets ☏207/646-5511), has been called "America's foremost summer theater" for most of its seventy years, and usually attracts a few big-name performers each season.

98 Provence 262 Shore Rd ☏207/646-9898. Lovingly prepared French cuisine in a country chic cottage away from the bustle of downtown. Dinner only (entrees start at $23), reservations recommended.

Amore Breakfast 178 Shore Rd ☏207/646-6661. Deservedly popular breakfast nook with an Americana kitsch vibe and Bananas Foster French toast ($9).

Arrows Restaurant Berwick Rd, just outside Ogunquit Square ☏207/361-1100. Excellent, though expensive (mains $40) New American cuisine in a Victorian house surrounded by gardens. Reservations recommended. They also run *MC Perkins Cove*, a sleek bar and fish eatery right on Perkins Cove (☏207/646-6263).

Barnacle Billy's Perkins Cove ☏207/646-5575. An Ogunquit stand-by, with a casual café next door. The lobster and fried fish are a bit overpriced (particularly when you factor in the valet parking), but it's still a good spot.

Blue Water Inn 111 Beach St ☏207/646-5559. Right on the river and a stone's throw from the beach, the *Blue Water Inn* serves up fresh seafood at amazing prices, such as grilled haddock with rice and veggies ($18).

Fisherman's Catch 134 Harbor Rd, Wells Harbor ☏207/646-8780. Pleasingly located in a marsh with great water views, the *Catch* offers great fried clams, haddock, and chocolate cream pie. Open daily in summer 11.30am–9pm.

Five-O 50 Shore Rd ☏207/646-5001. With its buttery interior, creative New American cuisine, and adjacent first-rate lounge, *Five-O* makes for a good evening splurge. They also run the delightful *Caffe Prego* (44 Shore Rd, ☏207/646-7734), which serves panini sandwiches and home-made gelato at lunch and dinner.

Jonathan's 92 Bourne Lane ☏207/646-4777. Live entertainment – musical and otherwise – on weekends from April to Oct, with a decent restaurant serving seafood, pasta, and creatively prepared meats. Reservations recommended.

Joshua's Restaurant 1637 Rte-1, Wells ☏207/646-3355. Inside this unassuming chocolate-colored house chef Joshua Mather grills, sears, and sautés some of Maine's best cuisine. Many of the dishes use ingredients from his own farm. Dinner only (entrees start at $21; reservations recommended.

Maine Diner 2265 Rte-1, Wells ☏207/646-4441. Serving diner food with a regional twist, this place is famed for its lobster pie and great Indian pudding ($3). The vinyl booth ambience is somewhat dampened by the long waits and beeper system, however.

North to Portland

North of Ogunquit, the coastal route meanders on a bit, with distances between towns lengthening. In the thirty-or-so-mile drive up to Portland, the main points of interest are in **Kennebunkport** and **Old Orchard Beach**.

The Kennebunks

There's a reason former presidents **George Herbert Walker Bush** (known locally as "41") and **George W. Bush** summer in **Kennebunkport** – it's beautiful, historical, and full of places to eat that even Barbara approves of. Maybe it's because of these political bigwigs, but **THE KENNEBUNKS** – comprised of Kennebunkport ("the Port") and Kennebunk – often get dismissed as hoity-toity. However, this upscale vibe is more imagined than real, and though you can easily step it up here with martinis and heels, it's just as acceptable to kick back on the beach with flip-flops, a locally made soda, and freshly fried clams.

Arrival and information

As with other southern coastal Maine towns, a car-free vacation is possible via **Amtrak**'s *Downeaster*, which pulls into neighboring Wells five times daily from Boston's North Station (one-way $19; ☎1-800/USA-RAIL, @www .amtrakdowneaster.com); in summer, there is also a useful **hotel shuttle** from the train station to Kennebunkport ($14; 48hr advance reservation required; ☎1-800/696-2463, @www.shorelineexplorer.com). From here you can use the **trolley** ($1); which stops around town and also continues south, providing access to Ogunquit and the Yorks. As an alternative, there is an Enterprise Rent-A-Car at 2204 Rte-1 in Arundel (☎207/985-7493).

Accommodation

Bufflehead Cove Inn Bufflehead Cove Rd (off Rte-35), Kennebunk ☎207/967-3879, @www.buffleheadcove.com. Located on a peaceful private way right on the Kennebunk River, *Bufflehead Cove* is noted for its blissful scenery, stellar breakfasts, and friendly innkeepers. **❼–❾**

Captain Fairfield Inn 8 Pleasant St, Kennebunkport ☎1-800/322-1928, @www.captainfairfield .com. A stylish 1813 sea captain's home with plush, contemporary furnishings; it's also quite walkable to downtown and the beach. **❾**

Franciscan Guest House 26 Beach Ave, Kennebunk ☎207/967-4865, @www .franciscanguesthouse.com. Situated on the scenic grounds of a monastery (of all things), the *Guest House* is a pleasant, affordable place to stay, with tasty breakfasts and a casual vibe. No daily maid service. **❺–❽**

The Town

Fortunately, Kennebunkport has been blessed with beaches as well as bluebloods. The best is **Goose Rocks Beach**, about three miles north of town on King's Highway (off Dyke Rd via Rte-9). It's a premium stretch of expansive sand, though you will need a parking permit to park here ($6 daily, $25 weekly; call the Kennebunkport police ☎207/967-2454). Kennebunk is home to a trio of lovely beaches: Kennebunk, Mother's, and Gooch's, all of which are located on Beach Avenue off Rte-9 South. You will also need a permit to park at any of these ($15 daily, $25 weekly; available 6am–10pm from HB Provisions, 15 Western Ave, Kennebunk ☎207/967-5762). If you're staying in town, your lodging should provide you with a free beach pass – check when you make reservations. If you want to get beyond the beach and onto the water, the *First/ Second Chance* (☎207/967-5507) does whale-watching and scenic lobster trips out of Kennebunkport.

Near Goose Rocks Beach, the **Seashore Trolley Museum**, 195 Log Cabin Rd, off Rte-9 or Rte-1 (daily mid-May to mid-Oct 10am–5pm; $8; ☎207/967-2712, @www.trolleymuseum.org), holds a surprisingly engaging display on the history of the trolley in northern New England. You can take a twenty-minute ride on a vintage car through the Maine woods and see a collection of old trolleys from around the world, including the original New Orleans trolley that ran along Desire Street, made famous by the Tennessee Williams play *A Streetcar Named Desire*. The **Brick Store Museum**, 117 Main St in Kennebunk (Tues–Fri 10am–4.30pm, Sat 10am–1pm; $5 suggested donation; ☎207/985-4802, @www .brickstoremuseum.org), showcases archival tidbits related to Kennebunk heritage and is also worth a whirl, if only to see its elegant paintings of Kennebunk notables, sea captains, and ships. Keep an eye out for the depiction of Captain James Fairfield, whose portrait was found at sea but amazingly made it home because of the letter in his hand addressed to Kennebunk, ME (his house is now a beautiful B&B; see opposite). Another fun diversion is the tiny Tom's of Maine outlet store at 52 Main St, Kennebunk (☎207/985-6331); the pleasantly aromatic space sells slightly dinged toothpaste "seconds" for only $2. One last landmark, the yellow **Wedding Cake House**, 105 Summer St (Rte-35), is also worth a mention. Although closed to the public, the house's gorgeous carved buttresses and gingerbread swirls are definitely good for a photograph on the way to Dock Square in downtown Kennebunkport.

Eating and drinking

Eating in Kennebunkport doesn't necessarily require a second mortgage – there's a nice range of tempting eateries, from the extremely upscale to the lowly (and loved) clam shack.

Alisson's 11 Dock Square, Kennebunkport ☎207/967-4841. A fun, relaxed, crowd-pleasing place to hang out and chow on seafood.

Bandaloop 2 Dock Square, Kennebunkport ☎207/967-4994. *Bandaloop* serves creative dinner entrees ($16-25) with a range of home-made sauces amidst a funky, stylish atmosphere.

Bennett's 200 Sea Rd (Rte-9), Kennebunk ☎207/967-5401. Amazing sub sandwiches to take to the beach, plus home-made sodas. May–Oct only.

Cape Arundel Inn 208 Ocean Ave, Kennebunkport ☎207/967-2125. You can glimpse the Bush compound while sipping a martini from *Cape Arundel's* elegant patio.

Clam Shack Just before the Kennebunkport bridge, Kennebunk ☎207/967-3321. With fried clams endorsed by Rachael Ray and Barbara Bush, and whoopee pies favored by Martha Stewart, the *Clam Shack* lives up to the hype with stellar fried fish and lobster rolls served from its takeout window.

Nunan's Lobster Hut 9 Mills Rd (Rte-9), Cape Porpoise ☎207/967-4362. Near Goose Rocks Beach, this lovable, casual eatery is the place to go for boiled lobster dinners. May–Oct only.

The Ramp 77 Pier Rd, Cape Porpoise ☎207/967-8500. Downstairs from the swanky *Pier 77* restaurant, this petite bar packs a lively punch with unbelievable water views and a cozy design that evokes the inside of a ship.

Old Orchard Beach

During the late nineteenth and early twentieth centuries, **OLD ORCHARD BEACH** ("OOB," in local parlance) stood alongside Ogunquit as a classic New England resort town, drawing upper-crust citizens from all over the eastern seaboard to stay in its massive seafront hotels. After World War II, its popularity and property values declined steadily, and in 1980 the town attempted to rectify the situation by refurbishing its decaying, carnivalesque pier. Almost overnight, OOB regained its status as a hotspot, though it resembled the spring break town of Fort Lauderdale more than the posh resort of old. Things have calmed down a bit, even if a slightly corny party atmosphere remains, especially along the waterfront.

The main draw here is the **beach**, a fantastic seven-mile strip of white sand. Unfortunately, its beauty means it can get intolerably crowded during summer and holiday weekends, in which case you'd do better to find another stretch of shore. The beach itself is free, but **parking** can be pricey; lots that charge $5–7 per day are reasonable. Just off the beach is the **pier**, which does a fireworks show on Thursdays at 9.30pm, and Palace Playland (☎207/934-2001), with classic amusement-park rides such as a Ferris wheel, bumper cars, and a vintage carousel dating from 1906. The entirety of **Old Orchard Street** (which leads down to the pier and beach) and **Grand Avenue** (which runs parallel to the ocean), are dotted with attractions, including instant-photo booths, cotton-candy vendors, and stores where you can design your own souvenir T-shirt. It's hopelessly tacky, but its campy carnival vibe does make an alternative to its sedate neighbors.

Practicalities

The **Old Orchard Beach Chamber of Commerce**, on First Street (Sept–June Mon–Fri 8am–4pm, July & Aug daily 9am–5pm; ☎207/934-2500, ⓦwww.oldorchardbeachmaine.com), operates an information center and can help arrange accommodation. **Amtrak**'s *Downeaster* pulls into OOB five times daily from Boston's North Station (one-way $24; ☎1-800/USA-RAIL, ⓦwww.amtrakdowneaster.com); the station is a two-minute walk from the beach. Although the town is packed with **places to stay**, it can fill to capacity; definitely call ahead for reservations. The seafront is dotted with pricey motels, though they sometimes have the advantage of owning a small strip of private beach – an invaluable respite from the maddening crowds. *White Lamb Cottages,* 3 Odessa Ave (☎978/815-6789, ⓦwww.whitelambcottages.com; ⑧), comprises a series of stand-alone beach cottages done up in 1940s-era style; the owners also run the well-appointed *Edgewater Inn,* right on the water at 57 W Grand Ave (☎207/934-3731 or 1-800/203-2034, ⓦwww.janelle.com; ⑧). The *Royal Anchor Resort,* 203 E Grand Ave (☎1-800/934-4521, ⓦwww.royalanchor.com; ⑦), and the *Echo Motel,* 8 Traynor St (☎207/934-5174, ⓦwww.echomotel.com; ⑨), are two other good, clean options also right on the beach.

Eating in OOB is not such a treat. You'll find an overabundance of pizza and burger joints crowding the main thoroughfares (in addition to the overrated *Pier Fries*), although there are a few nearby exceptions, most notably *Joseph's by the Sea,* 55 W Grand Ave (☎207/934-5044), whose deservedly expensive menu includes – but does not focus exclusively on – seafood, and the great ocean views are a bonus. *The Landmark Restaurant,* a stone's throw from the pier at 28 E Grand Ave (☎207/934-0156), does simple Maine fare like haddock with crumb topping. For cheap eats, head to *Rocco's,* 4 W Grand Ave (☎207/934-7552), which serves tasty New York-style slices. The *Oceanside Grille* at *The Brunswick,* 39 W Grand Ave (☎207/934-4873), is the place to go for drinking and dancing; there are also plenty of fun watering holes on the pier.

Portland

The largest city in Maine, with a population hovering around 65,000, **PORTLAND** was founded in 1632, at a superb point on the Casco Bay Peninsula. It quickly prospered, building ships and exporting its great supply of inland pines for use as masts. A long line of wooden **wharves** stretched along the seafront, with merchants' houses on the hillside above. When the **railroads** came, the Canada Trunk Line had its terminus right on Portland's quayside, bringing the produce of Canada and the Great Plains one hundred miles closer to Europe than it would have been at any other major US port. Some of the wharves are now taken up by sleek condo developments, though **Custom House Wharf** remains much as it must have looked when novelist Anthony Trollope passed through in 1861 and said, "I doubt whether I ever saw a town with more evident signs of prosperity."

As with much of New England, the good times didn't last through the mid-twentieth century. Grand Trunk Station was torn down in 1966, and downtown Portland appeared to be in terminal decline until a group of committed residents undertook the energetic redevelopment of the area now known as the

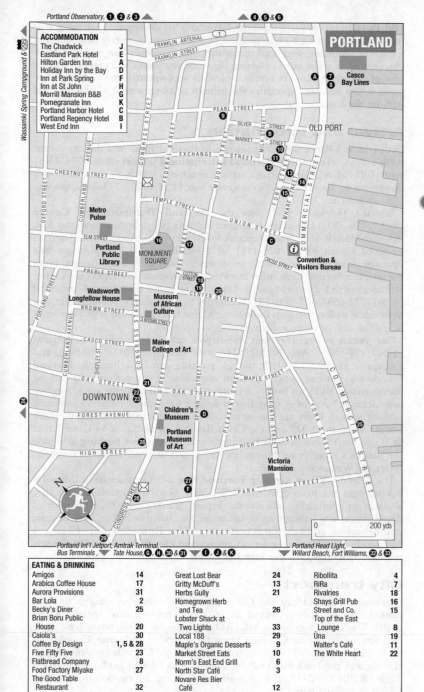

PORTLAND

Casco
Bay Lines

ACCOMMODATION

The Chadwick	J
Eastland Park Hotel	E
Hilton Garden Inn	A
Holiday Inn by the Bay	D
Inn at Park Spring	F
Inn at St John	H
Morrill Mansion B&B	G
Pomegranate Inn	K
Portland Harbor Hotel	C
Portland Regency Hotel	B
West End Inn	I

FRANKLIN ARTERIAL
FRANKLIN STREET

OLD PORT
PEARL STREET
SILVER STREET
MARKET STREET
MILK STREET
EXCHANGE STREET
FORE STREET
WHARF STREET
COMMERCIAL STREET

CHESTNUT STREET
OXFORD STREET
CUMBERLAND AVENUE
CONGRESS STREET
FEDERAL STREET
MIDDLE STREET

TEMPLE STREET
UNION STREET

Metro
Pulse

ELM STREET

Portland
Public
Library

MONUMENT
SQUARE

Convention &
Visitors Bureau

CROSS STREET

PREBLE STREET

Wadsworth
Longfellow House

BROWN STREET

Museum
of African
Culture

COTTON STREET
CENTER STREET

Maine
College of Art

CASCO STREET
SHEPLEY ST
OAK STREET

DOWNTOWN

FOREST AVENUE

Children's
Museum

Portland
Museum
of Art

MAPLE STREET
SPRING STREET
PLEASANT STREET
DANFORTH STREET
YORK STREET

HIGH STREET

Victoria
Mansion

PARK STREET

MAINE

⑧

N

0   200 yds

STATE STREET

EATING & DRINKING

Amigos	14	Great Lost Bear	24	Ribollita	4
Arabica Coffee House	17	Gritty McDuff's	13	RiRa	7
Aurora Provisions	31	Herbs Gully	21	Rivalries	18
Bar Lola	2	Homegrown Herb		Shays Grill Pub	16
Becky's Diner	25	and Tea	26	Street and Co.	15
Brian Boru Public		Lobster Shack at		Top of the East	
House	20	Two Lights	33	Lounge	B
Caiola's	30	Local 188	29	Ùna	19
Coffee By Design	1, 5 & 28	Maple's Organic Desserts	9	Walter's Café	11
Five Fifty Five	23	Market Street Eats	10	The White Heart	22
Flatbread Company	8	Norm's East End Grill	6		
Food Factory Miyake	27	North Star Café	3		
The Good Table		Novare Res Bier			
Restaurant	32	Café	12		

Old Port. In recent years, downtown Portland has undergone a renaissance of sorts, spurred by a high concentration of artists, some wise city planning, and a burst of innovative high-end restaurants. Such successes have revitalized the city, keeping it at the heart of Maine life – but you shouldn't expect a constant hive of energy. Portland is simply a pleasant, sophisticated, and very attractive town, where one can experience the benefits of a large city at a lesser cost and without the hassle.

Arrival and information

Both I-95 and Rte-1 skirt the peninsula of Portland, quite near the city center, while I-295 goes through it. **Portland International Jetport** (☎207/774-7301) abuts I-95. Most major carriers serve the airport, which is connected with downtown by the city **bus** (#5; no service Sun; $1.25; ☎207/774-0351, Ⓦwww .gpmetrobus.com).

Amtrak's *Downeaster* pulls into the **Portland Transportation Center** (☎207/828-3939) five times daily from Boston's North Station (one-way $24; ☎1-800/USA-RAIL, Ⓦwww.amtrakdowneaster.com). Also arriving here is Concord Coach (☎207/828-1151 or 1-800/639-3317), the principal **bus** operator along the coast, with frequent service from Boston and Bangor. From the terminal, located three miles from the city center at 100 Thompson's Point Rd, adjacent to I-295, city buses and taxis can ferry you downtown. Greyhound (☎207/772-6587 or 1-800/231-2222) runs to Montréal, New Hampshire, and Vermont as well as to points throughout Maine from its station at 950 Congress St, on the eastern edge of downtown.

Car rental is available from the airport offices of National and Alamo (☎207/775-0855), Avis (☎207/874-7500), Budget (☎207/775-6508), and Enterprise (☎207/772-0030), though **parking** can be a hassle in Portland – finding a spot can sometimes seem impossible. If you get one, the parking meters charge $0.25 for twenty minutes (although the city runs on a "forgiveness ticketing" system – your first ticket for an expired meter or overtime parking is free). There are also numerous parking garages, including the Fore Street Garage at no. 427, and the Casco Bay Parking Garage at 54 Commercial St. If you don't mind an 8- to 10-minute walk, there is **free parking** alongside the Eastern Cemetery on Mountfort Street, near the intersection of Congress Street and Washington Avenue.

The helpful **CVB of Greater Portland** is at 245 Commercial St (Mon–Fri 8.30am–5pm, Sat 10am–3pm; ☎207/772-5800, Ⓦwww.visitportland.com); they also staff an information office at the Jetport (☎207/775-5809). All manner of details concerning transportation within the area, whether by bus, boat, or train, can be found at Ⓦwww.transportme.org. The Portland Public Library, 5 Monument Square, at the corner of Congress and Elm (☎207/871-1700, Ⓦwww .portlandlibrary.com), has free **internet access**.

City transport

Downtown Portland and the Old Port are each compact enough to stroll around, though they're served by a comprehensive **bus** system ($1.25; ☎207/774-0351); stop by the METRO Pulse, the hub of the bus system, at the Elm Street Garage near Congress Street for a detailed route map. CycleMania, 59 Federal St (☎207/774-2933), rents **bicycles** for $25 a day, which you can ride around the city's hundreds of acres of undeveloped land. Call Portland Trails (☎207/775-2411, Ⓦwww.trails.org) for more information on the city's biking or walking trails.

Tour companies abound in Portland. Three of the most entertaining are Mainely/Eagle Island Tours, 170 Commercial St (May–Oct; ☎207/774-0808, ⓦwww.eagleislandtours .com), whose land & sea combo ticket ($29) combines a trolley trip with a lighthouse lover's cruise; the amphibious Downeast Duck Adventures, 177 Commercial St (May–Oct; $24; ☎207/774-DUCK), which whisks you through the historical Old Port and then takes you into Casco Bay to view the Calendar Islands; and Lucky Catch Cruises, 170 Commercial St ($22; ☎207/761-0941, ⓦwww.luckycatch.com), which allows you to throw on lobstermen's overalls and head out to catch your very own lobster. For tours of Portland's historic hotspots ($7–10), contact Greater Portland Landmarks, 165 State St (☎207/774-5561, ⓦwww.portlandlandmarks.org).

Out on the water, the Portland Schooner Co. has two vintage schooners that sail around the harbor and to the Casco Bay islands and lighthouses from the Maine State Pier on Commercial Street (daily in summer; 2hr trip $35, overnight trips $240; ☎207/766-2500 or 1-87/SCHOONER, ⓦwww.portlandschooner.com); Maine Sailing Adventures runs a similar jaunt from the same pier via its 74-foot windjammer *Frances* (daily in summer; 2hr trip $30; ☎207/749-9169, ⓦwww.mainesailingadventures.net). Casco Bay Lines runs a twice-daily **mail boat** all year, and additional **cruises** in summer, to seven of the scenic Calendar Islands in Casco Bay, from its terminal at Commercial and Franklin streets (one-way direct trip $7.75–11.50, scenic cruises $12–22.50; ☎207/774-7871, ⓦwww.cascobaylines.com). Long, Peaks, and Cliff islands all have accommodation or camping facilities. Four mornings a week between late May and mid-October, the high-speed **Cat ferry** (6hr; passengers $99 one-way, vehicles $164; ☎1-877/359-3760, ⓦwww.catferry.com) runs to Canada. You will need a birth certificate or an up-to-date passport to make the trip.

Accommodation

Finding a room in Portland is no problem if you book in advance – but you *need* to book in advance, especially in summer and fall. You'll generally pay more for **accommodation** in town than at one of the **budget motels** that cluster around Exit 48 off I-95. The extra cost can be worth it, however: Portland has some great old renovated hotels, and the city is both atmospheric and walkable. Many of the hotels are pricey, but a number of B&Bs have recently moved in to fill the mid-range accommodation gap. If you want to be right at the airport, there is an *Embassy Suites*, 1050 Westbrook St (☎207/775-2200, ⓦwww.embassysuites .com; ⑥) and a *Hilton Garden Inn,* 145 Jetport Blvd (☎207/828-1117, ⓦwww .hiltongardeninn.com; ⑥). The closest **campground** is *Wassamki Springs*, 56 Saco St in Scarborough, off Rte-22 towards Westbrook (☎207/839-4276; May to mid-Oct only; $43).

The Chadwick 140 Chadwick St ☎207/774-5141, ⓦwww.thechadwick.com. Tucked away in Portland's West End, this delightful B&B has four cozy rooms, a welcoming innkeeper, excellent breakfasts, wi-fi, and happy guests. ⑥–⑦
Eastland Park Hotel 157 High St ☎207/775-5411 or 1-888/671-8008, ⓦwww .eastlandparkhotel.com. Luxurious, centrally located accommodation that has a business center, wi-fi, and a rooftop cocktail lounge with sweeping views of the city. ⑧
Hilton Garden Inn 65 Commercial St ☎207/780-0780, ⓦwww.hiltongardeninn.com.

Fitness center, saltwater pool, and wi-fi, all in a snappy location overlooking the harbor. ⑨
Holiday Inn by the Bay 88 Spring St ☎207/775-2311 or 1-800/345-5050, ⓦwww .innbythebay.com. Fairly standard link in the Holiday Inn chain, with 239 rooms, many of which overlook Casco Bay. ⑧
Inn at Park Spring 135 Spring St ☎207/774-1059, ⓦwww.innatparkspring.com. Not quite as stylish as other B&Bs in town, but it's the most centrally located and has friendly innkeepers, scrumptious breakfasts, and repeat customers. ⑦

Inn at St John 939 Congress St ☎207/773-6481 or 1-800/636-9127, ⓦwww.innatstjohn.com. Just outside downtown in a slightly dodgy area near the Greyhound bus station, this elegant Victorian offers reasonably priced, comfortable rooms, some with shared baths. Breakfast included, no elevator. ⑤–⑧

Morrill Mansion B&B 249 Vaughan St ☎207/774-6900, ⓦwww.morrillmansion.com. Another well-loved West End B&B, this one set in a renovated 1880s townhouse. Seven nicely furnished rooms with modern fixtures, wi-fi, amazing breakfasts, and a friendly pup and innkeeper. ⑦–⑧

Pomegranate Inn 49 Neal St ☎1-800/356-0408, ⓦwww.pomegranateinn.com. The most upscale B&B of the bunch, with a vibrant color scheme – all whimsical wallpaper and contemporary artworks – in an elegant West End home. ⑧–⑨

Portland Harbor Hotel 468 Fore St ☎207/775-9090 or 1-888/798-9090, ⓦwww .portlandharborhotel.com. Pretty, but not exceptional rooms, in a great location near the waterfront; many rooms overlook the English garden. ⑨

Portland Regency Hotel 20 Milk St ☎207/774-4200 or 1-800/727-3436, ⓦwww .theregency.com. Fancy rooms – some with bay views – in a beautifully renovated building not far from the Old Port. ⑨

West End Inn 146 Pine St ☎1-800/338-1377, ⓦwww.westenddbb.com. Charming 1871 brick townhouse in the West End, recently purchased by the owners of the chic and cozy *Pomegranate Inn*. ⑦–⑧

The City

Central Portland consists of two main districts: the **Arts District**, where you'll also find several museums, the Civic Center, and a smattering of good restaurants, and the **Old Port**, to the southeast, which bustles with lively shops, bars, and eateries. Commercial Street runs along the water's edge, but Fore Street, just inland, has most of the area's attractions. Aim to visit the Arts District on the first Friday of the month, when galleries open to the public and museums are free (5–8pm; ⓦwww.firstfridayartwalk.org).

The Arts District

Portland's single best destination, the **Portland Museum of Art** (PMA), in the heart of downtown at 7 Congress Square (Tues–Thurs, Sat & Sun 10am–5pm, Fri 10am–9pm; June to mid-Oct also Mon 10am–5pm; $10, Fri free 5–9pm; ☎207/775-6148, ⓦwww.portlandmuseum.org), was designed in 1983 by I.M. Pei and Partners, and many parts of the museum afford superb views – on a clear day you can see all the way to Mount Washington in New Hampshire. One of the museum's highlights is its stunning collection of glass: European and American lamps and vases glow in a riot of color. Elsewhere, ships and images of the sea are prevalent, exemplified by Winslow Homer's contemplative seascapes. An earthy alternative to the maritime pieces is *Woodsmen in the Woods of Maine* by Waldo Peirce. Rich and dark, it was commissioned by the Westbrook Post Office in 1937 and is displayed here with the clouded-glass mailroom door still intact. There's also a strong collection of modernist works by the likes of Nevelson, Indiana, and Hartley. Adjoining the main building is the impressive Federal-style **McLellan House**, built for a city shipping magnate in 1801, and the **L.D.M. Sweat Memorial Galleries** (1911). The Sweat Galleries focus on American art (especially landscapes) through 1900. Scenes of Maine are well displayed in works by Frederic Church (see the romantic *Mount Katahdin from Millinocket Camp*) and Wyeth.

Just next door, the **Children's Museum**, 142 Free St (Tues–Sat 10am–5pm, Sun noon–5pm; open Mon in summer only; $8, first Fri of the month free 5–8pm; ☎207/828-1234, ⓦwww.childrensmuseumofme.org), is a great spot for little ones, with hands-on exhibits that include a lobster boat, a fire truck, and – everyone's favorite – an interactive mini grocery store.

Several excellent art galleries have recently taken hold downtown, including the buzz-worthy **Whitney Art Works**, 492 Congress St (Wed–Sat noon–6pm; free; ☏207/774-7011), and the well-tailored **Institute of Contemporary Art** at the Maine College of Art, 522 Congress St (Wed & Fri–Sun 11am–5pm, Thurs 11am–7pm; free; ☏207/879-5742), which showcases works demonstrating new perspectives and trends in contemporary art, such as William Pope. L's *eRacism*. Also worth a look is the **Museum of African Culture**, 13 Brown St (Tues–Sat 10.30am–4pm; free; ☏207/871-7188), the only museum in New England devoted exclusively to African art and culture. It houses an eye-catching collection of sub-Saharan masks with complete ceremonial regalia.

Not all that much of old Portland survives, thanks to some massive fires over the years (portions of the city were burned by Native Americans in 1675, the British in 1775, and slipshod 4th of July revelers in 1866), though grand mansions can still be seen along Congress and Danforth streets. A few of the oldest houses are open to the public, most notably the **Wadsworth-Longfellow House** at 485 Congress St (May–Oct Mon–Sat 10.30am–5pm, Sun noon–5pm; call for holiday hours in Dec, last tour leaves at 4pm; closed Jan–April; $8; ☏207/774-1822). Portland's first brick house, it was built in 1785 by Revolutionary War hero Peleg Wadsworth, grandfather of poet Henry Wadsworth Longfellow. Longfellow spent his boyhood here, and at age 13 published his first poem in the *Portland Evening Gazette*. The house is furnished with a hodgepodge of Federalist furniture, all original to the Longfellow family. Next door, at 489 Congress St, the **Maine Historical Society** (Tues–Sat 10am–4pm; free with admission to Wadsworth-Longfellow House, otherwise $4; ⊕www.mainehistory.org) has rotating exhibits of art and Maine-related artifacts, as well as an extensive library.

Another building that survived the fires, slightly west of downtown, is the Georgian **Tate House**, 1270 Westbrook St (mid-June to Oct tours on the hour Tues–Sat 10am–3pm, first Sun of every month 1–3pm; $7; ☏207/774-6177, ⊕www.tatehouse.org). As mast agent for the British Royal Navy, Tate found financial success marking pine trees as property of the king and using them for ship masts. The exterior of the building merits attention for its clerestory (an indented wall rising above the gambrel roof on the second story), while the interior reflects a style typical of a wealthy eighteenth-century official. Closer to the Old Port, the **Victoria Mansion**, 109 Danforth St (May–Oct Mon–Sat 10am–4pm, Sun 1–5pm; Nov 28–Dec 31 Tues–Sun 11am–5pm; $13.50; ☏207/772-4841, ⊕www.victoriamansion.com), grande dame of house museums, is an Italianate brownstone constructed in 1859 as a summer home for hotelier Ruggles S. Morse. The exquisite interior includes fresco-ornamented walls and ceilings, a freestanding staircase made of Santo Domingo mahogany, and floor-to-ceiling gold-leaf mirrors. The best time to visit is during the holiday season, when the mansion is bedecked in Christmas finery.

The Old Port

For relaxed wandering, the restored **Old Port** near the quayside, between Exchange and Pearl streets, is quite entertaining, with all sorts of red-brick antiquarian shops, bookstores, boutique clothing shops (especially on Exchange St), and other esoterica. Several companies operate **boat trips** from the nearby wharves (see box, p.467).

If you follow Portland's waterfront to the end of the peninsula, you'll come to the **Eastern Promenade**. Once the bastion of the town's wealthy families, (who've since moved to the **Western Promenade** and the wander-worthy **West End**), it became almost exclusively residential after the last major fire and is remarkably peaceful for being so close to downtown. A big beach lies below the headland, while above, at the top of Munjoy Hill at 138 Congress St, is the shingled, eight-sided 1807 **Portland Observatory** (June to mid-Oct 10am–5pm; $7), the oldest remaining signal tower in the country; you can climb its 103 steps for an exhilarating view of the bay and the city.

Cape Elizabeth

Across the harbor, in Cape Elizabeth (five miles south via Rte-77), lies the **Portland Head Lighthouse**, the oldest in Maine, commissioned in 1790 by George Washington. Still an active light, it also houses an excellent **museum** on the history of Maine's lighthouses (June–Oct daily 10am–4pm; April–May & Nov weekends only 10am–4pm; $2). The small but intelligent collection traces the signal lights back to 300 BC, when Ptolemy II of Egypt built one on the island of Pharos near Alexandria. Best are the displays combining lighthouse literature and art, such as Longfellow's paean *The Lighthouse* and reproductions of Edward Hopper's forlorn watercolors, both of which were inspired by Portland Head. A few miles south is another lighthouse commissioned by George Washington, **Cape Elizabeth Lighthouse**. This light is also still active, and the

▲ Portland Head Lighthouse

unpredictable, ear-splitting blasts from its horn jolt anyone in the vicinity. A short drive through the neighborhood of Cape Elizabeth, with its stately homes and comfortable spaces, is also pleasant. Nearby, **Two Lights State Park** has easy shoreside trails and picnic areas (day-use fee $3).

Eating

Portland is a town of foodies, and as such is packed with outstanding **restaurants**. People eat out a lot here, so inquire about reservations on weekends. The **Farmers' Market** in Monument Square (April–Oct Wed only) offers the perfect opportunity to sample local produce.

Portland

Aurora Provisions 64 Pine St ℡207/871-9060. Upscale market/deli with mouthwatering sandwiches, a full selection of coffees, drinks, pastries, salads, desserts, and a small seating area. The perfect place to stock up for picnics. Closed Sun.

Bar Lola 100 Congress St ℡207/775-5652. Off the beaten track in Portland's East End, this whimsical tapas gem utilizes lots of local ingredients in its tasty seasonal menu with Greek undertones. Open Wed–Sat; dinner only.

Becky's Diner 390 Commercial St ℡207/773-7070. Renowned, vintage Maine breakfast spot serving hearty portions, including home-made muffins and pies. Open 4am (for the fishermen) to 9pm.

Caiola's 58 Pine St ℡207/772-1110. This cozy West End neighborhood spot serves upscale comfort food – really good burgers, *paella* with chicken and chorizo, and excellent desserts. They also have a tasty (and cheaper) Sunday brunch.

Five Fifty Five 555 Congress St ℡207/761-0555. Upscale, organic dinner spot with mains like garlicky mussels and line-caught Atlantic swordfish, served in an airy dining room. Considered one of the best foodie spots in town. For a less expensive treat, check out their Sunday brunch.

Flatbread Company 72 Commercial St ℡207/772-8777. Tasty pizzas made with flatbread dough, their own sauce, and all-natural ingredients in a hip waterfront location.

Food Factory Miyake 129 Spring St ℡207/871-9170. There's a lot of good sushi in Portland, but this teeny West End spot garners a worthy buzz for dishes such as seared tuna sashimi with truffle oil (and the chef/owner harvests his own clams!) and BYOB ambience. Closed Mon.

Herbs Gully 55 Oak St ℡207/780-8080. Creatively constructed burritos ("hand-rolled fatties"), quesadillas, and side dishes. They also mix drinks like the "Kind Buzz" (banana, honey, vanilla, and bee pollen).

Local 188 685 Congress St ℡207/761-7909. A fun, affordable spot with a roomy blue dining room and the likes of Cuban pork sandwiches ($8) for lunch and seared shrimp over penne ($18) for dinner. They also do a mean weekend brunch.

Maple's Organic Desserts 151 Middle St ℡207/774-COOL. *Maple's* dishes out the best scoops in town: gelato crafted in small batches from local milk and served in yummy home-made waffle cones.

Market Street Eats 36 Market St ℡207/773-3135. This subterranean sandwich joint turns out awesome fare like the "Red Rooster" wrap (chicken, bacon, provolone, spicy mayo, and red onion; $6.75).

Norm's East End Grill 47 Middle St ℡207/253-1700. Crave-worthy barbecue joint satisfying a nice mix of customers. The classics (pulled pork, corn bread, barbecued chicken) are all well represented here, with some good veggie options too.

Ribollita 41 Middle St ℡207/774-2972. Reasonably priced, fresh pasta and other Italian fare in a cozy, narrow, brick-walled dining room. Closed Sun and Mon.

RiRa 72 Commercial St ℡207/761-4446. A more creative choice for dinner than you might expect from an authentic Irish pub, with shepherd's pie ($11) served alongside salmon filled with crab, shrimp, and brie stuffing ($21). Lunch, featuring some traditional Irish favorites, can be had for under $10.

Shays Grill Pub 18 Monument Square ℡207/772-2626. The place to go for Portland's best burgers and onion strings, as well as good martinis and beers in a relaxed ambience right on Monument Square.

Street and Co. 33 Wharf St ℡207/775-0887. A great special-occasion seafood spot where the cuts are grilled, blackened, or broiled to perfection. There are a few good non-fish items as well. Reservations recommended. *Fore Street*, their land-focused brother (288 Fore St, ℡207/775-2717), is another good upscale eatery.

Walter's Café 15 Exchange St ℡207/871-9258. New American cuisine in a high-ceilinged dining room with an open kitchen. Most entrees go for $13–20. Also makes an elegant lunch option.

Cape Elizabeth

The Good Table Restaurant 527 Ocean House Rd (Rte-77) ☎207/799-4663. Right by Two Lights State Park, this endearing, family-owned spot is open 8am–9pm (closed Mon) for casual salads, sandwiches, and hot cinnamon rolls in the morning.

🎿 **Lobster Shack at Two Lights** 225 Two Lights Rd ☎207/799-1677. Perhaps the best seafood-eating scenery in all of Maine – lighthouse to the left, unruly ocean to the right, and a scrumptious lobster roll on the plate in front of you.

Drinking and nightlife

The bar–restaurant distinction is blurry in Portland – most watering holes serve food, and many eateries have good microbrews and wine. There are a good many **bars** scattered throughout the Old Port, of which a number feature live rock music; note that ID policies are strict and bars aren't allowed to serve after 1am. **Cafés** are becoming increasingly popular with Portland's youthful population, and frequently offer internet access. On the weekends they're generally as crowded and lively as bars. Portland's **club scene** is pretty tame, but there are a few raucous dance and music venues.

Cafés

Arabica Coffee House 16 Free St ☎207/879-0792. Mellow café with numerous types of imported java. Comfortable but limited seating, and free wi-fi.

Coffee by Design 67 India St ☎207/780-6767; 620 Congress St ☎207/772-5533; and 43 Washington Ave ☎207/879-2233. This local chain roasts their own beans, and also stocks a wide assortment of teas and some tasty pastries.

Homegrown Herb & Tea 195 Congress St ☎207/774-3484. Like something from *Harry Potter*, the owner at this teeny shop handcrafts your cup of tea from wooden drawers of herbs. If you're in need, ask for the hangover cure. Closed Sun and Mon.

North Star Music Café 225 Congress St ☎207/699-2994. They offer frequent live tunes at this comfy coffee shop, featuring free wi-fi, bagel sandwiches, and beer and wine.

Bars

Amigos 9 Dana St ☎207/772-0772. All stripes of Portlanders squish into this low-key, centrally located bar. In summer it's a bit of a lust magnet, but that's not necessarily a bad thing.

Brian Boru Public House 57 Center St ☎207/780-1506. Traditional Irish pub serving Guinness and a big, if typical, menu. Great outdoor deck.

Great Lost Bear 540 Forest Ave ☎207/772-0300, ⓦwww.greatlostbear.com. One of the top ten beer bars in the US, according to *The Malt Advocate*. Try one from their 65 taps, including fifteen state microbrews. Decent pub grub, too.

Gritty McDuff's 396 Fore St ☎207/772-2739, ⓦwww.grittys.com. Portland's first brewpub,

making Portland Head Pale Ale and Black Fly Stout. Food, folk music, long wooden benches, and a friendly atmosphere, which can get rowdy on Sat nights.

Novare Res Bier Café 4 Canal Plaza, Suite 1 (enter through alleyway on lower Exchange St, by Keybank sign) ☎207/761-2437. A little tricky to find, this very cool Old Port beer spot sports over 200 brews with fifteen on tap, outdoor and indoor picnic tables, and tasty meat and cheese plates.

Rivalries 10 Cotton St ☎207/774-6044. Packed with energetic fans, this recent addition to Portland's scene is a hip sports bar.

Top of the East Lounge In the *Eastland Park Hotel* 157 High St ☎207/775-5411. Sophisticated rooftop lounge, with swanky martinis and great views of the city.

Úna 505 Fore St ☎207/828-0300. Rare for this neck of the woods: a sleek martini bar with chi-chi decor, all to the tune of a local DJ. They have great deals at happy hour (Mon–Sat 4.30–7pm).

The White Heart 551 Congress St ☎207/828-1900. Good-looking hipster bar that welcomes you into its red and black Art Deco interior with a lovely winged white neon heart. $2.50 PBRs, danceable DJs, and never a cover.

Clubs and live music venues

Geno's 625 Congress St ☎no phone. Rock venue featuring mostly local indie acts.

The Porthole 20 Custom House Wharf ☎207/780-6533. Right on the water, this Portland fixture has all sorts of cool features, including a great daily breakfast. Their summertime Sunday reggae shows, held on a sunny deck in the harbor, are seriously bumping.

SPACE Gallery 538 Congress St ☎207/828-5600, Ⓦwww.space538.org. Cool, artsy space that displays contemporary artworks and always has something interesting going on, whether it's films, music, art shows, or local bands.

Entertainment

There are several options for the **performing arts** in Portland. The free *Portland Phoenix* (Ⓦwww.portlandphoenix.com) has listings of all local events. Maine's biggest gigs take place each summer at Old Orchard Beach (see p.463), but some mid-level shows come to town at the Merrill Auditorium, 20 Myrtle St. Call PorTix (☎207/842-0800) for all area ticketing sales and information. Chamber music, opera, dance, and touring theater productions are often featured as part of the PCA Great Performances series, which is held at Merrill Auditorium (tickets ☎207/842-0800, Ⓦwww.pcagreatperformances .org), while the Portland Stage Company puts on larger-scale productions at the Portland Stage Co., 25A Forest Ave (☎207/774-0465). Portland Parks and Recreation (☎207/756-8130, Ⓦwww.ci.portland.me.us) sponsors free outdoor jazz and blues concerts at various locations throughout the city during the summer. You can find indie-type **films** at The Movies, 10 Exchange St (☎207/772-9600).

Sports fans should take a trip to Hadlock Field, an intimate baseball stadium on Park Avenue where the minor league **Portland Sea Dogs** (Ⓦwww .portlandseadogs.com; now affiliated with the Boston Red Sox) play from May to October. Tickets are wildly inexpensive (prices top out at about $9). Call ☎207/879-9500 for ticket and schedule information. At the time of writing, Portland had just signed a lease agreement to use the Expo Building for a **NBA Development League** basketball team; it is hoped the team will become an affiliation of the World Champion Boston Celtics. Other sporting choices: Portland Pirates hockey (☎207/828-4665) and harness racing in nearby Scarborough Downs (☎207/883-4331).

Shopping

Part of the fun of shopping in Portland is the scenery – errands here are complemented by pretty byways. The boutiques of the cobblestoned Old Port, particularly those along Exchange Street, are a great starting point for browsing. Below are a few spots worth checking out that you might not come across on your own.

Angela Adams 273 Congress St ☎207/774-3523. A Portland landmark in the East End, Angela Adams designs vibrant, imaginative wool and cotton rugs inspired by the Maine landscape.

Black Parrot 131 Middle St ☎207/221-6991. This beautiful Portland newcomer has carefully chosen racks of women's clothing that give real meaning to the word "design." Pricey but amazing.

Rogue's Gallery 41 Wharf St ☎207/553-1999. If you want your boyfriend to look like a stylish seafarer (who doesn't?) get thee to Rogue's Gallery, a small space loaded with artful nautical-meets-rocker wares.

The designs have a Manhattan look, but the shop's seaside roots lend a loving legitimacy to the brand.

Sea Bags 24 Custom House Wharf ☎207/780-0744. Now on sale from coast to coast, this is the warehouse where sea bags – stylish totes crafted from recycled sails – get made. Stop by to pick up an original design, or just to see how the magic happens.

Stonewall Kitchen 182 Middle St ☎207/879-2409. Less harried and more atmospheric than the flagship York location, this Stonewall sells all the signature jams, mustards, and grilling sauces for which these flavor kings are known. Great for take-home gifts.

Freeport

Sixteen miles north of Portland along Rte-1 and the coast, **FREEPORT** is simply one huge shopping mall, though the town was once one of Maine's primary shipbuilding centers. Huge logs were brought here that would ultimately be used for masts; this past is still evident in the wide shape of the town square at Main and Bow streets, which was fashioned to give the gigantic logs plenty of room to swing as the carts turned on the way to the mast landing. Freeport's prominence was such that the town's **Jameson Tavern** is believed (though not without dispute) to have been the place where the treaty separating Maine from Massachusetts was signed in 1820.

The shipping industry fell into disrepair following the Civil War, but Freeport managed a big comeback fifty years later when a fishing-boot maker by the name of **Leon L. Bean** planted the seeds of what has become an unbelievably successful outdoors-wear manufacturer – it's now Maine's number-one tourist destination. L.L. Bean's store stood alone along Freeport's Main Street for decades until the 1980s, when it was joined by factory outlets and the town developed its current commercial character.

Arrival and information

The best way to get to Freeport is by **car** – there's no public transport, and the closest buses come to Portland, from where you'll need to take a **taxi** the rest of the way. Try Brunswick Taxi (☏207/729-3688) or Freeport Taxi (☏207/865-9494). Drop by the incredibly complete Freeport Merchants' Association, in a restored old tower at 23 Depot St (☏207/865-1212 or 1-800/865-1994), for reams of area **information** as well as public restrooms and an ATM.

Accommodation

There's no shortage of quality **B&Bs** in town, but if you're low on cash, some cheap motels line Rte-1 south of town. (Better still, stay in Portland and make a quick trip through Freeport.) The best nearby **camping** is at the oceanside *Recompense Shores*, 134 Burnett Rd (☏207/865-9307; $21–44), near Casco Bay, which has 115 well-kept and -spaced sites.

Applewood Inn 8 Holbrook St ☏207/865-9705, ⓦwww.applewoodusa.com. Welcoming B&B with artful decor in a great setting just behind L.L. Bean (next door to Mr. Bean's former house, no less). Some rooms are fancier and have Jacuzzis, and there is one lovely suite that sleeps eight. ⓻–⓽

Brewster House 180 Main St ☏207/865-4121, ⓦwww.brewsterhouse.com. B&B set in a beautifully restored Queen Anne cottage with antique furnishings. ⓺–⓼

Harraseeket Inn 162 Main St ☏207/865-9377 or 1-800/342-6423, ⓦwww.harraseeketinn.com. Wonderful, albeit pricey, clapboard B&B inn with some eighty rooms, two good restaurants, and an indoor pool. ⑧–⑨

Hilton Garden Inn 5 Park St ☎207/865-1433, ⓦ www.hiltongardeninn.com. Well-situated new Hilton with a fitness center and wi-fi. ⑥

Maine Idyll Motor Court 1411 Rte-1 N ☎207/865-4201, ⓦ www.maineidyll.com. Basic

but romantic cottage quarters in a woodsy area a few miles north of town. Blueberry muffins in the morning. ④–⑤

Village Inn 186 Main St ☎207/865-3236 or 1-800/998-3649, ⓦ www.freeportvillageinn.com. Motel-style units in the rear building, with breakfast in the proprietors' home. ④

The Town

Freeport owes virtually all of its current prosperity to the invention by Leon Leonwood Bean, in 1912, of a funky-looking rubber-soled fishing boot, now favored by everyone from seasoned Mainers to Manhattan hipsters. The boot is still available (indeed, now there's a huge replica welcoming you into the store), and **L.L. Bean** has grown into a multinational clothing conglomerate, housed in an enormous 90,000-square-foot factory outlet building on Main Street (☎1-800/441-5713 or 207/552-6879, ⓦ www.llbean.com) that literally never closes. In theory, this is so that hunters can stock up in the pre-dawn hours; all the relevant equipment is available for rent or sale, and the store runs regular workshops from its worthy Outdoor Discovery School (ⓦ www.llbean .com/ods). In practice, though, the late-night hours seem more geared toward local high school students, who attempt to fall asleep in the tents without being noticed by store personnel. It's worth a spin through just to gawk at the four stories, which are packed with camping supplies and fleecy outerwear; there's also a full café and even a trout pond with a waterfall. There are plenty of other **outlet stores** nearby, with chic fashion stops (Cole Haan, Brooks Brothers, Burberry) alongside ones geared towards outdoorsmen (Patagonia, Timberland, North Face). The **Frost Gully Gallery**, 1159 Rte-1 N (Mon–Fri noon–5pm; ☎207/865-4505), usually has a fine display of oil paintings by both local and nationally known artists, and will provide a respite from the commercialism found elsewhere in town.

On Bow Street, the **Soldiers and Sailors Monument**, a lone reference to the city's life before Bean, was dedicated by Civil War general Joshua Chamberlain, and boasts cannons that were used at the Battle of Bull Run. To get even farther from the shops, however, head a mile south of Freeport to the sea, where the green cape visible just across the water is **Wolfe's Neck State Park**. In summer, for just $3, you can follow hiking and nature trails along the unspoiled fringes of the headland. For a more bizarre change of pace, check out the **Desert of Maine**, 95 Desert Rd, Exit 20 off I-295 (May to mid-Oct; $8.75; ☎207/865-6962, ⓦ www.desertofmaine.com), a vast expanse of privately owned sand deposited here by a glacier that slid through the area eleven thousand years ago. This tiny, self-contained desert spread, ultimately engulfing the surrounding homes and trees; you can still see them, half-buried in the sand.

Eating, drinking, and entertainment

Restaurants in the area are all done up to match the town's strict aesthetic zoning laws; even the *McDonald's* is disguised by a clapboard motif. As for nightlife, L.L. Bean runs a fun, free Saturday concert series in summer; check ⓦ www.llbean.com for a calendar of events.

Broad Arrow Tavern 162 Main St, in the *Harraseeket Inn* ☎207/865-9377. Gourmet pizzas, pulled-pork sandwiches, and a great lunch buffet. They also serve a good dinner.

China Rose 23 Main St ☎207/865-6886. Reputed to serve some of Maine's best Szechuan and Hunan cuisine. Also has a surprisingly good sushi bar upstairs.

Conundrum Wine Bistro 117 Rte-1 S (by the wooden Indian sculpture) ℡ 207/865-0303. South of downtown proper, and serving the best food in Freeport. Most people come for the swanky martinis, then they get hooked on the fresh, eclectic entrees.

Harraseeket Lunch & Lobster Co Off Rte-1 in South Freeport ℡ 207/865-4888. Extending on its wooden jetty into the peaceful bay, this makes a great outdoor lunch spot. Open May to Oct only.

Jacqueline's Tea Room 201 Main St ℡ 207/865-2123. Girly to the max, this tempting tea spot, all decked out in white wicker and roses, serves a scrumptious two-hour, four-course tea service. Reservations required, no credit cards. Closed Mon.

Lobster Cooker 39 Main St ℡ 207/865-4349. A casual seafood restaurant specializing in lobster and crabmeat rolls.

Mediterranean Grill 10 School St ℡ 207/865-1688. Really good, authentic Lebanese food like gyro kebabs ($8.95) and chicken *sarma* (chicken breast with rice and pistachios; $16.95).

The Mid-Coast

Maine's central coast, which stretches roughly from the quiet college town of **Brunswick** to blue-collar **Bucksport**, is a study in geographic, economic, and cultural contrasts. The shore here is physically different from the southern coast, with peninsulas such as the **Harpswells** and **Pemaquid Point** providing divergent alternatives to well-traveled Rte-1. Much of this region prospered in the late nineteenth century through shipbuilding and trading, as evidenced by

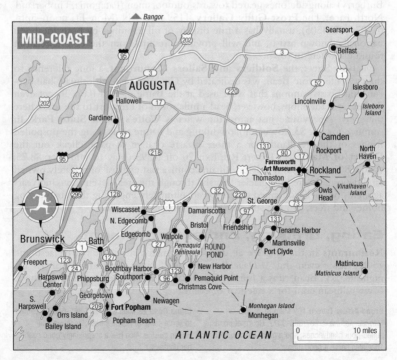

its wealth of attractive old captains' homes; today, only **Bath** remains as a ship manufacturer. Throughout, though, the focus is still unquestionably the sea, be it for livelihood, sustenance, or entertainment. Consequently, one of the best ways to see the area is by boat. Indeed, remote **Monhegan Island**, a lobstermen's hub and artists' retreat eleven miles offshore, is accessible only by boat. **Lobster-fishing** is also especially important to **Rockland**, home of the most active lobster industry in the state. Busy **Camden**, just beyond Rockland, is known for its fleet of recreational **windjammers**, while picturesque fishing villages such as **Round Pond** and **Tenants Harbor** – tiny windows into rustic Maine – can be found all along this stretch, somehow coexisting with summer resorts like **Boothbay Harbor**, which is all but deserted in the winter.

Brunswick and the Harpswells

A few miles north from Freeport is **BRUNSWICK**, home since 1794 to Bowdoin College. The town is attractive enough, with a concentration of old brick and clapboard homes and buildings, but apart from the small campus itself – at the south end of Maine Street – and a couple of unobtrusive cafés, there's little evidence of student life here. South of Brunswick, the scenic peninsulas that comprise the Harpswells make a worthy detour.

Arrival, information, and local transport

The **Southern Midcoast Maine Chamber of Commerce**, at 2 Main St in neighboring Topsham (☎207/725-8797, ⓦwww.midcoastmaine.com), is particularly helpful, with an array of brochures and a knowledgeable staff. **Public transportation** to and from Brunswick is fairly frequent: Greyhound stops at the depot at 206 Maine St (☎1-800/231-2222), from where you can catch **buses** to most other parts of New England. Concord Coach (☎1-800/639-3317) stops at the Mobil/Puffin Stop, 101 Rte-24, before continuing north to Bangor or south to Boston.

If you're moving on from Brunswick to Rockland, consider the **Maine Eastern Railroad** ($40 round-trip; ☎1-866/637-2457, ⓦwww.maineeasternrailroad.com), which runs scenic trips between the two towns (with stops in Bath and Wiscasset) in its restored Art Deco cars. The train is equipped with a lounge and dining area; in the latter you can sip wine and watch the coast go by – views are particularly stunning in the fall.

Accommodation

There are many **places to stay** in Brunswick, and most of the time you shouldn't have trouble finding a good-value room. If you have a self-contained camper, head to *Orrs Island Campground*, on the island of the same name in the **Harpswells** along Rte-24 (☎207/833-5595; end May to mid-Sept; weekly rentals only; $259).

Brunswick B&B 165 Park Row ☎207/729-4914 or 1-800/299-4914, ⓦwww.brunswickbnb.com. A gracious old inn decorated with antiques and quilts in the town center, within walking distance of the college. ⑥–⑧
Fairfield Inn 36 Old Portland Rd (Rte-1) ☎207/721-0300, ⓦwww.marriott.com. New,

clean, comfortable, very adequate motel digs right on Rte-1. ⑧
Harpswell Inn 108 Lookout Point, Harpswell ☎207/833-5509 or reserve at 1-800/843-5509, ⓦwww.harpswellinn.com. An exceedingly comfortable place with nine rooms and three suites overlooking the cove. ⑥–⑧

The Town

Free tours of **Bowdoin College** (ⓦwww.bowdoin.edu), which counts among its alumni Henry Wadsworth Longfellow, Nathaniel Hawthorne, and Franklin Pierce, begin at the Admissions Office (call for times ☎207/725-3100). After decades of disagreement, experts now generally conclude that former student Admiral Robert Peary was the first man to reach the North Pole in 1909; whatever the truth, his caribou fur parka, sled, and notebooks, found at the **Peary-MacMillan Arctic Museum** (Tues–Sat 10am–5pm, Sun 2–5pm; free; ☎207/725-3416), will be captivating to anyone who longs to experience ice floes. The college's **Museum of Art** (Tues–Wed & Fri–Sat 10am–5pm, Thurs 10am–8.30pm, Sun 1–5pm; free; ☎207/725-3275) is also worth a look, with some moody nineteenth-century paintings (including a lovely one by Albert Bierstadt) and a petite but intriguing collection of nineteenth- and twentieth-century African-American artworks.

Another distinguished alumnus of the college, Civil War hero General Joshua Chamberlain, graduated in 1852 and became a professor at the school in 1855. At the onset of the Civil War, and with no military training, he volunteered to serve, then went on to fight in 24 battles and receive the Congressional Medal of Honor; at the end of the war he was selected by Ulysses S. Grant to accept the formal surrender of the Confederate troops. He later became governor of Maine and, in 1871, president of Bowdoin College. The general's varied career is documented at the **General Joshua L. Chamberlain Museum**, 226 Maine St (May–Oct Tues–Sun 10am–4pm; $5; ☎207/729-6606). Tours of his restored home run twice hourly.

The Harpswells

South of Brunswick, a set of narrow, forested peninsulas, collectively known as the **HARPSWELLS**, make for a welcome escape from the bustle of Rte-1. The only problem is that once you get to the end of one of the thrusts of land, you have to turn around and retrace your tracks. Rte-123 weaves down the Harpswell Neck past Maine's **oldest meeting house** (1757) in Harpswell Center, then clear down to South Harpswell, where the Basin Cove Falls, created by tidal flows, are popular with canoeists and kayakers. Rte-24 heads down another long, finger-like strip to **Bailey Island** (one of Casco Bay Cruise

---

Harriet Beecher Stowe

Harriet Beecher Stowe (1811–96), a native of Litchfield, Connecticut, moved to Brunswick with her family from Ohio in the spring of 1850 when her husband, Calvin, took a position as professor of religion at Bowdoin College. It was here that Stowe formulated and wrote *Uncle Tom's Cabin*, the anti-slavery novel that would go on to become the bestseller of the century. The passage of the 1850 **Fugitive Slave Act**, which stipulated that it was illegal for citizens to assist escaped slaves, and demanded that escapees be apprehended and deported back to their "rightful" owner, outraged Stowe, who conceived of the death of Uncle Tom while sitting at worship in Brunswick's historic **First Parish Church**, 223 Maine St (pew no. 23; ☎207/729-7331). Encouraged by her husband, she published her violent story serially in the *National Era*, an abolitionist weekly. The book is credited with bringing respectability to the abolitionist cause, and when Abraham Lincoln met Stowe years later he reportedly remarked, "So you're the little lady who wrote the book that started the war." The **Harriet Beecher Stowe House** in Brunswick, at 63 Federal St, is now privately owned.

Line's stops), first crossing Orr's Island and then the **Cribstone Bridge**, which allows tides to flow right through it. Bailey Island's highlight is the **Giant Staircase**, off Rte-24 on the eastern shore of the island, a massive waterfront stone stairway good for exploring. On Orr's Island, H2Outfitters (☎207/833-5257, ⓦwww.h2outfitters.com) leads **kayak** trips of varying lengths. While in the area, don't miss a chance to sample the fish chowder at *Dolphin Marina* (515 Basin Point Rd, South Harpswell, ☎207/833-6000), a tiny restaurant that overlooks a working harbor.

Eating and drinking

For a small town, Brunswick has a great supply of enticing **restaurants**. In addition to the ones below, there are a few good Indian, Thai, and Japanese spots downtown.

111 Maine 111 Maine St ☎207/729-9111. Atmospheric café with gourmet soups, salads, and sandwiches like Tuscan ham & brie on a baguette ($8). They also have a weekend brunch with slamming frittatas (eggs, crab, caramelized onions, and Swiss cheese; $11).

Back Street Bistro 11 Town Hall Place ☎207/725-4060. Fine dining as well as inexpensive options in a side street off the square. Easily one of Brunswick's best restaurants, with the likes of bleu cheese-crusted steak and creative seasonal salads.

Fat Boy Drive-In 111 Bath Rd (Rte-24) ☎207/729-9431. This summertime landmark began in 1955 and still offers burgers, frappes, and lobster rolls; just turn on your lights for service.

Frontier Café 14 Maine St (in the Fort Andross Mill) ☎207/725-5222

ⓦwww.explorefrontier.com. Local foodies are all abuzz for this creative newcomer – a spacious café, cinema, and gallery all in one beautiful old mill space. Order one of the marketplates – charcuterie, cheeses, spreads, and breads served on square planks – and feast beside the mighty Androscoggin. Free wi-fi.

Gelato Fiasco 74 Maine St ☎207/607-4002. Life-changing gelato in creative flavors that range from a pudding-rich chocolate to pineapple to wasabi. Good coffee, too. There's another location in Freeport at 58 Main St.

Richard's 115 Maine St ☎207/729-9673. Tasty, good-value German and American cuisine. The German entrees are available in two sizes, the larger of which is huge; you can also get your favorite wursts by the pound. Excellent beer selection, too.

Bath

Crossing the bridge into **BATH** on Rte-1, it's hard to miss the enormous industrial cranes of the massive **Bath Iron Works** shipyard jutting into the skyline. The town has an exceptionally long history of **shipbuilding** – the first vessel to be constructed and launched here was the *Virginia* in 1607. Shipbuilding continued to be a major industry in the region throughout the eighteenth century, and between 1800 and 1830, nearly 288 ships set sail out of Bath's port. The Iron Works, founded in 1833, attracted job-seeking Irishmen in such numbers as to provoke a mob of anti-immigrant residents to burn down the local Catholic church in July 1854. Smaller trading vessels eventually gave way to larger ships, and in 1841, Clark & Sewall, one of the major builders at the time, launched the 1133-ton *Rappahannock*, at the time the world's largest ship. Despite changes in the shipbuilding market over the centuries, Bath's military contracts have never been in short supply, and during World War II more destroyers were built here than in all Japan. Today, it's very much worth a visit for its stellar **Maine Maritime Museum** and quaint downtown, with turn-of-the-century buildings and a pretty city hall espousing the authentic charm of this hard-working town.

Accommodation

Bath is not short on good-value **accommodation**, mostly of the inexpensive B&B variety. There's **camping** south of town along the water in Perry Cove at the *Meadowbrook Camping Area*, Meadowbrook Road (May–Sept; $30; ☎1-800/370-2267), as well as two sites farther south along the Phippsburg Peninsula: *Hermit Island* at the end of Rte-216 (late June to mid-Oct; $37–56; ☎207/443-2101), where you can rent small boats and camp near a white-sand beach, and *Ocean View Park*, near Popham Beach (mid-May to Sept; $42; ☎207/389-2564).

Benjamin F. Packard House 45 Pearl St
☎207/443-6004 or 1-866/361-6004,
☻www.benjaminfpackardhouse.com. Simple, prettily furnished rooms in a 1790 Georgian house, some with nice nautical accents; full breakfast included. ⑥–⑦

Coveside B&B 6 Gott's Cove Lane, 9 miles south in Georgetown ☎207/371-2807, ☻www.covesidebandb.com. This scenic hideaway, tucked between a boat-filled cove and a beautiful garden, has seven stylish rooms, friendly innkeepers, kayaking opportunities, and phenomenal breakfasts. Open May to Oct only. ⑥–⑧

Fairhaven Inn 118 North Bath Rd
☎207/443-4391 or 1-888/443-4391. You'll find a bit of rural flavor here – hiking and cross-country skiing trails are right nearby – plus a fine breakfast. ④–⑥

Galen C Moses House 1009 Washington St
☎207/442-8771, ☻www.galenmoses.com. A restored mansion whose proprietors are almost as eccentric as the fabulous decorations; a delicious gourmet breakfast is included. ⑥–⑨

Holiday Inn at Bath 139 Richardson St (just off Rte-1) ☎207/443-9741, ☻www.ichotelsgroup .com. A fairly unremarkable link in the Holiday Inn chain that's just off Rte-1. ⑨

Inn at Bath 969 Washington St ☎207/443-4294, ☻www.innatbath.com. An 1810 Greek Revival house with friendly service and tastefully decorated rooms, some with wood-burning fireplaces. ⑧

Kismet Inn 44 Summer St ☎207/443-3399, ☻www.kismetinnmaine.com. This turreted Queen Anne house features bright rooms, luxurious soaking tubs, body scrubs, and yoga classes one block from downtown. ⑥–⑨

The Town

With more than seven thousand employees, **Bath Iron Works**, two miles south of the town center, is the largest private employer in the state – and, thanks to a continuous stream of government contracts, the only shipbuilder remaining in Bath. Workers keep the factory running around the clock, so you should aim to avoid driving anywhere in Bath around 3.30pm, when shifts change and traffic slows. You can take a trolley tour of the Works (reservations recommended; $26) via the **Maine Maritime Museum**, 243 Washington St, next to the Iron Works (daily 9.30am–5pm; $10 for two days; ☎207/443-1316, ☻www.bathmaine.com). At the museum itself, you can also tour the old Percy & Small shipyard, explore several historic vessels, and browse the Maritime History Building, where galleries house an interesting range of ship-related paintings, photographs, and artifacts. Outside, there's an intriguing, 426ft steel sculpture of the *Wyoming* – the largest wooden vessel ever built in the US, made here in 1909 – that delineates the size

AMC huts on Georgetown Peninsula

The **Appalachian Mountain Club** (☎603/466-2727, ☻www.outdoors.org) maintains a couple of excellent low-budget **accommodations** on Georgetown Peninsula. At the *Knubble Bay Camp*, a friendly riverfront cabin with a nice porch and kitchen ($80 per day for three people, $12 each additional person), there's bunk space for up to fifteen people. The site is accessible by car, and parking is available ($1 per day). A much more primitive option is the secluded wilderness campground at Beal Island (closed in winter; $12 per night), which is accessible only by canoe or kayak.

▲ Maine Maritime Museum

of the ship. There's also a mini-pirate ship for little buccaneers to climb around on. The museum also runs a number of appealing **boat trips** and cruises (call for schedule and prices).

A pretty fourteen-mile drive south along Rte-209 leads to gorgeous **Popham Beach** ($4; ☎ 207/389-1335), at the end of the Phippsburg Peninsula, and part of a 529-acre state park. Outside of its scenic sands, you can explore **Fort Popham**, a nineteenth-century granite fort; it also has some nicely situated picnic benches facing the ocean. The **Georgetown Peninsula**, just east from Bath and down Rte-127, contains another superior beach at **Reid State Park** (☎ 207/371-2303), where the dunes flatten out into three miles of seashore.

Eating and drinking

The majority of Bath's **restaurants** are hearty, no-nonsense grub-holes that cater to off-duty BIW employees.

Beale Street Barbeque and Grill 215 Water St ☎ 207/442-9514. Hickory-smoked Memphis barbecue in an airy, modern dining room. Takeout available.

The Cabin 552 Washington St ☎ 207/443-6224. Near the museum, the *Cabin* dishes out some of Maine's best pizza in dark, wooden booths.

Five Islands Lobster Co. 1447 Five Islands Rd (off Rte-127), 12 miles south in Georgetown ☎ 207/371-2990. One of the coolest spots around to eat lobster or great fried clams. The picnic tables have amazing views that take in boats, islands, and a lighthouse. Open May to Oct only.

Montsweag Roadhouse 942 Rte-1, north of Bath in Woolrich ☎ 207/443-6563. If you're headed north on Rte-1, this is a fun stop – the *Roadhouse* seamlessly ranges from fine dining to biker

hangout and has a menu (think sandwiches, seafood, pizza, and steak) almost as big as its premises, a sprawling old house.

Robinhood Free Meetinghouse Robinhood Rd, Georgetown, north of Bath along Rte-127 ☎ 207/371-2188. This is one of Maine's premier restaurants, and worth the detour. Housed in Georgetown's former town hall, the creative American bistro integrates touches of Cajun, Italian, and Szechuan cuisine into its $25-and-up entrees. Don't miss the biscuits. Reservations recommended.

Solo Bistro Bistro 128 Front St ☎ 207/443-3373. Very hip bistro with bright, modern seating. Dinner is a tasty, seasonal, upscale affair with the likes of spiced pork tenderloin and gorgonzola polenta. There's also a cute wine bar downstairs.

Hunting for Maine's best lobster roll

There is a healthy amount of debate about where to find the "best" lobster roll in Maine. Eating at **Red's Eats** (Rte-1, Wiscasset; ☎207/882-6128) is certainly a Maine rite of passage – people line the block to get their hands on his using-the-entire-lobster roll – but some locals might question the waiting. Scenery is also a factor, and for this category **Two Lights** in Cape Elizabeth (see p.473), **Five Islands Lobster Co.** in Georgetown (see p.481), and **Shaw's Fish & Lobster Wharf** in New Harbor (see p.485), are perhaps the strongest contenders, with outstanding rolls further complemented by unbelievably scenic water views. At the end of the day, though, you can't go too wrong anywhere in the state. Just make sure the lobster is **fresh** – and by fresh we mean straight from the boat (anything advertised as "handpicked" is a good sign). You shouldn't stand for any tomfoolery with the ingredients, either: look for a roll that is dressed simply with mayo, salt, and pepper, and a perfectly grilled hot dog bun – remember that the lobster should be the star flavor.

Boothbay Harbor

Less than fifteen miles south of Rte-1 along Rte-27, several villages cluster near the end of the Boothbay Peninsula. The most active of these is **BOOTHBAY HARBOR**, a crowded, yet undeniably pretty, resort town on the peninsula's western edge. Much of the town's history as a prosperous fishing and shipbuilding center has been obscured by tourism, which has been an active pursuit here since the late nineteenth century, resulting in a wealth of predictable shops and restaurants. Nevertheless, the village is beautifully situated on a harbor, and has a lively town center, some good inns, and ample opportunities to explore the sea and surrounding coast. For a more genuine Maine experience, however, you might try the less popular neighboring Pemaquid Peninsula or even the Blue Hill Peninsula, closer to Bar Harbor.

Arrival, information, and local transport

The town is not easily reached via **public transport**. Concord Coach (☎1-800/639-3317) stops in nearby Wiscasset twice daily, from where you can catch a taxi on to Boothbay; try Platinum Plus (☎207/443-9166). Courtesy **trolleys** run frequently from the Meadow Mall, on Rte-27 across the street from the Chamber of Commerce (10am–5pm in summer), to various points in town. The Chamber itself (☎207/633-2353) is a very good source of **information**, with binders on local accommodation and a reservation service. The Boothbay Harbor Memorial Library, 4 Oak St (☎207/633-3112), has free **internet access**.

Though it's quite likely you'll have arrived by car, Boothbay Harbor is definitely not well designed for auto travel – the town's windy, narrow streets are packed with cars all summer long and **parking** can be a nightmare. It's a good idea to park farther out, along West, Howard, or Sea streets, or take the shuttle into town from the Meadow Mall.

Accommodation

You can always find some sort of **place to stay** in Boothbay Harbor, but in the summer, try to book at least a month in advance. In addition to several resort-style motels there are lots of B&Bs in the town center and on the eastern shore of the harbor. Prices are considerably lower at the beginning and end of the tourist season, and many places close down by mid-October.

Anchor Watch B&B 9 Eames Rd ☎207/633-7565, ⓦwww.anchorwatch.com. Pamper yourself in this cozy little B&B with an ocean view, just outside the town center. Open March–Nov. ❽

Captain Sawyer's Place 55 Commercial St ☎207/633-2290, ⓦwww.captsawyer.com. The rooms here are not huge, but the staff is very friendly and the rates are lower than at most of the other places on the strip. Full breakfast included. ❹–❻

Fisherman's Wharf Inn 22 Commercial St ☎1-800/628-6872, ⓦwww.fishermanswharfinn.com. Very centrally located motel (it's right on the wharf) with large, clean rooms, many with porches facing the harbor. Open May–Oct only. ❻–❽

Greenleaf Inn 65 Commercial St ☎1-888/950-7724, ⓦwww.greenleafinn.com. Fun, friendly B&B with an international crowd, lively and tasty breakfasts, a book and movie library, and appealing rooms right in the center of town. They also own the adjacent Admiral's Inn. ❽

The Thistle Inn 55 Oak St ☎207/633-3541, ⓦwww.thethistleinn.com. If you're willing to forego a water view, this vintage sea captain's home has beautiful rooms, unbelievable food, and fantastic innkeepers. ❺

Topside Inn 60 McKown St ☎207/633-5404, ⓦwww.topsideinn.com. Beautiful, stylish rooms in an old sea captain's house on the top of a hill, with great harbor views. Open May to mid-Oct only. ❻–❽

Welch House Inn 56 McKown St ☎1-800/279-7313, ⓦwww.welchhouseinn.com. This gabled clapboard house on a hill affords excellent views from its deck. Light and airy rooms are tastefully furnished and a buffet breakfast is included. ❻–❽

The Town

The town center runs along **Commercial Street** and **Townsend Avenue**, while the rest of the settlement spreads out around a tiny cove, thinning into residential neighborhoods southwest on Southport Island and southeast towards Ocean Point. Aside from taking a quick stroll around the town's hilly, shop-lined streets, Boothbay Harbor's main attraction lies in the inordinate number of **boat trips** on offer from the harbor behind Commercial Street. Some depart for Monhegan Island (see p.487), while others circle the coast, taking in the dramatic scenery. Balmy Days Cruises (☎207/633-2284 or 1-800/298-2284) is as good as any of the outfits on the waterfront, with all-day trips to Monhegan Island costing $32 and harbor tours for $14. The traditional windjammer *Eastwind* departs from the wharf three times daily (May–Oct; 2hr 30min round-trip; $25; ☎207/633-6598). Cap'n Fish's affable "Puffin Nature Cruises" (2hr 30min; $24; ☎207/633-3244 or 1-800/636-3244) offers glimpses of the brightly beaked birds – bring binoculars. If you'd rather explore the coast under your own power, contact the Tidal Transit Company (☎207/633-7140), which offers **kayak** rentals ($20 per hr) and tours ($35–80) and also rents **bikes** ($40 per day).

On foot, the most immediate view of the harbor is from the thousand-foot-long wooden **footbridge** that connects downtown to the east side of town. If you venture all the way across, head south along Atlantic Avenue to the pretty **Our Lady Queen of Peace** church, which holds its holy water in clam shells and has some fine architectural details. Unless you're on the move with small children, skip the rather unimpressive state-run **Marine State Aquarium** on McKown Point Road in West Boothbay Harbor (June–Sept daily 10am–5pm; $5; ☎207/633-9559), which houses a touch-tank in addition to a small number of other displays. A worthier visit is the Coastal Maine Botanical Gardens (daily 9am–5pm; $10; call for directions ☎207/633-4333; ⓦwww.mainegardens.org), which has pretty, bloom-filled trails that wind along the Sheepscot River.

Ocean Point and Southport Island

There's plenty of less crowded land to explore in the area surrounding the busy town. At the end of the pretty fifteen-minute drive south along Rte-96 to desolate **Ocean Point**, you are rewarded with views of the horizon across the ocean, interrupted only by Squirrel, Fisherman, and Ram islands, with its prominent lighthouse. A few miles north on the same peninsula, the **Linekin Preserve** maintains extensive **hiking trails** on nearly a hundred acres of wilderness between Rte-96 and the coast. On relatively deserted **Southport Island**, south on Rte-27, you can drive all the way to Newagen, with its views of the Cuckolds Lighthouse, a half-mile out to sea.

Eating and drinking

There are good eats to be had in Boothbay Harbor, ranging from vintage seafood joints to fairly stylish dinner spots. Many restaurants close between October and May.

Boathouse Bistro 12 The By-Way (Pier 1) ⊤207/633-0400. Excellent tapas – like Maine maple scallops ($6) or bacon-wrapped dates with pecans ($5) – in a fun, sunny, rooftop bar setting.
Blue Moon Café 54 Commercial St ⊤207/633-2220. Probably the least expensive of the places right on the water, serving a variety of delicious hot and cold sandwiches, including veggie specials. There's indoor and outdoor seating (with great views), and it's open for breakfast and lunch.
Ebb Tide 43 Commercial St ⊤207/633-5692. Cheap, utilitarian breakfasts and dinners are served all day at this vintage blue-collar joint right in the center of town. If you're here in the summer, don't miss the fresh peach shortcake.
Lobster Dock 49 Atlantic Ave ⊤207/633-7120. Ultra-fresh lobster rolls, crab cakes, and seafood

dinners, accompanied by great views of the harbor. Casual, beer-and-picnic-table vibe.
McSeagull's Pier 1 ⊤207/633-5900. Right in the center of town, this casual eatery has a large menu with the likes of seafood fettucine and crab and avocado quesadillas served on their harborside porch or spacious dining room. Takeout also available. Open until 10pm.
Ports of Italy 47 Commercial St ⊤207/633-1011. An excellent dinner spot, with authentic Northern Italian cuisine served in a cozy second-floor dining room. Reservations recommended.
The Thistle Inn 55 Oak St ⊤207/633-3541. One of the best restaurants in Boothbay, serving creative dishes like brandied lobster in puff pastry, perfectly seared tuna, fruit-infused martinis, and great crème brûlée. Reservations recommended.

Damariscotta

The compact town of **DAMARISCOTTA**, just off Rte-1 across the Damariscotta River from Newcastle, is a pretty entrance point into Maine's region of lakes and loons, with a quaint Main Street that's a good place to stop for lunch or a stroll. From town, River Road leads south to **Dodge Point**, where you can **hike** along several miles of trails or hang out on the sandy **beach** along the Damariscotta River in summer. It's also a popular spot for **fishing**, where anglers fish for striped bass, bluefish, and mackerel. You can dig for clams in the offshore tidal flats – contact the Newcastle Town Office (⊤207/563-3441) for rules and regulations.

Practicalities

Damariscotta is a pleasant place to stay while exploring the Pemaquid Peninsula, to the south, and it's host to the region's friendly **Chamber of Commerce**, 15 Courtyard St, Suite 2 (⊤207/563-8340). The best **accommodation** in the area, however, is at ⚑ *Blue Skye Farm* in neighboring Waldoboro at 1708 Friendship Rd (follow the signs from Rte-1; ⊤207/832-0300, ⊛www.blueskyefarm .com; ❹–❻). Open year-round, the B&B is favored for its surrounding acres of woodlands, well-priced, appealing accommodation, and fantastic proprietors. The *Newcastle Inn*, at 60 River Rd in Newcastle (⊤207/563-5685, ⊛www .newcastleinn.com; ❻), is another great spot with lots of character and fifteen unique rooms named for lighthouses. Also in Newcastle, the *Flying Cloud B&B*,

45 River Rd (☎207/563-2484, ⓦwww.theflyingcloud.com; ❹–❽), is an immaculately restored 1840s sea captain's home with five rooms and an elegant yet cozy atmosphere.

In terms of places to **eat** and **drink**, both *King Eider's Pub*, 2 Elm St (head for the downstairs bar area; ☎207/563-6008), and the *Salt Bay Café*, 88 Main St (☎207/563-3302), are two local favorites; the former is a fun pub complemented by creative entrees, and the latter has simple but fresh seafood, soups, sandwiches, and steaks. On Rte-1 east of town in **Waldoboro** is the legendary 🍴 *Moody's Diner* (☎207/832-7785), a Maine institution for more than eighty years. *Moody's* is the real deal, open late and oozing nostalgia, with inexpensive daily specials, soups, and fourteen types of pie – their four-berry is a must-have. Another local landmark in North Waldoboro is the amazing *Morse's Sauerkraut* 3856 Washington Rd/Rte-220 (☎207/832-5569; closed Wed), which offers tasty breakfasts and lunches and peddles chocolates, jams, meats, cheeses, and house-made sauerkraut from its endearing German foodstuffs store dating to 1918.

The Pemaquid Peninsula

From Damariscotta, the **PEMAQUID PENINSULA** (Pemaquid means "long finger" in the native language) points some fifteen miles south along routes 129 and 130, culminating in the rocky **Pemaquid Point**. Archeological studies have recently concluded that this was the site of an English settlement in 1626, making it the northernmost British colonial settlement. **Colonial Pemaquid**, a small state-run museum on the site, just west of New Harbor off Rte-130 (late May to early Sept daily 10am–7pm; $3; ☎207/677-2423), houses old pottery, farming tools, and other household items. Over the years, ongoing excavation has also unearthed stone walls and foundations dating back to the seventeenth century. Within the nineteen-acre historical site stands a 1908 replica of **Fort William Henry**, the original built in 1677 by English settlers to ward off pirates, the French, and Native Americans, who are believed to have inhabited the peninsula as early as two thousand years ago. Though the robust fortress was thought to be impenetrable, it was overrun three times in the seventeenth century. There are good **ocean views** from the top of the massive citadel.

Nearby, the sands of **Pemaquid Beach**, just off Snowball Hill Road, are some of the most inviting in the state, and are correspondingly crowded on sunny summer weekends. Nevertheless, it's a great place to catch some rays, and even though the water can be cold, swimming is not impossible (parking $2). There's another, smaller **beach** all the way around the bend near the end of Rte-129 on Rutherford Island at **Christmas Cove**, so named by Captain John Smith after the day on which he discovered it.

Just north of Pemaquid Beach, from 🍴 *Shaw's Fish and Lobster Wharf* (see box, p.482; ☎207/677-2200) in quaint **New Harbor**, Hardy Boat Cruises (☎207/677-2026) runs daily **boat trips** (9am & 2pm) out to Monhegan Island for $30 round-trip, in addition to seal watches ($12), well-recommended puffin watches ($22), and shorter scenic cruises ($12 and up).

South along Rte-130, at the tip of Pemaquid Point, the **Pemaquid Point Lighthouse** ($2) sits on a dramatic granite outcrop constantly battered by the violent Atlantic surf. You can wander around the small park for a good view of the salt-stained light, built in 1827 and still operational, but be careful not to get too close to the rocks at the water's edge. The adjoining keeper's quarters have been transformed into the small **Fishermen's Museum** (May–Oct 10am–5pm;

There are probably few better places to observe **lighthouses** than on Maine's coast, where some 68 of the structures direct ships of all sizes along the rocky coast from Kittery up to Quoddy Head. For centuries much of Maine's economy has centered on the sea, and its lighthouses have become symbols of this dependence (not to mention the saving grace of many a ship). Consequently, a series of museums serves to illustrate their history, none more prominent than the **Maine Lighthouse Museum** in Rockland's Chamber of Commerce (see p.489). Some of Maine's most dramatic lighthouses include the lonely **West Quoddy Head Light** (see p.510), a candy-striped beauty in Lubec and the easternmost point in the US; the scenic **Pemaquid Point Light**, south of Damariscotta (see p.485); and the **Cape Elizabeth Lighthouse** near Portland (see p.470), which was commissioned by none other than George Washington. **Lighthouse tours** are easy to come by – ask around locally to see what's available in your area. One good tour is run by the *Elms B&B* in Camden – call ☎207/236-6060 or 1-800/388-6000 for more information.

donation requested), containing exhibits related to the local fishing trade and, more interestingly, a map of Maine with a photo and description of each of the state's 68 lighthouses (see box above).

Another potential diversion on the Pemaquid Peninsula is the **Thompson Ice House**, Rte-129 north of South Bristol (July & Aug Mon, Wed, Fri & Sat 1–4pm; $1 suggested donation; ☎207/644-8551). Although modern refrigeration has eliminated the ice industry, this house was in operation for 150 years, harvesting ice from a nearby pond and shipping it to points as far away as South America. Business mostly halted here in 1986, but the building, which sports ten-inch-thick sawdust-insulated walls, has been restored into a museum and working ice-harvesting facility. In the summer, you can check out a display of the defunct trade's tools and gaze at photos depicting ice harvesters in action. In February, townspeople still gather to collect ice from a pond using old-fashioned tools before burying the blocks in hay until summer, when they are sold to local fishermen.

Practicalities

Just back from the Pemaquid Lighthouse, you can enjoy reasonably priced American **food** with a fine view of the water at the café that adjoins the Sea Gull Gift Shop (☎207/677-2374). If you're in the area, definitely stop in for breakfast at the *Cupboard Café*, 137 Huddle Rd in New Harbor (☎207/677-3911) – their cinnamon rolls will change your life. The *Anchor Inn* on Anchor Inn Road in Round Pond (☎207/529-5584) is another good bet, with crab cakes, stuffed lobster, pastas, and succulent steaks in a rustic dining room overlooking the harbor. There are also a number of traditional **lobster pounds** on the peninsula in New Harbor and Round Pond.

If you'd like to stay close to the lighthouse, the *Hotel Pemaquid*, only 100 yards away at 3098 Bristol Rd (Rte-130) (☎207/677-2312; open June–Oct; cash only; ④–⑤), offers Victorian furnishings in casual surroundings – some rooms share baths. Another option is the *Gosnold Arms* on Rte-32 in New Harbor (☎207/677-3727; ⑤–⑥), with country furnishings and superb harbor views. Basic **campsites** are available up the road near Pemaquid Beach at the *Sherwood Forest Campsite*, on Pemaquid Trail in New Harbor (☎207/677-3642 or 1-800/274-1593; $27–31), which has multiple aquatic options: the ocean is only 800ft away, plus they have their own pool.

Monhegan Island

Deliberately low-key **MONHEGAN ISLAND**, eleven miles from the mainland, has long attracted a hardy mix of artists and fishermen. It also attracts its fair share of tourists, but for good reason: it's the most worthwhile jaunt away from the mainland along the entirety of the Maine coast. Not much has changed since artist Robert Henri first came here in the early 1900s looking for tranquility and solitude – credit cards are not readily accepted, and there are only two public restrooms. Though there were already a few artists residing on the island at the time, Henri introduced the place to George Bellows and Rockwell Kent, establishing it as a genuine artists' colony. Edward Hopper also spent time here, and the youngest of the Wyeth family, Jamie, currently calls Monhegan his summer home.

The small village – occupying only twenty percent of the island – huddles around the tiny harbor, protected by Manana and Smutty Nose islands. Other than a few old hotels and some good restaurants, there's not much here. Some seventeen miles of **hiking trails** crisscross the eastern half of the island, leading through dense stands of fir and spruce to the headlands, 160ft above the island's eastern shore. Monhegan Associates publishes a reliable **trail map**, available at most island stores, which is quite handy.

The **Monhegan Island Lighthouse**, on a hill overlooking the village (and a great place to watch the sunset), was erected in 1824 and automated in 1959. You can check out the **Monhegan Museum** inside the former keeper's house (July–Sept daily 11.30am–3.30pm, Sept 1–30 daily 1.30–3.30pm; $4 donation), where there's also a building to house the work of Monhegan artists, including a few paintings by Rockwell Kent and Jamie Wyeth. Other rooms display artifacts, photographs, and documents relating to island history and natural features.

In summer, some of the artists in residence on the island open their **studios** to visitors. For times and locations, check the bulletin boards around town. You can also see works by local artists at one of several **galleries** – the Lupine Gallery (T 207/594-8131) at the end of Wharf Hill Road has a consistently good grouping of local works on display.

Practicalities

There's not a great deal of **accommodation** choice on the island, so you should plan on reserving a room well in advance. The largest place to stay is the *Island Inn* (T 207/596-0371; May–Oct; ⑧–⑨), an attractive 1807 structure

---

Getting to Monhegan Island

You can access Monhegan from three different towns: Port Clyde, Boothbay Harbor, and New Harbor. To ensure a spot with one of the three boat carriers connecting the mainland with Monhegan, make sure you call in advance. Boats depart from Port Clyde for Monhegan three times daily during the summer and less often during the winter, arriving about an hour later, depending on which boat is in service ($18 one-way, $30 round-trip; T 207/372-8848, W www.monheganboat.com). From Boothbay Harbor you can take the *Balmy Days III* (end of May to mid-Oct; $32 round-trip; T 207/633-2284 or 1-800/298-2284, W www.balmydayscruises.com), which departs once daily at 9.30am and takes ninety minutes. The *Hardy Boat* takes seventy minutes to get from Shaw's Wharf in New Harbor (see p.482) to Monhegan (late May & early Oct departs Wed, Sat & Sun at 9am; June–Oct daily at 9am and 2pm; $30 round-trip; T 207/677-2026 or 1-800/278-3346, W www.hardyboat.com).

with stylish rooms overlooking the harbor. Many of the rooms at the funky *Trailing Yew* (☎207/596-6194; May–Oct; cash only; ④), spread out among several buildings, do not have heat or electricity, while the guest accommodation at *Shining Sails B&B* (☎207/596-0041, ⊛http://shiningsails.com; ⑦–⑧) is modern, with private baths; some even have small decks with ocean views. The *Hitchcock House*, at the top of Horn's Hill (☎207/594-8137; ④–⑤), has two simple efficiencies with living and kitchen area and deck, as well as several private rooms.

The island's selection of sit-down **restaurants** are all good, hearty, and affordable affairs. At the *Island Inn* (see p.487), tasty breakfasts generally include the signature lobster casserole, while dinner is more upscale and shows off the water view. The *Monhegan House Café* (☎207/594-7983) has a menu featuring simple meat, fish, and vegetarian dishes. You can get soups and sandwiches as well as wine and groceries at *North End Market*, up the hill and to the right from the wharf (☎207/594-5546). For light **snacks and coffee**, head to the *Barnacle* (late May to mid-Oct), overlooking the wharf; it houses the only ATM on the island and serves salads, sandwiches, espresso drinks, and baked goodies.

Rockland

Driving down Main Street in seaside **ROCKLAND**, you might observe an old truck to your left and, a minute later, a shiny BMW to your right. Such is the socioeconomic make-up of the town, one of the more hip settlements in the state. Home to the annual Maine Lobster Festival (the first weekend of Aug; ☎1-800/LOB-CLAW, ⊛www.mainelobsterfestival.com) as well as the North Atlantic Blues Festival (mid-July; ☎207/596-6055, ⊛www.northatlanticbluesfestival .com), Rockland has historically been Maine's largest lobster distributor, and boasts the busiest working harbor in the state. This blue-collar vibe is anchored by a strong arts and cultural scene: Rockland is blessed with some remarkable museums and a happening Art Deco movie theater.

The town and around

The town's centerpiece is the outstanding **Farnsworth Art Museum**, 16 Museum St (late May to mid-Oct daily 10am–5pm; rest of year Tues–Sun 10am–5pm; $10; ☎207/596-6457), established in 1935 through the bequest of the reclusive Lucy Farnsworth, who rather surprised the town by leaving $1.3 million to build a museum in her father's honor. The museum comprises several buildings, including the **Wyeth Center**, a converted old church that holds two floors' worth of works by Jamie and N.C. Wyeth. Across the street (at the museum proper), the impressive collection spans two centuries of American art – much of it Maine-related. The focal point is the permanent "Maine in America" exhibit, which features landscapes and seascapes by Fitz Henry Lane, portraits by American Impressionist Frank Benson, watercolors by Winslow Homer, and, of course, dramatic canvases from the Wyeths. The museum does not own *Christina's World*, Andrew Wyeth's most famous work, but you can visit the field and home depicted in the painting at the **Olson House**, Hathorn Point Road, just outside of town in Cushing (late May to mid-Oct daily 11am–4pm; $4 or free with museum admission). Admission to the museum also gets you into the **Farnsworth Homestead**, tucked between museum buildings on Elm Street (late May to mid-Oct daily 10am–5pm), a fine example of Victorian opulence.

Rockland's other star attraction is the **Strand Theatre**, 345 Main St (tickets $8; ☎207/594-0070; ⓦwww.rocklandstrand.com), with diverse live acts, live Met Opera broadcasts, and contemporary and classic films. The lush theater was originally opened in 1923, closed rather mysteriously in 2000, and then reopened in 2005 after an extensive restoration. Another worthwhile museum, the **Maine Lighthouse Museum**, in the same building as the Chamber of Commerce, 1 Park Drive (Mon–Fri May–Oct 9am–5pm, Sat & Sun 10am–4pm; rest of year closed Sun; $5; ☎207/594-3301), allows you to peruse one of the largest collections of lighthouse memorabilia and artifacts in the country. It's fun to press the buttons that trigger various foghorns and bells, but the real attraction is the curator, who probably knows more about lighthouses than anyone in existence. The **Owls Head Transportation Museum**, three miles south of Rockland on Rte-73 at Owls Head (April–Oct daily 10am–5pm; rest of year daily 10am–4pm; $10; ☎207/594-4418, ⓦwww.ohtm.org), is a similarly niche-oriented spot, with a vintage (mostly working) collection of cars, motorcycles, and planes from a bygone era, including a full-scale replica of the Wright Brothers' 1903 *Flyer*. During the summer they also do great airplane shows. For **food**, head to the *Owls Head General Store*, 2 S Shore Drive near the airport (☎207/596-6038), which offers tasty bites like crab sandwiches and pumpkin whoopee pies.

The harbor

From Rockland's enormous **harbor**, a number of powerboat and **windjammer** companies compete for your business with offers of everything from leisurely morning breakfast cruises to week-long island-hopping charters. The majority set sail for three to six days at a time, costing a little more than $125 per night, including all meals. You really can't go wrong with any of the options, but a few boats to try include the luxurious 68-foot *Stephen Taber* (☎1-800/999-7352), the three-masted *Victory Chimes*, featured on the Maine state quarter (☎1-800/745-5651), or the 95-foot *Schooner Heritage* (☎1-800/648-4544). If you're having trouble finding what you want, stop by the Chamber of Commerce at 1 Park Drive, or call the Maine Windjammer Association (☎1-800/807-9463). As an alternative, **Captain Jack Lobster Boat Adventure** offers great lobstering trips captained by a former lobsterman ($25; ☎207/542-6852). Down the road at 517A Main St, the **Maine State Ferry Service** (☎207/596-2202 or 1-800/491-4883) runs modern vessels out to the summer retreats of Vinalhaven (75min; $12) and North Haven (1hr; $12), both of which make for relaxing day-trips.

For views of the water without actually boarding a boat, head to the **Rockland Breakwater**, a man-made granite structure jutting into the water and providing additional protection for the harbor. At its terminus lies the picturesque Rockland Breakwater lighthouse. To get there, take Waldo Avenue south from Rte-1 to Samoset Road. Go right on Samoset and the road will dead-end into Marie Reed Park, at the base of the breakwater.

St George Peninsula

South of Rockland, the lovely **St George Peninsula**, in particular the village of Tenants Harbor, inspired writer Sarah Orne Jewett's classic Maine novel *Country of the Pointed Firs*. Jewett describes the landscape so deftly that you can still pick out many of the sites depicted in the book, much of which was written in a tiny schoolhouse in Martinsville, since rebuilt. Boats sail from the hamlet of Port Clyde, at the tip of the peninsula, to **Monhegan Island** (see p.487) You may recognize Port Clyde's picturesque 1857 Marshall Point Lighthouse from the movie *Forrest Gump*; there's a small historical museum in the old keeper's house.

Practicalities

Thanks to Cape Air (☎1-800/352-0714), you can **fly** to Rockland's Knox County Regional Airport direct from Boston, for a mere $80 each way. The **bus station** is at the Maine State Ferry building, 517A Main St, just a short walk away from the **Chamber of Commerce** (same hours as Lighthouse Museum, see p.489; ☎207/596-0376), which has comprehensive listings and information. A fun day-trip is the **Maine Eastern Railroad** ($40 round-trip; ☎1-866/637-2457, ⓦwww.maineeasternrailroad.com), which provides scenic two-hour coastal trips between Rockland and Brunswick (including stops in Bath and Wiscasset), in its restored Art Deco railcars.

A good **place to stay** in the town center is the *Captain Lindsey House Inn*, 5 Lindsey St (☎207/596-7950 or 1-800/523-2145; ❻), snugly decorated with down comforters and puffy pillows. In a turreted Victorian mansion, the ⚡ *LimeRock Inn*, 96 LimeRock St (☎207/594-2257 or 1-800/LIMEROC, ⓦwww.limerockinn.com; ❼–❽) has elegant yet comfortable rooms, good breakfasts, and great proprietors. The endearing little *Ripples Inn* (☎207/594-5771, ⓦwww.ripplesinnattheharbor.com; ❼–❽) has bright rooms in a cozy old Victorian right near the center of town.

You won't go hungry in Rockland. Some of the best **food** in town can be had at funky and perennially crowded *Café Miranda*, tucked away at 15 Oak St (☎207/594-2034); the appetizing array of international entrees ranges from sea scallops with leeks and cream ($24) to lamb "wowie" in a curry spice mix ($21.50). Situated in expanded new digs at the corner of Ocean and Water streets, *Amalfi on the Water* (☎207/596-0012; closed Mon; reservations recommended) features creative seafood fare with some surprises (such as lobster pad thai) slipped onto its menu. *Primo*, 2 S Main St (☎207/596-0770), has some of the best food in the state (for less moderate prices) from its scenic Victorian digs. Another popular spot is the *Brass Compass Café*, 305 Main St (☎207/596-5960), with standout breakfast and lunch options – try the haddock club sandwich ($8). *Rock City Books & Coffee*, 328 Main St (☎207/594-4123), is a friendly place to eat pastries and drink locally roasted **coffee**. And finally, there's the irreplaceable *Conte's 1894 Restaurant*, in a sea shack right on the water (no phone, no credit cards, no printed menus), offering gruff service and incredibly fresh entrees ($8–25) from an irrepressible Italian cook.

Camden

The adjacent communities of Rockport and **CAMDEN** split into two separate towns in 1891 over a dispute as to who should pay for a new bridge over the Goose River, which runs between them. Since then Camden has clearly won the competition for tourists; indeed, it's one of the few towns in Maine that attracts visitors year-round (it helps that Rte-1 heads right through its downtown). Today the essential stop in town is **Camden Hills State Park**, which affords beautiful coastal views and has good camping. Camden's other highlight is its huge fleet of wind-powered schooners known as **windjammers**, many of which date back to the late nineteenth century, when the town was successful in the shipbuilding trade.

Arrival and information

Concord Coach's closest **bus** stop is in Rockport at the Maritime Farms Convenient Store on Rte-1. Once in Camden, downtown is actually compact

▲ Camden harbor

enough to be explored **on foot**. If you've got a car, know that **parking** can be a problem, but with patience you can usually find something on Chestnut Street or by the police station on Washington Street.

Camden's **information office**, down at 2 Public Landing (℡207/236-4404, Ⓦwww.camdenme.org), is usually a big help with finding a place to stay; they also stock a dizzying array of brochures. You can get free **internet access** at the Camden Public Library, located partially underground on Atlantic Avenue, across from Harbor Park. Published every Wednesday and available at many shops, *Steppin' Out* has comprehensive **listings** of all the goings-on in the area.

Accommodation

While **accommodation** in Camden is plentiful, it is not cheap – it is difficult to find a room for less than $125. The budget spots congregate along Rte-1 farther north in Lincolnville. There are over a dozen B&Bs in the immediate area, but you'd still be well advised to call in advance; Camden Accommodations runs a **reservation service** (℡207/236-6090) for longer-term accommodations such as house rentals. Most of the hotels and B&Bs stay open all year here. Camden Hills State Park (see opposite) is one of the best places to **camp** along the coast (℡207/236-3109).

The Belmont 6 Belmont Ave ℡207/236-8053 or 1-800-238-8053, Ⓦwww.thebelmontinn.com. Decorated with conservative elegance, this stately inn sits on a residential street just beyond the commercial district. ❼
Camden Maine Stay Inn 22 High St ℡207/236-9636, Ⓦwww.camdenmainestay.com. Beautiful, three-story white-clapboard 1813 inn, with eight inviting rooms. ❻–❽
Cedarholm Garden Bay Inn 2159 Atlantic Highway (Rte-1), Lincolnville ℡207/236-3886 or 1-800-540-3886, Ⓦwww.cedarholm.com. Pricey, but very beautiful secluded cottages built for two.

A great honeymoon spot, with lush gardens and wonderful water views. ❾
Captain Swift Inn 72 Elm St ℡207/236-8113 or 1-800-251-0865, Ⓦwww.swiftinn.com. Eight rooms in a restored Federalist house – ask for one in the rear if possible, as the traffic on Elm St (Rte-1) can be bothersome. ❻–❽
Ducktrap Motel Rte-1, Lincolnville ℡207/789-5400 or 1-877/977-5400, Ⓦwww.ducktrapmotel.com. Cute, basic budget option north of town. They also have an ocean-view cottage as well as two larger, family-sized rooms. ❺

The Elms B&B 84 Elm St ☎207/236-6060 or 1-800/388-6060, ⓦwww.elmsinn.net. A Colonial home at the southern end of Elm St. The rooms are cozy and the bubbly owners – lighthouse enthusiasts – offer a range of lighthouse tours. ⑦–⑧

The Hawthorn 9 High St ☎1-800/381-3647, ⓦwww.camdenhawthorn.com. Well situated by Camden Harbor and with nice views of Mount Battie, this favorite has lush gardens, a veranda, wi-fi, and a lovely, helpful proprietor. ⑧–⑨

Inn at Sunrise Point Fire Rd 9, off Rte-1, Lincolnville ☎207/236-7716, ⓦwww.sunrisepoint .com. This secluded, luxurious B&B frequently graces the pages of travel magazines, and with good reason – its indulgent rooms and stunning views continue to lure back guests. ⑨

The town and around

As in Rockland, Camden's speciality is organizing sailing expeditions of up to six days in the large schooners known as **windjammers**. Daysailers, which tour the seas just beyond the harbor, include the *Appledore* (☎207/236-8353), the *Surprise* (☎207/236-4687), and the *Olad* (☎207/236-2323). Sails on these boats cost anywhere from $30 to $80 and can often be booked on the same day – each vessel usually has an information table set up along the public landing. Longer **overnight trips**, including all meals, can cost from $550 to $1200 (for six days) and should be booked in advance; the ships stop at various points of interest along the coast, such as Castine, Stonington, and Mount Desert Island. Contact the Maine Windjammer Association (☎1-800/807-WIND) for information.

In the center of town, the immaculately maintained **Harbor Park**, right where the Megunticook River spills into the sea, is a good spot to relax after wandering the town's small shopping district, which runs south from Main Street along the water. Farther down Bayview Street, which holds many of the shops, tiny **Laite Beach** looks out onto the Penobscot Bay.

Camden Hills State Park

Just north of town, Rte-1 leads towards **Camden Hills State Park** ($3 entrance fee), the best spot around for **hiking** and camping. Rather than drive, pick up the **Mount Battie Trail** (45min) that begins at the intersection of Spring Street and Harden Avenue, a short walk from the town center. The panoramic views of the harbor and Maine coastline from the top of 790-foot Mount Battie are hard to beat; on the summit, you can climb to the top of a circular World War I memorial for the best vantage point. It was here that poet Edna St Vincent Millay (see box opposite) penned part of her poem, *Renascence*, which is commemorated with a small plaque. There's a variety of other trails in the area, including ones that head to the summits of **Ocean Lookout** and **Zeke's Lookout**; you can get a decent free hiking map at the ranger station in the parking lot at the park entrance just off Rte-1.

Eating and drinking

Camden has a good array of **eating and drinking** spots, from gourmet restaurants to casual seafood joints to busy bars. One thing is for sure: on summer weekends, they're all going to be full, so plan on waiting for a table.

Camden Bagel Café 25 Mechanic St ☎207/236-2661. Popular morning spot with tables in a sunny dining area, lots of fresh bagels, coffee, sandwiches, and salads.

Camden Deli 37 Main St ☎207/236-8343. Great variety of bulging, gourmet sandwiches and deli salads, right in the center of town overlooking the harbor. They also serve beer and wine.

Cappy's Chowder House 1 Main St ☎207/236-2254. This cramped, child-friendly bar and restaurant is the place to go in town for a casual drink or meal. They also have an adjacent bakery.

Francine 55 Chestnut St ☎207/230-0083. Elegant French bistro with tealights and aubergine walls. The menu changes daily, and

Edna St Vincent Millay

Edna St Vincent Millay came to Camden with her divorced mother and two sisters in 1900, when she was 8 years old. Her mother encouraged all the sisters in the arts, and Edna (she insisted on being called "Vincent") excelled in writing. As a young child, she had poems published in *St Nicholas*, a children's magazine, and by age 20 she had won international recognition for her poem, *Renascence*, which she first recited at the *Whitehall Inn*, 52 High St (☎207/236-3391 or 1-800/789-6565). Today, the inn maintains a small collection of writings and photos depicting her Camden childhood. Millay reputedly had a rather carefree adulthood, too: an acknowledged bisexual, she had many affairs with women, and when she finally did marry a man, it was on open terms. A lifelong smoker, she died of heart failure in 1950.

features fresh fare such as haddock with mint and tomato chutney ($23) or Charentaise melon salad with goat cheese, cucumbers, and crispy prosciutto ($8).
Lobster Pound Restaurant Rte-1, Lincolnville Beach ☎207/789-5550. Casual and wildly popular seaside restaurant serving heaps of the bright-red crustaceans.
Scott's Place 85 Elm St ☎207/236-8751. Two great Maine institutions at one location – cheap and tasty lobster rolls, served from a stand next to

hardware mainstay Reny's. They also have hot dogs, toasted sandwiches, and the like.
Waterfront Restaurant 44 Bayview St ☎207/236-3747. The delicious clam chowder, fisherman's stew, and fresh seafood pastas are a bit expensive, but you can't beat the dockside seating.
Whalestooth Pub & Restaurant Rte-1, Lincolnville Beach ☎207/789-5200. A few miles north of Camden, this year-round local favorite has a chatty ambience and enjoyable steak and fish fare.

Rockport

Just over the town line from Camden, Concord Coach (☎1-800/639-3317) has a **bus** stop in tranquil **ROCKPORT** at the Maritime Farms Convenient Store on Rte-1. A bit of the town's lime-producing past can be viewed via the decaying **lime kilns** in pleasant Marine Park, next to the harbor just off Rte-1. The park also houses a statue of Rockport's most famous former citizen, André the Seal. André was adopted in 1961 after Harry Goodbridge found the little seal pup abandoned out in the water. In his lifetime, André spent his winters at the Boston aquarium, and come fall, would find his way back home to the Goodbridge residence in Rockport (a distance of 150 miles). At one point he was made honorary harbor-master, and in 1978, helped to unveil this statue, done in his likeness.

Don't underestimate the magnetism of the Belted Galloway cows at **Aldermere Farm**, on Russell Avenue (☎207/236-2739, ⓦwww.aldermere.org). These endearing "Oreo cows" (so named for their black-white-black stripe pattern) have been amusing passers-by for ages. The farm doesn't currently have any public programming, but the cows are nearly always in view for camera-snapping fans.

The tiny town center holds a couple of intriguing galleries, such as the **Center for Maine Contemporary Art**, 162 Russell Ave (Tues–Sat 10am–5pm, Sun 1–5pm; winter closed Mon–Wed; $5; ☎207/236-2875), where local artists display their works, and the **Maine Media Workshops**, nearby at 2 Central St (☎207/236-8200), which is somewhat well known for its school of photography. Right across the street, the friendly *Corner Shop* (☎207/236-8361; closes 2pm) serves up one of the best **breakfasts** in the area, with big and cheap omelettes in a sunny room.

Belfast

Cozy **BELFAST** feels like the most liveable of the towns along the Maine coast. Here the shipbuilding boom is long since over, but the inhabitants have had the waterfront declared a historic district, sparing it from over-commercialization. A strong creative bent pervades the town these days, with many inviting galleries lining Main Street and a Gallery Walk every Friday in summer. As you stroll around, look out for the town's Greek Revival houses, particularly prevalent along the wide avenues between Church and Congress streets. At 70 Church St, in an unbelievable stroke of excessive historic puns, there once lived Mrs Wealthy Poor and her husband, who ran a drugstore on High Street (it's now a B&B). You can pick up a copy of the *Belfast Historic Walking Tour* at the convivial **information office** (℡207/338-5900), at the foot of Main Street by the bay.

Searsport, five miles north on Rte-1, is home to the atmospheric **Penobscot Marine Museum**, Rte-1 at Church Street (Mon–Sat 10am–5pm, Sun noon–5pm; $8; ℡207/548-2529), which features marine artworks and nautical artifacts that are spread between a number of historic buildings, including a nineteenth-century sea captain's home (which includes among its furnishings a very cool vintage record player and a piano with mother-of-pearl keys).

Practicalities

Up from the bay at 96 Main St, spacious ᴊ *Chase's Daily* (℡207/338-0555; closed Mon) is a great spot for **food**, with fresh eats like beet & bleu cheese salad and peach smoothies with ginger and lime as well as baked goods, produce, and fresh flower bouquets. *Three Tides*, 2 Pinchy Lane (℡207/338-1707), is a hip tapas spot right on the water that brews its own beer (and root beer) on site; their *Ship to*

Bucksport

Named after founder Colonel Jonathan Buck, quiet yet up-and-coming **BUCKSPORT** (20 miles north from Belfast on Rte-3) was first settled as a trading post in 1762. These days, it's known for its **Penobscot Narrows Observatory** (just across the river from Bucksport; daily 9am–5pm, summer 9am–7pm; $5; ℡207/469-7719), which whisks gleeful gazers up inside a 420ft viewing station. On a clear day you can see out to Mount Desert Island and Katahdin, but even if it's cloudy, it's still a thrill to look down and see traffic moving on the bridge 400 feet below you. Even if you have no particular interest in the military, the hulking **Fort Knox**, adjacent to the observatory (and where you buy your tickets; May–Oct daily 9am–sunset; admission included with observatory fee; ℡207/469-7719), still merits a wander round its castle-like structure. You can climb up and down circular stairways, stagger through tunnels that disappear into total darkness, investigate officers' quarters, and clamber to the top of the fort's thick granite walls, from where you can admire Bucksport's factory skyline. With all the cannon mounts – there are over 130 in all – it's hard to believe this place never saw any action, though it was manned from 1863 to 1865.

Northeast Historic Film, in the restored 1916 Alamo Theater building at 85 Main St in Bucksport (Mon–Fri 9am–4pm; ℡207/469-0924 and ℡207/469-6910 for event info, ⓦwww.oldfilm.org), is also worth a look. NHF collects and screens film and video related to the history and heritage of northern New England; this even includes your old family films, which they'll edit and store for free. Call in advance and ask about tours – they'll take you into their amazing (and freezing) climate-controlled film storage room, and show you the ins and outs of their film equipment setup.

Shore harbor store features lobster rolls and picnic provisions. Across the bay at 2 Fairview St, *Young's Lobster Pound* (℡207/338-1160) serves up fresh-boiled lobster dinners, among the best in the state, with sunset views. *Darby's*, 155 High St (℡207/338-2339), is a bit overpriced but nevertheless dishes out delicious food such as pecan haddock, pad thai, and filet mignon; they also have an adjoining **pub**. *Rollie's Bar and Grill*, back on the hill at 37 Main St (℡207/338-4502), is a rough-and-ready bar open until 1am every day of the year, that is (surprisingly) also pretty popular for breakfast.

For **accommodation**, try the *Alden House*, 63 Church St (℡207/338-2151, Ⓦ www.thealdenhouse.com; ⑤–⑦), a beautiful 1840 Greek Revival house run as a B&B by two genial hostesses; the comfortable *Penobscot Bay Inn*, 192 Northport Ave (℡207/338-5715 or 1-800/335-2370; ④–⑤); or the pretty Victorian *Jeweled Turret Inn*, 40 Pearl St (℡207/338-2304 or 1-800/696-2304; ④–⑦), with friendly hosts and good breakfasts. The *Garden Cottage Suites* 52 Main St, has two beautiful rooms right in the center of town that come complete with full kitchens, furnishings, and a washer/dryer; rooms can be rented nightly or weekly (℡207/338-0165; ⑥).

Down East Maine

So called because sailors heading east along the coast were also usually heading downwind, **Down East** Maine has engendered plenty of debate over its boundaries – some wish to draw its western line at Ellsworth, or Belfast, or even include the entire state in their definition. It's all a matter of pride, of course; to be a "downeaster" means to be tough and fiercely independent. For the purposes of this book, we've defined "Down East" as the Maine coast east of Bucksport, including the **Blue Hill Peninsula**, home to several gorgeous, secluded seaside towns; the extremely popular **Mount Desert Island**, the second most visited place in the state (after L.L. Bean); and the one hundred miles of nearly deserted shoreline stretching from Ellsworth to **West Quoddy Head**, the point farthest east in the US.

As you make your way up the coast – particularly once you pass Mount Desert Island and **Acadia National Park** – the terrain and the population become more rugged and less prone to tourism. Also noteworthy are the area's mesmerizing fogs – the coast near the Canadian border is normally enshrouded in a wispy pouf on and off for a good half of the year.

The Blue Hill Peninsula

It used to be that the **Blue Hill Peninsula**, extending south from Bucksport, was a sleepy expanse of land, too far off the primary roads to attract much attention. But word is slowly getting out about this beautiful area, blanketed with wild blueberry bushes and dotted with both dignified old towns like **Castine** and **Blue Hill** and fishing villages like **Stonington** and **Deer Isle**. Even farther off the established tourist trail, **Isle au Haut** is a remote outpost accessible only

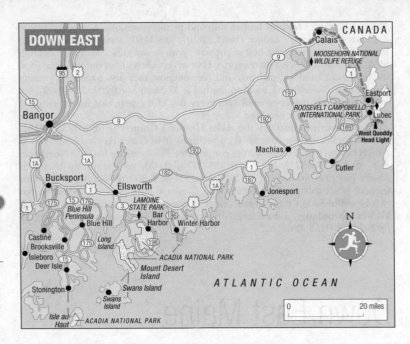

by mail boat. In the smaller towns between, you'll find close-knit communities which can trace their ties to the peninsula back for several generations. As you might expect, the main draw down here is the tranquility that comes with isolation, and while the area presents ample opportunities for exploration, you might find yourself content with a good book, an afternoon nap, a gourmet meal, and a night in a posh B&B.

Arrival, information, and local transport

The Blue Hill Peninsula is deceptively large, and, with somewhat indirect roads, it can take well over an hour to reach its southernmost point. It's a good idea to pick up a detailed DeLorme map (see p.474) before you set out – even some of the locally produced plans can't seem to keep all the different numbered roads straight. **Cycling** is a good way to get around. Your best bet for renting is probably at the Rocky Coast Outfitters, on Grindleville Road in Blue Hill (T207/374-8866); they also do kayak and canoe rentals. Public transport is not available, though if you're really in a bind, you can call a **taxi** through Airport & Harbor Taxi (T207/667-5995).

The Blue Hill Peninsula **Chamber of Commerce** is at 28 Water St, in Blue Hill proper (T207/374-3242). Most inns and shopkeepers are also well equipped to provide just about all the information you need, including regional maps. The local chambers of commerce maintain **websites** at Ⓦ www.bluehillme.com and Ⓦ www.deerislemaine.com.

Accommodation

There's a good variety of **accommodation** on the Blue Hill Peninsula, ranging from B&Bs to motels. Plan to spend $100 or more per night in summer; for a comparable amount, you may be able to rent a small house or cottage. *Greenlaws*, in Stonington (☎207/367-5049), has RV-oriented **campgrounds**.

Blue Hill and around

Blue Hill Inn Union St ☎207/374-2844 or 1-800/826-7415, ⓦwww.bluehillinn.com. Romantic 1830 inn with inviting rooms and decor. Guests are treated to outstanding gourmet meals. A small apartment, Cape House, is available in winter for $165 per night, two-night minimum. Open May–Nov. ⑧

Captain Isaac Merrill Inn 5 Union St ☎207/374-2555, ⓦwww.captainmerrillinn.com. Clapboard house in the center of town with fireplaces throughout and blueberry pancakes in the morning. Cheaper single rates available. ⑥

Oakland House 435 Herrick Rd, Brooksville ☎207/359-8521 or 1-800/359-7352, ⓦwww .oaklandhouse.com. Stay in the immaculately refurbished old stone inn or one of the well-maintained cottages strewn about the property, which is in a remote area along the Eggemoggin Reach. Follow the signs down Rte-15 to get here. ⑥

Castine

Castine Inn 1 Main St ☎207/326-4365, ⓦwww .castineinn.com. One of the few old inns (1898) in the state that was actually built as an inn, this Castine fixture now offers updated amenities and has friendly, helpful hosts. Open May–Sept. ⑤–⑨

Manor Inn Battle Ave ☎207/326-4861, ⓦwww .manor-inn.com. Constructed as a summer home for a yachting commodore, the *Manor* looks a little incongruously like a sort of castle. The inn offers fourteen rooms beautifully decorated in eclectic lodge style, plus immediate access to hiking and cross-country skiing trails, and yoga, in addition to fine dining and pub grub. ⑦–⑧

Pentagoet Inn 26 Main St ☎207/326-8616 or 1-800/845-1701, ⓦwww.pentagoet.com. A welcoming old 1894 inn with sixteen rooms restored by the antique-buff owners. The inn also has a quiet and sophisticated pub, *Passports*, a huge porch, and great fine dining. They'll even lend you a bicycle. Open May–Oct. ⑥–⑨

Stonington

Boyce's Motel 44 Main St ☎207/367-2421 or 1-800/224-2421, ⓦwww.boycesmotel.com. Centrally located, basic, clean rooms at the right prices. The very cool owner also offers apartments with kitchens and living rooms, for $540–780 per week. ③

Inn on the Harbor 45 Main St ☎207/367-2420, ⓦwww.innontheharbor.com. Stonington's fanciest (and priciest) accommodation, with beautiful rooms and good amenities (wi-fi, TVs, binoculars). It also has the best location, with a fine view of the harbor. Open all year; breakfast included. ⑥–⑧

Pres du Port B&B W Main St at Highland Ave ☎207/367-5007. Brightly wallpapered, whimsically furnished B&B with a great view from the rooftop deck and a berry-filled breakfast in the morning. Also has one endearing little room for only $40. Cash or check only. Open June–Oct.

Blue Hill

Plenty of folks come to **BLUE HILL**, at the intersection of routes 172, 176, and 15 adjacent to the Blue Hill Harbor, simply to relax, but there are livelier activities available, particularly with the town's bustling music scene – it runs a well-loved **chamber music festival** every summer (ⓦwww.kneisel.org), and is the self-proclaimed "Steel Drum Capital of Downeast Maine" (ⓦwww.peninsulapan.org). The best time to visit is Labor Day weekend, when oxen pulling, sheep dog trials, fireworks, and carnival rides are part of the **Blue Hill Fair** ($5; ⓦwww.bluehillfair .com), the basis for the country fair in E.B. White's *Charlotte's Web*.

Several well-known writers, among them E.B. White, have made their homes in the Blue Hill Peninsula. Blue Hill proper boasts two excellent bookstores. North Light Books, 58 Main St (☎207/374-5422), is a great source for **travel books** and maps as well as fiction, speciality titles, and art supplies. The larger Blue Hill Books, 26 Pleasant St (☎207/374-5632), is a more comprehensive independent bookseller.

It's a 30- to 45-minute walk up to the top of **Blue Hill Mountain**, from which you can see across the Blue Hill Bay to the dramatic ridges of Mount Desert Island. The trailhead is not difficult to find, halfway down Mountain

Road between routes 15 and 172. South on Rte-175, **Blue Hill Falls** is a good spot to give kayaking a try: the Activity Shop in Blue Hill at no. 61 Rte-172 (℡ 207/374-3600, ⓦ www.theactivityshop.com) has canoe and kayak rentals that they'll even deliver to your door ($25 a day and up; reservations recommended). In summer, the Marine Environmental Research Institute (**MERI**) at 55 Main St (℡ 207/374-2135) runs eco-cruises ($40, children $20) and island excursions ($60, children $40) during which you might spot a seal or pull lobster traps from an uninhabited shoreline.

Castine

CASTINE, nearly surrounded by water on the northern edge of the Penobscot Bay, is one of New England's most quietly beautiful towns, with nicely kept gardens, enormous elm trees, and a peaceful sophistication.

The town's small population is a mix of summer residents, a number of well-known poets and writers (Elizabeth Hardwick, founder of *The New York Review of Books*, lived here until her death in 2007), and year-round people, many of whom are employed by the **Maine Maritime Academy**, with buildings both along the water and back on Pleasant Street. It's pretty tough to miss the *State of Maine*, the huge ship that's usually docked at the landing (except in May and June) and used to train the academy's students, who give tours in the summer (call ℡ 207/326-4311 for schedules, or walk up the plank and ask). Take a stroll down **Perkins Street** to check out the string of enormous mansions looking out over the water. Between these ostentatious summer retreats are a number of old historic buildings, such as the 1665 **John Perkins House**, the town's earliest, which is occasionally open to the public. There is also the *Compass Rose Bookstore and Café*, 3 Main St (℡ 207/326-9366), a welcoming book-browsing space. When you tire of wandering around the town, Castine Kayak (℡ 207/866-3506) runs various **sea-kayaking** tours ($55–105, includes equipment and instruction) from Eatons Wharf at the public boat landing.

▲ Castine harbor

Deer Isle, Stonington, and Isle au Haut

DEER ISLE – all scenic inlets and serene woodlands – is one of the most beautiful areas in a state that's known for its beauty, and is reachable only by crossing a narrow, elevated suspension bridge. In the town proper, try out the preserves from **Nervous Nellie's Jams and Jellies**, set amidst a funky sculpture garden at 600 Sunshine Rd (☎1-800/777-6845, Ⓦwww.nervousnellies.com). Although you can't enter the studios at nearby **Haystack Mountain School of Crafts** (☎207/348-2306, Ⓦwww.haystack-mtn.org), you can stroll the campus down to its waterfront flagpole and contemplate whether you'd like to sign up for a blacksmithing or book arts class. They also have an artsy bookstore.

Few places are more remote than gorgeous **STONINGTON**, a fishing village whose residents have long had a reputation for superior seamanship. Over the past hundred years, the place, all the way at the end of Rte-15, has found hard-earned prosperity in the sardine-canning and granite-quarrying businesses; now it has turned to lobstering. Stonington's **Zone C Lobster Hatchery**, 43 School St (☎207/367-2708, Ⓦwww.penobscoteast.org), nurtures baby lobsters to learn whether they could grow up and survive in the wild; they offer tours of their science center ($10) on Tuesday and Wednesday in summer. For nightlife, the restored **Opera House** (☎207/367-2788, Ⓦwww.operahousearts.org) always has something going on, be it a first-run movie or a Shakespeare performance – during their annual Jazzfest, New Orleans bands parade with dancing crowds beside the town's scenic harbor.

Mail boats headed for **ISLE AU HAUT** (pronounced "I'll ah hoe") depart from the Stonington landing several times daily ($16 one-way; ☎207/367-5193 or 207/367-6516). On this lonely island, you can explore the trails of the less-visited part of **Acadia National Park**, highlighted by the rocky shoreline, bogs, and stands of spruce trees. Alternatively, you can charter your own boat for a reasonable price from Captain Bill at Old Quarry Ocean Adventures, in Stonington (☎207/367-8977, Ⓦwww.oldquarry.com), who, in addition to Isle au Haut, will take you anywhere on the Maine coast, and also runs excellent kayaking, boating, and camping trips and a highly recommended puffin trip.

Eating and drinking

There's a lot of good **food** to be had on the peninsula, but keep in mind that distances between towns are deceptively large. The appealing Blue Hill **farmers' market** is held Saturday mornings in the summer at the Blue Hill Fairgrounds on Rte-172.

Blue Hill and around

Arborvine 33 Main St ☎207/374-2119. Tasty, contemporary fare like mushroom and leek risotto and local Damariscotta River oysters, served in an 1800s-style home. Try the plum napoleon with whipped cream for dessert. They also have a more casual attached wine bar, *The Vinery*. Reservations recommended; closed Mon.

El El Frijoles 41 Caterpillar Hill Rd (Rte-15), Sargentville ☎207/359-2486. Worth visiting for the name alone (it's a riff on L.L. Bean), this casual, California-style taqueria serves up wicked good burritos and house-made *agua fresca*. Open Wed–Sat 11am–8pm; breakfast served Fri–Sun 8–11am.

Fish Net 162 Main St ☎207/374-5240. Soft-serve ice cream and really good lobster rolls, right in the middle of town.

Morning Moon Café 1 Bay Rd, at intersection of Rte-175 and Naskeag Point Rd, Brooklin ☎207/359-2373. South of Blue Hill and known as "The Moon," this is a popular spot for breakfast and lunch. Closed Mon; closes at 2pm rest of the week.

🎿 **The Wescott Forge** 66 Main St ☎207/374-9909. The best of both worlds: fabulous fine dining on a sunny deck and a plush bar that's open late. Lunch is less expensive and just as good.

Castine

Bah's Bakehouse and Stella's Jazz Nocturnal
26 Water St ⊕ 207/326-9710. Upstairs is a local
morning and lunch spot, with coffee, sandwiches,
and blueberry muffins; downstairs is a fun night-
time hangout, with live music on weekends and
elegant entrees like lobster cobb salad and great
brick-oven pizzas.

The Breeze Right on the waterfront ⊕ 207/326-
9200. It doesn't get much better than take-out pints
of fried clams and haddock, lobster rolls, burgers,
and Gifford's ice cream on picnic tables by the water.

The Pentagoet Inn Main St ⊕ 207/326-8616.
Lobster *bouillabaisse*, warm asparagus salad with
prosciutto crisps, and pistachio-dusted diver scallops,
served in an atmospheric, elegant dining room.

Stonington and Deer Isle

Maritime Café 27 Main St, Stonington
⊕ 207/367-2600. Pristine café featuring seafood
victuals, crêpes, and espresso. Ridiculously good
views of the harbor.

Harbor Café Main St, Stonington
⊕ 207/367-5099. A salty ambience – it's where
the fishermen come in the morning – with
sandwiches, coffee, and muffins; right in the
center of town.

Lily's Café and Wine Bar 450 Airport Rd at
Rte-15, Stonington ⊕ 207/367-5936. The sunny,
bloom-filled gardens welcome you in to this local
lunch and breakfast spot where you munch on
fresh sandwiches and home-made soups. Closed
weekends.

Whale's Rib Tavern In the *Pilgrim's Inn*, 20
Main St, Deer Isle ⊕ 207/348-5222. Tasty dinner
entrees ($13–20) in a wood-paneled, historic
barn with water views. The menu ranges from
haddock chowder to ribs to sticky toffee pudding.
Reservations recommended.

East to Mount Desert Island

Aside from a short strip of quaint brick gift shops and a couple of cafés
along the old part of Main Street (Rte-1), most of **ELLSWORTH** has
been overdeveloped into a disastrous sprawl of parking lots and chain stores.
There's predictably little to see, although you might check out the **Woodlawn
Museum**, on Rte-172 just south of Rte-1 (June–Sept Tues–Sat 10am–5pm,
Sun 1–4pm; May and Oct Tues–Sun 1–4pm; $7.50; ⊕ 207/667-8671), a huge
and splendid Federal period house with original furnishings amidst a pleasant
park and two miles of trails. Otherwise, stop only for provisions or a quick bite
to eat before you head south to Mount Desert Island. The beloved *Riverside
Café*, at 151 Main St (⊕ 207/667-7220), is a friendly local haunt for **breakfast**
or **lunch**, while just down the hill at no. 112, foodies rave about the tapas at
Cleonice (⊕ 207/664-7554).

If you're arriving in the Acadia region in high season (July & Aug) and the
traffic is unbearable along Rte-3, head off down Rte-184 to **Lamoine State
Park** ($3), just north of Mount Desert Island along the shores of Frenchman
Bay. There are no hiking trails, but there are plenty of beautiful spots to have a
picnic or wander the coast. The 62-site **campground** (mid-May to mid-Oct;
$20 per night; park info ⊕ 207/667-4778, reservations ⊕ 207/287-3824) here
is rarely full – maybe because it offers no hookups or hot showers – and has
some well-situated tent sites that offer views of the island. Nearby, Lamoine
Beach is the best **swimming** beach in the area.

Mount Desert Island

Considering that **Mount Desert Island** contains most of New England's only
national park, and that it boasts not only a genuine fjord but also the highest
headland on the entire Atlantic coast north of Rio de Janeiro, it is quite an
astonishingly small place, measuring just fifteen by twelve miles. Aside from

these claims, though, there are plenty of other reasons to visit: Mount Desert is the most accessible of the three hundred islands hugging the coast (it's been linked to the mainland by bridge since 1836), possesses the best facilities, and offers water- and land-based activities galore.

The island was named *Monts Deserts* ("bare mountains") by Samuel de Champlain in 1604, and then fought over by the French and English for the rest of the century. Although all existing settlements date from after the final defeat of the French, the name remains, still pronounced in French (more like *dessert*, actually). After painters Thomas Cole and Frederic Church depicted the island in mid-nineteenth-century works, word spread about its barren beauty, and by the end of the century, tourism was a fixture here. America's wealthiest families – among them the Rockefellers, Pulitzers, and Fords – erected palatial estates in **Bar Harbor**, and (under the leadership of Harvard University president Charles Eliot) established the organization that would later work to create Acadia National Park, the first national park donated entirely by private citizens. In 1947, a fire destroyed many of the grand cottages, including Bar Harbor's "Millionaires' Row," putting an end to the island's grand resort era. The fire didn't entirely tarnish the island's luster, however, and the place now attracts vacationing middle-class families and outdoor enthusiasts in addition to the frighteningly rich.

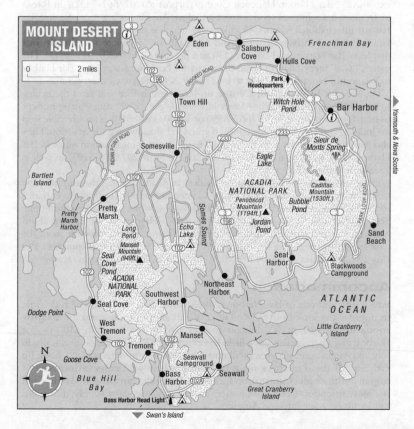

Somes Sound roughly divides the island in half; the east side is more developed and ritzy, holding the island's social center and travel hub, **Bar Harbor**, as well as **Northeast Harbor**, the site of huge summer homes for many CEOs. The west side, known to some as the "quiet side," is less harried, with a few fishing villages and year-round settlements like low-key **Southwest Harbor**, fast catching on as a popular destination in its own right. **Acadia National Park**, which covers much of the island, has great opportunities for camping, cycling, canoeing, kayaking, hiking, and birdwatching, though you're hardly ever very far from civilization.

Arrival, information, and local transport

If you're **driving**, Mount Desert is easy enough to get to from Rte-1 via Rte-3, although in summer roads on the island itself get congested (and the horse-drawn tours don't help). **Public transport** is minimal outside of Bar Harbor, though once you get there, take advantage of the free Island Explorer **shuttle buses** (Ⓦwww.exploreacadia.com/guide.html), which travel through Acadia to Bar Harbor, and even out to the airport.

West's Coastal Connections **buses** (Ⓣ207/546-2823 or 1-800/596-2823) travel between Bangor and the border town of Calais via Ellsworth. Mount Desert is also accessible via airplane. **Flights** into Bar Harbor are relatively infrequent and expensive – Bar Harbor/Hancock County Airport (Ⓣ207/667-7432), on Rte-3 in Trenton, has a limited service run by Colgan Air. Flights are more feasible via Bangor International Airport, 45 miles away, which is served by Northwest, Delta, Continental, US Airways Express, and Allegiant Air, and there is a **shuttle bus** that links Bar Harbor and Bangor ($30 and up, cash only; Ⓣ207/479-5911). The speedy "Cat" **ferry** takes two and three-quarter hours one-way from Bar Harbor to Yarmouth, Nova Scotia ($69; Ⓣ1-877/359-3760, Ⓦwww.catferry.com).

The **Acadia Information Center**, on Rte-3 just before you cross the bridge to Mount Desert Island (daily: May & June 9am–6pm, July & Aug 9am-8pm; Sept to mid-Oct 9am–6pm; Ⓣ207/667-8550 or 1-800/358-8550), is an advisable stop for lodging and camping information if you don't already have a reservation. They also have decent free maps of the island. There's a tourist information office in Bar Harbor in the municipal building on 93 Cottage St (Ⓣ207/288-5103), as well as a seasonal office at 1 West St.

There are numerous **information** outlets at Acadia during the summer, the best of which is the Hulls Cove Visitor Center, just off of Rte-3 at the entrance to the Park Loop Road (mid-April to June 8am–4.30pm; July & Aug 8am–6pm; Sept & Oct daily 8am–5pm; Ⓣ207/288-3338). Here you can inquire about hiking routes and purchase maps. You can also obtain more information about the park by writing or calling the National Park Service at **Park Headquarters**, PO Box 177, Bar Harbor, ME 04609 (Ⓣ207/288-3338, Ⓦwww.nps.gov/acad).

Accommodation

Rte-3 into and out of Bar Harbor is lined with budget motels, which do little to improve the look of the place but satisfy an enormous demand for **accommodation**. In season, it's difficult to find a room for less than $100 in Bar Harbor; elsewhere, prices are a little less exorbitant. Rates increase drastically in July and August, and sea views will cost a whole lot more. Many places book up early, so call ahead to check for availability. For help with **reservations**, call or stop in at the Acadia Information Center (see above). **Camping** in Acadia itself is a pleasant option (see box opposite) but spaces are in short supply; if possible, call in advance for July and August.

Camping on Mount Desert Island

There are three **campgrounds** in Acadia National Park, two public and one private. **Blackwoods**, near Seal Harbor (☎207/288-3274), is open all year, with reservations taken starting in February (through the National Park Service ☎1-877/444-6777, ⓦwww.recreation.gov; $20). At **Seawall**, off Rte-102A near Bass Harbor (mid-May to Oct; walk-in tent site $14; ☎207/288-3338), campsites are available on a first-come, first-served basis. The Appalachian Mountain Club maintains the private **Echo Lake Camp** (July to early Sept; $550 per week; ☎207/244-4747 and 603/466-2727, ⓦwww .amcecholakecamp.org), an extremely popular lakefront camp in Acadia National Park between Somesville and Southwest Harbor, with tent sites, cots, a dining room, kitchens, shared bathhouses with hot showers, canoes, and kayaks; rates here include three family-style meals a day. The following list of privately owned campgrounds on the island is not exhaustive but it should be sufficient; for a more complete guide, contact the information center (see opposite). Most charge about $30 per night, or more for a waterfront location. Also, the months they are open vary – call before setting out.

Bar Harbor 409 Rte-3, Bar Harbor ☎207/288-5185

Bar Harbor KOA 136 County Rd, Bar Harbor ☎207/288-3520

Bar Harbor Woodlands KOA 1453 Rte-3, Bar Harbor ☎207/288-3520

Bass Harbor Bass Harbor ☎207/244-5857

Mt. Desert Rte-198, Somesville ☎207/244-3710

Mt. Desert Narrows 1219 Rte-3, Bar Harbor ☎207/288-4782

White Birches 195 Seal Cove Rd, Southwest Harbor ☎207/244-3797

Bar Harbor

Acadia Hotel 20 Mount Desert St ☎207/288-5721 or 1-888/876-2463, ⓦwww.acadiahotel.com. One of the more affordable spots in town, with a central location. The rooms in this old hotel are newly renovated but a bit overdone. ⑤–⑥

Aysgarth Station 20 Roberts Ave ☎207/288-9655, ⓦwww.aysgarth.com. On a quiet sidestreet a short walk from the center of town, this small, country-style B&B offers friendly service and a laid-back atmosphere. ⑤–⑥

Bar Harbor Hostel 321 Main St ☎207/288-5587, ⓦwww.barharborhostel.com. Clean, friendly hostel right near the center of town with ten beds for ladies and ten for men. Dorm beds $25 a night (linens included), private room $80, or there are 3 tent platforms ($10 per person).

Bar Harbor Inn Newport Drive ☎207/288-3351 or 1-800/248-3351, ⓦwww.barharborinn.com. The grandest hotel in town, the inn has 153 rooms in three attractively decorated buildings with modern amenities. The eight-acre property is right on Frenchman Bay, and has excellent views from many rooms. ⑧–⑨

Bass Cottage Inn 14 The Field ☎207/288-1234, ⓦwww.basscottageinn.com. Off the beaten path yet still near the downtown, this gorgeous (but pricey) B&B has contemporary decor and lovely trimmings: whirlpool tubs, fireplaces, crisp linens, and decadent breakfasts. ⑧–⑨

Manor House Inn 106 West St ☎207/288-3759, ⓦwww.barharbormanorhouse.com. Eighteen rooms in a quaint old Victorian and three cottages near the center of town. The pleasant porches are nicely suited for afternoon tea. ⑦–⑧

Seacroft Inn 18 Albert Meadow ☎207/288-4669, ⓦwww.seacroftinn.com. No-frills B&B with welcoming innkeepers and affordable rooms, one with detached bath (and a cheaper rate). Great location, and Continental breakfast in the morning. ④–⑥

Ullikana B&B 16 The Field ☎207/288-9552, ⓦwww.ullikana.com. The place to go for a romantic splurge, *Ullikana* has brightly decorated rooms and sumptuous breakfasts served on a terrace overlooking the water. They also run the *Yellow House*, just across the way. ⑧–⑨

Southwest Harbor and the west side

Bass Harbor Inn 28 Shore Rd, Bass Harbor ☎207/244-5157, ⓦwww.bassharborinn.com. Three tasteful, affordable rooms (one a half bath, one a full bath, and one a studio with kitchenette that sleeps four) in a secluded spot overlooking the water. ⑤

The Claremont 22 Claremont Rd, Southwest Harbor ☎207/244-5036 or 1-800/244-5036, ⓦwww.theclaremonthotel.com. One of the most beautiful accommodations in all of Maine – if you can't afford it now, plan to honeymoon here. The classic old-fashioned hotel has tennis and croquet, an excellent shorefront, and boating. On Fri nights the tasty fine dining is accompanied by live piano-playing. They also have a number of cottages. Mid-May to mid-Oct. ❽–❾

The Inn at Southwest 371 Main St, Southwest Harbor ☏ 207/244-3835, Ⓦ www.innatsouthwest .com. Brilliant inn in the center of town with a cozy living room, cheery bedrooms, hearty breakfasts, and attentive proprietors. Cheaper off-season rates. ❼

Lindenwood Inn 118 Clark Point Rd, Southwest Harbor ☏ 207/244-5335 or 1-800/307-5335, Ⓦ www.lindenwoodinn.com. This first-class inn offers tastefully decorated rooms and African accents in a stylish turn-of-the-century captain's home. Breakfast included. ❼–❾

Bar Harbor

The town of **BAR HARBOR** began life as an exclusive resort – it was the summer home of both Vanderbilts and Astors – but a great fire in October 1947 destroyed their opulent "cottages" and changed the direction of the town's growth. Many of the old-money families rebuilt their summer estates in hyper-rich **Northeast Harbor**, southwest along Rte-3, and Bar Harbor is now firmly geared towards tourists – though it's by no means downmarket. To take in the scene, stroll around the village green (now a free wi-fi zone), and walk along the **Shore Path** past the headland of the *Bar Harbor Inn* and up the coast for views of the ocean and Frenchman Bay.

In high season, up to 21 different **sea trips** set off each day, for purposes ranging from deep-sea fishing to cocktail cruises. Among the most popular are

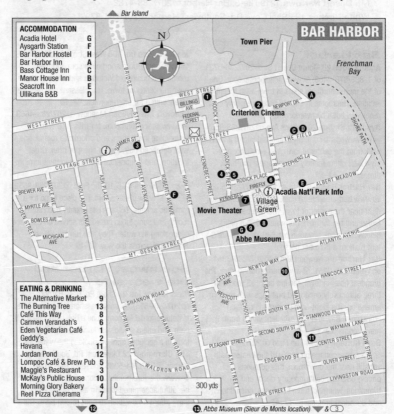

▲ Bar Island

BAR HARBOR

ACCOMMODATION
Acadia Hotel	G
Aysgarth Station	F
Bar Harbor Hostel	H
Bar Harbor Inn	A
Bass Cottage Inn	C
Manor House Inn	B
Seacroft Inn	E
Ullikana B&B	D

Town Pier

Frenchman Bay

Criterion Cinema

THE FIELD

Acadia Nat'l Park Info

Movie Theater

Village Green

Abbe Museum

EATING & DRINKING
The Alternative Market	9
The Burning Tree	13
Café This Way	8
Carmen Verandah's	6
Eden Vegetarian Café	1
Geddy's	2
Havana	11
Jordan Pond	12
Lompoc Café & Brew Pub	5
Maggie's Restaurant	3
McKay's Public House	10
Morning Glory Bakery	4
Reel Pizza Cinerama	7

0   300 yds

⑬, Abbe Museum (Sieur de Monts location) ▼ & ③

the **whale-watching**, puffin, and seal trips run by Bar Harbor Whale Watch Company, 1 West St (3hr; $53; ☎207/288-2386 or 1-888/WHALES-4). With Downeast Windjammer Cruises, you can enjoy a two-hour trip on the **schooner** *Margaret Todd* or a deep-sea fishing experience on the *Katherine* (leaving from the *Bar Harbor Inn* pier daily June–Oct; $32 and $39.50; ☎207/288-4585). Lulu Lobster Boat Rides ($27; ☎207/963-2341, ⓦwww.lululobsterboat.com) offers authentic **lobstering** trips wherein Captain John raises his traps and charms riders with nautical folklore and lighthouse sightings.

One of the town sights in its heyday was the "Indian Village," a summer encampment to which Native Americans came to sell pottery, necklaces, and trinkets to tourists. Nowadays, Wabanaki heritage – and current happenings – are preserved in a far more inspiring space: the **Robert Abbe Museum**, 26 Mount Desert St (mid-May to mid-Oct daily 9am–5pm, Thurs–Sat until 9pm; rest of year Thurs–Sun 10am–5pm; $6, children $2, admission includes Sieur de Monts location; ☎207/288-3519, ⓦwww.abbemuseum.org), which has a number of gorgeously constructed exhibit spaces full. Although the opening displays on Wabanaki culture are well put together, the Abbe's knockout piece is the "Circle of the Four Directions," a contemplative space built of cedar panels that span upward into an arced skylight. If that's not enough to wow you, they even have an original piece from glass wizard Dale Chihuly. The museum's original building, which shows Maine archeological findings and relates the history of the institution, is included in the admission price, and is just a couple of miles south of Bar Harbor at Sieur de Monts Spring, just off the Park Loop Road (daily mid-May to mid-Oct 9am–4pm).

Acadia National Park

Acadia National Park, which covers most of Mount Desert Island, the Schoodic Peninsula to the east (see box, p.507), and Isle au Haut (see p.499) to the south, is the most visited natural place in Maine. It's visually stunning, with dramatic rolling hills carving smooth silhouettes into the misty horizon. Dense stands of fir and birch trees hide over 120 miles of **hiking trails** (see box, p.506) that pop into view on the island's 26 summits. In fact, there's all you could want here in terms of mountains and lakes for secluded rambling, and sightings of **wildlife** such as seals, beavers, and bald eagles are not uncommon. The two main geographical features are the narrow fjord of **Somes Sound**, which almost splits the island in two, and **Cadillac Mountain**, an unbelievable place to watch the sunrise, though the summit of the 1530-foot mound offers tremendous ocean views at any time of the day (assuming clear weather). It can be reached either by a moderately strenuous climb – more than you'd want to do before breakfast – or by a very leisurely drive, winding up a low-gradient road.

The most enjoyable way to explore is to ride a **bicycle** around the 45 miles of gravel-surfaced "**carriage roads**," built by John D. Rockefeller, Jr as a protest against the 1913 vote that allowed "infernal combustion engines" onto the island. Keep an eye out for the ornate **granite bridges**, commissioned by Rockefeller and built by architects William Welles Bosworth and Charles Stonington. Three companies rent bikes for less than $30 per day: Bar Harbor Bicycle Shop, at 141 Cottage St on the edge of town (☎207/288-3886), and Acadia Bike & Canoe, across from the post office at 48 Cottage St (☎207/288-9605); Southwest Cycle does the same on Main Street in Southwest Harbor (☎207/244-5856 or 1-800/649-5856). All provide excellent maps and are good at suggesting routes. Be sure to carry water, as there are very few refreshment stops inside the park.

It's no secret that Mount Desert Island offers some of the most exhilarating **hiking** in New England. Though by no means exhaustive, the following list highlights some of the best hikes. If you plan on exploring extensively, get your hands on a copy of the detailed guide *A Walk in the Park*, published locally ($15) and available at the park visitors' center. The Southwest Harbor Chamber of Commerce (☎207/244-9264 or 1-800/423-9264) prints a decent free map of the west side of the park, including some two dozen hikes.

Easy

Flying Mountain Trail, five minutes north of Southwest Harbor, just off Rte-103 on Fernald Point Road. This 0.7-mile hike affords beautiful views at the top of 284-foot Flying Mountain (1hr).

Jordan Pond Shore Trail, from the Jordan Pond parking area. A 3.3-mile loop that roughly follows the water's edge (2hr).

Ship Harbor Nature Trail, at the southern end of the park off Rte-102A near the Bass Harbor Head Light. An easy 1.3-mile trail that loops out along the coast and back (45min).

Moderate

Bubble Rock Trail, starting at Bubble Rock parking area. Two one-mile forest loop trails, with some vistas of Jordan Pond (1hr).

Great Head Loop, beginning at Sand Beach on the Park Loop Road. Scenic 1.5-mile trail leading along towering cliffs right above the sea (45min).

South Ridge Trail, departing from Rte-3, near the *Blackwoods Campground*. This trail is the best way to get to the top of Cadillac Mountain, the highest point on the island (1530ft). The 7.4-mile round-trip is not particularly strenuous and very rewarding (5hr).

Strenuous

Acadia Mountain Trail, a few miles south of Somesville, on the east side of Rte-102. A relatively steep ascent to the top of the 700-foot mountain, with fine views of the Somes Sound. 2.5 miles round-trip (1hr 30min).

The Beehive, just north of the Sand Beach parking area. A short one-mile trip up iron rungs on exposed ledges. There's a swimming pond near the top called the Bowl (45min).

Mansell Mountain, at the south end of Long Pond, near Southwest Harbor. Trees impede the views from the 950-foot summit, but the two-mile hike along the Perpendicular Trail features stairways carved into the rock and unparalleled seclusion (2hr).

Penobscot Mountain, departs near the Jordan Pond House. This 2.6-mile trail (round-trip) affords panoramic views, second only perhaps to those from Cadillac Mountain (3hr).

If you'd prefer to get out on the water, you can take a four-hour guided **kayak tour** ($48) from May to October with National Park Sea Kayak Tours, 39 Cottage St (☎207/288-0342 or 1-800/347-0940, ⓦwww.acadiakayak .com), which also leads overnight trips. Just up the street at no. 48, Coastal Kayaking Tours offers similar trips, including overnight camping packages (☎207/288-9605 or 1-800/526-8615). With an abundance of rocky cliffs and overhangs, **rock climbing** is also popular here, and Acadia Mountain Guides (☎207/866-7562 or 1-888/232-9559) conducts half- and full-day climbs, with prices at $50–100 a head.

The park is open all year, with a summer-only **visitors' center** in Hulls Cove (May–Oct) at the entrance to the Loop Road north of Bar Harbor (see p.502), and one on the village green in Bar Harbor. The entrance fee is $20 per car for a seven-day pass, or $5 if you enter on bike or cycle. Many visitors do nothing more than drive the length of the 27-mile Park Loop Road, which admittedly winds through some of the park's most arresting areas, but you should also make the effort to get onto the trails. In addition to the fee collection station on Park Loop Road near **Sand Beach**, five miles south of Bar Harbor, there are several spots (including the aforementioned visitors' center in Bar Harbor) where you can purchase a pass.

Southwest Harbor and Bass Harbor

The western half of Mount Desert Island was for many years unflatteringly called the "Backside" by the well-heeled and snooty residents of Bar Harbor. These days, though, as Bar Harbor gets more and more touristy, the "quiet side" of Mount Desert is often a better place to be, with a less harried setting and (arguably) better restaurants and scenery.

SOUTHWEST HARBOR, along Rte-102 across from Northeast Harbor, is the center of this side's action, so to speak. The small "downtown" is graced with a couple of top-notch places to eat and the surrounding area has a smattering of cozy, out-of-the-way accommodation. If you plan on visiting neighboring Swans Island or Long Island, the state ferry is only a couple of miles away in Bass Harbor, and both Southwest and Northeast Harbor provide access to the Cranberry Islands.

South along Rte-102, **BASS HARBOR** is even further removed, the simple homes that line its streets reflecting the modest lifestyle of its residents. At the southernmost tip of the island, just off of Rte-102A, you'll find **Bass Harbor Head Light**, perched on the rocks and tucked behind the trees. Though the 1858 structure is not open to visitors, you can walk down a short seaside path for a good view of the lighthouse and the ocean. If you prefer to explore the water itself, take a three-and-a-half-hour **cruise** from Island Cruises ($27, lunch not included), to the fishing village of Frenchboro on Long Island, or a two-hour nature cruise aboard the forty-foot *R.L.Gott* (mid-June to mid-Oct; $23; ☎207/244-5785). The Maine State Ferry also runs **boats** between Bass Harbor, Swans Island, and Frenchboro several days a week (☎207/244-3254).

The Schoodic Peninsula

A small section of Acadia National Park lies isolated at the end of the **Schoodic Peninsula**, some eight miles south of Rte-1 along Rte-186, where Schoodic Point overlooks a rocky shoreline that spills out into the crashing surf, creating many natural picnic benches. Watch out for the menacing gulls, though, who easily quell their fear of humans in search of sandwiches.

The Point is the most scenic of stops on the peninsula, but there are plenty of other places to pull off Rte-186 and explore a bit of the coast on foot. The pleasant little village of **WINTER HARBOR**, northwest of the park along Rte-186, is a worthwhile stop. If you prefer, you can take the ferry over from Bar Harbor – there are five round-trips a day ($29; ☎207/288-2984). If you are in the area, don't miss the yearly **lobster festival** in Winter Harbor, held the second Saturday in August, when lobster lovers converge on the tiny town to down heaps of the tender meat, shop for crafts, listen to live music, and watch a parade.

Eating, drinking, and entertainment

Mount Desert's most memorable **eating** experiences are to be found in the many **lobster pounds** all over the island. For nightlife, people head to Bar Harbor, which is home to diversions like the Art Deco Criterion cinema at 35 Cottage St (℡207/288-3441), showing current favorites, and ImprovAcadia, on the second floor at 15 Cottage St ($15; ℡207/288-2503), with nightly comedy shows in summer. More unusual is the Great Maine Lumberjack Show (on Rte-3 in Trenton; mid-June to Aug nightly 7pm; $8.25; ℡207/667-0067, Ⓦwww.mainelumberjack.com). Hosted by Timber Tina, an international logging sports champion, it's campy family fun, with bits of history, humor, axes, and sawdust flying through the air.

Bar Harbor

The Alternative Market 16 Mt Desert St
℡207/288-8225. Bag lunches, big sandwiches, soups, smoothies, and fresh-squeezed juices.
The Burning Tree Rte-3, Otter Creek ℡207/288-9331. A few miles south of Bar Harbor, this outwardly unimpressive seafood restaurant spices up its brilliant entrees ($16–20) with tasty Southwestern and Caribbean touches. Reservations a must in July and Aug. Closed mid-Oct to mid-June, and Mon & Tues in Sept.
Café This Way 14½ Mt Desert St ℡207/288-4483. Fresh, creative breakfast options like the "Café Monte Cristo" (a French toast sandwich with eggs, ham, cheddar cheese, and syrup on the side), fresh orange juice, and eight omelet varieties. Expect a wait in summer. They also serve dinner.
Carmen Verandah's 119 Main St ℡207/288-2766. Above the less-exciting *Rupununi* bar, this fun-loving drinkery generally dissolves into a dance party that lasts til the wee hours. There's also pool and darts, and occasionally karaoke and live music. Sometimes a cover of around $5.
Eden Vegetarian Café 78 West St #A ℡207/288-4422. A well-loved dinner spot with inventive, international fare and an emphasis on organic, locally grown produce.
Geddy's 19 Main St ℡207/288-5077. You can't miss the glam-rock lobster claws jutting out from *Geddy's* exterior. The interior is better-looking, plus they serve up good family fare (steak, seafood, pasta) in a lively bar setting.
Havana 318 Main St ℡207/288-CUBA. American dining with a Latin sensibility, which translates into lemon- and cilantro-cured local salmon. Cool modern ambience, sometimes with low-key live music.
Jordan Pond Park Loop Rd, Acadia National Park ℡207/276-3316. Light meals, ice cream, and popovers (puffy egg muffins) in the heart of the park, between Bar Harbor and Northeast Harbor. Afternoon tea, an Acadia tradition, is served in the beautiful lakeside garden (11.30am–5.30pm; reservations recommended).

Lompoc Café & Brew Pub 36 Rodick St ℡207/288-9392. A healthy Middle Eastern menu for $14–20, with local Bar Harbor Blueberry Ale and other Atlantic Brewing Company beers on draft, complemented by a woodsy outdoor dining area and bocce ball court. Live music every Fri and Sat. Open 11.30am–1am.
Maggie's Restaurant 6 Summer St ℡207/288-9007. In a little blue house away from downtown, *Maggie's* serves fresh, well-composed seafood entrees such as lobster crêpes and salmon with cucumber-mint salsa. Reservations recommended. Closed Sun.
McKay's Public House 231 Main St ℡207/288-2002. The interior feels like your grandfather's den (assuming your grandfather has a good sense of modern esthetics), and the menu comprises slightly upscale, creatively prepared meats and fishes for lunch and dinner. Reservations recommended.
Morning Glory Bakery 39 Rodick St ℡207/288-3041. Fabulous fresh breads, coffee, and pastries, and take-out lunch options served at a purple-trimmed cottage. Closed Sun.
Reel Pizza Cinerama 35 Kennebec Place, right on the Village Green ℡207/288-3828 take-out, ℡207/288-3811 movie info. Eat pizza, drink beer, and watch artsy or blockbuster films on the big screen – it's fun when your food order comes up on the big bingo board. Movie tickets $6.

Southwest Harbor and around

Beal's Lobster Pier 182 Clark Point Rd, Southwest Harbor ℡207/244-7178. Fresh seafood for under $10 on a rickety wooden pier. You can pick out your own lobster from a tank, or choose from a small menu of other seafood choices. Closed Nov–April.
Eat a Pita & Café 2 326 Main St, Southwest Harbor ℡207/244-4344. A great casual, cozy, and affordable spot with delicious, healthful gourmet food (pastas, veggie entrees, paninis, burgers, seafood),

candlelit tables, and friendly service. Breakfast, lunch, and dinner served; there's also a full bar.

Maine-ly Delights 48 Granville Rd, Bass Harbor ☎207/244-3656. Don't sweat the corny name – this tasty take-out spot has incredibly good (and affordable) crab cake sandwiches, seafood baskets, and grilled sandwiches on picnic tables right by the water.

Red Sky 14 Clark Point Rd, Southwest Harbor ☎207/244-0476. Seasonal, new American cuisine served in a popular, fairly upscale eatery. Reservations recommended.

Thurston's Lobster Pound Steamboat Wharf Rd, Bernard ☎207/244-7600. Dine on your lobster of choice amidst a casual cafeteria-style layout overlooking Bass Harbor. Open late May to Oct.

XYZ Restaurant Bennett Lane, off Seawall Rd (Rte 102-A), Manset ☎207/244-5221. Slamming, legitimate Mexican entrees served in a bright, folk-artsy interior that will make you long for the southlands. Reservations (and the margaritas) strongly recommended. Dinner only, closed Sun.

East to Canada

Few travelers venture into the hundred miles of Maine lying east of Acadia National Park, mainly because it is sparsely populated, windswept, and remote. In summer though, the weather is marked by mesmerizing fogs, and the coastal drive is exhilarating – it runs next to the Bay of Fundy, which has the highest tides in the nation. Here, the air is so crisp and clean you will want to bottle it and take it with you. Tourism is not big business in these parts, but each village has a B&B or two and some low-priced restaurants. Outside of the rugged scenery, highlights include picturesque **West Quoddy Head Light**, the easternmost point in the United States; the artsy seaside town of **Eastport**; and the wild **blueberries** – ninety percent of the nation's crop comes from this part of Maine.

Machias and Cutler

MACHIAS, right on Rte-1, sports a little waterfall smack in the middle of town, and was the unlikely location of the first naval encounter of the Revolutionary War: in 1775, the townsfolk, brandishing pitchforks, swords, and firearms, commandeered the British schooner *Margaretta* after refusing to provide it with provisions. The attack was planned in the still-standing gambrel-roofed **Burnham Tavern**, Rte-192 just off Rte-1 (mid-June to early Sept Mon–Fri 9.30am–4pm; $2.50; ☎207/255-6930), which has been restored to approximate the tavern's original colonial setup. Aim to visit Machias the second week of August, when they have their annual blueberry festival (Ⓦwww.machiasblueberry.com), featuring craft fairs, fireworks, and general blueberry feasting.

Perhaps the best place to **eat** in town is the *Artist's Café*, 3 Hill St (☎207/255-8900), with its moderately priced and frequently changing menu; chicken parmesan and lobster linguini are typical offerings. Meals are also good value at the bluesy and fresh *Fat Cat Deli*, 50 Main St/Rte-1 (☎207/255-6777), and be sure you don't leave town without trying the blueberry pie at landmark *Helen's*, 28 E Main St/Rte-1 (☎207/255-8433). Nearby on Rte-1, the *Inn at Schoppee Farm* (☎207/255-4648, Ⓦwww.schoppeefarm.com; ❺–❾) is run by the owner of *Helen's*, overlooks the Machias River, and has two beautiful rooms as well as a family-sized guesthouse set in a restored barn.

East of town, Rte-191 heads along a regal and desolate portion of shoreline known as the **Bold Coast**. From the parking lot on Rte-191, four miles east of **CUTLER**, two **hiking loops** head out to the windswept coast. There's a small beach at Long Point Cove, and you can sometimes catch a glimpse of humpback whales from the cliffs. The Cobscook Trails Coalition (☎207/733-5509, Ⓦwww.qrlt.org) has information on the trails and campsites along the way. Also in Cutler, the Bold Coast Charter Co. runs spectacular puffin-sighting trips ($80;

$\textcircled{T}$207/259-4484, $\textcircled{W}$www.boldcoast.com), wherein its 40-foot *Barbara Frost* lands and actually lets passengers embark on tiny Machias Seal Island, home to thousands of the brightly beaked birds. Even if birding is not your thing, this is a unique and recommended experience.

West Quoddy Head, Lubec, and Campobello Island

With its distinctive red-and-white-striped lighthouse, **WEST QUODDY HEAD** is the easternmost point of the United States, jutting defiantly into the stormy Atlantic. You can see Canada just across the Bay of Fundy, though for a better view, take the three-mile east trail in **Quoddy Head State Park** that traces a winding line along precipitous cliffs and also diverges onto a fantastic bog trail.

Just beyond the turn-off for Quoddy Head, tiny **LUBEC** was once home to more than twenty sardine-packing plants. They're all gone now, but the restored **McCurdy's Fish Company**, on Water Street, now gives lively tours ($3); you might spot a seal as you stroll the main drag. Lubec also hosts the lively adult music camp Summer Keys ($\textcircled{W}$www.summerkeys.com). Of several B&Bs in town, the *Peacock House*, 27 Summer St ($\textcircled{T}$207/733-2403, $\textcircled{W}$www .peacockhouse.com; $\textcircled{6}$), is a fantastic place to stay, offering stylish and cozy furnishings. The *Home Port Inn*, 45 Main St ($\textcircled{T}$207/733-2077 or 1-800/457-2077; mid-June to mid-Oct; $\textcircled{6}$), an old 1880 house with seven guestrooms, is another worthy option. *Sunset Point Trailer Park*, on the west end of town, has scenic **campsites** overlooking the water ($\textcircled{T}$207/733-2272).

Campobello Island

Lubec is the gateway to **CAMPOBELLO ISLAND**, in New Brunswick, Canada, where Franklin D. Roosevelt summered from 1909 to 1921, before he became president, and to which he occasionally returned while in office. His barn-red cottage is now open to the public, furnished just as the Roosevelts left it. There is also a sleek and informative visitors' center, with additional exhibits relating to the Roosevelts, and some huge dahlias in a well-tended garden. The rest of **Roosevelt Campobello International Park** (mid-May to mid-Oct daily 9am–5pm; free; $\textcircled{W}$www.fdr.net), located on Canadian soil but held jointly with the United States, is good for a couple of hours' wandering. There are several coastal trails and picnic areas, and the drive out to **Liberty Point** is worth the effort. (Keep in mind, though, that you will need a birth certificate or valid passport to cross the border.)

Eastport

EASTPORT is incredible. Perched on Moose Island, between Cobscook and Passamaquoddy bays at the end of Rte-190, this artsy town is quite a way off the beaten track, but if you have the driving stamina, it's one of the coolest places you'll ever see, with an end-of-the-earth feel. Canada is only a few miles away, but the closest border crossing is twenty-eight miles north in Calais, and the bridge to Campobello Island in Lubec is forty miles from here by car – you have to drive all the way around Cobscook Bay or take the ferry ($\textcircled{T}$207/853-4166) to get there. The quiet town maintains the air of a remote outpost, with spotty weather, hills that slope gently toward a collection of Canadian islands just across the bay, and lots of old brick and clapboard buildings. Eastport can also claim the largest whirlpool in the western hemisphere, ignobly dubbed the "Old Sow." You can view the rushing waters safely from the terminus of Clark Street.

A result of an active local arts community, the Commons Gallery, 51 Water St (☎207/853-4123), is worth a spin, usually housing an interesting collection of works by Maine artists; the Tides Institute & Museum of Art (☎207/853-4047), across the street at no. 43, is an 1887 bank building with an appealing mix of exposed brick and contemporary artwork. If you're looking to get out on the water, the romantic windjammer *Sylvina W. Beal* (used in the film version of *The Age of Innocence*) and the *Halie Matthew* offer whale-watching, sunset, and overnight cruises (☎207/853-2500).

Practicalities

There are several good **restaurants** in town, two culinary landmarks, and some good-value **accommodation**. *The Pickled Herring*, 32 Water St (☎207/853-2323), has inviting options like shrimp and chorizo skewers ($9), grilled pizzas, burgers, and seafood under a pressed-tin ceiling. *Quoddy Bay Lobster*, 7 Sea St (May to Oct only, ☎207/853-6640), is the place to go for handpicked lobster rolls, while the *Eastport Chowderhouse*, 169 Water St (☎207/853-4700), dishes up wicked good fresh seafood. *Raye's Mustard*, 83 Washington St (☎207/853-4451), has been producing its "liquid gold" for over one hundred years – it's the country's last surviving stone mustard mill – while another local landmark, *Katie's on the Cove*, north of town on Rte-1, doles out unbelievably good confections from a little canary-yellow house (☎207/454-8446, ⓦ katiesonthecove.com). The *Chadbourne House*, an elegant Federalist home at 19 Shackford St (☎207/853-2727 or 1-888/853-2728; ❼), has spacious rooms, many with fireplaces, while the *Motel East*, 23A Water St (☎207/853-4747; ❺), has porches overlooking the bay. 🍴 *The Commons*, 51 Water St (☎207/853-4123, ⓦ www.thecommonseastport.com; weekly rentals $700) offers two inviting suites above an art gallery for one of the nicest **stays** in Maine; each suite comes with two bedrooms, a kitchen, dining room, internet access, laundry, and a front porch with barbecue setup and jaw-dropping views of the harbor into Canada. Halfway between Eastport and Lubec off Rte-1, **Cobscook Bay State Park** has some of the best **camping** around (mid-May to mid-Oct; ☎207/726-4412), with over a hundred beautifully situated campsites and good facilities and access to clam beds ($5 day fee).

Calais

The border between the United States and Canada weaves through the center of **Passamaquoddy Bay**; the towns to either side get on so well that they refused to fight in the US–UK War of 1812, and promote themselves jointly to tourists as the **Quoddy Loop**. It's perfectly feasible to take a two-nation vacation, but each passage through customs between **CALAIS** (pronounced "callous") in the States and **St Stephen** in Canada does take a while – and remember that they're in different time zones. No trace now remains of Samuel de Champlain's 1604 attempt to found a colony on the diminutive St Croix Island, which you can view via an International Historic site commemorating the explorer on Rte-1. In town, *Julianna's World Café*, 28 North St (☎207/454-2299), has fresh sandwiches and good Mexican entrees. West's Coastal Connections (☎207/546-2823 or 1-800/596-2823) runs a once-daily bus from Calais to Ellsworth and Bangor. The **visitors' center**, 39 Union St (☎207/454-2211), has loads of information on activities and accommodations and a helpful staff.

Nearby, the Baring division of the **Moosehorn National Wildlife Refuge**, between Rte-191 and Charlotte Road (☎207/454-7161), is a good place to catch a glimpse of a bald eagle or woodcock; they maintain some sixty miles of hiking trails, which are also good for cross-country skiing in winter.

Inland Maine

The vast expanses of the under-utilized **Maine interior**, stretching up into the far north, consist mostly of forests of pine, spruce, and fir, interspersed by white birches and maples responsible for some spectacular fall colors. Distances here are large. Once you get away from the two largest cities – **Augusta**, the capital, and **Bangor** – it's roughly two hundred miles by road to the northern border at **Fort Kent**, while the trip between the two most likely inland bases, **Greenville** and **Rangeley**, takes three hours or more. Driving (there's very little public transport) through this mountainous scenery can be a great pleasure, but you do need to know where you're going. There are few places to stay, even fewer gas stations, and beyond Millinocket many roads are tolled access routes belonging to the lumber companies: gravel-surfaced and vulnerable to bad weather.

If you have the time, this is great territory in which to **hike** – the **Appalachian Trail** starts its two-thousand-mile course down to Georgia at the top of Mount Katahdin – or **raft** on the swift **Penobscot** or **Kennebec** rivers. **Skiing**, too, is a popular activity, particularly at **Sugarloaf** or in the area around **Bethel**, near the New Hampshire border.

Especially around beautiful **Baxter State Park** and enormous **Moosehead Lake**, the forests are home to deer, beaver, a few bears, some recently introduced caribou, and plenty of **moose**. These endearingly gawky creatures (they look like badly drawn horses and are virtually blind) tend to be seen at early morning or dusk; in spring they come to lick the winter's salt off the roads, while in summer you may spot them feeding in shallow water. They do, however, cause major havoc on the roads, particularly at night, so aim to be at your destination before the sun sets – each year there are a significant number of moose-related collisions.

Augusta and Hallowell

The capital of Maine since 1831, **AUGUSTA**, thirty miles north of Brunswick, is much quieter and less visited now than it was a hundred years ago. The lumber industry took off here after the technique of making paper from wood was rediscovered in 1844, and Augusta also had a lucrative ice-making commerce at the time: each winter hundreds of thousands of tons, cut from the Kennebec River, were shipped as far as the Caribbean. There are informative displays on this past in the **Maine State Museum** (Mon–Fri 9am–5pm, Sat 10am–4pm, Sun 1–4pm; $2; ☎207/287-2301, ⓦwww.state.me.us/museum), inside the governmental complex shared by the Maine State Library and Archives, just south of the capitol on State Street. Walking through the hallways past the intriguing (if slightly outdated) "Twelve Thousand Years in Maine" exhibit, you actually get a good sense of how the state has developed over the centuries. Also of note is "Made in Maine," centered on a functional water-powered mill and including a fantastic collection of old looms and antique forms of transport.

Next door, the 180-foot dome of the imposing **Maine State House** (Mon–Fri 8am–5pm), a Charles Bulfinch design, is visible from nearly anywhere in Augusta. The rather impressive granite structure, completed in 1832, has been subject to several renovations that have nearly doubled its size. You can take a self-guided **tour**, or if you're so inclined, free guided tours can be arranged by calling the museum at ⊕207/287-2301. For other diversions, the brand-new Kennebec River Rail Trail (mastheads on Water St behind the Maine State Housing Authority and in Capital Park on Union St) winds 6.5 miles all the way to Gardiner and makes for great biking, walking, and contemplating.

Hallowell

Just two miles south of Augusta beside the gently sloping banks of the Kennebec River, the quaint haven of **HALLOWELL** is far more pleasant than its governmentally focused neighbor, especially along its main drag, **Water Street**, lined with some excellent **restaurants** and a couple of diverting bookstores and antique shops. Once a major port for lumber and granite, as well as a shipbuilding center, the place boasts a number of stately homes left over from those prosperous times, mostly perched in the hills above town. A small population of artists and craftsmen has arrived in recent years; for **information** on visiting the many studios in the area, contact the Kennebec Valley Chamber of Commerce (⊕207/623-4559).

Practicalities

If you plan to stay in the Augusta area, the best-value **accommodation** is the *Super 8 Augusta*, 395 Western Ave (Rte-202), Exit 109 off I-95 (⊕207/626-2888; ❸). There are a number of good **B&Bs** in Hallowell, including *Maple Hill Farm*, set on 62 acres on Outlet Road, off Shady Lane (⊕207/622-2708 or 1-800/622-2708, ⊛www.maplebb.com; ❻–❾), where you can feed the farm animals in the morning before enjoying a delicious breakfast; there is also the cozy-chic *Benjamin Wales House B&B* 49 Middle St (⊕1-877/323-4712, ⊛www.benjaminwales.com; ❺–❼).

For **food**, *Club OTR*, 349 Water St (⊕207/623-7625), is a fun bar with really good "Led Zeppelin" burgers. Along the short main drag of Hallowell, *Slates Restaurant*, 169 Water St (⊕207/622-9575), has a friendly atmosphere, fair prices, and original entrees like shrimp and scallops with coconut pie sauce over jasmine rice. Nearby, *Hattie's Chowder House*, 103 Water St (⊕207/621-4114), has lobster stew so good it is mail-ordered across the country. To the south, in neighboring Gardiner, the ⚓*A1 Diner*, 3 Bridge St/Rte-9/Rte-201 (⊕207/582-4804), serves eclectic entrees in a funky vintage diner car that's been there since 1946.

Bangor

BANGOR, 120 miles northeast of Portland at the intersection of Rte-1A and I-95, is not a place to spend much time, although its plentiful motels and the Bangor Mall on Hogan Road north of town make it a good last stop before the interior. As Maine's third largest city (32,000 people), the place is noticeably more urban and rough around the edges (for Maine, at least) than the state's smaller towns, serving as a major source of goods and services for the stretch of coast twenty miles south.

In its prime, Bangor was the undisputed "Lumber Capital of the World." Every winter its raucous population of "River Drivers" went upstream to brand the felled logs, which they then maneuvered down the Penobscot River as the thaw came in April, reaching Bangor in time to carouse the summer away in the grog shops of Peppermint Row. Bangor also exported ice to the West Indies – and got rum in return. The forests were thinning and the prosperous days were coming to an end, however, in 1882, when Oscar Wilde addressed a large crowd at the new Opera House and spoke of "such advancement. . . in so small a city." A devastating fire in 1911 leveled much of the city, although a fair number of the lumber barons' lavish mansions survived.

Arrival, information, and local transport

Many of the major airlines service the renovated **Bangor International Airport** (☎207/992-4600), on the western edge of town. Frequent **bus service** is available from Bangor to most other parts of the state. Concord Coach, which docks at the Transportation Center, 1039 Union St across from the airport (☎207/942-0807), can take you to Portland, Camden, and a number of smaller coastal cities. The CYR Bus Line (☎1-800/244-2335) stops at both the Coach and the Greyhound terminals and then heads north to Caribou, stopping in several small towns along the way. Greyhound has a terminal at 158 Main St (☎207/945-3000), from which you can travel to Boston via Portland and Portsmouth, NH or connect with Greyhound routes to other destinations. If you're spending any time at all in Bangor, you will find **BAT Community Connector** ($1, five tickets $4; ☎207/992-4670) to be a handy means of getting around – look for the red bus with the black and gray bat outline on the side. Pick up a route map from any bus driver.

There's a helpful **information** center at the Bangor Region Chamber of Commerce, 519 Main St (☎207/947-0307, ⓦwww.bangorregion.com), which has the typical collection of brochures and hotel information.

Accommodation

Bangor Super 8 Motel 462 Odlin Rd ☎207/945-5681, ⓦwww.super8.com. Clean, comfortable, budget motel accommodation close to the Hollywood slots. ❹

Fireside Inn and Suites 570 Main St ☎207/942-1234, ⓦwww.firesideinnbangor .com. Clean and friendly hotel, next to the Hollywood Slots and Bangor landmark *Geaghan's Restaurant and Irish Pub.* Continental breakfast included. ❹–❻

Lucerne Inn 2517 Main Rd, Dedham ☎1-800/325-5123, ⓦwww.lucerneinn.com. A somewhat grander experience that combines accommodation, access to golf facilities, a lakeside setting, three-course dinner, and Continental breakfast. ❻–❽

Nonesuch Farm B&B Hudson Rd (Rte-221; call for directions) ☎207/942-3631, ⓦwww .bangorsfirstbedandbreakfast.com. Three gorgeous, contemporary rooms on a sprawling working farm that dates to 1855. ❹

The town and around

One of the mansions that survives along West Broadway, complete with a spider-web-shaped iron gate, is now the suitably Gothic residence of horror author **Stephen King**, a Maine native who relocated here in 1980. You can browse the full collection of King's works, including some limited editions and collectibles, at Bett's Bookstore, 584 Hammond St (☎207/947-7052).

Bangor's other claim to fame, the 31-foot **Paul Bunyan** statue along Main Street south of downtown, is perhaps the largest such statue in the world

– excepting one or two in Minnesota – though it looks more like a brightly painted model airplane kit than a statue. Bunyan was allegedly born here in 1834, though several other prominent logging towns across the US dispute that claim. From mid-May until the end of July there's **harness racing** (☎207/947-6744) and year-round **Hollywood slot machines** (☎1-877/779-7771) at Bass Park on Main Street just behind the statue; admission is free but the potential to lose money is unlimited.

The **Cole Land Transportation Museum**, 405 Perry Rd (from I-95 follow signs to War Memorials; May to mid-Nov daily 9am–5pm; $6, children free; ☎207/990-3600), is packed with a fantastic collection of antique fire trucks, trains, and frighteningly large snowplows; the latter look like they could plow your house up along with the snow.

A few miles north of Bangor, the Maine Center for the Arts (☎207/581-1755), at the University of Maine in **Orono**, runs a series of big-name concerts each summer.

Eating and drinking

Bagel Central 33 Central St ☎207/947-1654. Fresh bagels and a huge selection of other kosher foods.
Bahaar 23 Hammond St ☎207/945-5979. Excellent, aromatic Pakistani food for lunch and dinner.
Dysart's Exit 180 off I-95 S in Hermon ☎207/942-5978. Beloved *Dysart's* has been a Maine institution for over 35 years. Essentially a 24hr truck stop, they have a roomy diner with great trucker food, showers, and even a barber shop.
Massimo's 96 Hammond St ☎207/945-5600. This Bangor newcomer serves amazing authentic Italian food at dinner time, try the pizza *patate* with thinly sliced potatoes, fontina, and truffle oil ($13).

New Moon 49 Park St ☎207/990-2233. Bangor's swankiest eating establishment, with tasty four-course meals serving loosely New American cuisine such as grilled pork chops with tomato butter, collard greens, and biscuits. There's also a sleek bar.
Thistle's Restaurant 175 Exchange St ☎207/945-5480. Family-owned, *Thistle's* serves up tasty, fairly upscale foods – grilled swordfish, Maine crab cakes, paella – for lunch and dinner.
Whig & Courier 18 Broad St ☎207/947-4095. This straightahead pub is the place to drink in town with really good cheesesteaks, burgers, and a wide variety of beers on tap.

Bethel and around

The remote, quintessentially New England town of **BETHEL**, nestled in the mountains about seventy miles north of Portland, may appear rather sleepy, but it's an excellent year-round base from which to explore the outdoors, most notably in the **White Mountains** and **Grafton Notch State Park**. Bethel has long attracted a rather academic and prosperous population; the prestigious Gould Academy is here, and the town was once home to the clinic of famous neurobiologist Dr John Gehring. Another town claim to fame is that they built both the world's tallest snowman and snowwoman – 113ft and 122ft, respectively.

Arrival, information, and local transport

Bethel is not accessible via public transit, though the **Sunday River Stage-coach** (☎207/357-5783, ⓦwww.srstage.com) makes local and out-of-town trips, going as far as Fort Kent. A similar service is operated by Airport Limo & Taxi (☎207/773-3433 or 1-800/517-9442). The particularly helpful **Chamber of Commerce**, on Cross Street (Mon–Fri 8am–5pm, Sat 10am–6pm, Sun noon–5pm; ☎207/824-2282 or 1-800/442-5826, ⓦwww.bethelmaine.com), can assist you if you need.

Accommodation

Bethel does have a good concentration of **places to stay** once you arrive. For **camping**, *Crocker Pond Campground* off Songo Pond Road (Rte-5) just south of town (first-come, first-served; $14; mid–May to mid–Oct), has seven secluded and rather primitive campsites maintained by the US Forest Service, while the more family-oriented *Bethel Outdoor Adventures*, 121 Mayville Rd/Rte-2 (☎207/824-4224 or 1-800/553-3607), has both RV and tent sites on the banks of the Androscoggin River.

Bethel Inn Resort and Country Club On the Common ☎207/824-2175 or 1-800/654-0125, ⓦwww.bethelinn.com. A full-service, four-season resort, complete with golf course, tennis courts, a health club, fine dining, and pub. In the winter, they have 25 miles of groomed cross-country ski trails. ❸–❾
Briar Lea Inn 150 Mayville Rd (Rte-2 east of Bethel Village) ☎207/824-7277 or 1-877/311-1299,

ⓦwww.briarleainn.com. Renovated 150-year-old Georgian farmhouse with a full-service English pub. ❺–❻
Chapman Inn On the Common ☎207/824-2657, ⓦwww.chapmaninn.com. Another fine B&B-like option, also with dorm beds ($33, including breakfast). ❻

Skiing and outdoor activities

Just a few miles north of Bethel off Rte-2 on Sunday River Road, the **Sunday River Ski Resort** (lift tickets $72; ☎207/824-3000 or 1-800/543-2754, ⓦwww .sundayriver.com), is one of the major alpine ski areas in New England, with eighteen lifts servicing eight mountain peaks.

Bethel is also known for its **cross-country skiing**, and there are several privately owned centers in addition to the trails maintained for snowmobiles (to which skiers have access) in the White Mountain National Forest and Grafton Notch State Park (see opposite). Some 40 kilometers of cross-country ski trails penetrate the wilderness at the beginner-oriented Sunday River Inn & Cross Country Ski Center, on Sunday River Road (☎207/824-2410). Don't miss the trail that leads to the 1872 Artist's Covered Bridge, off Sunday River Road, which is a good spot for swimming during the summer. You can also cross-country ski at Carter's Cross Country Farm & Ski Shop, with eighteen miles of trails at its location off Rte-26 in Oxford, and forty miles of groomed trails in Bethel on Intervale Road (☎207/539-4848).

For warm-weather activities, stop by Bethel Outdoor Adventures, on Rte-2 just east of Bethel Village (☎207/824-4224 or 1-800/533-3607). They have **bike rentals** ($25 per day) and route advice; they also rent **canoes** and **kayaks** and do guided trips. Fishing is another popular pastime; contact outdoor sports specialist Sun Valley Sports (☎1-877/851-7533) for fly-fishing, snowmobiling, kayaking, and canoeing trips.

Eating, drinking, and entertainment

Bethel's Best Rte-2, one mile west of Bethel Village ☎207/824-3192. Casual place for excellent pizza, also serving ice cream, clam chowder, lobster rolls, and hearty breakfasts.
DiCocoa's 119–125 Main St ☎207/824-5282. Bold vegetarian and creative specialities, wraps, soups, and espresso in a funky dining room. Their hours can be spotty – give them a call first.

Cho Sun 141 Main St ☎207/824-7370. Really good sushi in the center of town. Dinner only.
S.S. Milton 43 Main St ☎207/824-2589. Fairly casual spot with simple fare like tortellini alfredo and pan-seared sea bass. Open for lunch and dinner. In the summer, there's a sunny patio.
Sudbury Inn & Suds Pub 151 Main St ☎207/824-6558. The best of both worlds: incredible fine dining upstairs, drinking den downstairs,

with live entertainment five nights per week and a good selection of microbrews until 1am.
Sunday River Brewing Co. North of town along Rte-2 at Sunday River ☎ 207/824-4253.

Particularly popular with skiers, serving freshly brewed ales and hearty pub fare, with occasional live music. Open year round.

White Mountain National Forest

Bethel sits just on the edge of the fifty thousand acres of the **White Mountain National Forest** that fall within Maine's borders, the center of which is **Evans Notch**. Contact the Bethel Chamber of Commerce, (☎ 207/824-2282) for maps, hiking suggestions, and information on campsite and shelter availability. There are a number of **backcountry shelters** in the forest. All are at least a couple of miles from the trailheads (accessible only on foot), and are either free or have a nominal fee on a first-come, first-served basis. Particularly good **hikes** through the birch, maple, and pine stands include the moderately difficult 7-mile (about 5hr 30min) **Caribou Mountain Loop**, starting at the trailhead on Rte-113, following the Mud Brook Trail, and ending at the summit of Caribou Mountain, and the easier 1.8-mile (about 1.5hr) loop that begins on Rte-113, across the bridge just north of *Hastings Campground* and leads up to the **Roost**, a granite overlook providing views of the Wild River Valley and Evans Notch.

Grafton Notch State Park

North of Bethel, Rte-26 bisects beautiful **Grafton Notch State Park** (mid-May to mid-Oct; $2; ☎ 207/824-2912), a patch of rugged mountains, gurgling streams, cascading waterfalls, and bizarre geological formations. Among these, **Screw Auger Falls**, where the Bear River has carved out a gorge through the solid granite, is good for wading. Just north, easy trails lead to **Moose Cave Gorge** and through the 45-foot-deep **Mother Walker Falls Gorge**, which features several natural bridges. More difficult trails head up **Old Speck Mountain**, Maine's third highest. Follow the 3.9-mile (one-way) **Old Speck Trail**, which traces the Appalachian Trail from the Grafton Notch trailhead parking area up numerous switchbacks, past the Cascade Brook Falls to the Mahoosuc Trail, which eventually affords sweeping views at the summit. A somewhat shorter option is the **Table Rock Loop** (a 2hr jaunt with some very steep sections) that also departs from the main trailhead parking area up **Baldpate Mountain** to Table Rock, where you are treated for your efforts with mountain views. The Bethel Area Chamber of Commerce (see p.515) can provide you with maps and other necessary info. There are no campgrounds in Grafton Notch State Park.

Rangeley

RANGELEY is only just in Maine, a little way east of New Hampshire and fewer than fifty miles from the Canadian border, at the intersection of routes 4 and 16. Furthermore, as the sign on Main Street boldly declares, it is equidistant from the North Pole and the Equator (3107.5 miles), though that doesn't mean it's on the main road to anywhere. It has always been a resort, however, served in 1900 by two train lines and several steamships, with the attraction then being the fishing in the spectacularly named Mooselookmeguntic Lake. Today this cozy one-street town, nestled amid a complex system of lakes and waterways, serves as a base for summer explorations. There's still one unorthodox indoor attraction, the remote **Wilhelm Reich Museum**, on Dodge Pond Road, about halfway along the north side of

AMC mountain huts in western Maine

The Appalachian Mountain Club (ⓦwww.outdoors.org) maintains a number of **mountain huts** and **camps**, of which there's a concentration in western Maine near the White Mountains. If you have your own tent and stove, these well-kept facilities are excellent options, especially if you're kayaking or canoeing. If you have questions or want to make reservations, call the Pinkham Notch Visitor Center (ⓣ603/466-2727). Other AMC mountain huts in Maine are on Mount Desert Island and near Georgetown Island, south of Bath.

Cold River Camp, North Chatham, NH (late June to late Aug, weekly rate $545; late Aug to mid-Sept $60 per day). In the beautiful and undeveloped Evans Notch area of the White Mountain National Forest near the state border, this hundred-plus-acre site offers such as cabins, electricity, hot showers, linens, a recreation hall, and a screened tea house. Rates include meals and firewood (three nights' minimum stay in summer; cash only).

Swan's Falls Campground, Fryeburg (mid–May to mid-Oct; ⓣ207/935-3395; $6 per night non-members, $5 members). Eighteen tent sites, several shelters, canoe access, toilets, and hand-pumped water in a pine forest along the Saco River near the White Mountains. Some campsites are accessible by car and all are quiet during the week. Parking costs an additional $5 per day.

Rangeley Lake, a mile up on a side track off Rte-16 (July & Aug Wed–Sun 1–5pm; Sept Sun 1–5pm; $6; ⓣ207/864-3443, ⓦwww.wilhelmreichmuseum.org), where Wilhelm Reich eventually made his home after fleeing Germany in 1933. Although he was an associate of Freud in Vienna and the author of the acclaimed *Mass Psychology of Fascism*, Reich is best remembered for developing the orgone energy accumulator. He claimed it could concentrate atmospheric energy; skeptical authorities focused on the way in which it was said to collect and harness human sexual energy. In a tragic end to his career, Reich was imprisoned after a student broke an injunction forbidding the transportation of his accumulators across state lines, and he died in prison in Lewisburg, PA, in November 1957. He is buried here, amid the neat lawns and darting hummingbirds, and his house remains a museum for the reflection of his work.

South of town along Rte-17, it's worth seeking out **Angel Falls**, which, at ninety feet, are the highest in Maine. There's a good **swimming** spot at the base. Getting there is a bit complicated: take Rte-17 17.6 miles south of Oquossoc, turn west off Rte-17, cross the bridge, at mile marker 6102, turn right on the old railroad line, after 3.5 miles, turn left on the gravel road, and stay left through small gravel pits. Follow the marked trail, approximately one mile from this point. Nearby, in the old mining town of Byron, you can also swim in the clear waters of **Coos Canyon**, just off Rte-17.

Practicalities

The *Rangeley Inn*, 2443 Main St (ⓣ207/864-3341, ⓦwww.rangeleyinn .com; ❹), stands between Rangeley Lake and the smaller bird sanctuary of Haley Pond, so you can stay right in town and have a room that backs onto a scene of utter tranquility; there's also a gorgeous old wooden dining room. *Pleasant Street Inn*, 104 Pleasant St (ⓣ207/864-2440, ⓦwww.pleasantstreetinnbb.com; ❺), is a great second choice – ask for room no. 5. Otherwise, the Chamber of Commerce (see opposite) can provide lists of private home/condo rentals and "remote campsites" around the lake – which really are remote, several of them inaccessible by road. For **food**, try *The Shed*, 2647 Main St (Thurs–Sun; ⓣ207/864-2277), where pit boss

Martin gets up early to smoke his excellent pulled pork and ribs – "it's done when it's ready." The *Loon Lodge Inn*, 16 Pickford Rd (℡207/864-LOON), looks like a fancy log cabin, and while their food is a bit overpriced, their lake views can't be beat. *Sweet Dreams Bakery*, 2755 Main St (℡207/864-5678), is the place to go for breakfast, while the best food in the area is at the *Porterhouse Restaurant*, in Eustis (take Rte-16 E to Rte-27 N, four miles up on Rte-27 N; ℡207/246-7932). Set in a 1908 farmhouse, it offers exquisitely prepared entrees and an award-winning wine list.

Just south of the *Porterhouse* is the pretty *Cathedral Pines* **campground** (℡207/246-3491). Twenty miles north of Rangeley, the peaceful *Grants Camps* beside Kennebago Lake (℡1-800/633-4815) arranges fishing, canoeing, and windsurfing, with accommodation in comfortable cabins overlooking the lake, including all meals, costing around $185 per person per day; there are lower weekly rates. Rangeley Lakes' **Chamber of Commerce**, 6 Park Rd (℡207/864-5364 or 1-800/MT-LAKES, ⓦwww.rangeleymaine.com), has details of various activities, including snowmobiling and moose-watching **canoeing** expeditions.

Sugarloaf USA and Kingfield

The road east of Rangeley cuts through prime moose-watching territory – in fact, locals call Rte-16 "Moose Alley." After about fifty miles, in the Carrabassett Valley, looms the huge mountain of **SUGARLOAF USA**, Maine's biggest ski resort (lift tickets $69; ℡207/237-2000 or 1-800/THE-LOAF, ⓦwww.sugarloaf.com). A spectacular place for skiers of all abilities, with over 130 trails, this condo-studded center would be a more popular destination if it weren't for the fact that the nearest airport is a two-hour drive away in Portland. Summer activities include guided **mountain-bike tours** over the extensive trail system on the ski mountain; you can set one up, or just rent a bike, courtesy of the Sugarloafer Shop (℡207/237-6718). There's also a full complement of hiking, canoe trips, and cookouts, plus a **golf** course designed by Robert Trent Jones Jr.

Kingfield

A good base for Sugarloaf is fifteen miles south in the tiny town of **KINGFIELD**. The *Mountain Village Farm B&B Inn*, 164 Main St (℡207/265-2030; ⑤–⑦) has welcoming rooms and terrific views of Sugarloaf mountain from its sunny dining room. In the center of town, at 246 Main St, the *Herbert Grand Hotel*

Driving Maine's logging roads

While the majority of the **roads** in northern Maine are owned and maintained by huge logging and paper conglomerates, the public is often permitted access. On the **Golden Road**, for example, which connects Millinocket with the Canadian border, travelers can pay a $4 fee at one of several gates for the privilege of driving its 96-mile length. While most people don't usually get that far, a lot of folks do travel the toll-free section that stretches between Millinocket and Greenville. Keep in mind, however, that this mostly unpaved road is used primarily by logging trucks, and that services are few and far between. Use caution, do not travel at night or during bad weather, and always yield to trucks. Distances are great and poor road conditions dictate slow travel speeds; be sure to consult with a local resident and have a good map and plenty of gas before you set out.

(☎1-888/656-9922; ❹–❺) has less attractive but functional rooms and a restaurant. For **food**, the groovy *Orange Cat Café* at 329 Main St (7am–3pm daily; ☎207/265-2860) has fresh wraps, salads, espresso, and wi-fi, while *Tufulio's*, north of Kingfield on Rte-27 in the Carrabassatt Valley (☎207/235-2010), is a good year-round dinner spot with Italian treats like chicken marsala, pizza, and tiramisu served amongst stained-glass windows and sunny wooden booths.

Kingfield was the birthplace of twins Francis and Freelan Stanley, who invented, among other things, the famous Stanley Steamer car, and the dry-plate photographic process (which they sold to Kodak). The **Stanley Museum**, 40 School St (June–Oct Tues–Sun 1–4pm; Nov–May Tues–Fri 1–4pm; $4; ☎207/265-2729, ⓦwww.stanleymuseum.org), celebrates their story. Part of the main room is given over to their sister Chansonetta, a remarkable photographer whose studies of rural and urban workers have been widely published. Other exhibits include working steam cars from the early 1900s – if you're lucky, they might have one fired up when you arrive.

Moosehead Lake and around

Serene waters lap gently at the miles of deserted, thickly wooded shores around **Moosehead Lake**, which at 117 square miles is the largest lake in Maine. **Greenville** is the sole settlement of any size, and it makes a good base from which to explore the area, especially if you want to see moose or go white-water rafting, though **The Forks**, a sporty settlement along the **Kennebec River** and US-201, has emerged as the center of the whitewater industry. West of the lake along Rte-15, gritty **Jackman**, big with the **snowmobile** crowd in winter, is the last stop before the Canadian border.

Greenville and around

With a population of 1800, the rugged outpost of **GREENVILLE**, at the southern end of Moosehead Lake, is a nineteenth-century lumber town that now makes its living primarily from tourism. People come from all over to see wild **moose**, indigenous to the area, which the town has been quick to exploit; there is nary a business around here that doesn't somehow incorporate the animal into its name. For several weeks in May and June there's even a celebration, the creatively named **Moosemainea** (☎207/695-2702, ⓦwww.mooseheadlake.org). The *Birches Resort* (see opposite) offers, for $35 and up, moose-spotting cruises, where you're also likely to see eagles, bears, and peregrine falcons.

This tiny town is quite pretty and is also well positioned for explorations throughout the Maine woods. The main attraction here is the lake – a serene inky blot that shines silver at night, taking on the appearance of an enormous mirror. You can get out on the water via the restored **steamboat**, *Katahdin*, which tours the lake and serves as the floating Moosehead Marine Museum – watch out, ladies, no high heels or smoking on the ship (call for cruise times; $30–35; ☎207/695-2716). Near the dock, tiny **Thoreau Park** has a couple of picnic tables and a sign commemorating and describing the writer's 1857 visit to Moosehead Lake, of which he remarked "[looking into the depths of which] the beholder measures his own nature."

A good way to explore the area is on a **mountain bike**; you can rent them ($25 per day), along with canoes, kayaks, and camping equipment at North-woods Outfitters, on Main Street (☎207/695-3288 or 1-866/223-1380, ⓦwww.maineoutfitter.com). Greenville is also the largest **seaplane** base in

▲ Canoeing on Moosehead Lake

New England; contact Currier's Flying Service (☎207/695-2778) or Jack's Air Service (☎207/695-3020).

If you choose to wander, one spot worth a visit is **Kineo**, an isolated nature preserve in the middle of the lake. Island trails lead to the top of dramatic **Mount Kineo**, whose flint-like cliff face rises some 800ft above the lake's surface. Shuttle boats to Kineo leave from Rockwood (daily 8am–5pm; $10). Other good **hikes** in the area include the trip to **Gulf Hagas**, a 300-foot gorge fifteen miles east of town off Greenville Road; the walk to an old B-52 crash site on nearby Elephant Mountain; and difficult climbs to the summits of 3196-foot **Big Moose Mountain** and 3230-foot **Big Spencer Mountain**. Contact the Chamber of Commerce for more information.

Practicalities

The **Chamber of Commerce**, just south of town on Rte-6/15 (Mon–Sat 10am–4pm; ☎207/695-2702), has lots of information about area activities and accommodation. As an alternative, the **Maine Forest Service** (☎207/695-3721) can provide information on their many free campsites in the area. There's not too much in the way of **food** options here; one local favorite is *The Rod & Reel*, 77 Pritham Ave (☎207/695-0388), which serves fresh fish entrees on its outdoor patio. Also on Pritham Avenue, the *Stress Free Moose Pub & Café*, 65 Moosehead Lake Rd (☎207/695-3100), has tasty pub grub and a good selection of beers amidst fun sayings like "beauty is in the eye of the beer holder."

Accommodation is generally in the form of upscale wilderness retreats built for hunters, though there are exceptions. The *Birches Resort*, north of Greenville near the small village of Rockwood (☎1-800/825-9453, ⓦwww.birches.com; ❷–❾), for example, offers both rustic (tents, yurts) and first-class quarters along with a host of outdoor activities. There's also a fairly gourmet dining room overlooking the lake. More traditional choices in Greenville include the *Pleasant Street Inn*, on Pleasant Street (☎207/695-3400; ❺–❼), and the unbelievably well-appointed *Blair Hill Inn* (☎207/695-0224; ❾), which boasts lavish rooms, fabulous views of the lake, incredible fine dining (lit with original Tiffany lamps), and even an excellent summer concert series. *Little Lyford Pond Camps*, a remote AMC lodge and set of vintage cabins accessible via the logging roads (☎603/466-2727; ❷), offers showers, flush toilets, and hiking, biking, and outdoor activities galore.

Jackman

Fifty miles west of Greenville, gritty **JACKMAN** is a small frontier border town that was once a center for logging. Situated next to deserted Wood Pond, less than twenty miles from the Canadian border, its main attraction is as a haven for **snowmobiles**, which take over the parking lots and surrounding lumber roads in winter. You can rent one of the noisy crafts at Dana's Rentals on Main Street (☎207/668-7828) for about $180–270. **Ice-fishing** is also popular in winter and several local businesses sell non-resident licenses, bait, and tackle. In summer, a forty-mile circuit known as the Moose River **Bow Trip** is one of the better flat-water **canoe trips** in the state, with good fishing and several **campsites** scattered along the way. The Jackman Moose River Chamber of Commerce, Main Street (☎207/668-4171, ⓦwww.jackmanmaine.org), can help you locate a guide, if you so desire.

The refurbished *Bishop's Motel*, right in the center of town at 461 Main St (☎1-888/991-7669, ⓦwww.bishopsmotel.com; ❺), provides basic, clean **rooms** at reasonable rates. *Sally Mountain Cabins,* 9 Elm St (☎207/668-5621 or 1-800/644-5621; $32 per person), has rustic cabins along the lake with full kitchens and private baths. *Schmooses*, 513 Main St (☎207/668-7799), is a good place to **eat**, with tasty ginger macadamia shrimp served amidst pine-paneled environs. *Mama Bear's*, 420 Main St (☎207/668-4222), offers up good pub grub for three meals a day.

Millinocket

Farther north, **Millinocket** is a genuine company town, built on a wilderness site by the Great Northern Paper Company in 1899–1900 as the "magic city of the North." Public curiosity was so great that three hundred people came on a special train from Bangor to see what was happening. Nowadays, the town is best known as a base for exploring Baxter State Park. It's also a good place for moose sightings – try Mainely Photos' "Moose and Photo Tour," 353 Penobscot Ave, for a reliable moose safari (☎207/723-5465).

Next to **Millinocket Lake**, ten miles northwest, the splendidly ramshackle *Big Moose Inn* (☎207/723-8391, ⓦwww.bigmoosecabins.com; ❷) makes a great

---

Whitewater rafting

The **Penobscot** and the **Kennebec** are the two most popular rivers in Maine for the exhilarating sport of **whitewater rafting. The Forks** (population: 35), along Hwy-201 between Bingham and Jackman, is the undisputed rafting center, and the majority of the outfitters are based there, along with the deluxe lodges and camps they've built to house eager outdoors enthusiasts. Run from May to mid-October, most trips depart in the early morning and return by mid-afternoon and require advance reservations. Levels of difficulty vary, but the rafting companies insist that people of all athletic abilities are welcome on most trips, which, as dictated by state law, are all led by certified "Maine guides." However, many companies do have age requirements. Raft Maine (☎1-800/723-8633, ⓦwww.raftmaine.com) is an association comprised of several outfitters that can answer your questions.

place to stay, with cabins and an inn, and a wide range of activities. There's also an adjacent campground ($10 per person). A more standard place to stay is the Jacuzzi-enhanced *America's Best Value Heritage Inn*, 935 Central St/Rte-11 (℡207/723-9777, Ⓦwww.heritageinnmaine.com; ❹), or the clean *Gateway Inn*, Rte-11/157 just off I-95 at the Medway exit (℡207/746-3193, Ⓦwww.medwaygateway.com; ❸), where many rooms have decks with views of Katahdin. Next to Millinocket Lake, ten miles northwest, several whitewater rafting companies have set up lodgings and **campsites** as bases for their trips down the Penobscot River (see box opposite). Before heading off into the wilderness, grab a hot, hearty **meal** from the *Appalachian Trail Café*, 210 Penobscot Ave (℡207/723-6720).

Baxter State Park

By now you're approaching the southern end of sprawling and unspoilt **BAXTER STATE PARK** itself, with (on a clear day) the 5268-foot peak of imposing and beautiful **Katahdin** visible from afar. Entrance to the park, collected at the Togue Pond Gate on Park Tote Road, costs $13 per car, and you should plan to arrive early in the day, as only a limited number of visitors are permitted access to Katahdin trailheads. The enormous park – covering over 200,000 acres – was the single-handed creation of former Maine governor Percival P. Baxter, who, having failed to persuade the state to buy the imposing Katahdin and the land around it, bought it himself between the 1930s and 1960s and deeded it bit by bit to the state on condition that it remain "forever wild." A 4000-acre parcel was recently added which includes Katahdin Lake and a wildlife sanctuary, best accessed by Katahdin Lake Wilderness Camps (Ⓦwww.katahdinlakewildernesscamps.com) on the eastern side, a privately owned site that dates to 1885. The park's majestic green peaks (48 in all) and deserted ponds remain tremendously remote and pristine, and sightings of bears, bald eagles, and (of course) moose are not uncommon.

Hiking and camping

Hiking is the major pursuit here; indeed, the northern terminus of the **Appalachian Trail** is at the top of Katahdin, and in summer, many champagne-popping family and friends join hikers here to celebrate their completion of the trail. Among the park's 186 miles of trails, don't miss the **Knife Edge**, a thrilling walk across a narrow path that connects Katahdin's two peaks. The higher and typically more crowded of these, **Baxter Peak**, can also be reached via the **Hunt Trail** (5.2 miles, from Katahdin Stream), the **Cathedral Trail**, and the **Saddle Trail** (both around 2 miles, originating at Chimney Pond). For a less crowded but equally rewarding jaunt, head to the top of Hamlin Peak on the two-mile **Hamlin Ridge Trail**, which starts at Chimney Pond. Wherever you plan to hike, stop beforehand at either the headquarters in Millinocket, 64 Balsam Drive next to *McDonald's* (℡207/723-5140, Ⓦwww.baxterstateparkauthority.com), the visitors' center at Togue Pond (at the south entrance to the park – also a good place to **swim**), or at any of the park's campgrounds for a detailed **hiking map**. Water in the park is not treated.

There are ten designated **campgrounds** in Baxter, providing an array of options from basic tent sites to cabins equipped with beds, heating stoves, and gas lighting. Prices range from $10 to $27 per person per night and most sites are open from mid-May to mid-October. Reservations are accepted via regular mail for up to four months ahead of time, while phone reservations can only be made fourteen days in advance (contact park headquarters).

North to Canada

The northernmost tip of Maine is taken up by **Aroostook County**, which covers an area larger than several small states. Although its main activity is the large-scale cultivation of potatoes, it is also the location of the **Allagash Wilderness Waterway**, where several whitewater rafting companies put in boats (see box, p.522). Britain and the United States all but went to war over Aroostook in 1839; at **Fort Kent**, the northern terminus of Rte-1, the main sight is the solid cedar **Fort Kent Blockhouse**, which was built to defend American integrity and looks like a throwback to early pioneer days. If you happen to be driving along Rte-1 between Presque Isle and Houlton (just east of here), keep an eye out for the very cool, 40-mile long **solar system** model that was crafted entirely by Northern Maine residents and appears in scaled intervals here beside the highway. People come from all around to eat at *Eureka Hall*, 5 School St, off Rte-161 in Stockholm (☎207/896-3196), an institution of Aroostock County that serves up home-style meals and incredible desserts. Reservations are recommended for weekend meals.

Contexts

Contexts

History

I t's generally accepted that people of mixed Mongolian descent crossed the Bering Straits from northeast Asia to the American continent sometime between 12,000 and 25,000 years ago, then gradually spread eastwards over the next several millennia, arriving in the New England area between 9000 and 3000 BC. It's unclear whether or not these peoples were the ancestors of the Algonquins, who greeted the Europeans when they arrived in the sixteenth and seventeenth centuries, or whether they had died off before the tribes we consider "Native American" came here.

Native peoples and early Europeans

The first documented **Europeans** to visit these shores were the Norse. In about 1000 AD, Norway's King Olaf commissioned Leif Eriksson to bring Christianity to Greenland. Like many explorers, Eriksson was blown off course, and came ashore somewhere between Newfoundland and Massachusetts. Discovering a new land where wild grapes grew in abundance, he dubbed it "Vinland the Good."

It's unlikely that the native peoples encountered by early European settlers in the region had arrived much before the fourteenth or fifteenth centuries – not long before the Europeans, who applied the blanket term **Algonquin** to all the peoples they met. However, despite being linked by various dialects of the Algonquin tongue, and by common cultural ties, these groups were fiercely independent of each other. By 1600, there were only about 25,000 natives, broken into a dozen or so tribal nations, among them the **Narragansetts** of Rhode Island, the **Abnaki** of Maine, and smaller groups such as the **Niantics** and **Pequot** in Connecticut, all of whom used the land to hunt, fish, and grow crops such as beans, squash, tobacco, and corn.

The age of exploration

With the Spanish focusing almost exclusively on the southern regions of what is now North America, the Dutch, English, Portuguese, and French were left to explore the cooler and less hospitable shores of New England. In 1498, **John Cabot** nosed by the shores of New England while searching for the elusive Northwest Passage, which was believed to lead to the Orient and its treasures. Cabot, who landed somewhere in Labrador, claimed all of America east of the Rockies and north of Florida for England. Meanwhile, **Giovanni de Verrazano**, sailing for Francis I of France, traveled as far north as Rhode Island's Narragansett Bay, though the thought of establishing a settlement seems not to have crossed his mind.

Almost a century later, in 1583, **Sir Humphrey Gilbert** became the first Englishman to attempt to settle North America. Sailing from Plymouth, he aspired to set up a trading post at the mouth of the Penobscot River, but lost his life in a storm on the crossing over. More of his countrymen followed him: between 1602 and 1606, Bartholomew Gosnold, Martin Pring, and George Weymouth set out to tap New England's lucrative sassafras bark, regarded in Europe as a panacea for all ills. In 1606, King James I granted a charter to the **Virginia Company of Plymouth**, with permission to establish a colony between North Carolina and Nova Scotia. A year later, a hundred adventurous souls led by Pring, Sir Walter Raleigh, and Sir Fernando Gorges set out from Plymouth. Arriving on Parker's Island, off the coast of Maine, they made a short go of it, but were soon repelled by the winter weather. Despite their lack of success, they took home with them stories of a land of fast-flowing rivers, verdant forests, and friendly native peoples – so positive a picture, in fact, that the Plymouth Company commissioned distinguished surveyor **John Smith** to research the region's potential for development. Sailing along the Massachusetts coast in 1614, he named the region "**New England.**" It was his book, *A Description of New England*, which persuaded the Pilgrims to migrate to these shores. At the same time, farther north, the French were making inroads: in 1609, Samuel de Champlain traversed the lake that today bears his name.

The Pilgrims

By the early seventeenth century, Europe was in religious turmoil: on the continent, Luther, Calvin, and other Protestant reformers had begun a religious revolution against Roman Catholicism. The **Church of England**, created as a result of this revolution, claimed to be both Catholic and reformed in an attempt to appease the factions within its ranks. Religious zealots who opposed all aspects of Catholicism, called **Puritans**, enjoyed a degree of respectability during the reign of Elizabeth I. However, after the accession of a pro-Catholic king, James I, in 1603, the Puritans found themselves increasingly harassed by the authorities. As a result, 66 Puritans negotiated a deal with the Plymouth Company to finance a permanent settlement in North America, where they would be free to practice their own religion. Chartered by one John Carver, the vessel *Mayflower* had a passenger list that included the separatists plus hired help such as Myles Standish, professional soldier, and John Alden, cooper. In all, just over one hundred passengers set sail aboard the *Mayflower* from Southampton, England, on September 16, 1620. After two months at sea, they reached the North American coast at **Provincetown**, **Cape Cod**, on November 19. The same day, 41 men signed the **Mayflower Compact**, in which they agreed to establish a "Civic Body Politic" (temporary government) and to be bound by its laws. The Compact became the basis of government in the Plymouth Colony. The new arrivals had landed on a virtually barren stretch of the coast, and soon resettled across the bay, arriving at what is now Plymouth, Massachusetts, on December 26, 1620.

The early colonists

Only half the colonists survived their first **winter** on American soil. Unaccustomed to the extreme cold, many died from pneumonia; scurvy and other infections killed many more. It would have been even worse but for **Squanto**, a Native American who had spent time in England. He managed to enlist the support of Massassoit, the local Wampanoag sachem, who signed a Treaty of Friendship, and plied the visitors with food. Exactly a year after their arrival in Plymouth, the surviving colonists sat down with the Indians to enjoy a feast – an occasion still celebrated in America today, at the end of November, as Thanksgiving.

Weeks later, these first settlers were joined by 35 more, laden with provisions, and by 1624 Plymouth had become a thriving village of thirty cottages. News of the community's success reached England, and in 1629 another group, led by London lawyer John Winthrop, obtained a royal charter as the "Company of the Massachusetts Bay in New England." Winthrop had lofty goals for the town he was to settle in New England, aspiring that it would be a "city upon a hill" – a model Christian town that others would look to as an example. That summer Winthrop and more than three hundred settlers arrived at Salem; thousands more followed in the 1630s, as the persecution of Puritans in England intensified. Dozens of new communities were formed; many, such as Dorchester, Ipswich, and Taunton, were named after the towns and villages the settlers had left behind. By 1640, the **Massachusetts Bay Company** comprised around 10,000 colonists.

At this stage, new arrivals in the colonies were not limited to Massachusetts. In **Connecticut**, the Reverend Thomas Hooker established the community that would become Hartford, while Theophilus Eaton and John Davenport founded New Haven. But frictions were already developing among the settlers, many of whom were proving to be even less tolerant than their oppressors in England. The **Reverend Roger Williams**, hounded out of the Massachusetts Bay Colony for his liberal views, established a settlement at Providence, in 1638, on land made available by two Indian sachems. The new **State of Rhode Island and Providence Plantations**, in its 1663 charter, guaranteed religious freedom for all: Jews, Huguenots, even Quakers. Communities were also established in New Hampshire in 1638, and Maine in 1652.

As the colonial population grew, so did the perceived need for clergy, preferably trained in New England. In 1636, **Harvard College** was established for that specific purpose, while a General Court was formed to administer the colony's affairs, including justice. Meanwhile, zealous Puritans worked on **converting** the Indians to their faith, translating the Bible into Algonquin and setting up special communities for Christian Indians along the Connecticut River and on Cape Cod, which became known as "praying towns." Several Algonquins were sent to Harvard to train as Christian clergy – although only one completed the training – and by the 1660s, one fifth of all Indians were nominally Christian. However, the settlers' arrogant attempt to persuade the Indians to give up their native culture rapidly created profound unhappiness.

At first, the new settlers and the Native Americans had been able to coexist peacefully, though **diseases** introduced by the colonists may have been directly responsible for a plague which killed more than a third of all the Algonquins. As the colonists ventured south, they met growing resistance, particularly from the proud Pequot tribe, with whom war erupted in 1636, at Fort Mystic and Fairfield; many lives were lost on both sides. Then, in 1675, Narragansett leader Metacom, also known as Philip, persuaded feuding Algonquin groups, principally the Nipmucks, Narragansetts, and Wampanoags, to bury their differences and join in a concerted campaign against the settlers. Known as **King Philip's War**, hostilities culminated in the **Great Swamp Fight** in Kingston, Rhode Island. More than 2000 Indians were killed, including Metacom himself. More significantly, the outcome of the conflict signaled the breaking of the Indian will in New England.

The road to revolution

Until the middle of the seventeenth century, the colonies were largely left to take care of themselves, as England was preoccupied with domestic concerns (a bloody civil war, the beheading of Charles I, the establishment of Oliver Cromwell's parliamentary republic). To a certain extent, though, the colonists retained intimate cultural and economic ties to Great Britain, a relationship complicated further by often hostile dealings with the Native Americans and the **French**. The latter group maintained an active presence throughout North America up until the end of the **French and Indian War** (1754–63), when they ceded all land east of the Mississippi to Great Britain, with the exception of New Orleans. The exit of the French and the gradual decline of the Indian tribes set the stage for separatism, as the colonists no longer relied on Great Britain for defense. Defiance against an increasingly domineering Crown, fueled by unpopular laws and taxes, quickly escalated.

In 1686, King James II revoked the northern colonies' charters and attempted to create a **Dominion of New England** stretching from Maine to New Jersey. Allegedly a security measure to protect the English communities from the French and the Indians, it was in reality an attempt to keep tabs on an increasingly defiant populace. The king's first gubernatorial appointees were staunch Anglicans, which only increased the colonists' frustration. A new respect between the Crown and colonies was temporarily forged in 1689, when the "Glorious Revolution" brought Protestants William and Mary to the British throne, but conditions reverted in 1760, with the crowning of King George III. In a move designed not so much to raise revenue as to remind the colonists who was boss, he imposed the **Revenue Act of 1764**, which taxed sugar, silk, and wine. In reaction, colonists instituted a boycott of British goods and supplies. The situation deteriorated further in 1765, with the introduction of the **Stamp Act** and the imposition of taxes on commercial and legal documents, newspapers, and even playing cards. Protests erupted throughout New England. The bulk of the demonstrations were peaceful, but in Boston the houses of stampman Andrew Oliver and Governor Thomas Hutchinson were plundered. British prime minister William Pitt **repealed** the act in March 1766.

Then, in the summer of 1767, new prime minister Charles Townshend arrogantly taunted the colonies with the remark, "I dare tax America." The subsequent **Townshend Acts**, which introduced harsh levies on imports such as paper, glass, and tea, prompted the dispatch to Boston of two regiments of British soldiers, called "Redcoats" for their bright red uniform jackets. On March 5, 1770, a crowd of several hundred Bostonians gathered to ridicule a "lobster-back" guard outside the customs house. The scene turned ugly as stones and rocks were thrown, and seven nervous reinforcements arrived, one firing on the crowd without orders. In the panic, more shots followed. Three colonists were pronounced dead at the scene and two were mortally wounded in the event that was to become known as the **Boston Massacre**.

Things would have gone downhill more quickly but for the **economic prosperity** that New England, and particularly Boston, was beginning to enjoy. Eventually the Townshend acts were repealed, though not the tax on East Indian tea, which was boycotted by the colonists. Dutch blends were smuggled in, and a special brew called "Liberty Tea" was concocted from sage, currant, or plantain leaves. Britain responded in September 1773 by flooding the market with half a million pounds of its own subsidized blend. Resistance to the British tea focused on Boston, where the **Massachusetts Committee of Correspondence**, an unofficial legislature, and the local chapter of the **Sons of Liberty**, a pseudo-secret society, organized the barricading of the piers and wharves and demanded Governor Hutchinson send home the tea-filled ship *Dartmouth*. When Hutchinson refused, sixty men disguised as Mohawk Indians, Samuel Adams and John Hancock among them, surreptitiously climbed aboard and dumped 350 crates of the tea into Boston Harbor. The date was December 16, 1773, and the event captured the world's imagination as the **Boston Tea Party**.

This blatant act of defiance rattled Parliament, which introduced the so-called "**Coercive Acts**," among them the Boston Port Act, which sealed off the city with a massive naval blockade. Meanwhile, American patriots from Massachusetts, Rhode Island, and other states gathered in Philadelphia for the **First Continental Congress**, convened on September 5, 1774. Though British garrisons still controlled the major towns, such was the antagonism in rural areas that policing them was becoming virtually impossible. All the while locals continued to stockpile arms and munitions.

The Revolution

In April 1775, London instructed its Boston-based commander, General Thomas Gage, to put down rebellion in rural Massachusetts, where the provincial congress had assumed de facto political control. On the night of April 18, Gage dispatched seven hundred soldiers to destroy the arms depot in Concord, while at nearby Lexington seventy colonial soldiers, known as **Minute Men** (because they were prepared to fight at a moment's notice), lay in wait, having been warned of the plan by Paul Revere and William Dawes. On Lexington's Town Common, British musket fire resulted in the deaths of eight Americans. The British moved on to Concord, where they were repelled, and were eventually pushed back to Boston, losing 273 men on the way to the colonists' ambushes. As news of the Continental victory spread, rumors of plunder and pillage by British troops further fueled American resentment.

A couple of months later, the war intensified with the **Battle of Bunker Hill**, on Boston's Charlestown peninsula, which General Artemus Ward of the Continental Army had ordered to be fortified – though it was actually on nearby Breed's Hill, not Bunker, where the American forces were stationed. On June 17, the Redcoats attacked twice, and were twice rebuffed. The third attempt succeeded, because the Americans ran out of ammunition – the much-celebrated order "don't fire until you see the whites of their eyes" was given (some say by Colonel William Prescott, others by General Isaac Putnam) specifically to save bullets. Bunker Hill, with a thousand British casualties, was an expensive triumph for the Crown. Worn down by lack of manpower, low morale, and growing American resistance, less than a year later an embattled General Gage ordered a **British withdrawal** to Halifax, Nova Scotia.

The **Declaration of Independence** – with fifty-six signatories, fourteen of whom were from **Massachusetts**, **Connecticut**, **New Hampshire**, and **Rhode Island** – was adopted by the Continental Congress on July 4, 1776. The war, however, was far from over; hostilities between the colonists and the British continued throughout the next several years. In the fall of 1781, General George Washington, with significant French naval support, led a decisive victory against the British at the port of Yorktown, Virginia, essentially quashing British hopes for victory. In 1783, a series of settlements finally ended the war. Most important among them was the **Treaty of Paris**, which established the independence of the colonies from Great Britain. America was soon recognized as a sovereign state by the major European powers.

The thirteen colonies had hammered out an integrated union in 1781, though not without the concern that a centralized federal system would be just as bad as British rule. For that reason, heroes Sam Adams and John Hancock gave only grudging support to the Constitution, and representatives from Rhode Island consistently voted against it, relenting only after the Bill of Rights was added. Vermont remained an independent state until 1791, when it was admitted to the Union as the **fourteenth state**. **Maine's statehood** was not gained until 1820. According to the Missouri Compromise of 1820, Maine was admitted to the Union as a free (anti-slavery) state, balanced by Missouri, a slave state.

Nineteenth-century development

New England began as a predominantly **agricultural region**. However, apart from some parts of Vermont, the soil was generally rocky, making plowing difficult, and long, cold winters meant that the ground was frozen solid for a large part of the year. The land really lent itself to little more than subsistence farming, with small farms, wheat, corn, pigs, and cattle.

The region's true prosperity came first as a result of its **connection with the sea**: fishing, especially for cod, was important, as was the production of whale derivatives, especially oil, used for heating and lighting. More adventurous sea captains, many of them based in Boston or Salem, Massachusetts, ventured farther afield, and brought back great treasures from India and China, including tea, spices, silk, and opium. Several communities, including Newport and Providence, Rhode Island, flourished through the so-called **Triangular Trade**: ships unloaded West Indian molasses, reloaded with rum, then sailed to Africa, where the rum was exchanged for slaves, in turn shipped to the West Indies and traded for molasses. **Shipbuilding** industries flourished, particularly in places such as Essex, Massachusetts, which earned a reputation for manufacturing swift vessels. New Hampshire and Maine also developed important trades in timber, agriculture, and fishing, with some shipbuilding on the coast at Bath, Maine, and Portsmouth, New Hampshire. But the first two decades of the nineteenth century showed how volatile maritime trade was, especially with so many political uncertainties, notably the Napoleonic Wars, Thomas Jefferson's Embargo Acts (which prohibited all exports to Europe and restricted imports from Great Britain – a response to British and French interference with American ships), and the War of 1812. There was a clear need for New England to diversify its economy were its prosperity to grow.

The Industrial Revolution

In 1789, **Samuel Slater**, a skilled mechanic from England, sailed to New York disguised as a laborer (the emigration of skilled mechanics was forbidden by the British government, and there were also serious penalties against smuggling drawings of industrial machinery). Undaunted, Slater memorized the specifications, and with financial backing provided by Moses Brown, a Providence Quaker, he set up the nation's first successful **cotton mill** in Pawtucket, Rhode Island. Though an important milestone in the Industrial Revolution, working conditions at the mill were hellish, and these, together with poor pay, inspired the nation's first industrial strike in 1800.

▲ Lowell mills

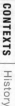

Another entrepreneur determined to duplicate British weaving feats was Bostonian **Francis Cabot Lowell**, a self-styled "industrial tourist" who set up a small mill with a power loom in Waltham, Massachusetts. Lowell's **Merrimack Manufacturing Company** proved extremely profitable, with sales at $3000 in 1815 and reaching $345,000 in 1822. In 1826, having already moved once to Chelmsford, the business relocated again, to a purpose-built community named "Lowell" after its founder.

New England was fast becoming the **industrial center** of the US, home to some two-thirds of the nation's cotton mills, half of which were in Massachusetts. Tiny Rhode Island processed twenty percent of the nation's wool, and in Connecticut **Sam Colt** and **Eli Whitney**, known for his invention of the cotton gin, manufactured the first firearms with interchangeable parts. Connecticut also became home to a thriving watch- and clock-making industry. In the fields of paper and shoe manufacture and metalworking, New England, in particular New Hampshire, was unsurpassed.

Culture and education

New England, particularly Boston, was a pioneer in **education**. The nation's first secondary school, Boston Latin, opened here in 1635, while the first university, Harvard, was established in 1636. Yale University was founded in 1701 in Connecticut, while Brown University, originally Rhode Island College, came into being in 1764. Farther north, New Hampshire's Dartmouth College dates from 1769, and Bowdoin College in Maine from 1796.

In 1639, America's first **printing press** was set up in Cambridge, where the *Bay Psalm Book* and *New England Primer* were among the first published works. The colonies' first newspaper came into being in 1690, succeeded by the popular *Boston News-Letter* in 1704. By the 1850s, more than four hundred periodicals were in print. Libraries such as Hartford's famous Wadsworth Atheneum and the Providence Athenaeum both came into existence in the mid-nineteenth century, while in 1854 the Boston Public Library, with 750,000 volumes, became the world's first free municipal library.

With these developments, New England came to occupy a prominent place in the American cultural landscape. Easily recognized names include Henry David Thoreau, the **transcendentalist** philosopher and essayist; the poet Emily Dickinson; novelists Nathaniel Hawthorne, Mark Twain, and Harriet Beecher Stowe; and numerous others. In Boston, the 1871 founding of the **Museum of Fine Arts** was followed a decade later by the Boston Symphony Orchestra and the Boston Pops. New Haven became an important focus for theater, with the establishment of the Long Wharf, Shubert, and Yale Repertory stages.

The Civil War

From the moment of its inception, the unity of the nation had been based on shaky foundations, including the question of how the practice of **slavery** was to be addressed. Great care went into devising a Constitution that balanced the need for a strong federal government with the aspirations for autonomy of its component states. That was achieved by giving Congress two separate chambers – the House of Representatives, in which the number of representatives from each state depended on its population, and the Senate, where each state elected two members, regardless of size. Thus, although in theory the Constitution remained silent on the issue of slavery, it allayed the fears of the less populated Southern states, that the voters of the North might destroy their economy by forcing them to abandon the "peculiar institution."

However, it soon became apparent that the system only worked so long as there were roughly equal numbers of "free" and slave-owning states. At first, it seemed possible that the balance could be maintained – in 1820, under the Missouri Compromise, Missouri was admitted to the Union as a slave-owning state at the same time as Maine was admitted as a "free" one. In 1854, the **Kansas–Nebraska Act** forced the issue to a head, allowing both prospective states self-determination on the issue. The situation only deteriorated further from this point forward.

Most New Englanders held ambivalent views about slavery, even though all the region's states had outlawed the practice. Nonetheless, when the **Civil War** began in earnest in 1861 the region sent thousands of men to bolster the Union cause, many of whom never returned. In the end, it was not so much the brilliance of the generals as sheer economic power that won the war for the Union. It was the North, with New England leading the way, that was able to maintain full trading with the rest of the world while diverting spare resources to the production of munitions.

Into the twentieth century

The Industrial Revolution and the Civil War created a sea of change for New England in the latter half of the nineteenth century. Meanwhile, the US frontier moved west, and other regions also began to play their part in the development of the nation. Despite a **diminishing influence** on the national stage, New England nonetheless maintained a strong tradition of social reform, paving the way in the fields of prison reform and health and mental health provision.

Meanwhile, the ethnic and religious make-up of New England was changing rapidly. No longer was it the preserve of white Anglo-Saxon Protestants; in the 1840s, following the potato famine, **Irish immigrants** began arriving. Soon more than a thousand Irish immigrants a month were landing in Boston, while catholics from Italy, French Canada, Portugal, and Eastern Europe accounted for two-thirds of the total population growth during the nineteenth century. Indeed, by 1907, seventy percent of Massachusetts' population could claim to be of non-Anglo-Saxon descent. Such waves of immigration provoked backlash, with the openly racist **Know-Nothing** party gaining governorships in Massachusetts, Rhode Island, Connecticut, and New Hampshire; membership of the American Protective Association and Immigrant Restriction League increased dramatically; and signs such as "No Irish Need Apply" were found on the doorsteps of many a business.

Still, immigrants found their way into the political system. In 1881, John Breen from Tipperary became the first Irishman to take up an establishment position, as mayor of Lawrence, Massachusetts. This had a profound motivating effect on his fellow countrymen, and three years later, Hugh O'Brien won the Boston mayorship, while Patrick Andrew Collin represented Suffolk County with a congressional seat in the nation's capital. By the turn of the twentieth century, immigrants were represented at all levels of government.

But political scandal and **corruption** were never far away. "Boss" Charlie Brayton and the *Providence Journal* ring bought their way to office in Rhode Island, with individual votes costing $2 to $5, and up to $30 in hotly contested elections. Others abused the support they enjoyed: **James Michael Curley**, elected Boston mayor four times, and governor of Massachusetts from 1934 to 1938, did much to improve the welfare of the poor, but also doled out jobs and money to community leaders who carefully manipulated the electorate.

With the huge influx of poor immigrants, especially from Catholic countries, a **"New Puritanism"** began to take hold. Encouraged by Catholic leader William Cardinal o'Connell and the closely associated **Watch and Ward Society**, moralists lobbied for the prohibition of, among other things, Hemingway's *The Sun also Rises* and a variety of plays and books.

The southern exodus

As time passed, other regions began to challenge New England's claim to be the manufacturing capital of the US. Many companies **moved south**, where costs were much lower, and by 1923 more than half of the nation's cotton goods were being woven there. Industrial production in Massachusetts alone fell by more than $1 billion during the 1920s, while unemployment skyrocketed in some towns. The **Great Depression** hit New England particularly hard and, with few natural resources to draw upon and human resources relocating, industry here never really recovered. By 1980, the region which had given birth to America's Industrial Revolution was headquarters to only fourteen of the nation's top five hundred companies.

Recent history

Political collaboration, instead of confrontation, between New England's "Brahmin" political set, and the second- and- third-generation sons and daughters of immigrants, began to pay off in a common quest to find an answer to New England's economic problems, and by the 1980s the region was beginning to experience something of a **resurgence**. New industries, such as the production of biomedical machinery, computer hardware and software, and photographic materials, sprang up throughout the region, but especially along Rte-128 west of Boston. During this period, Boston became the country's mutual fund capital, Hartford's insurance industry continued to flourish, and tourism asserted itself as the region's second largest source of income. New England became known for its political stability and, at the same time, for leading the way with anti-pollution laws, consumer rights, handgun controls, and civil rights legislation.

Though the nationwide **economic slump** in the late 1980s and early 1990s caused problems in those larger urban centers which had failed to address the social consequences of the demise of traditional manufacturing industries, the area managed to rebound again. Almost unparalleled prosperity accompanied by low unemployment, especially in the latter half of the 1990s, meant that more money was freed up for the benefit of long-neglected areas that needed attention: roads and infrastructure, crime prevention, schools, and social provision. At the same time **urban regeneration**, sometimes on a spectacular scale (in Providence, Rhode Island, for example), and the continued development of new industries have put the region more or less back on track. New England now lays claim to nearly thirty of the top five hundred companies in the US.

The present and the future

Like most of the country, New England took a hit with the slowdown of the economy in the wake of the bursting of the dot-com bubble and September 11, 2001. But some positive changes warrant optimism – several states have enacted significant measures to protect the environment, and in 2006 Massachusetts spearheaded major healthcare reforms. Politically, liberalism and, to an extent, libertarian values, remain prominent. In 2006, Massachusetts elected its first African-American governor, while Connecticut elected its first female Republican governor. Democrat **John F. Kerry**, the junior senator from Massachusetts, lost his bid for the presidency in 2004 against George W. Bush by a very narrow margin.

Though New England is not as liberal as the national press often makes it out to be (note that the current governors of Rhode Island, Connecticut, and Vermont are all Republican), it maintains an independent stance on several issues. Maine, Vermont, and Rhode Island have flouted federal statutes by making **medical marijuana** legal, and at the time of writing Massachusetts was on its way to decriminalizing the personal possession of less than one ounce of marijuana. In 2004, Massachusetts legalized same-sex marriage, and also recently opened its doors to couples from other states seeking to marry here; Connecticut legalized same-sex marriage in October 2008. Indeed, New England is more gay- and lesbian-friendly than most other regions in the country –Vermont and New Hampshire grant same-sex civil unions, while Rhode Island recognizes same-sex marriages performed in other states.

New England on film

New England's scenery is undeniably cinematic, and the region is rich in film narrative, drawing from a rich literary tradition. Films set here often adopt distinct, local subject matter – academia or witchcraft, for example. The following films are all set in New England, though many are filmed elsewhere.

The Actress George Cukor, 1953. A unique portrait of Boston in the early 1910s, based on a play by Ruth Gordon about her early life in nearby Wollaston. Stars Jean Simmons as Gordon and a deliciously cantankerous Spencer Tracy as her father.

Affliction Paul Schrader, 1998. Brooding tale of violence shattering the placid surface of a snowbound New Hampshire town. Nick Nolte is superb as the divorced small-town cop stumbling through middle age, whose father's legacy of abuse is too heavy a load to bear.

Alice's Restaurant Arthur Penn, 1969. Built around Arlo Guthrie's hit song of the same name, this quizzical elegy for counterculture brought the hippie nation to the Berkshire town of Stockbridge

All That Heaven Allows Douglas Sirk, 1955. Recounting the forbidden romance of a middle-aged widow (Jane Wyman) and her strapping, Thoreau-quoting gardener (Rock Hudson), this devastating portrait of the small minds of the local country-club set served to show seventeenth-century Puritanism alive in postwar New England.

Beetlejuice Tim Burton, 1988. Early Burton comedy in which a recently deceased couple (Geena Davis and Alec Baldwin) decide to haunt their historic New England home until its new tenants decide to leave; the couple gets some unwanted "help" from Beetlejuice (Michael Keaton). Shot in Vermont.

Between the Lines Joan Micklin Silver, 1977. Shot on location, this comedy-drama documents the dying throes of counterculture in late 1970s Boston by focusing on the ragtag staff of an underground newspaper (based on the real-life *Real Paper*).

The Bostonians James Ivory, 1984. In 1875 Boston, New England women's libbers and a Southern male chauvinist battle for the soul of one very pliable young woman in the drawing rooms of Cambridge, on the lawns of Harvard, and on the beaches of Martha's Vineyard.

Christmas in Connecticut Peter Godfrey, 1945. Barbara Stanwyck plays a Manhattan magazine writer who has faked her way to being the Martha Stewart of her day. When her publisher asks her to invite a war hero to her Connecticut farm for Christmas, Stanwyck has to conjure up the idyllic New England existence she'd only written about.

Cider House Rules Lasse Hallstrom, 1999. Adaptation of John Irving's novel (see p.544), in which a shifting Maine backdrop sets the stage for a somewhat didactic, if winning, meditation on love, suffering, and the thorny issue of abortion.

A Civil Action Steve Zaillian, 1998. A rainy, wintry vision of New England in which John Travolta struts his stuff as a cocky Boston lawyer who loses everything but regains his soul when he takes up the case of a group of families in a nearby town.

The Crucible Nicholas Hytner, 1996. Riveting adaptation of Arthur Miller's allegory of McCarthyism, set in 1692 Salem. Winona Ryder and her friends are spied dancing by firelight and accused of witchcraft; to save themselves they start naming names.

Dolores Claiborne Taylor Hackford, 1995. On a dreary island off the coast of Maine, Kathy Bates is suspected of killing her wealthy employer. Gothic sleeper adapted from a Stephen King novel.

The Europeans James Ivory, 1979. Shot against the gorgeous fall foliage of New Hampshire and Massachusetts, Merchant-Ivory's genial adaptation of Henry James's novella pits New England sobriety against the dizzy charms of a couple of European visitors.

Far From Heaven Todd Haynes, 2002. Haynes's ode to Douglas Sirk (See "All that Heaven Allows") stars Julianne Moore as a 1950s housewife in a conservative small Connecticut town, whose life unravels as she discovers her husband's deepest secret and her own love for her black gardener.

Good Will Hunting Gus Van Sant, 1997. This Oscar-winner for Best Screenplay tells of a South Boston townie who is a closet math wizard, and his transformation, with the help of a therapist friend.

The House of the Seven Gables Joe May, 1940. Fusty superstition battles liberal enlightenment in eighteenth-century Massachusetts in this histrionic adaptation of Nathaniel Hawthorne's Gothic family saga, starring George Sanders and Vincent Price.

The Ice Storm Ang Lee, 1997. Suburban living in 1970s Connecticut – alcoholic excess, adultery, alienation – is laid bare in all its formica-covered splendor in this disturbing adaptation of Rick Moody's novel. Starring Kevin Kline, Sigourney Weaver, and Joan Allen.

In the Bedroom Todd Field, 2001. Against the backdrop of Maine's small harbor-town lobster docks, a college-age boy begins seeing a local divorcee with an angry ex-husband. Tom Wilkinson wins the best-Maine-accent-by-a-foreigner award in this intense drama.

John Adams, 2008. Finely rendered TV mini-series about second US president John Adams (Paul Giamatti) and the birth of the nation, with an award-winning performance by Laura Linney as Adams's beloved wife Abigail, and vivid portrayals of other Founding Fathers.

Jaws Steven Spielberg, 1975. Toothsome blockbuster, in which a killer shark wreaks havoc on the shores of Martha's Vineyard (known here as Amity Island).

Leave Her to Heaven John M. Stahl, 1945. A stunning, too-little-known gem, in which Gene Tierney plays a woman who loves too much. Gorgeously colourful, with some indelible scenes set in Maine.

Legally Blonde Robert Luketic, 2001. A ditzy but charming sorority girl from California (Reese Witherspoon) follows her boyfriend to Harvard Law School, where she charms the cold town and clinches a murder trial defense on which she's assisting.

Little Women George Cukor, 1933; Gillian Armstrong, 1994. Louisa May Alcott's timeless classic, set in Concord, MA, has not one but two wonderful Hollywood adaptations. The first, Cukor's in 1933, stars a rambunctious Katherine Hepburn as Jo; the second, made some sixty years later by Gillian Armstrong, has Winona Ryder in the lead role and Susan Sarandon as the ever-wise Marmee.

Love Story Arthur Hiller, 1970. The Harvard preppie (Ryan O'Neal) and the working-class Radcliffe wiseacre (Ali McGraw) fall for each other against a backdrop of library stacks, falling leaves, and tinkling pianos, while tragedy makes its way into the air.

Malice Harold Becker, 1993. In a small college town in Massachusetts (the film was shot at Smith College in Northampton) the blissful life of newlyweds Bill Pullman and Nicole Kidman is rocked by the arrival of diabolically charismatic Harvard doctor Alec Baldwin.

Mermaids Richard Benjamin, 1990. Single mom Cher relocates her two daughters (Winona Ryder and Christina Ricci) to a small Massachusetts town. Elder daughter Winona, decides she wants to become a nun, and suffers various other growing pains, while Cher finds love with Bob Hoskins and becomes a better mother.

Misery Rob Reiner, 1990. Adaptation of popular Stephen King novel, with a chilling Kathy Bates as novelist James Caan's biggest fan. The dreary and ominous New England backdrop is perfect – though most action takes place inside a house.

Mystic Pizza Donald Petrie, 1988. The film that put both Julia Roberts and Mystic, Connecticut, on the national map. Shot on location in Mystic, CT and nearby Rhode Island, this film tells of the romantic travails of three young waitresses at a local pizza joint.

Mystic River Clint Eastwood, 2003. Dark, poignant indie classic based on Dennis Lehane's novel, telling of three childhood friends (Sean Penn, Kevin Bacon, Tim Robbins) in working-class Boston, reunited when the daughter of one is brutally murdered.

Next Stop Wonderland Brad Anderson, 1998. The title of this indie romance refers to the final stop of Boston's blue line subway, where luckless nurse Hope Davis finally crosses paths, after many a false start, with the man of her dreams.

On Golden Pond Mark Rydell, 1981. The namesake of this tearjerker is really Squam Lake in New Hampshire, where, one summer, a crabby Boston professor (Henry Fonda in his final film) and his wife (Katherine Hepburn) came to rediscover their marriage.

The Perfect Storm Wolfgang Petersen, 2000. George Clooney, Diane Lane, and Mark Wahlberg star in this adaptation of Sebastian Junger's bestseller about a New England swordfishing boat's doomed journey into the heart of the "storm of the century."

The Raid Hugo Fregonese, 1954. Based on a true story, this little-known gem tells of a band of escaped Confederate prisoners, who infiltrated a Vermont town intending to raze it to the ground. Anne Bancroft plays a beautiful Yankee widow.

Reversal of Fortune Barbet Schroeder, 1990. Opening with an aerial sequence of the mansions of Newport strung along the Rhode Island coastline, this witty film dramatizes the case of Claus von Bülow, who was convicted of attempting to murder his heiress wife.

The Russians Are Coming! The Russians Are Coming! Norman Jewison, 1966. A comic vision of Cold War paranoia in which a Russian submarine runs aground off fictional "Gloucester Island" somewhere on the New England coast, causing panic in the archetypally dozy community. Actually shot on the coast of Northern California.

The Scarlet Letter Victor Seastrom, 1926; Wim Wenders, 1973; Roland Joffe, 1995. Hawthorne's masterpiece has been treated about as well by Hollywood as Hester Prynne was treated by the people of Salem. The first, silent, adaptation of the book, starring Lillian Gish, is the best, though it reduces Hawthorne's work to a tragic pastoral romance. The 1973 version – filmed in Spain with German actors – is about as much fun as Salem on the Sabbath, while the 1995 Demi Moore vehicle includes some racy sex scenes and a rewritten ending.

Splendor in the Grass Eli Kazan, 1961. Though its handful of scenes set at Yale University are confined to studio sets, Kazan's Kansas melodrama bears mention for the pivotal role that New Haven's legendary pizza pie plays in the protagonists' romantic proceedings.

Starting Over Alan J. Pakula, 1979. Burt Reynolds leaves his marriage and swanky Manhattan pad to move to a cold-water Boston flat, for a new start. A wonderful, little-known comedy romance shot by Bergman's cinematographer Sven Nykvist.

State and Main David Mamet, 2000. A slick Hollywood film crew lands in uptight small-town Vermont after having been run out of New Hampshire for unknown, but undoubtedly lurid, reasons. Screwball comedy with some winning performances.

The Swimmer Frank Perry, 1968. A splendid curio adapted from John Cheever's short story of the same name, in which rural Connecticut is imagined as a lush Garden of Eden through which broad-chested Burt Lancaster makes his allegorical way home one summer afternoon.

There's Something About Mary Farrelly Brothers, 1998. If Rhode Island is to go down in the annals of cinema history it would have to be as the site of Ben Stiller's notorious pre-prom mishap in this funny opus.

Tough Guys Don't Dance Norman Mailer, 1987. Set in Provincetown, Mailer's bizarre retelling of his novel is a convoluted affair involving an intoxicated writer, a gay-bashing sheriff, a Southern millionaire, a gold digger, drug-dealing lobster men, and a severed head.

The Trouble with Harry Alfred Hitchcock, 1955. A black comedy painted in the reds and golds of a Vermont fall. The trouble with Harry is that he keeps turning up dead and everybody, including his young wife (Shirley MacLaine), thinks they may have killed him.

Vermont is for Lovers John O'Brien, 1993. A charming, semi-documentary comedy about a New York couple who came here to get married, come down with a bad case of cold feet, and turn to the locals – all real Vermonters and neighbors of O'Brien – for advice. Scene-stealing septuagenarian sheep farmer Fred Tuttle then had a spin-off in O'Brien's spoof of Vermont politics, *Man with a Plan* (1995).

Walk East on Beacon Alfred L. Werker, 1952. A matter-of-fact thriller about FBI agents ferreting out communists in Cold War Boston. The film tempers its pinko-bashing paean to Hoover's boys with the more engaging nuts and bolts of their activities.

White Christmas Michael Curtiz, 1954. Singing and dancing army buddies Bing Crosby and Danny Kaye take the train up to Vermont for a skiing holiday, only to find there hasn't been snow all year. One of the very few musicals to be set in New England, beloved for its Irving Berlin score, and that magical snowy finale.

The Witches of Eastwick George Miller, 1987. An arch, handsome, but ultimately hollow adaptation of John Updike's novel about three love-starved women who conjure up a rather unwelcome visitor to their sleepy Massachusetts town.

Books

N ew England is home to a rich literary tradition, from colonial times to the present day. For a general introduction, see the Literary New England" color section. **Malcolm Cowley's** *New England Writers and Writing* (University Press of New England) discusses New England writers of the last two centuries, while **William Corbett's** *Literary New England: a History and Guide* (Faber) highlights the literary haunts and trivia of the region. Below, publishers are listed after the title.

Poetry, prose, and drama

Emily Dickinson *The Complete Poems* (Little, Brown). The ultimate New England poet, who spent all her life in the same town (Amherst) – indeed the same house – and quietly recorded the seasons and her own inner contemplations.

Robert Frost *The Collected Poems* (Henry Holt). The master poet skillfully evokes the New England landscape, especially the collection *North of Boston*.

Donald Hall *Old and New Poems; Life Work; The Ox-Cart Man* (Mariner Books, Beacon Press, Puffin). Hall is a New England poet's poet; he lives in New Hampshire and was married to Jane Kenyon (see below) until her death in 1995. He has also written non-fiction about New England, and even a few children's books, including the much-loved *Ox-Cart Man*.

Jane Kenyon *Collected Poems* (Graywolf). Kenyon was New Hampshire's poet laureate when she died of leukemia in 1995. Her poems have New England themes, but also deal wisely with depression, a disease she had fought since childhood.

Maxine Kumin *Selected Poems; The Long Marriage; Inside the Halo* (W.W. Norton). Living on a horse farm in New Hampshire, Kumin is deeply rooted in the New England landscape, with these two collections

coming after her recovery from a near-fatal riding accident.

Henry Wadsworth Longfellow *Poems and Other Writings* (Library of America). Longfellow celebrated both common and heroic New Englanders in his sometimes whimsical verse; perhaps a bit light for some, but central to mid-nineteenth-century New England society.

Robert Lowell *Life Studies; For the Union Dead* (Noonday Press). Affecting stuff from arguably New England's greatest twentieth-century poet, tackling family and social issues.

Arthur Miller *The Crucible* (Penguin). This compelling play about the 1692 Salem witch trials is peppered with quotes from actual transcripts and loaded with appropriate levels of hysteria and fervor – a must for witch fanatics everywhere.

Wallace Stevens *The Palm at the End of the Mind* (Vintage). Aspiring to create a distinctly American idiom, Stevens used simple language, but is still considered difficult. Despite growing success, he never quit his job as a lawyer for an insurance firm in Connecticut.

Henry David Thoreau *Cape Cod; The Maine Woods; Walden* (Penguin US). Thoreau put his transcendentalist philosophy into practice by living a life of self-reliance in his cabin by Walden Pond, near Concord, Massachusetts. *Cape Cod* and *The Maine Woods*, published after his death, recounts the writer's walks in nature.

History, culture, and society

James Chenoweth *Oddity Odyssey* (Henry Holt US). Fun little book that points out the more intriguing and humorous episodes and myths surrounding the sights and major players in New England's history.

David Hackett Fischer *Paul Revere's Ride* (University of Massachusetts Press/Oxford University Press). An exhaustive account of the patriot's legendary ride to Lexington, related as a historical narrative.

Sean Flynn *3000 Degrees* (Warner). Gripping retelling of the 1999 four-alarm fire in Worcester, MA, that resulted in the deaths of six fire-fighters.

Mark Kurlansky *Cod* (Penguin). Does a fish merit this much obsessive attention? Only in New England. Kurlansky makes a good case for viewing the cod as one of the more integral parts of the region.

J. Anthony Lukas *Common Ground: a Turbulent Decade in the Lives of Three American Families* (Vintage US). A Pulitzer Prize-winning account of three Boston families – one Irish-American, one black, one white middle-class – against the backdrop of the 1974 race riots sparked by court-ordered busing to desegregate public schools.

David McCullough *John Adams* (Simon & Schuster) Bestselling 2002 biography of the country's second president and lesser-known founding father, who spent much of his life in Massachusetts.

Louis Menand The *Metaphysical Club* (Farrar, Straus and Giroux USA). Engaging study of four Boston literary heavyweights, this Pulitzer Prize-winning biography reveals the effect of their pragmatic idealism on American intellectual thought.

Children's literature

Perhaps because its rich history is taught in schools across the country, or maybe for more romantic reasons, New England has served as a muse for children's book **authors** throughout the years.

Some of the best are by **Robert McCloskey**, who wrote and illustrated the timeless *Make Way for Ducklings*, *Blueberries for Sal*, *One Morning in Maine*, and *Time of Wonder*, all of which employ New England's landscape and wildlife. The poet **Donald Hall** has written several New England-based children's books, each beautifully illustrated: *The Ox-Cart Man*; *Lucy's Summer*; *Lucy's Christmas*; and *The Man Who Lived Alone*.

For slightly older readers, Vermonter Robert N. Peck is famed for his *Soup* series, published in the 1970s about a small-town Vermont boy named Soup. One-word author Avi lived in the historic part of Providence for many years, a locale that inspired *Something Upstairs*, in which a 13-year-old boy befriends the ghost of a slave who lived in his attic hundreds of years ago. Lois Lowry wrote the much-loved series of books about Anastasia Krupnik, a spirited Boston adolescent, while another remarkable girl, Kit, is the protagonist of *The Witch of Blackbird Pond*, by Elizabeth Speare, set in idyllic, dark, seventeenth-century Puritan Connecticut.

Nathaniel Philbrick *In the Heart of the Sea: the Tragedy of the Whaleship Essex* (Penguin). Gripping, true story behind *Moby Dick*, exploring the Nantucket whaling industry through the *Essex* saga.

Dan Shaughnessy *The Curse of the Bambino; Reversing the Curse* (Penguin, Houghton Mifflin). Shaughnessy, a Boston sportswriter, exams the Red Sox's "curse" – no championships since 1918, until their triumphant 2004 win (*Reversing the Curse*) – that began just after they sold Babe Ruth to the Yankees.

Architecture and design

Mona Domosh *Invented Cities: the Creation of Landscape in Nineteenth-Century New York and Boston* (Yale University Press US). Fascinating historical account of how these very different cities were shaped according to the values, beliefs, and fears of their respective societies.

Elaine Louie and Solvi dos Santos *Living in New England* (Simon & Schuster). Well-illustrated coffee-table book on the interiors of New England homes.

Naomi Miller and Keith Morgan *Boston Architecture 1975–1990* (Prestel). Contextualizes Boston's transformation into a modern city, with emphasis on the building boom of the 1980s, but also detailing the early development and architectural trends of the centuries before.

Susan and Michael Southworth *AIA Guide to Boston* (Globe Pequot US). The definitive guide to Boston architecture, organized by neighborhood, City landmarks and dozens of notable buildings.

Nature and specific guides

Appalachian Mountain Club *Maine Mountain Guide: The Hiking Trails of Maine* (Appalachian Mountain Club). Meticulous hiking guide, with detailed color maps, that should get you through both the popular and more backwoods sections of the state.

Tom Wessels *Reading the Forested Landscape: Natural History of New England* (Countryman Press). Uniquely informative deconstruction of why the land and trees are like they are today.

Weekend Walks in Rhode Island (Countryman Press). Rhode Island local Ken Derry leads you on 40 trails along the coast and into the backwoods, meticulously selected and described.

Fiction

Louisa May Alcott *Little Women* (Puffin). A semi-autobiographical novel, drawing on family experiences, Alcott's novel remains a classic to this day.

Brunonia Barry *The Lace Reader* (William Morrow). Debut novel by a Salem local, introducing the town with a twist – it's inhabited by modern-day witches whose human activities include dealing with tourists and going to therapy.

Gerry Boyle *Lifeline* (Berkley). Hard-hitting suspense novel about an ex-big-city reporter looking for solace in small-town Maine, only to find that crime exists there, too.

James Casey *Spartina* (Vintage). Set in the fishing world of Rhode Island, this memorable, spare work on a man's inner struggles captured the National Book Award in 1989.

John Cheever *The Wapshot Chronicle* (Vintage). Cheever's first novel documents the weird doings of the Wapshot family, of St Botolph's, Massachusetts. The sequel, *The Wapshot Scandal*, continues the saga.

Bret Easton Ellis *The Rules of Attraction* (Picador UK; Vintage US). A sex, drug, and booze-driven narrative, charting the romantic progress of a few students through Vermont's fictional Camden College.

Mary Eleanor Freeman *A New England Nun and Other Stories* (Penguin Books). Relatively unknown these days, Freeman enjoyed quite a fashion about a century ago for her tales of rural New England life.

Elizabeth Graver *Unravelling* (Hyperion). In distinct and compelling fashion, Graver charts a young woman's progress on the bleaker edges of New England life: its farms and factory mills.

Nathaniel Hawthorne *The House of the Seven Gables; The Scarlet Letter* (Bantam). Born in Salem, Massachusetts, in 1804, Hawthorne was descended from a judge at the famous witch trials, which provides the setting for his two classic novels.

George V. Higgins *Penance for Jerry Higgins* (Abacus UK). Ace crime writer and former district attorney portrays the seamier side of Boston life in this and most of his other novels.

John Irving *The Cider House Rules* (Black Swan UK; Vintage US). Irving writes huge, sprawling novels set all over New England. This one, suitably Dickensian in scope, is neither his most popular (*The World According to Garp*) or beloved (probably *A Prayer for Owen Meany*). But it is perhaps his best – a fascinating meditation on abortion.

Henry James *The Bostonians; The Europeans* (Penguin). The first is a satire tracing the relationship of two fictional feminists in the 1870s; the second is an early James novella about Europeans who travelled to New England, to find the area's puritanical culture astounding.

Sarah Orne Jewett *A Country Doctor* (Bantam US). Late nineteenth-century account of life in rural Maine, about a woman who refuses marriage so she can pursue her ambitions to become a doctor.

Jack Kerouac *Maggie Cassidy* (Penguin). The protobeatnik grew up in New England; here, he traces the arc of a youthful romance in a small Massachusetts mill town, to fine effect.

Stephen King *Different Seasons; Dolores Clainborne* (Penguin). Born in Maine, horror-master King is incredibly prolific. These are two of his better books, which manage quite well to evoke his home state and region.

Dennis Lehane *Darkness, Take My Hand* (Avon). Lehane sets his mysteries on the working-class streets of South Boston; they are all excellent and evocative, but this is probably the cream of the crop. His *Mystic River* (William Morrow), now a movie (see p.539), is highly recommended, too.

H.P. Lovecraft *The Best of H.P. Lovecraft: Bloodcurdling Tales of Horror and the Macabre* (Ballantine). The best stories from the author whom Stephen King called "the twentieth century's greatest practitioner of the classic horror tale.

John Miller and Tim Smith (eds) *Cape Cod Stories* (Chronicle US). Well-selected stories, essays, and excerpts by prominent writers ranging from Thoreau to Updike.

Herman Melville *Moby Dick* (Penguin). The incomparable story of a man's obsession with a great white whale, with descriptions of the whaling industry evocative of old New Bedford and Nantucket.

Susan Minot *Folly*; *Monkeys* (Washington Square Press, Vintage). This obvious nod to Edith Wharton's *Age of Innocence* is set in 1917 Boston instead of New York, and details the proclivities of the Brahmin era.

Robert B. Parker *A Triple Shot of Spenser* (Berkley Trade). Parker, a prolific mystery author with more than forty novels behind him, is best known for his Spenser series, about the adventures of a Boston private eye.

Sylvia Plath *The Bell Jar* (Harper Perennial US). Angst-ridden, dark, autobiographical novel about a girl's mental breakdown. The second half is set in Boston suburbs and at that, a mental hospital.

Annie Proulx *Heartsongs* (Fourth Estate UK; Macmillan US). Finely crafted, gritty stories of life in rural and blue-collar New England.

Philip Roth *The Human Stain* (Vintage International). Set in a small New England college town, an English professor fired from his job actually carries a much deeper secret.

Richard Russo *Empire Falls* (Vintage). In the failing blue-collar town of Empire Falls, Maine, Miles Roby runs the town's most popular diner, which he hopes someday to inherit from its controlling owner.

George Santayana *The Last Puritan* (MIT Press). The philosopher's brilliant "memoir in the form of a novel," set around Boston, chronicles the short life and education of protagonist Oliver Alden coming to grips with Puritanism.

Zadie Smith *On Beauty* (Penguin). The young novelist rewrites *Howard's End* with interracial and cross-continental couples in her third novel, set on the campus of a fictional New England college.

Wallace Stegner *Crossing to Safety* (Penguin). The saga of two couples who form a lifelong bond, set partly in Vermont.

John Steinbeck *The Winter of Our Discontent* (Penguin). A late work by Steinbeck, published in 1961, examining the moral collapse of Ethan Hawley and his family in small-town New England in the 1950s.

Eleanor Sullivan *Murder in New England* (Castle). A collection of pulpy murder mystery stories by Isaac Asimov, Ed Hoch, and Brendan DuBois, among others.

Donna Tartt *The Secret History* (Penguin UK; Ballantine US). A small group of students at a fictional Vermont college (modeled after Bennington) discover the murderous turns their elite cadre takes.

John Updike *The Witches of Eastwick* (Ballantine). Satirical witchy tale set in rural 1960s Rhode Island and chock-full of hypocrisy, adultery, and wickedness; a fun read.

David Foster Wallace *Infinite Jest* (Little, Brown US). A whopping 1088-page hilarious opus, with some parts set at a tennis academy outside Boston and other nuggets involving a Cambridge store owner in a Canadian separatist-terrorist plot.

Dorothy West *The Wedding* (Anchor). 1995 re-appearance of the 1940s author, with a touching family saga that takes place among the wealthy black community vacationing on Martha's Vineyard.

Edith Wharton *Ethan Frome* (Penguin). A distilled portrait of stark, icy New England that belies the fiery emotions blazing underneath, set in rural Massachusetts.

Travel
store

UK & Ireland
Britain
Devon & Cornwall
Dublin **D**
Edinburgh **D**
England
Ireland
The Lake District
London
London **D**
London Mini Guide
Scotland
Scottish Highlands
& Islands
Wales

Europe
Algarve **D**
Amsterdam
Amsterdam **D**
Andalucía
Athens **D**
Austria
Baltic States
Barcelona
Barcelona **D**
Belgium &
Luxembourg
Berlin
Brittany & Normandy
Bruges **D**
Brussels
Budapest
Bulgaria
Copenhagen
Corsica
Crete
Croatia
Cyprus
Czech & Slovak
Republics
Denmark
Dodecanese & East
Aegean Islands
Dordogne & The Lot
Europe on a Budget
Florence & Siena
Florence **D**
France
Germany
Gran Canaria **D**
Greece
Greek Islands
Hungary

Ibiza & Formentera **D**
Iceland
Ionian Islands
Italy
The Italian Lakes
Languedoc &
Roussillon
Lanzarote &
Fuerteventura **D**
Lisbon **D**
The Loire Valley
Madeira **D**
Madrid **D**
Mallorca **D**
Mallorca & Menorca
Malta & Gozo **D**
Moscow
The Netherlands
Norway
Paris
Paris **D**
Paris Mini Guide
Poland
Portugal
Prague
Prague **D**
Provence
& the Côte D'Azur
Pyrenees
Romania
Rome
Rome **D**
Sardinia
Scandinavia
Sicily
Slovenia
Spain
St Petersburg
Sweden
Switzerland
Tenerife &
La Gomera **D**
Turkey
Tuscany & Umbria
Venice & The Veneto
Venice **D**
Vienna

Asia
Bali & Lombok
Bangkok
Beijing
Cambodia
China

Goa
Hong Kong & Macau
Hong Kong
& Macau **D**
India
Indonesia
Japan
Kerala
Korea
Laos
Malaysia, Singapore
& Brunei
Nepal
The Philippines
Rajasthan, Dehli
& Agra
Shanghai
Singapore
Singapore **D**
South India
Southeast Asia on a
Budget
Sri Lanka
Taiwan
Thailand
Thailand's Beaches
& Islands
Tokyo
Vietnam

Australasia
Australia
East Coast Australia
Fiji
Melbourne
New Zealand
Sydney
Tasmania

North America
Alaska
Baja California
Boston
California
Canada
Chicago
Colorado
Florida
The Grand Canyon
Hawaii
Honolulu **D**
Las Vegas **D**
Los Angeles &
Southern California
Maui **D**

Miami & South Florida
Montréal
New England
New York City
New York City **D**
New York City Mini
Orlando & Walt
Disney World® **D**
Oregon &
Washington
San Francisco
San Francisco **D**
Seattle
Southwest USA
Toronto
USA
Vancouver
Washington DC
Yellowstone & The
Grand Tetons
Yosemite

Caribbean
& Latin America
Antigua & Barbuda **D**
Argentina
Bahamas
Barbados **D**
Belize
Bolivia
Brazil
Buenos Aires
Cancùn & Cozumel **D**
Caribbean
Central America on a
Budget
Chile
Costa Rica
Cuba
Dominican Republic
Ecuador
Guatemala
Jamaica
Mexico
Peru
Puerto Rico
St Lucia **D**
South America on a
Budget
Trinidad & Tobago
Yucatán

D: Rough Guide
DIRECTIONS for
short breaks

ROUGH GUIDES

Small print and Index

A Rough Guide to Rough Guides

Published in 1982, the first Rough Guide – to Greece – was a student scheme that became a publishing phenomenon. Mark Ellingham, a recent graduate in English from Bristol University, had been traveling in Greece the previous summer and couldn't find the right guidebook. With a small group of friends he wrote his own guide, combining a highly contemporary, journalistic style with a thoroughly practical approach to travelers' needs.

The immediate success of the book spawned a series that rapidly covered dozens of destinations. And, in addition to impecunious backpackers, Rough Guides soon acquired a much broader and older readership that relished the guides' wit and inquisitiveness as much as their enthusiastic, critical approach and value-for-money ethos.

These days, Rough Guides include recommendations from shoestring to luxury and cover more than 200 destinations around the globe, including almost every country in the Americas and Europe, more than half of Africa, and most of Asia and Australasia. Our ever-growing team of authors and photographers is spread all over the world, particularly in Europe, the USA, and Australia.

In the early 1990s, Rough Guides branched out of travel, with the publication of Rough Guides to World Music, Classical Music, and the Internet. All three have become benchmark titles in their fields, spearheading the publication of a wide range of books under the Rough Guide name.

Including the travel series, Rough Guides now number more than 350 titles, covering: phrasebooks, waterproof maps, music guides from Opera to Heavy Metal, reference works as diverse as Conspiracy Theories and Shakespeare, and popular culture books from iPods to Poker. Rough Guides also produce a series of more than 120 World Music CDs in partnership with World Music Network.

Visit www.roughguides.com to see our latest publications.

Rough Guide travel images are available for commercial licensing at www.roughguidespictures.com

SMALL PRINT

Rough Guide credits

Text editor: Ella Steim
Layout: Nikhil Agarwal
Cartography: Animesh Pathak
Picture editor: Sarah Cummins
Production: Rebecca Short
Proofreader: Karen Parker
Cover design: Chloë Roberts
Photographer: Dan Bannister and Curtis Hamilton
Editorial: **London** Ruth Blackmore, Andy Turner, Keith Drew, Edward Aves, Alice Park, Lucy White, Jo Kirby, James Smart, Natasha Foges, Róisín Cameron, Emma Traynor, James Rice, Emma Gibbs, Kathryn Lane, Christina Valhouli, Monica Woods, Mani Ramaswamy, Alison Roberts, Harry Wilson, Lucy Cowie, Helen Ochyra, Joe Staines, Peter Buckley, Matthew Milton, Tracy Hopkins, Ruth Tidball; **New York** Andrew Rosenberg, Steven Horak, AnneLise Sorensen, Anna Owens, Sean Mahoney, Paula Neudorf; **Delhi** Madhavi Singh, Karen D'Souza, Lubna Shaheen
Design & Pictures: **London** Scott Stickland, Dan May, Diana Jarvis, Mark Thomas, Nicole Newman, Emily Taylor; **Delhi** Umesh Aggarwal, Ajay Verma, Jessica Subramanian, Ankur Guha, Pradeep Thapliyal, Sachin Tanwar, Anita Singh

Production: Vicky Baldwin
Cartography: **London** Maxine Repath, Ed Wright, Katie Lloyd-Jones; **Delhi** Rajesh Chhibber, Ashutosh Bharti, Rajesh Mishra, Jasbir Sandhu, Karobi Gogoi, Alakananda Roy, Swati Handoo, Deshpal Dabas
Online: **London** George Atwell, Faye Hellon, Jeanette Angell, Fergus Day, Justine Bright, Clare Bryson, Áine Fearon, Adrian Low, Ezgi Celebi, Amber Bloomfield; **Delhi** Amit Verma, Rahul Kumar, Narender Kumar, Ravi Yadav, Debojit Borah, Rakesh Kumar, Ganesh Sharma, Shisir Basumatari
Marketing & Publicity: **London** Liz Statham, Niki Hanmer, Louise Maher, Jess Carter, Vanessa Godden, Vivienne Watton, Anna Paynton, Rachel Sprackett, Libby Jellie, Laura Vipond; **New York** Geoff Colquitt, Nancy Lambert, Katy Ball; **Delhi** Ragini Govind
Manager India: Punita Singh
Reference Director: Andrew Lockett
Operations Manager: Helen Phillips
PA to Publishing Director: Nicola Henderson
Publishing Director: Martin Dunford
Commercial Manager: Gino Magnotta
Managing Director: John Duhigg

Publishing information

This fifth edition published June 2009 by
Rough Guides Ltd,
80 Strand, London WC2R 0RL
345 Hudson St, 4th Floor,
New York, NY 10014, USA
14 Local Shopping Centre, Panchsheel Park,
New Delhi 110017, India
Distributed by the Penguin Group
Penguin Books Ltd,
80 Strand, London WC2R 0RL
Penguin Group (USA)
375 Hudson Street, NY 10014, USA
Penguin Group (Australia)
250 Camberwell Road, Camberwell,
Victoria 3124, Australia
Penguin Group (Canada)
195 Harry Walker Parkway N, Newmarket, ON,
L3Y 7B3 Canada
Penguin Group (NZ)
67 Apollo Drive, Mairangi Bay, Auckland 1310,
New Zealand

Cover concept by Peter Dyer.

Typeset in Bembo and Helvetica to an original design by Henry Iles.

Printed and bound in China

© Rough Guides, 2009

568pp includes index
A catalogue record for this book is available from the British Library.
ISBN: 978-1-84836-062-4

Help us update

We've gone to a lot of effort to ensure that the fifth edition of **The Rough Guide to New England** is accurate and up to date. However, things change – places get "discovered", opening hours are notoriously fickle, restaurants and rooms raise prices or lower standards. If you feel we've got it wrong or left something out, we'd like to know, and if you can remember the address, the price, the hours, the phone number, so much the better.

Please send your comments with the subject line "**Rough Guide New England Update**" to ® mail@roughguides.com. We'll credit all contributions and send a copy of the next edition (or any other Rough Guide if you prefer) for the very best emails.

Have your questions answered and tell others about your trip at
® community.roughguides.com

SMALL PRINT

Acknowledgements

Sarah Hull would like to thank: her family, for rallying spectacularly for the cause, and Ella Steim, for being the jam editor. Much love goes to the Boston National Park Service, for making sure I got the history straight. A big, big thanks to Veronika V, Michael C, and the Bitons, as well as to Carter Long at the MFA. And to my Stuart Smalleys: Amber, Ali, Handel, and Bat-Sheva.

Stephen Keeling would like to thank: Sarah Hull for the excellent tips, Ella Steim for her masterful editing and invaluable local knowledge, and as always Tiffany Wu, without whose support this would not have been possible.

Zhenzhen Lu would like to thank: Catherine Sidor at the Fairfield County CVB and Janet Serra at the Northwest Connecticut CVB for all their help; and along with many others who pointed the way or provided great company, thanks to Marguerite on Block Island,

Bianca L of West Cornwall, and Mary Orlando of Goshen. Thanks to Jon Collete, Christoph Gorder, and Kathryn Renton for generously sharing your local digs. Thanks to Dad for the car, and to my family and roomies for bearing with my continual absence through the summer. Many thanks to Ella Steim for patience, guidance, and warm support.

The editor would like to thank: Sarah Hull, Stephen, and Zhenzhen, for their hard work, diligence, and enthusiasm; Mani, for the opportunity; Nikhil, for putting it all together beautifully; Sarah Cummins, for great picture research; Animesh, for patient map-making; and Karen Parker, for proofreading. Many thanks also to: Alison Roberts, Katie Lloyd-Jones, Umesh Aggarwal, Nicole Newman, Chloe Roberts, and Andrew Rosenberg, for all their help along the way; to Julia, for putting up with my clutter; and to the beautiful region of New England.

Readers' letters

Thanks to all the readers who have taken the time to write in with comments and suggestions (and apologies if we've inadvertently omitted or misspelt anyone's name): Kathie Cote, Stavros Fotiadis, Marika Green, Dave Ingram, and Mary Redmond.

SMALL PRINT

Index

Map entries are in color.

INDEX

I

INDEX

INDEX

561

INDEX

565

Map symbols

maps are listed in the full index using colored text

– – –	Chapter boundary	ⅵ	Marsh
–––·–	International boundary	ⅶ	Viewpoint
––––··	State boundary	∿	Spring/spa
95	Interstate	🗼	Lighthouse
2	U.S. Highway	🎿	Skiing
27	State Highway	ⓘ	Information office
73	Canadian Autoroute	★	Bus stop
——	Pedestrianized road	Ⓣ	Ⓣ station
= = =	4WD track	✈	International airport
·····	Tunnel	✗	Domestic airport
-----	Walking path/bicycle trail	🅿	Parking
——	River	) (	Bridge
— —	Ferry route	⊠—⊠	Gate
—•—•—	Railway	⊞	Hospital
•- - -•	Cable car	⊠	Post office
——	Wall	◆	Point of interest
⌂⌂	Mountain range	⊙	Statue
▲	Peak	⛺	Campground
𓃰	Rocks	◉	Accommodation
🜨	Waterfall	✝	Church
🏛	Stately home	▬	Building
🌳	Garden	⊹	Cemetery
♣	Museum	▒	Park/forest
🏛	Monument